Case Studies in Abnormal Psychology

Seventh Edition

Thomas F. Oltmanns
Washington University in St. Louis

Michele T. Martin, Ph.D.
Wesleyan College

John M. Neale
State University of New York at Stony Brook

Gerald C. Davison
University of Southern California

WILEY

John Wiley & Sons, Inc.

ACQUISITIONS EDITOR	Christopher Johnson
ASSOCIATE EDITOR	Jessica Bartelt
PUBLISHER	Jay O'Callaghan
PRODUCTION MANAGER	Pam Kennedy
SENIOR PRODUCTION EDITOR	Sarah Wolfman-Robichaud
MARKETING MANAGER	Jeffrey Rucker
DESIGNER	Hope Miller
CREATIVE DIRECTOR	Harry Nolan
EDITORIAL ASSISTANT	Lindsay Lovier
COPYEDITOR	Christine Cervoni

This book was set in 10/12 Times by Kelly Tavares and printed and bound by Courier Westford. The cover was printed by Courier Westford.

To order books or for customer service please, call 1-800-CALL WILEY (225-5945).

ISBN-13   978- 0-471-73112-2
ISBN-10   0-471-73112-9

Printed in the United States of America

10 9 8 7 6 5 4 3 2 1

To Gail, Sara, and Josh
TFO

To Matt, Caroline, Grace, and Thomas
MTM

To Gail and Sean
JMN

To Kathleen, Eve, and Asher
GCD

PREFACE

Most textbooks on abnormal psychology include short descriptions of actual clinical cases. However, those presentations are necessarily brief and too fragmented for students to gain a clear understanding of the idiographic complexities of a person's troubled life. They cannot describe the client's developmental history, the manner in which a therapist might conceptualize the problem, the formulation and implementation of a treatment plan, or the trajectory of a disorder over a period of many years. In contrast to such brief descriptions, a detailed case study can provide a foundation on which to organize important information about a disorder. This may enhance the student's ability to understand and recall abstract theoretical and research issues.

The purpose of *Case Studies in Abnormal Psychology,* 7e is therefore threefold: (1) to provide detailed descriptions of a range of clinical problems; (2) to illustrate some of the ways in which these problems can be viewed and treated; and (3) to discuss some of the evidence that is available concerning the epidemiology and etiology of the disorders in question. The book is appropriate for both undergraduate and graduate courses in abnormal psychology. It may also be useful in courses in psychiatric social work or nursing and could be helpful to students enrolled in various practicum courses that teach how best to conceptualize mental health problems and plan treatment. It may be used on its own or as a supplement to a standard textbook in abnormal psychology.

In selecting cases for inclusion in the book, we sampled from a variety of problems, ranging from psychotic disorders (e.g., schizophrenia and bipolar mood disorder) to personality disorders (e.g., paranoid and antisocial) to various disorders of childhood and aging (e.g., separation anxiety disorder). We focused deliberately on cases that illustrate particular problems that are of interest to students of abnormal psychology. We do not mean to imply, however, that all the cases fit neatly into specific diagnostic molds. In addition to describing "classic" behavioral symptoms (e.g., hallucinations, compulsive rituals, or specific fears), we emphasized the social context in which these disorders appear as well as life problems that are significant in determining the person's overall adjustment, even though they may not be relevant from a diagnostic standpoint. For example, our case on hypertension considers issues in etiology and treatment when the person is African American. Several of the cases include a consideration of marital adjustment and parent-child relationships.

Our coverage extends to examples of eating disorders, multiple personality, transsexualism, borderline personality, and posttraumatic stress disorder (following rape). Each of these disorders represents an area that has received considerable attention in the contemporary literature, and each has been the focus of theoretical controversy.

We have added one new chapter to this seventh edition, a new case of somatization disorder, which is characterized by a history of many somatic complaints that cannot be traced to physical impairments or other medical disorders. The new case provides important coverage of this difficult and complex topic, including a description of the challenging issues that are faced in the diagnosis and treatment of people suffering from this condition.

Our cognitive-behavioral perspective is clearly evident in most of these case discussions. Nevertheless, we have tried to present alternative conceptual positions. The cases can therefore be used to show students how a given problem can be reasonably viewed and treated from several different perspectives. Although most of the interventions described illustrate a cognitive-behavioral approach to treatment, we have also described biological treatments (e.g., medication, electroconvulsive therapy, and psychosurgery) when they are relevant to the case. In some cases, the outcome was not positive. We have tried to present an honest view of the limitations, as well as the potential benefits, of various treatment programs. Note also, that two of the cases were not in treatment. We believe that it is important to point out that many people who have psychological disorders do not see therapists.

Each case study concludes with a discussion of current knowledge about etiology. Some of these discussions are necessarily briefer than others. More research has been done on schizophrenia, for example, than on gender identity disorder (transsexualism) or paranoid personality disorder. We had two goals in mind for these discussions. First, we have tried to use the case material to illustrate the application of research to individual client's problems. Second, we alert readers to important gaps in our knowledge of abnormal psychology, our abiding belief being that realizing what we do not know is as important as appreciating what we do know. All of these discussions have been revised in the seventh edition to include new ideas and empirical evidence that are changing the way that particular disorders are viewed and treated.

We have included discussions of issues associated with gender, culture, and ethnicity in all of the previous editions of this book. For example, issues of race and psychotherapy are considered in the case of hypertension. Attention to these issues, particularly those involving gender, have been strengthened in this seventh edition. The case on social phobia discusses important issues related to race and gender. Our description of posttraumatic stress disorder (PTSD) following rape trauma also includes many issues that are particularly important for women (e.g., helpful and harmful ways in which other people react to the victim, decisions by the victim, her therapist, and her professor about whether to report the rapist, and so on). Our discussion of the etiology of major depression includes consideration of possible explanations for gender differences in this disorder. The chapters on dissociative identity disorder, borderline personality disorder, and bulimia nervosa all discuss the impact of prior sexual abuse on subsequent development of psychopathology. Both cases of eating disorder involve extended consideration of cultural attitudes that affect women's feelings and beliefs about themselves. These are only a few of the instances in which we have attempted to address gender issues in relation to the etiology and treatment of mental disorders. We are grateful to Patricia Lee Llewellyn (University of Virginia) for many helpful comments on these issues.

All of the cases in this book are based on actual clinical experience, primarily our own but, in some instances, that of our colleagues and students. Various demographic characteristics (names, locations, and occupations) and some concrete clinical details have been changed to protect the anonymity of clients and their families. In some instances, the cases are composites of clinical problems with which we have dealt. Our intent is not to put forth claims of efficacy and utility for any particular conceptualization or intervention but, instead, to illustrate the ways clinicians think about their work and implement abstract principles to help a client cope with life problems. The names used in the case studies are fictitious; any resemblance to actual persons is purely coincidental.

As in the first six editions of this book, we have not identified the authors of specific case studies. This procedure has been adopted and maintained in order to preserve the clients' anonymity. We are grateful to Serrita Jane, Ron Thompson, Kevin Leach, and Kimble Richardson, who provided extensive consultation on five of these cases. We also thank Elana Farace and Sarah Liebman for drafting two others.

We would like to thank the following reviewers for their helpful and constructive comments: Dorothy Bianco, Rhode Island College; Bernardo Carducci, Indiana University Southeast; Ron Evans, Washburn University; Jan Hastrup, SUNY at Buffalo; Russell Jones, Virginia Polytechnic Institute and State University; Patricia Lee Llewellyn, University of Virginia; Richard McNally, Harvard University; Janet Morahan Martin, Bryant College; Linda Musun Miller, University of Arkansas – Little Rock; Mark Pantle, Baylor University; Esther Rothblum, University of Vermont; Gary Sterner, Eastern Washington University; Sondra Solomon, University of Vermont; and John Wixted, University of California-San Diego.

We also want to express our sincere appreciation to the superb staff at Wiley, especially Jessica Bartelt, Assistant Editor, Psychology; Ryan Flahive, Executive Editor, Psychology; Lindsay Lovier, Editorial Assistant; and Sarah Wolfman-Robichaud, Senior Production Editor. Their conscientious efforts were essential to the successful completion of this revision.

Finally, we remain grateful to our families for their continued love and encouragement. Gail Oltmanns and Matt Martin have both provided invaluable support throughout the preparation of this new edition.

Thomas F. Oltmanns
Michele T. Martin
John M. Neale
Gerald C. Davison

CONTENTS

CHAPTER 1

Obsessive Compulsive Disorder

Karen Rusa was a 30-year-old married woman and the mother of four children. Although she had been having anxiety-related problems for a number of years, she had never sought professional help prior to this time. During the preceding three months, she had become increasingly depressed; her family physician finally suggested that she seek psychological services.

For the past several months Karen had been experiencing intrusive, repetitive thoughts that centered around her children's safety. She frequently found herself imagining that a serious accident had occurred, and she was unable to put these thoughts out of her mind. On one such occasion she imagined that her son, Alan, had broken his leg playing football at school. There was no reason to believe that an accident had occurred, but Karen brooded about the possibility until she finally called the school to see if Alan was all right. Even after receiving reassurance that he had not been hurt, she was somewhat surprised when he later arrived home unharmed.

Karen also noted that her daily routine was seriously hampered by an extensive series of counting rituals that she performed throughout each day. Specific numbers had come to have a special meaning to Karen; she found that her preoccupation with these numbers was interfering with her ability to perform everyday activities. One example was grocery shopping. Karen believed that if she selected the first item (e.g., a box of cereal) on the shelf, something terrible would happen to her oldest child. If she selected the second item, some unknown disaster would befall her second child, and so on for the four children. The children's ages were also important. The sixth item in a row, for example, was associated with her youngest child, who was 6 years old. Thus, specific items had to be avoided to ensure the safety of her children. Obviously, the rituals required continuing attention because the children's ages changed. Karen's preoccupation with numbers extended to other activities, most notably the pattern in which she smoked cigarettes and drank coffee. If she had one cigarette, she believed that she had to smoke at least four in a row or one of the children would be harmed in some way. If she drank one cup of coffee, she felt compelled to drink four.

Karen acknowledged the irrationality of these rituals but, nevertheless, maintained that she felt much more comfortable when she observed them conscientiously. When she was occasionally in too great a hurry to perform the rituals, she experienced considerable anxiety in the form of a subjective feeling of dread and apprehension. She described herself as tense, jumpy, and unable to relax during these periods. Her fears were most often confirmed because something unfortunate invariably happened to one of the children within a few days after each such "failure." The fact that minor accidents are likely to occur at a fairly high rate in any family of four children did not diminish Karen's conviction that she had been directly responsible because of her inability to observe the numerical rules.

In addition to her obsessive ideas and compulsive behaviors, Karen reported dissatisfaction with her marriage and problems in managing her children. Her husband, Tony, had been placed on complete physical disability 11 months prior to her first visit to the mental health center. Although he was only 32 years old, Tony suffered from a very serious heart condition that made even the most routine physical exertion potentially dangerous. Since leaving his job as a clerk at a plumbing supply store, he had spent most of his time at home. He enjoyed lying on the couch watching television and did so for most of his waking hours. He had convinced Karen that she should be responsible for all the household chores and family errands. Her days were spent getting the children dressed, fed, and transported to school; cleaning; washing; shopping; and fetching potato chips, dip, and beer whenever Tony needed a snack. The inequity of this situation was apparent to Karen, and extremely frustrating, yet she found herself unable to handle it effectively.

The children were also clearly out of her control. Robert, age 6, and Alan, age 8, were very active and mischievous. Neither responded well to parental discipline, which was inconsistent at best. Both experienced behavioral problems at school, and Alan was being considered for placement in a special classroom for particularly disruptive children. The girls were also difficult to handle. Denise, age 9, and Jennifer, age 11, spent much of their time at home arguing with each other. Jennifer was moderately obese. Denise teased her mercilessly about her weight. After they had quarreled for some time, Jennifer would appeal tearfully to Karen, who would attempt to intervene on her behalf. Karen was becoming increasingly distressed by her inability to handle this confusing situation, and she was getting little, if any, help from Tony. During the past several weeks, she had been spending more and more time crying and hiding alone in her bedroom.

Social History

Karen was raised in New York City by Italian immigrant parents. She was the first of four children. Her family was deeply religious, and she was raised to be a devout Roman Catholic. She attended parochial schools from the first grade through high school and was a reasonably good student. Her memories of the strict practices of the church and school authorities were vivid. The formal rituals of the church played an important role in her life, as they did for the other members of her family. Beginning at an early age, Karen was taught that she had to observe many specific guidelines that governed social behavior within the church (not eating meat on Fridays, going to confession regularly, and so forth). She was told that her strict adherence to these norms would ensure the safety of her immortal soul and, conversely, that transgressions would be severely punished.

The depth of her belief and the severity of its consequences can be seen in the following story, which Karen recalled during an early session. When she was 8 years old, Karen and her classmates at school were to receive their First Communion in the church. This is a particularly important and solemn occasion for Roman Catholics that signifies the child's advancement to adult status in the church community. Before the child is allowed to partake in communion, however, a complete confession must be made of *all* prior sins. Karen was told that she was to confess all her sins, regardless of their severity or the time of their occurrence, to her priest, who would prescribe an appropriate penance. She remembered her parents' and teachers' warnings that if she failed to mention any of her sins, her soul would be banished to hell for eternity. This threat was still vivid in Karen's mind many years later. Despite the terror aroused by these circumstances, Karen intentionally failed to tell the priest about one of her sins; she had stolen a small picture book from her classroom and was now afraid either to return it or to tell anyone about the crime. She lived with intense guilt about this omission for several years and could remember having occasionally terrifying nightmares that centered around imagined punishments for not providing a complete confession. In subsequent years, Karen intensified her efforts to abide by even the most minute details of church regulations, but she continued to harbor the conviction that she could never atone for this mortal sin.

Karen remembered her parents as having been very strict disciplinarians. Her mother was apparently a rather unemotional and rigid person who had insisted on the maintenance of order and cleanliness in their household. Beyond her unerring adherence to religious rules and regulations, Karen's mother kept the family on a tight schedule with regard to meals and other routine activities. When the children deviated from these guidelines, they were severely punished. Karen's most positive recollections of interaction with her mother centered around their mutual participation in prescribed church functions. She did not remember her parents ever demonstrating affection for each other in front of their children.

Karen married Tony after she graduated from high school, and she became pregnant two months later. During this pregnancy, she witnessed an unfortunate accident at her neighbor's apartment. While Karen was chatting with her friend, the woman's infant daughter crawled off the porch and was run over by another child riding a bicycle. The girl was seriously injured and remained in the hospital for several weeks. Shortly after this accident, Karen began experiencing repetitive, intrusive thoughts about injuring herself. At unpredictable but frequent intervals throughout the day, she would find herself thinking about jumping out of windows, walking in front of cars, and other similar dangerous behaviors. These thoughts were, of course, frightening to her, but she could not prevent their occurrence. When one of the thoughts did come into her mind, she attempted to get rid of it by quickly repeating a short prayer that she had learned as a child and then asking God for forgiveness for having entertained such a sinful impulse. This procedure was moderately successful as a temporary source of distraction, but it did not prevent the reappearance of a similar, intrusive thought several hours later. These thoughts of self-injury occurred less frequently and seemed less troublesome after the birth of her first child, Jennifer, perhaps because Karen was soon preoccupied with all of the responsibilities of caring for the baby.

During this same time, Karen began to be disillusioned with the church. Her distress centered around a number of reforms that had been introduced by Pope

John XXIII and the ecumenical council. The Mass, for example, was no longer said in Latin, and nonclerical persons were allowed to administer various rites of the church. Similarly, church members were no longer admonished to give up meat on Fridays, and other rituals were modified or completely eliminated. Most people found these changes refreshing, but Karen was horrified. The church's rituals had come to play a central role in her life. In de-emphasizing the importance of traditional rituals, the church was depriving Karen of her principal means of controlling her own destiny. She was extremely uncomfortable with these new practices and eventually stopped going to church altogether.

When Jennifer was 9 months old, Karen once again became pregnant. She and Tony decided to move to the suburbs, where they would be able to afford a house with a yard in which the children could play. Although she was proud of their new home, Karen began to feel depressed during this period because she missed her old friends.

Karen's situation showed little change throughout the next few years. By the time she was 25 years old, she had four children. She found this responsibility overwhelming and was generally unhappy most of the time. Her relationship with Tony had essentially reached a stalemate; they were not satisfied with their marriage, but they agreed to stay together for the children. Although they did not fight with each other openly, a sense of covert tension and estrangement pervaded their relationship. Tony refused to participate in what he considered to be unnecessarily rigid and complicated household regulations, particularly those dealing with the children's behavior. Karen had established very specific guidelines for meals, bedtime, and so on but found that she was unable to enforce these rules by herself. She remained distant from Tony and resisted most of his attempts to display physical affection. Thus, overall, Karen was chronically unhappy and generally dissatisfied with her life, but she nevertheless clung to her miserable surroundings and established patterns of behavior out of fear that any change would be for the worse.

This unhappy, yet tolerable, equilibrium was disturbed by Tony's deteriorating health. One day, while he was working at the store, he experienced sudden chest pains and numbness in his extremities. Recognizing these symptoms as serious in nature (he had had high blood pressure for years and was therefore well-informed in this regard), Tony asked a friend to drive him to the hospital. His experience was diagnosed as a mild heart attack. Further testing revealed serious structural abnormalities in his heart. He was eventually discharged from the hospital, given a complete medical disability, and laid off from his job.

Karen became more and more depressed after Tony began staying home during the day. It was during this time that her fears about the children's safety became clearly unreasonable, and she started performing her counting rituals. Karen realized that her situation was desperate because she felt that she had lost control of her own behavior and experienced considerable anxiety whenever she attempted to resist performing the rituals. At this point, she finally decided to seek professional help.

Conceptualization and Treatment

The therapist saw the ritualistic behavior as one part of Karen's overall difficult situation. Karen's counting compulsion represented her attempt to reintroduce a sense of personal control over her own life. In this sense, the rituals were being performed instead of either the more socially acceptable religious activities that she had employed as a child or more effective social skills that she had apparently never developed. For example, she was unassertive in her relationship with Tony. Instead of standing up for her rights, she would meekly acquiesce to even his most unreasonable demands. At the same time, she would become extremely frustrated and angry with him and would look for subtle ways to "even the score." She was similarly unable to convey her appreciation to him on those (admittedly rare) occasions when he did please her. Treatment was therefore initially aimed at the development of interpersonal skills that would give Karen more control over her environment. It was hoped that as she was able to create a more satisfactory relationship with her husband and children, her increased competence would eliminate the necessity of turning to admittedly superstitious, ineffective attempts to achieve self-control.

Karen quickly recognized her deficiency in this regard but was nevertheless unable to change her behavior spontaneously. She and the therapist therefore agreed to pursue a systematic program of assertion training. The initial sessions in this sequence were devoted to a careful assessment of the situations in which Karen was unassertive. She was asked to keep a daily notebook of such situations in which she noted the people involved, the nature of their interaction, and her perception of the situation, including what she thought would happen if she did behave assertively. Having identified typical problem situations, Karen and her therapist role-played several incidents as a way of introducing Karen to more appropriate responses. They also discussed Karen's irrational fears associated with assertion. These thoughts centered on her implicit belief that everyone should love her, and that if she stood up for her own rights people would reject her. These irrational self-statements were inhibiting the expression of assertive behaviors. After Karen became proficient with such exercises in the therapy sessions, she was asked to start practicing her new skills in real-life situations outside the clinic.

After assertion training had produced some positive results, the therapist began teaching Karen more effective child-management skills. These were based primarily on procedures associated with instrumental learning (also known as operant conditioning). She was taught, for example, to ignore her daughters when they were quarreling and to reinforce them positively for playing together appropriately. Her efforts were initially channeled toward behaviors that could be changed easily. The most difficult problems, such as getting the children to stop fighting at mealtimes, were left until Karen had mastered some of the general principles of child management.

In addition to these skill-training programs, the therapist also discussed Karen's concerns about religion. It was clear that the church was still important to her and that she experienced considerable guilt and anxiety over her failure to attend services regularly. The fact that her children were not involved in church activities was also troubling to Karen. She worried that if any harm came to one of them, God would not protect them. For these reasons, Karen was encouraged to visit several priests at churches in her area in an effort to find one who was more conservative and thus more compatible with her own views. Although most of the local priests had moved toward contemporary practices in their own churches, they did refer her to an older priest at a church somewhat farther from her neighborhood, who still adhered to several of the traditional rituals she had learned as a child. She made an appointment to visit this priest and was both pleased and relieved after their initial meeting. He was able to discuss with her some of the changes that had been made in the church. In some cases, he was able to explain the rationale behind a particular change in a way that was acceptable to her. This process was, no doubt, facilitated by the fact that he shared many of her concerns about abandoning traditional practices. Karen felt much more comfortable with this priest than she did with the liberal pastor who was in charge of the church in her immediate neighborhood. Within weeks she was once again attending church regularly with her four children.

The combination of assertion training, parent education, and a renewed interest in church activities did lead to an important improvement in Karen's mood. After three months of treatment, she reported an increased sense of self-confidence and an improvement in her family life. There was also some reduction in her anxiety level. She continued to observe her number rituals, but they were somewhat less frequent, and, when she did fail to perform the counting routines, she was not as distraught as she had been at the beginning of treatment.

At this point, Karen's rituals were addressed directly using a behavioral treatment method known as exposure and response prevention (ERP) (Steketee, 1994). This procedure involves purposely exposing the person to stimuli that provoke intense anxiety (either in imagination or in reality) for extended periods of time while preventing the person from performing anxiety-reducing rituals. Karen was asked to smoke a single cigarette at the beginning of a therapy session. When she was finished with the cigarette, she began to feel anxious and worry about her oldest daughter. She was then instructed to resist the temptation to smoke another cigarette. Thus, the response that she typically employed to neutralize her anxiety and to control the ruminations was prevented. The therapist believed that this type of prolonged exposure to the anxiety-provoking situation would lead to a reduction in Karen's anxiety. The procedure was carried out during four consecutive two-hour sessions. Karen was encouraged to practice the same response prevention procedure on her own between sessions. When she had mastered the cigarette-smoking problem, the procedure was extended progressively to other similar situations in which she had been concerned about numbers.

Treatment was terminated after 20 sessions. Karen was no longer depressed and had not engaged in her compulsive counting rituals for four weeks. The children were better behaved at home, and Karen had plans to institute further changes in this regard. Her relationship with Tony was somewhat improved. Although he had become quite upset initially when Karen began to assert herself, he became more cooperative when he saw an improvement in her adjustment.

Discussion

Obsessive Compulsive Disorder (OCD) is included in the *Diagnostic and Statistical Manual of Mental Disorders* (*DSM-IV-TR*, APA, 2000, pp. 462–463) under the general heading of Anxiety Disorders. It is defined by the following criteria:

A. Either obsessions or compulsions:

Obsessions as defined by (1), (2), (3), and (4):

1. Recurrent and persistent thoughts, impulses, or images that are experienced, at some time during the disturbance, as intrusive and inappropriate, and that cause marked anxiety or distress.

2. The thoughts, impulses, or images are not simply excessive worries about real-life problems.

3. The person attempts to ignore or suppress such thoughts, impulses, or images, or to neutralize them with some other thought or action.

4. The person recognizes that the obsessional thoughts, impulses, or images are a product of his or her own mind.

Compulsions as defined by (1) and (2):

1. The person feels driven to perform repetitive behaviors (e.g., handwashing, ordering, checking) or mental acts (e.g., praying, counting, repeating words silently) in response to an obsession, or according to rules that must be applied rigidly.

2. The behaviors or mental acts are aimed at preventing or reducing distress or preventing some dreaded event or situation; however, these behaviors or mental acts either are not connected in a realistic way with what they are designed to neutralize or prevent, or are clearly excessive.

B. At some point during the course of the disorder, the person has recognized that the obsessions or compulsions are excessive or unreasonable.

C. The obsessions or compulsions cause marked distress, are time consuming (take more than one hour a day), or significantly interfere with the person's normal routine, occupational (or academic) functioning, or usual social activities or relationships.

The most common types of obsessions have been described by Rasmussen and Eisen (1992), who recorded the frequency of specific symptoms in a sample of over 500 patients. The numbers in parentheses indicate the percentage of patients who exhibited each type of obsession. Most of the patients (72 percent) had multiple obsessions.

Fear of contamination (50 percent): A fear of exposure to stimuli such as dirt, germs, poison, or radiation. The person's concern may include fear that other people, as well as themselves, will become ill. Fear of contamination is most often coupled with compulsive handwashing.

Pathological doubt (42 percent): An inclination to worry that something bad is going to happen because a task has not been completed correctly. People with this symptom often develop counting rituals that may include a complex system of good numbers and bad numbers. They may repeat certain actions a particular magical number of times (as in Karen's case).

Somatic obsessions (33 percent): The irrational, persistent fear of developing a serious life-threatening illness (often indistinguishable from *hypochondriasis*, i.e., fear of having some disease despite reassurance from a physician that the disease is not present).

Need for symmetry (32 percent): An extreme need to have objects or events in a certain order or position, to do and undo certain motor actions in an exact fashion, or to have things exactly symmetric or "evened up."

Aggressive obsessions (31 percent): Recurrent, ghastly thoughts or images that the person has committed a violent or an inappropriately aggressive act.

Sexual obsessions (24 percent): Repeated, distressing thoughts about, or impulses to perform, inappropriate sexual behaviors.

In addition to provoking anxiety, sexual and aggressive obsessions are associated with exaggerated feelings of shame and guilt. People with this symptom may seek constant reassurance from friends (or therapists) that they are not really capable of performing such actions.

Compulsions represent patterns of ritualistic behavior and thinking that are usually performed in response to an obsession. Whereas obsessions lead to an *increase* in subjective anxiety, compulsions *reduce* the person's anxiety or discomfort. Compulsive behavior is designed to neutralize or to prevent discomfort or some dreaded event or situation. Most patients who seek treatment for obsessive symptoms also exhibit compulsive behaviors (Foa & Franklin, 2001; Parmet, Glass, & Glass, 2004). Compulsive patients fall into two primary groups: "cleaners" and "checkers."[1] Cleaning and washing rituals are associated with fear of contact with contaminating objects. For example, a patient who is afraid of contamination by germs or bodily secretions may spend hours each day bathing or disinfecting his or her home. This ritualistic behavior restores the patient's sense of safety. Repetitive checking, on the other hand, is more often motivated by a fear of some catastrophic event. For example, a patient who experiences obsessive thoughts about gas explosions may engage in compulsive checking of the burners on a gas stove.

Some other behaviors that take a repetitive form and are associated with either a decrease or increase in anxiety have also been considered "compulsive" in the popular media. These include problems such as gambling, drug addiction, and exhibitionism. There are, however, some important distinctions between these actions and truly compulsive behaviors. First, addictive behaviors involve a pleasure-seeking component that is absent in compulsive behaviors. Second, the anxiety that is associated with the performance of criminal activities (e.g., stealing) is appropri-

---

[1] Some investigators have suggested that there may be important differences between these two subgroups in terms of their etiology and response to treatment (e.g., Rachman & Hodgson, 1980). Cleaning compulsions may be more likely to develop in families in which the parents are overprotective, whereas checking rituals, which are more often associated with doubts and indecisiveness, are more often encouraged by parents who are excessively critical.

ate in light of social sanctions; obsessive compulsive patients experience anxiety that is inappropriate to the situation.

Obsessive Compulsive Disorder (OCD) should be distinguished from Obsessive Compulsive Personality Disorder (OCPD). The latter does not involve specific ritualistic behaviors; it is intended to refer to a general *personality style*. People with an obsessive compulsive personality are preoccupied with orderliness and perfectionism as well as mental and interpersonal control. They are inflexible and overly devoted to work to the point that they avoid leisure activities and ignore friendships.

The phobic disorders (i.e., specific phobia, social phobia, and agoraphobia) are similar to OCD because they involve severe anxiety and are characterized by behaviors that are designed to reduce that anxiety. Some obsessive compulsive patients also display phobic avoidance of situations associated with anxiety about dirt or contamination. There are, however, some important differences between OCD and the phobic disorders. For example, phobic patients do not show the same tendency toward superstitious or "magical" thinking that is often characteristic of obsessive compulsive patients, nor do they manifest compulsive symptoms. Also, for the phobic patient, the anxiety-inducing stimulus is unrelated to the content of any obsessions the patient may experience.

Obsessive thoughts should also be distinguished from delusional beliefs. Two criteria are important in this regard. First, patients with OCD try, often desperately, to resist their intrusive ideas, whereas delusional patients do not. Second, most OCD patients are ambivalent about their thoughts; they realize the essential absurdity of their obsessions and compulsions at the same time that they are preoccupied with them. Some OCD patients do have relatively poor insight regarding the senseless nature of their obsessions, but *DSM-IV-TR* requires for a diagnosis of OCD that, *at some point during the course of the disorder*, the person must recognize that the obsessions or compulsions are excessive or unreasonable (Eisen, Phillips, & Rasmussen, 1999; Foa & Kozak, 1995).

Depression is a common complication of OCD. Two out of every three patients with OCD have experienced at least one episode of major depression at some point during their lives. The relationship between these phenomena is unclear. Sometimes compulsive symptoms appear before the onset of depression; in other cases this relationship is reversed. The successful treatment or alleviation of depressive symptoms does not invariably lead to a reduction in the frequency of compulsive behaviors, and vice versa (Abramowitz et al., 2000).

Although OCD was previously thought to be relatively rare, results from the Epidemiologic Catchment Area (ECA) study suggest that milder forms of the disorder may affect between 2 and 3 percent of the general population at some point during their lives (Karno & Golding, 1991; Zohar et al., 1999). The disorder may be slightly more common among women than men. Prevalence rates among untreated community residents must be interpreted with caution, however. The validity of OCD diagnoses based on data collected by lay interviewers has been seriously questioned; the *false positive rate* (people who receive a diagnosis when they do not really have the disorder) may be quite high (Fireman et al., 2001; Nelson & Rice,

1997). Data from England suggest that the true prevalence of OCD in the community may be closer to 1 percent (Bebbington, 1998).

Relatively little information is available regarding conditions that set the stage for later development of OCD. Nevertheless, some interesting clues were provided in one classic study. Kringlen (1970) reported the results of a 20-year followup of 91 patients who had been hospitalized with obsessive compulsive disorder. More than 80 percent of these patients had exhibited nervous symptoms as children. They had typically been raised in strict, puritanical homes. The average age of onset for compulsive symptoms in female patients was between 10 and 20 years, although most of the women did not seek professional help until some years later. More than half of the patients showed an acute onset of symptoms following a specific stressful event. Marital problems were common among compulsive patients.

The prognosis for patients with OCD is mixed. Although the disorder can last many years, most patients do improve. One study conducted followup assessments with a group of patients 40 years after they had been treated in a hospital in Sweden (Skoog & Skoog, 1999). This was, of course, a group of severely disturbed patients because most people with OCD do not need to be treated in an inpatient setting. Nevertheless, the results suggest that many patients recover from OCD. At the time of the final followup, half of the patients had recovered from their disorder (defined as the absence of clinically relevant symptoms for at least five years). Another 30 percent showed some improvement, although they still experienced clinical symptoms. Similar data have been reported from a more recent five-year followup study with people who had been treated on an outpatient basis. These investigators found that 20 percent of their patients had recovered completely and another 50 percent showed partial remission of their OCD symptoms (Steketee et al., 1999). Both studies reported that approximately 20 percent of their OCD patients were either unchanged or had deteriorated at the time of followup.

Karen was in many ways a typical OCD patient. She had, in fact, been raised in a strict, puritanical family setting. As a child, she was generally anxious and quite concerned with order and rituals. Since midadolescence, Karen had experienced difficulty with intrusive, repetitive ideas that she found distressing. These problems would come and go without apparent reason. She was also prone to serious depression. Karen's family background is also consistent with the literature on OCD (e.g., Pauls et al., 1995). There is a relatively high incidence of psychiatric anomalies— particularly obsessional traits, anxious personalities, and mood disturbances— among the biological relatives of obsessive compulsive patients.

The similarity in behavior between many obsessive compulsive patients and their parents probably reflects the influence of both genetic and environmental variables (Hudziak et al., 2004; Wolff, Alsobrook, & Pauls, 2000). In Karen's case, her mother's rigid, moralistic behavior may have had an important influence on the development of later symptoms. Karen's mother provided a salient model for her daughter's subsequent compulsive behavior. She also reinforced early tendencies toward such response patterns.

Theoretical Perspectives and Treatment Implications

According to traditional psychoanalytic theory, compulsive symptoms are the product of the ego's unconscious attempt to fend off anxiety associated with hostile impulses. Freud (1909, 1925) argued that compulsive patients had experienced overly harsh toilet training and were therefore fixated in the anal-sadistic stage of development. Such individuals presumably suffer serious conflict over the expression of anger. Since these feelings are dangerous, or unacceptable to the ego, the anticipation of their expression is seen as anxiety provoking. This anxiety is dealt with primarily through the defense mechanism known as *reaction formation*, in which the original impulse (anger) is transformed into its antithesis (love or oversolicitude). This conceptual approach is not incompatible with Karen's situation. Her principal symptoms were compulsive rituals that were intended to protect her children from harm. But her feelings about her children were, in fact, ambivalent. It would not be unreasonable to assume that she was most often very angry with them, perhaps to the point that she might have considered doing them physical harm. Of course, this impulse would be anxiety provoking to the ego, which would convert it to its opposite form. Thus, instead of injuring the children, she would spend a good deal of her time every day performing irrational responses aimed at *protecting* them.

Most contemporary therapists agree that people with OCD have trouble expressing anger (Osborn, 1998). Some recognition was given to these considerations in the treatment that was employed. Karen's anger and frustration were identified as central features of her adjustment problems, but the therapeutic procedures went beyond the goal of insight-oriented treatment. Karen's recognition of her anger and hostility was not sufficient to effect change; specific training procedures were used to help her develop more adaptive responses.

Learning theorists would view Karen's problems in a distinctly different fashion. Within this general model, two factors would be given primary consideration. Both involve the principle of *negative reinforcement,*[2] which states that the probability of a response is increased if it leads to the termination of an aversive stimulus. Consider, for example, the net effect of Karen's rituals. Their performance ensured that she would be away from her home for extended periods of time. If she went to her neighbor's house for coffee, she would be gone for at least two hours before she could consume enough cups and smoke enough cigarettes to satisfy the rituals. Grocery shopping, which she did by herself, had also turned into a long, complicated process. Given that being at home with her family was mostly an aversive experience for Karen, her rituals might be seen as an operant response that was being maintained by negative reinforcement.[3]

A behavioral clinician would be most likely to point to the anxiety reduction associated with the performance of the rituals. Whenever Karen was engaged in an activity that reminded her of numbers and, consequently, her children, she became

---

[2] Negative reinforcement should be distinguished from punishment, in which the *appearance* of an aversive stimulus is made contingent on the emission of a response, so the probability of the response is therefore *reduced*.

[3] This phenomenon would be labeled *secondary gain* by a psychoanalyst, who would give primary emphasis to the ego-defensive nature of the symptom.

anxious. She was able to neutralize this anxiety temporarily by counting the appropriate number of boxes, and so on. This ritual was therefore reinforced and maintained by the reduction of anxiety. This notion is similar to the psychoanalytic view in that the symptom is produced as a means of reducing tension. The two theories differ in that the behavioral view does not see her anxiety as being directly attributable to the unconscious urge to harm her children, nor does the behavioral view hold that the anxiety reduction is mediated by an unconsciously activated defense mechanism.

Some elements of the behavioral view were incorporated into the treatment procedure followed with Karen. In particular, by teaching her to be more assertive and to manage her children more effectively, the therapist was able to make her home life less aversive. She now experienced more pleasurable interactions with her children and her husband, and one important source of negative reinforcement for her rituals was removed. Unfortunately, this view of human behavior is fairly limited. In particular, it does not account for the importance of cognitive events. By focusing exclusively on environmental events, behaviorists may ignore important factors associated with the client's perceptions, beliefs, and attitudes. These variables also seemed to play an important role in Karen's problem.

Cognitive theories regarding the etiology of OCD emphasize the importance of excessive feelings of responsibility and guilt (Rachman, 2002; Salkovskis & Forrester, 2002). This viewpoint begins with the recognition that most normal people experience intrusive thoughts from time to time, especially when they have been exposed to stress or negative mood states. Most intrusive thoughts do not become persistent or troublesome because people do not assign special meaning to them. According to the cognitive model, obsessions may develop if people interpret their intrusive thoughts as proof that they will be responsible for harm (to themselves or others) if they do not do something immediately to correct the thought. People most likely to develop OCD may be those who (1) learned a broad sense of responsibility and high level of conscientiousness at an early age, (2) were exposed to rigid and extreme codes of conduct and duty (e.g., have learned that some thoughts are particularly dangerous or unacceptable), and (3) experienced a critical incident in which their action (or inaction) or their thoughts seemed to be connected to a harmful incident that affected them or someone else. Alarmed by the intrusive appearance of forbidden thoughts, the person may struggle to avoid them, but cognitive events are difficult to control. In fact, active attempts at thought suppression often backfire and increase the severity of the problem (Wegner, 1994). This vicious negative feedback loop magnifies feelings of helplessness and loss of control and also serves to focus attention on the content of unwanted thoughts. The person's anxiety level continues to escalate, and compulsive rituals are employed in an attempt to regain control over mental events as well as life experiences.

The relevance of this perspective to Karen's case is clear. She had experienced frequent intrusive thoughts related to her children's safety, and she did believe that a failure to act in response to these thoughts would result in harm coming to her children. As a child, Karen had been taught that certain thoughts and ideas were bad and that strict observation of the rituals of the church would guarantee her salvation and prevent harm from coming to her. These rituals became the primary means for controlling her fate and ensuring her safety. As an adult, Karen found herself stripped of these control mechanisms. The church now maintained that salvation (or the protection of one's soul) depended more on faith than on the performance of specific overt behaviors. When Karen experienced the critical incident in which her friend's infant daughter was injured, and she began to experience intrusive thoughts about harming herself, she turned to the use of private prayers in an attempt to protect herself. In some ways, Karen's subsequent development of counting rituals represented a substitute for the formal religious practices she had learned as a child. She admitted that they were irrational and probably unnecessary, but they did reduce her immediate anxiety in much the same way that going to church had left her with a comforting feeling as a child.

Karen's treatment addressed various cognitive factors, including efforts to improve her sense of self-control. Treatment was aimed initially at reducing the level of stress, improving Karen's mood, and giving her alternative means of controlling her environment, such as assertion training and instruction in parenting skills. Considering her deeply ingrained religious beliefs, it was also judged necessary to help her reestablish contact with the church. After these procedures had achieved some modest success, it was possible to attack the counting rituals directly through the use of exposure and response prevention. A cognitive therapist would view the process of exposure and response prevention as a kind of "behavioral experiment" in which the person is given an opportunity to disconfirm her exaggerated beliefs about responsibility (i.e., "if I do not count the cereal boxes, something bad will happen to my children").

An extensive body of evidence indicates that behavior therapy is effective in treating compulsive disorders (Abramowitz, Brigidi, & Roche, 2001; Franklin et al., 2000). The most useful procedure seems to be in vivo (i.e., in the natural environment) exposure coupled with response prevention (ERP). Studies that have compared ERP with control treatments, such as applied relaxation, have found that patients who receive ERP (typically between 15 and 20 sessions) are more likely to experience substantial improvement. There are, of course, some patients who refuse to enter or who drop out of behavioral treatment, perhaps because it is initially anxiety provoking. But among those who do complete ERP, approximately 80 percent have been classified as improved, and most OCD patients maintain these improvements several months after the end of treatment (Stanley & Turner, 1995).

Cognitive therapy is another psychological approach to the treatment of OCD (Salkovskis, 1999). It is concerned primarily with the meanings that a person assigns to intrusive thoughts, images, and impulses. Symptoms of OCD are presumably more likely to occur if the person interprets the thoughts as an unquestionable sign that he or she is responsible for either causing or preventing harm that might come to oneself or other people. Cognitive therapy helps the person develop and use different interpretations of intrusive thoughts that do not require or motivate the person to continue to engage in compulsive rituals which are clearly ineffective and self-defeating. Treatment outcome studies report that this type of cognitive therapy can be an effective form of treatment for people with OCD (McLean et al., 2001).

Medication is also beneficial for many patients. Clomipramine (Anafranil®) has relatively specific effects in reducing OCD symptoms; its therapeutic effects cannot be attributed solely to a reduction in comorbid depressive symptoms (Abramowitz, 1997). Sustained improvement depends on continued use of the drug. Most patients experience a return of OCD symptoms within four weeks after they stop taking medication. The newer generation of antidepressant drugs known as selective serotonin reuptake inhibitors (SSRIs), including fluoxetine (Prozac®), fluvoxamine (Luvox®), and sertraline (Zoloft®), has also been used with OCD patients. Controlled studies indicate that these drugs are also effective in the treatment of OCD (Hollander & Allen, 2001). The SSRIs are often preferred to other forms of medication because they have fewer side effects.

Several issues will need to be addressed in future studies of treatment outcome. Direct comparisons of medication and ERP have not been reported. It is not clear whether one form of treatment is, in general, more effective than the other. And, perhaps more importantly, it is not currently possible to predict whether a particular patient will respond better to ERP or to medication. In actual clinical practice, medication is often used in combination with behavioral therapy for the treatment of OCD. Two studies have reported that the combination is more beneficial than either treatment alone, but this conclusion must be considered tentative in the absence of better data (Eddy, Dutra, Bradley, & Westen, 2004).

When both psychotherapy and medication fail, one other form of treatment may be considered: neurosurgery, which refers to techniques in which neural pathways in the brain are surgically altered in an effort to change the person's behavior. Although neurosurgery was originally intended to be used with psychotic patients, clinical research indicates that it may be most effective with obsessive compulsive disorder (see Jenike, 1998; Mathew et al., 1999). One longitudinal study described 26 patients who had received neurosurgery after failing to respond to all other forms of treatment. In comparison to similar OCD patients who had not received surgery, 10 of the 26 patients were obviously improved several years after the procedure was performed. Six others showed mild improvement, six were unchanged, and four had gotten worse (Hay et al., 1993). Since the duration of illness prior to surgery was several years for all of the patients in this study, the reported rates of improvement are probably not due to placebo effects or spontaneous remission.

These results cannot be ignored, but they should also be interpreted with considerable caution. First, it is virtually impossible to conduct a double-blind[4] evaluation of neurosurgery. Second, surgical procedures have varied widely across studies, thus making general statements about neurosurgery questionable. Third, and perhaps most important, neurosurgery may produce general changes in the patient's intellectual and emotional capacities. These changes remain unpredictable and poorly understood. Thus, most investigators agree that such radical procedures should be considered only when the patient's symptoms are chronic and severely disturbing and when other treatment programs have already been unsuccessful.

---

[4] A double-blind procedure is used to reduce the biasing effects of the expectations of the patient and the therapist. In drug studies, patients and therapists can be kept "blind" to the patient's treatment status by assigning some patients to a placebo control group.

CHAPTER 2

Panic Disorder with Agoraphobia

Dennis Holt was 31 years old, divorced, and a successful insurance salesman. He had experienced panic attacks on several occasions during the past 10 years, but he did not seek psychological treatment until shortly after the last incident. It happened while Dennis and his fiancée, Elaine, were doing their Christmas shopping at a local mall. Their first stop was a large department store where Elaine hoped to find a present for her mother. Dennis was in a good mood when they arrived at the store. Although he was usually uneasy in large crowds of people, he was also caught up in the holiday spirit and was looking forward to spending the bonus that he had recently received from his company. Ten minutes after they began shopping, Dennis suddenly felt very sick. His hands began to tremble uncontrollably, his vision became blurred, and his body felt weak all over. He experienced a tremendous pressure on his chest and began to gasp for breath, sensing that he was about to smother. These dramatic physical symptoms were accompanied by an overwhelming sensation of apprehension. He was terrified but did not know why. Without saying anything to Elaine, he whirled and dashed from the store, seeking refuge in their car, which was parked outside. Once there, he rolled down the windows to let in more air, lay down on the back seat, and closed his eyes. He continued to feel dizzy and short of breath for about 10 minutes more.

Elaine did not find him for more than an hour because she had been browsing in an adjacent aisle and had not seen him flee from the store. When she noticed that he was gone, she looked for him in other stores before she realized that something was wrong and finally decided to check the car. This was the first panic attack that Dennis had experienced since he and Elaine had begun dating several months previously. After they returned to his apartment, he explained what had happened and his past history of attacks in somewhat greater detail; she persuaded him to seek professional help.

When Dennis arrived at the psychological clinic for his first appointment, he was neatly dressed in an expensive suit. He was five minutes early, so the receptionist asked him if he would like to take a seat in the large, comfortably furnished waiting room where several other clients were sitting. Politely indicating that he would prefer to stand, Dennis leaned casually against the corridor wall. Everything about his physical appearance—his posture, his neatly trimmed hair, his friendly smile—conveyed a sense of confidence and success. Nothing betrayed the real sense of dread with which he had struggled since he had promised Elaine that he would consult a psychologist. Was he, in fact, crazy? He wanted help, but he did not want anyone to think that he was emotionally unstable.

The first interview was not very productive. Dennis cracked jokes with the psychologist and attempted to engage in an endless sequence of witty small talk. In response to the psychologist's persistent queries, Dennis explained that he had promised his fiancée that he would seek some advice about his intermittent panic attacks. Nevertheless, he was reluctant to admit that he had any really serious problems, and he evaded many questions pertaining to his current adjustment. Dennis seemed intent on convincing the psychologist that he did not have a serious psychological problem. He continued to chat on a superficial level and, at one point, even began asking the psychologist whether she had adequate life insurance coverage.

In subsequent sessions it became clear that the panic attacks, which never occurred more than two or three times per year, were simply the most dramatic of Dennis's problems. He was also an extremely tense and anxious person between attacks. He frequently experienced severe headaches that sometimes lasted for several hours. These generally took the form of a steady, diffuse pain across his forehead. Dennis also complained that he could not relax, noting that he suffered from chronic muscle tension and occasional insomnia. His job often required that he work late in the evening, visiting people in their homes after dinner. When he returned to his apartment, he was always "wound up" and on edge, unable to sleep. He had tried various distractions and popular remedies, but nothing had worked.

Dennis was very self-conscious. Although he was an attractive man and one of the most successful salespersons in his firm, he worried constantly about what others thought of him. This concern was obvious in his behavior both before and after sessions at the clinic. At the end of every session, he seemed to make a point of joking loudly so that anyone outside the psychologist's office would hear the laughter. He would then open the door, as he continued to chuckle, and say something like, "Well, Alicia [the therapist's first name], that was a lot of fun. Let's get together again soon!" as he left her office. The most peculiar incident of this sort occurred prior to the fourth treatment session. Dennis had avoided the clinic waiting room on past visits, but this time it happened that he and his therapist met at a location that required them to walk through the waiting room together in order to reach her office. Thinking nothing of it, the therapist set off across the room in which several other clients were waiting, and Dennis quickly followed. When they reached the middle of the long room, Dennis suddenly clasped his right arm around her shoulders, smiled, and in a voice that was slightly too loud said, "Well, Alicia, what's up? How can I help you today?" The therapist was taken completely by surprise but said nothing until they reached her office. Dennis quickly closed the door and leaned against the wall, holding his hand over his heart as he gulped for air. He was visibly shaken. Once he had caught his breath, he apologized profusely and explained that he did not know what had come over him. He said that he had always been afraid that the other people in the clinic, particularly the other clients, would realize that he was a client and therefore think that he was crazy. He had become extremely uncomfortable as they walked across the waiting room and had been unable to resist the urge to divert attention from himself by seeming to be a therapist.

This preoccupation with social evaluation was also evident in Dennis's work. He became extremely tense whenever he was about to call on a prospective client. Between the point at which an appointment was arranged and his arrival at the person's home, Dennis worried constantly. Would he or she like him? Could he make the sale? His anxiety became most exaggerated as he drove his car to the person's home. In an effort to cope with this anxiety, Dennis had constructed a 45-minute recording that he played for himself on the cassette deck in his car. The tape contained a long pep talk, recorded in his own voice, in which he continually reassured and encouraged himself: "Go out there and charm 'em, Dennis. You're the best damn salesman this company's ever had! They're gonna be putty in your hands. Flash that smile, and they'll love you!" and on and on. Unfortunately, the net effect of the recording was probably to increase his tension. Despite this anxiety, he managed to perform effectively in the selling role, just as he was able to project an air of confidence in the clinic. But, on the inside, he was miserable. Every two or three months he would become convinced that he could no longer stand the tension and decide to quit his job. Then he would make a big sale or receive a bonus for exceeding his quota for that period and change his mind.

Social History

Dennis was an only child. His father was an accountant, and his mother was an elementary-school teacher. No one else in his family had been treated for adjustment problems.

Dennis and his mother got along well, but his relationship with his father had always been difficult. His father was a demanding perfectionist who held very high, probably unrealistic, expectations for Dennis. When Dennis was in elementary school, his father always wanted him to be the best athlete and the best student in his class. Although Dennis was adequate in both of these areas, he did not excel in either. His father frequently expressed the hope that Dennis would become an aeronautical engineer when he grew up. Now that Dennis was working as an insurance salesman, his father never missed an opportunity to express his disapproval and disappointment. He was also unhappy about Dennis's previous divorce. When his parents came to visit, Dennis and his father usually ended up in an argument.

Dennis remembered being shy as a child. Nevertheless, he enjoyed the company of other children and always had a number of friends. When he reached adolescence, he was particularly timid around girls. In an effort to overcome his shyness, he joined the high school drama club and played bit parts in several of its productions. This experience provided an easy avenue for meeting other students with whom he became friends. He also learned that he could speak in front of a group of people without making a fool of himself, but he continued to feel uncomfortable in public speaking and social situations.

After graduating from high school, Dennis attended a private liberal arts college for two years. Although he had been a reasonably good student in high school, he began to experience academic problems in college. He attributed his sporadic performance to test anxiety. In his own words, he "choked" on examinations. Shortly after he entered the classroom, the palms of his hands would begin to perspire profusely. Then his breathing would become more rapid and shallow and his mouth would become very dry. On the worst occasions, his mind would go blank.

Some of his instructors were sympathetic to the problem and allowed him to take extra time to finish examinations; others permitted him to turn in supplementary papers that were written out of class. Nevertheless, his grades began to suffer, and by the end of his first year he was placed on academic probation.

During his second year in college, Dennis began to experience gastrointestinal problems. He had always seemed to have a sensitive stomach and avoided rich or fried foods that often led to excessive flatulence or nausea. Now the symptoms were getting worse. He suffered intermittently from constipation, cramping, and diarrhea. He would frequently go for three or four days without having a bowel movement. During these periods, he experienced considerable discomfort and occasional severe cramps in his lower abdominal tract. These problems persisted for several months until, at the urging of his roommate, Dennis finally made an appointment for a complete gastrointestinal examination at the local hospital. The physicians were unable to find any evidence of structural pathology and diagnosed Dennis's problems as "irritable bowel syndrome." They prescribed some medication, but Dennis continued to suffer from intermittent bowel problems.

Dennis had several girlfriends and dated regularly throughout high school and college. During his sophomore year in college, he developed a serious relationship with Mary, who was a freshman at the same school. She and Dennis shared some interests and enjoyed each other's company, so they spent a great deal of time together. At the end of the academic year, Dennis decided that he had had enough of college. He was bored with his classes and tired of the continual pressure from his parents to get better grades. An older friend of his had recently landed a well-paying job with an insurance firm, so Dennis decided that he would complete applications with a number of companies. He was offered a position in sales with a company in a nearby state. Mary decided that she would also drop out of school. She and Dennis began living together; they were married two years later.

Dennis and Mary were reasonably happy for the first three years. He was successful at his job, and she eventually became a licensed realtor. As they were both promoted by their respective firms, they found themselves spending more and more time working and less and less time with each other. Their interests also began to diverge. When Mary had some time off or an evening free, she liked to go out to restaurants and parties. Dennis liked to stay home and watch television.

Dennis's first real panic attack occurred when he was 24 years old. He and Mary were at a dinner theater with three other couples, including Mary's boss and his wife. The evening had been planned for several weeks, in spite of Dennis's repeated objections. He was self-conscious about eating in public and did not care for Mary's colleagues; he had finally agreed to accompany her because it seemed that it would be important for her advancement in the firm. He was also looking forward to seeing the play, which would be performed after the meal was served. As the meal progressed, Dennis began to feel increasingly uncomfortable. He was particularly concerned that he might experience one of his gastrointestinal attacks during dinner and be forced to spend the rest of the evening in the men's restroom. He did not want to have to explain the problem to all of Mary's friends. In an attempt to prevent such an attack, he had taken antispasmodic medication for his stomach and was eating sparingly. Just as everyone else had finished eating dessert, Dennis began to experience a choking sensation in his throat and chest. He could not get his breath, and it seemed certain to him that he was going to faint on the spot. Unable to speak or move, he remained frozen in his seat in utter terror. The others quickly realized that something was wrong, and, assuming that he had choked on some food, Mary began to pound on his back between the shoulder blades. There was now a sharp pain in his chest, and he began to experience heart palpitations. Dennis was finally able to wheeze that he thought he was having a heart attack. Two of the other men helped him up, and a waiter directed them to a lounge in the building where he was able to lie down. In less than 30 minutes, all of the symptoms had passed; Dennis and Mary were able to excuse themselves from the others and drive home.

Dennis was frightened by this experience, but he did not seek medical advice. He was convinced that he was in good physical condition and attributed the attack to something he had eaten or perhaps to an interaction between the food and medication. He did, however, become even more reluctant to go to restaurants with Mary and her friends. Interestingly, he continued to eat business lunches with his own colleagues without apparent discomfort.

The second panic attack occurred about six months later, while Dennis was driving alone in rush-hour traffic. The symptoms were essentially the same: the sudden sensation of smothering, accompanied by an inexplicable, intense fear. Fortunately, Dennis was in the right lane of traffic when the sensation began. He was able to pull his car off the road and lie on the seat until the experience was over.

By this point, Dennis was convinced that he needed medical help. He made an appointment with a specialist in internal medicine who gave him a complete physical examination. There was no evidence of cardiovascular or gastrointestinal pathology. The physician told Dennis that the problem seemed to be with his nerves and gave him a prescription for alprazolam (Xanax®), a high-potency benzodiazepine often used in treating anxiety disorders and insomnia. Dennis took 2 milligrams of Xanax three times per day for four months. It did help him relax and, in combination with his other medication, seemed to improve his gastrointestinal distress. However, he did not like the side effects (such as drowsiness and lightheadedness) or the feeling of being dependent on medication to control his anxiety. He saw the latter as a sign of weakness and eventually discontinued taking the Xanax (decreasing his daily dosage gradually, as recommended by his physician).

Mary asked Dennis for a divorce three years after they were married (two years after his first panic attack). It came as no surprise to Dennis; their relationship had deteriorated considerably. He had become even more reluctant to go out with her in the evening and on weekends, insisting that he needed to stay home and rest his nerves. He was very apprehensive in crowded public places and also careful about where and when he drove his car. He tried to avoid rush-hour traffic. When he did drive in heavy traffic, he always stayed in the right lane, even if it was much slower, so that he could pull off the road if he had an attack. Long bridges made him extremely uncomfortable because they did not afford an opportunity to pull over; he dreaded the possibility of being trapped on a bridge during one of his "spells." These fears did not prevent him from doing his work. He continued to force himself to meet new people, and he drove long distances every day. The most drastic impact was on his social life. These increased restrictions led to greater tension between Dennis and Mary. They had both become more and more irritable and seldom enjoyed being with each other. When she decided that she could no longer stand to live with him, he agreed to the divorce.

After Mary left, Dennis moved to an apartment in which he was still living when he entered treatment five years later. His chronic anxiety, occasional panic attacks, headaches, and gastrointestinal problems persisted relatively unchanged, although they varied in severity. He had a number of friends and managed to see them fairly frequently. He did, however, avoid situations that involved large crowds. He would not, for example, accompany his friends to a professional football game, but he did like to play golf, where he could be out in the fresh air with very few people and lots of open space around him. He met Elaine four years after the divorce. She was slightly older than he and much less active socially than Mary had been. They enjoyed spending quiet evenings watching television and occasionally got together with one or two other couples to play cards. Although they planned to get married, neither Dennis nor Elaine wanted to rush into anything.

Conceptualization and Treatment

When Dennis entered treatment, he expressed a desire to learn how to control his anxiety, particularly when it reached its most excessive proportions in the form of panic attacks. He did not feel comfortable taking medication because he considered it to be an artificial "crutch." He had read about cognitive-behavioral approaches to the treatment of anxiety and was looking for a psychologist with whom he could follow such an approach. He had, in fact, found such a person.

The difficulties that Dennis had experienced over the last several years included a complex blend of generalized anxiety and occasional panic attacks. His therapist viewed Dennis's problems as being the result of an interaction between vulnerability to stress and various cognitive and behavioral responses that exacerbate and maintain high levels of anxiety. Like many other patients with panic disorder, Dennis had experienced his first panic attack during an event that he perceived to be very stressful (the dinner with his wife's boss). After that traumatic experience, he became increasingly afraid of (and tried to avoid) situations in which he might have another attack. This avoidance was maintained, in part, by distorted and unrealistic things that he said to himself about future events and his interactions with other people. For example, Dennis believed that it would be a catastrophe if someone did not like him. He also insisted to himself that he had to be the *best* salesperson in this firm—and, if he was not, then he would be a failure. These maladaptive attitudes had most likely been instilled in Dennis by his father, who had continually emphasized his demand for perfection and whose affection seemed to hinge on its attainment. More useful self-statements would have to be substituted for these maladaptive demands before Dennis would feel more comfortable in social situations, particularly those that involved his work.

The therapist agreed to help Dennis reduce his generalized anxiety as well as to help him to eliminate panic attacks. In Dennis's case, this was particularly important because his panic attacks were relatively infrequent. The reduction in general-ized anxiety would be accomplished by teaching him more appropriate ways of coping with, and thinking about, his environment. Treatment would include applied relaxation training and cognitive restructuring. Once these skills were learned, ther-apy sessions would turn to situational exposure aimed at decreasing Dennis's avoidance of situations in which he feared having another panic attack. The process of discussing this conception of the problem and arriving at a treatment plan was accompanied by an obvious change in Dennis's behavior toward the therapist. He became much less defensive and dropped his annoying, superficial displays of bra-vado, when he realized that the psychologist intended to function as a teacher, not as a judge who would rule on his sanity.

The therapist decided to begin treatment with training in relaxation. Her pur-pose at the outset was not to eliminate the occurrence of any more panic attacks. They were, of course, the most dramatic and perhaps the most difficult of Dennis's problems. But their infrequency also meant that even if Dennis learned to control them, he would not be able to notice any improvement in his adjustment for a long time. Therefore, the therapist's first goal was to select a simpler problem and an area in which Dennis could see rapid improvement, thus enhancing his motivation for further change efforts. The most suitable place to begin, therefore, was his in-ability to relax when he returned to his apartment after work.

Relaxation training was introduced to Dennis as an active coping skill that he could use to control muscular tension. The therapist explained that she would begin by teaching Dennis how to use the procedure in the clinic setting. Dennis would be expected to practice relaxation at home on a daily basis for several weeks. He was cautioned against expecting a sudden change in his anxiety level and was told that, for most people, the development of relaxation skills takes considerable effort.

Relaxation training began during the sixth treatment session. The therapist asked Dennis to stretch out in a comfortable reclining chair and then demonstrated the procedure, which involved the alternate tensing and relaxing of a sequence of muscle groups. The therapist drew Dennis's attention to his pattern of breathing and asked him to take deep, slow breaths. When Dennis was comfortable, the therapist asked him to lift his forearms off the arms of the chair and tighten his hands into fists. He was instructed to hold that position for five seconds, noting the muscle tension, and then let go. This cycle was repeated through a sequence of several other groups of muscles. Throughout this process, the therapist reminded Dennis to breathe slowly and deeply.

Dennis responded positively to relaxation training. He felt awkward and self-conscious at the beginning of the procedure but quickly overcame his apprehension. Although he did not think that he had reached a state of complete relaxation, he did feel much more relaxed than he had when he arrived for the session; he indicated that he was looking forward to practicing the procedure during the coming week. The therapist explained a subjective rating scale that he could use to keep track of his progress. Using a 10-point scale, with 1 being complete relaxation ("similar to the quiet, drifting feeling that you have before you go to sleep") and 10 being maximum tension ("like you feel when you've already had a tough day and a potential client has just decided against buying a policy"), Dennis was asked to keep a record of his subjective level of tension before and after each practice session.

Dennis was faithful in completing his homework assignment. His average self-rating of tension was about 6 or 7 before practice and 3 or 4 at the end of each session. He enjoyed the exercise and was pleased finally to be learning a skill to help him cope with his tension. His outlook was clearly hopeful. The therapist expressed confidence in Dennis's ability to overcome his anxiety and also noted that Dennis's willingness to practice outside of their weekly sessions was a good prognostic sign.

The next three sessions were mostly spent discussing Dennis's progress with his relaxation training. By the end of the first month of training, Dennis was consistently able to reduce his subjective tension to a level of 1 or 2 at the end of each practice session. His only problem arose in trying to use the procedure during periods of very high tension. For example, during the second week of practice, he had tried unsuccessfully to use the exercise to eliminate a severe headache that had developed in the afternoon and persisted throughout the evening. The therapist pointed out that Dennis should not be discouraged because he had not reached a stage of proficiency that would allow him to deal with the most serious levels of stress. She also noted that the object of relaxation was primarily to teach Dennis to be aware of muscular tension before it had progressed to such an advanced level. Relaxation could therefore be seen as a kind of preventive procedure, not as a way of coping with problems like headaches after they became severe.

After Dennis was making satisfactory progress with relaxation, the therapist shifted the focus of their discussions to introduce a process known as *cognitive restructuring*. She began with the observation that emotions, or feelings, are influenced by what people say to themselves. In other words, it is not necessarily the objective situation with which we are confronted, but rather what we tell ourselves about the situation that determines our emotional response. For example, a woman who is fearful when speaking in front of a large group of people is not in physical danger. It is probably what that woman is telling herself about the audience ("They'll all think that I'm stupid," or "I'm sure none of them will like me") that leads to undue levels of anxiety. The therapist explained the general principles behind cognitive restructuring while carefully avoiding specific reference to Dennis's own experience.

Once Dennis understood the assumptions behind cognitive restructuring, the therapist outlined several cognitive distortions that are associated with severe anxiety. One example, called "probability overestimation," refers to the tendency to overestimate the probability that a negative event will occur. Another form of cognitive distortion, called "catastrophic thinking," refers to the tendency to exaggerate the consequences of negative events. People who engage in this type of thinking act as though an imagined event would be completely devastating when, in fact, it would be more accurate to say it would be unpleasant but tolerable.

Dennis was intrigued by these notions and, throughout the discussion, often thought of examples of situations in which other people (such as his former wife, Mary) seemed to be making themselves unhappy by engaging in cognitive distortion. As they talked further, the therapist asked Dennis if he could think of examples in which he engaged in this kind of thinking. Initially, this was difficult. The therapist noted that we are often unaware of the distorted thoughts; they have been so deeply instilled and overlearned that they become automatic. Confronted with an audience, the person with public speaking anxiety does not actually whisper, "I have to be perfect in everything I do, including public speaking, and it is imperative that they all think that I am witty and clever. If they do not, I am a miserable failure." The only subjective experience may be an immediate sensation of overwhelming fear. Nevertheless, that emotional response may be mediated by these self-statements. Furthermore, if that person could learn to think in a less distorted fashion (e.g., "I hope that I will do well and that many of the people will enjoy my talk, but if they do not, it's not the end of the world"), anxiety could be controlled.

These discussions filled the next several sessions. Much of the time was spent taking specific experiences that had been anxiety provoking for Dennis and analyzing the self-statements that might have accompanied his response. Many centered around contacts with clients. The applicability of the cognitive restructuring approach to these situations was particularly evident given the tape recording that he had made to coach himself before appointments. The therapist pointed out that Dennis had been on the right track in this attempt to cope with his anxiety, but many of the statements in the tape created unrealistic expectations that probably exacerbated his problem. Instead of assuring himself that the client would like him because he was the best salesperson in the company, Dennis would have been better able to control his anxiety if he had reduced the demands that he placed on himself and recognized that the success or failure of his career did not depend on the outcome of a single client contact.

Dennis gradually became proficient in noticing the distorted thoughts that led to his anxiety in various situations. At first, he could only dissect these situations in discussions with his therapist. Together, they challenged his catastrophic thoughts and substituted more realistic, evidence-based reasoning. Dennis found it helpful to recognize that the impact of negative events (such as being turned down by a client) would be manageable and short-lived. The goal, of course, was to help him practice this skill until he could employ adaptive self-statements as a coping response before and during stressful experiences. In order to facilitate this process and provide for generalization of these new cognitive responses outside of the therapy sessions, the therapist asked Dennis to begin a diary. Each night, he was to take a few minutes to describe any situation in which he had become particularly anxious during the day. He was instructed to note distorted thoughts that might have been associated with his anxiety as well as complementary self-statements that would have been more appropriate. After keeping this record for four weeks, Dennis noted that he was beginning to feel less anxious in social situations and during sales visits.

The final step in treatment was concerned with Dennis's avoidance of situations that had been previously associated with panic attacks. He had not experienced an attack in the three months since his first visit to the psychologist, probably because he had refused to accompany Elaine to any movies, restaurants, or department stores. He was now able to achieve a state of relaxation quickly and without the aid of the formal tension-relaxation procedure. The therapist therefore decided to begin a program of exposure to feared and avoided situations. This would be accomplished in vivo (i.e., in the natural environment), by having Dennis purposefully enter situations that had previously led to feelings of apprehension and dread and then remain there until he had successfully demonstrated to himself that he would not have a panic attack. At the beginning of treatment, this procedure would have been likely to fail because Dennis did not believe that he could handle such situations. The therapist noted that he had now acquired new skills with which he would be able to cope with whatever anxiety, if any, he might experience.

They intentionally began with a fairly easy situation and arranged for Elaine to accompany Dennis. He indicated that her presence would make him feel less vulnerable. His assignment for the week was to go to a specific department store, during the morning on a weekday when there would not be a large crowd present, and spend 15 minutes browsing in the men's department, which was located just inside the front entrance. When this task had been successfully accomplished, Dennis and the therapist designed a hierarchy of stressful situations to which he would expose himself in sequence and for increasing amounts of time. These began with more simple situations, such as the first one at the men's department, and continued on to those that had previously been most difficult for him. The latter included activities such as attending a play with Elaine and sitting in the middle of a center row (where he did not have easy access to an aisle or exit).

The treatment sessions were terminated after six months. Dennis had made considerable progress during that time. He had successfully mastered all of the situations in the exposure hierarchy and had not experienced a panic attack since the one that provoked his entry into treatment. His general anxiety level was also considerably reduced. He continued to experience occasional tension headaches, particularly after especially busy days, but they were less frequent (perhaps two or three each month) and less severe than they had been in the past. His insomnia had disappeared completely. Whenever he did have trouble sleeping, he would utilize the formal tension-relaxation procedure. In this way, he was able to eliminate muscular tension and simultaneously distract himself from whatever problems he was worrying about. Unfortunately, his gastrointestinal problems remained. He still suffered from intermittent constipation and diarrhea and continued to use medication to relieve these discomforts on an ad hoc basis.

Discussion

Disorders in which anxiety is the most prominent symptom are quite common. During any given year, 17 percent of the people in the United States may suffer from at least one form of anxiety disorder, although only one out of four of these people receives treatment for the problem (Narrow et al., 2002). *DSM-IV-TR* (APA, 2000) recognizes eight disorders that involve anxiety and avoidance:

1. Panic Disorder (with or without Agoraphobia)
2. Agoraphobia without History of Panic Disorder
3. Specific Phobia
4. Social Phobia
5. Obsessive Compulsive Disorder (OCD)
6. Posttraumatic Stress Disorder (PTSD)

7. Acute Stress Disorder

8. Generalized Anxiety Disorder (GAD)

Many people exhibit a mixture of symptoms and meet the criteria for more than one disorder (panic disorder and generalized anxiety disorder, in Dennis's case). Most patients who meet the diagnostic criteria for GAD also qualify for a diagnosis of at least one other type of anxiety disorder or major depression (Barlow, 2002).

The *DSM-IV-TR* (APA, 2000) description and organization of anxiety disorders pay special attention to the presence or absence of panic attacks. These extraordinarily frightening experiences, which seldom last more than a few minutes, are discrete periods of apprehension or fear, accompanied by sensations such as shortness of breath, palpitations, chest pains, choking or smothering sensations, dizziness, perspiring, and trembling or shaking. Some patients, like Dennis, experience only one or two attacks a year, whereas others may have them on a daily basis.

The *DSM-IV-TR* definition of a panic attack includes the following criteria: A discrete period of intense fear or discomfort, in which four (or more) of the following symptoms develop abruptly and reach a peak within 10 minutes:

1. Palpitations, pounding heart, or accelerated heart rate

2. Sweating

3. Trembling or shaking

4. Sensations of shortness of breath or smothering

5. Feeling of choking

6. Chest pain or discomfort

7. Nausea or abdominal distress

8. Feeling dizzy, unsteady, lightheaded, or faint

9. Derealization (feeling of unreality) or depersonalization (being detached from oneself)

10. Fear of losing control or going crazy

11. Fear of dying

12. Paresthesias (numbness or tingling sensations)

13. Chills or hot flushes

The *DSM-IV-TR* criteria for Panic Disorder require that the person experience recurrent, unexpected panic attacks. At least one of these attacks must be followed by a period of at least one month in which the person has worried about having further attacks or else changes his or her behavior as a result of the attacks.

In phobic disorders, the most important element is a persistent, irrational fear of a specific object or situation that the person goes out of his or her way to avoid. *Agoraphobia* is defined as an exaggerated fear of being in situations or places from which escape might be difficult, or in which help, if needed, might be unavailable. It is among the most common and debilitating of the phobic disorders. In severe cases of agoraphobia, the person becomes entirely housebound—unable to venture outside for fear of experiencing intense anxiety. Agoraphobics frequently report fear of becoming physically ill, fainting, having a heart attack, or dying, particularly during a panic attack. These fears increase if the person's access to support (e.g., a companion) or an avenue of escape is blocked or impaired. Most cases of agoraphobia begin with the experience of panic attacks.

In contrast to the circumscribed fears seen in phobic disorders, Generalized Anxiety Disorder (GAD) is characterized by unrealistic and excessive worry and anxiety occurring more days than not for at least six months. The person must exhibit three or more of the following symptoms in association with these worries: restlessness or feeling keyed up or on edge, being easily fatigued, difficulty concentrating, irritability, muscle tension, and sleep disturbance (Ballenger et al., 2001).

Dennis met the criteria for both Panic Disorder with Agoraphobia and GAD. Although his panic attacks were not especially frequent, he was persistently afraid of having another. His behavior met the criteria for agoraphobia in that he was apprehensive about being in public places from which escape might be difficult. He had occasionally forced himself to enter such situations, but the constriction of his social activities had a very negative impact on his life. Dennis's fear was not so severe that he was entirely housebound, but he did avoid public places from which he was afraid he might not be able to escape.

Dennis also met *DSM-IV-TR* criteria for GAD (APA, 2000). His muscle tension was clearly evidenced by his inability to relax, his frequent tension headaches, and the constant fatigue from which he suffered. His irregular bowel movements and diarrhea were further signs of autonomic difficulties. He experienced continual apprehension and frequently had difficulty sleeping.

Data regarding the frequency of specific anxiety disorders in the community have been reported by investigators involved in a large-scale epidemiological study, known as the ECA study, concerned with the distribution of mental disorders in five American cities (Robins & Regier, 1991). Approximately six out of every one hundred people interviewed in a 12-month period reported some form of phobic disorder; some people fit more than one subcategory. Specific phobias were the most common (about 5 percent), followed by agoraphobia (about 3 percent), and social phobias (about 2 percent). Specific phobias and agoraphobia were more common among women than men; gender differences are less pronounced for social phobias. GAD was also relatively common among people in this study, with a 12-month prevalence rate of 4 percent. Panic Disorder, on the other hand, was the least common form of anxiety disorder. Slightly more than 1 percent of the subjects in the ECA study qualified for a diagnosis of Panic Disorder during the 12-month period immediately prior to their interview.

Depression and drug abuse are often associated with anxiety disorders (Goodwin, 2002). At least half of all patients with an anxiety disorder have also experienced an episode of major depression at some point. Alcoholism and barbiturate abuse are common results of attempts to use drugs to cope with chronic tension and generalized anxiety. In fact, some patients become addicted to minor tranquilizers that have been prescribed by physicians. Fortunately, Dennis did not become dependent on the use of medication. Although Xanax did make him feel more relaxed, he resisted its use because it made him feel even less in control of his own emotions.

When people with panic disorder decide to seek treatment, most begin by going to a general medical clinic rather than a mental health facility (Zaubler & Katon, 1998). They are among the heaviest users of medical care. Dennis became convinced that he needed help after having a panic attack while driving in rush-hour traffic. Rather than consulting a psychologist or a psychiatrist, he visited a specialist in internal medicine. This pattern is important for a number of reasons. In order to avoid the use of inappropriate and expensive medical tests and treatments, primary care physicians must be alert to the possibility that many of their patients are suffering from mental disorders, especially anxiety and depression. Identification and effective treatment of problems such as panic disorder can simultaneously minimize the distress experienced by patients and reduce the overall cost of medical services.

Unfortunately, it is sometimes difficult to make the distinction between anxiety disorders and other medical disorders. Patients with panic disorder experience a broad range of medical symptoms, including headaches, cardiovascular problems, and gastrointestinal difficulties (Eaton, et al., 1998). Again, Dennis's experience is consistent with the literature on these points, including his chronic gastrointestinal problems. There is a strong connection between panic disorder and irritable bowel syndrome, which is the most common type of functional gastrointestinal disorder (Mayer et al., 2001).

Etiological Considerations

Several twin studies have found that genetic factors are influential in the transmission of anxiety disorders, especially those that involve the experience of panic attacks (e.g., Hettema, Neale, & Kendler, 2001; van den Heuvel et al., 2000). A somewhat inconsistent picture has emerged with regard to the influence of genetic factors in the etiology of GAD. The data indicate that GAD is somewhat less heritable than other forms of anxiety disorder. Studies of the distribution of various psychological disorders in families also suggest that the etiology of some forms of anxiety and depression may be related. First-degree relatives of patients diagnosed as having both major depression and panic disorder show markedly increased rates of depression, anxiety disorders, and alcoholism in comparison to relatives of normals and those of depressed patients without anxiety disorder. Thus, biological factors appear to be important in the etiology of anxiety disorders, but environmental events are also influential.

Traditional psychological views of anxiety have been based on psychoanalytic and learning theories. Although there are obvious differences between these points of view, both theories treat anxiety as a signal of some expected negative event. Neither draws an important distinction between chronic anxiety and panic attacks. A psychoanalytically-oriented therapist would have viewed Dennis's chronic anxiety as a symptom of unconscious conflict between the ego and previously punished id impulses (Compton, 1992). These impulses are usually presumed to be sexual or aggressive in nature and traceable to early childhood experiences. It might have been argued, for example, that Dennis secretly harbored violent impulses toward his father, who criticized and belittled him. Since he was also afraid of his father (a classic assumption of psychoanalytic theory) and since he would be punished if he harmed his father, these impulses were anxiety provoking and therefore repressed. But when he entered situations in which he might be evaluated by other people, he was reminded of his father's criticism. The hostile impulses then became more intense, and his anxiety would increase proportionately. There was, however, no clear evidence to support this notion. Dennis did not hide his resentment of his father. They argued openly and frequently about every imaginable topic.

The conditioning model would view Dennis's problem as a fear response that had been learned through the association of previously neutral stimuli (e.g., a crowded theater) with a painful or frightening stimulus. Once Dennis had learned to fear particular situations, his avoidance of them would presumably be reinforced by the reduction in anxiety that he experienced after he fled. There are a number of problems with this model (see Mineka & Zinbarg, 1995). One is that very few patients with anxiety disorders can remember having experienced a traumatic event. In Dennis's case, his first panic attack was certainly a terrifying experience, and the fear that he experienced may have become paired with the stimuli that were present when it occurred. This process might explain the maintenance of his desire to avoid crowded public places, but it does not explain the original onset of his intense fear.

Cognitive perspectives on anxiety disorders emphasize the way in which people interpret information from their environment (Roth, Wilhelm, & Pettit, 2005). Maladaptive emotions such as chronic, generalized anxiety are presumably products of self-defeating cognitive schemas. Some people make themselves unnecessarily anxious by interpreting events in a negative fashion. They view the world in a distorted manner that is biased against themselves. The negative thoughts and images that are triggered by environmental events lead to persistent feelings of threat and insecurity.

One cognitive theory of panic disorder was proposed by Clark (e.g., Clark et al., 1997), who argued that panic disorder is caused by catastrophic misinterpretation of bodily sensations. An anxious mood presumably leads to a variety of bodily sensations that accompany negative emotional reactions (changes in heart and respiration rates, dizziness, and so on). This process is accompanied by a narrowing of the person's attention focus and increased awareness of bodily sensations. Next, the person misinterprets the bodily sensation as a catastrophic event.

Consider how this approach might explain one of Dennis's panic attacks. After he had his first attack, Dennis became highly vigilant, watching for the slightest indication that he was having another one. If he became short of breath, for whatever reason, he would interpret the experience as being a sign that he was about to have another attack. This reaction ensured continued operation of the feedback loop, with the misinterpretation enhancing Dennis's sense of threat and so on until the process would spiral out of control. Thus, according to Clark's model, cognitive misinterpretation and biological reactions associated with the perception of threat are both necessary for a panic attack to occur.

Treatment

The therapist who treated Dennis combined the use of relaxation with a cognitive approach to his problems (e.g., Craske & Barlow, 2001). She hypothesized that Dennis's perceptions of social events and the things that he said to himself about these events played an important role in the maintenance of his anxiety. The therapist helped Dennis recognize the general kinds of self-statements that were associated with his anxiety and then modeled more appropriate statements that he would be able to use to cope more effectively with stressful situations. The latter component of the process is particularly important. In addition to helping Dennis gain "insight" into his problem, the therapist taught him specific cognitive skills (adaptive self-statements) that had previously been absent from his repertoire of coping responses. If insight had been sufficient, Dennis would have experienced a decline in his anxiety level as soon as he recognized that he engaged in distorted thinking, but he did not. Positive change was evident only after a prolonged period of practice employing more realistic self-statements, both in and out of therapy sessions.

It should also be noted that the therapist did not rely solely on the cognitive form of intervention. In addition to talking with Dennis about his problem, the therapist helped him learn specific behavioral responses (e.g., applied relaxation) and insisted that he confront various situations in the natural environment. This approach was founded on the realization that although cognitive variables may play an important role in the change process, the most effective treatment programs are performance based. This was clear in Dennis's case. His apprehension in crowded public places was not significantly reduced until he had actually mastered a series of such situations following the exposure procedure.

One version of cognitive-behavioral treatment for panic disorder includes some additional procedures that were not employed in Dennis's case. "Panic control treatment" typically follows a 12-session sequence and incorporates three specific methods (Barlow, 1997). First, *cognitive restructuring* is used to correct the person's erroneous appraisals of physical sensations and to reduce the frequency of catastrophic thinking. Second, *breathing retraining* is used to help the person avoid hyperventilation (a common trigger for panic). Third, *structured exposure to bodily sensations* is employed to reduce the person's sensitivity to cues that have come to be associated with panic attacks (e.g., increased heart and respiration rates). This is accomplished by having the person participate in a series of exercises such as running in place or breathing through a narrow straw. If the person has also developed agoraphobic avoidance, in vivo exposure is also incorporated into the treatment program.

Panic disorder can also be treated with various forms of medication. Selective serotonin reuptake inhibitors (SSRIs), which are widely employed in the treatment of depression, are also used for the treatment of panic disorder (Simon & Pollack, 2000). These drugs include fluoxetine (Prozac®) and fluvoxamine (Luvox®). In comparison to high-potency benzodiazepines such as alprazolam (Xanax®), patients are less likely to become addicted to an SSRI, and they experience fewer problems when the medication is withdrawn. Tricyclic antidepressants, such as imipramine (Tofranil®), are also effective in the treatment of panic disorder. Patients often prefer the SSRIs because they produce fewer side effects than tricyclic antidepressants.

Anxiety disorders are also treated with minor tranquilizers from the class of drugs known as benzodiazepines, which includes alprazolam (Xanax®) and diazepam (Valium®). Dennis had taken Xanax for a few months after his second panic attack. The benzodiazepines reduce many symptoms of anxiety, especially vigilance and subjective somatic sensations, such as increased muscle tension, palpitations, increased perspiration, and gastrointestinal distress. They have relatively less effect on the tendency to worry and ruminate. Some psychiatrists consider alprazolam to be the drug of choice for patients with panic disorder because it leads to more rapid clinical improvement than antidepressant medication and it has fewer side effects. Several placebo-controlled outcome studies indicate that alprazolam is an effective form of treatment for patients with panic disorders (Davidson, 1997).

There are, of course, some side effects associated with the use of benzodiazepines. These include sedation accompanied by mild psychomotor impairment as well as problems in attention and memory. Dennis discontinued taking Xanax because he was bothered by these side effects. The most serious adverse effect of benzodiazepines is their potential for addiction. Approximately 40 percent of people who use benzodiazepines for six months or more will exhibit symptoms of withdrawal if the medication is discontinued (Shaner, 2000).

Controlled outcome studies indicate that cognitive-behavioral procedures and medication are effective forms of treatment for the anxiety disorders. One report compared several forms of intervention for panic disorder patients (Barlow et al., 2000). More than 300 clients were randomly assigned to one of five forms of treatment: cognitive-behavior therapy (CBT); antidepressant medication (imipramine); CBT plus medication; placebo medication; or CBT plus placebo. Clients were treated weekly for three months. Those who improved during this period were then treated once a month for six more months and followed up six months after treatment had been terminated. Medication and CBT were both found to be superior to placebo by the end of treatment. Panic attacks were significantly reduced in both groups. There were no significant differences between CBT alone and medication alone, although more patients dropped out of the medication group because of unpleasant side effects. Overall, the results of this study suggest that cognitive-behavioral procedures and antidepressant medication are effective forms of intervention for patients with panic disorders.

CHAPTER 3

Posttraumatic Stress Disorder: Rape Trauma

Jocelyn Rowley, a 20-year-old single woman, was a sophomore at a midwestern university. She had always been a good student, but her grades had fallen recently and she was having trouble studying. Her academic difficulties, coupled with some problems with relationships and with sleeping, had finally led Jocelyn to see a therapist for the first time. Although she was afraid of being alone, she had no interest in her current friends or boyfriend. She told the therapist that when she was doing everyday things like reading a book, she sometimes was overcome by vivid images of violent events in which she was the victim of a mugging or an assault. These symptoms had begun rather suddenly, and together they made her afraid that she was losing her mind.

Most of Jocelyn's symptoms had begun about two months before she visited the university's counseling service. Since then she had been having nightmares almost every night about unfamiliar men in dark clothing trying to harm her. She was not having trouble falling asleep, but she was trying to stay awake to avoid the nightmares. During the day, if someone walked up behind her and tapped her unexpectedly on the shoulder, she would be extremely startled, to the point that her friends became offended by her reactions. When she was studying, especially if she was reading her English textbook, images of physical brutality would intrude on her thoughts and distract her. She had a great deal of difficulty concentrating on her schoolwork.

Jocelyn also reported problems with interpersonal relationships. She and her boyfriend had argued frequently in recent weeks, even though she could not identify any specific problems in their relationship. "I just get so *angry* at him," she told the therapist. Her boyfriend had complained that she was not emotionally invested in the relationship. He had also accused her of cheating on him, which she denied. These problems were understandably causing her boyfriend to distance himself from her. Unfortunately, his reaction made Jocelyn feel abandoned.

Jocelyn was afraid to walk alone to the library at night. She could not bring herself to ask anyone to walk with her because she didn't know if she could feel safe with anyone. Her inability to study in the library intensified her academic problems. Jocelyn's roommates had begun to complain that she was unusually sensitive to their teasing. They noticed that she cried frequently and at unexpected times.

In the course of the first few therapy sessions, the psychologist asked a number of questions about Jocelyn's life just prior to entering therapy. Because the symptoms had such a rapid onset, the therapist was looking for a specific stressful event that might have caused her symptoms. During these first few sessions, Jocelyn reported that she had begun to feel more and more dissociated from herself. She would catch a glimpse of herself in the mirror and think, "Is that me?" She would walk around in the midwestern winter with no gloves on and be relieved when her hands hurt from the cold, because "at least it's an indication that I'm alive."

After several sessions, Jocelyn mentioned to her therapist that she had been raped by the teaching assistant in her English literature course. The rape occurred two months before she entered therapy. Jocelyn seemed surprised when the therapist was interested in the event, saying "Oh, well, that's already taken care of. It didn't really affect me much at all." The therapist explained that serious trauma such as rape is rarely resolved by itself, especially not quickly. When it became apparent that Jocelyn had not previously reported the rape to anyone else, her therapist strongly advised her to contact the police. She refused, citing a number of reasons ranging from her conviction that no one would believe her (especially two months after the incident) to the fear of facing cross-examination and further humiliation. Without Jocelyn's consent, the therapist could not report the rape because the information she had obtained from her was protected by *confidentiality* (the ethical obligation not to reveal private communications, in this case between psychologist and client).[1]

Jocelyn gradually revealed the story of the rape over the next few sessions. She had needed help writing an English paper, and her T.A. had invited her to his house one night so that he could tutor her. When she arrived at the house, which he shared with several male graduate students, he was busy working. He left her alone in his room to study her English textbook. When he returned, he approached her from behind while she was reading and grabbed her. The T.A. forced her onto his bed and raped her. Jocelyn said that she had not struggled or fought physically because she was terrified and stunned at what was happening to her. She had protested verbally, saying, "No!" and, "Don't do this to me!" several times, but he ignored her earnest objections. She had been afraid to yell loudly because there were only other men in the house, and she was not sure whether or not they would help her.

After the rape, the T.A. walked Jocelyn back to her dorm and warned her not to tell anyone. She agreed at the time, thinking that if she never told anyone what had happened, she could effectively erase the event and prevent it from having a negative effect on her life. She went up to her dorm room and took an hour-long hot shower, trying to scrub away the effects of the rape. While describing these events to the therapist, Jocelyn shook and her voice was breathy. She kept saying, "You believe me, don't you?"

For several days after the rape occurred, Jocelyn believed that she had been able to keep it from affecting her everyday life. The more she tried not to think about it, however, the more times it came to mind. She began to feel stupid and

---

[1] There are some rare exceptions to this ethical principle. State laws require mental health professionals to break confidentiality and report cases of child abuse. Psychologists are also required to report clients who are imminently dangerous to themselves or others.

guilty for having gone to a T.A.'s house in the first place and, because she had not been able to anticipate the rape, Jocelyn wondered whether her own behavior had contributed to the rape: Had she dressed in some way or said something that indicated a sexual invitation to him? She was ashamed that she was not strong enough to have prevented the rape or its negative consequences.

Jocelyn had initially believed that only one aspect of her life changed after the rape; she no longer attended discussion sections for her English course. Unfortunately, several other problems soon became evident. Her exaggerated startle response became more and more of a problem because her friends were puzzled by her intense reactions to their casual, friendly gestures. Frequent nightmares prevented her from getting any real sleep, and she was having trouble functioning academically. She had no further contact with her T.A. unless she saw him while walking across campus. When that happened, she would duck into a doorway to avoid him. She also began to withdraw from relationships with other people, especially her boyfriend. He responded to this retreat by pressuring her sexually. She no longer had any interest in sex and repeatedly rejected his physical advances. All these problems finally made Jocelyn believe that she was losing control of her feelings, and she decided to seek professional help.

Social History

Jocelyn had grown up in a small midwestern town 100 miles away from the university. She was the oldest of three children. Both of her parents were successful in their professional occupations, and they were involved in the community and their children's schools. Jocelyn had attended public schools and was mostly an A student. She was involved in several extracurricular activities. In high school, she had some trouble making friends, both because she was shy and because it was considered "nerdy" to be an A student. It wasn't until she enrolled at the university that she was able to form a relatively large peer group.

Jocelyn's parents were strict about dating and curfews. She had not been interested in attending large parties or drinking when she was in high school. She did have a boyfriend during her junior and senior years. They began dating when they were both 16 years old and became sexually involved a year later. That relationship had ended when they left their hometown to attend different colleges.

Jocelyn recalled that her high school boyfriend had occasionally pressured her into having sex when she thought it was too risky or when she was not interested. She denied having previously been a victim of sexual assault, although one incident that she described did sound abusive to the therapist. When she was about 13 years old, Jocelyn went to a summer music camp to play the trombone, an instrument not usually played by a female. One day after rehearsal, the boys in her section ganged up on her, teasing her that, "girls can't play trombones!" One boy began to wrestle with her, and in the melee placed a finger inside her shorts into her vagina. Jocelyn remembered yelling at him. The boy let her go, and then all the boys ran away. Jocelyn had never viewed that event as being assaultive until she thought about it in reference to being raped.

Jocelyn's adjustment to college had been good; she made several friends, and most of her grades were good. She had never before sought psychological help. Jocelyn felt as if she had the world under control until she was raped by someone she knew.

Conceptualization and Treatment

As Jocelyn began to address her anxiety symptoms, additional problems were caused by other people's reactions to the account of her rape. These difficulties kept the focus of treatment away from her primary anxiety symptoms. After telling her psychologist that she had been raped, Jocelyn began to tell other people in her life, including her boyfriend and her roommates. Her roommates were understandably frightened by what had happened to her, and they tried to divorce themselves from the possibility that it might happen to them. They did this by either accusing her of lying or pointing out differences between them: "I never would have gone to a T.A.'s house," or, "You've slept with more people than me; he must have sensed that," or, "You didn't *look* beat up; you must not have fought back hard enough." The absence of meaningful support from her friends fueled Jocelyn's progressive withdrawal. Her anxiety symptoms became more pronounced, and she also became depressed.

Her boyfriend's unfortunate and self-centered reaction to the description of her rape quickly led to the end of their relationship. He sought help to cope with his own feelings about her rape by talking to some mutual friends. Jocelyn had specifically asked him not to discuss the attack with other people she knew. Jocelyn's general feelings of being out of control of her life were exacerbated by her apparent inability to contain the spread of gossip about her assault. One specific event, which would have been trivial under ordinary circumstances, led to a series of heated exchanges between Jocelyn and her boyfriend. He approached her from behind and playfully put his arms around her. When she jumped and screamed in fright, he tightened his grip, preventing her escape. After arguing about this incident a number of times, they decided not to see each other anymore.

Jocelyn finally approached her English professor and told her that she had been sexually assaulted by the T.A. The professor's reaction progressed from shock to outrage. She recommended that Jocelyn report the attack to the appropriate campus office. Unfortunately, Jocelyn still refused. She was not ready to report her attacker to the university or to press legal charges, in part because she felt that she could not bear being in the same room with him for any reason. The professor did assign Jocelyn to a different T.A. so that she could continue to go to discussions for the class. She also told Jocelyn that she was uncomfortable letting the matter drop. She asked whether Jocelyn would mind if she discussed the situation with the Dean and with campus police. Jocelyn agreed reluctantly, only after the professor promised not to use Jocelyn's name in any of these conversations.

Treatment during this time focused primarily on giving Jocelyn an opportunity to express her considerable anger and frustration about her situation. Jocelyn frequently railed to her therapist against the unfairness of the situation. For example, in order to deal with her fear of walking alone after dark, she was trying to find someone to walk with her. It seemed bitterly ironic, however, that she wanted a friend to protect her from violence from strangers. It was, after all, someone she knew rather well who had raped her.

Jocelyn also felt a great deal of guilt over not having been able to prevent her assault. Perhaps she hadn't fought hard enough. Maybe she had unknowingly flirted with him. Did he assume that she knew he was inviting her to his house for sex? Was she a fool for not having recognized that implicit invitation? She also felt guilty about the effect of her situation on her boyfriend and roommates. Was she responsible for the fact that she had made them fearful and resentful?

In one session, the therapist pointed out that the intrusive images that Jocelyn now experienced while reading her English textbook might result from the fact that she had been reading that textbook when her attacker grabbed her from behind. Jocelyn was relieved to hear this explanation, because she had worried that she really was going crazy. This insight did not immediately diminish the frequency of her intrusive images, however, and she remained frustrated and depressed.

By this time, Jocelyn's nightmares had become increasingly severe. The content of her dreams was more and more obviously rape related. The dream would begin with Jocelyn in a crowded parking lot. Then a shadowy male in dark clothing would approach her, tell her he wanted to rape her, and proceed to attack her. She remembered trying to fight off the attack in her dream, but her limbs felt as if they were in thick glue and her struggles were ineffective. The other people in the parking lot stood watching, clapping and cheering for her assailant. Jocelyn would wake up in the middle of the room, crouched as if awaiting attack. These experiences terrified Jocelyn, and they also frightened her roommates.

The therapist's treatment strategy moved to a focused, cognitive-behavioral intervention that had two main parts. The first part was to address the cognitive processes that prolong a maladaptive view of traumatic events. Specific procedures included self-monitoring of activities, graded task assignments (such as going out alone), and modification of maladaptive thoughts regarding the event (such as guilt and self-blame) (Foa & Rothbaum, 1997). This part of the treatment procedure had actually begun as soon as Jocelyn entered therapy. It was continued in parallel with the second part of the therapy, which is based on prolonged exposure.

In prolonged exposure, the victim reexperiences the original trauma in a safe situation in order to decrease slowly the emotional intensity associated with memory of the event. This step is based on the notion that repeated presentation of an aversive stimulus will lead to habituation (defined as the process by which a person's response to the same stimulus lessens with repeated presentations). Jocelyn had, of course, experienced many fleeting and terrifying images of the rape during the weeks after it happened. This form of "reliving" the traumatic experience is symptomatic of the disorder. It presumably does not lead to improvement in the person's condition because the experiences are too intensely frightening and too short-lived to allow negative emotions to be processed completely. In the therapy, Jocelyn was asked to relive the rape scene in her imagination. She described it aloud to the therapist in the present tense. The therapist helped Jocelyn repeat this sequence many times during each session. The sessions were recorded on audiotape, and Jocelyn was required to listen to the tape at least once every day.

As the end of the semester approached, Jocelyn was able to resume her studies. This was an important sign of improvement. Flunking out of school would have been the ultimate proof that the rape had permanently affected her life, and she struggled not to let that happen. She ended the semester by passing three of her four classes, including English. Therapy was terminated somewhat prematurely after 16 sessions (twice weekly for eight weeks) because the semester was ending and Jocelyn was going home for the summer. The psychologist could not convince her to continue therapy during the summer, although she still suffered from occasional nightmares and other symptoms. Jocelyn refused to see a therapist in the summer because she would have to tell her parents, and she was not ready to do that.

A followup call to Jocelyn when she returned the following spring, after having taken a semester off, revealed that Jocelyn had finally told her parents about the rape. They were much more supportive than Jocelyn had anticipated. She had continued treatment with another therapist, and her symptoms had diminished slowly over time. She now had nightmares only on rare occasions, and they were usually triggered by a specific event, such as viewing a sexually violent movie or when someone physically restrained her in a joking manner. Jocelyn decided not to return to therapy at the university's counseling service, saying that she was tired of being preoccupied by the rape. She believed that it was time for her to concentrate on her studies.

Ten-Year Followup

Jocelyn performed well in school and on the job in the years following her rape. She completed college and then earned her master's degree in Library Science. She enjoyed her work as a librarian at a small college in her hometown. Her social life recovered more slowly. Jocelyn experienced residual symptoms of Posttraumatic Stress Disorder (PTSD) intermittently for several years. She no longer met the formal diagnostic criteria for PTSD, however, because her symptoms were not sufficiently frequent or severe. In the following pages, we describe her experiences during this time.

Jocelyn still suffered from occasional nightmares if she watched a movie or a TV show with a scene containing sexual violence. Rape scenes did not have to be overtly graphic in order to cause a nightmare. In fact, scenes in which a rape was alluded to rather than depicted on screen were just as disturbing to Jocelyn. She tried to avoid movies or TV shows with sexual violence. This decision might be interpreted as avoiding stimuli associated with her rape trauma (a symptom of PTSD). Her avoidance was also the product of Jocelyn's conscious decision not to support the segment of the entertainment industry that profits from depicting such scenes.

Other examples of lingering mild PTSD symptoms included hypervigilance and increased startle response. Jocelyn was hypervigilant in situations that might present a threat to her own safety. For example, when speaking with a male colleague in his office, she was often concerned about the distance to the door and the proximity of assistance if she called for it. Of course, we all protect ourselves by being cautious and alert. But Jocelyn found herself worrying too much about potential threats when none existed. This hypervigilance occasionally intruded on Jocelyn's professional career. It could make her appear unnecessarily suspicious and aloof to her coworkers, especially the men. Jocelyn also continued to be quite jumpy if someone touched her from behind, though the degree of her startle response had diminished greatly since college.

The residual effects of the rape trauma could also be seen in the way that Jocelyn struggled to control her temper, which had become quite volatile. When provoked, the intensity of her *subjective response* was often out of proportion to the situation. Events that would annoy or irritate most people (such as being treated rudely by a boss) would cause her to become enraged. Because she knew that the intensity of her anger was often inappropriate, she almost always suppressed it. Jocelyn was afraid of what might happen if she acted on her feelings. Suppressing her anger interfered with her ability to have discussions or arguments with other people. If Jocelyn was involved in a discussion, she would often concede a point with which she disagreed, in order to avoid "blowing up." She became unnecessarily timid about stating her opinions.

Jocelyn's relationships with men were also affected by the lingering impact of her rape. For a period of time in her early 20s (immediately following the rape), Jocelyn avoided intimate contact with men entirely. She referred to this time as her "celibacy" years. Jocelyn avoided intimacy with men in order to sort through her own feelings about herself, her remaining guilt surrounding her rape, and her feelings about men. Several young men found her attractive during this time (perhaps because she was uninterested in them), but she rejected their overtures. Jocelyn's parents and friends were afraid that surviving the rape had "turned her into a lesbian" because she was not interested in dating men. Perhaps in rebellion against her parents' concerns, Jocelyn joined a women's poetry cooperative and a women's music group which included women of all sexual orientations. She found this community to be warm and supportive. She made several close female friends, but she never felt any sexual attraction to them. This was a difficult time in which Jocelyn forged new friendships and also reestablished relationships with her previous social support network whenever possible.

When Jocelyn eventually began dating again, she seemed to choose relationships that allowed her to avoid emotional intimacy. She pursued men who were inappropriate for her (such as someone who lived a thousand miles away, or someone who was already married). Her affairs were brief and even exciting, but they did not result in significant, long-term relationships. At times, she could not imagine having a meaningful emotional relationship with a partner. Establishing clear consent to have intercourse prior to engaging in any type of sexual foreplay was of ultimate importance to her. Therefore, her sexual relationships tended to be "all or nothing"; she either had intercourse with the man she was dating or did not share any physical intimacy at all. Jocelyn realized later that she probably conducted her relationships in this fashion so that decisions of consent were as unambiguous and unemotional as possible.

Recognition of these ongoing difficulties led Jocelyn to decide to go back into therapy with a local psychologist. She had just met a new boyfriend and seemed to sense something special about this relationship from the beginning. Jocelyn wanted to work on issues involving intimacy, trust, and sexuality, in the hope that progress in these areas would help her to forge a better relationship with her new boyfriend (who did eventually become her husband).

During this therapy, Jocelyn acknowledged that she felt very close to her boyfriend, but she had a great deal of difficulty learning to trust him. She found it hard to believe him when he said that he loved her. They were also having some trouble in their sexual relationship. Many forms of touching, if the touch was not gentle enough, were upsetting to Jocelyn. If her partner accidentally did anything that caused her discomfort during physical intimacy, Jocelyn would think to herself: "This is it. He's been good until now, but now he's going to hurt me." Because of these irrational thoughts, Jocelyn frequently interrupted sexual contact with her boyfriend abruptly. He found these reactions confusing, and their relationship was becoming strained.

Similar distorted thoughts interfered with Jocelyn's ability to have discussions with others, especially men. Part of the problem was being afraid of her own temper. But when Jocelyn got involved in an argument with someone, she often had thoughts like: "What if he hits me?" and "Don't make him mad, you don't know what he might do." She knew that these thoughts were irrational, but she was unable to ignore or fight them.

Jocelyn's therapist used cognitive therapy to address these problems. Her goal was to eliminate the systematic biases in thinking that were responsible for Jocelyn's maladaptive feelings and behavior. She treated Jocelyn's distorted patterns of thinking and her biased conclusions as being "testable hypotheses." She used their therapy sessions as an opportunity to identify, test, and challenge these hypotheses. Several strategies were employed. Her distorted thoughts were either "decatastrophized" (developing "what if" strategies to deal with feared consequences), "reattributed" (considering alternative causes of events), or "redefined" (changing the perspective of the problem so that the person feels some control over it). For example, Jocelyn's reactions to painful stimuli during physical intimacy with her boyfriend were "reattributed" (could your discomfort be the result of something other than his desire to hurt you?). Her fears during normal verbal arguments with men were "decatastrophized" (what is the worst thing that could really happen?).

Therapy also included some elements of *anger management training* (Novaco, 1995). In the initial phase of this process, Jocelyn learned to monitor her own anger and the situations that triggered it. Applied relaxation was employed to help her learn to regulate arousal in situations that were potentially provocative. The same cognitive restructuring procedures that had been used to address her anxiety and fear were now used to help her modify distorted thoughts and misinterpretations of events that sometimes led to inappropriate anger. Finally, the therapist helped her to rehearse assertive communication skills that would allow Jocelyn to express herself clearly in situations that had previously led to withdrawal or the suppression of her true feelings.

Cognitive therapy and anger-management training helped Jocelyn improve her communication skills with others, including her boyfriend, as well as people at work. Her mood was more stable, and she felt better about herself. She also developed a deeper, more meaningful relationship with her boyfriend. They were married soon after the therapy was completed.

The fact that Jocelyn's PTSD symptoms persisted for several years after the rape may seem discouraging. Nevertheless, beyond her subtle relationship problems, the long-term impact of the rape was not devastating. Jocelyn was able to complete school, have a successful career, regain closeness with family and friends, and (with a little additional help in therapy) form an intimate and lasting relationship with a loving partner. She occasionally mourns the loss of her 20s because her relationships were so chaotic, but she also has many important plans and hopes for the future.

Discussion

Rape is an alarmingly frequent problem on college campuses and in other areas of our society (Elliott, Mok, & Briere, 2004). Consider, for example, the results of the National Health and Social Life Survey, the first large-scale examination of sexual behavior in the United States since the Kinsey reports (Laumann, Gagnon, Michael, & Michaels, 1994). In this national probability sample of women between the ages of 18 and 59, 22 percent reported that they had been forced by a man to do something sexually that they did not want to do. Only 4 percent of these coercive sexual acts were committed by a stranger.

Unfortunately, most rapes are never reported to the police. One national survey of rape victims found that only 16 percent had filed an official complaint against their attackers (Kilpatrick et al., 1998). Victims like Jocelyn, whose immediate reactions to the rape included intense fear, helplessness, avoidance, and emotional detachment, may be particularly unlikely to contact legal authorities.

Should other people have reported Jocelyn's rape when they heard about it? Her therapist was clearly prevented from filing a complaint by the ethical principle of confidentiality. If her therapist had reported the rape against Jocelyn's objections, the therapist would have violated her trust and seriously damaged their therapeutic relationship. Her English professor, on the other hand, was not strictly bound by this professional obligation. Policies guiding the behavior of faculty members in this circumstance currently vary from one university to the next and are the topic of heated debate. Some might argue that Jocelyn's professor should have reported the rapist to police or campus administrators, even if it meant acting against Jocelyn's own wishes. One justification would be to protect other students. Other people might believe that Jocelyn's decision not to report the rape should be respected so that she would not feel even more helpless or out of control. Would she be exposed to further danger if charges were filed without her knowledge? What would happen if the rapist tried to retaliate and Jocelyn did not know that he had been confronted by authorities? What action could be taken against him without Jocelyn's direct testimony, and how would his right to due process be protected? These are all difficult questions. We encourage people to seek advice on these matters from local police officials and from sexual assault resource agencies. Just as many state laws now require therapists to break confidentiality to warn potential victims of violence, new regulations may be passed to deal with the plight of rape victims and the need to report this heinous crime.

One frequent outcome of rape is Posttraumatic Stress Disorder (PTSD). PTSD is included in the *Diagnostic and Statistical Manual of Mental Disorders* (*DSM-IV-TR*, (APA, 2000 pp. 467–468) under the general heading of Anxiety Disorders. It is defined by the following criteria:

A. The person has been exposed to a traumatic event in which both of the following were present:

    1. The person experienced, witnessed, or was confronted with an event or events that involved actual or threatened death or serious injury, or a threat to the physical integrity of self or others

    2. The person's response involved intense fear, helplessness, or horror

B. The traumatic event is persistently reexperienced in one (or more) of the following ways:

    1. Recurrent and intrusive distressing recollections of the event, including images, thoughts, or perceptions

    2. Recurrent distressing dreams of the event

    3. Acting or feeling as if the traumatic event were recurring

    4. Intense psychological distress at exposure to cues that symbolize or resemble an aspect of the traumatic event

    5. Physiological reactivity on exposure to cues that symbolize or resemble an aspect of the traumatic event

C. Persistent avoidance of stimuli associated with the trauma and numbing of general responsiveness (not present before the trauma), as indicated by three (or more) of the following:

    1. Efforts to avoid thoughts, feelings, or conversation associated with the trauma

    2. Efforts to avoid activities, places, or people that arouse recollections of the trauma

    3. Inability to recall an important aspect of the trauma

    4. Markedly diminished interest or participation in significant activities

    5. Feeling of detachment or estrangement from others

    6. Restricted range of affect (such as being unable to have loving feelings)

    7. Sense of a foreshortened future (for example, does not expect to have a career, marriage, children, or a normal life span)

D. Persistent symptoms of increased arousal (not present before the trauma), as indicated by two (or more) of the following:

    1. Difficulty falling or staying asleep

    2. Irritability or outbursts of anger

    3. Difficulty concentrating

    4. Hypervigilance

   5.   Exaggerated startle response

E.   Duration of the disturbance is more than one month

F.   The disturbance causes clinically significant distress or impairment in social, occupational, or other important areas of functioning

The rape, and the fear surrounding it, were clearly responsible for provoking the symptoms that Jocelyn experienced. One of the key elements of PTSD is the recurrence or reexperience of stimuli associated with the event. Jocelyn initially experienced this symptom in the form of intrusive, violent images that came to mind whenever she opened her English textbook. Her recurrent nightmares were another symptom linked to reexperiencing the event. Whenever one of these images or dreams occurred, Jocelyn would become extremely fearful and distract herself (escape) as quickly as possible. This type of reexperiencing of the trauma should be distinguished from the procedures used in cognitive-behavioral treatment. The latter is designed to ensure prolonged exposure in the context of a safe and supportive environment, which allows the person's intense emotional response to diminish gradually.

Avoidance of rape-related stimuli has been shown to differentiate rape victims with PTSD from those rape victims who did not develop PTSD. Jocelyn's avoidance was manifested by withdrawal from her friends, her decision against reporting the rape, and perhaps her reluctance to return to therapy for several years. Her feelings of dissociation, such as asking "Is that me?" when looking into the mirror, were another sign of Jocelyn's avoidance.

Jocelyn's increased arousal was consistent with the *DSM-IV-TR* (APA, 2000) description of PTSD. Her exaggerated startle response, irritability in interpersonal relationships, difficulty studying, and sleep disturbance are all signs of the heightened arousal that is associated with this disorder. The length of time that had elapsed since the initial appearance of her symptoms and the obvious impact that these symptoms had on her adjustment also indicate that Jocelyn met the formal diagnostic criteria for PTSD.

The term *Posttraumatic Stress Disorder* was introduced to the formal diagnostic manual with the publication of *DSM-III* in 1980 (APA, 1980). The concept of a severe and maladaptive reaction to a traumatic event was recognized many years earlier, but it was described in different terms. The disorder had been observed among soldiers returning from World War II and was known as Traumatic Neurosis of War in *DSM-I* (APA, 1952). The category was dropped in the next edition of the diagnostic manual, *DSM-II* (APA, 1968), even though the phenomenon had been well documented in combat veterans. *DSM-III* (APA, 1980) returned the concept to the manual and listed it with other types of anxiety disorders. This version of the manual expanded the range of possible stressors from a limited focus on combat experiences to the consideration of any traumatic event that was "outside the range of usual human experience" (*DSM-III*, APA, 1980, p. 247). In other words, people who had been victims of a crime or survivors of a natural disaster might also develop the symptoms of PTSD.

Following the publication of *DSM-III*, clinicians reported that many victims of rape suffered from the symptoms of PTSD. There were problems, however, with the way in which the disorder was described in the diagnostic manual. For example, epidemiological studies indicated that rape was not "outside the range of usual human experience": Rape is *not* an uncommon event. The *DSM-III* (APA, 2000) criteria also put the therapist in the difficult position of having to make a judgment about the expected or usual impact of an environmental event. The authors of *DSM-IV* (APA, 1994) corrected some of these problems when they revised the criteria for PTSD. The traumatic event is now described as one in which the person experienced a threat of death or serious injury and responded with intense fear. This description clearly includes rape as a traumatic event.

The classification of PTSD has been criticized on a number of grounds (McNally, 2003; Resick & Calhoun, 1996). Some scientists suggest that PTSD may not be a mental disorder because it is a reaction to an event that would be distressing for almost anyone. Thus, perhaps PTSD should be separated from anxiety disorders and placed in an etiologically-based category along with other disorders that follow traumatic events. This grouping would include adjustment disorders and enduring personality changes that may follow trauma. This approach is currently used in the *International Classification of Diseases* (*ICD*; World Health Organization, 1990).

Further questions about the classification of PTSD as an anxiety disorder involve the nature of its core symptoms (Feeny, 2000). Some symptoms in PTSD do involve anxiety, such as recurrent, intrusive images, avoidance, hypervigilance, and startle responses. These are similar to the symptoms of Obsessive Compulsive Disorder, Phobic Disorder, and Generalized Anxiety Disorder. But PTSD also shares many symptoms with Dissociative Disorders such as amnesia, fugue, and multiple personality. These include flashbacks, memory impairment, and body dissociation. These classification issues will need to be addressed in future versions of the *DSM*.

It is difficult to estimate the true prevalence of PTSD from epidemiological studies because the disorder is precipitated by traumatic events. These events may be personal, affecting one person at a time, as in the case of rape, but they may also be events that affect a large number of people simultaneously, as in the case of a hurricane. How many people in the general population are exposed to traumatic events that might trigger PTSD? The National Comorbidity Study (NCS) found that 60 percent of men and 51 percent of women reported at least one such traumatic event at some time during their lives (Kessler et al., 1999). Many of these people had been exposed to more than one traumatic event. The most frequently reported traumatic events were witnessing someone being badly injured or killed, being involved in a natural disaster, being involved in a life-threatening accident, and being the victim of an assault or robbery. These alarming numbers indicate that traumatic events are unfortunately a relatively common experience in our society.

The overall rate of PTSD in the general population is higher for women (10 percent) than for men (5 percent) (Kilpatrick & Acierno, 2003). This pattern may be surprising in light of the fact that men are somewhat more likely to be exposed to traumatic events. How can it be explained? The NCS investigators suggest that, in comparison to men, women may be more likely to be exposed to traumatic events that are *psychologically* catastrophic. Rape is one example. Women are much more likely to be raped than men, and the rate of PTSD (for *both* male and female victims) is much higher following rape than following any other type of traumatic event. What are the distinguishing features of rape that account for its devastating impact? In comparison to many other traumatic events, rape involves directed, focused, intentional harm that is associated with the most intimate interpersonal act (Calhoun & Wilson, 2000).

The prevalence rate for symptoms of PTSD is highest immediately after the traumatic event. Most rape victims (95 percent) show symptoms of PTSD within one or two weeks of the crime (although the person cannot technically meet the *DSM-IV-TR* criteria until after the symptoms have been present for at least one month) (Foa, 1997). The rate tapers off over time, with 48 percent of the victims meeting the criteria for PTSD three months after the rape. For many people, PTSD can become a chronic condition. Data from the NCS epidemiological study indicate that at least one out of every three people with PTSD (resulting from various types of trauma) still experiences some symptoms several times a week after 10 years (Kessler et al., 1999). Jocelyn certainly experienced some symptoms of PTSD for many years, even though her overall condition had improved and she no longer met the formal criteria for the disorder.

Etiological Considerations

Not all victims of trauma develop PTSD. What determines whether or not a victim will develop PTSD following a traumatic event? There do not appear to be systematic differences between crime victims who develop PTSD and those who do not in terms of demographic characteristics such as race, employment, education, and income. One common line of investigation is whether or not rape victims who developed PTSD had different premorbid personality characteristics or a different pattern of adjustment that may have contributed to developing PTSD. Some evidence suggests a relationship between precrime depression, the level of stress associated with the crime (e.g., an attack with life threat, actual injury, or completed rape), and the probability of developing of PTSD. If the victim is depressed before the assault, and if the victim is assaulted in a particularly severe manner, then she is more likely to suffer from PTSD following the crime in comparison to victims of lower stress crimes (Ozer & Weiss, 2004).

Cognitive factors may also influence whether a rape victim will develop PTSD. A perceived life threat may be present even in situations that are not overtly violent. In fact, the severity of *perceived* life threat, rather than *actual* life threat, may be the best predictor of whether a person will develop PTSD (Basoglu & Paker, 1995). The person's beliefs about whether she or he can control future events are also important. Victims who perceive (perhaps with justification) that future negative events are uncontrollable are much more likely to have severe PTSD symptoms than those victims who perceive some future control (Basoglu & Mineka, 1992; Kushner, Riggs, Foa, & Miller, 1992). This indication is particularly important when viewed in light of the finding that 41 percent of the women who were raped reported that they expect to be raped again (Koss et al., 1987).

Risk for persistent problems following a traumatic event is also increased by avoidance of emotional feelings and rumination about the traumatic event. Victims who suppress their feelings of anger may have an increased risk of developing PTSD after a rape (Foa & Riggs, 1995). Intense anger may interfere with the modification of the traumatic memory (to make it more congruent with previous feelings of safety). Anger also inhibits fear, so the victim cannot habituate to the fear response. Jocelyn's ongoing problems with the experience of anger may have helped to prolong her other symptoms of PTSD such as nightmares and hyperarousal.

Protective factors such as the person's level of social support may help to prevent or limit the development of PTSD and other psychological consequences of rape (Andrews, Brewin, & Rose, 2003; Keane et al., 1994). Unfortunately, simply having a social support network may not be enough. The tendency of the victim to withdraw and avoid situations is an inherent part of the disorder. This avoidance may mean that victims do not take advantage of social support, even if it is available to them. In Jocelyn's case, the reactions of her friends often led to further problems and made her feel less in control and more alienated from other people. This kind of problem may help to explain why some studies do not find that social support serves as a protective factor.

The moderating effects of social support may also be quite complex. Consider, for example, the evidence regarding traumatic stress responses among survivors of torture (Basoglu et al., 1994). Those victims with extensive social support networks were less likely to be anxious or depressed, but social support did not specifically reduce the frequency or severity of PTSD symptoms. This pattern suggests that the needs of trauma survivors must be addressed broadly. In other words, factors that alleviate some of the more general consequences of exposure to trauma may not have a direct impact on the more focal symptoms of PTSD, such as avoidance and numbing, reexperiencing, and increased arousal.

Attitudes that society holds toward victims of sexual assault are also important in relation to social support (Feldman et al., 1998; Ullman & Filipas, 2001). Some people apparently believe that certain women somehow deserved to be raped. These women undoubtedly receive less social support than other victims. People may also be more supportive after hearing the details of an assault that was clearly nonconsentual—one in which the victim violently fought back when attacked by a stranger—than when the circumstances surrounding the assault were more ambiguous (the woman's protests were verbal and not physical). Myths about rape, especially about acquaintance rape, may decrease the amount of social support received by victims of these crimes.

Jocelyn's case also highlights another frequent consequence of rape trauma. Many victims develop sexual dysfunctions. These problems include decreased motivation for sexual activity, arousal difficulties, and inhibited orgasm (DeSilva, 1999). Their onset is undoubtedly mediated by a complex interaction of emotional responses to the rape, including anxiety, depression, and guilt. They can be exacerbated by interpersonal difficulties with, and lack of support from, sexual partners, as illustrated by Jocelyn's boyfriend at the time of her rape. Sexual difficulties may be an important consideration in planning treatment for some victims of sexual trauma (Barnes, 1995).

Treatment

The most effective forms of treatment for PTSD involve the use of either cognitive-behavior therapy or antidepressant medication, alone or in combination (Ballenger et al., 2000; Yehuda, 2002). The psychological intervention that has been used and tested most extensively is prolonged exposure (Taylor et al., 2003). This procedure starts with initial sessions of information gathering. These are followed by several sessions devoted to reliving the rape scene in the client's imagination. Clients are instructed to relive the assault by imagining it and describing it to the therapist, as many times as possible during the 60-minute sessions. Sessions are tape-recorded, and patients are instructed to listen to the tape at least once a day. Patients are also required to participate in situations outside the therapy sessions that are deemed to be safe but also elicit fear or avoidance responses. An adapted form of this treatment was used in Jocelyn's therapy.

Cognitive therapy is another effective psychological approach to the treatment of PTSD (Tarrier et al., 1999). It can be used on its own or in combination with prolonged exposure. Perceived threat, more than actual threat, is a better predictor of many of the symptoms of PTSD. Cognitive therapy can address maladaptive ways of perceiving events in the person's environment. It can also be used to change unrealistic assumptions and beliefs that lead to negative emotions such as guilt. For example, in Jocelyn's case, her therapist might have used cognitive-therapy procedures to reduce her feelings of guilt about the assault and its consequences (that is, blaming herself for the rape). Cognitive therapy and prolonged exposure are both effective and approximately equal in their effects on reducing symptoms of PTSD (Bradley et al., 2005).

Various types of antidepressant medication are also effective forms of treatment for PTSD (Ballenger et al., 2000). Carefully controlled outcome studies indicate that selective serotonin reuptake inhibitors, such as sertraline (Zoloft®) and paroxetine (Paxil®), lead to a reduction in PTSD symptoms for many patients within a period of six weeks. In actual practice, cognitive-behavior therapy is often combined with the use of medication.

Final Comments

We have used the term *victim* rather than *survivor* to describe a person who experienced a traumatic event. This choice was made primarily because *victim* is the term used in the scientific literature on PTSD. We also want to point out, however, that many rape victims prefer to think of themselves as survivors in order to enhance their sense of control over events in their environments. Further information and resources are also available in Robin Warshaw's book *I Never Called It Rape* (1988). Her descriptions are less technical than this case, and they may provide additional sources of support.

CHAPTER 4

Social Phobia

This patient was seen for training purposes in a graduate therapy class. Personal details have been altered. The therapist saw the patient for one semester for her "panic attacks." The patient was not charged for the sessions, and she readily gave consent, hoping that her treatment record might help others. Because the treatment was focused and time-limited, little information was collected on her past history.

Presenting Clinical Picture

Ling was a 39-year-old mother of two, a second-generation Chinese American living in a large metropolitan area in southern California. A social worker referred her to the training clinic of a clinical psychology Ph.D. program for treatment of her "panic attacks." The social worker, who had been seeing the patient for 10 months, described Ling as a full-time high school drama teacher and part-time actress with episodes of extreme anxiety marked by elevated heart rate, perspiration, and what the patient called "mind-fucking" cognitions. The social worker described the patient as having low self-esteem and a high need for approval.

Conceptualization and Treatment

Before even meeting the patient, the therapist wondered whether her "panic attacks" were cued or uncued and whether they were a part of a panic disorder. Recurrent uncued attacks and worry about having attacks in the future are required for the diagnosis of panic disorder. Exclusive cued attacks most likely are due to a phobia. Initially the therapist set out to determine whether there were any cues or life events that might be triggering her episodes of anxiety.

If the diagnosis was panic disorder, the therapist would teach the patient not to catastrophize internal sensations and to control them with relaxation and other anxiety-reduction techniques. However, if the diagnosis was a phobia, behavioral treatment would identify the environmental triggers of the fear.

In discussing the case with the social worker before treatment, the therapist clarified when the attacks occurred and were most severe. They occurred when Ling was being evaluated or criticized, often during auditions for acting roles, and in dealings with her husband, who was critical of some of her behavior at home. Ling had a long history of sensitivity to criticism, dating back to childhood experiences with her hypercritical mother. The therapist hypothesized that criticism could be an important cue for Ling's episodes, which raised the following questions: Does she react with this extreme anxiety when she perceives she might not do well in auditions? Are there situations not relating to auditions in which she experiences the anxiety? Answers by the social worker and, later in the session, by the patient herself, indicated that criticism, or social evaluation, might be a powerful cue for the extreme bouts of anxiety, and that these high levels of anxiety were being mislabeled as panic attacks by both the social worker and the patient.

Ling readily engaged the therapeutic situation with energy and intelligence. She was an attractive, intelligent, and articulate person who was strongly motivated to work to reduce her "panic attacks." She showed considerable emotional lability in this session as she was tearful one moment, reflective and composed the next. The therapist investigated whether specific situations could in fact be linked to the feelings of intense anxiety. Some excerpts from the first session will illustrate:

Therapist: Are there things that trigger greater or lesser degrees of anxiety? For instance, I understand that you feel anxious during auditions.

Patient: Auditions or any other kind of situation when people might criticize me.

Therapist: Would you describe yourself as sensitive to criticism? Can a negative remark stay with you for hours, even a day or two?

Patient: Definitely. I have always been that way since I was a child. My mother was very critical . . . . I can hear her nagging . . . .

Therapist: Can you recall a recent situation that was very troubling? One in which you were very anxious about criticism?

Patient: Yeah, a few months ago I auditioned for a part in a television commercial. When I got there, I heard that everything had gone wrong that day. There were technical problems and [problems also with] the house they chose for the location. I got very anxious and worried about doing a good job so everyone would feel better. I could feel my heart pounding and my hands were sweating.

The therapist began to discuss with the patient the possibility of viewing her primary problem as what *DSM-IV-TR* (APA, 2000) calls "social phobia," that was specific to social situations involving evaluation or criticism. The patient agreed with the therapist's description of her sensitivity to criticism as "thin-skinned." She reported many childhood experiences with her nagging mother. She also tended to blame herself for anything around her going awry. For example, if technicians at a shoot were unhappy, she would see it as her fault and her responsibility to make things right. Critical—but also neutral—reactions from people to her presence or to her actions were perceived as signs of rejection and even danger.

Ling was certain that the "panics" she experienced never occurred out of the blue, and by the end of the second session she began referring to them as anxiety feelings rather than as panicky feelings. Making links between her anxieties and specific events in her environment relieved her fear that she was losing her mind, a common concern of people who suffer high levels of anxiety that seem to come out of nowhere.   For years Ling had been extremely concerned about pleasing others and very fearful of being criticized by them.

The therapist explained to Ling that her extreme anxiety in response to social evaluation was understandable, given that she was an actress often going to auditions. As the therapist learned in succeeding sessions, auditions and acting in general provide a very thin schedule of positive reinforcement and a very concentrated schedule of punishment. However, both agreed that Ling's anxiety reactions were much greater than the situations warranted and that they were interfering with her performance in the auditions.

Designing an Intervention Based on the Reformulation

Systematic desensitization is an effective form of treatment for anxiety. Ling was a good candidate for systematic desensitization because she had done Hatha Yoga and was proficient at achieving a state of relaxation. Her background as an actor suggested that she would have no trouble in the imaginal role-playing essential in desensitization, where the feared event has to be imagined.

During the second session, the therapist asks Ling to tell more about her fear of the unknown:

Therapist: Does the fear of the unknown have anything to do with not knowing what to do, a fear of harm that might befall you?

Patient: I'm aware of something physiologically that happens to me, the excessive sweating, the adrenaline flowing, and I don't know why that happens. I think it comes down to "they won't like who or what I am." I don't know what any other actors' insides are like, but I can't imagine spending the rest of my life feeling what I have over the past year. I always compare myself to other people. I look around and see that they all seem fine and I'm about to pass out. I am dying inside from the anticipation. One way I judge the appropriateness of how I feel is to see how others are feeling.

Ling had great difficulty expressing her needs and disagreeing with others. The therapist believed that reducing her concern about the opinions of others would increase her assertiveness.[1]

---

[1] Nonassertive patients will say they agree with interpretations and other statements of the therapist when, in fact, they don't. It is helpful to encourage them to express their needs and disagree openly in session. In this therapy we watched for opportunities for the patient to disagree. For example, during the relaxation training, Ling described problems she was occasionally having with at-home practice sessions that did not result in her feeling more relaxed. Also, there were many occasions when she expressed a difference of opinion about the therapist's interpretation of an event. Another sign that the patient was becoming more assertive was a comment in the 12th session when she reported that listening to the desensitization tape the previous week had been "boring" and that she had trouble working with it on a daily basis. The therapist construed her boredom as a positive sign, that the hierarchy items were becoming easier for her to cope with. Ling's openness in discussing her boredom was a sign of her progress in therapy.

At the end of the second session, the therapist asked Ling to write down situations or events where she found herself getting more anxious "than you believe the event warrants." Feelings of anxiety, therefore, were construed for her as useful tools for treatment, signals that would help in the design of a therapy that would target her excessive anxiety in reaction to a range of specific situations.

The therapist asked the patient what she thinks when she becomes anxious, laying the groundwork for a cognitive-therapeutic approach to add to the desensitization. Ling was therefore monitoring external events that triggered excessive anxiety as well as her thoughts while she experienced it. The following exchange illustrates how this self-monitoring assessment was presented to the patient:

Therapist: What someone says or does is the external situation, so write that down [in the coming week as soon as possible after it happens]. But an important part is also what *you* bring to the situation. It's very important and useful to know what the thoughts are when you feel anxious. Start from your anxious feelings and use them as a signal to gather data. Include your "self-statements" or things you say to yourself.

Patient: Subtext. In acting we call it subtext.[2]

The therapist distinguished between useful and maladaptive anxiety so that Ling would not worry that she would "lose her edge" in behaving under the pressure of acting auditions. The goal of the therapy would not be to eliminate her concern about the quality of her performance, leaving her unable to "get up for" an acting challenge, but would be to teach her ways to avoid the debilitatingly high degrees of anxiety that had been preventing her from performing at her best and that had been making her life as an aspiring actress little better than a living hell. The therapist explained that optimal performance occurs with moderate arousal: too little arousal can contribute to a lackadaisical performance while too much can interfere with the expression of the person's talents and skills. This made sense to Ling and helped her adopt a realistic and adaptive view of therapy.

The goal of therapy was reducing her overly high levels of performance anxiety and her sensitivity to criticism. To make maximum use of the limited time, the therapist used a two-pronged approach: systematic rational restructuring, an imagery-based strategy for implementing Beck's cognitive therapy (see Goldfried & Davison, 1976, 1994, Chapter 8); and taped systematic desensitization, an imagery-based method for reducing anxiety (Wolpe, 1958) adapted for audiotaped presentation.

The cognitive component would alter cognitions to lessen Ling's catastrophizing and absolutist attitudes toward acting and other situations in which she could be unfavorably evaluated or criticized. The desensitization component would break the links between anxiety-provoking situations and autonomic reactions that had been classically conditioned to the situations.

---

[2] The patient immediately grasped the importance of a person's ongoing dialogue with herself. The therapist emphasized the connections and similarities between what was going on in their therapy together and what an actor is familiar with and uses to enhance her work.

For the desensitization component, a 19-item anxiety hierarchy representing her anxiety was constructed. The numbers in parentheses represent the patient's rating of the aversiveness of the item on a 100-point scale, 1 indicating no anxiety at all if the situation occurred, and 100 indicating that it would be as anxiety-provoking as imaginable.

> At school, you are having a production meeting for the musical. You've done your work, and other people are reporting being on schedule, too. (15, easiest item)
>
> Arriving for the shooting of the industrial [a training film], you are parking your car on the street near the house where the shoot is going to be. (30)
>
> As you enter the house for the shooting of the industrial, the casting director asks you who you are. You tell her who you are. (40)
>
> At home, you are putting on your makeup as you get ready to leave for the production company audition. (48)
>
> You've just arrived at the production company audition, and you're scoping out the competition. (59)
>
> You're walking down a long hall in heels on your way to the production company audition room. (62)
>
> At the reading for the play, you're a few beats late with your first entrance. (65)
>
> At the industrial shoot, the director is yelling at you to get together with the continuity director and clean up the dialogue. (68)
>
> You're sitting around your dining room table with Kathy, Marion, and your daughter. You, Marion, and your daughter are smoking. Your husband comes in, quickly turns on his heel, goes into the kitchen, and slams the cabinet door shut after getting a glass to show his displeasure. (80)
>
> At the reading for the play, you're making an entrance and realize that you didn't turn the page and you now have to find your place in the script. (92)
>
> At the industrial shoot, you're working with the continuity director to clean up the dialogue, and she is having you repeat each sentence often until you get it correct. (95, most difficult item)

The cognitive intervention focused on Ling learning to decatastrophize negative events and on internal monologues and assumptions that reflect an overly demanding, perfectionistic attitude toward herself and the environment. The desensitization component entailed instructing the patient to relax away even the slightest degree of tension elicited by an aversive image. The cognitive component involved first providing the patient with, and then later encouraging her to develop on her own, self-statements that reflected a less demanding, less absolutistic view of her interactions with others. For example, to deal with the item, "You're calling your friend Jane to borrow an outfit for the production company audition," the therapist asked her to cope cognitively with the tension by saying silently to herself, "While it would be nice for the outfit to be great and for the audition to go well, it's not a catastrophe if things don't go perfectly." The patient imagined each item twice, the first time using relaxation to lessen her anxiety, the second time using a coping self-statement to control her tensions.

This combined treatment was designed to give her *choice*. We proposed to her that one of the most frightening consequences of being so sensitive to negative evaluation—especially when one's life is full of such challenges, as hers was because of her acting—was that she felt tugged at by external events. Learning ways to cope with such anxiety should lessen her feelings of helplessness. Another feature of the cognitive therapy is that the patient can learn to choose to *construe* the world in a particular way, thereby increasing the range of choices she might have. Ling began to cry during this discussion of choice during the fourth session because she felt hope that she could achieve more freedom in her emotional life.

A number of events took place during the therapy that indicated that our view of the patient's problems and the intervention based on it were proving useful. In the fourth session, when she came in with a report of an audition that week having gone well because she had tried not to "beat up on myself" as she usually did when things were not going as well as they "should." She found herself realizing that she would be unlikely to get the part because she looked too young for it. She thought as well that her Asian American ethnicity might make her less attractive to the producers than a European American actress. With this pressure removed, she was able to relax and ended up auditioning very well. This experience, unplanned by the therapist, showed Ling how helpful it was to use self-talk and not to pressure herself with feelings that she should or must perform in a certain way. It also showed that she would respond well to therapy using a cognitive approach.

Ling was better and better able to refrain from demanding perfection of herself, and this made practicing relaxation with audiotapes easier. She reported in the seventh session that she was able to not worry about how well she was doing with the practice and was able to see it as less of a challenge to be perfect and more as something to enjoy, focusing on the process and not the desired outcome.

In the ninth session, she reported a good audition and attributed it to two factors: She knew beforehand that she had the part, and she saw that it was someone else's role that was to be decided on during the audition, not hers. During the 13th session, she recounted being able to deal with some stressors in a less agitated way than usual and made the following comment:

Patient: The good side of all this [dealing with stressful situations] is that I feel so good about situations that come up that before would have made me very nervous and very anxious that haven't. I've had very quick clarity on the ability to put it into perspective and judge what my role is . . . . I'm not getting emotional and I know I couldn't have done that last year . . . . I was at a party where everyone was singing. One of the songs was an audition song of mine and everyone stopped singing because I was singing so well. When they stopped, I could feel my anxiety just go right up, but I was able to continue singing and bring it down again.

In the 15th session, Ling commented that the hierarchy items she had worked with the preceding week seemed "silly" to get upset by. These were items that she had earlier ranked as moderately anxiety provoking. In the second to last session,

Ling said she was on her way to an audition and was, to her pleasure, looking forward to it as an occasion to apply her newly learned relaxation and cognitive restructuring skills.

While the time-limited therapy focused on her anxiety, other themes were discussed during the 17 sessions. Each could have been relevant to the anxiety episodes. One was problems the patient and her husband were having with the one of Ling's daughters, a 17-year-old suffering from an eating disorder, which added to Ling's stress. Also a source of concern was conflicts with her husband, centered on his overbearing attitude toward family finances. Coupled with this was a lack of assertiveness in the patient, something she herself traced to her traditional Chinese upbringing, constraints, and limitations that she chafed under as a coequal breadwinner in the marriage. These issues would typically have been a focus in the treatment but were entrusted to the social worker in her continuation of therapy.

The last session took place five months after the initial consultation and included the social worker in a review of the course of the treatment. The social worker confirmed that Ling's general anxiety level had decreased and that her ability to deal with stressful situations had improved greatly. The audition that Ling had gone to immediately following the preceding session, along with a second one that week, had both gone very well. As she put it: "I just nailed both those auditions. I feel the anxiety creeping up and I use it for the auditions. It's just not unmanageable."

At this wrap-up, the therapist encouraged Ling to practice with the relaxation tapes about once a week and also with the last couple of desensitization tapes (which dealt with the most difficult hierarchy items) in order to keep these newly acquired cognitive skills fresh and available to apply to the stressors that are a part of everyone's life. "It's like staying in good physical condition . . . . It takes repetition and drill," the therapist observed. Ling would begin seeing her social worker once again to work on her marital stress, and a two-month followup session was scheduled.

Followup

Two months later, Ling was continuing to have good auditions and was even getting some paid acting jobs. She commented jokingly that on one voice-over she was doing, she was feeling so relaxed that the director told her to "put more of an edge on it." Her home situation continued to pose major challenges—her daughter's bulimia and ongoing conflicts with her husband—but she expressed confidence that, with the continuing help of her social worker, she would be able to cope adequately. In general, she saw herself as less of a pawn and more of an assertive person with legitimate rights and the means to achieve them.

During a second followup session seven months after completion of the therapy, improvements were intact. Ling was continuing to audition and to get jobs, and was planning to leave her teaching job in order to focus more on her acting career. She described her marriage in very positive terms and was having less frequent sessions with the social worker. At the end of the session, she was reminded that slip-ups were inevitable and that she would be well advised to see them as temporary and a part of normal daily life.

A letter 18 months later and a phone call two years after that, or about three years after termination, confirmed that things continued to be going well. She asserted that her social evaluative anxiety was gone. This had given her, she said, a sense of self-empowerment that was having generalized positive effects in her life.

Discussion

This case study illustrates how a presenting complaint of panic attacks was reformulated into a theme of social evaluative anxiety or social phobia. This construction of the patient's problem led to a two-pronged approach: systematic desensitization and rational-emotive behavior therapy, combined in an imaginal therapeutic procedure done mostly with audiotapes made over several sessions and used in daily at-home practice by the patient. In this procedure, relaxation and positive self-statements were applied by the patient as ways to ease tension in a range of social evaluative situations, most especially auditions for this part-time actress. As with most people in psychotherapy, this patient had other problems as well, among them a bulimic daughter, problems of nonassertiveness, and a marriage that showed some signs of strain. These issues improved with the anxiety-reduction procedure as much as did the social phobia that was the target for intervention. Treatment gains were being maintained even after almost three years and the patient was succeeding in coping well with life's inevitable stressors.

Social Phobia

Social phobia is defined as a persistent, irrational fear generally linked to the presence of other people (Turk, Heimberg, & Hope, 2001). It is sometimes referred to as social anxiety disorder, since many people with these sensitivities do not avoid social evaluative situations, because either they have no choice but to deal with other people or, as in Ling's case, they have compelling reasons to not want to avoid these situations (in her case, she wanted to get acting jobs).

Social phobia can be extremely debilitating. Individuals usually try to avoid particular situations in which they might be evaluated and reveal signs of anxiousness or behave in an embarrassing way. Speaking or performing in public, eating in public, using public lavatories, or virtually any other activity that might be carried out in the presence of others can elicit extreme anxiety. It is not surprising that such a problem would cause particular hardship for a person who, like Ling, works in a field that requires performances that are critically evaluated.

Social phobias can be either generalized or specific, depending on the range of situations that are feared and avoided. People with the generalized type have an earlier age of onset, more comorbidity with other disorders, such as depression, other anxiety disorders, and alcohol abuse, and more severe impairment (Chartier,

Walker, & Stein, 2003; Wittchen, Stein, & Kessler, 1999). In many instances, depression and substance abuse are consequences of the phobia. Depression can often result from the isolation from others caused by the phobia and its effects on self-esteem, and substance abuse can result from efforts to self-medicate the symptoms of anxiety.

Social phobias are fairly common, with a lifetime prevalence of 11 percent in men and 15 percent in women (Kessler et al., 1994; Magee et al., 1996). They have a high comorbidity rate with other disorders and often occur in conjunction with generalized anxiety disorder, specific phobias, panic disorder, avoidant personality disorder, and mood disorders (Chartier et al., 2003; Kessler et al., 1999). In a large epidemiological study using a representative sample, Chartier et al. (2003) found that 52 percent of people that had social phobia during their lifetime had at least one other mental disorder, and 27 percent had three or more mental disorders. Onset is generally during adolescence, when social awareness and interaction with others are particularly important. Such fears are sometimes found in children as well, however. Adults with social phobia sometimes have a history of social phobia during adolescence and problems with anxiety during childhood (Rapee & Spence, 2004). Bögels and Tarrier (2004) call for more research into early onset social phobia and suggest that severe social anxiety may be evident in the first two years of life. As is the case with specific phobias (for example, fear of animals like dogs and snakes), social phobias vary somewhat cross-culturally. For example, in Japan, fear of giving offense to others is very important, whereas in the United States, fear of being negatively evaluated by others is more common.

Etiology of Phobias
Psychoanalytic, behavioral, cognitive, and biological theorists have all proposed explanations for why social phobias, or phobias in general, develop.

Psychoanalytic Theories Freud was the first to attempt to account systematically for the development of phobic behavior. According to Freud, phobias are a defense against the anxiety produced by repressed id impulses. This anxiety is displaced from the feared id impulse to an object or situation that has some symbolic connection to it. These objects or situations—for example, elevators or closed spaces—then become the phobic stimuli. The phobia is the ego's way of warding off a confrontation with the real problem, a repressed childhood conflict.

Behavioral Theories Behavioral theories focus on learning as the way in which phobias are acquired. Several types of learning may be involved.

The main behavioral account of phobias is that such reactions are *learned avoidance responses*. The avoidance-conditioning formulation is based on the two-factor theory (Mowrer, 1947) that phobias develop from two related sets of learning:

1. Via classical conditioning a person can learn to fear a neutral stimulus (the CS, conditioned stimulus) if it is paired with an intrinsically painful or frightening event (the UCS, unconditioned stimulus).

2. The person can learn to reduce this conditioned fear by escaping from or avoiding the CS. This second kind of learning is assumed to be operant conditioning; the response is maintained by its reinforcing consequence of reducing fear (negative reinforcement).

Outside the laboratory, the evidence for the avoidance-conditioning theory is mixed. Some clinical phobias fit the avoidance-conditioning model rather well. A phobia of a specific object or situation has sometimes been reported to have developed after a particularly painful experience with that object. Some people become intensely afraid of heights after a bad fall; others develop a phobia of driving after experiencing a panic attack in their car (Munjack, 1984). Other clinical reports suggest that phobias may develop without a prior frightening experience. Many individuals with severe fears of snakes, germs, airplanes, and heights have had no particularly unpleasant experiences with any of these objects or situations (Ost, 1987).

Some phobias may instead be acquired by modeling, *learned through imitating the reactions of others*. A wide range of behavior, including emotional responses, may be learned by witnessing a model (e.g., Bandura & Rosenthal, 1966).

People tend to fear only certain objects and events, such as spiders, snakes, and heights, but not others, such as lambs (Marks, 1969). Certain neutral stimuli are more likely to become classically conditioned stimuli (*prepared learning*). For example, rats readily learn to associate taste with nausea but not with shock when the two are paired (Chambers & Bernstein, 2003). This biological preparedness may reflect fears that would be adaptive, or advantageous to an organism's survival.

Diathesis-Stress But why do some people who have traumatic experiences not develop enduring fears? The difference is that those who do, focus on and become anxious about the possible occurrence of similar events in the future. Thus, a cognitive diathesis—believing that similar traumatic experiences will occur in the future—may be important in developing a phobia. Another possible psychological diathesis is a history of not being able to control the environment (Mineka & Zinbarg, 1996). Others suggest a combination of biological vulnerability or diathesis (inherited tendency to be anxious and inhibited) and psychological vulnerability or diathesis (early life experiences that lead to a reduced sense of control) combine with a specific environmental stress and result in social phobia (Bitran & Barlow, 2004). Adverse social experiences in childhood, such as being humiliated, criticized, or bullied, may be linked to the development of social phobia, and there is some suggestion that parents of socially phobic adults were more controlling and less warm (Neal & Edelmann, 2003; Rapee & Spence, 2004). People with social phobia are more likely than people with agoraphobia or those with no mental disorders to report childhood experiences where their parents socially isolated them or used shame for discipline. With respect to Ling, it may be that her Asian background and her having had what she described as a hypercritical mother contributed to her social phobia.

Social-Skills Deficits in Social Phobias Inappropriate behavior or a lack of social skills may have a lot to do with the development of social anxiety. According to this view, people with social phobias have not learned how to behave so that they feel comfortable with others, or they repeatedly commit social blunders, are awkward and socially inept, and are often criticized by social companions. A person's lack of social skills may actually *contribute to* the creation of punishing interpersonal situations. Support for this model comes from findings that socially anxious people are indeed rated as being low in social skills (Twentyman & McFall, 1975) and that the timing and placement of their responses in a social interaction, such as saying thank you at the right time, are impaired (Fischetti, Curran, & Wessberg, 1977). While the evidence for social-skills deficits is mixed among adults, it is consistent in indicating that children with social phobia have poorer social skills (Rapee & Spence, 2004).

Note how this social-skills deficit perspective relates to the avoidance-conditioning theory reviewed above. For example, not knowing how to respond politely yet assertively to the demands of another can offend, leading to awkward interpersonal situations and even tense conflicts. Being punished by others can be expected to make a person more fearful of interacting with them. In Ling's case, it is doubtful that social-skills deficits are relevant. When not blocked by debilitating anxiety, Ling was very effective in dealing with others in social situations.

Cognitive Theories   Cognitive views of anxiety focus on how people's thought processes can serve as a diathesis and on how thoughts can maintain a phobia. Anxiety is related to being more likely to attend to negative stimuli, to interpreting ambiguous information as threatening, and to believing that negative events are more likely to occur in the future (Turk et al., 2001). People with social phobia are hypervigilant, or selectively attentive to threat-related rather than neutral stimuli, and have heightened self-focused awareness (Bögels & Mansell, 2004). Socially-phobic individuals are hypervigilant in their visual scanning of faces, particularly angry faces, and are less likely to look directly at the eyes in photographs (Horley, Williams, Gonsalvez, & Gordon, 2004). This gaze aversion may be to signal to others that they do not pose a threat or challenge and thus to avoid retaliation. This cognitive perspective appears to apply well to Ling, who focused on the negative, construed even innocuous situations as fearsome, and expected that if anything could go wrong, it probably would.

Socially-anxious people are more concerned about evaluation than are people who are not socially anxious (Goldfried, Padawer, & Robins, 1984), are more aware of the image they present to others (Bates, Campbell, & Burgess, 1990), and tend to view themselves negatively even when they have actually performed well in a social interaction (Wallace & Alden, 1997). A study by Davison and Zighelboim (1987) provides further evidence for these conclusions. This experiment compared, as they role-played participation in both a neutral situation and one in which they were being sharply criticized, the thoughts of undergraduate volunteers with those of undergraduates referred from the counseling center who were described by their therapists as shy, withdrawn, and socially anxious. The thoughts articulated by the socially-anxious students in both stressful and neutral situations were more negative than were those of the control subjects. Some of the thoughts expressed by socially-anxious students as they imagined being criticized included: "I've been rejected by these people," "There is no place to turn to now," "I think I am boring when I talk to people," "I often think I should not talk at all."

Others have found that people with social phobia engaged in more negative rumination about their performance after giving a speech than did nonanxious people (Abbott & Rapee, 2004). Nonanxious people tended to see their performance in a more positive light over time, and socially-phobic people tended to see their performance in a more negative light. This tendency to ruminate in a negative manner was significantly improved after cognitive-behavioral treatment.

Christensen, Stein, and Means-Christensen (2003) tested two different models to explain why socially-anxious people think they are seen negatively by other people. The first model is that other people actually view them negatively, and that the socially-anxious person accurately perceives the opinions of others. The second model is that they see themselves negatively and expect that other people will, too. They found that although others were able to detect the socially anxious people's anxiety and discomfort in a social setting, they did not view them negatively. Rather, the socially-anxious people had a global negativity, rating themselves more negatively, and therefore expecting that others will do the same, and also viewing others more negatively. So, the data supported the second model.

Predisposing Biological Factors In addition to the psychological diatheses mentioned above, investigators have studied biological diatheses for the development of phobias. Why do some people acquire unrealistic fears when others do not, given similar experiences? After all, the criticism and evaluation to which Ling was subjected as an actress and a wife are probably no worse than what most people experience without developing social phobia. Perhaps those who are adversely affected by stress have a biological malfunction that somehow predisposes them to develop a phobia following a particular stressful event. Research has examined several different areas: brain and autonomic nervous system activity and genetic factors.

People with social phobia have distinctively different patterns of electrophysiological activity in their brains, which suggest hyperarousal, than people with other types of anxiety disorders or than people without any mental disorders (Sachs, Anderer, Dantendorfer, & Saletu, 2004). Neuroimaging studies of brain activity in socially-phobic people have pointed toward the amygdala and basal ganglia as key areas of importance (Talbot, 2004). Hyperarousal in the autonomic nervous system is suggested by the finding that people with social phobia often fear they will blush or sweat heavily in public (sweating and blushing are controlled by the autonomic nervous system). However, most of the evidence does not find that individuals with phobias differ much from controls on various measures of autonomic activity, even when in situations such as public speaking, in which we would have expected to find differences. It may be that *fear* of blushing or sweating is as important as *actual* blushing or sweating. For example, a recent study assessed blushing during three different stress tasks in three groups of people: those with social phobia who reported that they blushed a lot, those with social phobia who did not report excessive blushing, and controls. Participants with social phobia self-reported more blushing during each of the three stress tests, but they actually blushed more than the controls during only one test (watching a videotape of themselves singing a children's song). The people with social phobia who had earlier reported blushing did not actually blush more than the people with social phobia who did not report blushing (Gerlach, Wilhelm, Gruber, & Roth, 2001). Therefore, while autonomic overactivity is relevant to social phobia, the fear of its consequences may be more important.

Genetic factors are being investigated in the cause of social phobia. For both social and specific phobias, prevalence is higher than average in first-degree relatives of patients and twin studies show higher concordance for monozygotic than dizygotic pairs (Hettema, Neale, & Kendler, 2001). In their review, Rapee and Spence (2004) conclude that genetic factors are modest contributors to social phobia and social anxiety.

Inhibition or shyness during childhood may also be important (Kagan, Snidman, Zentner, & Peterson, 1999). Some infants as young as four months become agitated and cry when they are shown toys or other stimuli. This behavior pattern, which may be inherited (Arnold, Zai, & Richter, 2004), may set the stage for the later development of phobias. In one study, for example, inhibited children were more than five times more likely than uninhibited children to develop a phobia later in life (Biederman et al., 1990).

It is important to note that this data does not indicate that only genetic factors are involved. Although close relatives share genes, they also share environments. The fact that a son and his father are both afraid of heights may indicate a genetic component, the son's direct imitation of the father's behavior, or both. It is misleading at times to consider the effects of genes without considering the interplay of genes with particular environments. Certain genes may only result in mental disorders in the presence of certain types of environmental experiences (Arnold et al., 2004). Although there is reason to believe that genetic factors may be involved in the etiology of phobias, it is not yet clear how important they are.

Treatment of Phobias

Psychoanalytic Approaches Psychoanalytic treatments of phobias attempt to uncover the repressed conflicts that are assumed to underlie the extreme fear and avoidance characteristic of these disorders. Because the phobia itself is regarded as symptomatic of underlying conflicts, it is usually not dealt with directly.

The analyst uses psychoanalytic techniques to reduce the repression. During free association, in which the patient says whatever comes to mind without censoring, the analyst listens carefully for any references to the phobia. An orthodox analyst will look for conflicts related to sex or aggression, whereas an interpersonal analyst will encourage patients to examine their generalized fear of other people (Arieti, 1979). People with social phobia often report feelings of shame and guilt, which may relate to an unconscious desire to be in the center of attention and receive positive feedback from others (Gabbard, 1992). However, feelings of shame emerge related to imagined disapproval of parents or parent-figures, and fear of this disapproval fuels the avoidance of social situations. There is support for the effectiveness of interpersonal psychotherapy in treating social phobia (Lipsitz & Markowitz, 1999).

Behavioral Approaches Systematic desensitization was the first major behavioral treatment to be widely used in treating phobias (Wolpe, 1958). The individual with a phobia imagines a series of increasingly frightening scenes while in a state of deep relaxation. Clinical and experimental evidence indicates that this technique is effective in eliminating, or at least reducing, phobias (Barlow, Raffa, & Cohen, 2002). Most contemporary clinical researchers regard in vivo (or actual) exposure as superior to techniques using imagination, but imagery is more readily controlled, and any kind of situation can be constructed for the patient.

Learning social skills can help people with social phobias who may not know how to act in social situations. Some therapists encourage patients to role-play or rehearse interpersonal encounters in small therapy groups (Heimberg & Juster, 1994; Marks, 1995). Several studies document the effectiveness of such an approach (e.g., Heimberg et al., 1998; Turner, Beidel, & Cooley-Quille, 1995). Such practices may also expose the shy person, even when there is no social-skills deficit, to anxiety-provoking cues, such as being observed by others, so that through real-life exposure, extinction of fear takes place (Hope, Heimberg, & Bruch, 1995).

Modeling is another technique that uses exposure to feared situations. In modeling therapy, fearful clients are exposed to filmed or live demonstrations of other people interacting fearlessly with the phobic object, for example, handling snakes or petting dogs. Flooding is a therapeutic technique in which the client is exposed to the source of the phobia at full intensity. The extreme discomfort that is an inevitable part of this procedure has until recently tended to discourage therapists from employing it, except perhaps as a last resort when graduated exposure has not worked.

Behavior therapists who favor operant techniques downplay the importance of the fear and attend instead to the overt avoidance of phobic objects and to the approach behavior that must replace it. They treat approach to the feared situation as any other operant and shape it according to the principle of successive approximations. Real-life exposures to the phobic object are gradually achieved, and the client is rewarded for even minimal successes in moving closer to it.

Cognitive Approaches Cognitive methods—sometimes combined with social-skills training—are useful in treating social phobia. Learning to more accurately appraise people's reactions to them (a frown from my teacher may have less to do with disapproval of me than with something the teacher is preoccupied with that has nothing to do with me) and to rely less on approval from others for maintaining a sense of self-worth (just because I have been criticized does not mean that I am a worthless nonentity) reduces the phobia. With the recognition in recent years that many people with social phobias have adequate social skills but are inhibited by self-defeating thoughts from showing them, there has been increasing emphasis on cognitive approaches (Abbott & Rapee, 2004; Turk et al., 2001).

The effectiveness of cognitive-behavioral treatment in treating social phobia was directly compared to exposure therapy in a study by Hofmann, Moscovitch, Kim, and Taylor (2004). They compared the two types of therapy to a waitlist control group in terms of their ability to reduce the number of negative thoughts reported by participants while they were waiting to engage in a socially stressful situation. They found that both types of therapy reduced negative self-focused thoughts and reduced social anxiety. Some advocate the use of numerous techniques to address different aspects of a particular patient. For example, Feeney (2004) employed a combination of self-monitoring, cognitive restructuring, muscle relaxation, breathing retraining, paradoxical intention, and exposure in her treatment of a woman with social phobia. Huppert, Roth, and Foa (2003) recommend tailoring different components of cognitive-behavioral therapy into individualized programs to address each patient's particular needs.

All the behavioral and cognitive therapies for phobias have the common theme of the need for the patient to begin facing the feared object or situation. We saw this in Ling's case.[3] Thus, all these therapies reflect folk wisdom that tells us that we must face up to what we fear. As an ancient Chinese proverb puts it, "Go straight to the heart of danger, for there you will find safety."

Biological Approaches Researchers are increasingly exploring the use of psychoactive medications in treating phobias. Drugs that reduce anxiety are referred to as sedatives, tranquilizers, or anxiolytics. Barbiturates were initially used to treat anxiety disorders, but are highly addictive. Propanediols and benzodiazepines (e.g., Valium ® and Xanax ®) are widely used today and are effective with some anxiety disorders, although not with phobias. Furthermore, benzodiazepines are addictive and produce a severe withdrawal syndrome (Schweizer, Rickels, Case & Greenblatt, 1990).

In recent years, antidepressants have become popular in treating many of the anxiety disorders, phobias included. Monoamine oxidase (MAO) inhibitors are more effective in treating social phobia than a benzodiazepine (Gelernter et al., 1991), and in another study were as effective as cognitive-behavior therapy at a 12-week follow-up (Heimberg et al., 1998), but can lead to weight gain, insomnia, sexual dysfunction, and hypertension. The selective serotonin reuptake inhibitors (SSRIs), such as fluoxetine (Prozac ®), were also originally developed to treat depression and have shown some promise in reducing both specific and social phobia in double-blind studies (Benjamin, Ben-Zion, Karbofsky, & Dannon, 2000; van Ameringen et al., 2001). The SSRIs are currently considered to be the first-choice medication in the treatment of social phobia (Kuzma & Black, 2004).

Asian Americans and Psychological Intervention

Cultural diversity is important to consider, particularly in very heterogeneous countries, such as the United States and Canada. Despite our increasing understanding of the role of biological factors in mental illness and how to prevent and treat many disorders, social circumstances cannot be ignored. Because of Ling's ethnicity, we close this case study with a consideration of some diversity issues in psychotherapy.

It is generally assumed that patients do better with therapists who are similar to them in cultural and ethnic background. Therapists of similar background and the same gender may better understand the patient's life circumstance and will be better able to build rapport with them. In psychoanalytic terms, similarity between patient and therapist may strengthen the therapeutic alliance.

Extensive research on modeling provides some justification for these assumptions. Participants in studies of learning through observation are found to acquire information more readily from models that are perceived as credible and relevant to them; similarity of age and background are important determinants of credibility

---

[3] Ling engaged in little avoidance behavior. Because of her strong motivation to succeed as an actress and a teacher, she entered situations that she knew would cause her extreme anxiety. Viewing her problems as phobic is appropriate because confronting her demons triggered the kind of anxiety that would have led less motivated people to avoidance.

and relevance (Rosenthal & Bandura, 1978). Yet it has not been demonstrated that better outcomes are achieved when patient and therapist are similar in race or ethnicity (Beutler, Machado, & Neufeldt, 1994). The jury is out on this question. There are certainly many successful cases involving therapists and patients of different ethnic background and different gender, including Ling's case. Research in this area involves making generalizations about the reactions of groups of people to psychotherapy, which runs the risk of oversimplifying or stereotyping people. Nonetheless, ethnic and cultural factors are increasingly being recognized as important.

Because Ling was Chinese American, some general comments on therapy with Asian Americans are offered here. But first it is important to bear in mind that Asians living in the United States and Canada, as well as other parts of the world, comprise more than two dozen distinct subgroups (e.g., Filipino, Chinese, Japanese, Vietnamese) and differ on such dimensions as how well they speak English, whether they immigrated or came as refugees from war or terrorism in their homeland, and how much they identify with their native land (or that of their parents if they were born in the United States) (Yoshioka et al., 1981, as cited in Sue & Sue, 1992). In general, Asian Americans are more ashamed of emotional suffering, more reluctant to seek professional help, and are less assertive than European Americans.

Asian Americans have been stereotyped as being highly educated, wealthy, and emotionally well-adjusted, but in actuality have been the target of severe discrimination (Sue & Sue, 1999). For example, over 100,000 Japanese Americans were imprisoned in concentration camps for several years during World War II without any evidence that they posed a security threat. Recently, discrimination has been more subtle but nonetheless hurtful. For example, after the skating competition between Michelle Kwan and Tara Lipinski in the 1998 Olympics, MSNBC reported "American beats Kwan" (Sue & Sue, 1999, p. 260). The irony, of course, is that while Michelle Kwan's family tree originates in China, Tara Lipinski's originates in eastern Europe. Recall that Ling suspected that her failure to get a particular part might have been due to her race. It is never easy to know such things for certain, but the very fact that the possibility exists—whether in reality or only in the person's mind—is bound to take a psychological toll.

Many suggestions have been made for conducting psychotherapy with Asian Americans. Sue and Sue (1999) advise therapists to be sensitive to the personal losses that many Asian refugees have suffered and, especially in light of the great importance that family connections have for them, to the likelihood that they are very stressed from these losses. Therapists should also be aware that Asian Americans have a tendency to "somaticize"—to experience and to talk about stress in physical terms, such as headaches and fatigue, rather than to view their stress in psychological terms, which they often see as equivalent to being crazy or inferior (Nguyen, 1985). Asian values are also different from the Western values of the majority culture in the United States. For example, Asians are more likely to respect structure and formality in interpersonal relationships, whereas a Western therapist is likely to favor informality and a less authoritarian attitude. Respect for authority may take the form of agreeing readily to what the therapist does and proposes, and perhaps, rather than discussing differences openly, just not showing up for the next session. Psychotherapy as a way to handle stress is less accepted among Asian Americans, who tend to see emotional duress as something to be handled on one's own and through willpower (Kinzie, 1985). Asian Americans may also consider some areas off-limits for discussion with a therapist, such as the nature of the marital relationship and especially sex.

Asian Americans born in the United States are often caught between two cultures. One way to resolve this is to identify vigorously with majority values and denigrate anything Asian, a kind of racial self-hate. This occurs in other ethnic groups that have been discriminated against, like African Americans and Jews. Others, torn by conflicting loyalties, experience rage at a discriminatory Western culture, but at the same time question aspects of their Asian background. Finally, therapists may have to be more directive and active than they otherwise might be, given the preference of many Asian Americans for a structured approach over a reflective one (Atkinson, Maruyama, & Matsui, 1978; Iwamasa, 1993).

Where does Ling fit in here? Like many offspring of immigrants, she had largely acculturated to dominant U.S. culture. It is not clear whether cultural factors or individual personality traits, or a combination of the two, contributed to her symptoms. It could be that, had the therapy not been time-limited and focused on the episodes of anxiety, more would have emerged about the influence of her cultural background on her presenting problems. When therapists remain sensitive to cultural issues, they will be more likely to be effective in treating their patients' problems.

CHAPTER 5

Hypertension in an African American Man

John Williams had been complaining to his wife of dizziness, fatigue, and occasional light-headedness that almost caused him to faint one day at the water cooler in the law office where he worked downtown. His boss had been after him for weeks to see a physician, but John had stubbornly refused and felt angry that his boss was being condescending. He was frightened, though, because he felt something must be wrong.

His first clear knowledge of having hypertension, or high blood pressure, came during a visit to his dentist. Before taking X-rays of his mouth, the dental assistant wound a black blood pressure cuff around John's right arm, pumped it full of air until the blood stopped flowing, and then slowly released the valve, noting when the first and the last sounds of the pulse could be heard through the stethoscope pressed to the vein in his arm beneath the cuff. Alarmed at the reading—165/110—she took the pressure reading again after doing the X-rays and found it to be almost exactly the same. She tried to smile pleasantly and reassuringly, but found this difficult, especially when she noticed John's worried expression.

He did not ask about the blood pressure reading until he was sitting across from the dentist in the consulting room to discuss treatment plans. His dentist asked how he had been feeling lately, whether he had been feeling tired, irritable, or under pressure. John searched his dentist's face for some hint of what was going on, but he already knew that his blood pressure must be much too high. Finally, he just asked for the numbers, thanked the dentist, and went home.

It took him 30 minutes to reach his condominium in the suburbs. As he unlocked the door, he wondered how, or whether, he would raise the issue with his wife. Although he wasn't a physician himself, he knew what the kind of high blood pressure he seemed to have might mean to a 40-year-old like himself, especially someone who was so driven to succeed professionally and financially. Certainly he would have to slow down and perhaps also take some medication. But what else, he wondered.

Social History

John Williams was the only child of an upper-middle-class African American family in Atlanta. His father was a successful attorney, and his mother was a high-school music teacher. Life was sweet in his childhood, and he had many friends.

Although he was raised in a segregated city, he seldom felt excluded from anything important. John was taught during countless dinnertime conversations that there were plenty of opportunities for success; he had superior intelligence, an engaging wit, and a degree of ambition that matched that of his hard-working father.

In high school, John excelled at everything he attempted. A straight-A student, he was also a varsity athlete in three sports, dated the most popular girls, and was senior class president. He graduated from high school during the middle 1950s, well before the Civil Rights Movement. John wanted to leave Georgia for college, and this created anxiety in John's mother and anticipatory pride in his father. Mr. Williams wanted his son to have a college education with "class," as he put it. With the encouragement of his guidance counselor and the urging of his father, John applied to several Ivy League schools. He was accepted at Harvard University.

Years later, John's college roommate Bill confided to him that a month before school started their freshman year, he had received a letter from the housing office indicating that he had been assigned to room with a Negro student, but only if he had no objection. Bill, a Jew from Brooklyn, New York, was outraged at the discrimination and prejudice of this inquiry. Their discussion was the first of many about the pressures on members of ethnic minority groups who tried to succeed in society, especially in the elite circles of a private, selective college.

One night a handwritten invitation to join a fraternity was slipped under John's door. Fraternities at Harvard differed from their Greek-letter counterparts on other campuses in that they were not residential. All undergraduates were affiliated with a house, modeled after the "colleges" of Oxford and Cambridge, in which they lived and took all their meals. The fraternities operated outside the house system and were by invitation only. Some of them bore names of winged and sharp-toothed animals such as bats and wolves, others the more familiar Greek initials. John had felt sure that he would be excluded from these clubs, although he hated even thinking about it. Thinking implied that he cared, and to care about the clubs was to accord them a legitimacy and importance he desperately resisted. As he picked up the engraved envelope, he could feel the blood pound in his ears.

When he looked back on things, this single moment crystallized much of the conflict he felt about his blackness in a white world. John knew he and his race had come far from the days a fair-skinned youngster might hope to "pass" for white. He had grown up proud of the fact that he was African American and felt that whatever barriers there might be in succeeding in a white society could not outweigh his self-respect. But as he lingered over breakfast coffee with Bill the morning the invitation arrived, he felt it was strange that one of the prestigious clubs wanted him as a member. Bill had an uneasy feeling about it all, but he kept it to himself, wondering whether he was just jealous that he had not been invited.

John agonized all day over whether to attend the reception for newly solicited members. He was tempted to call his parents, but what would he tell them, and how? Was there something to celebrate? Would his father smile quietly to himself as he heard the news, confirming his own good judgment in sending his son to one of the bastions of eastern elitism? In the end, John did not call. He feared that his father would either congratulate him on the invitation or chide him for even considering it. No way to win, he told himself. At some level he knew that it was his own conflict he was wrestling with, not his father's reaction.

The day of his initiation, John awoke with a screaming headache. He took three aspirins—a habit he had gotten into since coming to college—and told himself to stop worrying about the party that evening. Perhaps he need not have worried. The welcome he received seemed genuine. And yet he could not shake the feeling that his new "brothers" were being nicer to him than they were to the other initiates, too nice somehow. His wine glass was never empty, always filled by a brother who, it struck John, smiled a bit too ingratiatingly. In fact, it seemed to him that his new friends must have suffered from aching mouths, so broadly did they smile whenever they talked to him. He tried to reassure himself that the cordiality was real, and maybe it was. The problem, he knew, was that he did not really know, nor could he devise a practical way to find out.

His membership in the club turned out to be a boon to his social standing but an emotional disaster. Headaches and feelings of pressure in the brain were more regularly part of his existence than ever before. He hated himself for even being in the club, yet he prided himself on being the only African American member. He was furious at the fact that so few Jews were members and was also suspicious that there were no other African Americans, but he found the young men in the club congenial and enjoyable to spend time with, and he did experience a thrill whenever he donned the club necktie. His friends from the club were certainly no less bright than his other classmates, no less interested in abstract ideas and "deep" conversations over sherry after dinner. But the clubs were by nature exclusionary, and John was coming to realize that he might be seen as the quintessential Uncle Tom. He began to think of himself as the "club nigger."

His anger at himself and at his brothers grew to an intensity that was frightening. To Bill, in whom he confided his doubts, fears, guilt, and rage, there seemed to be no way for John to win. To express his concerns to his club brothers seemed out of the question. But not to do so, at least to one of them, had begun to make the thought of going to the handsome Georgian building for the evening a challenge, almost a dare. He dreaded the possibility of someone making a racist remark. How should he react? He had learned to let it pass, but the muscle tension that mounted in his body told him this was not the best thing for him to do. Once a club member used the word "niggardly," and he felt himself blush. How infantile to react that way, he told himself. And yet, maybe the word was used to taunt him. But how inane to think that. Sure, Uncle Tom, he concluded.

The four years of college passed quickly. As his family and friends expected, John did very well academically and also managed to earn a varsity letter in baseball. He was admitted to a first-rate law school, although John's problem by this time was his uncertainty as to whether he had been admitted solely on his academic merits, or whether the several prestigious schools, like the club, wanted him primarily for his color. And so his internal conflicts continued through law school. By this time, they took the form of John's having to excel to what even his ambitious father regarded to be an unreasonable degree. John just had to prove he was good enough, indeed, that he was the best.

John became engaged to an African American woman from a prominent family, but the joys of the relationship were dulled by his relentless drive for excellence and perfection. One major change was that his problems with hypertension were now impossible to hide. She insisted that he have a complete physical examination, something he had consciously avoided since entering college. The reading was 130/85, something the doctor called "high normal," high enough to cause concern because he was a young man and in very good physical condition. His fiancée was convinced that John's grim pursuit of straight As, law review, and all the rest were the cause. But she did not know the reasons behind his near-obsessive push.

John graduated at the top of his law school class. It was now the middle 1960s, and the developing social turmoil surrounding Vietnam and the Civil Rights Movement affected him deeply. On the one hand, he felt that he should be out protesting, but his studies and his new job at a top law firm took precedence. He tried to assuage his guilt by donating money to civil rights groups, but it did not seem to help. He had cast his lot with the white world, he told himself, and his wife and his own family back in Atlanta supported that decision. Middle- and upper-middle-class professional African Americans had their role to play, his father continually reminded him, and who could better play that role than him? The sense he had that it was, indeed, a *role* turned out to be important in the psychotherapy he began after the alarmingly high blood pressure reading in the dentist's office.

Conceptualization and Treatment

Choosing a therapist is never easy. For John it presented special difficulties. Though he lived near a large city, there were few African American psychiatrists or psychologists. As he had grown accustomed to doing in most other areas of his life, John decided to work with a white person, but was uncertain whether he could relate openly to a European American. His only really close white friend was his old college roommate, Bill, and even then he sometimes held back his thoughts and feelings about race. Would this same problem arise in a therapeutic relationship? In fact, was race even an issue?

"Well, what do you really want out of life?" asked Dr. Shaw, a distinguished and experienced clinical psychologist. "The same thing everyone else is after," was his reply. "But what is that?" questioned the psychologist.

The first couple of sessions were like this: Dr. Shaw trying to get John to examine what he really wanted, and John sparring with him, fending off the probes with generalities about "all other people." In Shaw's mind, John Williams did not want to confront the conflicts of playing a role in the white professional world. He identified with being African American, Shaw believed, but he sensed a falseness about his life. Racial slurs went by without comment. He took pride in the fact that his wife wore her hair straight but at the same time castigated himself for feeling this way. He hid from his colleagues the fact that he was a member of several civil rights groups and that he considered Martin Luther King to have been too moderate. But what was *he* doing about it? King and others had risked personal safety in freedom marches, but John was terrified of being seen in one. What would the people in the firm think of him? Would they want a "radical" in the office?

Dr. Shaw thought to himself during these early sessions that he should pressure his client more and realized he was holding back in a way he would not with a white client. Was it his right to suggest to John that he was at the same time proud and ashamed of his racial heritage, and that he despised himself for hiding his feelings? Indeed, was it his duty? But how could Shaw be certain, and wouldn't it be terrible if he suggested something to John that was off base? But that, too, was something he worried far less about with his white clients. No therapist is infallible, but somehow he believed that with John he had to be more certain about his interpretations.

Dr. Shaw routinely referred clients with medical or psychophysiological problems to an internist. This doctor prescribed some antihypertensive medication for John to take daily. But the physician also hoped that this relatively young patient would not come to rely on the drug. In an extended consultation, Shaw and his medical colleague agreed that John's high-pressure lifestyle was a major factor in his hypertension. What they could not agree on was what role the man's race played. There was no family history of hypertension; they agreed that, for whatever reason, John's particular response to stress was hypertension, more specifically essential hypertension, because a medical evaluation had ruled out physical causes.

A crisis took place in the fifth and final session. For months afterward Dr. Shaw wondered whether he had blundered so badly that his client was driven from therapy.

Dr. Shaw: John, I've been wondering about what you've told me about your college days.

John (a bit suspiciously): What aspect of them?

Dr. Shaw: Well, I guess I was thinking about the club. (Shaw noted to himself that he seldom said "I guess" in such circumstances. Stop pussyfooting, he told himself.)

John (feeling his ears becoming warm): Well, what about the club?

Dr. Shaw: Your feelings of being the only black.

John: Well, I felt really good about it. I used to daydream about what my high school friends would think.

Dr. Shaw: And what would they have thought?

John: They'd have envied me to the utmost. I mean, I must be doing something right to get into one of the Greeks.

Dr. Shaw: Yes, I know you were quite proud about it. . . . But I wonder if you had any other feelings about it.

John (definitely on edge, wary): What do you mean?

Dr. Shaw: Well, lots of times people are conflicted about things that are important to them. Like the nervous bridegroom on the wedding day. He's eager for the honeymoon, but he knows he's giving up something.

John: What do you think I was giving up?

Dr. Shaw: You feel you were giving up something by being in the club?

John: Come on, Doc, don't play games. You know damn well that *you* think I gave up something. What did I give up?

Dr. Shaw: John, if anything was given up, it was you who gave it up, not I. (That sounded too harsh, he told himself immediately, but maybe it was time to apply more pressure on him. Otherwise he might never move.)

John: I resent what you're implying.

Dr. Shaw: Okay, but can you explore it, just hypothetically?

John (suspicion mounting, almost a feeling of panic setting in): Okay, Shaw, let me think of what I gave up.

At this point there was a lengthy silence. John stared at his feet, Dr. Shaw at his notes, occasionally glancing up at John but not wanting to look at him too much. John began to dwell on the thoughts he had never shared with anyone, not even with his roommate, Bill. Oreo cookie, he called himself, black on the outside and white on the inside. Who needs the damned club? If they were serious about being democratic, I would not be the only African American. Just me, and oh, that Chinese kid, whose family just happened to own half of Hong Kong. Yeah, David and me, the two typical minority members. And they can congratulate themselves for being so damned liberal. And I can congratulate myself for making it in the door. But how would they have reacted if I had dated a white woman? Or worn my hair in an Afro? Or put on a dashiki? Ha! How do you wear a club tie with a dashiki? Even the one overt sign of club membership conflicts with a dashiki! What am I doing with them? How hypocritical can I be?[1]

Dr. Shaw: John, can you share some of your thoughts with me?

John: Doc, I can't do it. You're one of them.

Dr. Shaw: One of whom?

John: Doc, I can't talk to a white man about this. I can't talk to a black man about this. I'm too ashamed, too mixed up (beginning to sob). I can't handle this.

Dr. Shaw: This is hard for you, I know, John. But this is a place you can use to look at those feelings. Try to sort them out. Try to figure out what you really want—

John (interrupting the psychologist): No! It's not for you to tell me what I should be doing. *I'm* the one who has to decide. (long silence again)

Dr. Shaw: John?

John just stares at his feet, jaws clenched, that familiar tightness in his head. My blood pressure must be soaring, he told himself. I can't handle this. If I'm not careful, I'll be a psychological success, but I'll die from a stroke. No, that's an exaggeration. Or is it? I'm bullshitting myself so much that I don't even know what I want, or think, or feel . . .

Dr. Shaw: John, perhaps that's enough for today.

John (relieved): Yes, that's right. That's enough . . . for today.

Dr. Shaw: See you next week, same time.

---

[1] Dr. Shaw learned later on something of what was going through John's mind during these lengthy silences.

John (knowing he would break the appointment): Yeah. Thanks. I'll see you next week.

Discussion

It has been known for thousands of years that mental and emotional states can affect the functioning of the body. When a person is under emotional strain, there are numerous physiological changes, such as increases in heart rate and in blood pressure; these changes are usually temporary, diminishing when the stressor is removed. But in some individuals the changes persist; when this happens over a long period of time, a psychophysiological disorder can result.

Many medical illnesses are caused in part, or are markedly affected by, psychological factors. A disease such as hypertension can be life threatening even when a person's emotions seem to be playing a major role in causing the sustained high blood pressure. Psychophysiological disorders are sometimes grouped in terms of the organ system affected. Some of the major ones are:

1. Skin disorders: Neurodermatitis and hyperhydrosis (dry skin)
2. Respiratory disorders: Bronchial asthma, hyperventilation (breathing very rapidly, often leading to fainting)
3. Cardiovascular disorders: Migraine headache and high blood pressure (hypertension)
4. Gastrointestinal disorders: Ulcerative colitis, heartburn

Theories about psychophysiological disorders attempt to explain why only some people exposed to stress develop them and which type of disorder will be produced. Both biological and psychological theories have been proposed.

Biological Theories

The *somatic weakness theory* states that a particular organ—for genetic reasons or because of poor diet or earlier illnesses—can be weak and thus vulnerable to stress. For example, a congenitally weak respiratory system might predispose a person to develop asthma under stress. Thus, the connection between stress and a particular psychophysiological disorder is a weakness in a specific bodily organ.

According to the *specific-reaction theory*, individuals respond to stress in their own idiosyncratic ways, and the bodily system that is the most responsive becomes a likely candidate for the locus of a subsequent psychophysiological disorder. For example, someone reacting to stress with elevated blood pressure may be more susceptible to essential hypertension.

A third biological theory asserts that the biological changes that stress produces are adaptive in the short run, for example, mobilizing energy resources in preparation for physical activity, but that the body pays a price if it must constantly adapt to stress (McEwen, 1998). This can take the form of difficulties "shutting down" the biological stress response, for example, by exhibiting an unusually high level of cortisol secretion even after the stress has abated.

A fourth theory focuses on the body's immune system, which is involved in fighting off infections. Stress can weaken the functioning of the immune system and thereby play a role in such diseases as cancer and allergies as well as autoimmune diseases such as rheumatoid arthritis, in which people's immune systems actually attack their own bodies. Many stressors produce negative effects on the immune system—exams in school, bereavement, divorce, looking after a relative with Alzheimer's disease, and natural disasters (Cohen & Herbert, 1996).

Psychological Theories

Psychophysiological disorders have sometimes been viewed as symbolic manifestations of unresolved repressed conflicts. Environmental causes have also been examined. Our autonomic nervous systems are equipped to respond to danger with either fight or flight, and the healthy body prepares itself by increasing the rate of breathing, diverting blood into the muscles, and releasing sugar into the bloodstream. When danger has passed, this burst of sympathetic nervous system activity subsides. People respond in this way to *psychological* dangers as well. Thoughts can activate our autonomic nervous systems, thereby maintaining our bodies in a state of hyperarousal, as if we are runners in a 100-yard dash crouched at the starting line and tensely ready for the race, expectant and highly aroused.

People can stir themselves up with regrets from the past and worries about the future. Appraisal, one characteristic of our cognitive activity, is important: One person can judge a particular situation as dangerous while another views it as challenging and interesting. The autonomic and motoric activity arising from these contrasting cognitions is different.

Investigators have to consider both physical diatheses, or predispositions, and highly specific psychological ways of reacting to stress. One person might have a genetically determined tendency to react to emotional situations with elevated blood pressure and thus be at risk for hypertension, but will not develop it without a stressful life. Another person might have a constitution that is not disposed to react in an abnormal way to stress and have blood pressure that declines rapidly once a stressor is removed.

Essential Hypertension

High blood pressure, or hypertension, is involved in many deaths each year and is occurring in younger and younger age groups. Despite better treatments, there has recently been a 3 percent increase in Americans' hypertension-related deaths (Farag & Mills, 2004). If blood pressure remains at an elevated level—readings above 140/90 are regarded as high—a strain is placed on the cardiovascular system and, over a period of years, there is an increased risk of stroke or heart attack. Only about 10-15 percent of all cases of hypertension in the United States are attributable at this time to an identifiable physical cause; the other 85-90 percent have *essential* or *primary hypertension*. Hypertension is more likely in developed, industrialized societies than in traditional, less-developed societies (Dressler, 2004).

According to recent estimates, 20 percent of adults in the United States have varying degrees of hypertension; it is twice as frequent in African Americans as in European Americans. As many as 10 percent of college students have hypertension; most are unaware of their illness. Unless people have their blood pressure checked, they may go for years without knowing they are hypertensive. This disease is referred to as the "silent killer" because over time it is dangerous to a person's physical health and it can be present for years without the person knowing it. Sometimes symptoms do develop, however, as we saw in John's case: fatigue, nervousness, dizziness, heart palpitations, headaches, and, for some, even a feeling of pressure in the head.

A number of psychosocial factors are thought to contribute to hypertension: job stress, anger and hostility, depression, social isolation, and effects of racism. These factors tend to cluster in low socioeconomic groups, and compound the risk for cardiovascular disease (Williams, Barefoot, & Schneiderman, 2003). Research on each will be examined.

The first factor examined is stress, which increases blood pressure in the short term. Kasl and Cobb (1970) found that people who knew that their jobs would be terminated in two months had higher blood pressure during that period as well as two years following the loss of the job than those whose employment remained constant. Other types of work stress can also affect blood pressure. People who report low levels of control in their jobs, like not being able to control when they take breaks, have higher blood pressure (Steptoe & Willemsen, 2004).

The next psychosocial factor to be considered is anger. Of various negative emotions, anger is most strongly linked to elevated blood pressure (Faber & Burns, 1996). People with Type A behavior patterns (competitive, achievement-oriented, and hostile) were found to be more likely to have hypertension, and further research has pinpointed anger/hostility as the key element. Time urgency or impatience and hostility predicted hypertension 15 years later (Yan et al., 2003). Experiencing anger has been conclusively linked to higher blood pressure, but expressing anger is linked to lower blood pressure (Schum, Jofgensen, Verhaeghen, Sauro, & Thibodeau, 2003). People with essential hypertension may have a social skills deficit, an inability to be assertive when angry (Larkin & Zayfert, 2004). Assertive, constructive responses to anger are linked to lower blood pressure (Hogan & Linden, 2004).

More directly relevant to John Williams is laboratory research (Hokanson & Burgess, 1962) where college students were given a task but were then made angry by a confederate of the experimenter. Half were given the opportunity to retaliate against their harasser, but the others were not. Results showed that being harassed raised blood pressure, and students who could retaliate showed larger decreases in their elevated blood pressure than those who were denied that opportunity.

Applying these findings to John Williams, we can hypothesize that his habit of inhibiting anger and his resentment of racial discrimination played a role in his high blood pressure. Additionally, of the students who retaliated, blood pressure decreases were found only when they aggressed against a fellow college student, not when their harasser was presented as a visiting professor. Expressing resentment and anger to a high-status source of frustration, then, did not reduce blood pressure.

In John's case, if he *had* asserted himself more, this might not have helped *if* he perceived the people angering him as higher in status. This is where issues of race and status enter, because the therapist would have had to discuss with John his underlying feelings about the status of European Americans.

Depression has also been examined for its contributions to hypertension. Negative mood states have been linked to hypertension (Pollard & Schwartz, 2003). People who are depressed are more likely to have hypertension (Bosworth, Bartash, Olsen, & Steffens, 2003). In a study of African American men with hypertension, depression was linked to poorer adherence to treatment and to alcohol and tobacco use (Kim, Han, Hill, Rose, & Roary, 2003). Depression and social isolation may interact in contributing to hypertension. Social support may serve as a protective factor. People in cohesive, supportive marriages had lower levels of hypertension (Baker, Szalai, Paquette, & Tobe, 2003). In addition, depression likely directly impacts hypertension through sympathetic nervous system activity and cortisol levels (Scherrer, Xian, Bucholz, Eisen, Lyons, Goldberg, et al., 2003).

While racism and discrimination probably contribute to the especially high incidence of hypertension among African Americans, additional causes may be found in social factors, especially having to deal continually with social stress (Neighbors & Jackson, 1996; Sherman, 1994). Harburg et al. (1973) studied two areas of Detroit; one was a poor neighborhood with a high crime rate, much crowding, and many marital breakups, and the other was a middle-class neighborhood. In both, black and white married men had their blood pressure taken several times in their homes, and they were also asked how they would respond to various stressful situations. For example, they were asked how they would react if a landlord refused to rent an apartment to them because of their race or religion. Results showed that blood pressure was higher among African Americans than among whites. But African Americans living in the poor neighborhood had higher blood pressure than those living in the middle-class area. High blood pressure among African Americans may be related to the socially created stress under which they live (Anderson & Armstead, 1995). Furthermore, results from the stressful situation test indicated that for most subjects, holding anger in was related to high blood pressure. Unexpressed anger is key in the development and maintenance of high blood pressure.

Perceived racism against African Americans may increase the risk for hypertension, but the type of coping mechanism the person uses may make a difference (Brondolo, Rieppi, Kelly, & Gerin, 2003). One hypothesis to explain the higher risk for hypertension among African Americans is the *John Henryism hypothesis*, based on a legend about a man of that name. It suggests that people who face socioeconomic adversity and inequity with active coping strategies of commitment to hard work and a strong determination to succeed are actually at higher risk for high blood pressure (Fernander, Durán, Saab, & Schneiderman, 2004). This type of coping strategy was linked with higher blood pressure among African American men with high education and African American women with low education. John Williams fits this hypothesis particularly well. His constant striving for perfection exacerbated his level of stress, over and above the pressure probably created by the prejudice he sometimes encountered. His blood pressure was apparently increased as well by the tremendous conflicts he experienced as an African American man who felt he was being false to himself, who compromised his beliefs and his ideals in order to succeed in white society.

A diathesis-stress model is useful in understanding risk for hypertension. John Williams's life was full of emotionally stressful events. But it was a psychophysiological disorder that he developed, not any of the many other problems that people under duress are subject to, such as mood disorders or anxiety disorders. Furthermore, given that it was a psychophysiological problem, he had essential hypertension, not asthma, hives, or any of the other such disorders. Did he have a somatic weakness in his cardiovascular system, or was his system somehow predisposed to overreact to stress, as in the specific reaction theory? We do not know in John's case. Evidence suggests that reactivity to stress may be important in hypertension (Rutledge & Linden, 2003). In one study (Hodapp, Weyer, & Becker, 1976), the blood pressure of hypertensive and nonhypertensive people was measured while resting, while viewing slides of landscapes, and while performing a demanding intellectual task (the stressor). All participants showed blood pressure increases during the stress, but hypertensives maintained that increase even when the stressor was removed. It is as though some people's cardiovascular systems are preset to be elevated and to maintain that elevation once they are stressed.

In a longitudinal study, Wood et al. (1984) followed up with people who had had their blood pressure monitored during a stress task many years earlier. Those who had reacted strongly were five times more likely to be hypertensive. Further support for the importance of reactivity comes from high-risk research comparing individuals with and without a positive history for hypertension (Hastrup, Light, & Obrist, 1982). As anticipated, people with a positive family history showed greater blood pressure reactivity to stress. Coupled with other research showing the heritability of blood pressure reactivity (Matthews & Rakaczky, 1987) and the heritability of hypertension, blood pressure reactivity becomes a good candidate for a genetically transmitted diathesis. Recent evidence points to cardiovascular reactivity as a diathesis for hypertension, that is, the extent to which blood pressure and heart rate increase in response to stress. People differ on this factor, some being very reactive, and others less so. More reactive people are more likely to have higher blood pressure over time (Light, Dolan, Davis, & Sherwood, 1992). Of particular relevance to our case, African American children have been found to be higher in blood-pressure reactivity than whites, a fact that may help explain the high incidence of hypertension among blacks (Murphy, Stoney, Alpert, & Walker, 1995).

The Psychological Treatment of Hypertension

Medications to lower blood pressure are effective. But the undesirable side effects of these medications—drowsiness, light-headedness, and in men, erectile difficulties—as well as the growth of behavioral approaches to treatment have led many investigators to explore nonpharmacological treatments for borderline essential hypertension. Those with more severe hypertension usually take drugs to control its deleterious long-term effects. However, studies looking at large numbers of patients in the community who have taken medication for many years found increased rather than decreased mortality, and there is increasing interest in nonpharmacological treatments (Linden, 2003).

Regular exercise as well as losing weight through sensible diet continues to be part of any comprehensive approach to controlling high blood pressure (Whelton et al., 1998). But these medical measures also involve psychological change components (Dubbert, 1995). Most therapists agree that anxiety, and sometimes anger, must be reduced to lessen the sympathetic nervous system arousal that plays a role in maintaining blood pressure at abnormally high levels. Therapy can help the client cope better with pressures and anxiety and thereby reduce blood pressure.

Client-centered therapists would focus on John's denial of his inner self, his not marching to the beat of his own drum, his compromising his ideas and deeply felt beliefs in order to meet with favor and acceptance from others (especially his father), or "conditions of worth" (Rogers, 1951). Dr. Shaw was operating in this framework, but we have seen that he did not get further than suggesting to John that he might be acting against his own self.

The transcript provided earlier shows the kind of empathic listening and reflection common in client-centered therapy. Note, however, that Dr. Shaw did not merely reflect back to John what he had just said, but empathizes:

John: Doc, I can't talk to a white man about this. I can't talk to a black man about this. I'm too ashamed, too mixed up (beginning to sob). I can't handle this.

Dr. Shaw: This is hard for you, I know, John . . . .

Dr. Shaw acknowledges that he appreciates how difficult it is for John to be talking about his private thoughts. The hope is that the relationship will be strengthened and that John will be encouraged to continue exploring his feelings. In another part of the session, however, Dr. Shaw goes beyond what John has expressed, restating to him what Dr. Shaw believes is going on with John. He makes an *inference*, an interpretation about what is troubling the client in the hope of helping John view himself in a new, better perspective, one that will generate movement and greater self-honesty (Dr. Shaw has asked John how he felt about being the only African American in his club at college).

Dr. Shaw: [I'd like to know about] your feelings of being the only black.

John: Well, I felt really good about it . . . . My high school friends would've envied me to the utmost. . . .

Dr. Shaw: Yes, I know you were quite proud about it . . . . But I wonder if you had any other feelings about it.

This statement was too confrontational. Dr. Shaw was on target, but John was too frightened, too angry to consider the interpretation. This error in pushing too quickly for movement may have been because of Dr. Shaw's impatience with himself for dancing too gingerly around John's problems for fear of sounding bigoted.

Relaxation training and meditation have also been used with some success in efforts to control hypertension (Yung & Keltner, 1996). When relaxation was compared with an information-only treatment, anger and hostility were reduced more by the relaxation, and this was accompanied by a reduction in blood pressure (Davison, Williams, Nezami, Bice, & DeQuattro, 1991). There has also been interest in biofeedback, a technique that uses a highly sensitive electronic apparatus to inform a person of bodily changes that are usually too subtle to be detected. John might have been taught when his blood pressure had passed a certain level and then been reinforced for bringing it down below that level. Statistically significant changes have been achieved with both normals and hypertensives in laboratory settings (Blanchard, 1990; Blanchard et al., 1996), but success may be due to relaxation (McGrady, Nadsady, & Schumann-Brzezinski, 1991). Attention to the person's driven lifestyle also seems to be essential if anything like biofeedback is going to play a significant role in lowering blood pressure.

Teaching clients coping skills for handling stress and encouraging meditation have been effective treatments (Williams et al., 2003). Some clinicians target Type A behavior directly, to reduce hostility and time urgency. Others advocate psychopharmacology treatment of depression to improve hypertension.

African American urban residents have particularly low levels of adherence with medication therapy and are sometimes suspicious and distrustful of their physicians (Lukoschek, 2003). For urban, African American men who are at high risk for hypertension but are often underserved by the health-care system, an intensive team approach that incorporated education, home visits, and telephone checks produced more reductions in hypertension than a traditional medical approach (Hill et al, 2003). In one study, some African American patients expressed concern that they would become addicted to their medication and would only take them if they felt symptoms (Ogedegbe, Harrison, Robbins, Mancuso, & Allegrante, 2004).

Issues of Race and Psychotherapy

African American clients report higher levels of rapport with, prefer, and are more satisfied with African American therapists than with white therapists (Atkinson, 1983; 1985). African American clients engage in more self-exploration with black counselors (Jackson, 1973). At the same time, studies suggest that racial differences are *not* insurmountable barriers to understanding between counselor and client (Beutler et al., 1994). Therapists with high levels of empathy are perceived as more helpful by clients, regardless of ethnic background. Therapists report that when they address race with their clients who are a different race, it has positive effects on the therapy (Knox, Baurkard, Johnson, Suzuki, & Ponterotto, 2003). Talking openly about these issues improves rapport.

Therapists need to understand that virtually all African Americans have encountered prejudice and racism, and many must often wrestle with their anger and rage at a majority culture that is sometimes insensitive to and unappreciative of the emotional consequences of growing up as a feared, resented, and sometimes hated minority (Hardy & Laszloffy, 1995). On the other hand, as Greene (1985) cautions, therapists' sensitivity to social oppression should not translate into a paternalism that removes personal responsibility and individual empowerment from their client. These issues are vividly illustrated in the case of John Williams, both throughout his life and in his brief dealings with his therapist.

Mention has already been made of how being African American might contribute to high blood pressure. John Williams's race also played a role in the therapy he terminated prematurely. Not adequately appreciated in the psychotherapy literature are the social conditions under which African Americans have been living in this country as well as the sometimes subtle, unconscious biases existing in the primarily white investigators who offer the generalizations (Comas-Diaz, 1992).

Complicating the matter is the difficulty a white therapist can experience with a black client. Therapists have to get past their prejudices and relate to their African American clients as to any other client, and to place race in a context that will promote a fruitful assessment and intervention instead of impeding them.

These issues are to be seen in the case of John Williams. Should the therapist have encouraged a more assertive stance toward the prejudices that seemed to be oppressing him? Or should the therapist have promoted an adjustment to the situation, an attitude that he really had things good, that life is imperfect, and perhaps he should just find a way to make the best of it? Did John Williams wish that he were white? Should John have declined the invitation to the club at Harvard? Was his wish to be accepted by his white classmates an unhealthy one, or could it be seen as no less healthy than the wish a white initiate would have? Was John really "Uncle-Tomming" by joining the exclusive group while fearing that true acceptance would ultimately be denied him? Was he not "truly" accepted by his club members? If people were being nice to him, was it because he was African American and they were trying to demonstrate their liberalism and open-mindedness? How was he to know if they really liked him?

Dr. Shaw was reluctant to push John more than he would have a white client. It has been suggested that some white therapists are overly sympathetic toward their African American clients, to avoid seeming to be expressing racial prejudice (Greene, 1985). There is a general issue in psychotherapy about how much pressure a therapist should place on a client. In one study of group therapy (Yalom & Lieberman, 1971), casualties occurred most often when the group leader was confrontative and authoritative. Clearly, clients can be hurt if their therapists demand more of them than they are capable of giving. On the other hand, the art of therapy requires that therapists encourage movement on the part of their clients that might not occur otherwise. After some hesitation, Dr. Shaw did apply such pressure, but he seemed to misread his client's readiness to explore his conflicts and lost the opportunity to work further with him. By most standards, Dr. Shaw failed with John Williams, even though he saw him for only five sessions.

Dr. Shaw should have anticipated the difficulties in establishing rapport. John was suspicious and hostile, wondering whether Dr. Shaw would be able to empathize with his suffering. Will he truly be able to appreciate the tensions I am under? How will he judge my desires to be accepted by whites for what I am, my fierce pride in being African American, especially as I succeed in a white world? Will he see me as copping out or decide that my inhibition of resentment is adaptive and healthy? Indeed, will and can the therapist help me explore within myself what *I* really want? Must I want only what other African Americans want in order to be a whole person?

CHAPTER 6

Dissociative Identity Disorder: Multiple Personality

The instructor in Paula's human sexuality course suggested that she talk to a psychologist. Several factors contributed to his concern: Although Paula was a good student, her behavior in class had been rather odd on occasion. Every now and then, it seemed as though she came to class "high." She participated actively in the discussions, but she did not seem to be familiar with the readings or previous lecture material. Her scores on the first two exams had been As, but she failed to appear for the third. When he asked her where she had been, Paula maintained with apparent sincerity that she couldn't remember. Finally, she had handed in an essay assignment that described in rather vague, but sufficiently believable, terms the abusive, incestuous relationship that her father had forced upon her from the age of 5 until well after she was married and had had her first child. All of this led her professor to believe that Paula needed help. Fortunately, she was inclined to agree with him because there were a number of things that were bothering her. She made an appointment to talk to Dr. Harpin, a clinical psychologist at the student health center.

Paula Stewart was 38 years old, divorced, and the mother of a son 18 years of age and a daughter who was 15. She was about 90 pounds overweight, but in other ways her appearance was unremarkable. For the past five years, Paula had been taking courses at the university and working part time at a variety of secretarial positions on campus. She and her daughter lived together in a small, rural community located about 20 miles from the university—the same town in which Paula had been born. Her son had moved away from home after dropping out of high school. Paula's mother and father still lived in their home just down the street from Paula's.

Over a series of sessions, Dr. Harpin noticed that Paula's behavior was often erratic. Her moods vacillated frequently and quickly from anger and irritability to severe depression. When she was depressed, her movements became agitated, and she mentioned that she experienced sleep difficulties. She threatened suicide frequently and had, on several occasions, made some attempts to harm herself. In addition to these emotional difficulties, Paula frequently complained of severe headaches, dizziness, and breathing problems.

It also seemed that Paula abused alcohol, although the circumstances were not clear. This situation was a source of distress and considerable confusion for Paula. She had found empty beer cans and whiskey bottles in the back seat of her car, but she denied drinking alcoholic beverages of any kind. Once every two or three weeks, she would wake up in the morning with terrible headaches as though she were hung over. Dr. Harpin believed that her confusion and other memory problems could be explained by her alcohol consumption.

Paula's relationships with other people were unpredictable. She would explode with little provocation and often argued that no one understood how serious her problems were. On occasion, she threatened to kill other people, particularly an older man, Cal, who lived nearby. Paula's relationship with Cal was puzzling to both of them. They had known each other since she was an adolescent. Although he was 15 years older than she and had been married to another woman for more than 20 years, Cal had persistently shown a romantic interest in Paula. He would frequently come to her house saying that she had called. More often than not, this made Paula furious. She maintained that she was not at all interested in him and would never encourage such behavior. At other times, however, she insisted that he was the only person who understood and cared for her.

Paula's father was still alive, but she did not spend any time with him. In fact, he behaved as though she didn't exist. She was able to recall and discuss some aspects of the incestuous relationship her father had forced upon her in previous years, but her memory was sketchy, and she preferred not to discuss him.

Throughout the first year of treatment, Paula's memory problems became increasingly severe. The notes she wrote during classes were often incomplete, as though she had suddenly stopped listening in the middle of a number of lectures. She sometimes complained that she lost parts of days. On one occasion, for example, she told Dr. Harpin that she had gone home with a severe headache in the middle of the afternoon and then couldn't remember anything until she awakened the following morning. Another time she was eating lunch, only to find herself hours later driving her car. Her daughter asked her about a loud argument Paula had had with her mother on the phone, and she couldn't remember even talking to her mother that day. These unexplained experiences were extremely frustrating to Paula, but the therapist continued to believe that they were induced by alcohol.

One day, Dr. Harpin received a message from his secretary saying that a woman named Sherry had called. She had identified herself as a friend of Paula's and had said that she would like to discuss the case. Before responding directly to this request, Dr. Harpin decided to check with Paula to find out more about this friend and determine whether she would give her consent for this consultation. Paula denied knowing anyone named Sherry, so Dr. Harpin did not return the call. It did strike him as odd, however, that someone knew that he was Paula's therapist.

Two weeks after receiving this call, Dr. Harpin decided to use hypnosis in an attempt to explore the frequent gaps in Paula's memory. They had used hypnosis on one previous occasion as an aid to the process of applied relaxation, and it was clear that Paula was easily hypnotized. Unfortunately, it didn't help with the memory problem; Paula couldn't remember anything else about the time she had lost.

Upon waking out of a trance, Paula complained of a splitting headache. She gazed slowly about the room as though she were lost. Dr. Harpin was puzzled. "Do you know where you are?" he asked. She said she didn't know, so he asked if she knew who he was. Rather than providing a quick answer, she glanced around the room. She noticed his professional license hanging on the wall, read his name, and finally replied, "Yes. You're Dr. Harpin, the one who's working with Paula." This switch to her use of the third person struck Dr. Harpin as being odd and roused further curiosity about her state of mind.

"How do you feel?"
"Okay."
"Do you still have a headache?"
"No. I don't have a headache."

The way she emphasized the word "I" was unusual, so Dr. Harpin said, "You make it sound like somebody else has a headache." He was completely unprepared for her response:

"Yes. Paula does."

Pausing for a moment to collect his wits, Dr. Harpin—who was simultaneously confused and fascinated by this startling exchange—decided to pursue the identity issue further.

"If Paula has a headache, but you don't, what's your name?"
"Why should I tell you? I don't think I can trust you."
"Why not? Don't you want to talk to me?"
"Why should I? You wouldn't talk to me when I called last week!"

Dr. Harpin finally remembered the call from Sherry, who had wanted to talk to him about Paula's case. He asked the woman, once again, what her name was, and she said, "Sherry." After they talked for a couple of minutes, Dr. Harpin said, "I'd like to talk to Paula now."

"Oh, she's boring."
"That doesn't matter. She's my client, and I want to talk to her to see how she feels."
"Will you talk to me again?"
"Yes."
"Why should I believe you? You wouldn't talk to me before."
"Now I know who you are. Please let me talk to Paula."

At that point, she closed her eyes and waited quietly for a few moments. When her eyes opened, Paula was back and her headache was gone, but she could not remember anything about the last half hour. Dr. Harpin was stunned and incredulous. Although he was aware of the literature on Dissociative Identity Disorder (DID) and a few well-known cases, he could not believe what Paula had said.

When Paula appeared for their next appointment, she still could not remember anything that had happened and seemed just as she had before this remarkable incident. Dr. Harpin decided to attempt to discuss with Paula a traumatic incident that had happened a number of years ago. Paula had frequently mentioned a day when she was 15 years old. She couldn't remember the details, but it was clearly a source of considerable distress for her and seemed to involve her father.

Dr. Harpin asked Paula to describe what she could remember about the day: where they were living at the time, what time of year it was, who was home, and so on. Paula filled in the details slowly and as best she could. Her father had grabbed her, hit her across the face, and dragged her toward the bedroom. No matter how hard she tried, she couldn't remember anything else. Paula said that she was getting a headache. Dr. Harpin suggested that she lean back in the chair and breathe slowly. She paused for a moment and closed her eyes. In a few moments, she opened her eyes and said, "She can't remember. She wasn't there. I was!" Sherry was back.

Paula's appearance had changed suddenly. She had been very tense, clutching the arms of the chair and sitting upright. She also had had an annoying, hacking cough. Now she eased down in the chair, folded her arms, and crossed her legs in front of her. The cough was completely gone. Sherry explained why Paula couldn't remember the incident with her father. As Sherry put it, when Paula was dragged into the bedroom, she "decided to take off," leaving Sherry to experience the pain and humiliation of the ensuing rape. Dr. Harpin translated this to mean that Paula had experienced a dissociative episode. The incident was so extremely traumatic that she had completely separated the experience and its memory from the rest of her consciousness.

After discussing the rape in some detail, Dr. Harpin decided to find out as much as he could about Sherry. She provided only sketchy information, admitting that she was in her thirties but denying that she had a last name. Sherry's attitude toward Paula was contemptuous. She was angry because Paula had so frequently left Sherry to experience painful sexual encounters. They discussed numerous incidents dating from Paula's adolescence to the present, but none of Sherry's memories traced back prior to the incident with Paula's father. Since that time, Sherry was apparently aware of everything that Paula had done. Paula, on the other hand, was completely oblivious to Sherry's existence.

Toward the end of this conversation, Dr. Harpin asked whether it was Sherry or Paula who had been responsible for the beer bottles Paula found in her car. Sherry said, "Oh, we did that." Intrigued by the plural pronoun, Dr. Harpin asked whom she meant to describe, and the patient said, "Oh, Janet and I."

"Who's Janet?"
"You don't want to talk to her. She's always angry. You know how adolescents are."

By this point, Dr. Harpin knew that Sherry found it easier than Paula to switch back and forth among these personalities, so he encouraged her to try. Sherry agreed, somewhat reluctantly, and soon there was another dramatic change in Paula's appearance. She fidgeted in her chair, pulled at her hair, and began to bounce her leg continuously. She was reluctant to talk, but adopted a coy, somewhat flirtatious manner. She claimed to be 15 years old.

Several sessions later, Sherry presented Dr. Harpin with a request. She said that she and Janet were extremely concerned about Caroline, who was presumably only

5 years old and had been crying a lot lately. Sherry and Janet wanted Dr. Harpin to talk to Caroline. He agreed to try. Sherry closed her eyes and effortlessly transformed her posture and mannerisms to those of a little girl. She pulled her legs up onto the chair and folded them under her body. Holding her hand in a fist clenched close to the side of her mouth almost as if she were sucking her thumb, she turned sideways in the chair and peered at Dr. Harpin bashfully out of the corner of her eye. She seemed to be rather frightened.

"Will you talk to me, Caroline?" Dr. Harpin began.

After an extended pause, Caroline asked, "What's your name? I don't know you." Her voice seemed higher and weaker than it had been moments before.

"I'm Dr. Harpin."
"Do you know my mommy and daddy?"
"No. But I'm a friend of Sherry's. She asked me to talk to you. Do you know
   Sherry?"
"Yes. She watches me. She takes care of me."
"Do you know Janet?"
"She's big. She has fun!"
"Do you know her very well?"
"Not really. She gets mad easy."
"Sherry told me that you've been feeling sad. Why is that?"
"I'm a bad girl."
"Why do you think you're bad?"
"Mommy told me I'm bad. That's why she has to punish me."
"I don't think you're a bad girl."
"Yes I am. If I'm not bad, why would they punish me?"
"What do they punish you for?"
"I don't know. They just do. They hurt me. Once I pinched my brother when he
   took my toy puppy. Then they took my puppy away, and they won't give it
   back! Grandpa gave it to me. He's good to me."

At their next session, Dr. Harpin asked Paula if she remembered ever having a stuffed puppy when she was a child. A fond smile of recognition followed several moments' reflection. She had indeed had such a toy. He asked if she knew what had happened to it. She insisted that she had no idea. It had been almost 30 years since she remembered seeing it, but she agreed to look around in the attic of her mother's house.

Much to everyone's surprise, Paula was able to find the puppy, which was known as Jingles because of the sound made by a small bell sewn into its tail. Unfortunately, it became the source of considerable aggravation for Paula. The first day she found it, she left it in the living room before she went to bed. When she woke up in the morning, Jingles was in bed with her. This happened two nights in a row. On the third night, she locked the puppy in her car, which was kept in the garage, and went to bed. Once again, the puppy was in bed with her when she woke up in the morning. She was annoyed and also a bit frightened by this strange turn of events. In subsequent sessions, Sherry provided the following explanation for what had happened. Caroline would wake up in the middle of the night crying, wanting to hold her stuffed animal. In an effort to console her, Sherry would then retrieve Jingles from the living room or garage. Of course, Paula would not remember what had happened.

Thus far there were four names: Paula, Sherry, Janet, and Caroline. The clinical picture was as fascinating as it was unbelievable. Dr. Harpin felt that he needed help as much as his client. In his 15 years of clinical experience, he had never seen a case that resembled Paula's in any way. It fit closely with some of the published cases of DID, but he had never really believed that this sort of thing happened, except in fiction. Surely it was the product of the therapist's imagination, or the client's manipulative strategy, he had believed. He sought advice from colleagues about a plan for the treatment of this complex set of problems. His contacts with Paula continued to deal largely with day-to-day crises.

He asked Paula if she had read any of the well-known books or watched any of the popular films dealing with DID (which was formerly called multiple personality). She had not. Since she was not familiar with other examples of this phenomenon, it seemed unlikely that she had simply invented the alter personalities as a way of attracting attention or convincing others of the severity of her problems. In an attempt to help Paula—who was not aware of the alters—understand the problems that she faced, Dr. Harpin asked her to read *The Three Faces of Eve*, the book upon which the famous film was based. She reacted with interest and disbelief. What did it have to do with her situation? She was still completely unable to remember those times when she spoke as if she were Sherry, Janet, or Caroline. Later, however, there were times when Sherry discussed the book with Dr. Harpin, and Janet was also reading it. To make matters more confusing, they all seemed to be reading at a different pace. Paula might be two-thirds of the way through the book, but Janet— an adolescent who did not read as quickly—was aware of only the first part of the book.

Dr. Harpin also used videotape to help Paula understand the problem. With her consent, he recorded her behavior during a sequence of three therapy sessions. She alternated among the various personalities several times during the course of these tapes. Paula was then asked to view the tapes and discuss her reactions to her own behavior. Again, she was surprised, interested, and puzzled, showing no signs of previous awareness of this behavior. She would often ask, "Did *I* say that?" or "Who am I? *What* am I?"

Another unusual set of circumstances led to the identification of still another personality, Heather. Paula had complained on numerous occasions that a loaded shotgun, which belonged to her father, kept appearing at her house. She had no use for guns, and their presence upset her, so she would take the gun back to her father's house. Several days later, she would find it again at her house. Her parents and daughter adamantly denied knowing anything about the gun. Recognizing that Paula was frequently unaware of things that she did as the other personalities, Dr. Harpin discussed the gun with Sherry and Janet. Both denied any knowledge of these incidents. Janet said, "I know you think it's me, but it's not!" Finally, Sherry suggested that it might be someone else. "You mean there might be others?" Dr. Harpin asked. Sherry acknowledged the possibility, but said that she was not aware of any others.

At the beginning of the next session, Dr. Harpin decided to use hypnosis in an effort to see if he could identify more alters. While Paula was in the trance, he asked if anyone else, with whom he had not yet spoken, was able to hear what he was saying. This was when Heather emerged. She was presumably 23. It was she who had been bringing the gun to Paula's house, and it was she who had been calling Cal. Heather told Dr. Harpin that she was in love with Cal. If she couldn't marry him, she wanted to kill herself. This was the first alter with whom Sherry did not have co-consciousness, and her existence explained several important inconsistencies in Paula's behavior and gaps in her memory.

Heather's affection for Cal illustrates another important characteristic of the dissociative identity phenomenon. There were important, and occasionally radical, differences among Paula, Sherry, and the other alters in terms of tastes and preferences as well as mannerisms and abilities. Heather loved Cal (she couldn't live without him), but the others hated him. In fact, Paula's most remarkable reaction to videotapes of her own behavior centered around one conversation with Heather. Paula insisted that it was not she. "I would *never* say those things!" she said. Paula's attitude toward her parents was also at odds with those of some of the alters, and this inconsistency undoubtedly explained some of the erratic shifts in her behavior and relationship with other people. Sherry didn't like Paula's children and was inconsiderate in her behavior toward them. She frequently promised them things to keep them quiet and then failed to honor her commitments.

Social History

Paula grew up in a small rural community. She had one older brother. Her mother was an outspoken, dominant woman who maintained firm control of the family. Both parents were strict disciplinarians. The parents of Paula's mother lived nearby. This grandfather was the only sympathetic adult figure throughout Paula's childhood. It was he who gave her the stuffed puppy, Jingles, which became such an important source of comfort to her until her parents took it away. When Paula was upset, her grandfather was the only person who was able to console her and stop her crying (although she never dared to tell him about the things that her father forced her to do).

Paula's father was a shy, withdrawn, unaffectionate man who did not have many friends. For the first few years of her life, he ignored her completely. Then, when she was 5 years old, he began to demonstrate physical affection. He would hug and kiss her roughly, and when no one else was around, he would fondle her genitals. Paula didn't know how to respond. His touches weren't pleasant or enjoyable, but she would accept whatever affection he was willing to provide.

When she was 15, their sexual encounters started to become violent. The pretense of affection and love was obviously dissolved; he wanted to hurt her. In one incident, which Paula and Dr. Harpin had discussed repeatedly, her father dragged her into his bedroom by her hair and tied her to the bed. After slapping her repeatedly, he forced her to have intercourse with him. The incest and physical abuse continued until she was 20 years old.

Paula's mother was a strict disciplinarian who often punished Paula by putting her hands in scalding hot water or locking her in a dark closet for hours on end. Mrs. Stewart did not realize—or seem to care—that her husband was abusing Paula sexually. If she did know, she may have been afraid to intervene. Mr. Stewart may also have abused his wife as well as his daughter, but Paula could not remember witnessing any violence between her parents.

Perhaps in an effort to tear herself away from this abusive family, Paula pursued relationships with other men at an early age. Many of these men were older than she, including teachers and neighbors. The longest relationship of this sort was with Cal, the owner of a small construction business. Paula was 16 and Cal was 31 when they started seeing each other. Although he took advantage of Paula sexually, Cal was a more sympathetic person than her father. He did listen to her, and he seemed to care for her. On numerous occasions, Cal promised that he would marry her. For Paula, he was a "rescuer," someone who offered a way out of her pathological family situation. Unfortunately, he didn't come through. He married another woman but continued to pursue Paula's affection and sexual favors. She continued to oblige, in spite of the strong feelings of anger and betrayal that she harbored.

A few incidents that occurred while Paula was in high school were probably precursors of the memory problems and dissociative experiences that she later encountered as an adult. They suggest that the problem of alter personalities began during adolescence, although it was not discovered until many years later. People sometimes told Paula about things that she had done, things that she could not remember doing. Most of these involved promiscuous behavior. Paula was particularly upset by a rumor that went around the school when she was a sophomore. Several other girls claimed that Paula had been seen in a car with three men. They were parked in a remote picnic area outside of town, and Paula presumably had intercourse with all of them. She couldn't remember a thing, but she also didn't know where she had been that night.

After graduating from high school, Paula enrolled in the university's school of education, but she dropped out after one year. For the next few years, she worked at various clerical jobs, while living either at home with her parents or in apartments that she rented nearby. She was married briefly, gave birth to her children, and was then divorced. Paula decided to return to the university many years later, after her son left home.

Conceptualization and Treatment

Dr. Harpin's initial diagnostic impression, before the emergence of the alter personalities, was that Paula fit the *DSM-IV-TR* (APA, 2000) criteria for both dysthymia (a long-lasting form of depression that is not sufficiently severe to meet the criteria for major depressive disorder) and borderline personality disorder. Throughout the first year of treatment, his approach to the problem was focused primarily on the management of frequent, specific crises. These included numerous transient suicidal threats, fights with her mother and daughter, confusion and anger over her relationship—or lack of a relationship—with Cal, difficulties in her schoolwork and with professors teaching her classes, and a variety of incidents involving her employers. When immediate problems of this sort were not pressing, Paula usually wanted to talk about the way her father had abused her. Her focus was on both the anger and the guilt that she felt about these incidents. She wondered whether in some way she hadn't encouraged his sexual advances.

After the appearance of the alter personalities, Dr. Harpin's initial hypothesis was that Paula was malingering, that is, feigning a dramatic set of symptoms in an effort to gain some benefit from him or her family. This explanation was attractive for several reasons, including his skepticism regarding the existence of a phenomenon such as DID. Nevertheless, he eventually abandoned this view. One problem was the apparent absence of information that would have been necessary for Paula to fake this disorder. She had not read or seen any of the popular descriptions of the disorder, and it was therefore unlikely that she would be able to create or imitate the problem in such a believable, detailed fashion. The other problem was the lack of a clear motive. She was not, for example, facing criminal charges that might be avoided by the existence of a severe form of mental illness. Nor was she able to avoid personal or family responsibilities by the onset of these conditions, because she continued to go to school, work, and take care of her daughter after the emergence of the alters. The only thing she might stand to gain was increased attention from Dr. Harpin. It seemed unlikely that this would explain the problem, since he had already been spending an inordinate amount of time and energy on the case as a result of the previous suicidal gestures, and he had repeatedly conveyed to Paula his concern for her problems.

It eventually became clear that Paula was experiencing a genuine disruption of consciousness that was usually precipitated by stressful experiences. Faced with an extremely threatening or unpleasant circumstance, Paula would often dissociate— entirely blot out (or repress) her awareness of that event. This pattern of cognitive activity could apparently be traced to the violent abuse that she received from her father during adolescence. By her own description, when these events began, Paula would usually "leave" the situation and Sherry would be left to face her father. The turbulent nature of these years and the concentration of abuse during this time might account for the fact that the ages of most of the alters seemed to cluster between 15 and 23. Over time, the extent of this fragmentation of conscious experience became more severe, and her control over changes in her patterns of awareness eroded progressively.

One approach to the resolution of these dissociative episodes might involve the recall and exploration of previous traumatic experiences that seemed to be responsible for particular splits in Paula's consciousness. Perhaps the most salient of these episodes was the rape scene involving Paula's father. The existence of Sherry suggested that the split could be traced to about this period of time, and it was an incident that Sherry mentioned repeatedly. Previous accounts of DID suggest that the patient's disturbance in consciousness might improve if the repression of such memories can be lifted. Unfortunately, this approach did not seem to be useful in

Paula's case. She and Dr. Harpin spent many hours discussing this incident—from the perspectives of both Paula and Sherry—but it only seemed to make things worse.

A different approach was needed. Dr. Harpin had two principal goals in mind during the next several months of treatment: to discourage further fragmentation of Paula's conscious experience and to facilitate the integration of information across the divisions of conscious experience. In other words, without encouraging or crystallizing the existence of separate personalities, Dr. Harpin wanted to help Paula recognize the nature of the problem and the way her behavior patterns changed in association with loss of memory for these incidents. This was done, in part, by having her read and discuss *The Three Faces of Eve* and allowing her to view videotapes of her own behavior. Dr. Harpin's hope was that the videotapes might jog Paula's memory and begin to break down the barriers that had been erected to prevent the exchange of information between the subdivisions of her conscious working memory.

Ten-Year Followup

Paula remained in treatment with Dr. Harpin for several years during which they were able to establish a strong working relationship. Paula trusted Dr. Harpin, and, based on their extended discussions, she eventually accepted his diagnosis of her problem. Treatment continued to follow an interpersonal, problem-solving approach, in which Paula was encouraged to learn and use new, nondissociative coping skills to deal with stressful events. Emphasis was placed on the identification of strong feelings and the recognition of logical connections between these feelings and specific life events.

Paula's relationship with Cal, the older businessman, illustrates the utility of this approach. Their disagreements, and the confusion associated with their on-and-off affair, had been a source of considerable anxiety and anger for many years. Although it had originally seemed that Cal might rescue Paula from her terrible family situation, he had betrayed her by marrying another woman. Many people experience this type of bitter disappointment; most find a way to resolve their strong, ambivalent feelings and move on to other relationships. Unfortunately, for more than 20 years, Paula had responded to her encounters with Cal using dissociative responses. She continued the romance through one of her alters, Heather. Switching between Paula and Heather, she would alternately threaten to kill Cal and then herself. After many extended discussions of this situation with Dr. Harpin, Paula was finally able to recognize that Cal provided one of the consistent triggers for her dissociative episodes. She confronted Cal and ended their relationship. Shortly after this success, Heather stopped appearing. That particular alter had apparently been integrated with Paula, the host personality.

Paula's relationship with her children had been another source of considerable stress over the years. Arguments with them, and with her mother over her role as a parent, may also have served as a stimulus for dissociative responses. Her son and daughter, now young adults, remained angry for many legitimate reasons. They had been left alone frequently and inconsistently while they were growing up. They had also been bitterly disappointed on numerous occasions when Paula had failed to honor promises that she made to them. Previous attempts to discuss these feelings had been fruitless, in large part because Paula did not recognize her dissociative disorder as the root of the problem with these relationships. Paula had to accept responsibility for her own inconsistent and occasionally harmful parenting behaviors. The children also had to understand her disorder. Many sessions were devoted to discussions of these issues and to face-to-face meetings between Paula and her daughter (her son lived too far away to be included in this process). This aspect of Paula's family situation improved a great deal.

As treatment progressed, Dr. Harpin made an effort to avoid, whenever possible, speaking directly to the alters. For example, he sometimes received phone calls from Sherry, usually to report something inappropriate that Paula had done. Whenever the caller identified herself as one of the alters, Dr. Harpin would ask to speak to Paula. He also began to discourage their appearance in sessions. Over a period of several months, some of the alters stopped making appearances and seemed no longer to influence Paula's behavior. When asked about them, Paula and Sherry (the alter who had been most aware of the others) would reply, "Oh, she's not around anymore."

As the number of alters decreased, Dr. Harpin also noticed a shift in Sherry's attitude toward Paula. She had originally been contemptuous and hostile, but she gradually became compassionate and protective. Dr. Harpin sometimes felt that Sherry had become something like a surrogate therapist. Paula became increasingly aware of Sherry's attitudes and feelings, which were sometimes more adaptive or appropriate than Paula's because they were informed by a more complete understanding of her experience (Janet's being more fragmented by dissociative experiences). Some of the tangible distinctions between these personalities also seemed to fade. For example, the voices in which Paula and Sherry spoke had always been easy to distinguish. Paula was usually distressed when she called, and her voice was often agitated and shrill. Over time, it became softer and more stable in tone. Their accents and vocabularies had also been different (with Sherry using a more prominent rural dialect).

Discussion

The complex and puzzling nature of Dissociative Identity Disorder (DID) is illustrated in the controversy surrounding its name. It was formerly known as Multiple Personality Disorder because most descriptions of the syndrome have emphasized the diagnostic importance of several alter personalities. One unfortunate consequence of this approach has been a tendency toward public sensationalism and a preoccupation with counting the exact number of alters exhibited by any patient. These estimates have occasionally reached preposterous numbers, with some clinicians claiming to see patients who have hundreds of personalities. The dissociative disorders committee for *DSM-IV* (APA, 1994) felt strongly that a different approach should be encouraged. The chairperson of that committee, David Spiegel, explained that "there is a widespread misunderstanding of the essential psychopathology in this dissociative disorder, which is failure of integration of various aspects of identity, memory, and consciousness. The problem is not having *more than one personality*; it is having less than one personality" (cited in Hacking, 1995 p. 18). For this reason, the name was changed, and it is called Dissociative Identity Disorder (DID) in *DSM-IV-TR* (APA, 2003).

Dissociative Identity Disorder is a rare phenomenon. Prior to 1980, fewer than two or three hundred cases had been reported in the professional literature (Fahy, 1988). This number is incredibly small compared to the millions of patients who suffer from disorders such as schizophrenia and depression at any point in time. Some investigators have suggested that DID appears more frequently than previously assumed (e.g., Ross, 1997a), but these claims have been disputed (e.g., Lilienfeld & Lynn, 2003; Piper & Merskey, 2004). One small but careful study suggests that the prevalence of DID in the general population is much less than 1 percent (Akyuez et al., 1999).

DID has attracted considerable attention, partly because a few dramatic cases have received widespread publicity through popular books and films. These include *The Three Faces of Eve* (Thigpen & Cleckley, 1957) and *Sybil* (Schreiber, 1973). Sybil was one of the most famous cases in psychiatry during the twentieth century; interest surrounding the book and the film fueled an enormous increase in interest in this fascinating phenomenon throughout the 1970s and 1980s. The authenticity of the Sybil case has been seriously questioned, however. Some critics contend that the therapist influenced this patient to adopt alternate personalities by employing different names to identify her varying mood states (Acocella, 1999; Rieber, 1999). Unfortunately, for many years, case studies such as these were our best source of information about the disorder. A few investigators have managed to identify samples of patients with DID for the purpose of research. Their descriptions have made significant contributions to the base of knowledge that is now available regarding this enigmatic disorder.

Among the cases of DID that have been reported, a few patterns stand out. First, most cases of DID are women, with the ratio of women to men being at least five to one. Most DID patients are first assigned that diagnosis in their late twenties or early thirties. Many of these people have already received mental health services while receiving a different diagnosis, often some type of mood disorder, substance-use disorder, schizophrenia, or borderline personality disorder (Putnam, 1989; Ross, 1997a).

DSM-IV-TR (APA, 2000) lists the following diagnostic criteria for Dissociative Identity Disorder:

A.   The subject exhibits two or more distinct identities or personality states (each with its own relatively enduring pattern of perceiving, relating to, and thinking about the environment and self)

B.   At least two of these identities or personality states recurrently take control of the person's behavior

C.   The subject is unable to recall important personal information that is too extensive to be explained by ordinary forgetfulness

D. The disorder is not due to the direct physiological effects of a substance (such as blackouts or chaotic behavior during alcohol intoxication)

The manual also notes that the transition between different personalities is usually sudden and often beyond voluntary control.

Memory disturbances are perhaps the most important feature of this disorder (Dorahy, 2001; Eich et al., 1997). Most people behave differently, or may seem to be somewhat different people, as a function of the environmental stimuli with which they are confronted, but the changes are seldom as dramatic or complete as those seen in cases of DID. Furthermore, very few people forget what they have done or who they are whenever they alter their pattern of behavior. In DID, the original personality is presumably unaware of the existence of the alters. It is not unusual for the person to express concern about large chunks of time that seem to be missing or unaccounted for. The alter personalities may, or may not, be aware of one another or "co-conscious." At any given moment only one personality is controlling the person's behavior and interacting with the environment, but other personalities may simultaneously perceive, and subsequently remember, events that are taking place. Of course, the inability to recall personal information is based almost exclusively on self-report. There is a serious need for the development of more objective measures of memory impairment in DID (Allen & Iacono, 2001).

The boundaries of this diagnostic category are difficult to define (Dell, 2001; Spiegel, 2001). Some clinicians have argued that it should be considered broadly, while others would prefer that the term be applied only to severe or classic cases. Putnam (1993), author of the most authoritative book on DID (Putnam, 1989), has recommended that clinicians make a diagnosis of DID only after they have: (1) witnessed a switch between two alter personality states, (2) met a given alter personality on at least three separate occasions, so that they can evaluate the degree of uniqueness and stability of the alter personality state, and (3) established that the patient has amnesias, either by witnessing amnesic behavior or by the patient's report.

Because the disorder is rare and clinicians are not routinely familiar with its manifestations, some patients have probably been misdiagnosed as suffering from other disorders, most notably schizophrenia and borderline personality disorder. Several diagnostic signs might alert a clinician to suspect that a patient may be experiencing DID (Greaves, 1980). These include:

1. Reports of time distortions or time lapses
2. Reports of being told of behavioral episodes by others that are not remembered by the patient
3. Reports of notable changes in the patient's behavior by a reliable observer, during which time the patient may call him- or herself by different names or refer to him- or herself in the third person
4. Elicitability of other personalities through hypnosis
5. The use of the word "we" in the course of an interview in which the word seems to take on a collective meaning rather than an editorial "we"

6. The discovery of writing, drawings, or other productions or objects among the patient's personal belongings that he or she does not recognize and cannot account for

7. A history of severe headaches, particularly when accompanied by blackouts, seizures, dreams, visions, or deep sleep

Paula exhibited almost all of the signs included on this list. Time lapses and headaches were a frequent source of concern when she began treatment at the student health center. She had been told about incidents that she could not remember as far back as high school. Her children and at least one professor had noticed marked changes in her behavior that were not easily explained by environmental circumstances. It should be emphasized, of course, that none of these problems, alone or in combination, can be considered sufficient evidence to diagnose DID if the patient does not also meet other specific diagnostic criteria such as those listed in *DSM-IV-TR* (APA, 2000).

Etiological Considerations

A variety of hypotheses have been proposed to account for the development of Dissociative Identity Disorder. One simple explanation is that the patient produces the symptoms voluntarily, or plays the role of having several different personalities, in an effort to attract attention or avoid responsibility. The intentional production of false symptoms is called *malingering*. A few widely publicized criminal trials in which the defendant claimed innocence by reason of insanity have indicated that the syndrome can be faked rather convincingly (Brown et al., 1999; James, 1998).

The best known example of malingering involves the case of Kenneth Bianchi, also known as the Hillside Strangler. Several experienced clinicians interviewed Bianchi after he was arrested. With the aid of hypnosis, they discovered an alter personality, Steve, who proudly claimed responsibility for several brutal rape-murders. The prosecution called Martin Orne, a psychiatrist at the University of Pennsylvania, as an expert witness to examine Bianchi. Orne raised serious questions about the case by indicating that the defendant was probably faking hypnosis during the interviews and by demonstrating that Bianchi's symptoms changed dramatically as a result of subtle suggestions (Orne, Dinges, & Orne, 1984). He proposed that the defendant was faking symptoms of DID in an attempt to avoid the death penalty. The court found Orne's skepticism persuasive, and Bianchi was eventually convicted of murder. These circumstances are clearly rather extreme; very few patients have such an obvious motive for feigning a psychological disorder. Although the Bianchi case should not be taken to mean that all patients who exhibit signs of DID are malingering or faking, it does indicate that therapists should be cautious in evaluating the evidence for any diagnostic decision, particularly when the disorder is as difficult to define and evaluate as DID (Labott & Wallach,, 2002; Thomas, 2001).

The sociocognitive model holds that DID is a product of the therapist's influence on the client (Lilienfeld et al., 1999; Spanos, 1996). This is not to say that the patient is faking the disorder, but rather that DID patients respond to cues that are provided during the course of assessment and treatment. Clinicians have frequently noted, for example, that patients with DID are easily hypnotized and that the alter personalities are often "discovered" during hypnosis, a process that is capable of inducing phenomena such as amnesia, one important symptom of dissociative disorders. According to this view, some therapists may provide their patients with information and suggestions about DID, subtly and unconsciously encouraging them to behave in ways that are consistent with these expectations, and rewarding them with extra attention and care when they adopt the role. In this regard, it is interesting to note that, while the vast majority of clinicians work an entire career without seeing a single case of DID, a small handful of therapists claim to have treated large numbers of these patients (Modestin, 1992). This radically disproportionate distribution of cases is consistent with the hypothesis that some clinicians find (and perhaps encourage the development of) symptoms in which they are particularly interested.

Are all patients with DID simply trying to please their therapists or responding to subtle suggestions? The sociocognitive model may explain some cases, but it does not provide a convincing explanation for many others. The model has a number of serious limitations (Gleaves et al., 2001). In many cases, important symptoms have been observed before the patient enters treatment. In Paula's case, the phone call from Sherry (which was the first clear-cut evidence of an independent alter personality) occurred before the use of hypnosis. Furthermore, most therapists are not looking for DID. Dr. Harpin, for example, had never seen a case of this sort before treating Paula. He went out of his way to consider other explanations of her behavior before considering the diagnosis of DID.

If DID is, in fact, a genuine psychological phenomenon involving a disturbance in consciousness and loss of volitional control, how can we account for its development? Current etiological hypotheses focus on two primary considerations: (1) the impact of repeated, overwhelming trauma during childhood—especially sexual abuse, and (2) individual differences in the ability to enter trancelike states (Forrest, 2001).

One influential model, proposed by Putnam (1989), starts with the proposition that the behavior of all human infants (less than 12 months old) is organized in a series of discrete behavioral states, which are characterized by marked contrasts in emotion and behavior. As the child matures, these states become more integrated. Transitions among them become less abrupt and increasingly subject to voluntary control. Failure to accomplish this integration can set the stage for DID. Putnam also assumes that children are able to enter dissociative states spontaneously. Some children may find this process easier than others. Those who are adept at it can presumably escape into trances as a way of protecting themselves from the psychological impact of intense trauma. This mechanism allows the child to contain painful memories and emotions outside normal conscious awareness. Alter personalities become stronger, more elaborate, and solidified as the child repeatedly enters particular dissociative states. The child eventually loses control of the process and is unable to stop it or recognize that it is happening. DID is the final product of these tragic events.

The credibility of Putnam's developmental model rests on a number of assumptions. Perhaps most important is the presumed connection between repeated traumatic events during childhood, particularly sexual abuse, and the subsequent onset of dissociative symptoms. Does the repetition of severe trauma lead inevitably to dissociative disorders? Are patients with DID always victims of prior sexual abuse? Are patients' memories always authentic? The answers to these questions are open to question (Hacking, 1995; Hornstein & Putnam, 1996). Evidence regarding DID is particularly difficult to evaluate because it is based largely on individual cases. Since the 1970s, most published cases have involved patients who reported being sexually abused as children. Paula is one example. The frequency of such reports has persuaded many clinicians that repeated sexual abuse is a necessary and sufficient condition in the etiology of DID. But how do we know that the patients' memories are accurate? This is an extremely controversial issue. Efforts to confirm patients' memories of prior abuse meet with mixed results; some can be confirmed while others cannot (Kluft, 1995; Yeager & Lewis, 1997). Cautious skepticism seems to be warranted with regard to the etiological link between abuse and DID.

Treatment

Most efforts to treat patients with Dissociative Identity Disorder have focused on two principal strategies: Stabilize the most functional or competent personality or integrate the disparate personalities into one. The former approach was employed initially by Thigpen and Cleckley (1957) in treating the patient described in *The Three Faces of Eve*. Followup reports on this case, which described the subsequent emergence of numerous additional personalities, illustrate the difficulties and possible futility of this method.

Most experts agree that integration is presently the treatment of choice (Kluft, 1999; Putnam, 1989). Dr. Harpin employed a number of techniques in trying to help Paula fuse the various alters. The first step involves facilitating recognition by the patient of the existence of alter personalities. One approach might be to use videotapes of the alter behavior in an effort to help the patient recognize radical changes that are otherwise unknown. It may also be important to help patients understand the general nature of the problem as it has appeared in others' lives so that they can gain perspective on their own dilemma. This was the goal that Dr. Harpin had in mind when he asked Paula to read *The Three Faces of Eve*. Fusion may eventually be accomplished if the main personality comes to share the memories and emotions of the alters. Finally, the most important step involves learning to react to conflict and stress in an adaptive fashion rather than engaging in the avoidance behaviors associated with dissociative states (Fine, 1999).

While working toward the process of integration, it is also important that the therapist avoid further fragmentation of the patient's behavior or personality. Unfortunately, this is a difficult caveat to heed. The existence of independent personalities of such different tastes and styles is fascinating, and the therapist is easily tempted to explore and discuss every exotic detail of the patient's experience. Extended and persistent questioning of this sort may encourage additional dissociative experiences and impede integration. The use of separate names to describe and address alter personalities may also serve to stabilize and condone their existence. Finally, although hypnosis can be a useful tool in attempting to facilitate the patient's recall of forgotten events, it can also lead to the emergence of additional personalities. None of these problems is easy to avoid. They all suggest that therapists who are confronted with patients exhibiting symptoms of Dissociative Identity Disorder must be extremely cautious in planning their interventions. They must attend to the unique features of the patient's dissociative experience without ignoring other potentially crucial aspects of the person's problem (Ross, 1997b).

The outcome of treatment for DID is sometimes very positive. Many patients respond well to extensive and prolonged psychological treatment (Maldonado et al., 2002). In that respect, Paula may also be a typical case. Optimistic impressions about the prognosis for this disorder are based largely on clinical impressions because we do not have data from long-term outcome studies with this disorder. One two-year followup study of 54 patients found that many were substantially improved (Ellason & Ross, 1997). Unfortunately, randomized clinical trials comparing the efficacy of treatments and placebo programs have not been conducted. The effective ingredients of therapy have not been identified. Treatment research in this area is well behind that in most other areas of mental health services.

CHAPTER 7

Major Depressive Disorder

Janet called the mental health center to ask if someone could help her 5-year-old son, Adam. He had been having trouble sleeping for the past several weeks, and Janet was becoming concerned about his health. Adam refused to go to sleep at his regular bedtime and also woke up at irregular intervals throughout the night. Whenever he woke up, Adam would come downstairs to be with Janet. Her initial reaction had been sympathetic, but as the cycle came to repeat itself night after night, Janet's tolerance grew thin, and she became more argumentative. She found herself engaged in repeated battles that usually ended when she agreed to let him sleep in her room. Janet felt guilty about giving in to a 5-year-old's demands, but it seemed like the only way they would ever get any sleep. The family physician was unable to identify a physical explanation for Adam's problem; he suggested that Janet contact a psychologist. This advice led Janet to inquire about the mental health center's series of parent training groups.

Applicants for the groups were routinely screened during an individual intake interview. The therapist began by asking several questions about Janet and her family. Janet was 30 years old and had been divorced from her husband, David, for a little more than one year. Adam was the youngest of Janet's three children; Jennifer was 10 and Claire was 8. Janet had resumed her college education on a part-time basis when Adam was 2 years old. She had hoped to finish her bachelor's degree at the end of the next semester and enter law school in the fall. Unfortunately, she had withdrawn from classes one month prior to her appointment at the mental health center. Her current plans were indefinite. She spent almost all of her time at home with Adam.

Janet and the children lived in a large, comfortable house that she had received as part of her divorce settlement. Finances were a major concern to Janet, but she managed to make ends meet through the combination of student loans, a grant-in-aid from the university, and child-support payments from David. David lived in a nearby town with a younger woman whom he had married shortly after the divorce. He visited Janet and the children once or twice every month and took the children to spend weekends with him once a month.

Having collected the necessary background information, the therapist asked for a description of Adam's sleep difficulties. This discussion covered the sequence of a typical evening's events. It was clear during this discussion that Janet felt completely overwhelmed. At several points during the interview, Janet was on the verge of tears. Her eyes were watery, and her voice broke as they discussed her response to David's occasional visits. The therapist, therefore, suggested that they put off a further analysis of Adam's problems and spend some time discussing Janet's situation in a broader perspective.

Janet's mood had been depressed since her husband had asked for a divorce. She felt sad, discouraged, and lonely. This feeling had become even more severe just prior to her withdrawal from classes at the university (one year after David's departure). When David left, she remembered feeling "down in the dumps," but she could usually cheer herself up by playing with the children or going for a walk. Now she was nearing desperation. She cried frequently and for long periods of time. Nothing seemed to cheer her up. She had lost interest in her friends, and the children seemed to be more of a burden than ever. Her depression was somewhat worse in the morning, when it seemed that she would never be able to make it through the day.

Janet was preoccupied by her divorce from David and spent hours each day brooding about the events that led to their separation. These worries interfered considerably with her ability to concentrate and seemed directly related to her withdrawal from the university. She had been totally unable to study assigned readings or concentrate on lectures. Withdrawing from school precipitated further problems. She was no longer eligible for student aid and would have to begin paying back her loans within a few months. In short, one problem led to another, and her attitude became increasingly pessimistic.

Janet blamed herself for the divorce, although she also harbored considerable resentment toward David and his new wife. She believed that her return to school had placed additional strain on an already problematic relationship, and she wondered whether she had acted selfishly. The therapist noted that Janet's reasoning about her marriage often seemed vague and illogical. She argued that she had been a poor marital partner and cited several examples of her own misconduct. These included events and circumstances that struck the therapist as being very common and perhaps expected differences between men and women. For example, Janet spent more money than he did on clothes, did not share his enthusiasm for sports, and frequently tried to engage David in discussions about his personal habits that annoyed her and the imperfections of their relationship. Of course, one could easily argue that David had not been sufficiently concerned about his own appearance (spending too *little* effort on his own wardrobe), that he had been too preoccupied with sports, and that he had avoided her sincere efforts to work on their marital difficulties. But Janet blamed herself. Rather than viewing these things as simple differences in their interests and personalities, Janet saw them as evidence of her own failures. She blew these matters totally out of proportion until they appeared to her to be terrible sins. Janet also generalized from her marriage to other relationships in her life. If her first marriage had failed, how could she ever expect to develop a satisfactory relationship with another man? Furthermore, Janet had begun to question her value as a friend and parent. The collapse of her marriage seemed to affect the manner in which she viewed all of her social relationships.

The future looked bleak from her current perspective, but she had not given up all hope. Her interest in solving Adam's problem, for example, was an encouraging sign. Although she was not optimistic about the chances of success, she was willing to try to become a more effective parent.

Social History

Janet was reserved socially when she was a child. She tended to have one or two special friends with whom she spent much of her time outside of school, but she felt awkward and self-conscious in larger groups of children. Although her friends were important to her and she enjoyed spending time with them, Janet waited for them to contact her. She did not initiate activities and hesitated to express her own preferences when they were trying to decide what to do. In retrospect, Janet attributed this lack of assertiveness to her fear that her friends would abandon her or ridicule her interests. She was also self-conscious about her weight. She was not obese, but she tended to be a bit plump and was therefore afraid that the others would tease her if she drew attention to herself.

This friendship pattern persisted throughout high school. She was interested in boys and dated intermittently until her junior year in high school, when she began to date one boy on a regular basis. Janet was certain that she was in love with him and soon lost all contact with the few girlfriends with whom she had been close. She and her boyfriend spent all of their time together. Janet remembered that the other kids teased them about acting as if they were married. This criticism troubled Janet, even though she fully expected that they would be married shortly after they graduated from high school.

Her marriage plans did not work out, however. She and her boyfriend broke up during Janet's first year in college. Janet met David a few weeks afterward, and they were married the following summer. Janet later wondered whether she had rushed into her relationship with David primarily to avoid the vacuum created by her previous boyfriend's sudden exit. Whatever her motivation might have been, her marriage was followed shortly by her first pregnancy, which precipitated her withdrawal from the university. For the next seven years, Janet was occupied as a full-time mother and housekeeper.

When Adam was two years old and able to attend a day-care center, Janet decided to resume her college education. Her relationship with David became increasingly strained. They had even less time than usual to spend with each other. David resented his increased household responsibilities. Janet was no longer able to prepare meals for the family every night of the week, so David had to learn to cook. He also had to share the cleaning and drive the children to many of their lessons and social activities. A more balanced and stable relationship would have been able to withstand the stress associated with these changes, but Janet and David were unable to adjust. Instead of working to improve their communications, they bickered continuously. The final blow came when David met another woman to whom he was attracted and who offered him an alternative to the escalating hostility with Janet. He asked for a divorce and moved to an apartment.

Janet was shaken by David's departure, in spite of the fact that they had not been happy together. Fortunately, she did have a few friends to whom she could turn for support. The most important one was a neighbor who had children of approximately the same ages as Janet's daughters. There were also two couples with whom she and David had socialized. They were all helpful for the first few weeks, but she quickly lost contact with the couples. It was awkward to get together as a threesome, and Janet had never been close enough with the women to preserve their relationships on an individual basis. That left the neighbor as her sole adviser and confidante, the only person with whom Janet felt she could discuss her feelings openly.

For the next few months, Janet was able to continue her studies. With the children's help she managed the household chores and kept up with her work. She even found time for some brief social activities. She agreed to go out on two blind dates arranged by people with whom she and David had been friends. These were generally unpleasant encounters; one of her dates was boring and unattractive, and the other was obnoxiously aggressive. After the latter experience, she discontinued the minimal efforts she had made to develop new friendships.

As time wore on, Janet found herself brooding more and more about the divorce. She was gaining weight, and the children began to comment on her appearance. To make matters worse, Claire became sick just prior to Janet's midterm exams. The added worry of Claire's health and her concern about missed classes and lost studying time contributed substantially to a decline in Janet's mood. She finally realized that she would have to withdraw from her classes to avoid receiving failing grades.

By this point, one month prior to her appointment at the mental health center, she had lost interest in most of her previous activities. Even casual reading had come to be a tedious chore. She did not have any hobbies because she never had enough time. She also found that her best friend, the neighbor, was becoming markedly aloof. When Janet called, she seldom talked for more than a few minutes before finding an excuse to hang up. Their contacts gradually diminished to an occasional wave across the street or a quick, polite conversation when they picked up their children from school. It seemed that her friend had grown tired of Janet's company.

This was Janet's situation when she contacted the mental health center. Her mood was depressed and anxious. She was preoccupied with financial concerns and her lack of social relationships. Adam's sleeping problem, which had begun about one week after she withdrew from her classes, was the last straw. She felt that she could no longer control her difficult situation and recognized that she needed help.

Conceptualization and Treatment

The therapist and Janet discussed her overall situation and agreed that Adam was only a small part of the problem. They decided to work together on an individual basis instead of having Janet join the parent-training group.

Janet's depression was clearly precipitated by her divorce, which had a drastic impact on many areas of her life. Increased financial burdens were clearly part of this picture, but interpersonal relationships were even more meaningful. Although the marriage had been far from ideal in terms of meeting Janet's needs, her relationship with David had been one important part of the way in which Janet thought about herself. She had lost one of her most important roles (as a wife). The therapist believed that an enduring improvement in her mood would depend on her success in developing new relationships and expanded roles for herself. And she would eventually need to learn parenting skills that would allow her to perform her maternal role more successfully. In other words, the therapist adopted a problem-solving approach to Janet's situation. He was particularly concerned about the passive and ruminative way in which she had begun to respond to the circumstances in her life. The therapist decided to encourage her to engage more actively with her environment while also teaching her to perform specific behaviors more effectively.

As an initial step, the therapist asked Janet to list all of the activities that she enjoyed. He wanted to shift attention away from the unpleasant factors with which Janet was currently preoccupied. Most of the activities Janet mentioned were things that she had not done for several months or years. For example, prior to her return to school, her favorite pastime had been riding horses. She said that she would like to begin riding again, but she felt that it was prohibitively expensive and time consuming. With considerable prodding from the therapist, Janet also listed a few other activities. These included talking with a friend over a cup of coffee, listening to music late at night after the children were asleep, and going for walks in the woods behind her home. In some cases, Janet indicated that these activities used to be pleasant, but she did not think that they would be enjoyable at the present time.

Despite Janet's ambivalence, the therapist encouraged her to pick one activity that she would try at least twice before their next meeting. A short walk in the woods seemed like the most practical alternative, considering that Adam might interrupt listening to music and she did not want to call Susan. The therapist also asked Janet to call the campus riding club to inquire about their activities.

At the same time that the therapist encouraged Janet to increase her activity level, he also began to concentrate on an assessment of her interactions with other people. For several sessions, they covered topics such as selecting situations in which Janet might be likely to meet people with whom she would be interested in developing a friendship, initiating a conversation, maintaining a conversation by asking the other person a series of consecutive questions, and other elementary issues. Having identified areas that were problematic for Janet, they discussed solutions and actually practiced, or role-played, various social interactions.

During the first few weeks of treatment, Janet's mood seemed to be improving. Perhaps most important was her luck in finding a part-time job at a local riding stable. She learned of the opening when she called to ask about the campus riding club. They were looking for someone who would feed and exercise the horses every morning. The wages were low, but she was allowed to ride as long as she wanted each day without charge. Furthermore, the schedule allowed her to finish before the girls returned from school. The money also helped her return Adam to the day-care center on a part-time basis. Janet still felt depressed when she was at home, but she loved to ride and it helped to know that she would go to work in the morning.

An unfortunate sequence of events led to a serious setback shortly after it seemed that Janet's mood was beginning to improve. Her financial aid had been discontinued, and she could no longer cover her monthly mortgage payments. Within several weeks, she received a notice from the bank threatening to foreclose her mortgage and sell her house. Her appearance was noticeably changed when she arrived for her next appointment. She was apathetic and lethargic. She cried through most of the session, and her outlook had grown distinctly more pessimistic. The therapist was particularly alarmed by an incident that Janet described as happening the previous day. She had been filling her car with gas when a mechanic at the service station mentioned that her muffler sounded like it was cracked. He told her that she should get it fixed right away because of the dangerous exhaust fumes. In his words, "that's a good way to kill yourself." The thought of suicide had not occurred to Janet prior to this comment, but she found that she could not get it out of her mind. She was frightened by the idea and tried to distract herself by watching television. The thoughts continued to intrude despite these efforts.

The therapist immediately discussed several changes in the treatment plan with Janet. He arranged for her to consult a psychiatrist, who prescribed fluoxetine (Prozac ®), an antidepressant drug. She also agreed to increase the frequency of her appointments at the clinic to three times a week. These changes were primarily motivated by the onset of suicidal ideation. More drastic action, such as hospitalization or calling relatives for additional support, did not seem to be necessary because her thoughts were not particularly lethal. For example, she said that she did not want to die, even though she was thinking quite a lot about death. The idea frightened her, and she did not have a specific plan arranged by which she would accomplish her own death. Nevertheless, the obvious deterioration in her condition warranted a more intense treatment program.

The next month proved to be a difficult one for Janet, but she was able to persevere. Three weeks after she began taking the medication, her mood seemed to brighten. The suicidal ideation disappeared, she became more talkative, and she resumed most of her normal activities. The people who owned the riding stable were understanding and held Janet's new job for her until she was able to return. The financial crisis was solved, at least temporarily, when her father agreed to provide her with substantial assistance. In fact, he expressed surprise and some dismay that she had never asked him for help in the past or even told him that she was in financial trouble. The problem-solving and social skills program progressed well after Janet began taking medication. Within several weeks, she was able to reestablish her friendship with Susan. She was able to meet a few people at the riding stable, and her social network seemed to be widening.

After Janet's mood had improved, the issue of Adam's sleeping problem was addressed. The therapist explained that Janet needed to set firm limits on Adam's manipulative behavior. Her inconsistency in dealing with his demands, coupled with the attention that he received during the bedtime scene, could be thought of as leading to intermittent reinforcement of his inappropriate behavior. Janet and the therapist worked out a simple set of responses that she would follow whenever he got up and came downstairs. She would offer him a drink, take him back to his room, tuck him in bed, and leave immediately. Ten days after the procedure was implemented, Adam began sleeping through the night without interruption. This rapid success enhanced Janet's sense of control over her situation. Her enthusiasm led her to enroll in the parent training program for which she had originally applied. She continued to improve her relationship with her children.

Janet's individual therapy sessions were discontinued nine months after her first appointment. At that point, she was planning to return to school, was still working part time at the riding stable, and had started to date one of the men she met at work. Her children were all healthy, and she had managed to keep their house. She continued to take antidepressant medication.

Discussion

A sad or dysphoric mood is obviously the most prominent feature of clinical depression. Depressed patients describe themselves as feeling discouraged, hopeless, and apathetic. This dejected emotional state is usually accompanied by a variety of unpleasant thoughts that may include suicidal ideation. Beck (1967) has described these cognitive features of depression as the *depressive triad*: a negative view of the self, the world, and the future. Depressed people see themselves as inadequate and unworthy. They are often filled with guilt and remorse over apparently ordinary and trivial events. These patients hold a similarly dim view of their environment. Everyday experiences and social interactions are interpreted in the most critical fashion. The future seems bleak and empty. In fact, some extremely depressed patients find it impossible to imagine any future at all.

Clinical depression is identified by changes in several important areas in the person's life. In addition to a prominent and relatively persistent dysphoric mood, *DSM-IV-TR* (APA, 2000, p. 356) lists several features for major depressive episodes. Specifically, at least five of the following symptoms must have been present for at least two weeks if the patient is to meet the criteria for this diagnostic category:

1. Depressed mood most of the day, nearly every day, as indicated either by subjective report (e.g., feels sad or empty) or observation made by others (e.g., appears tearful)
2. Markedly diminished interest or pleasure in all, or almost all, activities most of the day, nearly every day (as indicated either by subjective account or observation by others)
3. Significant weight loss when not dieting or weight gain (for example, a change of more than 5 percent of body weight in a month), or decrease or increase in appetite nearly every day
4. Insomnia or hypersomnia (prolonged sleep) nearly every day
5. Psychomotor agitation or retardation nearly every day (observable by others, not merely subjective feelings of restlessness or being slowed down)
6. Fatigue or loss of energy nearly every day
7. Feelings of worthlessness or excessive or inappropriate guilt (which may be delusional) nearly every day (not merely self-reproach or guilt about being sick)
8. Diminished ability to think or concentrate, or indecisiveness, nearly every day (either by subjective account or as observed by others)
9. Recurrent thoughts of death (not just fear of dying), recurrent suicidal ideation without a specific plan, or a suicide attempt or a specific plan for committing suicide

Janet clearly fit these criteria. Her mood had been markedly depressed since her separation from David. She had gained considerable weight—25 pounds in nine months. Her concentration was severely impaired, as evidenced by her inability to study and her loss of interest in almost everything. Excessive and inappropriate guilt was clearly a prominent feature of her constant brooding about the divorce. Although she did not actually attempt to harm herself, she experienced a distressing period of ruminative suicidal ideation. Sleep impairment may also have been a problem, but it was difficult to evaluate in the context of Adam's behavior. Prior to her first visit at the clinic, Janet had been sleeping less than her usual number of hours per night, and she reported considerable fatigue. It was difficult to know whether she would have been able to sleep if Adam had not been so demanding of her attention throughout the night.

Most therapists agree that it is important to recognize the difference between clinical depression and other states of unhappiness and disappointment. Consider, for example, people who are mourning the loss of a friend or relative. *DSM-IV-TR* (APA, 2000) suggests that a diagnosis of major depressive episode should be made only if bereavement persists for more than two months (assuming that the person meets the diagnostic criteria for this condition). Is this a qualitative or a quantitative distinction? Are patients who might be considered clinically depressed simply more unhappy than their peers, or are these phenomena completely distinct? This is one of the most interesting and difficult questions facing investigators in the field of mood disorders. The present diagnostic system handles the problem by including an intermediate category, dysthymia, that lies between major depressive disorder and normal mood. This category includes patients who exhibit chronic depressed symptoms that are not of sufficient severity to meet the criteria for major mood disorder.

Etiological Considerations

Several psychological models have been proposed to account for the development of major depression. Each model focuses on somewhat different features of depressive disorders (e.g., interpersonal relations, inactivity, or self-deprecating thoughts), but most share an interest in the role of negative or stressful events in the precipitation of major depression.

Freud's explanation for the development of depression began with a comparison between depression and bereavement (Freud, 1917, 1925).[1] The two conditions are similar. Both involve a dejected mood, a loss of interest in the outside world, and an inhibition of activity. One principal feature distinguishes between the person who is depressed and the person who is mourning: a disturbance of self-regard. Depressed people chastise themselves, saying that they are worthless, morally depraved, and worthy of punishment. Freud noted the disparity between such extreme negative views and the more benign opinions of other people who do not hold the depressed person in such contempt. In other words, the depressed person's view

---

[1] Freud pointed out that his account was intended to apply to only a subset of depressed patients and that biological factors were probably more important in other cases.

does not seem to be an accurate self-perception. Freud went on to argue that depressed people are not *really* complaining about themselves but are, in fact, expressing hostile feelings that pertain to someone else. Depression is therefore the manifestation of a process in which anger is turned inward and directed against the self instead of against its original object.

Why would some people direct hostility against themselves? Freud argued that the foundation for this problem is laid in early childhood. For various reasons, people who are prone to depression have formed dependent interpersonal relationships. This dependency fosters frustration and hostility. Because these negative feelings might threaten the relationship if they are expressed openly, they are denied awareness. Problems then arise when the relationship is ended, for whatever reason. The depressed person's ego presumably identifies with the lost loved one. The intense hostility that had been felt for that person is now turned against the self, or *introjected*. Following this model, treatment would consist of an attempt to make the client aware of these unconscious, hostile impulses. Their more direct expression would presumably eliminate the depression.

At least one aspect of this model seems consistent with Janet's situation. She had, in fact, formed a series of intense, dependent relationships with men, beginning in high school. One might argue that her depression was precipitated by the loss incurred during her separation and divorce from David. She resented the separation deeply. Her guilt might be seen as a criticism of David's behavior. Other aspects of Janet's behavior, however, are inconsistent with Freud's model. Although Janet was critical of herself, she was also quite vocal in David's presence. They fought openly several times, both before and after the divorce, and he was fully aware of Janet's anger and resentment. It therefore seems unlikely that Janet's depression was a simple manifestation of misdirected hostility. It is also unlikely that her depression would be relieved by simply encouraging her to express her feelings more openly.

More recent attempts to explain the development of depression in psychological terms have borrowed and extended various aspects of Freud's psychoanalytic model. One important consideration involves his observation that the onset of depression is often preceded by a dependent personality style and then precipitated by the loss of an important relationship. Personality factors and relational distress may help to explain the fact that women are twice as likely as men to develop major depression.[2] Dependent people base their self-esteem on acceptance and approval by others. Some authors have suggested that, throughout their social development, women are frequently taught to think this way about themselves (Gilligan, 1982; Notman & Nadelson, 1995). Stereotypes of female roles include descriptions of personality traits such as being passive, dependent, and emotional (while men are presumably more often encouraged to be aggressive, autonomous, and rational). An extension of this hypothesis holds that women are more likely than men to define themselves in terms of their relationships with other people. Women would then presumably be more distressed by marital difficulties and divorce. In Janet's case, the loss of her relationship with David was certainly an important consideration in

---

[2] Specific epidemiological evidence regarding the prevalence of unipolar and bipolar mood disorders is presented in Chapter 8 (p. 129).

the onset of her depression. Her sense of self-worth was severely threatened by the divorce, in spite of the fact that her marriage had been far from ideal.

Stressful life events play a causal role in the etiology of depression (Kendler et al., 2003; Monroe & Harkness, 2005). One classic study has received considerable attention because it led to the development of a model that begins to explain the relationship between environmental conditions and the onset of depression. Brown and Harris (1978) found an increased incidence of stressful events in the lives of depressed women, but only with regard to a particular subset of such events—those that were severe and involved long-term consequences for the woman's well-being. Divorce and marital separation were prominent among these events, which also included events such as illness, loss of a job, and many other types of personal adversity. The impact of a stressful event apparently depends on the meaning that the event has for the person. Severe events that occur in the context of ongoing difficulties (such as a chronically distressed marriage) and events that occur in areas of a woman's life to which she is particularly committed (such as a child's health or the development of a career) are most likely to lead to the onset of depression (Brown, 2002).

The association between stressful life events and depression is apparently bidirectional. Stress may cause depression, but depression also causes stress. In comparison to women who are not depressed and women with medical disorders, depressed women generate higher levels of stress, especially in interpersonal relationships such as marriage (Hammen, 2005). This result indicates the operation of a dynamic process. Stressors that are not related to the person's own behavior may precipitate the onset of a depressed mood. The depressed person may then engage in maladaptive ways of coping with the immediate situation, and these dysfunctional behaviors may lead to even higher levels of stress.

Several of these concepts are consistent with Janet's situation. She had clearly experienced a high level of stress in the months before she entered therapy. The divorce from David is one obvious example. Her difficulties with the children may be another instance. When Claire's illness eventually forced her to withdraw from the university, there were important long-term consequences for her graduation and subsequent plans to enter law school.

Stressful life events are likely to precipitate depression, particularly in the absence of adequate social support. The manner in which these experiences combine to take their effect, however, is currently a matter of dispute and speculation. It is important to remember that most people experience stressful events at one time or another, but most people do not become seriously depressed. What factors make some people more psychologically vulnerable? Do people who are prone to depression respond differently than others to the problems of everyday life? Are they less likely than other people to establish or maintain a protective social support network? These questions have been addressed by other etiological models.

Social learning theorists (Joiner, Coyne, & Blalock, 1999) also emphasize the importance of interpersonal relationships and social skills (cf. narcissism and dependence) in the onset and maintenance of depression. This model provides an interesting account of the way in which depressed people respond to stressful life events and the effect that these responses have on other people. Others respond empathically and are initially attentive when the depressed person talks about depressing experiences, yet, the long-range result of this process is usually negative. The depressed person's few remaining friends eventually become tired of this behavior and begin to avoid further interactions. Whatever sources of social support may have been available are eventually driven away. One important factor in this regard is a deficit in social skills. Depressed people may be ineffective in their interactions with other people. An important aspect of treatment would therefore be to identify specific skills in which the person is deficient and to teach the person more effective ways of interacting with others.

Several aspects of this model are consistent with the present case. After her separation from David, Janet had become isolated. Her long discussions with her neighbor had eventually soured their relationship and eliminated one of her last sources of social support. When Janet and her therapist discussed things that she might do to meet new friends, she seemed lost. The few attempts that she had made, such as her blind dates, had gone badly, and she did not know where else to begin.

Another consideration in social learning views of depression involves the way in which people respond to the onset of a depressed mood. Some people try to distract themselves from negative emotions by becoming involved in some activity. Others respond in a more passive fashion and tend to ruminate about the sources of their distress. Nolen-Hoeksema (2002) proposed that people who respond in a passive, ruminative way will experience longer and more severe periods of depression. She also suggested that this factor may account for gender differences in the prevalence of depression because women are more likely than men to employ this response style. Janet's behavior following her divorce fits nicely with Nolen-Hoeksema's conceptual framework. Although Janet initially tried to cope actively with her various problems, she soon relinquished most of her efforts to find new friends or to keep up with her studies. She frequently found herself brooding about the divorce and the hopeless nature of her circumstances. Her therapist encouraged Janet to engage more frequently in pleasant activities in an effort to break this cycle of passive, ruminative behavior.

In addition to the social and behavioral aspects of depression, it is also important to consider the way in which depressed people perceive or interpret events in their environment. What do they think about themselves and things that happen in their world? More specifically, how do they explain the experience of negative events? Beck (1987)[3] has proposed that certain negative cognitive patterns play a prominent role in people who are prone to the development of depression. The hopelessness theory of depression presents a similar view (Alloy et al., 2004). According to this theory, the perceived occurrence of negative life events may lead to the development of hopelessness, which in turn causes the onset of symptoms of depression. Two cognitive elements define the state of hopelessness: (1) the expectation that highly desired outcomes will not occur or that highly aversive outcomes will occur, and (2) the belief that the person cannot do anything (is *helpless*) to change the likelihood that these events will occur.

---

[3] Specific epidemiological evidence regarding the prevalence of unipolar and bipolar mood disorders is presented in Chapter 8 (p. 129).

Why do some people become hopeless after negative experiences while others do not? The theory holds that the likelihood of developing hopelessness will depend on the person's inferences regarding three factors: the cause of the event, the consequences of the event, and the implications of the event with regard to the self. For example, hopeless depression is likely to occur if the person views a negative event as being important and also attributes the event to factors that are enduring (stable) and likely to affect many outcomes (global). The theory also recognizes that the perceived consequences of the negative event may be as important as inferred causes. If the person views the negative consequences of the event as important, persistent, and wide-ranging, depression will be more likely to develop than if the consequences are viewed as unimportant, short-lived, or limited in scope. The third and final consideration involves negative inferences about the self. Depression is a more likely outcome if the person interprets a negative event to mean that she or he is a less able, worthy, or desirable person.

Depressed people do express an inordinately high proportion of negative statements about themselves and how they relate to the world. Janet's verbal behavior provided several clear examples of the negative schemas that Beck has described, and her interpretation of the events leading up to and surrounding her divorce fit nicely with the hopelessness theory. She believed that the disintegration of her marriage was her own fault rather than David's; she argued that her failure in that relationship was characteristic of her interactions with all other men rather than specific to one person; and she maintained that she would never be able to change this pattern of behavior.

No one doubts that depressed people express negative thoughts. The difficult question, and one that is currently a matter of considerable controversy, is whether cognitive events play a central, formative role in the development of depression. Are they antecedents or consequences of emotional changes? Cognitive theorists have reported a considerable amount of empirical evidence in support of their position (e.g., Gotlib & Neubauer, 2000).

Treatment

Janet's treatment involved a combination of psychotherapy and antidepressant medication. Following the social learning/interpersonal model, her therapist focused on increasing Janet's activity level and helping her learn new social skills. By encouraging activities such as riding, the therapist hoped to interrupt and reverse the ongoing, interactive process in which social isolation, rumination, and inactivity led to increased depression, depression led to further withdrawal, and so on. Through the development of new response patterns, particularly those involving interpersonal communication and parenting skills, he hoped to enable Janet to deal more effectively with future stressful events. Increased social activity and more effective communication would also lead to a more supportive social network that might help reduce the impact of stressful events.

The therapy that Janet received was, in many respects, quite similar to another psychological approach to treating depression that is known as interpersonal psychotherapy, or IPT (Frank, 1996; Mufson et al., 2004). The focus of IPT is the connection between depressive symptoms and current interpersonal problems. Relatively little attention is paid to long-standing personality problems or developmental issues. The treatment takes a practical, problem-solving approach to resolving the sorts of daily conflicts in close relationships that can exacerbate and maintain depression. Deficits in social skills are addressed in an active and supportive fashion. The depressed person is also encouraged to pursue new activities that might take the place of relationships or occupational roles that have been lost. Therapy sessions often include nondirective discussions of social difficulties and unexpressed or unacknowledged negative emotions as well as role-playing to practice specific social skills.

Antidepressant medication was introduced when the risk of suicide became apparent. Janet's suicidal ideation was not extremely lethal. She had not planned a particular method by which she might end her life, and she reported that the idea of harming herself was frightening. The risk would have been much greater if she did have more specific plans and if she had really wanted to die. Nevertheless, her morbid ruminations marked a clear deterioration in her condition that called for more intensive treatment. Three general classes of drugs are useful in the treatment of depression: selective serotonin reuptake inhibitors (SSRIs), tricyclics (TCAs), and monoamine oxidase (MAO) inhibitors. Improvements in the patient's mood and other specific affective symptoms are typically evident after two to four weeks of drug treatment. Their continued administration also reduces the probability of symptomatic relapse.

Janet was given fluoxetine (Prozac), which is an SSRI. Selective serotonin reuptake inhibitors were developed in the 1980s and now account for most prescriptions written for antidepressant medication (Hirschfeld, 2001). Additional examples of SSRIs include fluvoxamine (Luvox®), sertraline (Zoloft®), and paroxetine (Paxil®). The SSRIs inhibit the reuptake of serotonin into the presynaptic nerve ending and therefore increase the amount of serotonin available in the synaptic cleft. SSRIs have fewer side effects (such as weight gain, constipation, and drowsiness) than TCAs or MAO inhibitors; they are easier to take (one pill a day instead of experimenting for weeks to find the proper dosage); and they are less dangerous if the patient takes an overdose. This does not mean that they are without side effects of their own. Some patients experience nausea, headaches, fatigue, restlessness, and sexual side effects such as difficulty in reaching orgasm. Controlled outcome studies indicate that Prozac and other SSRIs are at least as effective as traditional forms of antidepressant medication (Kroenke et al., 2001). Medication and psychotherapy are both effective forms of treatment for people who suffer from major depression (Hollon, Thase, & Markowitz, 2002).

One obvious disadvantage associated with both medication and psychotherapy is the extended delay involved in achieving therapeutic effects. In the face of a serious suicidal threat, for example, the therapist may not be able to wait several weeks for a change in the patient's adjustment. There are also many patients who do not respond positively to medication or psychosocial treatment approaches. Another form of intervention that may be tried with depressed patients, particularly if they exhibit profound motor retardation and have failed to respond positively to antidepressant medication, is electroconvulsive therapy (ECT). In the standard ECT procedure, a brief seizure is induced by passing an electrical current between two electrodes that have been placed over the patient's temples. A full course of treatment generally involves the induction of six to eight seizures spaced at 48-hour intervals. The procedure was first introduced as a treatment for schizophrenia, but it soon became apparent that it was most effective with depressed patients. Many studies have supported this conclusion (Husain et al., 2004).

Much of the controversy surrounding ECT is based on misconceptions concerning the procedure and its effects. Although it is often referred to as "shock therapy," ECT does not involve the perception of an electrical current. In fact, a short-acting anesthetic is administered prior to the seizure so that the patient is not conscious when the current is applied. Many of the deleterious side effects of ECT have been eliminated by modifications in the treatment procedure, such as the use of muscle relaxants to avoid bone fractures during the seizure (Abrams, 2002). The extent and severity of memory loss can be greatly reduced by the use of unilateral electrode placement. If both electrodes are placed over the nondominant hemisphere of the patient's brain, the patient can experience less verbal memory impairment, but the treatment may be less effective in terms of its antidepressant results. There is, of course, the serious question of permanent changes in brain structure and function. Some critics of ECT have argued that it produces irreversible neurological impairment. Proponents of ECT maintain that the evidence for this conclusion is inadequate (Abrams, 2002). Most of the objections to the use of ECT are based on misconceptions. The evidence supporting its therapeutic efficacy seems to justify the continued use of ECT with some severely depressed patients who have not responded to less intrusive forms of treatment.

CHAPTER 8

Bipolar Mood Disorder

By the time he was admitted to the hospital, George Lawler was talking a mile a minute. He harangued the other patients and ward staff, declaring that he was the coach of the U.S. Olympic track team and offering to hold tryouts for the other patients in the hospital. His movements were rapid and somewhat erratic as he paced the halls of the ward and explored every room. At the slightest provocation, he flew into a rage. When an attendant blocked his entrance to the nursing station, he threatened to report her to the president of the Olympic committee. He had not slept for three nights. His face was covered with a stubbly growth of beard, and his hair was scattered in various directions. His eyes were sunken and bloodshot, but they still gleamed with an intense excitement.

His life had taken a drastic change over the past two weeks. George was 35 years old, married, and the father of two young children. He worked at a small junior college where he taught physical education and coached both the men's and women's track teams. Until his breakdown, the teams had been having an outstanding season. They were undefeated in dual competition and heavy favorites to win the conference championship. The campus was following their accomplishments closely because it had been many years since one of the school teams had won a championship. In fact, track was the only sport in which the school had a winning record that season.

This was not the first time that George had experienced psychological problems. His first serious episode had occurred during his junior year in college. It did not seem to be triggered by any particular incident; in fact, things had been going well. George was playing defensive back on the university football team. He was in good academic standing and fairly popular with the other students. Nevertheless, during the spring semester, George found that he was losing interest in everything. It was not surprising that he did not look forward to classes or studying. He had never been an outstanding student. But he noticed that he no longer enjoyed going out with his friends. They said he seemed depressed all the time. George said he just did not care anymore. He began avoiding his girlfriend, and, when they were together, he found fault with almost everything she did. Most of his time was spent in his apartment in front of the television. It did not seem to matter what program he watched because his concentration was seriously impaired. He kept the set on as a kind of distraction, not as entertainment. When he did not show up for spring football practice, the coach called him to his office for a long talk. George told his coach that he did not have the energy to play football. In fact, he did not feel he could make it through the easiest set of drills. He did not care about the team or about his future in sports. Recognizing that George's problem was more than a simple lack of motivation, the coach persuaded him to visit a friend of his—a psychiatrist at the student health clinic. George began taking antidepressant medication and attending individual counseling sessions. Within several weeks he was back to his normal level of functioning, and treatment was discontinued.

George had also experienced periods of unusual ambition and energy. As a student, he had frequently spent several days cramming for exams at the end of a semester. Many of his friends took amphetamines to stay awake, but George seemed able to summon endless, internal reserves of energy. In retrospect, these periods seemed to be clear-cut hypomanic episodes, but, at the time, they went relatively unnoticed.[1] George's temporary tendency toward excess verbosity, his lack of need for sleep, and his ambitious goals did not seem pathological. In fact, these energetic intervals were quite productive, and his behavioral excesses were probably adaptive in the competitive university environment.

There had been two subsequent episodes of depression with symptoms that were similar to those of the first episode. The most recent incident had occurred eight months prior to his current hospitalization. It was September, two weeks after the start of the fall semester. George had been worried about his job and the team all summer. Who would replace his star sprinter who had transferred to the state university? Would his high jumper get hurt during the football season? Could they improve on last year's winning record? Over the past month, these concerns had become constant and consuming. George was having trouble getting to sleep; he was also waking up in the middle of the night for no apparent reason. He felt tired all the time. His wife and children noticed that he was always brooding and seemed preoccupied. Then came the bad news. First, the athletic department told him that he would not get an increase in travel funds, which he had expected. Then he learned that one of his assistant coaches was taking a leave of absence to finish working on her degree. Neither of these events would have a drastic effect on the upcoming season, but George took them to be disasters. His mood changed from one of tension and anxiety to severe depression. Over several days, George became more and more lethargic until he was almost completely unresponsive. His speech was slow and, when he did say more than a word or two, he spoke in a dull monotone. Refusing to get out of bed, he alternated between long hours of sleep and staring vacuously at the ceiling. He called the athletic director and quit his job, pointing to minor incidents as evidence of his own incompetence. He believed, for example, that the assistant coach had quit because of a brief argument that he had had with her six months earlier. In fact, they had a positive relationship, and she had always planned to return to school at one time or another. She was leaving earlier than she had expected for personal reasons. George seemed to be blaming himself for everything. He apologized profusely to his wife and children for failing them as a husband and father. His despair seemed genuine. Suicide appeared to be the only reasonable solution. He threatened to end it all if his family would only leave him alone.

---

[1] "Hypomania" refers to an episode of increased energy that is not sufficiently severe to qualify as a full-blown manic episode.

George's wife, Cheryl, called the psychiatrist who had treated him during his last episode (two years earlier) and arranged a special appointment. The psychiatrist decided to prescribe lithium carbonate, a drug that is used to treat manic episodes but that is also an effective antidepressant with bipolar patients (those who show both manic and depressed phases of disturbance). Although George had never been hospitalized for a manic episode, the psychiatrist suggested that his past history of "manic-like" behavior (increased energy, sleeplessness, inflated self-esteem, and so on) and his positive family history for bipolar mood disorder (his uncle Ralph) were both consistent with the diagnosis of bipolar disorder. The lithium seemed to be effective. Three weeks later, George was back at work. Maintenance doses of lithium were prescribed in an attempt to reduce the frequency and severity of future mood swings.

His first fully developed manic period began suddenly near the end of the next spring track season. The team was having a good year, and a few team members had turned in remarkable individual performances. Two days before the conference meet, Cheryl noticed that George was behaving strangely. There was a driven quality about his preparation for the meet. He was working much longer hours and demanding more from the athletes. When he was home, he talked endlessly about the team, bragging about its chances for national recognition, and planning intricate strategies for particularly important events. Cheryl was very worried about this change in George's behavior, but she attributed it to the pressures of his job and assured herself that he would return to normal when the season was over.

George was clearly losing control over his own behavior. The following incident, which occurred on the day of the conference meet, illustrates the dramatic quality of his disturbance. While the men's team was dressing in the locker room prior to taking the field, George paced rapidly up and down the aisles, gesturing emphatically and talking at length about specific events and the virtues of winning. When the men were all in uniform, George gathered them around his own locker. Without Cheryl's knowledge, he had removed a ceremonial sword from their fireplace mantel and brought it with him that morning. He drew the sword from his locker and leaped up on a bench in the midst of the men. Swinging the sword above his head, he began chanting the school fight song. The athletes joined in, and he led them out onto the field screaming and shaking their fists in the air. A reporter for the school newspaper later described the incident as the most inspirational pre-game performance he had ever seen in a locker room. Without question, the team was driven to an exceptional emotional peak, and it did go on to win the meet by a huge margin. In fact, George was later given the school's annual coaching award. His behavior prior to the meet was specifically cited as an example of his outstanding leadership qualities. Unfortunately, the action was also another manifestation of psychopathology and a signal of further problems that would soon follow.

George did not return home after the meet. He stayed in his office, working straight through the night in preparation for the regional meet. Cheryl was finally able to locate him by phoning his friend who worked in the office next door. She and his colleagues tried to persuade him to slow down, but he would not listen. The next morning George was approached by a reporter from the school newspaper. Here, George thought, was the perfect opportunity to expound on his ability as a coach and to publicize his exciting plans for future competition. The interview turned into a grandiose tirade, with George rambling uninterrupted for three hours. The reporter could neither interrupt nor extract himself from this unexpected and embarrassing situation.

The interview turned into a professional disaster for George. Among other things, George boasted that he was going to send the star high jumper from the women's team to the NCAA national meet in Oregon. He planned to go along as her chaperon and said that he would pay for their trip out of the proceeds of a recent community fund-raising drive. This announcement was startling in two regards. First, the money in question had been raised with the athletic department's assurance that it would be used to improve the college's track facilities and to sponsor running clinics for local children. George did not have the authority to reroute the funds. His announcement was certain to anger the business leaders who had organized the drive. Second, the prospect of a married male coach chaperoning a female athlete, who also happened to be quite attractive, promised to raise a minor scandal in their small, conservative community. Recognizing the sensitive nature of these plans, the reporter asked George if he might want to reconsider his brash announcement. George replied-asking the reporter to quote him—that it was not every year that he had the opportunity to take a free trip with a pretty girl, and he was not about to pass it up. He added that this might blossom into a genuine romance.

The article appeared, along with a picture of George, on the front page of the school paper the next morning. His disheveled appearance and outrageous remarks raised an instant furor in the athletic department and the school administration. The head of the department finally located George in his office making a series of long-distance calls. The director demanded an explanation and immediately found himself in the midst of an ear-shattering shouting match. George claimed that he had just been named head coach of the Olympic track team. He was now calling potential assistant coaches and athletes around the country to organize tryouts for the following month. Any interference, he claimed, would be attributed to foreign countries that were reluctant to compete against a team led by a coach with such a distinguished record.

The department head realized that George was not kidding and that he could not reason with him. He returned to his own office and phoned Cheryl. When she arrived, they were unable to convince George that he needed help. They eventually realized that their only option was to call the police, who then took George to a psychiatric hospital. Following an intake evaluation, George was committed for three days of observation. Because he did not recognize the severity of his problems and refused to cooperate with his family and the hospital staff, it was necessary to follow an involuntary commitment procedure. The commitment order was signed by a judge on the following day, after a hospital psychiatrist testified in court that George might be dangerous to himself or others.

Social History

In most respects George's childhood was unremarkable. He grew up in a small, midwestern town where his father taught history and coached the high school football team. He had one older brother and two younger sisters. All of the children were fair-to-average students and very athletic. George loved all sports and excelled at most. When he accepted a football scholarship to the state university, everyone expected him to go on to play professional ball.

He was always popular with his peers. They looked to him for leadership, and he seemed to enjoy the role. He and his friends were mischievous but were never serious discipline problems. Although some of his friends began drinking alcohol during high school, George always refused to join them. His father had been a heavy drinker, and he did not want to follow the same path. After several years of problem drinking, George's father had joined Alcoholics Anonymous and remained sober. Everyone agreed that the change in his behavior was remarkable.

George's uncle (his mother's brother) had also experienced serious adjustment problems. This uncle was several years older than George's mother, and the principal incidents occurred before George was born. George was therefore uncertain of the details, but he had been told that his uncle was hospitalized twice following periods of rather wild behavior. A later search of hospital records confirmed that these had, in fact, been manic-like episodes. Although the uncle had been assigned a diagnosis of "acute schizophrenic reaction," contemporary diagnostic criteria would certainly have required a diagnosis of bipolar mood disorder.

Conceptualization and Treatment

When George was admitted to the hospital, he was clearly out of control. He was racing in high gear despite the fact that he had not slept for several days. He was nearing a state of physical exhaustion. The psychiatrist immediately prescribed a moderate dosage of haloperidol (Haldol®), an antipsychotic drug that is also used to treat schizophrenia. George was supposed to have been taking lithium carbonate prior to the onset of the episode, but a check of his blood-lithium level indicated that he had not been following the prescribed procedure. He was therefore started on a dose of 900 milligrams of lithium on the first day. This was increased to 1800 milligrams per day over the next two weeks. The hospital nursing staff took blood tests every third day to ensure that the blood lithium level did not exceed 1.4 milliequivalents per liter—the point at which toxic effects might be expected. After three weeks, the Haldol was discontinued and George continued to receive maintenance doses of lithium (2100 milligrams per day).

George and Cheryl were, once again, given specific instructions pertaining to the potential hazards of taking lithium. The importance of a proper diet, and particularly a normal level of salt intake, was stressed. They were also told about the early warning signs of lithium intoxication (e.g., nausea, gastrointestinal distress, muscular weakness), so that they could warn George's psychiatrist if the dosage needed to be reduced.

In addition, George was involved in a number of other therapeutic activities. He and the other patients on the ward met daily for sessions of group psychotherapy. There were also several recreational and occupational activities that the patients could choose according to their own interests. Visits by family members and close friends were encouraged during the evening hours. When George's behavior improved, he was taken off restricted status and allowed to leave the ward for short periods of time.

George was discharged from the hospital after three weeks. His behavior had improved dramatically. The first few days in the hospital had been difficult for everyone concerned. He had been so excited that the entire ward routine had been disrupted. Mealtimes were utterly chaotic, and, when the patients were supposed to go to sleep for the night, George shouted and ran around like a child going to his first slumber party. The physical exertion finally took its toll. He fell into a state of nearly complete exhaustion. After sleeping for the better part of three days, George's demeanor was somewhat more subdued. He had given up the grandiose notion about Olympic fame and seemed to be in better control of his speech and motor behavior. But he had not returned to normal. He was still given to rambling speeches and continued to flirt with the female staff members. His mood was unstable, fluctuating between comical amusement and quick irritation. In contrast to most of the other patients, George was gregarious and energetic. He organized group activities and saw himself as a hospital aide, not as a patient.

These residual symptoms dissipated gradually over the next two weeks. He was switched to voluntary status and now recognized the severity of his previous condition. In retrospect, the events that had struck him as exhilarating and amusing seemed like a nightmare. He said that his thoughts had been racing a mile a minute. He had been totally preoccupied with the conference meet and upcoming events. The locker room incident caused him considerable concern as he admitted the possibility that he could have seriously injured someone with the sword.

Following discharge from the hospital, George was kept on a maintenance dosage of lithium. He attended an outpatient clinic regularly for individual psychotherapy, and his blood levels of lithium were carefully monitored. George and Cheryl also began conjoint therapy sessions with a dual purpose in mind. They needed to work on improving their own relationship, and they also wanted to acquire more effective means of interacting with and controlling their children. This aspect of the treatment program was unsuccessful. Cheryl had been seriously embarrassed by George's behavior during the manic episode. The cruelest blow came with the newspaper article in which George had announced his affection for another woman. That incident seemed to leave an insurmountable wall of tension between George and Cheryl, even though they both made a serious effort to improve their relationship. The therapist noticed an improvement in their interactions during therapy sessions, but they continued to have periodic, heated fights at home. Cheryl finally decided that the situation was hopeless and, six months after George was discharged from the hospital, she filed for a divorce.

George was, of course, shaken by this development, but he managed to avoid becoming seriously depressed. His friends from work were an important source of social support, particularly during the first weeks after Cheryl and the children moved to another apartment. He also met more frequently with his therapist during this period and continued to take lithium carbonate.

Discussion

Mood disorders are characterized by a serious, prolonged disturbance of the person's emotional state. These disturbances may take the form of depression or elation. They are accompanied by a host of other problems, including changes in sleep patterns, appetite, and activity level.

Several classification systems have been used to subdivide this broad category into more homogeneous groups. The classification system that currently seems most useful and that is represented in *DSM-IV-TR* (APA, 2000) draws a distinction between bipolar and unipolar mood disorders. In bipolar disorders the patient experiences periods of extreme elation (and/or irritability) known as manic episodes. These periods usually alternate with periods of normal mood and periods of severe depression to form a kind of unpredictable emotional cycle that some patients liken to a roller-coaster ride. Unipolar patients, on the other hand, experience serious depression without ever swinging to the opposite extreme. George had exhibited manic as well as depressive symptoms, so his problem would be diagnosed as a bipolar mood disorder.

DSM-IV-TR (APA, 2000, p. 362) lists the following criteria for a manic episode:

1. A distinct period of abnormally and persistently elevated, expansive, or irritable mood lasting at least one week (or any duration if hospitalization is necessary)

2. During the period of mood disturbance, three (or more) of the following symptoms have persisted (four if the mood is only irritable) and have been present to a significant degree:

    A. Inflated self-esteem or grandiosity

    B. Decreased need for sleep, for example, feeling rested after only three hours of sleep

    C. More talkative than usual or pressure to keep talking

    D. Flight of ideas or subjective experience that thoughts are racing

    E. Distractibility, for example, attention too easily drawn to unimportant or irrelevant external stimuli

    F. Increase in goal-directed activity (either socially, at work or school, or sexually) or psychomotor agitation

G. Excessive involvement in pleasurable activities that have a high potential for painful consequences; for example, the person engages in unrestrained buying sprees, sexual indiscretions, or foolish business investments

3. The mood disturbance is sufficiently severe to cause marked impairment in occupational functioning or in usual social activities or relationships with others, or to necessitate hospitalization to prevent harm to self or others

Bipolar mood disorders should be distinguished from schizophrenia as well as from unipolar mood disorders. Kraepelin (1919, 1971) recognized that manic and schizophrenic (dementia praecox) patients often exhibit similar symptoms. These include disorganized speech, flight of ideas, and delusional thinking. He argued that the difference between the two disorders became apparent on examination of their long-term course. Most patients who fit Kraepelin's definition of schizophrenia showed a progressive deterioration without periods of recovery. Manic-depressive patients, on the other hand, frequently followed a remitting course. Although they might have repeated episodes of psychotic behavior, their adjustment between episodes was relatively unimpaired. This distinction has continued to be one of the most important considerations in the classification of serious mental disorders.

A less severe form of bipolar mood disorder is experienced by people who go through episodes of expansive mood and increased energy that are not sufficiently severe to be considered manic episodes. These are called *hypomanic episodes*. According to *DSM-IV-TR* (APA, 2000), a person who has experienced at least one major depressive episode, at least one hypomanic episode, and no full-blown manic episodes, would be assigned a diagnosis of Bipolar II Disorder. A hypomanic episode is defined in terms of the same symptoms as those that describe a manic episode. The distinction between manic and hypomanic episodes is based on duration and severity. The minimum duration of symptoms for a hypomanic episode is four days, as opposed to one week for a manic episode. In a hypomanic episode, the mood change must be noticeable to others, but it must not lead to impairment in social or occupational functioning or require hospitalization. If the mood change becomes that severe, it is considered a manic episode.

Another type of mood disorder is known as *cyclothymia*, which is a chronic but less severe form of bipolar disorder. People who meet the criteria for cyclothymia experience several hypomanic episodes and several periods of minor depression during a period of two years. They do not, however, experience periods of disturbance that are sufficiently severe to meet the criteria for major depressive episode or manic episode during the first two years of their disturbance. After the initial two years of cyclothymia, full-blown episodes of mania or major depression will require that an additional diagnosis, such as Bipolar I Disorder or Bipolar II Disorder, be superimposed on the Cyclothymic Disorder.

Estimates of the prevalence of mood disorders in the general population indicate some fairly consistent patterns (Kessler, 2002; Waraich et al., 2004). In the Epidemiologic Catchment Area (ECA) study, lifetime prevalence was 0.8 percent for Bipolar I Disorder and 0.5 percent for Bipolar II Disorder. The lifetime prevalence for major depression was much higher: 4.9 percent overall. Gender differences are not found in the risk for bipolar mood disorders, but there are important gender differences in the rates for men and women for major depression. In the ECA study, women had a 7.0 percent lifetime prevalence for major depression, while the comparable rate for men was 2.6 percent.

There are also important differences between unipolar and bipolar disorders in terms of both the age of onset and the course of the disorder (Angst, Sellaro, & Angst, 1998; Johnson & Kizer, 2002). Bipolar patients tend to be younger than unipolar patients at the time of their first episode of disturbance, usually between the ages of 20 and 30. Bipolar patients also tend to experience a greater number of psychotic episodes during subsequent years. One large-scale followup study examined the psychosocial consequences of bipolar and unipolar mood disorders at the time that patients were seeking treatment and again five years later (Coryell et al., 1993). The results indicated that both types of mood disorder were frequently associated with serious and pervasive declines in occupational and social functioning. The absence of overt symptoms did not necessarily mean that patients returned to expected levels of functioning. Profound interpersonal impairments were even evident among those patients whose clinical condition had remained improved throughout the final two years of followup.

George's case was typical of the classic picture of manic-depressive illness. He showed an early onset of symptoms and a relatively complete remission between episodes. On the other hand, his experience was also consistent with that of many patients in the followup study described above. His behavior was so disruptive during each manic episode that it had long-term, negative consequences for his social and occupational adjustment. He had serious problems with his job, and his marriage ended in divorce.

Etiological Considerations

The fact that George's maternal uncle had also experienced manic episodes is consistent with the literature concerning genetic factors in mood disorders. Several family studies have found that the biological relatives of patients with mood disorders are more likely to develop mood disorders than are people in the general population. These data are usually reported in terms of "morbid risk," or the probability that given individuals will develop the disorder during their lifetimes. Several studies have now reported that the relatives of unipolar depressives are at increased risk for unipolar depression but that they are unlikely to exhibit bipolar mood disorder (Berrettini, 2000; McGuffin et al., 2003). The relatives of bipolar patients, on the other hand, typically demonstrate an increased risk for both unipolar and bipolar disorders. These data have generally been taken to indicate that the bipolar and unipolar subgroups are genetically distinct. George's positive family history for bipolar disorder thus may be taken as further validation of his bipolar diagnosis and was, in fact, helpful in the decision to try lithium carbonate prior to his first full manic episode.

The role of genetic factors in the etiology of mood disorders would be clearer if a specific model of genetic action could be identified. Polygenic models of transmission have not been ruled out, but many investigators are currently placing their bets on a single-locus model in order to take advantage of exciting technological advances in a procedure known as *linkage analysis*. This technique involves studying the occurrence of mood disorder across a family pedigree and simultaneously assessing some other characteristic—a genetic marker for which the mode of transmission is fully understood (e.g., red-green color blindness is known to result from mutations on the X chromosome). When the genes are linked, that is, when they are sufficiently close together on a chromosome, the family pedigree will tend to show that the two traits being examined are inherited together. Several groups of investigators have reported successful linkage analyses with regard to bipolar mood disorder. Recent information points toward chromosome 18 (e.g., McMahon et al., 2001) as well as several other chromosomes (Blackwood, Visscher, & Muir, 2001). Unfortunately, other laboratories have failed to find evidence for genetic linkage in bipolar disorder. What should we make of these inconsistencies? One possible conclusion is that the mood disorders are genetically heterogeneous (i.e., they are produced by different genes in different people with similar disorders). Further evidence is needed from additional linkage studies, and the next few years will undoubtedly witness exciting reports in this area of research (Goldman & Mazzanti, 2002).

Although genetic factors play some role in the development of bipolar mood disorder, they cannot account for it completely. Various experiences throughout the person's life must also influence the onset or expression of psychotic symptoms as well as the course of the disorder (Johnson & Roberts, 1995). The generally accepted diathesis-stress model would suggest that bipolar patients inherited some unidentified form of predisposition to the disorder and that the expression of this predisposition then depends on subsequent environmental events. Stressful life events frequently play an important role in the course of the disorder, particularly in triggering relapse (Cohen et al., 2004).

In George's case it would be reasonable to wonder whether the highly competitive atmosphere associated with college coaching might have triggered the onset of his manic symptoms or his depressive episodes. The weeks preceding his manic episode were busier than usual. His teams had been winning, and the athletic department's administration seemed to be putting considerable emphasis on the final meets of the season. Viewed from George's perspective, this amounted to enormous pressure. The job situation was also compounded by his family responsibilities. As he began to spend more and more time with his team, his wife became increasingly discontent and irritable. Her demands, coupled with his coaching responsibilities, placed George in a difficult position; he could reduce the amount of time spent planning and supervising workouts, thus increasing the probability that the team would lose, or he could reduce the amount of time spent with his wife and children, thus increasing the probability that she would ask for a divorce.

George's relationship with his family illustrates the complex interactive nature of mood disorders. Although his marital problems may not have been caused by his mood disorder symptoms, they certainly made an already difficult situation virtually impossible. The marital adjustment of bipolar patients has received considerable attention in the research literature, which indicates that bipolar patients are much more likely than unipolar patients or people in the general population to be divorced

(Coryell et al., 1993). The emotional atmosphere within a family is also related to the patient's social functioning and the course of the disorder. Miklowitz and his colleagues (1995) examined family members' attitudes toward the problems of their relatives who had recently been hospitalized with manic disorders. The investigators also assessed patterns of interaction between the patients and their relatives. The patients' adjustment was then evaluated during a nine-month period following their discharge from the hospital. Patients who lived in a stressful family environment (as indicated by high ratings on either measure) were much more likely to relapse than patients from families that were rated low on both factors.

George's situation was probably typical of the problems experienced by manic patients. Cheryl was forced by his erratic behavior to act as a buffer between George and the community. When he acted strangely at work, his colleagues called her to see if she could explain his behavior. She often found herself making up excuses for him in order to avoid the unpleasant necessity of disclosing the personal details of his problems. Her efforts were then "rewarded" by his continued excesses. Cheryl gradually came to see herself as a victim. The incident with the undergraduate student was the last straw. George's behavior was even more difficult for Cheryl to understand and accept because of his inconsistency. She argued that if he were always irrational or out of control, she could easily attribute these problems to a psychiatric disorder. However, between episodes, and most of the time, George was a very reasonable, considerate person. Cheryl found it difficult to believe that he could change so drastically over such a short period of time. Her first inclination was always to attribute his wild, manic behavior to some malicious intent on his part. When he became depressed, she often blamed herself. Eventually, the problem was simply more than she could handle.

Treatment

Lithium is the treatment of choice for bipolar mood disorders. The therapeutic effects of lithium salts were first reported in 1949 by John Cade, an Australian psychiatrist. Cade had been studying the toxic effects of uric acid in guinea pigs and the possibility that the lithium ion might reduce this toxicity. He was not initially interested in behavioral effects, but he happened to notice that guinea pigs that had been injected with lithium carbonate became lethargic and unresponsive to stimuli despite remaining fully conscious. This unexpected finding led Cade to wonder whether lithium carbonate might have beneficial effects for psychotic patients who were extremely excited. He used the drug with a sequence of 10 manic patients and obtained remarkable results. Even chronic patients who had been considered untreatable responded favorably within a period of several days. Furthermore, several patients with schizophrenia who had previously been markedly restless and excited became quiet and amenable. When lithium was discontinued, the patients generally returned to their previous patterns of wild behavior.

Other clinicians soon began to experiment with the use of lithium and met with similar results. Their favorable impression of lithium's effects were later confirmed by a number of controlled double-blind studies (Geddes et al., 2004). In fact, lithium can be beneficial for patients who are depressed as well as for those who are manic. This is particularly true for bipolar patients. Several studies that used double-blind procedures and placebo control groups have concluded that lithium is effective in preventing the recurrence of manic episodes and probably effective in preventing recurrent depression in bipolar patients (Kleindienst & Greil, 2000).

Other forms of medication can also be useful in treating bipolar mood disorders. For example, certain anticonvulsant drugs such as carbamazepine (Tegretol®) and valproic acid (Depakote®), often lead to improvement in patients who have not responded to lithium. This is an important consideration because about 40 percent of bipolar patients do not show an adequate clinical response to lithium alone. These are often patients whose moods cycle rapidly (defined in *DSM-IV-TR* APA, 2000 as bipolar patients with four or more separate episodes or depression, mania, or hypomania within 12 months). The anticonvulsants may be used either on their own or in combination with lithium (Walden et al., 1998).

George responded favorably to lithium during his brief stay in the hospital, and he returned to his job soon after discharge. It is possible that the episode might have been partially caused by his failure to take the medication regularly. This is a serious problem with all forms of psychopharmacological treatment. It is particularly severe with psychotic patients who characteristically lack insight into the severity of their problem. Every effort is usually made to educate the patient in this regard. The cooperation of family members is often enlisted to assist in the regulation of daily doses. The dangers of lithium also require that patients being treated on an outpatient basis be seen regularly to monitor levels of lithium in the blood. In spite of these precautions, many patients fail to follow medication schedules designed to prevent relapse.

Psychotherapy is also an important part of treatment for many patients with bipolar mood disorder (Craighead & Miklowitz, 2000; Jones, 2004). Used in combination with lithium or other types of medication, psychotherapy can help patients cope with social circumstances that may trigger further episodes. These include family conflict and stressful life events. Treatment may be aimed at improving the person's communication skills and problem-solving abilities in order to strengthen interpersonal relationships (Frank, Swartz, & Kupfer, 2000). Psychological interventions can also be used to increase medication compliance by identifying and addressing patients' reservations about taking lithium and other drugs.

CHAPTER 9

Somatization Disorder

Meredith Coleman opened her eyes, groggy from the anaesthesia, and blinked several times. She began to moan softly. The nurse turned toward her and asked how she was feeling. She felt queasy and cold, so the nurse gently pulled the blanket up to her chin. She was 25 years old and had just had a hysterectomy because for the past year she had suffered from heavy menstrual bleeding and constant uterine pain. Her physician was very reluctant to do the operation because Meredith was young and had never had any children, but her frequent visits to his office and complaints of pain and heavy flow had finally convinced him to go ahead. He was optimistic that the procedure would improve her condition, and she was eager for relief from the bleeding and repeatedly expressed her desire to have the surgery.

Meredith spent a restless night in the uncomfortable hospital bed, her pain from the surgery only partly eased by pain medication. The next morning her gynecologist came in to check on her. Meredith was worried about the pain she still felt in her abdomen, but her doctor assured her it was normal and that she should expect the pain to continue until she had healed fully which would take weeks. At her checkup six months after the surgery, she had experienced no improvement at all in the uterine pain, despite that fact that her uterus had been removed. If anything, the pain was a little worse. The doctor assured her that it could not be uterine pain, and that nothing was wrong with her. Meredith was unsatisfied after this checkup and scheduled an appointment with her regular doctor, Dr. Griffin.

Meredith, in fact, had a number of physicians treating her for many different physical problems. She had been in poor health since she was a teenager. She had severe, stabbing pain that radiated down both of her legs nearly every day. The pain seemed to originate in her lower back, and was somewhat unpredictable. It would seem to "burst" in her toes. Sometimes it would occur only once a day and last just a few minutes, and other times it would last for hours and bring her to tears. The pain was ruining her life.

She vaguely remembered sharp pains in her calf muscles when she was in high school, but her legs really started bothering her when she was a sophomore in college. In the beginning, the pain only occurred occasionally, but now it was a constant problem. Over the past three years, her legs had also become progressively weaker. The muscles in her legs would at times be so weak she could barely stand. She could not walk any distance at all due to this weakness. She had begun using her grandmother's old wheelchair that had been stored in the family's attic since her grandmother died. It was especially helpful when she was going to the mall where she would have to walk long distances. On certain days, her legs would completely give out and she would fall to the ground. She had been to many specialists to try to find the cause of the problem with her legs, but nobody had been able to figure it out. She had been evaluated by neurologists and had MRIs but there was no evidence of any condition that could be responsible for her symptoms. She was frequently tearful and despairing about her health, and her emotional outbursts worried her parents.

She had a number of other physical problems. Since puberty, she had suffered from frequent headaches that were characterized by sharp pain. They did not fit the typical symptom pattern of migraine headaches. She also had chest pains and often thought she was going to have a heart attack. The chest pains were her most recent symptom, only occurring over the last six months. One day, she went to the emergency room because of the chest pain and had a full workup to rule out a heart attack. The emergency physician told her anxiety was causing her chest pains, and that her heart was normal and healthy. She was surprised and insulted by these comments, because it was clear to her that she wasn't going crazy and that her chest pains were not in her head.

After meals she frequently experienced abdominal distention and uncomfortable bloating. She ate infrequently because of the bloating and because she often had nausea that made food very unappetizing. When she did eat, she would often have to lie down because of the bloating and stomachaches so severe she doubled over in pain. She had been tested extensively to rule out an ulcer or food allergy, but no cause had been discovered. Her gallbladder had been removed two years ago, but that did not relieve her symptoms.

Meredith met her husband, Steve, in college. He was a year older, and they married when he graduated from college and started his job as an insurance agent. At the time, Meredith was 21 years old. After the wedding, she never finished her degree, and her grades were suffering when she left college because her headaches made it difficult to study. Steve left her two years later, and she worked as a secretary to support herself. She lost her job after about a year when her health problems had caused her to miss too much work. So at 24 years old, she moved back in with her parents.

She did not go out very often anymore because she had trouble walking any distance and was afraid her legs would give out. She accompanied her parents to church but always wanted to hold onto her father's arm to steady herself. Her mother did all her laundry and prepared the meals. Her parents were both very concerned about their daughter's well-being. They were frustrated that no doctor could solve her problems.

When she went in for the appointment with Dr. Griffin that she made after her gynecologist told her nothing was wrong with her, she discussed her continuing uterine pain, her headaches, and her leg pains. The doctor listened sympathetically, but eventually interrupted Meredith and told her that she didn't understand what was going on. She said she could try another medication to help manage Meredith's digestive problems, to see if that would work. When Dr. Griffin handed her the prescription and opened the door of the examining room to leave, Meredith became very upset with her for giving her 12 months worth of refills. To her, that made it clear that Dr. Griffin did not want to see her back for another 12 months. When she began to cry about that, Dr. Griffin suggested that she see a psychologist for an evaluation. Meredith became indignant and angry at the suggestion of a psychologist, accusing Dr. Griffin of suggesting that she was insane. The doctor explained to Meredith that sometimes emotions complicate medical problems, and suggested that a psychological evaluation would help her determine the best course of medical treatment. Meredith finally agreed to be seen by a psychologist.

Social History

Meredith grew up in a small town where her father was a bank president and her mother was a homemaker. She was the youngest of three children. Her brother Wallace was five years older. Wallace was a natural athlete, popular, and a good student. He played baseball throughout his childhood and in college. He had attended law school and was now married and busy working to establish his law practice. Her sister Claire was two years older, and had been a cheerful, calm-natured girl who loved to ride horses. During high school, she had spent all her free time at the stables. Claire was now married to her high-school sweetheart and busy with five-year-old twins.

During Meredith's childhood, her father's mother lived with the family. She had survived a stroke that had left her very debilitated, and she had trouble walking. Meredith's mother, Evelyn, spent a lot of time caring for her. Evelyn would prepare special meals for her and would feed her because the stroke affected the use of her hands, which she could not hold steady. Evelyn was quite devoted to her mother-in-law and made sure she had everything she needed. Unfortunately, she died when Meredith was 12 years old. Meredith later told all her friends in college about her grandmother and how traumatic it had been when she died. She described her feelings of grief and the funeral in a dramatic fashion.

Evelyn was outgoing like Wallace, and she had a lot of friends. She had a busy social life, and was active in church groups and in civic organizations. As early as she could remember, Meredith never felt like she fit in. She was large-framed and tall for her age, not pretty and petite like her mother or sister. Meredith was somewhat outspoken and bossy with the other children and did not have many friends. Her mother always seemed a little embarrassed by her. However, her mother clearly was very proud of Wallace. She went to every one of his Little League games and was always bragging about his accomplishments to her friends. Meredith always felt "insignificant" and ignored, and it seemed to her that her mother had time for everybody else but her. When Meredith would try to talk to her mother about feeling left out at school with the other girls, her mother would tell her to pray about it and not to feel sorry for herself.

When Meredith began having headaches shortly after her grandmother died, her mother was very sympathetic. She would tell her to lie down and would bring her a cool compress for her head. That seemed to ease the pain some. When Meredith complained of bloating and nausea, her mother recommended that she eat blander foods that might be easier on her stomach. She began to prepare special foods for Meredith when the family meal might be too spicy or hard to digest.

In high school, Meredith became active in choir. She was very talented and had a beautiful voice. Through her singing, she began to find a measure of acceptance with other students. The choir hung out together, and Meredith was included in their activities. She continued to sing in college and decided to become a music major. She hoped for a career as an opera singer, and her professors encouraged her to develop her voice, which showed a great deal of promise. She met Steve when he asked her out after he saw her perform in a college production. He was enthralled by her voice and her stage presence. They quickly fell in love and were engaged three months later.

After they married, he was protective and tender toward her when she would take to bed with a headache or other ailment. She adored him and tried to be the perfect wife. She spent lots of time decorating their first apartment and fixed him gourmet meals. He threw himself into work, trying to establish his clientele. Meredith found it somewhat difficult to adjust to his long hours at work and his preoccupation with success. Increasingly during the day when he was gone, she would have problems with her legs. Eventually she brought her grandmother's wheelchair from home to their apartment to help her cope with getting around and to keep from falling when she felt weak. This bothered Steve. He began to criticize her and started to complain about the cost of medical bills from her frequent doctor's appointments. They continued this way for the rest of their marriage, with increasingly frequent arguments. One day, Steve announced that he wanted a divorce and that he had fallen in love with someone else. Meredith was completely devastated, but she could not convince him to stay. When he moved out and filed for divorce, she stayed in their apartment and got a job, and tried to cope until eventually she moved back with her parents.

Treatment

Meredith reluctantly made an appointment with the clinical psychologist recommended by Dr. Griffin. The psychologist, Dr. Edwards, conducted an extensive interview and tried to construct a medical history. It was difficult to get clear dates from Meredith about when her various symptoms had begun. With her written consent, Dr. Edwards obtained Meredith's medical records from Dr. Griffin and all the other physicians who had treated her. He needed to use these records to construct the chronology. They would also allow him to evaluate whether there was any medical basis to explain her numerous physical complaints. He was struck by Meredith's distress over her divorce, and her despair and sadness over her physical problems. He scheduled a followup appointment with her so he could propose a plan of treatment after he had reviewed all the medical records.

When reviewing the reams of medical records from all her treatments and evaluations, Dr. Edwards discovered that physician after physician had been unable to establish any physical basis for her numerous symptoms. Meredith's symptoms met criteria for Somatization Disorder. A person with this disorder has numerous physical symptoms that are not due to medical problems but have a psychological origin.

At their next session, he proposed a course of treatment to address her depressed mood and her somatic symptoms. Unfortunately, Meredith refused to agree to treatment. She became tearful again and told him that the only reason she agreed to see him was to help Dr. Griffin in planning her medical treatment. She didn't believe she needed a psychologist because she wasn't crazy. None of Dr. Edwards' rationales for entering psychological treatment could convince her. He eventually agreed to call Dr. Griffin with his findings to help with her medical treatment.

He described the findings of his evaluation to Dr. Griffin and suggested that she attempt to manage Meredith's problems by providing counseling in her medical practice. They discussed a general treatment plan in which Dr. Griffin would schedule regular appointments with Meredith. Meredith would also meet biweekly with Dr. Griffin's nurse. The nurse would record her symptoms, check her vital signs, and provide support and encouragement (especially for spending fewer days in bed and decreasing her wheelchair use). Dr. Griffin would meet every other month with Meredith and would review the nurse's notes on their sessions. Meredith seemed relieved by this plan, and readily agreed. Dr. Griffin also prescribed an antidepressant which she convinced Meredith to take by discussing the role of emotional upset in exacerbating pain. Dr. Edwards also encouraged Dr. Griffin to stop sending Meredith to specialists, and Meredith agreed not to contact any other physicians. After a few months, they were to decrease the frequency of these regularly scheduled sessions.

Meredith responded well to this treatment strategy. She continued to have problems with her symptoms, but with the predictable contact with her physician and the increased support and reassurance, she was somewhat less distressed by them. She kept her word about not going to other physicians. Her depressed mood improved, and she did not have any more emergency room visits. The frequency of her contact with physicians decreased and the weakness in her legs subsided. She eventually began another job, and made plans to find a new apartment of her own.

Discussion

Somatization disorder is one of the somatoform disorders, a category that also includes conversion disorder, hypochondriasis, pain disorder, and body dysmorphic disorder. Somatoform disorders are characterized by physical symptoms that appear to be due to a somatic (bodily) disease or disorder that cannot be medically explained and that frequently lead to visits to physicians for diagnosis and treatment. Many researchers believe that the physical symptoms originate in psychological distress and that somatization is a psychological mechanism in which physical symptoms express psychological distress (Hurwitz, 2004). People with a somatoform disorder do not intentionally or consciously produce the symptoms, as in malingering, which is pretending to have symptoms in order to avoid military service or legal responsibility for a crime, or for financial gain in a lawsuit, or for disability benefits. People with a somatoform disorder also differ from those with factitious disorder, which is pretending to have symptoms in order to assume the sick role. Instead, they actually experience the symptoms, such as feeling pain, experiencing weakness or seizures, or feeling bloated or nauseous, and fully believe they have a bodily medical condition. They typically seek treatment from physicians rather than psychologists or psychiatrists (Hurwitz, 2004).

Somatization disorder is defined in the *Diagnostic and Statistical Manual of Mental Disorders (DSM-IV-TR,* APA, 2000, pp. 486-490) by the following criteria:

1. A history of many physical complaints beginning before age 30 years that occur over a period of several years and result in treatment being sought or significant impairment in social, occupational, or other important areas of functioning.

2. Each of the following criteria must have been met, with individual symptoms occurring at any time during the course of the disturbance:

    a. Four pain symptoms: a history of pain related to at least four different sites or functions (e.g., head, abdomen, back, joints, extremities, chest, rectum, during menstruation, during sexual intercourse,[1] or during urination)

    b. Two gastrointestinal symptoms: a history of at least two gastrointestinal symptoms other than pain (e.g., nausea, bloating, vomiting other than during pregnancy, diarrhea, or intolerance of several different foods)

    c. One sexual symptom: a history of at least one sexual or reproductive symptom other than pain (e.g., sexual indifference, erectile or ejaculatory dysfunction, irregular menses, excessive menstrual bleeding, vomiting throughout pregnancy)

    d. One pseudoneurological symptom: a history of at least one symptom or deficit suggesting a neurological condition not limited to pain (conversion symptoms such as impaired coordination or balance, paralysis or localized weakness, difficulty swallowing or lump in throat, aphonia (inability to speak), urinary retention, blindness, deafness, seizures; dissociative symptoms such as amnesia; or loss of consciousness other than fainting)

3. Each of the symptoms in Criteria 2 cannot be fully explained by a known general medical condition or the direct effects of a substance, or when there is a related general medical condition, the physical complaints are in excess of what would be expected from the history, physical examination, or laboratory findings.

People with somatization disorder often have histrionic, excessively emotional, dramatic, vague, or attention-seeking ways of describing their physical symptoms. They are hopeful about receiving a diagnosis that will give meaning to their symptoms. The symptoms they experience fit the patient's beliefs about disease rather than actual disease process and characteristics of physiology, so they appear un-

---

[1] Some experts on sexual disorders propose that vaginismus and dyspareunia be classified as pain disorders rather than as sexual disorders (e.g., Binik, 2005; Binik, Reissing, Pukall, Flory, Payne, & Khalife, 2002).

usual or bizarre to the physician (Hurwitz, 2004). For example, a person with a somatoform disorder might experience loss of touch in a hand that affects the area covered by a glove rather than the areas of the hand and arm actually controlled by individual nerves.

When the concept of somatizing was originally developed, symptoms were thought to symbolize the patient's emotional problem (Merskey, 2004), such as a patient's aphonia (inability to speak) symbolically enacting their feeling of stifling their emotions to avoid interpersonal conflict. This speculation, rooted in psychoanalytic theories of repression, was not supported by empirical data. Current theories of pain downplay dualism, or mind-body separation, and argue that the mind and body are the same. Research indicates that the experience of pain is always the result of input both from the site of the pain and from the central nervous system, which is affected by emotions and interpersonal conflicts. It is therefore difficult to untangle the physical and psychological contributions to the experience of pain (Kirmayer, Groleau, Looper, & Dao, 2004). Emotional stress may impact a person's physical health in subtle ways through chronic activation of the hypothalamic-pituitary-adrenocortical axis or by interfering with normal sleep, which can produce physical symptoms. Immune function is also compromised by stress.

Very often people with somatoform disorders are not identified as having a psychological disorder. One study conducted a followup of patients with somatic symptoms. Years later, they continued to have somatic symptoms and continued to have frequent visits to physicians. Their general practice physician would not find any medical cause for their symptoms. After running some of their own diagnostic tests, they would refer them to specialists, who also found no cause. Eventually, the patient switched to a new general practitioner and began the course of diagnostic tests and referrals anew (Crimlisk, Bhatia, Cope, David, Marsden, & Ron, 2000). Even after many unproductive medical visits, few patients believed that psychological factors caused their symptoms. If they had depression or anxiety, they typically viewed it as a reaction to their symptoms. Some continued to believe they had a diagnosis that physicians had definitively ruled out. Very few patients ever received a referral for mental health treatment or evaluation.

The underdiagnosing of somatization disorder is very costly to both the patient and to society. The patient is at real risk for iatrogenic harm, illnesses or damage caused by medical treatment. For example, a patient who undergoes a spinal tap could be harmed by the procedure. Being hospitalized to run a battery of tests could expose the patient to infectious diseases that patients sometimes contract in hospitals, like staph infections. Social costs include the significant burden to the health-care system of repeated, unnecessary diagnostic procedures and emergency room visits in addition to loss of productivity at work.

The extent of unnecessary medical procedures that were conducted on patients with somatization disorder was examined in an important study by Fink (1992). He identified people between the ages of 17 and 49 years who had been hospitalized at least 10 times during an 8-year period. Somatizers were identified as those for whom no clear diagnosis had been established. The somatizers were compared to the rest of the patients in the sample for whom a clear diagnosis, such as diabetes mellitus or cancer, had been found. The somatizers actually had received more surgeries than the medically ill control group. Nine percent of the somatizers had more than 20 unnecessary surgeries. The most frequently performed types of surgery for the somatizers were gynecological procedures such as uterine curettage and hysterectomy, gastrointestinal surgeries, appendectomies, and laparoscopies. Almost none of the hysterectomies resulted in the patient's symptoms being resolved. In terms of providing symptom improvement, the success rate for all the surgical procedures performed on the somatizers was about 25 percent, about the same as the placebo effect. This study clearly documents the risks and costs of failing to recognize a patient's somatoform disorder. These costs were evident for Meredith. She had gallbladder surgery and a hysterectomy by the age of 25. Both were medically unnecessary and occurred because different physicians were only aware of some of her difficulties. If her gynecologist had been aware of all her other medical history, he may have decided against surgery.

Physicians and mental-health professionals must be equally cautious about overdiagnosing somatoform disorders. Medically unexplained symptoms are common and account for up to 30 percent of all primary care visits (Kirmayer et al., 2004). Medical knowledge is certainly far from perfect and complete. Nevertheless, physicians may be reluctant to admit they do not know the cause of a symptom, and they may shift the blame for the symptom to the patient's emotional state by invoking a somatoform diagnosis.

Researchers have found that 5 times as many women as men meet the criteria for somatization disorder (Karvonen, Veijola, Jokelainen, Läksy, Järvelin, & Joukamaa, 2004). From 0.2 percent to 2 percent of women and fewer than 0.2 percent of men qualify for a diagnosis of somatization disorder at some point in their lives (Mai, 2004). Somatization disorder is more common among people with lower income and lower social status (Ladwig, Marten-Mittag, Erazo, & Gündel, 2001). It is also more common among people with high emotional distress. People with the disorder often have a history of marriages that ended in divorce (Tomasson, Kent, & Coryell, 1991).

A number of people with somatization disorders also meet diagnostic criteria for a personality disorder. In one study, 72 percent had a personality disorder, most commonly dependent and histrionic types (Stern, Murphy, & Bass, 1993). This was a higher rate of co-existing personality disorders than for any other mental illness. A number of people with somatization disorder also meet criteria for an anxiety or depressive disorder (Leibbrand, Hiller, & Fichter, 2000). People with somatization disorder are significantly more likely to make a suicide attempt, even when comorbid depression and anxiety are controlled (Chioqueta & Stiles, 2004). This may be due to the greater likelihood that they have poor social functioning, marital instability, emotional distress, and impulsive, histrionic personality traits. For some people, diagnosing and providing appropriate treatment for somatization disorder is a matter of life or death.

Although patients with somatization disorder experience chronic somatic symptoms over many years, the specific symptoms they experience frequently shift. At one point in time, the patient will experience one type of problem, but a year later that symptom may have disappeared while another has developed (Simon & Gureje, 1999). In one 2-year followup of individuals with somatization, only one-third continued to have the same symptoms (Craig, Boardman, Mills, Daly-Jones, & Drake, 1993).

People with somatization disorder have many impairments in their ability to function, at rates that rival the impairments of people with schizophrenia (Bass, Peveler, & House, 2001). Up to 10 percent in one sample were confined to a wheelchair. Overall, people with somatization disorder spend an average of 7 days a month in bed. Often they are unable to hold a job. Some of these impairments were evident in Meredith's life, although she was not as disabled as others with the disorder.

Etiological Considerations

Psychodynamic theorists have suggested that somatization disorder is related to the use of the psychological defense mechanism of denial. People with the disorder presumably substitute somatic symptoms for the direct expression of psychological distress. Some early reports indicated that people from non-Western cultures found it more acceptable to express their feelings in somatic rather than psychological terms. Less sophisticated people who were not particularly psychologically minded, or people from cultures that did not promote a psychological focus, were thought to be more likely to somatize (Gureje, Simon, Ustun, & Goldberg, 1997). However, investigators who conducted a study of over 25,000 patients in 14 countries on 5 continents found that there were no differences among the different countries in the relationship between psychological and physical symptoms (Simon, VonKorff, Piccinelli, Fullerton, & Ormel, 1999). Many patients with depression who reported a lot of somatic symptoms were also able to acknowledge and describe their psychological phenomena, so they did not seem to manifest somatization as denial of psychological distress. Denial may play a role for some, but not all, people with somatic complaints.

Even though somatization disorder occurs in cultures all around the world, cultural factors must still be considered in the development of these symptoms. Certain cultural groups have specific syndromes consisting of somatic, and sometimes emotional, symptoms (Kirmayer & Young, 1998). Among people of Korean descent, *hwa-byung* consists of feelings of heaviness or burning in the throat, headaches, muscle aches, dry mouth, insomnia, indigestion, and heart palpitations. Koreans view this syndrome as being caused by suppressed rage, particularly at interpersonal or social injustice. In Nigeria, *brain fag* consists of heat or heaviness in the head associated with studying, typically among students with high levels of pressure for success. The *DSM-IV-TR* (APA, 2000) requires careful consideration of any cultural factors that may explain symptom presentation.

The personality style of alexithymia is a concept first described by psychodynamically oriented clinicians but now receiving acceptance by a broader group of researchers as a predisposing factor for somatization disorder. Alexithymia is a difficulty in identifying and describing one's emotions. This difficulty could lead people to focus on and misinterpret the bodily states associated with emotional arousal, therefore heightening them, and leading to somatization. A review of the research literature concluded that there is a moderate relationship between alexithymia and somatization (De Gucht & Heiser, 2003). Meredith had some trouble being aware of and expressing her emotions. Her family did not allow her to talk about feelings, and she was not encouraged to think about or discuss her emotions.

Another psychodynamic concept that has been tested empirically is secondary gain, the idea that symptoms provide situational benefits that reward their expression.[2] Some examples of secondary gain would be sympathy from family members, relief from chores or work, or attention from physicians. In an in-depth study comparing somatizers with physically ill, psychologically distressed, and healthy controls, Craig, Drake, Mills, and Boardman (1994) evaluated the role of stressful life events in somatic symptoms and their potential for secondary gain if the person developed illness symptoms. Situations with high potential for secondary gain involved rejection by another person, personal failures, and situations with obligations or commitments. For example, if a spouse threatens to terminate the marriage, symptoms of physical illness might elicit guilt, sympathy, care-giving behavior, and a renewed commitment to the relationship. These would all constitute secondary gain. Both the somatizers and the psychologically distressed group had significantly higher levels of stressful life events directly preceding the onset of symptoms than the physically ill or healthy controls. This supports the idea that emotional distress and other psychiatric symptoms are related to somatizing. Moreover, the somatizers were more likely to have experienced a life crisis with the potential for secondary gain and were much less likely to make attempts to solve the conflict directly. Active problem solving would publicize their emotional distress to others and eliminate the effectiveness of somatic complaints in obtaining secondary gain.

Somatization disorder may be viewed as learned illness behavior based on observing a sick parent or other family member (Mai, 2004). The child may identify with the ill person, who then models the behavior. The child's behavior is, in turn, reinforced by parents, teachers, or health-care professionals who give the child more attention or sympathy. The child may subsequently attempt to meet emotional or social needs through behaviors such as taking medicine, going to the doctor, going to bed, and acting as a patient. Children and adolescents with a number of somatic complaints are more likely to have a family member with a chronic physical illness (Fritz, Fritsch, & Hagino, 1997). They also are more likely to have family members who use illness for stress reduction. Meredith clearly had this risk factor. Her grandmother was quite disabled after her stroke, and Meredith grew up observing the special treatment and attention she received from Meredith's mother. Meredith probably longed for this special attention.

Childhood adversity may also play a role in the development of somatization disorder. A history of childhood sexual abuse has been implicated in adult somatization disorder (Fritz et al., 1997). The relationship between childhood sexual abuse and adult somatization may be due to dissociation (a disintegration of consciousness with experiences of amnesia, depersonalization, and derealization).

---

[2] In psychodynamic theory, primary gain refers to the main function of a symptom of protecting the ego from anxiety-provoking thoughts or feelings by disguising them as symptoms.

People who were sexually abused as children are more likely to somatize, but only those who also dissociate (Salmon, Skaife, & Rhodes, 2003).

People with somatization are more likely to have a history of childhood illness requiring surgery or hospitalization (Craig et al., 1993). However, this history of childhood illness was only related to adult somatizing when it was combined with parental neglect, or with parental illness which interfered with the parent's availability for caregiving. More often than not, the parental neglect came before the childhood illness. This suggests that for some people, the childhood illness may have resulted in the attention the child wanted desperately from an unresponsive or withdrawn parent. This experience may teach the child that the only way to have emotional needs met is through being nursed and cared for when sick. A striking example of this is the experience of one of the women with a somatoform disorder who participated in the study by Craig and his colleagues (1993). When she was 12 years old she had been institutionalized and did not see her mother even for visits. The only contact she ever had again with her mother was when she was hospitalized with kidney disease at the age of 15 and her mother visited her.

While Meredith was not neglected, she always felt excluded from the family and unimportant to her mother. She received the most loving attention from her mother when she complained of physical symptoms. This pattern clearly contributed to the development of her somatization.

Some studies have examined specific somatic symptoms. Harris (1989) interviewed women seeking medical treatment for menorrhagia (abnormally excessive menstrual bleeding) to evaluate how life events might relate to this symptom. The 98 women with menorrhagia were compared with 224 control women. Over half of the women with menorrhagia experienced a severe life event in the 12 months preceding the onset of their menstrual disorder, such as a divorce or the loss of a relationship with a boyfriend, compared to 30 percent of the other group. The menorrhagic women focused on their pain and devastation in describing their responses to the loss. They reported that they became depressed after the loss and before the onset of the menorrhagia. A hysterectomy was conducted on 58 percent of the women with heavy bleeding. Of the women who had hysterectomies, 40 percent had completely normal uteruses with no sign of any organic pathology. An additional 32 percent had conditions that were not known to cause excessive bleeding. It is unclear whether women seeking treatment for menorrhagia actually have more menstrual flow or just perceive that they do. Some researchers have speculated that autonomic nervous system arousal associated with emotional distress could induce dilation of the blood vessels, which could increase the blood flow.

Meredith's menorrhagia began after her husband divorced her. She reacted to this loss with depression and acute distress, and there was no evidence of any pathology in her hysterectomy. It is likely that the loss of her marriage and her subsequent depression were related to her heavy menstrual bleeding.

Genetic factors may also play a role in somatization disorder. Women whose biological parents had criminal or psychotic behavior and who were adopted by nonrelatives had higher rates of somatizing (Mai, 2004). Fathers of women with somatization disorder are more likely to have antisocial personality disorder. However, results from twin studies have been mixed. Preliminary investigations indicate that people who somatize have abnormalities in tryptophan levels in their bloodstream (Rief, Pilger, Ihle, Verkerk, Scharpe, & Maes, 2004). Tryptophan is an amino acid which is used in the brain to manufacture serotonin. Serotonin is involved with mood and with inhibitory processes from the central nervous system to the peripheral nervous system. The exact relationship between tryptophan levels and somatizing is not yet clear, and more research is needed.

Treatment

Research on psychopharmacological treatments for somatization disorder suggests that antidepressants are useful in reducing pain and other somatic symptoms and associated disability (Mai, 2004; Menza, Lauritano, Allen, Warman, Ostella, Hamer, et al., 2001). Antidepressants appear to be effective even with patients who do not have a depressed mood. Some patients are resistant to taking an antidepressant, though, because of the implication that their somatic symptoms are psychiatric. When the patient with somatization disorder has co-existing depression or anxiety, those conditions can also be treated, either with medication or psychotherapy.

Like Meredith, patients with somatization disorder are often reluctant to follow recommendations by their physicians to seek psychiatric treatment. When the psychiatrist and the physician work together, patient compliance and satisfaction are more likely. Successful medical management involves one (and no more) thorough medical evaluation to rule out organic conditions; the use of treatments that are not dangerous, such as vitamins, lotions, and slings, to allow the patient to "save face;" and moving the patient away from focusing on obtaining a diagnosis (Fritz et al., 1997). The physician should schedule regular visits to evaluate any new symptoms and physically examine the patient while refraining from using testing and medical treatments (Looper & Kirmayer, 2002). This strategy reduces doctor shopping and health-care expenditures, as well as reducing the patient's risk of injury or complications due to testing or treatment. Dr. Griffin used this strategy effectively with Meredith. A schedule of regular appointments gave Meredith a chance to have new symptoms evaluated without resorting to seeing specialists and being subjected to unnecessary and potentially dangerous medical procedures.

Often patients feel that their physician is denying the reality of their symptoms (Salmon, Peters, & Stanley, 1999). This occurs when their doctor says she does not know what is causing them or that everything is fine. Patients are also unsatisfied when their physician simply agrees with their proposed explanation for the symptoms' cause, which undermines their trust in their physician's competence and openness. The most successful patient-physician interactions occur when the physician legitimizes the patient's suffering and provides an explanation that allows the patient to escape blame for the condition (but which allows them a way to manage it).

Group cognitive-behavioral therapy is also effective in treating somatization disorder (Lidbeck, 2003; Looper & Kirmayer, 2002). Treatment typically focuses on relaxation training, problem solving, coping with stress, health education, assertiveness training, and encouraging emotional expression. Individual cognitive-behavior therapy has been documented to be effective in decreasing somatizing. In one study, patients received both individual and group cognitive-behavior therapy in which therapists focused on the emotions, thoughts, and behaviors related to somatic symptoms (Hiller, Fichter, & Rief, 2003). Dysfunctional thoughts and perceptions were modified and misinterpretations by the patients relating to their symptoms were challenged. The treatment was effective at significantly reducing health-care costs, symptom distress, anxiety, depression, and dysfunctional health beliefs, and improving psychosocial functioning. It is also important to reinforce coping behavior to reduce the secondary gain the patient receives through the sick role (Fritz et al., 1997).

CHAPTER 10

Schizophrenia: Paranoid Type

Bill McClary made his first appointment at the mental health center reluctantly. He was 25 years old, single, and unemployed. His sister, Colleen, with whom he had been living for 18 months, had repeatedly encouraged him to seek professional help. She was concerned about his peculiar behavior and social isolation. He spent most of his time daydreaming, often talked to himself, and occasionally said things that made little sense. Bill acknowledged that he ought to keep more regular hours and assume more responsibility, but he insisted that he did not need psychological treatment. The appointment was finally made in an effort to please his sister and mollify her husband, who was worried about Bill's influence on their three young children.

During the first interview, Bill spoke quietly and frequently hesitated. The therapist noted that Bill occasionally blinked and shook his head as though he was trying to clear his thoughts or return his concentration to the topic at hand. When the therapist commented on this unusual twitch, Bill apologized politely but denied that it held any significance. He was friendly yet shy and clearly ill at ease. The discussion centered on Bill's daily activities and his rather unsuccessful efforts to fit into the routine of Colleen's family. Bill assured the therapist that his problems would be solved if he could stop daydreaming. He also expressed a desire to become better organized.

Bill continued to be guarded throughout the early therapy sessions. After several weeks, he began to discuss his social contacts and mentioned a concern about sexual orientation. Despite his lack of close friends, Bill had had some limited and fleeting sexual experiences. These had been both heterosexual and homosexual in nature. He was worried about the possible meaning and consequences of his encounters with other males. This topic occupied the next several weeks of therapy.

Bill's "daydreaming" was also pursued in greater detail. It was a source of considerable concern to him, and it interfered significantly with his daily activities. This experience was difficult to define. At frequent, though irregular, intervals throughout the day, Bill found himself distracted by intrusive and repetitive thoughts. The thoughts were simple and most often alien to his own value system. For example, he might suddenly think to himself, "Damn God." Recognizing the unacceptable nature of the thought, Bill then felt compelled to repeat a sequence of self-statements that he had designed to correct the initial intrusive thought. He called these thoughts and his corrective incantations "scruples." These self-statements accounted for the observation that Bill frequently mumbled to himself. He also admitted that his unusual blinking and head shaking were associated with the experience of intrusive thoughts.

Six months after Bill began attending the clinic regularly, the therapist received a call from Bill's brother-in-law, Roger. Roger said that he and Bill had recently talked extensively about some of Bill's unusual ideas, and Roger wanted to know how he should respond. The therapist was, in fact, unaware of any such ideas. Instead of asking Roger to betray Bill's confidence any further, the therapist decided to ask Bill about these ideas at their next therapy session. It was only at this point that the therapist finally became aware of Bill's extensive delusional belief system.

For reasons that will become obvious, Bill was initially reluctant to talk about the ideas to which his brother-in-law had referred. Nevertheless, he provided the following account of his beliefs and their development. Shortly after moving to his sister's home, Bill realized that something strange was happening. He noticed that people were taking special interest in him and often felt that they were talking about him behind his back. These puzzling circumstances persisted for several weeks during which Bill became increasingly anxious and suspicious. The pieces of the puzzle finally fell in place late one night as Bill sat in front of the television. In a flash of insight, Bill suddenly came to believe that a group of conspirators had secretly produced and distributed a documentary film about his homosexual experiences. Several of his high school friends and a few distant relatives had presumably used hidden cameras and microphones to record each of his sexual encounters with other men. Bill believed that the film had grossed over $50 million at the box office and that this money had been sent to the Irish Republican Army to buy arms and ammunition. He therefore held himself responsible for the deaths of dozens of people who had died as the result of several recent bombings in Ireland. This notion struck the therapist and Bill's brother-in-law as being quite preposterous, but Bill's conviction was genuine. He was visibly moved as he described his guilt concerning the bombings. He was also afraid that serious consequences would follow his confession. Bill believed that the conspirators had agreed to kill him if he ever found out about the movie. This imagined threat had prevented Bill from confiding in anyone prior to this time. It was clear that he now feared for his life.

Bill's fear was exacerbated by the voices that he had been hearing for the past several weeks. He frequently heard male voices discussing his sexual behavior and arguing about what action should be taken to punish him. They were not voices of people with whom Bill was personally familiar, but they were always males and they were always talking about Bill. For example, one night when Bill was sitting alone in his bedroom at Colleen's home, he thought he overheard a conversation in the next room. It was a heated argument in which one voice kept repeating "He's a goddamned faggot and we've got to kill him!" Two other voices seemed to be asking questions about what he had done and were arguing against the use of such violence. Bill was, of course, terrified by this experience and sat motionless in his room as the debate continued. When Roger tapped on his door to ask if he was all right, Bill was certain that they were coming to take him away. Realizing that it was Roger and that he had not been part of the conversation, Bill asked him who was in the next room. Roger pointed out that two of the children were sleeping in the next room. When Bill went to check, he found the children asleep in their beds. These voices appeared at frequent but unpredictable intervals almost every day. It was not clear whether or not they had first appeared before the development of Bill's delusional beliefs.

The details of the delusional system were quite elaborate and represented a complex web of imaginary events and reality. For example, the title of the secret film was supposedly *Honor Thy Father*, and Bill said his name in the film was Gay Talese. *Honor Thy Father* was, in fact, a popular novel that was written by Gay Talese and published several years prior to the development of Bill's delusion. The actual novel was about organized crime, but Bill denied any knowledge of this "other book with the same title." According to Bill's belief system, the film's title alluded to Bill's disrespect for his own father and his own name in the film was a reference to his reputation as a "gay tease." He also maintained that his own picture had been on the cover of *Time* magazine within the past year with the name Gay Talese printed at the bottom.

An interesting array of evidence was marshaled in support of this delusion. For example, Bill pointed to the fact that he had happened to meet his cousin accidentally on a subway in Brooklyn two years earlier. Why, Bill asked, would his cousin have been on the same train if he were not making a secret film about Bill's private life? In Bill's mind, the cousin was clearly part of a continuous surveillance that had been carefully arranged by the conspirators. The fact that Bill came from a very large family and that such coincidences were bound to happen did not impress him as a counterargument. Bill also pointed to an incident involving the elevator operator at his mother's apartment building as further evidence for the existence of the film. He remembered stepping onto the elevator one morning and having the operator give him a puzzled, prolonged glance. The man asked him if they knew each other. Bill replied that they did not. Bill's explanation for this mundane occurrence was that the man recognized Bill because he had obviously seen the film recently; he insisted that no other explanation made sense. Once again, coincidence was absolutely impossible. His delusional system had become so pervasive and intricately woven that it was no longer open to logical refutation. He was totally preoccupied with the plot and simultaneously so frightened that he did not want to discuss it with anyone. Thus, he had lived in private fear, brooding about the conspiracy and helpless to prevent the conspirators from spreading knowledge of his shameful sexual behavior.

Social History

Bill was the youngest of four children. He grew up in New York City where his father worked as a firefighter. Both of his parents were first-generation Irish Americans. Many of their relatives were still living in Ireland. Both parents came from large families. Bill's childhood memories were filled with stories about the family's Irish heritage.

Bill was always much closer to his mother than to his father, whom he remembered as being harsh and distant. When his parents fought, which they did frequently, Bill often found himself caught in the middle. Neither parent seemed to make a serious effort to improve their relationship. Bill later learned that his father had carried on an extended affair with another woman. His mother depended on her own mother, who lived in the same neighborhood, for advice and support and would frequently take Bill with her to stay at her parents' apartment after particularly heated arguments. Bill grew to hate his father, but his enmity was tempered by guilt. He had learned that children were supposed to respect their parents and that, in particular, a son should emulate and revere his father. Mr. McClary became gravely ill when Bill was 12 years old, and Bill remembered wishing that his father would die. His wish came true. Years later, Bill looked back on this sequence of events with considerable ambivalence and regret.

Bill could not remember having any close friends as a child. Most of his social contacts were with cousins, nephews, and nieces. He did not enjoy their company or the games that other children played. He remembered himself as a clumsy, effeminate child who preferred to be alone or with his mother instead of with other boys.

He was a good student and finished near the top of his class in high school. His mother and the rest of the family seemed certain that he would go on to college, but Bill could not decide on a course of study. The prospect of selecting a profession struck Bill as an ominous task. How could he be sure that he wanted to do the same thing for the rest of his life? He decided that he needed more time to ponder the matter and took a job as a bank clerk after graduating from high school.

Bill moved to a small efficiency apartment and seemed to perform adequately at the bank. His superiors noted that he was reliable, though somewhat eccentric. He was described as quiet and polite; his reserved manner bordered on being socially withdrawn. He did not associate with any of the other employees and rarely spoke to them beyond the usual exchange of social pleasantries. Although he was not in danger of losing his job, Bill's chances for advancement were remote. This realization did not perturb Bill because he did not aspire to promotion in the banking profession. It was only a way of forestalling a serious career decision. After two years at the bank, Bill resigned. He had decided that the job did not afford him enough time to think about his future.

He was soon able to find a position as an elevator operator. Here, he reasoned, was a job that provided time for thought. Over the next several months, he gradually became more aloof and disorganized. He was frequently late to work and seemed unconcerned about the reprimands that he began receiving. Residents at the apartment house described him as peculiar. His appearance was always neat and clean, but he seemed preoccupied most of the time. On occasion he seemed to mumble to himself, and he often forgot floor numbers to which he had been directed. These problems continued to mount until he was fired after working for one year at this job.

During the first year after finishing high school, while working at the bank, Bill had his first sexual experience. A man in his middle forties who often did business at the bank invited Bill to his apartment for a drink, and they became intimate. The experience was moderately enjoyable but primarily anxiety provoking. Bill decided not to see this man again. Over the next two years, Bill experienced sexual relationships with a small number of other men as well as with a few women. In each case, it was Bill's partner who took the initiative. Only one relationship lasted more than a few days. He became friends with a woman named Patty who was about his own age, divorced, and the mother of a 3-year-old daughter. Bill enjoyed being with Patty and her daughter and occasionally spent evenings at their apartment watching television and drinking wine. Despite their occasional sexual encounters, this relationship never developed beyond the casual stage at which it began.

After he was fired from the job as an elevator operator, Bill moved back into his mother's apartment. He later recalled that they made each other anxious. Rarely leaving the apartment, Bill sat around the apartment daydreaming in front of the television. When his mother returned from work, she would clean, cook, and coax him unsuccessfully to enroll in various kinds of job-training programs. His social isolation was a constant cause of concern for her. She was not aware of his bisexual interests and encouraged him to call women that she met at work and through friends. The tension eventually became too great for both of them, and Bill decided to move in with Colleen, her husband, and their three young children.

Conceptualization and Treatment

Bill's adjustment problems were obviously extensive. He had experienced serious difficulties in the development of social and occupational roles. From a diagnostic viewpoint, Bill's initial symptoms pointed to schizotypal personality disorder. In other words, before his delusional beliefs and hallucinations became manifest, he exhibited a series of peculiar characteristics in the absence of floridly psychotic symptoms. These included several of the classic signs outlined by Meehl (1964): anhedonia (the inability to experience pleasure), interpersonal aversiveness, and ambivalence. Bill seldom, if ever, had any fun. Even his sexual experiences were described in a detached, intellectual manner. He might indicate, for example, that he had performed well or that his partner seemed satisfied, but he never said things like, "It was terrific," or "I was really excited!" He strongly preferred to be alone. When Colleen and Roger had parties, Bill became anxious and withdrew to his room, explaining that he felt ill.

Bill's ambivalence toward other people was evident in his relationship with his therapist. He never missed an appointment; in fact, he was always early and seemed to look forward to the visits. Despite this apparent dependence, he seemed to distrust the therapist and was often guarded in his response to questions. He seemed to want to confide in the therapist and was simultaneously fearful of the imagined consequences. Bill's pattern of cognitive distraction was somewhat difficult to interpret. His "scruples" were, in some ways, similar to obsessive thoughts, but they also bore a resemblance to one of Schneider's (1959) first-rank symptoms of schizophrenia-thought insertion. Considering this constellation of problems, it was clear that Bill was in need of treatment, but it was not immediately obvious that he was psychotic. The therapist decided to address Bill's problems from a cognitive-behavioral perspective. The ambiguity surrounding his cognitive impairment seemed to warrant a delay regarding biological interventions such as medication.

The beginning therapy sessions were among the most difficult. Bill was tense, reserved, and more than a bit suspicious. Therapy had been his sister's idea, not his own. The therapist adopted a passive, nondirective manner and concentrated on the difficult goal of establishing a trusting relationship with Bill. In the absence of such an atmosphere, it would be impossible to work toward more specific behavioral changes.

Many of the early sessions were spent discussing Bill's concerns about homosexuality. The therapist listened to Bill's thoughts and concerns and shared various bits of information about sexuality and homosexual behavior in particular. As might be expected, Bill was afraid that homosexual behavior per se was a direct manifestation of psychological disturbance. He also wondered about his motivation to perform sexual acts with other men and expressed some vague hypotheses about this being a reflection of his desire to have a closer relationship with his father. The therapist assured Bill that the gender of one's sexual partner was less important than the quality of the sexual relationship. In fact, the therapist was most concerned about Bill's apparent failure to enjoy sexual activity and his inability to establish lasting relationships. Instead of trying to eliminate the possibility of future homosexual encounters or to impose an arbitrary decision based on prevailing sexual norms, the therapist tried to (1) help Bill explore his own concerns about the topic, (2) provide him with information that he did not have, and (3) help him develop skills that would improve his social and sexual relationships, whether they involved men or women.

As their relationship became more secure, the therapist adopted a more active, directive role. Specific problems were identified, and an attempt was made to deal with each sequentially. The first area of concern was Bill's daily schedule. The therapist enlisted Colleen's support. Together with Bill, they instituted a sequence of contingencies designed to integrate his activities with those of the family. For example, Colleen called Bill once for breakfast at 7:30 A.M. If he missed eating with everyone else, Colleen went on with other activities and did not make him a late brunch as she had done prior to this arrangement. In general, the therapist taught Colleen to reinforce appropriate behavior and to ignore inappropriate behavior as much as possible. Over the initial weeks, Bill did begin to keep more regular hours.

After several weeks of work, this home-based program began to produce positive changes. Bill was following a schedule closer to that of the rest of the family and was more helpful around the house. At this point, the therapist decided to address two problems that were somewhat more difficult: Bill's annoying habit of mumbling to himself and his lack of social contacts with peers. Careful interviews with Bill and his sister served as a base for a functional assessment of the self-talk. This behavior seemed to occur most frequently when Bill was alone or thought he was alone. He was usually able to control his scruples in the presence of others; if he was particularly disturbed by a distracting thought, he most often excused himself and retired to his room. Colleen's response was usually to remind Bill that he was mumbling and occasionally to scold him if he was talking loudly. Given the functional value of Bill's scruples in reducing his anxiety about irreverent thoughts, it seemed unlikely that the self-talk was being maintained by this social reinforcement.

The therapist decided to try a stimulus-control procedure. Bill was instructed to select one place in the house in which he could daydream and talk to himself. Whenever he felt the urge to daydream or repeat his scruples, he was to go to this specific spot before engaging in these behaviors. It was hoped that this procedure would severely restrict the environmental stimuli that were associated with these asocial behaviors and thereby reduce their frequency. Bill and the therapist selected the laundry room as his daydreaming room because it was relatively secluded from the rest of the house. His bedroom was ruled out because the therapist did not want it to become a stimulus for behaviors that would interfere with sleeping. Colleen was encouraged to prompt Bill whenever she noticed him engaging in self-talk outside of the laundry room. The program seemed to have modest, positive results, but it did not eliminate self-talk entirely.

Interpersonal behaviors were also addressed from a behavioral perspective. Since moving to his sister's home, Bill had not met any people his own age and had discontinued seeing his friends in New York City. Several avenues were pursued. He was encouraged to call his old friends and, in particular, to renew his friendship with Patty. The therapist spent several sessions with Bill rehearsing telephone calls and practicing conversations that might take place. Although Bill was generally aware of what things he should say, he was anxious about social contacts. This form of behavioral rehearsal was seen as a way of exposing him gradually to the anxiety-provoking stimuli. He was also given weekly homework assignments involving social contacts at home. The therapist discussed possible sources of friends, including a tavern not far from Colleen's home and occasional parties that Colleen and Roger had for their friends. This aspect of the treatment program was modestly effective. Bill called Patty several times and arranged to stay with his mother for a weekend so that he could visit with Patty and her daughter. Although he was somewhat anxious at first, the visit was successful and seemed to lift Bill's spirits. He was more animated during the following therapy session and seemed almost optimistic about changing his current situation.

It was during one of their visits to the neighborhood tavern that Bill first mentioned the imagined movie to Roger. When the therapist learned of these ideas, and the auditory hallucinations, he modified the treatment plan. He had initially rejected the idea of antipsychotic medication because there was no clear-cut evidence of schizophrenia. Now that psychotic symptoms had appeared, an appointment was arranged with a psychiatrist who agreed with the diagnosis and prescribed risperidone (Risperdal®), one of the atypical (or "second-generation") antipsychotic drugs. Because Bill's behavior was not considered dangerous and his sister was able to supervise his activities closely, hospitalization was not necessary. All of the other aspects of the program were continued.

Bill's response to the medication was positive but not dramatic. The most obvious effect was on his self-talk, which was reduced considerably over a four-week period. Bill attributed this change to the virtual disappearance of the annoying, intrusive thoughts. His delusions remained intact, however, despite the therapist's attempt to encourage a rational consideration of the evidence. The following example illustrates the impregnable quality of delusional thinking as well as the naiveté of the therapist.

One of Bill's ideas was that his picture had been on the cover of *Time* magazine. This seemed like a simple idea to test, and Bill expressed a willingness to try. Together they narrowed the range of dates to the last eight months. The therapist then asked Bill to visit the public library before their next session and check all issues of *Time* during this period. Of course, Bill did not find his picture. Nevertheless, his conviction was even stronger than before. He had convinced himself that the conspirators had seen him on his way to the library, beaten him there, and switched magazine covers before he could discover the original. Undaunted, the therapist recommended two more public libraries for the next week. As might have been expected, Bill did not find his picture at either library but remained convinced that the cover had appeared. Every effort to introduce contradictory evidence was met by this same stubborn resistance.

Over the next several weeks, Bill became somewhat less adamant about his beliefs. He conceded that there was a *chance* that he had imagined the whole thing. It seemed to him that the plot probably did exist and that the movie was, in all likelihood, still playing around the country, but he was willing to admit that the evidence for this belief was less than overwhelming. Although his suspicions remained, the fear of observation and the threat of death were less immediate, and he was able to concentrate more fully on the other aspects of the treatment program. Hospitalization did not become necessary, and he was able to continue living with Colleen's family. Despite important improvements, it was clear that Bill would continue to need a special, supportive environment, and it seemed unlikely that he would assume normal occupational and social roles, at least not in the near future.

Discussion

The diagnostic hallmarks of schizophrenia are hallucinations, delusions, and disturbances in affect and thought. *DSM-IV-TR* (APA, 2000, p. 312) requires the following to support a diagnosis of schizophrenia:

1. **Characteristic Symptoms:** Two (or more) of the following, each present for a significant portion of time during a one-month period (or less if successfully treated):

   A. Delusions

   B. Hallucinations

   C. Disorganized speech

   D. Grossly disorganized or catatonic behavior

   E. Negative symptoms, such as affective flattening, alogia, or avolition
   Note: Only one of these symptoms is required if delusions are bizarre or hallucinations consist of a voice keeping up a running commentary on the person's behavior or thoughts, or two or more voices conversing with each other.

2. **Social/Occupational Dysfunction:** For a significant portion of the time since the onset of the disturbance, one or more major areas of functioning such as work, interpersonal relations, or self-care are markedly below the level achieved prior to the onset.

3. *Duration:* Continuous signs of the disturbance persist for at least six months. This six-month period must include at least one month of symptoms that meet Criterion 1 (active phase symptoms) and may include periods of prodromal or residual symptoms. During these prodromal or residual periods, the signs of the disturbance may be manifested by only negative symptoms or two or more symptoms listed in Criterion 1 present in an attenuated form (such as odd beliefs, unusual perceptual experiences).

Bill clearly fit the diagnostic criteria for schizophrenia. Prior to the expression of his complex, delusional belief system, he exhibited several of the characteristics of a prodromal phase. He had been socially isolated since moving to his sister's home. Although he did interact with his sister and her family, he made no effort to stay in touch with the few friends he had known in New York City, nor did he attempt to meet new friends in the neighborhood. In fact, he had never been particularly active socially, even during his childhood. His occupational performance had deteriorated long before he was fired from his job as an elevator operator. Several neighbors had complained about his peculiar behavior. For example, one of Colleen's friends once called to tell her that she had been watching Bill as he walked home from the grocery store. He was carrying a bag of groceries, clearly mumbling to himself, and moving in a strange pattern. He would take two or three steps forward, then one to the side onto the grass next to the sidewalk. At this point, Bill would hop once on his left foot, take one step forward, and then step back onto the sidewalk and continue the sequence. Thinking that this behavior seemed similar to games that children commonly play, Colleen asked Bill about his walk home. He told her that each of these movements possessed a particular meaning and that he followed this pattern to correct scruples that were being placed in his head as he returned from the store. This explanation, and his other comments about his scruples, would be considered an example of magical thinking. Overall, Bill's delusional beliefs and auditory hallucinations can be seen as an extension of the deterioration that began much earlier.

Schizophrenia is a relatively common disorder, affecting approximately 1 to 2 percent of the population (Jones & Cannon, 1998; Keith, Regier, & Rae, 1991). It is found equally in men and women. Onset usually occurs during adolescence or early adulthood, but somewhat later for women than for men. The prognosis is mixed. When Emil Kraepelin first defined the disorder (originally known as *dementia praecox*), he emphasized its chronic deteriorating course. Many patients do, in fact, show a gradual decline in social and occupational functioning and continue to exhibit psychotic symptoms either continuously or intermittently throughout their lives. However, a substantial number of patients seem to recover without signs of residual impairment. Much of the most informative data pertaining to prognosis have come from the World Health Organization's International Pilot Study of Schizophrenia (Leff, Sartorius, Jablensky, Korten, & Ernberg, 1992). Compared to people with other mental disorders, such as mood disorders, schizophrenics tended to have a worse outcome five years after being hospitalized. There was substantial overlap between the groups, however, and considerable variability within the schizophrenic patients. The results of this study and several others indicate that roughly 60 percent of schizophrenic patients follow a chronic pattern and approximately 25 percent recover within five or six years after the initial onset of the disorder (Heiden & Häfner, 2000).

Although people with schizophrenia share some important common characteristics, they are also an extremely heterogeneous group. This feature was emphasized in the title of Eugen Bleuler's classic monograph, *Dementia Praecox or the Group of Schizophrenias* (1911/1950). Kraepelin and Bleuler both outlined subtypes of schizophrenia, including catatonic, paranoid, hebephrenic, and simple types. Each of these subtypes was defined in terms of a few characteristic symptoms. *Catatonic* patients were identified by their bizarre motor movements and the unusual postures they would assume. Their motor behavior might include either a rigid posture with total immobility or undirected, manic-like excitement. *Paranoid* patients were those who expressed delusions of persecution and reference. The primary features of *hebephrenia* were taken to be inappropriate affect and florid symptomatology (e.g., bizarre delusions and hallucinations). *Simple* schizophrenia was a category originally proposed by Bleuler to describe patients without the more obvious symptoms such as hallucinations and delusions. The latter category has been eliminated from the schizophrenic disorders in *DSM-IV-TR* (APA, 2000) and is now listed as Schizoid Personality Disorder. Bill would clearly be included in the paranoid subcategory of schizophrenic disorders.

Symptomatically defined subgroups possess a certain intuitive appeal, but they have not proved to be particularly useful in other respects (Helmes & Landmark, 2003; Kendler et al., 1994). One major problem has been a lack of reliability in assigning patients to subcategories. Because of problems in identifying the general category of schizophrenia, it is not surprising that the subtypes present further difficulties. Inconsistency is another drawback; patients who exhibit a particular set of prominent symptoms at one point in time may exhibit another set of features during a later episode. The symptomatically defined subgroups have also not been shown to possess either etiological or predictive validity. For example, a specific treatment that is more or less effective with catatonic patients in comparison with hebephrenics has not been found.

Another system for subdividing schizophrenic patients is based on the use of three symptom dimensions: psychotic symptoms, negative symptoms, and disorganization (Andreasen et al., 1995; O'Leary et al., 2000). Psychotic symptoms include hallucinations and delusions. Negative symptoms include blunted or restricted affect, social withdrawal, and poverty of speech. Verbal communication problems, such as disorganized speech and bizarre behavior are included in the third symptom dimension, which is called disorganization. The distinctions among psychotic, negative, and disorganized symptom dimensions have generated a considerable amount of interest and research.

Etiological Considerations

Genetic factors are clearly involved in the transmission of schizophrenia (Tsuang, Glatt, & Faraone, 2003). The most persuasive data supporting this conclusion come from twin studies and investigations following various adoption methods. Twin studies depend on the following reasoning: Monozygotic (MZ) twins develop from a single zygote, which separates during an early stage of growth and forms two distinct but genetically identical embryos. In the case of dizygotic (DZ) twins, two separate eggs are fertilized by two sperm cells, and both develop simultaneously. Thus, DZ twins share only, on average, 50 percent of their genes, the same as siblings who do not share the same prenatal period. Based on the assumption that both forms of twins share similar environments, MZ twins should manifest a higher concordance rate (i.e., more often resemble each other) for traits that are genetically determined. This is, in fact, the pattern that has now been reported for schizophrenia over a large number of studies (Gottesman, 1991). For example, one study conducted in Finland reported a concordance rate of 46 percent for MZ twins and only 9 percent among DZ twins (Cannon et al., 1998). This substantial difference between MZ and DZ concordance indicates the influence of genetic factors. On the other hand, the absence of 100 percent concordance among the MZ twins also indicates that genetic factors do not account for all of the variance. The development of the disorder must therefore depend on an interaction between a genetically determined predisposition and various environmental events. This general view is known as a *diathesis-stress model* and is the most widely accepted notion regarding the etiology of schizophrenia.

We do not know how genetic factors interact with environmental events to produce schizophrenia. This problem is enormously complex because the environmental events in question might take any of several different forms (Walker et al., 2004). Some investigators have focused on factors such as nutritional deficiencies or viral infections. One hypothesis suggests that prenatal infections increase vulnerability to schizophrenia by disrupting brain development in the fetus (e.g., Brown & Susser, 2002). Another approach to environmental events and vulnerability to schizophrenia has focused on interpersonal relations within the family. Adverse family circumstances during childhood may increase the probability of subsequently developing schizophrenia among people who are genetically predisposed toward the disorder (Schiffman et al., 2001).

In addition to questions about the *causes* of the disorder, a considerable amount of research has also stressed the family's influence on the *course* of the disorder. These studies follow the progress of patients who have already been treated for schizophrenia, and they are concerned with *expressed emotion* (EE), or the extent to which at least one family member is extremely critical of the patient and his or her behavior. The patients are typically followed for several months after discharge from the hospital, and the outcome variable is the percentage of patients who return to the hospital for further treatment. Relapse rates are much higher for patients who returned to high EE homes (Butzlaff & Hooley, 1998).

The data regarding expressed emotion are consistent with Bill's experience. Bill remembered that when he and his mother were living together, they made each other anxious. His descriptions of her behavior indicate that her emotional involvement was excessive, given that he was an adult and capable of greater independence; she was always worried about his job, or his friends, or what he was doing with his time. Her constant intrusions and coaxing finally led him to seek refuge with his sister's family.

The supportive environment provided by Colleen and her family and their willingness to tolerate many of Bill's idiosyncrasies were undoubtedly helpful in allowing Bill to remain outside of a hospital during his psychotic episodes.

Treatment

There are several important variables to consider in selecting a treatment for acute schizophrenic disturbance. Antipsychotic drugs have become the principal form of intervention since their introduction in the 1950s (Bradford, Stroup, & Lieberman, 2002; Kane, 2001). A large number of carefully controlled studies have demonstrated that these drugs have a beneficial effect for many patients with schizophrenia. They lead to an improvement in symptoms during acute psychotic episodes. Antipsychotic medications also reduce the probability of symptom relapse if they are taken on a maintenance basis after the patient has recovered from an episode. Unfortunately, some patients, perhaps as many as 25 percent, do not respond positively to antipsychotic medication.

Antipsychotic medication seems to have a specific effect on many psychotic symptoms, such as hallucinations and disorganized speech. In Bill's case, medication did have a positive effect. The administration of antipsychotic medication was associated with an improvement in his most dramatic symptoms.

Despite these positive effects, there are also several limitations and some problems associated with the use of antipsychotic drugs. One problem, which was evident in Bill's case, is that medication is only a partial solution. Once the most dramatic symptoms have improved, most patients continue to suffer from role impairments that are not the direct product of hallucinations and delusions. In short, medication can sometimes relieve perceptual aberrations, but it does not remove deficiencies in social and occupational skills.

Another problem arises with treatment-refractory patients. Approximately 10 to 20 percent of schizophrenic patients do not benefit from typical forms of antipsychotic medication (Kane, 1996). Others who respond initially will relapse repeatedly during maintenance drug treatment. Therefore, pharmaceutical companies have continued to develop new forms of medication. Clozapine (Clozaril®) and risperidone (Risperdal®) are examples of the so-called second generation of antipsychotic drugs. They are also known as *atypical antipsychotic* drugs because they produce fewer adverse side effects and seem to have a different pharmacological mode of action than more traditional antipsychotic drugs. Controlled studies of clozapine and risperidone have found significant improvement in approximately 30 percent of patients who were previously considered "treatment resistant" (Lindenmayer et al., 2004). The availability of these new forms of medication offers new hope for many patients and their families.

A final problem has been the development of long-term side effects, most notably a serious, involuntary movement disorder known as *tardive dyskinesia*. The most obvious signs of tardive dyskinesia include trembling of the extremities, lip smacking, and protrusions of the tongue. These symptoms can be disconcerting to both patients and those with whom they interact. Fortunately, atypical antipsychotic drugs are much less likely to lead to the development of motor side effects such as tardive dyskinesia (Kane, 2004).

Psychosocial treatment programs are also beneficial for patients with schizophrenia (Bustillo et al., 2001). Perhaps most important is the use of family-based programs in conjunction with maintenance medication. Several studies have evaluated treatment programs designed to help patients with families that are rated high in expressed emotion (Falloon et al., 1999; Schooler et al., 1997). In addition to antipsychotic medication, treatment typically includes two principal components. First, the therapist provides family members with information about schizophrenia, on the assumption that some hostility and criticism result from failure to understand the nature of the patient's problems. Second, the therapist focuses on enhancing the family's ability to cope with stressful experiences by working on problem-solving and communication skills. Results with this type of family intervention have been very encouraging.

In Bill's case, his sister's family was not high in expressed emotion. Direct treatment focused on family patterns of communication was therefore unnecessary. The therapist did, however, spend time talking with Colleen and Roger about Bill's situation in an effort to help them cope with his idiosyncratic behavior. Bill's therapist also directed his attention to the development of social skills. These efforts met with mixed success. Social skills programs are often useful with schizophrenics who are being treated on an outpatient basis (Pilling et al., 2002).

There is also some reason to be cautious about the use of active psychological approaches to the treatment of patients who are socially withdrawn and exhibiting other negative symptoms (e.g., Kopelowicz, Liberman, Mintz, & Zarate, 1997). Programs that increase the level of social interaction among chronic schizophrenic patients may have adverse effects on other areas of the person's adjustment. Patients with severe, persistent negative symptoms and those who are not on medication may not be able to cope with the increase in stress that is associated with an active, directive form of social intervention. This effect may have been evident in Bill's case. He was not receiving medication until after the therapist became aware of his extensive delusional system. His response to the behavioral program seemed to be more positive after the introduction of antipsychotic medication. Prior to that point, the role-playing that was attempted during sessions and the homework assignments during the week actually seemed to increase his level of anxiety.

CHAPTER 11

Psychotic Disorder (NOS), Substance Dependence, and Violence

This case illustrates several difficult and confusing issues that are faced by mental-health professionals working in community mental-health settings. The woman in this case had been homeless for many months, perhaps several years. Many details of her life history were missing because of her chaotic lifestyle. Her own descriptions of herself and the events in her life were inconsistent and unreliable. She was often psychotic, and she apparently used drugs on a fairly regular basis. Because contact with clients who are homeless and seriously mentally ill is often sporadic and unpredictable, cases such as this one are hard to describe and even more difficult to manage. The information presented in this chapter is based on intermittent therapeutic contacts with the woman as well as one meeting with her brother, one phone conversation with her daughter, and one discussion with a woman who let her stay with her on occasion.

Angela was 36 years old and had apparently experienced nearly constant auditory hallucinations for the past 20 years. It was difficult to know very much about the nature of these experiences because she did not like to talk about the topic. Angela said that she heard several different voices, mostly males, talking about her. The volume, clarity, and emotional tone of the voices varied tremendously. Sometimes they were quite distinct, loud, and angry. Most of the time, they seemed almost like a dull, rumbling noise, running day and night in the background of her mind. At times, it seemed like listening to a radio talk show with the volume turned down.

Angela also had a long-standing problem with substance dependence, especially crack cocaine and heroin. Her heavy use of drugs started a few years after she had been experiencing hallucinations, and she sometimes used the drugs to try to drown out the voices. Angela's pattern of drug use escalated when her living circumstances were most chaotic, when she was least stable emotionally, and when her voices were most intrusive. Of course, it is impossible to untangle the direction of these effects; increased stress might have caused Angela to increase her consumption of drugs, but she also might have become more disorganized because she was using more drugs.

Many of the people with whom Angela spent her time were people who used drugs frequently. She had been drawn into (and also sought out) a social world that was dangerous, threatening, and hostile. She frequently spent periods of several days at a time hanging out in dirty, abandoned buildings with groups of other people who were also taking drugs. Her descriptions of these experiences were both confusing and frightening. Angela claimed that she had witnessed many assaults and more than one murder in such circumstances. Many of the other people also engaged in sexual activities, often as a way of earning money to purchase drugs or in exchange for drugs. According to Angela's description of her own behavior, she was able to obtain heroin and crack by conning other people. She denied being a prostitute and said that she did not exchange sex for drugs.

She had been in and out of drug rehabilitation programs many times. She had also been arrested once for possession of a small amount of cocaine and another time for stabbing a man in the stomach (see below). She had spent 18 months in prison for the assault before being released on parole and finding her way back onto the streets.

Her typical pattern in rehabilitation was to find a way—usually a desperate suicidal threat or gesture—to enter a program, go through detoxification quickly, and then leave after a few days (without completing the therapeutic program). These experiences usually allowed her to escape an unpleasant circumstance, such as living temporarily with a friend who had grown tired of her company. They also allowed her to get some relatively undisturbed sleep and to eat a few nourishing meals.

Angela was the mother of three children, two daughters and a son, who ranged in age from 20 to 15. They were all raised by Angela's mother—who lived in a neighboring state—because of Angela's long-standing problems with mental illness as well as her legal difficulties. Angela had been unable to visit them for many years because one of the conditions of her parole was that she could not travel to another state. The oldest child, a daughter, was an honors student at an elite, private college. Although Angela had not been able to spend much time with her children, she was very proud of them and kept track of their lives through intermittent conversations with her mother and one of her brothers.

Social History

Angela was born in Philadelphia, the second of four children in a lower middle-class, single-parent family. Her mother had been addicted to heroin as a young adult, but she had been free of drugs for many years, certainly since Angela and her siblings were small children. The family lived on disability payments that her mother collected as the result of a chronic problem with back pain. Angela's mother was a strong, dependable, and conscientious parent. Her children all attended public schools, and they all graduated from high school, even though the family endured many difficult financial times.

Like many of the other students in her high school, Angela drank alcohol and smoked marijuana as a teenager. She gave up drinking early because she said it "didn't do anything for her." She had hoped that it would make the voices go away, but it didn't. She did continue to smoke pot.

Angela graduated from high school, one year after the birth of her first child. Although her behavior was often impulsive and unpredictable, she was considered to be a very bright student. She was talkative in class and made intelligent, though occasionally obscure, comments in discussions with other students. Angela also liked to write. Teachers in her English classes said that she wrote interesting poetry; it was often ethereal and concerned with depressing themes.

Following graduation, she worked for short periods of times, but never at the same job for more than six months. One of her first jobs was as a clerk for a drug store. She was fired for stealing money that she used to buy marijuana. She also held several lower level secretarial positions. Her second and third children were born within three years after she graduated. Her relationships with the men who were the fathers were not stable, and both of these men disappeared from her life soon after she learned that she was pregnant.

Angela's use of drugs escalated dramatically after the birth of her third child, when she was 22. She began smoking crack and heroin. At first, she used these drugs separately. Later she began to combine cocaine and heroin into a mixture known as a *speedball* that could be injected. This process seemed to enhance the positive subjective feelings. Two motives seemed responsible for this change in her use of drugs. One was that her hallucinations had become more prominent and distressing. Angela took more drugs to try to quiet the voices. The other reason involved a process that she called "chasing the first high." None of her drug experiences ever seemed quite as wonderful as the feeling that she had had the first time she smoked crack. In an effort to be able to feel that way again, she kept taking increased doses and different combinations of drugs.

Her behavior became increasingly erratic. She would sometimes show up, unannounced, at her mother's house, asking to spend a few days with the children. Then she would disappear again. Her mother and her brothers and sister were extremely upset as they watched her health deteriorate, but they were unable to persuade her to change.

When she was 24 years old, Angela's mother finally persuaded her to make a serious attempt to stop using heroin. She had tried before unsuccessfully, both on her own and with friends. She always went back to using within a couple of days, unable to bear the symptoms of drug withdrawal. This time, she was accepted into a community treatment program. She went to meetings (Narcotics Anonymous) as well as a day treatment program, which included group therapy specifically directed at substance abuse and dependence. While she was participating in these meetings, she met a man who was also in the program. They became romantically involved, and, after a few months, Angela began living with him at his apartment. She had been off drugs for four months at that point. Unfortunately, he was a difficult person with many demons of his own, including a violent temper. He began to abuse her physically.

An Episode of Violence

Angela lived with this man and endured his beatings for a few months. She was constantly afraid and physically exhausted. Her voices were becoming more prominent once again, as the level of stress increased. At times, they warned her about things that her boyfriend was planning to do to her. The voices also urged her to protect herself and to get even with him. Frightened and confused, Angela left the apartment and began wandering the streets, looking for a way to get money so that she could buy heroin and drown out the voices.

She found herself in a busy area of the city, late at night. The street was lined with bars, tourist shops, and all-night markets. Cars were jammed at the intersection while many pedestrians were crowded onto the sidewalk. It was very noisy—horns honking, people shouting, and music blaring from car stereos and the bars. Angela was becoming increasingly agitated, while also feeling frustrated and angry about the way she was being treated. Her boyfriend was beating her. Now the people on the street were bumping and pushing and jumping in front of her. Everyone seemed to be taking advantage of her in one way or another. As her desperate search for money and drugs wore on, she was feeling more irritated, vigilant, and on edge.

A middle-aged man, who had clearly consumed a lot of alcohol, suddenly walked out of a bar and stumbled toward Angela. His speech was slurred and his balance and vision seemed impaired. He mumbled that he would give Angela $20 if she hailed a cab for him. She did that. The man moved toward the cab and started to get in without giving Angela the money that he had promised. Feeling angry because she had been manipulated by him, Angela grabbed his arm and demanded her money. He laughed, called her a name, and started to pull away, falling backward toward the door of the cab. She became enraged, pulled a small knife out of her jacket, and stabbed him in the stomach. As the man screamed and collapsed onto the sidewalk, several other people grabbed Angela and pulled her to the ground.

The police arrived within seconds. Angela was handcuffed and driven to the nearest police station. Her behavior was wild and erratic. Her mood was unstable, vacillating quickly between anger, fear, and sadness. Many of the things that Angela said were incoherent. She was interviewed by a court appointed psychiatrist who met with her once and prescribed antipsychotic medication that could be administered by injection (so that they would be certain that she took it). Her mood and behavior improved after she had been in jail for about ten days.

Several days later, the judge ordered a competence evaluation. She had been charged with aggravated assault, and conviction would carry a sentence of up to five years in prison (depending on any prior convictions). Before she could stand trial, the court had to determine whether Angela was able to understand the charges against her and participate in her own defense. The central question in this decision was whether or not she was still actively psychotic. By the time this interview was conducted, her speech was coherent and her mood was stable. She denied hearing voices because she did not want to be sent, on an involuntary basis, to a state facility for criminal defendants with mental disorders. The psychiatrist who conducted the evaluation recommended that she was competent to stand trial.

With consultation from the public defender who had been assigned to her case, Angela decided to plead guilty to a reduced charge. By this point her victim had recovered from his painful wound. She was sentenced to 18 months in jail, with the possibility of release on parole for good behavior. Angela was very upset during her first few days at the women's prison. According to the guards, she "went crazy." She had to be put in solitary confinement after she attacked another prisoner in her cell. She was not allowed to leave her cell to eat meals because she threw food and trays of dishes and could not be restrained. On the third day, she set fire to her own cell. Because of her wild, uncontrolled behavior, she was transferred to another institution with a psychiatric ward for people convicted of violent crimes.

The psychiatrist at the prison prescribed antipsychotic medication. Angela's behavior was extremely agitated for the first few days that she was living on the ward. She was belligerent and argumentative, frequently picking fights with staff members and other patients. Some of her time was spent in physical restraints because there was no other way to control her behavior. The medication eventually helped her calm down.

Because of her violent and disruptive behavior, Angela served the full 18-month sentence, some of it in the psychiatric unit and other times in the regular prison population. When she was finally discharged, she was 26 years old and homeless.

She was released from jail on probation and was required to check with her parole officer once a week. Another condition of her parole was that she had to remain in treatment for her mental health problems.

Angela went to live with her brother for a while, but her behavior was too disruptive. She argued with him and his wife several times a day. Her schedule was completely unpredictable. Some days, she would leave home in the late afternoon and not return for two or three days. Other times, she would stay in her room for several days, refusing to talk to anyone else. Her brother eventually asked her to leave because the stress associated with Angela's presence was causing too much conflict in his family. He and his wife were also extremely worried about the possible negative impact that Angela might have on their young children.

Community Treatment

For the next 10 years, Angela moved from place to place. She lived with friends at times, and sometimes she stayed on the streets or in community shelters. Now and then, she would find a way to gain entrance to another rehabilitation program. Access to treatment was not easy. For a person without health insurance or any other way to pay for services, Angela had to rely on public programs, and these often have extremely long waiting lists and strict criteria for admission. Very few beds are available in the detoxification programs run by most large cities. Angela found two methods that would usually result in immediate admission. One was to appear at a public mental health clinic and make a serious suicide threat. Once she told the counselor that she was going to jump off a bridge. She was admitted later that day.

Angela continued working on her poetry when she wasn't too high and could find a quiet place to write. She showed some of these poems to her counselor, who was impressed with the quality of her writing. Most of them were concerned with the use of drugs, especially how she felt when she stopped taking them (loneliness, emptiness, darkness, and so on).

After her release from prison, Angela began to experience occasional periods of severe depression. These episodes would last anywhere from two weeks to a month or more. Feelings of hopelessness and guilt would overwhelm her, and she would retreat from interactions with other people. Her inability to care for her children became a major preoccupation for her during these times. Although she was usually a prolific writer, she lost all interest in her journals during these episodes. Her appetite was also very poor when she was depressed, but it was difficult to know whether that was a symptom of depression or the result of the fact that she usually stopped taking drugs when she was severely depressed (perhaps because she didn't have the energy to go out and hustle the money she would need to buy the drugs).

Angela may have also experienced episodes of mania or hypomania. This is another issue that was difficult to understand, based on her own description of events. There were definitely periods of several days in a row when she would sleep very little and become extremely active. However, these were also times when she increased her use of illegal drugs, and it is difficult to know whether her manic-like behavior was the simple product of cocaine and other stimulants.

When she was admitted to the community treatment program, Angela was assigned two diagnoses on Axis I of *DSM-IV-TR* (APA, 2000): psychotic disorder not otherwise specified (NOS) and substance dependence (opioids). The diagnosis of psychotic disorder NOS is used to describe psychotic symptoms when there is not enough information to make a specific diagnosis, such as schizophrenia, or when there is contradictory information. For example, the clinician may not be able to determine whether the person's psychotic symptoms are caused by the ingestion of psychoactive substances. It is difficult for clinicians to draw the distinction between different diagnostic categories, such as schizophrenia and major depressive disorder with psychotic features when the person's self-report is unreliable and when it is not clear what she's like when she is not taking drugs.

Angela's behavior also raised a number of questions about the possible diagnosis of one or more personality disorders. Paranoid, antisocial, and narcissistic personality disorders all seemed to be possible diagnoses. She did not trust anyone, including members of her own family. Of course, the hostile and threatening world in which she had lived for most of her adult life made it difficult to determine whether her vigilance and suspicions were justified. Is this pattern entirely irrational for a person who had lived in such difficult circumstances? She had undoubtedly been abused and been taken advantage of for many years. Unfortunately, her pervasive mistrust also made it difficult to establish a relationship with her in therapy. Her speech was guarded and she did not confide easily in her therapist.

Because there was no evidence that Angela showed signs of conduct disorder as a child, she would not meet the formal diagnostic criteria for antisocial personality disorder. Nevertheless, she did exhibit several other features of the disorder, such as a failure to conform to social norms with respect to lawful behavior. She lied frequently, to her therapist and to her family as well as to the people with whom she spent time on the streets. She was often irritable, aggressive, and irresponsible.

Angela took great pride in her ability to con and manipulate others. For example, she once told her therapist that she was terribly afraid of dying. She said that she was feeling that her physical health was even worse than usual, and she cried at great length about this concern. Her specific concern was pancreatic cancer, which she claimed to be the cause of death for two close relatives. Preliminary tests indicated that she did have a very low glucose level. Upon further testing, however, physicians at the clinic were able to determine that Angela was intentionally taking too much insulin and thereby inducing these symptoms in an effort to gain admission to the hospital.

As with many of her other problems, it was impossible to know whether these characteristics played an active role in the original onset of her mental disorder or whether they were the consequences of living in a dangerous and chaotic environment.

Impulsive and hostile behaviors were also serious problems for Angela. Her inability to maintain regular clinic appointments provided only one example. She would come to appointments whenever she wanted to be there, and she would storm out if the therapist asked her to wait until she was finished with her current appointment. Then she would disappear for a few weeks. Her impulsivity was also evident in decisions about housing. She would leave where she had been living without giving any thought to where she would go next. Her therapist once spent weeks finding a new home for Angela, and she immediately provoked a fight with another woman who lived there. She was thrown out within a week because she wouldn't follow any of the rules (not coming in at the right time; refusing to help with cleaning and cooking).

Discussion

Many people who are seriously mentally ill qualify for more than one specific diagnosis. The term *dual diagnosis* has often been used to describe people who would meet the diagnostic criteria for both schizophrenia and substance use disorder (Drake & Mueser, 2000). Some estimates indicate that 50 percent of patients with schizophrenia also have a substance use disorder of some kind (Lewis, 2002). The concept of dual diagnosis has drawn needed attention to these issues, but it may fail to reflect the overwhelming range of problems that are faced by people like Angela (Marshall, 1998). In addition to her problems with psychosis and drug dependence, Angela experienced difficulties involving legal issues, physical illness (including increase risk of exposure to HIV), and homelessness. The combination of psychosis and substance dependence decreases the probability that a person will respond positively to treatment and amplifies the severity of social and occupational impairment associated with either type of disorder on its own. Substance use disorders are often associated with schizophrenia and depression, especially among people who are homeless (North et al., 1997).

Homelessness is an important and difficult problem that is often associated with mental disorders. Substance abuse and medication noncompliance (failure to take prescribed drugs) are both associated with an increased risk for homelessness among patients with schizophrenia (Opler et al., 2001). Being homeless leaves the person more vulnerable to many other negative environmental events. Women like Angela who are seriously mentally ill and homeless are often victims of sexual assault and physical violence (Gearson et al., 2003).

According to *DSM-IV-TR* (APA, 2000), people who exhibit psychotic symptoms but do not meet the specific criteria for a disorder, such as schizophrenia, may be given a diagnosis of Psychotic Disorder "not otherwise specified" (NOS). One example is the presence of persistent auditory hallucinations in the absence of other features of schizophrenia. Angela admitted hearing voices on a continuous basis for several years, but she did not like to talk about them, and her descriptions of these experiences were rather vague. Criterion 1 for schizophrenia requires that the person exhibit two or more types of psychotic symptoms, such as hallucinations, delusional beliefs, disorganized speech, catatonic behavior, or negative symptoms (such as affective flattening). Angela did not exhibit any of these other symptoms of schizophrenia. According to *DSM-IV-TR* (APA, 2000), only one symptom is required in Criterion 1 if the hallucinations conform to a certain description, such as a voice keeping up a running commentary on the person's behavior. This might have been true in Angela's case, but it was difficult to be certain of their character. Therefore, the diagnosis remained ambiguous, and psychotic disorder NOS provided the most accurate description of her condition.

Similar NOS options are available for mood disorders, eating disorders, personality disorders, and most of the other general headings in the diagnostic manual. The NOS categories are used to describe people who experience significant distress or social impairment but whose symptoms fall outside the official diagnostic boundaries. These options indicate that the categories defined in the manual do not provide an exhaustive description of all forms of mental disorder.

Another possible diagnosis for Angela's condition would have been schizoaffective disorder. This concept is used to describe patients who present a mixture of symptoms that fall on the boundary between schizophrenia and mood disorder with psychotic features (Averill et al., 2004; Frances, First, & Pincus, 1995). In *DSM-IV-TR* (APA, 2000), the diagnosis of schizoaffective disorder is restricted to the description of a single episode rather than a lifetime diagnosis. Therefore, when her condition was viewed from a broad perspective over a period of several years, Angela's diagnosis would be psychotic disorder NOS or perhaps schizophrenia. If a clinician looked only at a specific episode, however, she might have been assigned a diagnosis of schizoaffective disorder. The *DSM-IV-TR* criteria for schizoaffective disorder (APA, 2000, p. 323) include the following:

1. An uninterrupted period of illness during which, at some time, there is either a Major Depressive Episode, a Manic Episode, or a Mixed Episode concurrent with symptoms that meet Criterion 1 for Schizophrenia.

2. During the same period of illness, there have been delusions or hallucinations for at least two weeks in the absence of prominent mood symptoms.

3. Symptoms that meet criteria for a mood episode are present for a substantial portion of the total duration of the active and residual periods of the illness.

4. The disturbance is not due to the direct physiological effects of a substance (e.g., a drug of abuse, a medication) or a general medical condition.

Angela would have fit this description during some of her episodes of depression, when she also experienced auditory hallucinations. Note that this diagnosis would require the inference that she met Criterion 1 for the definition of schizophrenia (which was uncertain because of the ambiguous nature of her auditory hallucinations).

Etiological Considerations

Research studies indicate that schizoaffective disorder is a heterogeneous category (Evans et al., 1999). Most of the evidence suggests that genetic factors play a role in its development. Family history studies suggest that schizoaffective disorder does, in fact, represent a form of psychosis that is intermediate between schizophrenia and mood disorders. The first-degree relatives of people with schizoaffective disorder show an increased risk for schizophrenia, compared to the relatives of people with mood disorders. They also show an increased risk for mood disorder, compared to relatives of people with schizophrenia (Bertelsen & Gottesman, 1995; Tsuang, 1991).

Angela's case also raises interesting questions about the analysis of specific symptoms rather than global diagnosis categories. Her most long-standing symptoms were auditory hallucinations; she had been hearing voices that were not really there for many years. Hallucinations, or perceptual experiences in the absence of external stimulation, are associated with many kinds of disorders, including some that are mental disorders and many that are not. They are also found in some people without mental disorders. One study of people in the general population (that is, people who are not patients) found that 39 percent reported some type of hallucinatory experience, when that category was defined broadly to include hallucinations in any sensory modality (hearing, vision, taste, and smell) as well as "out of body experiences." Most people who reported hallucinations said that they had this type of experience less than once a month. Only 2 percent experienced hallucinations more than once a week (Ohayon, 2000).

The mechanisms that are responsible for auditory hallucinations are not entirely clear. Clinical scientists who study hallucinations have focused on two complementary views of these phenomena. Each view is focused on a different level of analysis. One focuses at the level of neurochemical events in the brain. Brain imaging studies indicate that auditory hallucinations are associated with abnormal patterns of neural activation in extended auditory pathways of the brain (Woodruff, 2004). These include areas of the temporal lobes and the prefrontal cortex. Another approach to studying hallucinations has focused on psychological factors or the mental mechanisms that are associated with neural activities. Cognitive studies suggest that patients who experience hallucinations make errors in attributing internal sensations to external events (Baker & Morrison, 1998). In other words, these people may have trouble distinguishing between their own thoughts and voices coming from other people (Johns et al., 2001; Morrison, Wells, & Nothard, 2000).

Violence and Mental Disorders

The connection between mental disorders and violence has been a controversial topic for many years. Unfortunately, many laypeople hold the mistaken belief that most people with disorders such as schizophrenia are more likely to commit crimes of violence, such as murder and assault (Link et al., 1999; Pescosolida et al., 1999). This belief may be partially responsible for the stigma—a sign of shame or discredit leading to social rejection—associated with mental disorders. Of course, most people with schizophrenia and other major forms of mental disorder are not violent or unusually aggressive, and most violent crimes are committed by people who do not have a mental disorder (Stuart & Arboleda-Florez, 2001).

It is not accurate to say, however, that mental disorders are not associated with an increased risk for violence. People who have been treated for mental disorders represent an extremely heterogeneous group. Some specific combinations of symptoms are associated with greater risk for violence. For example, patients with diagnoses of schizophrenia and mood disorders are not more violent than others living in the same community, unless they also have substance use disorders. Problems with substance dependence and abuse increase the rate of violence in both groups, especially people with mental disorders (Steadman et al., 1998). People who have co-occurring problems with major mental disorders and drugs or alcohol are much more likely to engage in aggressive or violent behavior. It is therefore the combination of these problems, rather than schizophrenia or depression alone, that leads to a serious increase in dangerousness (Walsh et al., 2004).

Personality disorders are also related to the risk for violent behavior. Patients with a major mental disorder, such as schizophrenia, who also exhibit features of antisocial personality disorder are more likely to be violent toward other people (Monahan, 2001; Nestor, 2002). In addition to antisocial traits, people who meet the diagnostic criteria for paranoid and borderline personality disorder may also be more aggressive and dangerous than others, particularly in the presence of problems with alcohol and drug use (Tardiff, 2001). Angela had exhibited features of antisocial personality, especially aggression and impulsiveness, for many years. Her impulsiveness seemed to contribute to her substance dependence. It also exacerbated problems encountered by her therapist in attempting to maintain consistent contact with Angela and trying to arrange for stable housing and employment.

Men are much more likely to be aggressive and violent than women. Nevertheless, research studies indicate that the association between mental illness, drugs, and violence applies to both men and women (Thomson et al., 2001). For example, one study conducted in Finland (a country with a low crime rate compared to the United States) examined rates of mental disorder among women who had been convicted of murder. These women were more likely than women in the community to meet the criteria for schizophrenia. Problems with substance dependence and antisocial personality disorder were also common in this group of women (Eronen, 1995).

Specific types of psychotic symptoms also seem to be associated with violent behavior. Prominent among these are command hallucinations—in which the person hears a voice telling him or her to perform a particular action. Patients who hear a voice telling them to harm someone else may follow that instruction (Braham, Trower, & Birchwood, 2004). Violent behavior is particularly likely when a patient is agitated and actively psychotic and is also using drugs and not receiving treatment for his or her condition (Swanson et al., 1997). Some experts also believe that patients with paranoid delusions are more dangerous than other patients. Delusions can influence a person's propensity toward violence because they shape his or her interpretation of situations. People who feel threatened by others may believe that a violent response is justified. Although Angela did not report paranoid delusions, it seems likely that she did feel threatened by the man she stabbed. It is, of course, impossible to know what her voices might have seemed to be saying to her in that moment.

The victims of acts of violence committed by people with mental disorders are most often family members and friends. Angela's assault was therefore somewhat unusual. It is also understandable, however, in the sense that the man she stabbed had provoked her. This is not to say the assault was justified, but rather that he had, in fact, taken advantage of her. When she protested, he responded in a hostile and disrespectful manner. She was in a desperate emotional state. She was not high on drugs at the time, but she was going through withdrawal and actively seeking the drug. This was a particularly unfortunate time for him to take advantage of her and then insult her.

Treatment

Many men and women who are seriously mentally ill are often confined to jails rather than treated in hospitals. Fazel and Danesh (2002) reviewed a large number of studies that examined the prevalence of psychopathology among prison inmates in 12 different countries (more than 22,000 prisoners) and found that 3 to 7 percent of male prisoners and 4 percent of female prisoners had psychotic disorders. Ten percent of men and 12 percent of women in prison suffered from major depressive disorder. In another study in the United States of more than 1200 incarcerated women who were awaiting trial, more than 80 percent met the criteria for at least one type of mental disorder, with the most common diagnosis being substance abuse or dependence (Teplin et al., 1996). These data indicate the dramatic need to identify people with mental disorders in jails and prisons and to provide them with treatment for their disorders.

Patients like Angela require a broad array of treatment services. Because most patients continue to experience occasional episodes of acute psychosis, hospital beds are necessary. The typical duration of a hospital admission is less than two weeks, so mental-health services must also be available in the community following discharge. Many states have closed public psychiatric hospitals. One paradoxical effect of these closings is that the cost of care for patients who are seriously mentally ill has increased because they must be admitted to emergency facilities at other hospitals (Rothbard et al., 1998).

Treatment guidelines for patients with schizoaffective disorder indicate that symptoms of psychosis, such as hallucinations, and symptoms of mood disorder should be given equal emphasis in planning the patient's treatment (Levinson et al., 1999). Antipsychotic medication is obviously one important consideration in this regard. Atypical antipsychotic drugs, such as clozapine, olanzapine, and risperidone have been shown to be effective for patients with schizoaffective disorder (Baethge, 2003; Janicak et al., 2001). The newer, atypical forms of antipsychotics are beneficial in treating both psychotic symptoms and mood disorder symptoms. Nevertheless, many patients receive more than one type of medication, and combination treatments have increased in recent years. Patients with schizophrenia are often prescribed antidepressants and mood stabilizers in addition to antipsychotic drugs. As many as 25 percent may also receive more than one type of antipsychotic medication at the same time (Clark et al., 2002).

Failure to take antipsychotic drugs as prescribed (a problem known as "medication noncompliance") is often associated with repeated episodes of psychosis and the need for readmission to the hospital (Perkins, 2002). Many of these patients are admitted after they have engaged in highly disruptive or dangerous behaviors (such as exhibiting extremely bizarre behavior, attempting suicide, or threatening other people). The use of atypical antipsychotic medication may help to reduce noncompliance because the side effects associated with these drugs are much less troublesome than those associated with traditional or classic forms of antipsychotic medication.

Violent patients present an important risk to mental health workers while the patients are in treatment. They are also more likely than other patients to be aggressive and violent after they return to the community. The most direct approach to treating violent patients with mental disorders is to address their psychotic symptoms. This is often done through the use of medication. Outcome studies indicate that atypical antipsychotic drugs, especially clozapine, produce a reduction in violent behavior at the same time that patients show an improvement in their clinical condition (Citrome & Volavka, 2000; Dalal et al., 1999).

The management of substance dependence among psychotic patients is an extremely difficult problem and one that has received increased attention in recent years (Kavanagh et al., 2002). Unfortunately, treatment services for these two domains—psychosis and substance use disorders—are often not integrated. Too often, patients must work within two separate systems, with different goals and different staff members. They may attend an outpatient mental-health clinic to receive antipsychotic medication and psychosocial rehabilitation aimed at symptoms associated with schizophrenia. And they may be expected to participate in self-help or 12-step programs, such as Narcotics Anonymous or Alcoholics Anonymous, for their problems with drugs or alcohol. The latter type of program may present special problems for people with a psychotic disorder because they have an inflexible goal (total abstinence from drugs and alcohol) and because they are sometimes opposed to the use of medication. Important efforts are underway to develop special, integrated treatment programs that can simultaneously address the many complex needs of patients like Angela.

CHAPTER 12

Alcohol Dependence

Dr. Lawton received a phone call from Grace Patterson. Her husband, Michael, had a history of heavy drinking, and it had escalated recently. Dr. Lawton suggested that she talk to Michael about her concerns. He emphasized that she should pick a time when Michael had not been drinking. She should tell him that she had spoken to a psychologist who had agreed to see Michael for an evaluation. After the evaluation, the psychologist would give them some advice about what they might do.

Grace called again several weeks later. She had spoken to Michael, and he refused to entertain the possibility of coming in for an evaluation. Grace had no idea what to do next, so Dr. Lawton scheduled an appointment to see her alone. They discussed ways Grace could change how she interacted with Michael that might motivate him to enter treatment. She was instructed to explain calmly to him the negative consequences of his drinking and to express how concerned she was about it. Grace and Dr. Lawton identified several recent incidents and rehearsed how she could respond. For example, several weeks ago Michael and Grace had dinner plans with another couple, but by late afternoon Michael was too drunk to go out. Grace had to call the other couple and make an excuse about canceling the dinner. That evening they had a huge argument about his drinking. Whenever Michael was really drunk, it was impossible to have a reasoned conversation with him, especially about his drinking. In the future, Grace was to wait until the next morning and then express her concerns about the drinking and how this pattern might cause them to lose some good friends. The problem was ruining their marriage.

A month later, Grace called Dr. Lawton to say that there had been no change in Michael's drinking. She described several occasions in which she had explained to Michael that his drinking was having destructive effects on their lives. Although Grace was discouraged, Dr. Lawton persuaded her to continue the plan. Three weeks later, Grace called to make an appointment for both her and Michael to come in for an evaluation. She told Dr. Lawton that she and Michael had had a terrible fight the previous evening; Michael had raised his hand to hit her but held back at the last second. This incident apparently alarmed Michael as much as it frightened Grace, and it led him to finally agree to see Dr. Lawton.

Dr. Lawton greeted Michael and Grace in the waiting room and invited them into his office. One primary goal of the initial session was to avoid scaring Michael out of therapy. Dr. Lawton explained that he understood his reluctance to come in. He told him that the purpose of this session was to gather information about his drinking habits and any problems that alcohol might be causing. Toward the end of the session, if Michael wanted to, they could discuss treatment options.

Michael was drinking heavily on a daily basis, beginning after work and continuing into the evening. On weekends he typically started to drink around noon and was quite intoxicated by dinner time. He recognized that his drinking was out of control and that it was indeed having adverse effects on both him and his wife. They had begun arguing frequently. On several occasions, Michael had broken dinnerware and punched holes in walls. The couple now saw friends infrequently. Michael's high blood pressure had been worsened by the alcohol. Toward the end of the session, when the issue of treatment was raised, Michael indicated that he knew he should cut back on his drinking but that he did not really want to stop entirely. He knew that abstinence was usually the goal of alcohol treatment programs like Alcoholics Anonymous (AA), and he did not want to become totally abstinent. At this point, Dr. Lawton pointed out that some treatments are focused on making changes that lead to moderate drinking. Michael seemed interested in this possibility. The session ended with Michael agreeing to consider entering treatment. A week later, he called and scheduled another appointment.

Social History

Michael's childhood was rather uneventful. His father was an electrical engineer and his mother worked part time in a local library once Michael and his older brother, James, were in school. Michael's mother and father were very light drinkers—an occasional beer or glass of wine. Michael recalled that his older brother was closer to their father than Michael. James shared his father's interest in electronic projects, and the two of them often worked together. Michael, in contrast, had little interest and even less aptitude for electronics. He was more interested in reading, particularly history.

Michael made excellent grades in both elementary and high school. In high school he was also on the wrestling team. He began drinking in high school, typically at house parties on weekends. He recalled that he found drinking relaxing and that it reduced the anxiety he sometimes felt in social situations. He remembered that his anxieties were greatest when around women; he often felt tongue-tied and was unable to sustain conversations.

He graduated from high school and went to a small college where he majored in history and education. His goal was to become a high school history teacher. His drinking increased somewhat in college, both in amount and frequency. His drinking was no longer confined to weekends, and he typically drank six or more beers at a sitting. As he had said about his drinking in high school, he reported that he drank mostly to relax. He maintained a decent GPA but recalled that his anxieties around women persisted. He met Grace at college in an art history class. They were immediately attracted to each other. Grace's social and conversational skills put Michael at ease, and they began seeing each other regularly. They married at the end of college.

Michael took a job teaching high school history, and Grace found work at a jewelry store. They lived in an apartment for two years, saving toward the down payment on a house. Because he aspired to become head of the history department or perhaps get into administration, Michael enrolled in an evening M.A. program at a local university. Michael recalled that these were very happy times. He and Grace were deeply in love.

He was drinking regularly now, a couple of scotches before dinner on weekdays and the usual scotches plus wine with dinner on the weekends. Grace joined her husband in a scotch before dinner, but only one. Michael remembered that when he and Grace went out for dinner with friends, he would wolf down two drinks before dinner while everyone else had only one. And when they were at a party, Michael would generally drink considerably more than anyone else. He claimed he needed the alcohol to feel at ease in social situations.

This drinking pattern continued for several years. During this time, Michael received his M.A., and he and Grace had a child, Ethan. The couple bought a small house, and life continued smoothly for the most part. Four years later, the position of head of the history department opened, and Michael applied for the post. When he didn't get the position, he was both crushed and very angry. His drinking began to increase. He would secretly freshen up his scotch when Grace was out of the room, so he was probably having three or four instead of his usual two. After a while Grace noticed that they were buying liquor more often than usual and began to suspect that Michael was drinking heavily. When she confronted him, Michael angrily denied it and changed his drinking pattern.

Now he began drinking on the way home from work. He would stop at a liquor store, buy a half pint of brandy, and drink it on the way home. He was careful to vary the liquor stores he stopped at and took back routes home to reduce the chance of being stopped by a police officer. Before getting home, he put the empty bottle in the trunk of his car, freshened his breath, and was ready to greet Grace and start in on the scotch. He began to fall asleep, possibly passing out, regularly after dinner. His after-work drinking led him to give up his afternoon racquetball games, and he no longer was able to engage in any activities after dinner. He started forgetting appointments he had made. For example, friends might call to invite Michael and Grace to a movie or dinner, but the next day Michael had no memory of the call. The number of calls from friends began to decrease. During this period, Grace was becoming increasingly upset. She was having less and less interaction with Michael, and she was coming to believe that Michael must be drinking secretly.

After several months, Grace became fairly certain that Michael must be drinking outside the home. One day she checked his trunk and found a dozen brandy bottles. Beside herself with anger and anxiety, she confronted Michael, and an ugly argument ensued—the first of many. Michael became even more secretive about his drinking, now throwing the empties away before arriving home, but his drinking did not decrease. He realized his drinking was out of control and made several attempts to cut back. Unfortunately, his resolve typically lasted only a day or two.

Treatment

During the first session, Dr. Lawton and Michael discussed treatment options in more detail. Michael was adamant that he wanted to cut down rather than aim for abstinence. Dr. Lawton told him that while he thought abstinence was a better goal, he was willing to help Michael reduce his consumption. Dr. Lawton indicated that in order to regain control of drinking, a month of abstinence would be necessary. While Michael showed signs of increased tolerance for alcohol, he had not experienced withdrawal symptoms; therefore, quitting "cold turkey" appeared to be a safe procedure. Michael reluctantly agreed to this period of abstinence. They also discussed the positive and negative consequences of Michael's drinking. Somewhat surprisingly, Michael was hard pressed to come up with much in the way of positives. He said that alcohol had allowed him to cope with stress in the past, but now it had just become a habit, a way of filling time. Their discussion of negative consequences produced a long list—marital problems, loss of friends, giving up activities, and the fact that his high blood pressure was undoubtedly worsened by alcohol. Dr. Lawton also provided normative information about the amounts people typically drank. Michael was surprised at how much he deviated from the average.

Both Grace and Michael were present for the next session. They discussed ways for Michael to cope with abstinence. Dr. Lawton pointed out that urges to drink would pass with time, especially if Michael could engage in some alternative activities. Michael was taught to think past the urge and to focus on the longer-term consequences of heavy drinking. In therapy sessions, he practiced how to imagine longer-term consequences of getting drunk, such as being arrested for driving while intoxicated, ruining his marriage, and losing friends. Together they planned a number of activities to engage Michael in the hours after work. Michael decided to help out with the wrestling team at school and also return to playing racquetball. If neither of these activities was possible on a given day, Michael was to stay later at work and grade papers or revise lectures. If he was having difficulty controlling his urges, he was to call Grace. Michael agreed to have Grace remove all alcohol from their home, and the couple came up with a list of activities that they could engage in to fill the time that Michael would have typically spent drunk or "asleep." Essentially these involved social activities like going to the movies with friends, renting a film to watch at home, playing bridge, and going out for dinner.

Over the next several weeks, Michael met with Dr. Lawton twice a week, with Grace present at some of the sessions. Michael was able to maintain abstinence and followed through on the plan to become involved in alternative activities. He reported that he experienced cravings, mostly after work and in the evening, but that they were not too severe. The cravings were nothing like those he had experienced when he had quit smoking several years previously. He described them as rather vague hungers, "like when you're sort of hungry but don't know what you really want." During these sessions, Michael was also taught deep muscle relaxation as a way to cope with the negative emotions that he experienced with the urge to drink.

Once the abstinence period was over, alcohol was reintroduced to the home. Michael agreed to have no more than two drinks per day, which had to be carefully measured in contrast to his earlier practice of just filling a highball glass with scotch. He also agreed to drink only in Grace's company. Drinks were now to be sipped, and a 20-minute waiting period had to elapse between drinks. Michael reported that he was enjoying the activities in which he was now engaging, especially the racquetball and renewing old friendships.

The moderate drinking pattern seemed well established in about a month, so the frequency of sessions was reduced. Over the next months, Michael and Dr. Lawton continued to discuss Michael's efforts to cope with urges. They also began to discuss the possibility of relapse. Dr. Lawton distinguished between a *lapse*—drinking too much on a single day—and *relapse*—returning completely to his old pattern. Dr. Lawton pointed out that while lapses would likely occur, a lapse would not mean that all of Michael's progress had been lost. They also discussed the need for continuing treatment and attending meetings of a local group of recovering alcohol abusers. The group was somewhat similar to AA but with fewer religious overtones and less emphasis on abstinence as the only solution to alcohol abuse. Michael agreed to attend meetings and treatment was ended.

Followup

Three years later, Dr. Lawton received another call from Grace, who told him that Michael had returned to heavy drinking. She and Michael had discussed returning to treatment, but he was reluctant, saying that it clearly hadn't worked the first time. Dr. Lawton suggested that she try to get Michael to call him. Michael called several days later and reiterated his belief that treatment had failed. He said that he had started drinking heavily when he had again been passed over for a promotion and then had just slipped back into his old pattern. Dr. Lawton pointed out that maintaining moderate drinking for several years was not really a failure. He told Michael that he believed that treatment could again help but that they would need to attend more carefully to maintaining treatment gains this time. Sensing his continuing reluctance to return to treatment, Dr. Lawton told him that because his drinking had only been out of control for a short time, a period of abstinence would not be necessary this time. Michael agreed to come for a session with Grace.

Grace was the first to speak. Tearfully, she explained that Michael was drinking heavily again. Michael sat quietly, head down, as Grace related recent events. She indicated that she wasn't sure she could get through another prolonged episode of the problems that always seemed to occur when Michael was drinking. She was considering divorce. Michael didn't disagree with anything Grace said. He wanted to try treatment again and would make an effort to stay sober.

Treatment was similar to before, but there was no period of abstinence. Michael was quickly able to reestablish a pattern of moderate drinking. In addition, a good deal of time was spent discussing Michael's reaction about being passed over for promotion. Michael's view of this event was that it was a catastrophe and proved how worthless he was. Dr. Lawton worked with Michael to try to get him to see it as unfortunate but not a complete disaster. During these meetings Michael told Dr. Lawton that after therapy had terminated he had not followed through with the suggestion to attend group meetings. As with the first therapy, the last sessions were spent discussing maintenance of the gains that had been achieved. Michael insisted that he would attend group meetings this time, and Dr. Lawton agreed to continue to see him once a month. Michael was also told to call Dr. Lawton and schedule a meeting if he drank heavily for more than two days in a row.

Michael continued to see Dr. Lawton for the next six months. Although he had a couple of lapses, for the most part he maintained moderate drinking and attended group meetings regularly. But then he began to cancel appointments and missed several without calling. At the end of a year, Dr. Lawton closed the case.

Two years later, Grace called to say the old pattern had returned. This time Michael was unwilling even to call Dr. Lawton. Grace was filing for divorce. She felt depressed and wanted to schedule some therapy sessions. These sessions dealt mostly with her feelings about Michael. Grace did not seem to be clinically depressed, but she was indeed experiencing considerable distress. Michael continued to drink heavily, and Grace finally ordered him out of the house. Shortly thereafter, Michael had a major heart attack and died. Therapy with Grace continued for several months, focusing on her distress and guilt over Michael's death.

Discussion

According to *DSM-IV-TR* (APA, 2000), the maladaptive use of various substances falls into two categories: substance dependence and substance abuse. Alcohol dependence is diagnosed if the person meets three of the following criteria:

- Withdrawal symptoms (negative psychological and physical effects) appear if the person stops drinking.
- Tolerance develops. The person needs to drink more and more alcohol to produce the desired effect.
- The person uses more alcohol than intended or uses it for a longer time than intended.
- The person wants to reduce alcohol consumption and may have unsuccessfully tried to cut down or stop.
- Much time is spent trying to obtain alcohol or recover from its effects.
- Alcohol use continues despite psychological or physical problems caused by it.
- Participation in many activities (work, recreation, social) is reduced because of the drug.

Alcohol dependence can be diagnosed as being accompanied with physiological dependence if either tolerance or withdrawal is present. Physiological dependence is what many people mean when they use the term addiction.

Alcohol abuse, a less serious disorder, is diagnosed if one of the following is present:

- Failure to fulfill major obligations due to recurrent drinking, for example, absences from work.
- Repeated exposure to physical dangers while drinking, such as driving while intoxicated (DWI).
- Legal problems due to drinking, such as disorderly conduct or DWI.
- Continued drinking despite persistent social problems, such as arguments with spouse.

Michael clearly met the criteria for alcohol dependence. He had developed tolerance, recognized that he was drinking too much, had unsuccessfully tried to cut back, given up activities that he had previously enjoyed, and continued to drink despite knowing that it was creating serious marital problems and contributing to his high blood pressure.

Lifetime prevalence rates for alcohol dependence are about 20 percent for men and 8 percent for women (Kessler et al., 1994), making it one of the most prevalent mental disorders. Alcohol dependence is less common than alcohol abuse (Somers, Goldner, Waraich, & Hsu, 2004). The path to the development of alcohol problems is somewhat variable. Some people, like Michael, progress steadily from moderate use to heavy use and then to abuse and dependence. But for many others the pattern is less regular. For example, some people become alcohol abusers during a time of stress and then return to light drinking when the stress has resolved (Langenbucher & Chung, 1995; Vaillant, 1996). Once a person becomes dependent, however, the disorder is sometimes chronic. For example, in one study two-thirds of men with alcohol dependence were still dependent when reassessed five years later (Schuckit et al., 2001). Some people who are dependent are able to stop drinking without treatment (Bischof, Rumpf, Hapke, Meyer, & John, 2003). Those who maintain abstinence from alcohol for three years are very likely to remain abstinent for the rest of their lives (Vaillant, 2003). Heavy drinkers were more likely to report that negative consequences from their drinking led them to stop, while those with less severe alcohol use reported that they stopped drinking due to changes in their living situations, such as a move, getting older, or having children (Cunningham, Blomqvist, Koski-Jännes, & Cordingley, 2005).

Many people with alcohol dependence have comorbid major depression (Wang & El-Guebaly, 2004), especially those who are divorced, separated, or widowed, and those with lower incomes. The more alcohol one consumes, the higher the risk for a number of health problems, including cancer (of the mouth, esophagus, liver, and breast), stroke, heart disease, and diabetes (Room, Babor, & Rehm, 2005). This is reflected in Michael's fatal heart attack. Many people who are dependent on alcohol have malnutrition and vitamin deficiencies because calories from drinking replace calories from food (Manari, Preedy & Peters, 2003). Chronic alcohol dependence can result in shrinking of the brain, particularly in frontal lobe areas contributing to problem-solving, judgment, and reasoning (Rosenbloom, Sullivan, & Pfefferbaum, 2003).

Etiological Considerations

Alcohol abuse and dependence has a genetic diathesis. Research clearly shows that problem drinking runs in families, with higher than expected rates among relatives (Chassin, Pitts, DeLucia, & Todd, 1999). Twin studies showing higher concordance in MZ (monozygotic) than DZ (dizygotic) pairs and adoption studies demonstrating high rates of problem drinking among people who were adopted and not raised by their alcoholic parents add further support to the importance of genetics (Cadoret, Yates, Troughton, Woodworth, & Stewart, 1995a; McGue, Pickens, & Svikis,

1992). Liu et al. (2004) found evidence for substantial heritability of alcohol dependence among men, and Whitfield et al. (2004) found comparable and substantial heritability of alcohol dependence for men and women. Nurnberger et al. (2004) found higher rates of drug abuse, antisocial personality disorder, anxiety disorder, and depression among relatives of people with alcohol dependence. Luczak et al. (2004) argue that the different rates of alcohol dependence found in different ethnic groups, such as European Americans and Chinese Americans, are due to the protective presence of a specific gene found much more often in Chinese Americans. Michael did not have a clear family history of problem drinking. Neither his parents nor his brother drank heavily, but he had an uncle who always seemed to be drunk at family parties.

The ability to tolerate alcohol may be what is inherited as a diathesis (Goodwin, 1979). This idea has been pursued in research studying young nonalcoholic adults who have an alcohol-abusing parent and similar individuals who do not have a positive family history for the disorder. Two variables, when measured in young adulthood, were found to predict the onset of alcohol abuse 10 years later: (1) self-report of a low level of intoxication after a dose of alcohol and (2) less body sway, a measure of steadiness while standing, after drinking (Schuckit, 1994; Schuckit & Smith, 1996). The largest difference between the two groups occurred when their blood alcohol levels were declining. While this small response to alcohol in people who later became abusers may at first seem puzzling, it fits with the idea that you have to drink a lot to later become a problem drinker. During the period when blood alcohol levels are declining, alcohol acts as a depressant and often produces unpleasant emotions. Future alcohol abusers may experience fewer of these punishing side-effects, setting the stage for heavier drinking. Furthermore, other research shows that sons of alcoholics experience more positive effects of alcohol on their mood when their blood alcohol levels are on the rise, making alcohol more positively reinforcing for them (Newlin & Thompson, 1990).

Recent evidence also suggests that prenatal exposure to alcohol is an additional risk factor for drinking in young adulthood, separate from the contribution of family history of alcohol use (Baer, Sampson, Barr, Connor, & Streissguth, 2003). The chance of a 21-year-old offspring reporting mild or more severe alcohol dependence was tripled by maternal heavy drinking during that pregnancy.

The principal psychological theory of alcohol abuse is that it is used to alter mood. Alcohol use might therefore be reinforcing, either by reducing negative emotions or by enhancing positive ones. Heavy alcohol use is then seen as a way of regulating mood and may reflect a failure of other means of coping with emotional states. Note that the theory focuses on a variable that might lead someone to drink heavily but does not attempt to deal with questions concerning how heavy drinking might later lead to abuse or dependence. This tension-reduction idea does fit the clinical information we presented on Michael. He began heavy drinking when faced with major disappointments in life.

Much of the work in this area has focused on the tension-reducing properties of alcohol. Alcohol use does seem to be related to other negative moods such as sadness and hostility, but there are fewer data on them (Hussong, Hicks, Levy, & Curran, 2001). Alcohol reduces tension among people who are not heavy drinkers

(Sher & Levenson, 1982). Similarly, research in which people recorded their moods and drinking on a daily basis has shown that nervousness predicts increased use of alcohol (Swendsen et al., 2000).

The situation in which alcohol is consumed impacts its effects on mood. Alcohol may reduce tension by altering cognition and perception. Alcohol impairs cognitive processing and narrows attention to immediately available cues, what Steele and Josephs (1988) call alcohol myopia—intoxicated people have less cognitive processing capacity for both ongoing activity and worry. If a distracting activity is available, intoxicated people focus on it instead of worrying about their stress. But alcohol can also increase negative moods if no distractors are present; in this case, intoxicated people focus their limited cognitive capacity only on the unpleasant source of worry and feel even worse. The tension-reducing effects of alcohol may only be found among some people. The relationship between alcohol use and negative moods has been found to be stronger among males, people who lack alternative ways of coping with stress, and those who expect alcohol to alleviate their negative moods (Cooper, Frone, Russell, & Mudar, 1995; Kushner, Abram, & Borchardt, 2000). Similarly, the relationship is stronger among people with less intimate and supportive social relationships (Hussong et al., 2001).

Treatment

Many people with drinking problems do not believe they have a problem and therefore, are unwilling to enter treatment. Therefore, as with Michael, initial treatment efforts are often focused on motivating the person to change. This is what Dr. Lawton tried to accomplish by having Grace point out the negative consequences of Michael's drinking and later drawing up a list of the negative consequences of drinking during treatment. Providing Michael with feedback about how far his drinking departed from national norms was also part of this process (as recommended by Sobell & Sobell, 1976).

Once the person has decided to enter treatment, many options are available. Hospitals provide detoxification, supervised withdrawal from alcohol, and a variety of group and individual therapies. Benzodiazepines are used to manage alcohol withdrawal (Myrick & Anton, 2004). In general, however, hospital treatment does not appear to be superior to outpatient therapy, except for people with few sources of social support and other psychological problems (Finney & Moos, 1998; Holder, Longabaugh, Miller, & Rubonis, 1991). Two medications, disulfiram and naltrexone, are used to prevent relapse (Myrick & Anton, 2004). Disulfiram interacts with alcohol to produce unpleasant side effects, so the person feels sick if they drink. However, patients often will not take the disulfiram as prescribed to avoid this effect. Naltrexone may reduce cravings, but is only modestly effective in preventing relapse. Psychopharmacological treatment of anxiety and depression in people with alcohol dependence is important to consider to improve the success of treatment of the drinking (Mann, 2004). However, treatment of depression alone does not improve the person's drinking (Nunes & Levin, 2004).

Self-help groups figure prominently in treatment. AA, the best known, runs regular meetings at which new members announce they are alcoholics, and older members relate stories about their problem drinking and how their lives have improved since giving up alcohol. The group provides emotional support, understanding, and a social life to relieve isolation. There is a heavy religious emphasis; one of the 12 steps is: "Make a decision to turn our will and our lives over to the care of God." Members are encouraged to call on one another for companionship or encouragement not to relapse. AA promotes the idea that alcoholism is a disease that can never be cured. Complete abstinence is necessary because it is believed that a single drink can trigger a complete relapse. Evidence shows that AA can be an effective treatment (Gossop et al., 2003; Kahler et al., 2004). In a longitudinal study of men, Vaillant (2003) found that AA attendance predicted sustained abstinence.

After his treatment with Dr. Lawton, Michael was encouraged to join a local group that had many features of AA but without the religious overtones and without the emphasis on abstinence. Many similar groups (such as Rational Recovery) now exist throughout the country. Outpatient group therapy is effective in reducing drinking. Litt, Kadden, Cooney, & Kabela (2003) found that cognitive-behavioral group therapy and interactional group therapy, which focuses on the patient's relationship patterns, produced significant gains even 18 months later. Both of these treatments were more effective than AA.

The treatment Michael received drew on the work of the Sobells (1976), who initiated moderate drinking as a treatment goal and demonstrated the effectiveness of such an approach. Patients are taught to respond adaptively to situations in which they might otherwise drink excessively. Social skills, relaxation, and assertiveness training (especially regarding how to refuse a drink) can be part of the treatment. Other strategies include increasing exercise, reducing the presence of cues for drinking (for example, taking a new route home that does not go by a bar), sipping rather than gulping drinks, and imposing a delay between drinks. Relapse prevention, pioneered by Marlatt (1985), is also part of the package. As was done with Michael, a distinction is drawn between a lapse and a relapse. Patients are encouraged to believe that a lapse does not signal a total relapse. A lapse should be regarded as a learning experience, not as a sign that the battle has been lost.

This case did not have a happy ending. Michael's fatal heart attack was probably related to his high blood pressure, which was worsened by his chronic alcohol abuse. Stress also plays a role in raising blood pressure, and Michael certainly experienced a lot of it, related both to his job and his marriage.

CHAPTER 13

Sexual Dysfunction: Female Orgasmic Disorder

Barbara Garrison was concerned about a number of problems when she arrived for her first appointment at the mental health center. Her principal complaint was an inability to achieve orgasm during sexual intercourse with her husband, Frank. They were both 33 years old and had been married for 15 years. Frank was a police detective, and Barbara had recently resumed her college education. Their children, Bonnie and Dennis, were 15 and 12, respectively.

Barbara's orgasmic problem was situational in nature. She had experienced orgasms through masturbation, and she masturbated an average of once or twice a week; however, she had never reached orgasm during sexual activity with Frank. The problem did not involve sexual desire or arousal. She found Frank sexually attractive, wanted to enjoy a more satisfying sexual relationship with him, and did become aroused during their sexual encounters. They had intercourse two or three times each month, usually late at night after the children had gone to sleep and always at Frank's initiative. Their foreplay was primarily limited to genital manipulation and seldom lasted more than five minutes. Frank always reached orgasm within a minute or two after penetration and often fell asleep shortly thereafter, leaving Barbara in a frustrating state of unfulfilled sexual arousal. On many occasions, she resolved this dilemma by slipping quietly out of the bedroom to the TV room, where she would secretly masturbate to orgasm. Frank realized that Barbara did not experience orgasms during intercourse but chose not to discuss the problem. He did not know that she masturbated.

This situation was distressing to Barbara. She felt considerable guilt over her frequent masturbation, particularly after sexual intercourse, because she believed that masturbation was a deviant practice. She was also concerned about the sexual fantasies she had during masturbation. She often imagined herself in a luxurious hotel room having sexual intercourse with a sequence of 8 or 10 men. They were usually men she did not know, but she would sometimes include men to whom she had been attracted, such as classmates from the university and friends of her husband. Barbara believed that these promiscuous fantasies proved that she was a latent nymphomaniac. She feared that she could easily lose control of her own desires and worried that she might someday get on a train, leave her family, and become a prostitute in a large city.

Her anxiety regarding sexual interests and arousal was also a problem during intercourse with Frank. He had, in fact, made numerous efforts to find out what she found arousing, but she remained uncommunicative. She was afraid to tell him what she liked because she thought that he would then realize that she was "oversexed." She was self-conscious during sexual activity with Frank. She worried about what he would think of her and whether she was performing adequately. Questions were continually running through her mind, such as "Am I paying attention to the right sensations?" or, "Will it happen this time?" The combination of fear of loss of control of her sexual impulses and continual worry about her inadequacy as a sexual partner finally persuaded Barbara to seek professional help.

In addition to Barbara's inability to reach orgasm during intercourse, Barbara and Frank were not getting along as well as they had in the past. Several factors were contributing to the increased strain in their relationship. One involved Barbara's decision to resume her education. Frank had not completed his college education, and the possibility that Barbara might finish her degree was threatening to him. He was also uncomfortable around the friends Barbara had met at the university. His job as a detective seemed to increase this tension because relations between students and the police had been strained by campus arrests for use of drugs and alcohol. Frank believed that Barbara's younger classmates saw him as an unwelcome authority figure who could present a threat to their independence. He resented changes in the way she dressed and also attributed their increasingly frequent disagreements to the influence of the university environment.

They also had more financial concerns than in previous years. Barbara's tuition and other fees amounted to a considerable amount of money each semester, and, within three years, their daughter, Bonnie, would be old enough to go to college. They had also taken out a substantial loan to build an addition onto their home. In order to make more money, Frank had been working many more overtime hours. Considering that he was away from home so often, Barbara resented the fact that he spent most of his spare time working on the new rooms in their house.

Bonnie and her friends were another major problem. She was a freshman in high school, and her boyfriend, John, was a senior. Barbara did not like most of Bonnie's friends. She wanted Bonnie to be one of the leaders of the school—a good student, active in school organizations—but Bonnie did not fit in that mold. She was a marginal student, did not care for group activities, and spent most of her time with John and her other friends at a local mall. John was not a good student either. He worked part time at a service station and planned to become a mechanic after graduation. Barbara and Bonnie argued continuously, mostly about Bonnie's relationship with John.

Barbara was preoccupied with the possibility that Bonnie might get pregnant. They did not talk about sex openly because the topic was too anxiety provoking for Barbara. She made every effort to prevent Bonnie and John from being by themselves. Bonnie had asked on several occasions whether John could come over to their house to watch television and listen to music. Barbara would allow John to be in the house only if she or Frank was in the same room with them. The net effect of this rule was to ensure that Bonnie and John spent most of their time away from the Garrisons' home. It also led to arguments between Barbara and Frank because he believed that Barbara was being too severe. Frank thought that the problem was mostly in Barbara's imagination. These problems were, in most ways, typical of the conflict that parents experience with teenage children. In the Garrisons' case, the tension was compounded by Barbara's sexual difficulty and their financial and educational worries.

Despite their frequent arguments and differences of opinion, Barbara and Frank were both seriously committed to their marriage. Neither of them was particularly happy, but they were not considering a divorce. Barbara believed that their relationship would be markedly improved if she could overcome her orgasmic dysfunction. Frank was less concerned about that particular issue but agreed that Barbara might feel better if a therapist could "help her understand *her* problem." He also hoped that a psychologist might be able to improve the relationship between Barbara and Bonnie.

Social History

Barbara's parents were both in their middle forties when she was born. They had one other child, a boy, who was five years older than Barbara. Her father was a police officer, and her mother was a homemaker. Barbara's parents clearly cared for each other and for the children, but they were not openly affectionate. She could not remember seeing them embrace or kiss each other except for occasional pecks on the cheek or top of the head; nor, on the other hand, could she remember hearing them argue. It was a quiet, peaceful household in which emotional displays of any kind were generally discouraged.

Barbara's parents and her older brother were unusually protective of her. She was "the baby of the family" and was always closely supervised. It seemed to Barbara that she was not allowed to do many of the things that her friends' parents permitted. When she was young, she was not allowed to leave their yard. When she was older and in high school, she was not allowed to go out on school nights and had to be home by 10 P.M. on weekends. Her parents insisted on meeting all of her friends and, in some cases, forbade her to associate with certain other children. Until she was 16 years old, Barbara was not allowed to go to parties if boys were also invited.

She remembered her first date as an awkward experience that occurred during her junior year in high school. A boy whom she had admired for several months had finally asked her to go to a movie. Her parents agreed to allow her to go after her father asked several of his friends about the boy and his parents. When he picked her up before the movie, Barbara's parents asked so many questions that they were finally late for the show. Later, as they were leaving the theater, Barbara realized that her brother and his girlfriend, who both attended a local junior college, had been sitting several rows behind them. Their parents had called him and asked if he would keep an eye on her "to be sure everything was okay." He did not intend to be secretive and, in fact, asked Barbara if she and her friend would like to go out for hamburgers and Cokes after the show. This carefully arranged supervision did not ruin the experience. Everyone had a good time, and Barbara went out with this same boy several times in the next year. Nevertheless, the protective manner in which Barbara's family treated her prevented her from developing close relationships with boys her own age and later left her feeling uncomfortable when she was alone with men.

Barbara's knowledge about and experiences with sexual activity were extremely limited during childhood and adolescence. Neither of her parents made an effort to provide her with information about her own body or reproductive functions. Her mother did discuss general issues such as romance and marriage with Barbara, but only at the most abstract level. All of the books and magazines in their home were carefully screened to avoid exposing the children to suggestive literature or photographs. Barbara was not able to learn much about these matters from her friends because she was so closely supervised. After she began menstruating at the age of 11, her mother gave her a book that explained the basic organs and physiology associated with the human reproductive system and, once again, avoided any personal discussion of Barbara's concerns about sexuality. The implicit message conveyed by her parents' behavior and attitudes was that sex was a mysterious, shameful, and potentially dangerous phenomenon.

After she graduated from high school, Barbara began taking classes at the local junior college. She continued to live at home with her parents and maintained several of the same friends she had had in high school. During her first semester, Barbara met Frank, who was then a student at the police academy. After several weeks, they began to see each other regularly. Her parents liked Frank, perhaps because her father was also a policeman, and they gradually began to allow her greater freedom than they had when she dated in high school. Frank and Barbara were both 18 years old, but he was much more mature and experienced. He had been dating regularly since he was 15 and had had sexual intercourse for the first time when he was 17.

Their sexual relationship progressed rapidly. Although she was initially apprehensive and shy, Barbara found that she enjoyed heavy petting. She refused to have intercourse with Frank for several months; finally she gave in one evening after they had both been drinking at a party. She later remembered being disappointed by the experience. Frank had climaxed almost immediately after penetration, but she had not reached orgasm. Her guilt was replaced by utter shock when she realized several weeks later that she was pregnant. They did not discuss the pregnancy with her parents and agreed they should be married as soon as possible. Bonnie was born less than six months after their marriage. Despite the obvious "prematurity" of the birth, Barbara's parents never mentioned the issue of premarital intercourse or pregnancy. Barbara dropped out of college before Bonnie was born and did not return to school for many years.

Barbara and Frank's sexual relationship did not change much over the next few years, although their frequency of intercourse declined markedly during their second year of marriage. Intercourse continued to be a pleasurable experience for both of them, even though Barbara was not able to experience orgasm. Her first orgasm occurred after they had been married for more than three years and both of their children had been born. Following their typical pattern, Frank had fallen asleep after intercourse and Barbara was lying in bed, half awake and very much aroused. She was lying on her stomach, and some of the blankets happened to be bunched up under her pelvis and between her legs. Without recognizing what she was doing, Barbara began rocking rhythmically from side to side. She was relaxed and noticed that this motion created a pleasurable sensation. Several minutes after she began rocking, she experienced an intense, unmistakable orgasm. It was an extremely pleasurable phenomenon restrained only by her fear of waking Frank. After her accidental discovery of masturbation, Barbara experimented further with various styles of self-manipulation and was soon masturbating regularly. She was afraid to describe these experiences to Frank, however, because she believed that masturbation was an immoral and selfish act, and her ability to reach orgasm by self-stimulation did not generalize to intercourse with Frank. Barbara also avoided conversations about sex when she was talking to other women. She believed that masturbation and sexual fantasies were immoral, and she was convinced that none of her friends had ever had such experiences.

Conceptualization and Treatment

In approaching the sexual problem described by Barbara, the therapist focused on Barbara and Frank as a couple, not on Barbara as an individual. She was principally concerned with the things Barbara and Frank did and said when they were together. It was clear from Barbara's description of the problem that she knew very little about sexual behavior. Her reports also indicated that she and Frank were not communicating effectively during sexual activity and were not engaging in effective sexual behaviors. In order to focus on the relationship, the therapist asked Barbara to bring Frank with her to the second treatment session.

Frank was initially reluctant to join Barbara in treatment because he had always believed that the problem was primarily hers. Nevertheless, he agreed to talk to the therapist at least once, and, during this interview, he indicated that he was also dissatisfied with their sexual relationship. On further questioning, he even admitted that he had secretly worried that he was to blame for Barbara's orgasmic difficulty. This thought had caused him considerable anxiety from time to time, particularly when he was also worried about his performance in other roles such as work and his relationship with the children.

The therapist asked Frank to describe their sexual activity from his perspective and noted, as Barbara had previously indicated, that little emphasis was placed on foreplay. Two considerations seemed to be particularly important in this regard. First, Frank said that he did not know what sorts of activity might be more pleasurable for Barbara, since she had never expressed any feelings in this regard. Second, Frank indicated that he generally felt unsure of his own ability to delay ejaculation and therefore preferred to insert his penis in Barbara's vagina before he "lost control." This concern was related to his belief that intercourse was the most mature form of sexual activity and his fear that Barbara would begin to question his virility if he were unable to accomplish intercourse. Although he realized that Barbara was not entirely happy with their sexual relationship, Frank privately conceded that he would rather not draw attention to his own difficulty. The therapist responded in a reassuring manner, emphasizing that she did not want to ascribe responsibility to either partner. The primary concern of treatment, she said, would be to increase both partners' satisfaction with their sexual relationship. She also noted that most forms of sexual dysfunction, particularly premature ejaculation, are amenable to brief, behavioral forms of therapy. Given this explanation of the problem and considering the optimistic prognosis, Frank agreed to work together with Barbara toward a solution to their problems.

During her initial interviews with both Barbara and Frank, the therapist made an effort to consider various factors that might contribute to sexual dysfunction, such as depression, fatigue, and marital distress. None of these seemed to account for the problem. Both partners were somewhat unhappy, but neither was clinically depressed. Although their relationship had been strained by the sexual problem, they were both committed to the marriage. Neither was involved in an extramarital relationship, which might detract from their involvement in treatment or their interest in change, and both Barbara and Frank expressed affection for each other. It was interesting to note that they were more willing to express their positive feelings for the other person when they were talking with the therapist than when they were interacting directly. Overall, the sexual dysfunction did not seem to be secondary to other adjustment problems.

Before beginning a psychological approach to their sexual problem, Barbara and Frank were also asked to obtain complete physical examinations. This assessment was recommended in an effort to rule out the possibility that their difficulty could be traced to a physical disorder. Various diseases that affect the central nervous system, hormone levels, and vascular functions can influence sexual arousal and performance. Abnormalities in the musculature and tissue structure of the genital area can also be problematic. None of these factors was evident in this particular case.

During the third session, the therapist explored many of Barbara's and Frank's attitudes and beliefs about sexual behavior. Her purpose was to improve their communication with each other about sexual matters and to open a discussion in which they could acquire additional knowledge and correct mistaken beliefs. Several issues were particularly important and seemed to be related to their failure to engage in more satisfying sexual behavior. For example, both Barbara and Frank believed that vaginal stimulation should be the principal source of sexual pleasure for women and that orgasm during coitus is dependent solely on such stimulation. The therapist explained that the clitoris is, in fact, more sensitive than the vagina. Female orgasm depends on both direct and indirect stimulation of the clitoris during both masturbation and intercourse.

Considerable time was also spent discussing the Garrisons' attitudes toward and use of sexual fantasies. The topic was broached cautiously by the therapist. She commented in a matter-of-fact tone that most normal adults engage in sexual fantasies; she then asked Frank to describe one of his favorite fantasies. Despite some initial embarrassment, and much to Barbara's surprise, Frank told Barbara and the therapist that he often pictured himself working late at night and being seduced in the detectives' lounge by an attractive female colleague. This was the first time that Barbara and Frank had discussed sexual fantasies. While Barbara expressed some mild jealousy that Frank would think about another woman, she was relieved to learn that he also used sexual fantasies. His self-disclosure lowered her anxiety on the topic. She then shared a description of one of her own fantasies—admittedly one that was less provocative than her thoughts of having intercourse with several men in a row. Having explored these and other issues at length, the therapist recommended a few books that the Garrisons should read in order to learn more about human sexuality. One of the books was *Becoming Orgasmic: A Sexual and Personal Growth Program for Women* (Heiman & LoPiccolo, 1988). It was hoped that this information would reduce their anxiety about their own interests and practices and, at the same time, suggest new activities that they had not yet tried.

The next step in treatment was to eliminate some of the obstacles that were interfering with Barbara's ability to become totally aroused and, to teach her and Frank to engage in more enjoyable sexual behavior. This could be accomplished only in a totally nondemanding atmosphere. Because of their history of sexual difficulty and dissatisfaction, Barbara and Frank had become self-conscious about their sexual behavior. Barbara felt considerable pressure, which was mostly self-imposed, to reach orgasm; Frank was secretly concerned about whether he could delay ejaculation long enough for Barbara to become more aroused. From the point at which Frank initiated sexual activity, both of them tended to assume a detached perspective as they observed what they were doing and how they were feeling. The therapist attempted to eliminate pressure to perform by telling Barbara and Frank that they were *not* to attempt sexual intercourse under any circumstances during the next few weeks. She told them that she was going to ask them to practice an exercise known as "sensate focus" in which their only goal would be to practice giving and receiving pleasurable sensations.

Sensate focus is a touching exercise in which the partners simply take turns gently massaging each other's body. The therapist instructed them to begin by finding a quiet time when they would not be disturbed or distracted and they were not overtired. Having removed their clothes, Barbara was to lie on her stomach across the bed while Frank massaged her back and legs. She was encouraged to abandon herself to whatever pleasures she experienced. Barbara's instructions were to concentrate on the simplest sensations—warm and cold, smooth and rough, hard and soft—and to let Frank know what she enjoyed and what she wanted to change. Stimulation of Barbara's breasts and genital area was expressly prohibited to avoid demand for increased sexual arousal. They were asked to practice sensate focus at least four times before their next session.

Barbara and Frank both responded positively to this initial exercise. They described these extended periods of touching and caressing as relaxing and pleasurable; they both said that they had felt a sense of warmth and closeness that had disappeared from their relationship years ago. Barbara also expressed relief that she was able to focus on the pleasure of Frank's touch without worrying about whether she would have an orgasm or whether he would ejaculate quickly and leave her stranded in a state of unfulfilled arousal. With this positive beginning, the therapist suggested that they move on to the next step. They were to change positions for the next week. Frank would sit on the bed with his back against the headboard and his legs spread apart. Barbara would sit in front of him, facing in the same direction, with her back resting against his chest and her legs resting over his. In this position, Frank would be able to touch and massage the front of her body; the restrictions against touching her breasts and genitals were removed. He was told, however, to avoid direct stimulation of the clitoris because it can be irritating and in some cases painful. Barbara was instructed to rest her hand gently on his and to guide his touch to convey the sensations that were most pleasurable to her, including location, pressure, and rhythm of movement. The therapist emphasized that Barbara was to control the interaction. As before, they were asked to practice at least four times in the following week.

At the beginning of the next session, minor problems were noted in the progress of treatment. Barbara reported that she had become somewhat self-conscious with the new exercise. She found the experience pleasant and arousing, but her mind wandered and she was unable to achieve a state of total abandon. Frank had also encountered difficulty with ejaculatory control. On the third evening of practice, he had become totally absorbed in the process and, without completely realizing what he was doing, he had rubbed his erect penis against Barbara's back and reached orgasm. The therapist reassured Frank that this experience was not unexpected and could, in fact, be seen as the predictable outcome of his immersion in the sensate focus exercise. It was also clear, however, that additional changes should be made in the process to help Frank gain more control and to reduce Barbara's tendency toward detachment.

The therapist addressed the issue of ejaculatory control by recommending that Barbara and Frank practice the "start-stop" procedure. Frank was instructed to lie on his back so that Barbara could stimulate his erect penis manually. His task would be to concentrate on his own level of arousal and signal Barbara when he experienced the sensation that immediately precedes ejaculation. At this point, Barbara would discontinue stimulation. When Frank no longer felt that ejaculation was imminent, she would resume stimulation until he again signaled that he was experiencing the urge to ejaculate. They were asked to repeat this cycle four or five times initially and to work toward achieving 15 to 20 minutes of continuous repetitions.

The sensate focus exercise was also continued with additional instruction. Barbara was encouraged to engage in her favorite sexual fantasies while guiding Frank's hands over her body. Frank's acceptance and support were particularly helpful in this regard because of Barbara's guilt about the use of sexual fantasies. By concentrating on these images, she would be able to avoid other mental distractions that had impaired her ability to become completely involved in the exercise.

The next two weeks of practice were very successful. Frank was able to control his ejaculatory urges within four or five days; Barbara found that the start-stop exercise was also quite pleasurable for her. In the past, Frank had always discouraged her from stroking or playing with his erect penis because he was afraid that he would ejaculate prematurely. It was becoming clear that their improved communication about what they enjoyed and when to start and stop various activities resulted in considerably greater freedom and pleasure than their previously constricted interactions had allowed. Barbara was now able to reach orgasm through Frank's manual stimulation of her breasts and clitoris. She was much less inhibited about directing his touch, and he noted he had learned a lot about Barbara's erotic zones. Much of the tension and inhibition had been reduced.

The final step was to help Barbara experience orgasm during intercourse. The prohibition against intercourse was lifted, and a new procedure was introduced. As before, they were instructed to begin their exercises by alternating in sensate focus. When they were both moderately aroused, Frank would lie on his back and Barbara would sit on top of him with her knees drawn toward his chest and insert his penis into her vagina. She would then control the speed and rhythm of their movements. Emphasis was placed on moving slowly and concentrating on the pleasurable sensations associated with vaginal containment. If Frank experienced the urge to ejaculate, Barbara was instructed to withdraw his penis until the sensation had passed. If she became less aroused during intercourse, they would also separate, and Frank would once again employ clitoral stimulation until Barbara reached a stage of more intense arousal, at which point they would resume coitus.

Barbara and Frank practiced this procedure many times over the next few weeks. It was an extremely pleasurable experience, and they noticed that they had made considerable progress, most notably Frank's ability to delay ejaculation throughout 20 to 30 minutes of intercourse with Barbara in the superior position. Nevertheless, Barbara was not able to reach orgasm through penile stimulation alone. They continued to alternate periods of insertion with manual stimulation of the clitoris, but Barbara's orgasms were limited to the latter intervals. The therapist noted that this was not uncommon and encouraged them to begin experimenting with other positions for intercourse that would also allow manual stimulation of her clitoris during coitus. The Garrisons were perfectly satisfied with this solution.

Fifteen weeks after their initial visit, Barbara and Frank had made significant changes in their sexual adjustment. Both of them were pleased with these developments, which included Frank's confidence in his ability to control ejaculation and Barbara's ability to reach orgasm during intercourse. Perhaps most important, these changes were not specifically limited to their sexual interactions. They reported that they also talked more frequently and openly about other areas of their lives and felt closer to each other than they had at the beginning of treatment. Thus, the new lines of communication that had been developed in sexual activities did generalize, or transfer, to other situations.

Even though some of the Garrisons' peripheral problems were resolved spontaneously after the successful treatment of Barbara's orgasmic inhibition, other difficulties remained. Several were addressed directly in further treatment sessions. Their relationship with Bonnie, for example, continued to be a source of frequent irritation. They argued with her individually and as a couple and sometimes fought with each other when she was not present. Most of these arguments centered on the issues of freedom and responsibility. Could Bonnie stay out past 10 P.M. on weekdays? Should she and her boyfriend be alone in the house when Barbara and Frank were out? What chores was she expected to do, and how often should she do them? All of these questions were addressed in conjoint family sessions in which the therapist served as a mediator. Bonnie and her parents negotiated a mutually acceptable agreement that specified what she could expect from them and, in turn, what they could expect from her. The agreement also included contingencies that would go into effect when and if anyone failed to fulfill his or her commitments. The level of conflict in the Garrison home was substantially reduced by these discussions.

Discussion

Sexual dysfunctions are defined by interference with any phase of the sexual response cycle. This cycle may be thought of as a continuous sequence of events or sensations, beginning with sexual excitement and ending with the decrease in tension following orgasm. This cycle can be roughly divided into three phases that are characteristic of both men and women. During the *excitement phase*, the person begins to respond to sexual stimulation with increased flow of blood to the genital area. This engorgement leads to erection in the male and vaginal lubrication in the female. Various physiological changes, including more rapid breathing and an increase in heart rate and blood pressure, occur throughout the excitement phase. These changes reach their maximum intensity during the *orgasmic phase*, a brief period of involuntary response. In males, the orgasmic phase occurs in two stages, beginning with the collection of sperm and seminal fluid in the urethra (creating a sensation of inevitability, or "point of no return") and ending with ejaculation. In females, the orgasmic phase involves rhythmic contractions in the outer third of the vagina. From a subjective point of view, the orgasmic phase is the point of peak physical pleasure. It is followed by a rapid dissipation of tension. The period following orgasm, known as the *resolution phase*, encompasses the return of bodily functions to a normal resting state (LeVay & Valente, 2003).

Interference with sexual response may occur at any point and may take the form of subjective distress (such as the fear of losing ejaculatory control) or disrupted performance (such as the inability to maintain an erection sufficient for intercourse). *DSM-IV-TR* (APA, 2000, pp. 535-558) provides the following definitions of problems experienced by men and women:

Hypoactive Sexual Desire Disorder: Persistently or recurrently deficient (or absent) sexual fantasies and desire for sexual activity

Sexual Aversion Disorder: Persistent or recurrent extreme aversion to, and avoidance of, all (or almost all) genital sexual contact with a sexual partner

Female Sexual Arousal Disorder: Persistent or recurrent inability to attain, or to maintain until completion of the sexual activity, an adequate lubrication-swelling response of sexual excitement

Male Erectile Disorder: Persistent or recurrent inability to attain or maintain, until completion of the sexual activity, an adequate erection

Female Orgasmic Disorder (Inhibited Female Orgasm): Persistent or recurrent delay in, or absence of, orgasm following a normal sexual excitement phase

Male Orgasmic Disorder: Persistent or recurrent delay in, or absence of, orgasm following a normal sexual excitement phase during sexual activity

Premature Ejaculation: Persistent or recurrent ejaculation with minimal sexual stimulation before, on, or shortly after penetration and before the person wishes it

Dyspareunia: Recurrent or persistent genital pain in either a male or a female before, during, or after sexual intercourse

Vaginismus: Recurrent or persistent involuntary spasm of the musculature of the outer third of the vagina that interferes with sexual intercourse

All these problems may be general or situational in nature. In the case of male erectile disorder, for example, the person may never have been able to attain or maintain an erection until completion of the sex act. On the other hand, he may have been able to do so in the past, or with a different partner, but cannot do so presently.

Most people with hypoactive sexual desire retain the capacity for physical sexual response, but they are generally unwilling to participate and are unreceptive to their partner's attempts to initiate sexual relations. Lack of interest in sexual activity may be an important source of distress, particularly for the spouse or partner of such an individual, but it is also a difficult problem to define. What is a normal sexual appetite? Instead of establishing an arbitrary standard, *DSM-IV-TR* (APA, 2000) has opted for a flexible judgment in this area that depends on a consideration of factors that affect sexual desire such as age, sex, health, intensity and frequency of sexual desire, and the context of the individual's life.

Diagnostic judgments in the area of sexual dysfunction often depend on subtle considerations. Is the problem sufficiently persistent and pervasive to warrant treatment? And, if it is, does the problem center on one partner or the other? These may be difficult questions. In the Garrisons' case, for example, it was not clear whether Barbara's inability to reach orgasm during intercourse could be attributed to Frank's difficulty in delaying or controlling his ejaculatory response. On the other hand, if she had been able to reach orgasm quickly, he might not have worried about the question of control. Two conclusions can be drawn from these considerations. First, sexual dysfunction is most easily defined in the context of a particular interpersonal relationship. The couple, not either individual, is the focus for assessment and treatment. Second, the identification of sexual dysfunction rests largely with the couple's subjective satisfaction with their sexual relationship and not with absolute judgments about typical, or normal, levels of performance.

Various forms of sexual dysfunction are quite common (Simons & Carey, 2001; Warnock, 2002). The best information on the epidemiology of sexual dysfunction comes from the National Health and Social Life Survey (NHSLS) (Laumann, Gagnon, Michael, & Michaels, 1994). These investigators used probability sampling to select people for their study. They interviewed nearly 3500 men and women between the ages of 18 and 59 throughout the United States. Each person was asked whether, during the past 12 months, he or she had experienced "a period of several months or more when you lacked interest in having sex; had trouble achieving or maintaining an erection or (for women) had trouble lubricating; were unable to come to a climax; came to a climax too quickly; or experienced physical pain during intercourse." For men, the most frequent form of sexual dysfunction was premature ejaculation, affecting 29 percent of the men in the study. Arousal problems were reported by 10 percent of the men overall (and 20 percent of those over the age of 50). For women, the most frequently reported difficulties were low sexual desire (33 percent), lack of orgasm (24 percent), and arousal problems (19 percent). Fourteen percent of the women (and 3 percent of the men) indicated that they had recently experienced a period of several months during which intercourse was painful.

The NHSLS data regarding the prevalence of sexual dysfunction should be interpreted with caution because they are not based on diagnostic judgments made by experienced clinicians. Participants' responses may overestimate the prevalence of sexual dysfunction. Consider, for example, the frequency of female orgasmic disorder. One fact is relatively clear: Approximately 10 percent of adult women report a total lack of previous orgasmic response (Stock, 1993). Does this failure to experience orgasm automatically indicate a dysfunction or the absence of the *capacity* to reach orgasm? Some women voluntarily refrain from sexual activity. Others may not have engaged in activities, such as masturbation, that are likely to result in orgasmic response. The *DSM-IV-TR* (APA, 2000) definition of female orgasmic disorder stipulates that the delay or absence of orgasm *must follow a normal sexual excitement phase*. The diagnosis is to be made only if the clinician decides that the woman's orgasmic capacity is "less than would be reasonable for her age, sexual experience, and the adequacy of sexual stimulation she receives" (*DSM-IV-TR*, APA, 2000, p. 547). Based on this more restrictive definition, fewer women would meet the criteria for this disorder.

Another important diagnostic consideration involves the issue of personal distress. Is the person upset about diminished sexual responsiveness? The NHSLS investigators asked people whether they had experienced a period of time in which they had lost interest in sexual behavior or had trouble becoming aroused or reaching orgasm. The *DSM-IV-TR* (APA, 2000) definition considers whether the person experienced subjective distress or interpersonal difficulty as a result of the lack of sexual response. Recommendations regarding further refinements in the classification of female sexual dysfunction have placed increased emphasis on personal distress as a necessary feature in the definition (Basson et al., 2000).

Etiological Considerations

Some cases of sexual dysfunction may be the result of other forms of physical or mental disturbance. Human sexual response involves a complicated and delicate system that may be disrupted by many factors. Several physical conditions and medical disorders, including diseases of the central nervous system, head and spinal cord injuries, drug ingestion, and fatigue, can impair the person's interest in sexual activity or the ability to perform sexual responses (Burns et al., 2001; Lambert & Waters, 1998). Other psychological adjustment problems can also lead to disturbances in sexual activity. Depression, for example, is commonly associated with a drastic decline in a person's interest in sex. People who are taking antidepressant medication, including selective serotonin reuptake inhibitors, may also experience sexual dysfunctions as a side effect (Clayton & West, 2003). These factors should be considered before a psychological treatment approach is attempted.

Many different psychological explanations have been proposed to account for the development and maintenance of sexual dysfunction (McConaghy, 2005). Psychoanalytic theory traces sexual problems to an inadequate resolution of the Oedipal conflict. In Barbara's case, for example, a psychoanalyst might have argued that her inability to reach orgasm during intercourse was associated with fear of success in the sense that being successful in her adult sexual relationship might be analogous to succeeding in the Oedipal situation. According to this notion, Barbara wanted to have intercourse with her father and was thus in competition with her mother. But she was also afraid that if she succeeded her mother would punish her severely. To the extent that her husband was symbolic of her father and reaching orgasm during intercourse with him was equivalent to "winning" the struggle with her mother, Barbara's orgasmic inhibition could be determined by this unconscious mental conflict. The treatment approach that follows from this theoretical position would involve long-term, individual psychotherapy with Barbara in which the goal would be to help her achieve insight into her frustrated sexual desire for her father, her consequent fear of her mother, and the relationship between this conflict and her current relationship with her husband.

Certain aspects of this theory are consistent with the present case. Most notable might be the resemblance between her father and her husband, Frank. They were both police officers and shared various interpersonal characteristics, such as conservative social and political beliefs. Barbara's current relationship with her mother might also be raised as evidence in support of a psychoanalytic approach to the case. Her father had died shortly after Barbara and Frank were married. Barbara and her mother continued to see each other often. Barbara admitted privately that her mother was usually more of an annoyance than a help, meddling in their daily activities and criticizing the manner in which Barbara and Frank handled the children. Barbara was markedly unassertive with her mother and usually acquiesced to her demands. A psychoanalyst might have argued that this close, ongoing interaction exacerbated and maintained Barbara's rivalry with her mother.

Barbara's problems with her teenage daughter could also be explained in psychoanalytic terms. Barbara's concerns about Bonnie's sexual behavior could be seen as the projection of her fear that she would lose control of her own sexual desires (as was evident in her discussion of her sexual fantasies and the fear that she might flee to Los Angeles to become a prostitute). There are, however, more parsimonious explanations for these phenomena. Her parental behavior may have been a simple reflection of the pattern modeled by her parents; they were overly protective of her when she was young, and she was now protective of Bonnie.

Learning theorists have also stressed the importance of past events in determining present sexual adjustment, but they have emphasized the importance of conditioning procedures, not unconscious mental conflict and sexual desire for one's parents. From a behavioral perspective, many forms of sexual dysfunction can be seen as the product of learned inhibitions that are acquired as a result of unsuccessful, early sexual experiences (Tollison & Adams, 1979). In some cases, these may have been traumatic events such as being raped or molested (Leonard & Follette, 2002).

Behavioral models of sexual dysfunction emphasize the importance of learned, anticipatory anxiety that is associated with sexual stimulation and the development of avoidance responses that serve to reduce this anxiety. This aspect of the model is weak; there is little scientific evidence indicating that either classical or operant conditioning plays an important role in learning sexual responses (Letourneau & O'Donohue, 1997). On the other hand, behavioral models also stress the importance of social skills, in this case knowing how to engage in effective sexual behaviors. They focus on what the people do during sexual activity instead of on the symbolic meaning of the act. This aspect of the behavioral approach has had important implications for the development of psychological treatments for sexual dysfunctions.

Several elements of Barbara's case are compatible with a social skills approach to sexual dysfunction. Her parents' inability to display physical affection (at least in front of the children), their failure to provide her with any information about sexual behavior, and the implicit message that sexual activity was somehow shameful or disgusting, were all important factors that contributed to both her anxiety regarding sexual activity and her lack of appropriate heterosexual social skills. Prior to her relationship with Frank, Barbara had no sexual experience other than brief kisses and hugs after dates. She and Frank, at his insistence, progressed rapidly in their own sexual relationship without giving Barbara sufficient time to extinguish gradually her fear of physical intimacy. Furthermore, their first experience with intercourse was generally unpleasant. This unfortunate event, coupled with their subsequent realization that Barbara had become pregnant, added to her discomfort in sexual activity. Instead of addressing the problem directly and learning more enjoyable ways of interacting sexually, Barbara and Frank tried to ignore the problem. They had intercourse infrequently and shortened the occasions when they did have sex to the briefest possible intervals.

Response patterns that provoke and exacerbate sexual problems tend to fall into four general categories. The first is *failure to engage in effective sexual behavior*. This category includes practices such as rushing to the point of penetration before the woman is sufficiently aroused, as was the Garrisons' habit. This sort of error is almost always the result of ignorance about human sexual responses and not the product of deeply ingrained neuroses or personality disorders. Frank and Barbara did not know that most women take longer than men to reach an advanced stage of sexual arousal and, as a result, neither of them had made a serious effort to improve or prolong their activity during foreplay.

The second type of maladaptive response is *sexual anxiety*, which includes subjective factors such as the pressure to perform adequately and fear of failure. This type of interference was clearly present in the Garrisons' case. Frank had been concerned for a number of years about losing control of his ejaculatory response. Because of this fear, he continued to rush through the initial stages of sexual activity and resisted any subtle efforts that Barbara made to slow things down. She, on the other hand, was troubled by a double-edged concern. Although she always *tried* very hard to have an orgasm (and was, in fact, quite self-conscious about her failure to reach a climax), she was simultaneously worried about getting carried away. Barbara was convinced that if she really abandoned herself completely and followed her "raw sexual instinct," she would lose control of herself. In so doing, she feared that she would risk losing Frank completely because he would be repulsed by her behavior. This was truly a vicious dilemma. If she did not relax and let herself go, she would not have an orgasm, thus perpetuating her own unhappiness as well as Frank's conviction (as she imagined it) that she was an inadequate lover. On the other hand, if she did relax and let herself go, she would lose control and run the risk of alienating him completely.

The third set of factors that maintain sexual dysfunctions include *perceptual and intellectual defenses against erotic feelings*. Sexual responses are not under voluntary control. The surest way to lose an erection, for example, is to think about the erection instead of the erotic stimuli. Nevertheless, some people engage in a kind of obsessive self-observation during sexual activity and, as a result, become spectators, not participants, in their own lovemaking. Laboratory studies have provided further insight regarding this phenomenon, and they have suggested a few interesting distinctions between sexually functional and dysfunctional people (Wiegel, Wincze, & Barlow, 2002). The arousal levels of sexually functional subjects are typically enhanced by performance-related erotic cues, such as the presence of a highly aroused partner. The same kind of stimulation can distract people who are sexually dysfunctional. The cognitive interference that they experience in response to these stimuli leads to a decrease in their sexual arousal. This problem was particularly characteristic of Barbara's behavior. She often found herself ruminating during sexual activity and asking herself questions about her own performance and desires (Will I come this time? What would happen if Frank knew what I have been thinking about?).

Failure to communicate is the final category of immediate causes of sexual dysfunction. Women suffering from orgasmic disorder report that, in addition to holding negative attitudes toward masturbation and feeling guilty about sex, they are uncomfortable talking to their partner about sexual activities, especially those involving direct clitoral stimulation (Kelly, Strassberg, & Turner, 2004). The Garrisons' failure in this regard was painfully obvious. Both were unwilling to talk to the other person about their desires and pleasures. In Barbara's case, her inhibitions could be traced to the environment in which she was raised. Her parents explicitly conveyed the message that decent people did not talk about sex. If she could not talk to her own mother about basic matters such as menstruation and pregnancy, how could she expect to discuss erotic fantasies with her husband? Consequently, Barbara and Frank knew little about the kinds of stimulation and fantasies that were most pleasing to their partner.

Treatment

The widely publicized work of Masters and Johnson (1970) had an important impact on the development and use of direct psychological approaches to the treatment of sexual dysfunction. Although questions have been raised about the way in which they evaluated and reported the results of their treatment program, their apparent success created an optimistic and enthusiastic environment in which further research and training could be accomplished. Instead of treating the problem as a symbol of unconscious turmoil, sex therapists are primarily concerned with the problem itself and the current, situational determinants that serve to maintain it. This is clearly a cognitive-behavioral approach. Therapists seek to eliminate sexual anxiety by temporarily removing distracting expectations (intercourse is typically forbidden during the first several days of treatment) and substituting competing responses. The sensate focus exercise, for example, is employed to create an erotic atmosphere devoid of performance demands, in which couples can learn to communicate more freely. In later sessions, couples are instructed in the use of specific exercises designed to foster skills related to their specific sexual problem (Bach, Wincze, & Barlow, 2001; McCarthy, 2004).

The "start-stop" procedure for treating premature ejaculation is a good example of this approach. The male partner is taught to attend to important sensations that signal the imminence of ejaculation and to interrupt further stimulation until the urge passes. Frank's experience indicates that there are important cognitive changes that accompany the physiological and behavioral components of this technique. As he became more successful in controlling his ejaculatory responses, Frank experienced less apprehension during extended periods of foreplay. His increased confidence and willingness to communicate were, in turn, important assets in addressing Barbara's orgasmic difficulty. Considerable success has been achieved with this approach (Grenier & Byers, 1995).

Antidepressant medication provides another useful approach to the treatment of premature ejaculation. Double-blind, placebo-controlled studies have shown that selective serotonin reuptake inhibitors (SSRIs), such as paroxetine (Paxil®), can lead to a significant delay in ejaculation after three or four weeks of treatment (Waldinger et al., 2001).

The prognosis for orgasmic dysfunction in women is also quite good (McCabe, 2001). For example, one study reported a 95 percent rate of success for directed masturbation training with 150 women who had never had an orgasm prior to treatment (LoPiccolo & Stock, 1986). Approximately 85 percent of the women were also able to reach orgasm if they were stimulated directly by their partners. It is also important to note, however, that only 40 percent of these women were able to reach orgasm during intercourse. With few exceptions, all women can learn to experience orgasm, but a substantial percentage cannot reach climax through the stimulation afforded by intercourse alone. As in Barbara's case, many women require additional stimulation beyond that associated with the motion of the erect penis in the vagina. These women should not be considered treatment failures. Orgasm during intercourse does not have to be the ultimate measure of treatment success (Stock, 1993).

Research studies have tended to focus on certain aspects of sexual performance, such as ability to delay ejaculation and orgasmic responsiveness. It must be remembered, however, that performance variables represent only one aspect of sexual adjustment. Factors such as subjective arousal, personal satisfaction, and feelings of intimacy and closeness with one's partner are also important considerations. Barbara and Frank were happy with their sexual relationship despite the fact that she could not achieve orgasm through intercourse alone. They had made remarkable changes in their ability to communicate and share sexual pleasure and were content to utilize positions that allowed either Frank or Barbara to stimulate Barbara's clitoral area manually while they were having intercourse. With this limitation in mind, direct approaches to orgasmic dysfunction have been quite successful (Bancroft, 1997; Rosen & Leiblum, 1995).

CHAPTER 14

Paraphilias: Exhibitionism and Frotteurism

Pete began therapy in November with a clinical psychologist. During the initial interview Pete, a 34-year-old married man, explained that he was coming for therapy concerning a sexual problem that he had had for years. He was seeking treatment now because he had been arrested in September for a sexual assault. He had been driving home, taking a shortcut along some back roads, when he saw a car with its hood up and a woman looking at the engine. He stopped to offer assistance. The woman had stopped because her alternator light had come on. Pete was able to correct the problem by adjusting the fan belt. When the woman thanked him, he pulled her close to him, trying to fondle her buttocks. As she pushed him away, he exposed himself and started masturbating. The woman ran to her car and drove off. Pete made no attempt to follow. Later that night the police came to his home and arrested him. An initial hearing was held the next day and bail was set. Pete's wife attended the hearing and paid the bail. At his subsequent trial Pete was allowed to plead guilty to a reduced charge of attempted assault and was put on probation for two years. Part of the probation agreement was that he enter psychotherapy.

This was not the first time that Pete's sexual behaviors got him into trouble. He had a long history of sexual deviance, since early adolescence. His deviant sexual practices took two forms. One was getting himself into crowded places—shopping centers or subway trains—moving up close behind a woman, and rubbing his pelvis against her buttocks. This type of activity is called frottage; the disorder is called frotteurism. Pete's other deviant sexual practice was exhibitionism. Sometimes he would park his car in a place where many women were walking, remain seated behind the wheel, and masturbate as he watched them. He did not expose himself directly but hoped that the passing women would look into his car and see him. Other times he would masturbate under a raincoat in a place frequented by women. Teenagers with "cute little behinds" were his preferred target for both activities.

Pete had engaged in both of these activities since adolescence. The first time he clearly remembered doing either was as a 16-year-old high school student. He was at a football game on a drizzly Saturday afternoon and had on a raincoat, one in which the pockets allow a hand to go from the outside all the way through the coat to the body. Sitting next to a female acquaintance, he found himself sexually aroused and masturbated to orgasm, his actions apparently undetected by anyone.

When he got his driver's license later that year, he began to openly masturbate in his car. Since then he had engaged in either frottage or exhibitionism fairly regularly—an average of 15 to 20 times per year. Pete reported that the urge to do so usually increased when he was under stress, such as during exams in high school and college or while under work pressures in adulthood. His sexual behavior had worried him for some time. He had been in therapy for brief periods on three previous occasions. Each time he dropped out after several sessions because it seemed to him that little progress was being made. This time Pete could not drop out of therapy because doing so would violate the terms of his probation.

Other important facets of his problem were explored over several sessions, including his sexual fantasies, which were a mirror of his deviant sexual practices. During the day, he often imagined rubbing against or masturbating in front of young women. His masturbatory fantasies also had the same content. He reported that the frequency of his sexual fantasies had been increasing lately. But there was an important difference between his fantasies and his actual sexual experiences. In real life, he had never succeeded in arousing a woman by rubbing against her or publicly masturbating. Women he rubbed against moved away from him or, less frequently, threatened to call for help if he persisted. When women saw him masturbating in his car, their reaction was shock or disgust. In his fantasies, however, Pete's frottage or masturbation usually served as a prelude to intercourse. The young women of his dreams became aroused as he rubbed against them or when they saw his erect penis. His fantasy would then expand to include a more conventional sexual encounter. Fantasies limited only to conventional intercourse, however, were not stimulating to Pete.

Pete also had problems in other areas of his life. Although he was a college graduate, he had never been able to find a job that he found satisfying. His interests in painting and music had never been profitable. He had held a long series of jobs he regarded as dull. His longest period of employment in the same job was 18 months. He was currently working as a bartender in a topless bar, which was not a good choice for someone with paraphilias.

Pete and Helen married when he was 24 and she was 22 after dating for six months. They had a 5-year-old son. Helen was a high school graduate and worked as an executive secretary for the vice president of an engineering firm. She had held this relatively high-paying and responsible job for four years. Pete reported that their marriage had gradually gone downhill. They did not fight or argue much, but he felt that Helen had become less affectionate, less interested in sex, and did not seem to care as much for him as she once had. Currently, he said, she found excuses to avoid most of his sexual advances. The frequency of intercourse had dropped to less than once per month. He reported that he did enjoy sex with his wife. Foreplay usually involved rubbing his penis on her bare buttocks, and intercourse was in the rear entry position. As with his fantasies, however, frottage was a necessary prelude to arousal and subsequent intercourse. According to Pete, the birth of their son seemed to coincide with the beginning of Helen's decline in interest in him. Pete was initially uninvolved and refused to help with feedings and diaper changes. More recently he was beginning to feel and act more like a father.

Social History

The origins of Pete's current problems seemed to lie in his childhood. He reported he had been "emotionally deprived" as a child. His father never held jobs for very long; consequently, the family moved a great deal. For this reason, Pete felt that he never had a chance to develop close childhood friendships. Furthermore, he felt rejected by his father. He reported that they never played or went on outings together and that his father always seemed cold and distant. Pete's father died when he was 12 years old.

Pete felt that his relationship with his mother was warm, but he thought that she was overprotective and somewhat smothering. After the death of Pete's father, his mother never dated and seemed to invest all of her emotional needs in her children, especially Pete. For example, she continued to bathe him until he was 15 years old. During these baths in Pete's early adolescence, she took great care in cleaning his penis, stroking it with the wet bar of soap and seeming to enjoy the erections that were often produced.

When Pete was 13 years old, he and his family were living in an apartment complex. His principal playmates were three slightly older female teenagers. The four often engaged in rough-and-tumble play like wrestling. During one of these play sessions, Pete had his first orgasm. He was wrestling with one of the girls and was on top of her, his genitals against her buttocks. While moving, he became erect and continued thrusting until he climaxed. He was able to keep his orgasm secret from his friends and went home quickly to clean up.

After this initial pleasurable experience, Pete began sexually abusing his 8-year-old sister. At night whenever he had the opportunity, he would go to her bed, take off her pajama bottoms, and rub his penis against her bare buttocks until he reached orgasm. He continued this practice regularly for the next couple years and stopped only after his sister threatened to tell their mother. When he stopped the frottage with his sister, he turned to regular masturbation with fantasies of both rubbing and conventional intercourse during his self-stimulation. When he was 15 years old, an opportunity for conventional intercourse presented itself. Pete had heard stories for some time about the sexual exploits of a 17-year-old girl who lived in the same apartment building as he did. He went out of his way to get to know her, did errands and favors for her, and finally was invited to have sex with her one night in a nearby park. Although he became aroused as they kissed and petted, he lost his erection when he attempted intercourse. Thereafter Pete reported that he became afraid to approach women. His first instance of public masturbation occurred the next year.

On a social level, adolescence was not much better for Pete than childhood had been. He did hang around with a group, but he did not develop any really close relationships. He did not date much and reported that being around popular and attractive women made him anxious. He also indicated that it was difficult for him to participate in conversations. He felt that most often people talked only about trivialities and that he was just not interested in that.

After graduating from high school, Pete attended a local community college and then a university, and graduated with a bachelor's degree in psychology. He then drifted through a series of jobs and casual affairs until meeting his wife. She was the first woman with whom he had ever had a lasting relationship.

Another perspective on Pete, and particularly on his marriage, was gained through a marital assessment conducted in separate sessions with Pete and Helen. Pete's main complaints about Helen centered on her lack of affection and their poor sexual relationship. He also reported that they argued about how to spend their leisure time. Helen liked to socialize with friends, but Pete found most of them boring. Helen did not know about Pete's long history of unconventional sexuality. She thought that Pete's trouble with the law was the only time he had ever engaged in such activity, and could not understand why he had done it. She was extremely upset and repulsed by the entire incident but stood by him. She also made it clear that another such incident would end their marriage.

Helen's description of the problems in their marriage was similar to Pete's. She recognized that infrequent sex, absence of affection, and disagreements about socializing with friends were serious problems. She had tolerated Pete's frottage before intercourse but did not find it appealing. Helen also complained about Pete as a father and husband. She resented the fact that he was less than a full partner in the marriage, sharing only minimally in parenting and other household duties. Her resentment was increased because she worked all day and then had to come home to cook, clean, and take care of their son while Pete did little but watch television. Even when Pete was not working, which was frequently, he made little attempt to help out. She had lost respect for him because of his failure to share in the marriage and because of his job history and consequent inability to make much of a financial contribution. She was currently somewhat ashamed of Pete's job as a bartender in a topless bar and suspected that he might be having an affair. Indeed, she attributed most of her inability to be affectionate and her declining interest in sex to this loss of respect. She added that she wished Pete would not always follow the same routine in their sexual encounters.

Conceptualization and Treatment

Initially, Pete's therapist needed to implement some procedures to increase the likelihood that Pete would be able to stop both the public masturbation and the frottage and thus avoid being jailed. He had not engaged in either for almost two months, the longest period for which he had refrained since adolescence. But Pete reported that the urges were still there and that they would appear unexpectedly. Because the frottage and public masturbation were linked to particular situations—parking lots, shopping centers, and subways—Pete was told to avoid these situations as much as possible. In addition, Pete was taught how to handle an urge if it arose. Because his urges were linked to heightened arousal, he was instructed about how to relax himself by imagining that he was on a beach, feeling drowsy, and enjoying the warm sun. In this and subsequent therapy sessions, Pete practiced imagining typical situations that would generally elicit the urge to exhibit or engage in frottage, but instead of acting on his urges he relaxed and imagined that he overcame the urge.

Over subsequent sessions several other components were added to the therapy. First, an attempt was made to try to change Pete's sexual fantasies, both when masturbating and when he felt attraction to or arousal by any woman. Second, marital therapy seemed necessary, both for the marriage itself and, more specifically, for the sexual relationship between Pete and Helen. Both aspects of the therapy were directed toward increasing the frequency and attractiveness of intercourse.

The first step in trying to make conventional intercourse more attractive to Pete was to have him masturbate while fantasizing only about intercourse. Initially, Pete reported that he was unable to develop a full erection unless he imagined frottage or public masturbation. He was first instructed to arouse himself with any fantasy (for him this was most often frottage or public masturbation), to begin masturbating and, when he was close to orgasm, to switch to an intercourse scene. He was able to do this easily. After a week of practice, he was told to switch to the intercourse fantasy closer to the start of masturbation. He was able to do so with no loss of arousal. By the fourth week, he was able to initiate and complete masturbation with no fantasies of frottage or public masturbation.

As this part of the therapy was progressing, Pete also began to work on altering fantasies elicited by women. His usual response to seeing a young woman, particularly one in tight jeans or slacks, was to begin imagining rubbing against her buttocks. A treatment was devised to help Pete change these fantasies. Initially during a therapy session, Pete was shown a series of pictures of young women in tight jeans. For each stimulus he was asked to generate a nonsexual fantasy, such as trying to guess the woman's occupation. He was encouraged to focus on the woman's face instead of her buttocks as he thought about the picture. Over a series of trials in which Pete verbalized his thoughts, a repertoire of distracting thoughts and fantasies were developed, with the therapist guiding Pete and providing feedback. This repertoire would help him have nonsexual thoughts when he encountered an attractive woman. Over the next several weeks, Pete continued to practice his new fantasies, both in session and at home. As this skill became better established, Pete was also encouraged to use it in his day-to-day life. He soon reported that he was beginning to have fewer and fewer thoughts of frottage when he encountered attractive young women.

Pete's fantasies regarding women responding positively to his sexual advances were also addressed. Although he had never succeeded in arousing a woman by exhibiting or rubbing, in his fantasy life he had continually imagined that his advances led to sexual contact. The therapist pointed out the striking inconsistency between his fantasies and real life. With this point beginning to sink in, Pete was also encouraged to reflect on how these incidents actually affected his victims. Pete was guided to have a more empathic sense of the unpleasant emotions his advances actually created.

Marital therapy was then initiated. At first the focus was on the nonsexual problems in the marriage. With the therapist functioning as a mediator and facilitator, the couple was instructed to talk about the various difficulties they were experiencing. The first problem they discussed was Pete's failure to help out with household chores. He acknowledged that he had not helped out very much but added also that when he did try to do something, Helen usually found fault with his efforts.

Helen agreed in part with Pete's analysis. For example, when Pete did the laundry he would leave the clothes in the dryer and they became wrinkled and would need ironing. From Helen's perspective, she was therefore not really saved from any work; if she had done the laundry herself, she would have quickly folded the clothes and not had to iron them. From Pete's viewpoint, his efforts had gone unappreciated. With the therapist's guidance Helen and Pete were able to realize the aspects of the situation that were creating the problem. Neither was feeling good about what the other had done. To solve the problem, Pete agreed to do the laundry and fold it immediately, and Helen agreed to be sure to let Pete know that she appreciated his efforts. A similar system was instituted for several other household chores (cooking, vacuuming, general cleaning) in which Pete had previously tried to be helpful, but his efforts had failed to elicit Helen's approval.

Next the therapist directed the couple to consider Pete's belief that Helen was not affectionate toward him. But the therapist was not able to limit the discussion to this problem; Helen was soon talking about her general lack of respect for Pete. The session became highly emotional. Pete, understandably somewhat defensive, argued that he had always done the best he could to be a provider for the family. This issue was not even close to resolution by the end of the session; the therapist instructed Pete and Helen not to talk about it further over the coming week but to think about it and be ready to discuss it the next week.

Two days later Pete called the therapist to request an extra session. Pete was visibly tense when they met the next day. He said that he had really been shaken by the last session, that he had no idea that Helen had come to view him so negatively. This realization, he said, had a profound effect on him, and he felt compelled to let the therapist know something that he had previously not told anyone. Over the past several years, he had engaged in a series of casual sexual experiences with young women, principally dancers at the bar. During most of them, he had not been able to complete intercourse satisfactorily. The pattern was similar to his initial attempt at intercourse. He would first become aroused and fully erect but later would lose his erection. He said that he wanted to start over now, to stop the affairs and do more to please Helen.

At the next session with Pete and Helen, Pete quickly announced that he had decided to change jobs, was job hunting, and had several promising leads. Seeing that Pete was serious about improving the marriage, Helen was obviously delighted. She also reported that he was helping out more around the house. She was beginning to believe that he was serious about improving their marriage, and she felt good about expressing her appreciation toward him. The next week Pete landed a job as a camera salesperson in a department store. Helen was very pleased. The two of them stated that they were ready to deal with sex.

Before beginning this phase of therapy, the therapist met individually with Pete to check on his progress in dealing with the urge to masturbate publicly or engage in frottage. Pete had continued to masturbate successfully to fantasies of conventional intercourse. Furthermore, he reported that seeing an attractive young woman no longer led automatically to thoughts of frottage and that he had not really experienced any of his old urges.

From this point on the therapy progressed quickly. Because Helen was beginning to feel better about Pete, she said that she would not resist his sexual advances. They discussed with the therapist their sexual likes and dislikes and agreed to plan several sexual experiences over the next week. Pete was told to refrain from his usual foreplay (rubbing his penis against Helen's buttocks). The couple agreed on manual and oral stimulation to take its place. They had intercourse four times the next week. Over the next few sessions, the couple continued working on their marital problems. Progress was excellent. They reported that their sexual interactions were both frequent and pleasurable. Occasional sessions with Pete alone revealed that he no longer felt the urge to masturbate publicly or engage in frottage.

Discussion

Pete's problems fall within the *DSM-IV-TR* (APA, 2000) category of *paraphilias*—frequently occurring sexual urges, fantasies, or behaviors that involve unusual objects and activities. The diagnosis is made only if the person is distressed by the urges or behavior or if social or occupational functioning is impaired. *DSM-IV-TR* lists nine paraphilias, as follows:

1.   Fetishism: the repeated use of nonliving objects to produce sexual excitement

2.   Transvestic fetishism: recurrent cross-dressing to produce sexual arousal

3.   Pedophilia: sexual activity with prepubescent children

4.   Voyeurism: repetitive looking at unsuspecting people, either while they are undressing or engaging in sexual activity

5.   Sexual masochism: the production of sexual arousal by being made to suffer

6.   Sexual sadism: the production of sexual arousal by inflicting physical or psychological suffering on someone else

7.   Paraphilia not otherwise specified: a heterogeneous group of unconventional activities (e.g., coprophilia—obtaining sexual gratification from handling feces; and necrophilia—being sexually intimate with a corpse)

The remaining two paraphilias, exhibitionism and frotteurism, were Pete's specific problems. In *exhibitionism*, the person repeatedly exposes his genitals to a stranger for the purpose of achieving sexual excitement. Like the other paraphilias, exhibitionism is practiced almost exclusively by men. It is the most common sexual offense for which people are arrested, accounting for about one-third of all such arrests. Exhibitionism can involve either the exposure of a flaccid penis or an erect one, accompanied by masturbation, as in Pete's case. The motivation for exhibiting seems to vary as the disorder progresses. When it begins in adolescence, it is sexually exciting, but in adulthood, exhibiting is accompanied by general arousal rather than by sexual excitement (McConaghy, 1994). At the time of the act, the adult exhibitionist typically feels both cognitive and physiological signs of arousal—nervousness, palpitations, perspiring, and trembling. Many report that the urge becomes so powerful that they lose control and even some awareness of what they are doing. Although clinical lore suggests that exhibitionists typically do not seek further sexual contact with their victims, more recent data indicate that, like Pete, some do get arrested for crimes involving actual sexual contact. For example, Sugarman, Dumugn, Saad, Hinder, & Blugass (1994) followed a large sample of exhibitionists and found that 26 percent subsequently were convicted for sexual crimes, including rape. Others have found about half of exhibitionists that were caught reoffended over the five years following their initial arrests, and a significant number of them go on to commit violent sexual offenses (Rabinowitz-Greenberg, Firestone, Bradford, & Greenberg, 2002). Some researchers report that exhibitionism often co-occurs with frotteurism (Tan & Zhong, 2001).

People with paraphilias often have other psychological disorders as well. Kafka and Hennen (2002) evaluated 88 men who voluntarily sought outpatient treatment for paraphilias and found that 17 percent reported a childhood history of physical abuse, and 18 percent reported a history of childhood sexual abuse; 61 percent had been arrested (not always related to the paraphilia), and 25 percent had been hospitalized for psychiatric problems. Exhibitionism was the most common paraphilia in the sample, followed by pedophilia and voyeurism. The most common comorbid lifetime psychiatric diagnoses were mood disorders: 69 percent met criteria for dysthymic disorder, 39 percent for major depression, and 7 percent for bipolar disorder; 42 percent had substance abuse, 42 percent had attention-deficit/hyperactivity disorder, 39 percent had an anxiety disorder, and 22 percent had a conduct disorder. Others have also found that people with a paraphilia were very likely to also have a substance abuse disorder, a mood disorder, or antisocial personality disorder (Dunsieth et al., 2004).

The rates of comorbid psychological disorders among 30 men with a paraphilia arrested for hands-on sexual offenses (pedophilia and sexual sadism) were examined by Leue, Borchard, and Hoyer (2004). Seventy-three percent met criteria at some point in their lives for an anxiety disorder, 57 percent for a substance abuse disorder, 30 percent for a mood disorder, and 74 percent for a personality disorder (most commonly antisocial personality disorder or avoidant personality disorder).

In their review of paraphilias, Saleh and Berlin (2003) note that they typically emerge in adolescence, and once established, are usually stable and long-lasting. Most people with paraphilias do not voluntarily seek treatment but are court-mandated to attend or receive treatment while incarcerated. Animal studies and a few human studies have suggested abnormalities in the hypothalamic-pituitary-gonadal axis that could be related to deviant sexual behaviors or thoughts, particularly for pedophiles. However, these findings are tentative.

Often people with paraphilias do not freely admit to the extent of their deviant sexual behavior. When questioned during polygraph (lie detector) testing, sexual offenders admitted to greater numbers of episodes of paraphilic behavior and significantly earlier ages of onset than was known from probation records (Wilcox & Sosnowski, 2005). They admitted to twice as many episodes of exhibitionism and public masturbation. Moreover, none of the probation records contained references to frottage, but half of the men admitted under polygraph examination that they had committed frottage. This suggests that the frequency and scope of deviant sexual behavior of sexual offenders is much larger than might be suspected. In addition, the men admitted that they began their sexual offending an average of 14 years before they were arrested for it.

The penile plethysmograph, a device that measures the circumference of the penis, was used in a study of male exhibitionists to determine whether they are sexually aroused by stimuli that do not arouse nonexhibitionists (Fedora, Reddon, & Yeudall, 1986). Compared with normal men and with sex offenders who had committed violent assaults, the exhibitionists showed significantly greater arousal to slides of fully clothed women in nonsexual situations, such as riding on an escalator or sitting in a park; they showed similar levels of sexual interest in erotic and sexually explicit slides. These results suggest that exhibitionists misread cues in the courtship phase of sexual contact, in the sense that they construe certain situations to be sexual that are judged to be unerotic by people without exhibitionism. In a more recent study using similar methods, it was found that exhibitionists also showed relatively more sexual arousal to scenes of violence, consistent with the fact that some of them do commit violent offenses (Seto & Kuban, 1996).

Exhibitionists also prefer to exhibit to people with whom they are unfamiliar (Freund & Watson, 1990). Clinical accounts suggest that the exhibitionist derives much gratification from the reaction of the victim, which is generally shock, fear, or disgust. In a laboratory study of sexual arousal in exhibitionists, however, they were not particularly aroused by filmed depictions of female anger or fear (Kolarsky & Madlafousek, 1983). According to data from court referrals, exhibitionism usually begins in adolescence, continues into the twenties, and declines thereafter. Whether the frequency truly declines or whether older exhibitionists are arrested less frequently is unknown.

Educationally and intellectually, exhibitionists do not seem to differ from the average person (Mohr, Turner, & Jerry, 1964). About 75 percent of exhibitionists over the age of 21 are married. Forgac and Michaels (1982) compared the personality characteristics of exhibitionists who do and do not participate in other criminal activities. Consistent with expectation, the criminal exhibitionists were more psychopathic and had higher levels of psychopathology.

Comparing Pete to the usual descriptions of exhibitionists, we can see that he is atypical in some respects. Instead of exposing himself openly, as is usually the case, Pete stayed in his car, hoping that he might be seen. He also indicated that he hoped his exposure would lead to a sexual contact; this is atypical because most authors regard exhibitionists as actually fearing sexual contact with their victims.

Some features of Pete's background, however, are quite similar to characteristics of exhibitionists in general. Many exhibitionists grow up in families in which there is a considerable amount of disturbance (Murphy, 1997). Furthermore, their marriages tended to be dysfunctional, with special difficulties in sexual adjustment. Interpersonally, exhibitionists tend to be socially isolated, with few close friends. And, like Pete, exhibitionists tend to be more active in their sexual behavior during periods of stress (Witzig, 1968).

Frotteurism involves intense sexual urges and sexually arousing fantasies involving touching and rubbing against a nonconsenting person. It is the touching, not the coercive nature of the act, that is sexually exciting. Little is known about frotteurism although clinical reports indicate that it does not often occur in isolation and commonly appears in conjunction with other paraphilias such as exhibitionism (Krueger & Kaplan, 1997).

Pete also had an incestuous relationship with his sister. Incest is sexual relations between close family members, and is listed in the *DSM-IV-TR* (APA, 2000) as a form of pedophilia. As with Pete, incest is most common between brother and sister.

Etiological Considerations

In psychoanalytic theory, the various paraphilias are viewed as defenses against the anxiety aroused by conventional sexual intercourse. Fenichel (1945), for example, saw the exhibitionist as a person who did not successfully resolve the Oedipal conflict. Instead of giving up his mother as his love object, getting over his fear of castration by the father, and identifying with him, the exhibitionist continues to fear castration, which is presumably associated with conventional intercourse. The act of exposing is thought to confirm to the exhibitionist that he does have a penis and has not been castrated. Furthermore, Fenichel argued that the exhibitionist unconsciously hopes that the women to whom he exhibits will expose themselves to him, because seeing that they have no penis would reduce his own castration anxiety. Psychoanalytic theory would regard Pete's frotteurism and exhibitionism as substitute ways of expressing sexual impulses. Although some of these speculations ring true for certain aspects of Pete's case (his seductive mother, his early sexual experiences with his younger sister), there are few data that would allow us to evaluate them better. Furthermore, the fact that Pete had been able to complete intercourse successfully is not easily explained by the psychoanalytic position.

People incarcerated for paraphilias are more likely to have been emotionally, physically, and sexually abused as children; were more likely to have had behavior problems as children; and were more likely to have come from dysfunctional families than people incarcerated for nonviolent and nonsexual crimes (Lee, Jackson, Pattison, & Ward, 2002). However, when examining data for only the exhibitionists, history of child sexual abuse was actually less likely than among the other paraphilias. Exhibitionism in particular was linked to childhood emotional abuse, family dysfunction, and childhood behavior problems.

Others have speculated that sexual offenders have a deficit in social skills, which makes it difficult for them to form intimate romantic relationships. Emmers-Sommer et al. (2004) examined ten studies of sex offenders to evaluate their social skills. They found that sex offenders have poorer social skills. In Pete's case, this is consistent with his difficulties in forming peer relationships and his difficulties relating in his marriage.

A learning-based conceptualization of Pete's case, which in part guided his therapy, involves the following considerations. First, during early adolescence Pete experienced a chance conditioning trial in which orgasm was linked to rubbing. Although a single experience like this one would not likely produce a durable effect, the link between rubbing and orgasm may have been strengthened through the many similar experiences he arranged between himself and his sister and the repetition of these encounters in his masturbation fantasies. His initial failure in conventional intercourse, coupled with his lack of social skills and infrequent dates, maintained his interest in frottage and set the stage for the development of exhibitionism. Finally, his unsatisfactory sexual relationship with his wife did not provide him with an opportunity to give up his old behavior patterns.

This account is still incomplete in many respects. Why did Pete reinforce his habit of frottage with his younger sister? What led him to exhibit instead of trying to develop skills that might have enabled him to date and to enjoy more conventional sexual pleasures? Why did his sexual fantasies involve the idea that exhibiting or rubbing would sexually arouse women? The theory also implies that early sexual experiences have very durable effects, but it appears that early sexual experiences need not have lifelong effects. The point has been clearly made in a study of the Sambia tribe in New Guinea (Stoller & Herdt, 1985). All male members of the tribe are exclusively homosexual from age 7 to marriage. During a first stage from 7 years old to puberty, the boys perform fellatio on older boys as often as possible because it is their belief that they have to drink a lifetime's supply of semen. From puberty to marriage, women are taboo, and the young men are fellated often by the younger boys. After marriage, the tribesmen become completely heterosexual. Their early homosexual experiences apparently have had little effect on their capacity for and interest in heterosexual arousal.

Treatment

There are very few controlled studies of the effectiveness of particular therapies in treating exhibitionism, frotteurism, and the other paraphilias. A major reason for the lack of controlled studies is the ethical problem that would be created by withholding treatment from the control group. Results from the studies that do exist are highly variable, with success rates from about 30 to 90 percent (Marshall et al., 1991).

Psychoanalytic therapy follows from the etiological model discussed previously. Using the standard techniques of psychoanalysis—free association, dream analysis, and interpretation—the exhibitionist is encouraged to explore the unconscious impulses (e.g., castration fears or incestuous impulses) that are assumed to be causing the problem. In addition, analysts (e.g., Karpman, 1954) recommend making changes in the patient's life situation, such as moving out of his mother's home or improving the sexual relationship between the exhibitionist and his wife.

Cognitive-behavioral interventions have evolved from focusing on the application of single techniques to more multidimensional treatments. As examples of the former, exhibitionism has been treated with systematic desensitization to reduce fears of conventional sexual contact (Wickramsekera, 1977) and with aversion therapy to reduce the attractiveness of exhibiting (Marshall, Eccles, & Barbaree, 1991).

Pete's therapy illustrates the use of multiple procedures. One component of the therapy was similar to a procedure originally developed by Davison (1968) in treating a case of a young man who required sadistic fantasies to produce sexual arousal. As in the present case, Davison had the client initiate sexual arousal with a sadistic fantasy and then masturbate while looking at a picture of a nude woman. If arousal began to wane, he could return to his sadistic images, but he was told to ensure that orgasm was associated only with the picture. As therapy progressed, the sadistic fantasies were relied on less and less until the client could masturbate to orgasm relying only on the stimulation produced by the nudes. Like Davison's client, Pete learned to become fully aroused and reach orgasm by changing his masturbatory fantasies from exhibiting and frottage to conventional intercourse.

Changing the masturbation fantasies of the person with a paraphilia is a common type of treatment. Dandescu and Wolfe (2003) examined the use of fantasy among people with exhibitionism and pedophilia who were in mostly court-ordered treatment. Of the 82 participants in their sample, 25 were exhibitionists. The majority of both experienced deviant masturbatory fantasies prior to engaging in their first sexual experience related to their paraphilia. For the exhibitionists, 76 percent had deviant masturbatory fantasies before their first offense, and 88 percent did after their first offense. The average number of deviant fantasies increased after the first offense. This suggests that deviant masturbatory fantasies are a critical part of the etiology and maintenance of paraphilias for most but not all men with paraphilias.

Another procedure used with Pete is called alternative behavioral completion (Maletzky, 1997). It involves imagining a scene in which the urge to exhibit appears but is overcome by relaxation. In addition, Pete came to change the fantasies that attractive women elicited by practicing new ones, first with pictures and then with women he encountered in the natural environment. Attempts were also made to alter his distorted cognitions and increase his empathy toward his victims. Finally, a reduction in marital conflict and an improved sexual relationship between him and his wife likely contributed to the overall success of the therapy.

Biological interventions have also been employed. Case studies suggesting positive outcomes have been reported for antidepressants and antianxiety drugs (Abouesh & Clayton, 1999; Terao & Nakamura, 2000). Researchers have evaluated an antiandrogen cyproterone acetate for treatment of paraphilia, which decreases all sexual behavior. In studies with exhibitionists, it was found to be effective in completely eliminating deviant behavior for some even after its discontinuation, but it does have side effects (Bradford, 2001). Several studies have also been conducted with medroxyprogesterone acetate, a drug that reduces testosterone levels and thereby lowers sexual arousal. Although effective in reducing recidivism when taken regularly, the disorders recur when the treatment is discontinued (Meyer, Cole, & Emory, 1992). This is problematic because the drug produces a number of unpleasant side effects that are likely to lead to discontinuation. A newer testosterone lowering medication, leuprolide acetate, has shown promise in the treatment of paraphilia and has fewer side effects (Saleh, Niel, & Fishman, 2004).

CHAPTER 15

Gender Identity Disorder: Transsexualism

Chris Morton was a 21-year-old senior in college. In most respects, she was an exceptionally well-adjusted student, successful academically and active socially. Her problem involved a conflict in gender identity—a problem so fundamental that it is difficult to decide whether to refer to Chris as he or she, although Chris used the masculine pronoun. We have somewhat arbitrarily decided to use the feminine pronoun in relating this case because it may be less confusing to the reader. And in many respects this is a confusing case. It calls into question one of the most fundamental, and seemingly irrefutable, distinctions that most of us make—the distinction between men and women.

Chris's physical anatomy was that of a woman. But this distinction was not made easily on the basis of overt, physical appearance. She was tall and slender: 5'8" inches and about 130 pounds. Her hips were narrow and her breasts, which she wrapped with an Ace bandage under her clothes, were small. Chris's face was similarly androgynous; her skin had a soft, smooth appearance, but her features were not particularly delicate or feminine. Her hair was cut short, and she wore men's clothes. A typical outfit included Levi's and a man's shirt with a knit tie and a sweater vest. She wore men's underwear and men's shoes, often Oxfords or penny loafers. She also wore a man's ring on her right hand and a man's wrist watch. Her appearance was generally neat and preppy. At first glance, it was not clear whether Chris was a man or a woman. Listening to Chris's voice did not provide any more useful clues because it was neither deep nor high pitched. Many people assumed that she was a man; others were left wondering.

On the basis of her own attitudes and behaviors, Chris considered herself to be like men. Like other transsexuals, she described herself as being a man trapped in a woman's body. She did not consider herself to be confused about her gender identity. From a biological point of view, Chris recognized that she was not a man. She knew that she had breasts and a vagina. She menstruated. But there was more to it than physical anatomy. In every other way possible, and for as long as she could remember, Chris had always felt more male than female. When she tried to explain this feeling to others, she would say, "You can think what you want—and I know that most people don't want to believe this—but if you spend time with me, talk to me, you will see what I mean. You'll know that I am not a woman." The details of this subjective perception, the experiences that served as support for Chris's belief, lie at the core of our notions of what is feminine and what is masculine.

Chris felt a sense of camaraderie in the presence of men. She wasn't sexually attracted to them, and it never would have occurred to her to flirt with them. She wanted to be buddies with them—to swap stories about adventures and compare notes on sexual exploits with women. They were her friends. In her behavior toward women, Chris was often characteristically masculine and excessively polite; she liked to hold doors for women, to pull out their chairs when they sat down to eat, to stand up when they entered a room. This is, of course, not to say that these behaviors are innately masculine, for they are learned as part of our upbringing. Chris felt more comfortable behaving this way because it made her feel masculine, and she said it seemed natural.

People responded in a variety of ways when meeting Chris for the first time. Most assumed that she was a man, but others took her to be a woman. Chris usually corrected people if they happened to address her as a woman. For example, if an instructor used a feminine pronoun when addressing or describing Chris during an initial meeting, she would quickly say "he" or "his." In situations that might arouse curiosity or attract attention, Chris tried to adopt exaggerated male postures or vocal patterns to overcome the observer's sense of ambiguity. One example occurred when she walked into a small seminar for the first time. Chris sauntered across the room, sat down so her legs crossed with one heel on the other knee, and then slouched down in the chair, adopting a characteristically masculine posture. When answering the phone, she usually tried to lower the pitch of her voice.

Chris was sexually attracted to women and, consistent with her male gender identity (her conviction that she was more like men than women), she considered herself to be heterosexual. In fact, she had had two long-term, intimate relationships, and both were with other women. Her present lover, Lynn, was a 26-year-old bisexual who treated Chris as a man and considered their relationship to be heterosexual. Lynn said that when they first met, she thought that Chris was a woman and she was attracted to her as a woman. But as their relationship developed, Lynn came to think of Chris as a man. Part of this impression could be traced to physical behaviors. Lynn agreed that making love with Chris was more like making love with a man than a woman. Although this impression was difficult to describe in words, it seemed to revolve around the way Chris held her and touched her. Perhaps more important were the emotional and intellectual qualities that Lynn noticed. Chris cried about different things than Lynn cried about and seemed unable to empathize with many of Lynn's experiences—experiences that seemed characteristically feminine. She was surprised, for example, at Chris's apparent inability to empathize with her discomfort during menstruation. And Lynn was often surprised by Chris's questions. Once when they were making love, Chris asked Lynn what it felt like to have something inside her vagina. It was a sensation Chris had never experienced (and never wanted to experience).

Chris's parents had known about her gender identity conflict since her senior year in high school. This was a difficult issue for them to address, but they both assured Chris that their love for her was more important than their concern about the problems she would face as a transsexual. Their reactions were also very different. Chris's mother accepted the problem and made every effort to provide emotional support for Chris. Her father, on the other hand, seemed to deal with the issue at a more intellectual level and continued to believe that it was merely a phase that she was going through. Both were opposed to her interest in physical treatment procedures that might permanently alter her appearance.

Although Chris's life was going well in most respects, she wanted to do something about her body to make it more compatible with her masculine gender identity. Several options seemed reasonable. First, she wanted to have her breasts removed. She also wanted to begin taking male hormones so that her voice would deepen and she would grow facial hair. Finally, she wanted to have surgery to remove her uterus and ovaries, primarily because their continued presence might conflict with the consumption of testosterone. Although she would also have preferred to have a penis, she did not want to go through genital surgery because it would not leave her with a functional male organ. Furthermore, the possibility of "mutilating" her existing organs and losing her capacity for orgasm through clitoral stimulation frightened her.

One interesting feature of Chris's masculine identity was revealed in her discussion of the advantages and disadvantages of the physical procedures involved in changing her body. Lynn mentioned, for example, the possible traumatic consequences of losing the capacity to bear children. What if Chris decided in a few years that she had been mistaken and now wanted to raise a family? The idea was totally foreign to Chris! It was a concern that never would have occurred to her. For Chris, the justification for the change was primarily cosmetic. Her concern involved plans for the future. "Right now I can pass for a young man. That's okay when I'm 21, but what happens when I'm 40 and still look like I'm 20 because I don't have facial hair? I can't date 20-year-old women all my life. I wouldn't be happy."

During her senior year in college, Chris made an appointment to see a psychologist at the student health center on campus. She wanted to talk about her desire to take male hormones and alter her body surgically. Although she had thought about the decision for a long time and discussed it with several other people, she wanted to get the opinion of a mental-health professional.

Social History

Chris was the oldest of four children. She had one brother, who was one year younger than she, and two younger sisters.

Chris said that she had always felt like a boy. Other people viewed her as a typical "tomboy," but Chris recognized the difference. When she was very young, she and her brother and their father played together all the time. Sports were a central activity in the family, especially basketball. Mr. Morton spent numerous hours teaching Chris and her brother Rick to dribble and shoot baskets on their driveway. These were pleasant memories for Chris, but she also remembered feeling excluded from this group as she and her brother grew older. For example, at that time, Little League rules prohibited girls from participating, and Chris found that she was generally discouraged from playing with boys in the organized games that became more common when they were 9 or 10 years old. She and her brother both played on organized youth teams, and their father served as a coach for both of them. But

Chris had to play on girls' teams and she didn't think that was fair, either for her or to the other girls. She remembered thinking to herself that, although she was always the best player on the girls' team, she would have been only an average player on a boys' team, and that was where she felt she belonged. When she got to high school, she finally quit the team, in spite of the fact that she was one of the best players, because she didn't want her name or picture to appear in the paper as being part of a girls' team.

Although Chris spent a great deal of time with her father and brother, she also had a good relationship with her mother, whom she remembers as being a source of emotional support and sympathy in difficult times. Her mother was not athletically inclined, so she didn't participate in the activities of Mr. Morton and the children, but she and Chris did spend time talking and shopping together. On the other hand, Chris was never interested in many of the other activities that some girls share with their mothers, like cooking.

She also wasn't interested in playing with toys that many other girls preferred. She and Rick shared most of their favorite toys, including slot cars, toy soldiers, and baseball cards. She and a friend did play with Barbie dolls for a while, but they only did so when combining them with G.I. Joes and weaving them into mock wars and sexual adventures.

When she started school and began meeting other children in public situations, Chris began to confront and think about issues that are taken for granted by virtually everyone else. How many children, for example, ever think twice about which bathroom to use? As early as the first and second grade Chris could remember feeling uncomfortable about using the girls' room. In the first grade, she attended a parochial school in which the girls were required to wear uniforms. She wore the dress and had her hair long and in a pony tail, but that changed as soon as she reached the second grade. After their parents arranged for Chris and Rick to transfer to a public school, Chris cut her hair very short and began wearing slacks and shirts that made her indistinguishable from the boys.

Similar issues centered around locker rooms. When Chris was 9 years old, her mother arranged for her and Rick to take swimming lessons at a public pool. Chris developed a crush on a cute girl in her class. She remembered feeling ashamed and embarrassed at being in the same locker room with the other girls and being seen in a girl's swimming suit.

Chris's sex play as a child involved little girls rather than little boys. When she was 9 years old, Chris spent long hours "making out" with an 11-year-old neighbor girl, who also experimented sexually with many of the young boys in their neighborhood. Thus, even at this fairly young age, Chris was sexually attracted to girls rather than boys. She had numerous opportunities to play sex games with young boys, who occasionally asked Chris to "mess around," but she wasn't interested. Girls were more attractive and interesting.

By the time she reached junior high school, Chris had begun systematically to avoid using her given name, Christine. She also came to dislike Chris, because although it is a name that is used by both men and women, she thought of it as being more feminine. She came instead to be known by her nickname, "Morty," which sounded more masculine to her.

Adolescence presented a difficult turning point for Chris. The separation of the sexes became more obvious. All of the girls wanted to wear dresses and date boys. Chris wanted to wear pants and date girls. The situation became even more frustrating in high school as her body began to change in obvious ways. The onset of menstruation was awkward, and the development of her breasts presented an even more difficult situation because their presence could be noticed by other people. As soon as her breasts began to enlarge, Chris began binding them tightly with a skin-colored belt that would not show through her shirt. The belt often left bruises on her chest. When she had to change clothes for gym class, she always had to find an isolated locker, away from the other girls, so that no one would see her taking off the belt. Nevertheless, the discomfort and pain associated with this procedure were preferable to the embarrassment of having other people realize that she was developing a woman's body.

Chris continued to have a lot of friends and to be active in academic and extra-curricular activities in spite of her discomfort with gender-specific roles and behaviors. In fact, she was so popular and well respected by the other students that she was elected president of her freshman class in high school. Although she dressed in masculine clothes, everyone knew that she was a girl because she was forced to take the girls' gym class at school. Many of the social activities in which Chris and her friends engaged centered on roller skating in the evening and on weekends. Large numbers of teenagers from their own school and several others in the city gathered at the roller-skating rink to skate to rock music, eat pizza, and have a good time. Because she was a good athlete and enjoyed physical activity, these were pleasant times for Chris. There were awkward moments, however, such as when the disc jockey would announce "girls only" or "boys only." In either case, Chris would leave the rink; she didn't want to be seen with the girls and wasn't allowed to be with the boys.

Chris's parents separated and were eventually divorced when she was a sophomore in high school. Because their parents had concealed the fact that they were not getting along, the news came as a shock to all of the children. In retrospect, Chris said that she should have known that something was going on because her parents had been spending so much time together talking quietly in their room; her parents had usually been content to go their separate ways. There were, of course, hard feelings on both sides, but the arrangements for the separation were made to minimize the children's involvement in the dispute. They continued to live with their mother and visited their father on weekends.

When Chris was 17, she finally decided to have a talk with her mother about her discomfort with femininity. She told her mother that she wanted to be a boy. Her mother's reply was, "I know you do. I was also a tomboy when I was your age, but you'll grow out of it." Her mother tolerated her masculine dress but didn't seem to comprehend the depth of Chris's feelings.

Chris's best friends in high school were three boys who spent most of their time together. They were the liberal intellectuals of the class. These boys accepted Chris as one of their group without being concerned about her gender. One of her friends later told her, "I never really thought of you as a girl. I guess it wasn't important. You were just Morty." She did attract some attention, however, from other children and teachers. She wore men's pants and shirts, and sometimes ties and sport coats. Chris and her friends were also good dancers and spent a lot of time on weekends at a local club. They were the life of the party. When they arrived, everyone else started dancing and having fun.

Sex presented an extremely frustrating dilemma for Chris. She was attracted to girls, as were all of her male friends. When the boys talked—in the usual crude adolescent way—about girls they knew, Chris wanted to join in. But all of her friends knew that she was a girl. She was particularly attracted to one girl, Jennifer, who had moved to their school the previous year. Jennifer was bright, attractive, and engaging. Her appearance and manners were quite feminine. She spent a lot of time with Chris and her friends, but she was going with a boy who was the captain of the basketball team. Chris and Jennifer began to spend more and more time together as the school year wore on. They talked on the phone every night for at least an hour and were virtually inseparable on weekends.

During their junior year, Jennifer's boyfriend moved away to go to college. The relationship began to deteriorate, but Jennifer didn't know how to break things off. Chris became her principal source of emotional support during these difficult months. Chris became very fond of Jennifer and recognized that she was sexually attracted to her but feared that she might destroy their relationship if she mentioned these feelings to Jennifer.

This all changed rather abruptly one Saturday evening. They went to see a movie together, and, as they were sitting next to each other in the darkened theater, Jennifer became conscious of the strong emotional attraction that she felt toward Chris. She sat wishing that Chris would put her hand on her leg or put her arm around her. Jennifer explained these feelings to Chris as they drove home after the film was over, and Chris, in turn, made an effort to explain her feelings for Jennifer. They continued the discussion inside Jennifer's house, and eventually retired to Jennifer's bedroom where they spent the rest of the night talking and making love.

Their physical relationship—which both Chris and Jennifer considered to be heterosexual in nature—was an exceptionally pleasant experience for both of them. It was not without its awkward moments, however. For example, Chris would not let Jennifer touch her breasts or genitals for the first six months after they began having sex. She touched Jennifer with her mouth and hands, but did not let Jennifer reciprocate beyond holding and kissing. In fact, Chris always kept her pants on throughout their lovemaking. This hesitation or resistance was primarily due to Chris's sense that she was in the wrong body. If she allowed Jennifer to touch her, they would both be reminded that she had a woman's body. This was frustrating for both of them, but especially for Jennifer, who by this point was not concerned about whether Chris was a man or a woman. She was simply in love with Chris as a person and wanted a complete, reciprocal relationship. Chris was also frustrated because she continued to feel—in spite of Jennifer's frequent protests to the contrary—that she could not satisfy Jennifer in the way that Jennifer most wanted because she did not have a penis. Their relationship gradually extended to allow more open physical reciprocity, primarily as a result of Jennifer's gentle insistence. Chris found that she enjoyed being stimulated manually and orally by Jennifer and had no trouble reaching orgasm.

Chris and Jennifer were able to continue their intimate relationship without interference from their parents because their parents viewed Chris as a girl and never considered the possibility that she and Jennifer were lovers. They frequently spent nights together at Jennifer's house without arousing any serious suspicion. Jennifer's mother occasionally made comments and asked questions about Chris's masculine wardrobe and manners, but she was totally oblivious to the complexities of Chris's behavior and to the nature of her daughter's involvement.

Despite Jennifer's obvious affection for Chris, their relationship created problems as Jennifer became increasingly sensitive to the reactions of other people. Part of the problem centered on gossip that spread quickly through their school, despite attempts by Chris and Jennifer to conceal the fact that they were dating. Other students had always been reasonably tolerant of Chris's masculine behavior, but their criticism became more overt when a close friend, in whom they had confided, let it become known that Chris and Jennifer were dating each other. That seemed to step beyond most other students' limit for acceptable behavior.

Their sexual relationship ended during Chris's freshman year at college. Jennifer's mother discovered some intimate love letters that Chris had written to Jennifer, who was also in college. She was furious! She threatened to discontinue financial support for Jennifer's education and refused to let her be in their home as long as Jennifer continued to see Chris. The pressure was simply too much. Chris and Jennifer continued to be good friends, but the romantic side of their relationship had to be abandoned. Jennifer dated two or three men afterwards and was eventually married.

After breaking up with Jennifer, Chris met and dated a few other women before starting her relationship with Lynn. One of these encounters is particularly interesting, because it also provides some insight into Chris's sexual orientation and gender identity. One of her male friends from high school, Robert, was also a freshman at the university. They continued to spend a lot of time together and eventually talked openly about Chris's "story" and the fact that Robert was gay. Both admitted considerable interest regarding sexual response in bodies of the opposite sex—responses that neither had had the opportunity to observe. In order to satisfy their curiosity, they decided to have sex with each other. Chris later described it as a pleasant experience, but one that felt uncomfortable. They engaged in mutual masturbation, but Chris did not allow him to penetrate her vagina with his penis. Chris had never experienced a sexual encounter with a male before, and her principal interest was in observing Robert's behavior. She wanted to watch him become aroused and reach orgasm. She had always sensed that her own sexual behavior was more like that of a man than a woman, and this would give her a chance to decide. She ended the evening convinced more than ever that her own behavior was masculine and that she was not sexually attracted to men.

Chris strongly preferred monogamous relationships. This was in part a matter of convenience, because it was obviously very difficult for her to get to know someone with sufficient intimacy to begin a sexual relationship. It was also a matter of choice. She did not understand, for example, how some people—particularly males—could be so promiscuous.

During her sophomore year in college, Chris stumbled across some literature on transsexualism. This was the first time that she realized that other people experienced the same feelings that she had and that the condition had a formal label. In addition to the comfort that she was not alone in this dilemma, she also obtained some useful information. For example, she learned that many transsexual females use Ace bandages, rather than belts, to bind their breasts. She felt much more comfortable after the change. She also learned about the possibilities of hormonal treatments and various surgical procedures that might be used to alter the appearance of her body. Recognition of these alternatives led Chris to pursue extensive reading at the university library. Having decided that she would like to change the appearance of her body, she made an appointment at the student health center.

Conceptualization and Treatment

When Chris came to see a psychologist at the student health center, she did not indicate that she wanted to change her behavior. Extended consultation with a mental-health professional is generally considered to be a prerequisite for the other procedures that might be used to alter her appearance. Chris sincerely wanted to learn as much as possible about her feelings and motivations for change before embarking upon a difficult set of procedures that carried some possibility for health hazards. She knew, for example, that the hormone treatments might lead to the development of acne and that the hair on the top of her head might begin to thin out. Although she felt strongly about her masculine gender identity, she was willing to consider the possibility that she needed psychological treatment rather than the sex-change procedure.

Chris's exceptional social adjustment was an important consideration in the evaluation of her condition. She was clearly functioning at a high level; her grades were good, and she had lots of friends—many of whom knew her only as a man—and she was satisfied with her current sexual relationship, which was based on her masculine identity. Even if procedures were available to alter her gender identity and convince Chris to act and feel like a woman, it did not seem likely that she could be any better adjusted. And, in all probability, she would have been miserable. Therefore, the psychologist decided that she would not try to persuade her that her problem regarding gender identity was the manifestation of more deeply ingrained psychopathology. She played a supportive role as Chris made her own decision about the pending medical procedures.

Fifteen-Year Followup

In the following pages, we describe many important experiences that Chris has had since this case was originally written. Chris is now living as a man. This successful transition leads us to use the masculine pronoun, "he," when referring to Chris in this update.

Chris attended psychotherapy on a regular basis for approximately two years. As Chris had hoped, the psychologist referred him to an endocrinologist (a physician who specializes in disorders of the hormonal system) after the first year of psychotherapy. The doctor asked Chris to complete a battery of psychological tests and a psychiatric evaluation prior to beginning hormone therapy. The doctor wanted this information so that he could be certain that transsexualism was the correct diagnosis.

The psychological test profile and psychiatrist's report indicated that Chris was an intelligent person who was able to evaluate the external world objectively. There was no evidence of psychotic thinking. The endocrinologist therefore granted Chris's request for hormone therapy. Chris was 22 years old and in his first year of graduate school. He can recall with vivid detail the first injection of a synthetic male hormone he received at the medical center. The prescription was Depo-Testosterone 300 mg (1-1/2cc) every three weeks. He looked at his face in the mirror and wondered how he might change physically and emotionally. Would he be satisfied with the results? What if he didn't feel "like himself?"

The first major physical change came two months later with the cessation of the menstrual period. There would be no more obvious monthly reminders that he was physically female. The other changes were more gradual. His voice deepened and cracked just like the voices of pubescent boys. His fat distribution changed, especially around the hips and thighs. He became more muscular and his breast tissue shrank so he no longer had to wear the Ace bandage to conceal his breasts. It would take at least five years for the torso bruising (from the bandaging) to disappear completely. Chris grew more hair on his arms, legs, stomach, and chest. The hair on his face took longer to grow. In the beginning, he shaved every four to five days. He now shaves every other day and sports a handsome mustache and goatee.

Chris had not anticipated a change in his feelings about sex. He had always seemed to have a normal sex drive. Nevertheless, his sex drive skyrocketed during the first two years of hormone therapy. He felt as though he was experiencing puberty all over again. His "first puberty" was spent daydreaming of kissing girls and holding hands. Now he could understand the urges adolescent boys feel for sex. It was often difficult to think of anything other than sex and how to get it. Fortunately, his age and maturity afforded him some control over such impulses. Chris developed sexual relationships with three women during graduate school. He noticed his orgasms were more intense. He was becoming much more comfortable with his own body and could even enjoy masturbating.

Chris could no longer hide the physical changes from his family. People were asking questions about his voice, and the hair on his legs was quite noticeable. Chris enlisted the help of his father and stepmother, who agreed to explain his transsexualism to most of his relatives. But he wanted personally to discuss the situation with his brother and sisters. To Chris's surprise and great relief, not one family member rejected or ridiculed him. Some did not understand his psychosexual disorder, but all professed their love as well as admiration for his courage in pursuing his dream. He had always enjoyed a great deal of support from his friends. Now, with his family's blessing, he no longer had to pretend to be a woman in any aspect of his life. He would now be known as a man.

Chris received a master's degree and landed his first professional job in the crisis department of a major metropolitan hospital. He was initially anxious about being discovered as a transsexual because he was living near the area where he grew up. Fortunately, this never happened. Over the next two years, he grew to trust several colleagues and eventually told them his story. His colleagues readily accepted his situation—although his male work friends often joked that he was "turned the wrong way" in the restroom stalls.

Many transsexuals resort to creative means to pass for the gender they wish to be. Chris frequently had to think fast on his feet to escape awkward situations. He demonstrated considerable ingenuity when he decided it was time to have the gender changed on his driver's license. This is normally a formal process that requires a court order and official documents, which he did not possess. He devised another approach. He began by renewing his current license, allowing his old information to be transferred to the new one. His gender was listed as "F" for female. A few days later, he returned to the same license branch and nonchalantly explained that someone must have made an honest error in recording his gender. He noted that it was a common mistake. Sometimes people would just look at the name "Chris," assume the person was female, and record it as such. The clerk apologized profusely and immediately issued a new license. He said it was obvious "just by looking" that Chris was male.

Chris was functioning as a male at work and with his friends. At 25 years of age, it was time to consider officially changing his name and gender. Chris hired an attorney to help guide him through the legal system. Chris asked his psychologist, physician, employer, and friends to write letters of endorsement to the court attesting to his stature as an upstanding citizen in the community who was living and functioning as a man. Several months later, after a five-minute hearing, the judge lowered his gavel and declared Christine to be now Christopher and legally male. This was done without any surgeries to remove organs (uterus, ovaries, breasts) or to add them (creation of a penis and scrotum).

To date, Chris has opted to forgo surgical interventions. He accepts his body, even though he is not entirely satisfied with it. He wishes that he had been born with a penis, but he does not need one to live, function, and be accepted as male. He will need medication for the rest of his life, although he now requires less testosterone to maintain his outward appearance. He does acknowledge some concern about the medication because the long-term effects of hormone use for female-to-male transsexuals have not been studied extensively. If Chris were to stop the injections for several months, the menstrual cycle would resume, body fat would redistribute, and his facial hair would be lost. His voice would retain its low pitch. Once the vocal cords thicken as the result of male hormones, they will remain so unless surgically altered. Chris has no plans to stop the medication.

Important developments have also taken place in Chris's social life. He had always loved Jennifer, his high school sweetheart, despite his involvement in other romantic relationships. Jennifer was married, but Chris never lost hope of renewing his relationship with her. As luck would have it, they became reacquainted while working on their high school five-year reunion committee. Their friendship picked up where it left off. Jennifer confided to Chris that she was unhappy in her marriage and was contemplating divorce. Chris hoped that their renewed friendship would evolve into something more intimate, but he did not want to be the cause of Jennifer's divorce. Jennifer believed that she would have been divorced eventually regardless of her relationship with Chris.

Jennifer was introduced to Chris's circle of friends and was invited to their social events. Jennifer began to spend occasional nights at Chris's apartment, although they slept separately. After a few months, their relationship became sexual. Sex was now more satisfying to them than it had been before, perhaps because Chris was more comfortable with his own body. In spite of the excitement and happiness that they found in their new romance, Chris and Jennifer felt uneasy having an illicit affair. One year after they became reacquainted, Jennifer filed for divorce and moved into an apartment near Chris. Soon, they moved in together. Chris's dream of marrying his high school sweetheart was going to come true. They had been living together for four years when he proposed to Jennifer.

Now they had lots of planning to do. Could they apply for a marriage license? Who would marry them? Would they need to disclose the fact that Chris was transsexual? They struggled with these and many other issues. Their relationship had faced many obstacles over the years, but could it survive planning a wedding? They were confronted with even more stressful situations during that year. Jennifer graduated from nursing school and took her licensing board examination. Some of Chris's extended family members refused to attend the wedding because of their religious beliefs. In spite of these hurdles, they obtained a wedding license, found a judge, and had a beautiful ceremony.

Chris's life was normal in most ways. He and Jennifer both had successful careers. They bought a house. However, Jennifer felt something was missing. She wanted children. Despite a few reservations about parenthood, they forged ahead with the process of artificial insemination. They chose an anonymous donor who matched Chris's physical characteristics and personality type. Two years later, Jennifer was pregnant . . . with twins!

Chris and Jennifer faced some unique circumstances, above and beyond all the normal anxieties that come with first-time parenthood. Preparing for the births of their son and daughter made them wonder how they would handle Chris's transsexuality. How would they deal with their own nudity? How would they respond to the children's normal curiosity about sex? As it turned out, the most pressing issues during the first year of parenthood were finding time for sleep and keeping enough diapers on hand.

It would have been impractical to expect that the children would never see Chris's body, though he tried his best to be discreet. Jennifer and Chris decided to respond to the children's questions about sexuality with honest, age-appropriate explanations. They learned quickly that all their rehearsed responses could be easily thwarted by their children's brutal honesty. For example, Chris recalled a dinner table conversation in which his 3-year-old son announced that "when I grow up, I want to be a man without a penis, like Daddy." Perhaps the most interesting implication of this bold declaration is the fact that Chris's son viewed him as a man, in spite of his physical anatomy. In fact, neither child ever confused Chris with a woman. Their daughter sometimes announced proudly to her brother,

"Mommy and I are girls, and you and Daddy are boys." To date, Chris only once has explained his genitalia to the children. He said, "Daddy's penis didn't get made all the way. But your penis and vagina were made just fine." Chris knows that the issue will come up again; simple explanations will not always be sufficient.

Chris's transsexuality is with him everyday, but it is no longer the focal point in his life. The issues arise infrequently now. Although the old anxieties of rejection and ridicule can still be evoked from time to time, he accepts himself and lives a full and happy life. Chris does not think of his transsexualism as a disorder from which he can be cured. He views it as a condition that he has learned to integrate and manage.

Discussion

Because the discussion of this case involves a number of subtle and frequently controversial issues, it may be helpful to begin with the definition of some elementary terms. *Gender identity* involves a person's belief or conviction that he or she is a male or a female. The public expression of this belief involves role-specific behaviors associated with masculinity and femininity. *Sexual orientation*, on the other hand, represents the person's preference for male or female sexual partners. In the infinite variety of human behavior, there can be endless combinations of gender identity, gender-role behaviors, and sexual orientations (Kessler & McKenna, 2000; Newman, 2002).

People with gender identity disorders vary considerably with regard to the severity and persistence of their problems. Relatively few children who exhibit gender identity problems continue to experience similar problems as adults (Bradley & Zucker, 1997; Green, 1987). In *DSM-IV-TR* (APA, 2000), the term *transsexualism* is used to describe severe gender identity disorder in adults.

Why is gender identity disorder a controversial topic? Perhaps because it raises such difficult questions about the way in which we view ourselves and our world. Perhaps because the attitudes of many transsexuals, as well as the surgical procedures that have been used to help them attain their goals, are inconsistent with popularly held notions about men and women.

> *Transsexuals raise a larger issue, in an era of wholesale efforts to relax rigid sex roles and give men and women more freedom to behave in ways that have traditionally been labeled "masculine" or "feminine." For, by their insistence on surgery—which gives them the form if not always the function of the sexual apparatus they desire—transsexuals seem to reassert the primacy of genital forms in defining sex and gender.* (Restak, 1979, p. 20)

The following discussion focuses on clinical and scientific issues involved in the study of transsexualism rather than its political and social implications.

In *DSM-IV-TR* (APA, 2000), Gender Identity Disorder is listed in a general section with sexual dysfunctions and paraphilias. There is, of course, an important difference between Gender Identity Disorders and Sexual Disorders. The latter are defined primarily in terms of problems that interfere with the capacity for recipro-cal, affectionate sexual activity. Chris's situation illustrates why Gender Identity Disorders are not considered sexual disorders. Although she was uncomfortable with her anatomic sex and wanted to live as a man, she was sexually functional and actively involved in a mutually satisfying relationship.

DSM-IV-TR (APA, 2000, pp. 581-582) description of Gender Identity Disorder can apply to children, adolescents, or adults. In fact, most transsexuals report that their discomfort with their anatomic sex began during childhood. The disorder is defined by the following criteria:

1.   A strong and persistent cross-gender identification (not merely a desire for any perceived cultural advantages of being the other sex)

     In children, the disturbance is manifested by four (or more) of the following:

     A.   Repeatedly stated desire to be, or insistence that he or she is, the other sex

     B.   In boys, preference for cross-dressing or simulating female attire; in girls, insistence on wearing only stereotypical masculine clothing

     C.   Strong and persistent preferences for cross-sex roles in make-believe play or persistent fantasies of being the other sex

     D.   Intense desire to participate in the stereotypical games and pastimes of the other sex

     E.   Strong preference for playmates of the other sex

     In adolescents and adults, the disturbance is manifested by symptoms such as a stated desire to be the other sex, frequent passing as the other sex, desire to live or be treated as the other sex, or the conviction that he or she has the typical feelings and reactions of the other sex.

2.   Persistent discomfort with his or her sex or sense of inappropriateness in the gender role of that sex

3.   The disturbance is not concurrent with a physical intersex condition

4.   The disturbance causes clinically significant distress or impairment in social, occupational, or other important areas of functioning

Because discomfort with one's anatomic sex and the desire to be rid of one's own genitals form a central part of this definition, it is important to point out that transsexuals are not the only people who seek sex reassignment surgery. Meyer (1974) described a number of subtypes among those individuals seeking sex change surgery at the Johns Hopkins Sexual Behaviors Consultation Unit. These include self-stigmatized homosexuals who believe that they should be punished, schizoid and psychotic individuals, and sadomasochists who derive sexual pleasure from inflicting and experiencing physical pain.

Disturbances in gender identity should also be distinguished from two related but generally distinct conditions. First, it would be misleading to say that transsexu-als are, by definition, delusional. There are, of course, a few transsexuals who are psychotic, but the vast majority are not. They acknowledge the inconsistency between their anatomy and their gender identity. A delusional man might argue, for example, that he is a woman; a transsexual would be more likely to say, "I am not a woman *anatomically*, but I am a woman in almost every other way." Furthermore, unlike delusional patients whose beliefs are completely idiosyncratic, transsexuals are frequently able to convince other people that they are right. In Chris's case, for example, Jennifer and Lynn concurred with the belief that Chris was more like a man than a woman.

Second, there is an important difference between transsexualism and transvestic fetishism, but the two conditions are not mutually exclusive (Zucker & Bradley, 2000). Transvestic fetishism is a disorder in which heterosexual (or bisexual) men dress in women's clothing for the purpose of sexual excitement. The gender identity of transvestic fetishists is typically not inconsistent with their anatomic sex, and many transsexuals do not become sexually excited by cross-dressing. Nevertheless, a substantial proportion of male-to-female transsexuals do become sexually aroused at least occasionally when they dress in women's clothing (Blanchard & Clemmensen, 1988), and some transvestic fetishists do seek sex reassignment surgery (Wise & Meyer, 1980). According to *DSM-IV-TR* (APA, 2000), males who meet the criteria for both gender identity disorder and transvestic fetishism should be assigned both diagnoses.

Precise epidemiological data regarding transsexualism are difficult to obtain. Estimates of the prevalence of the disorder are based on the number of people who apply for treatment rather than comprehensive surveys of the general population. We do know that transsexualism is a relatively infrequent problem and that it may be more common among men than women. Early studies reported a male-to-female ratio of approximately three to one, but the proportion of females may be increasing. One study computed prevalence estimates on the basis of the number of patients seeking treatment at the only gender treatment center in the Netherlands. The investigators reported a prevalence of 1 transsexual in every 12,000 males and 1 in 30,000 females (Bakker, van Kesteren, Gooren, & Bezemer, 1993). More recent data suggest that, when narrow diagnostic criteria are employed, the incidence of new cases may be roughly equivalent in men and women (Landen, Walinder, & Lundstrom, 1996; Olsson & Moller, 2003).

There appear to be some fairly consistent differences between male and female transsexuals in terms of psychological characteristics. For example, female transsexuals tend to report better relationships with their parents, more stable relationships with sexual partners, and greater satisfaction with their sexual experiences prior to treatment (e.g., Lewins, 2002; Verschoor & Poortinga, 1988).

Many male transsexuals, perhaps as many as half of those seeking treatment, experience additional psychological problems. The most common symptoms are depression, anxiety, and social alienation (Bower, 2001; Campo et al., 2003). Some exhibit severe personality disorders, but very few are considered psychotic. The level of psychopathology observed in female transsexuals, on the other hand, does not seem to be different from that seen in the general population. Chris may therefore be similar to other female transsexuals. Aside from the issue of gender identity, he was well-adjusted in terms of his mood as well as his social and occupational functioning.

The relationship between transsexualism and homosexuality has been the source of some controversy (Chivers & Bailey, 2000). Some people have argued that transsexuals are simply homosexuals who use their cross-gender identity as a convenient way of escaping cultural and moral sanctions against engaging in sexual behavior with members of their own sex. There are a number of problems with this hypothesis. First, unlike transsexuals, homosexual men and women are not uncomfortable with their own gender identities. Lesbians, for example, are typically proud of their status as women and would be horrified at the suggestion that they want to be men. Second, many transsexuals, like Chris, are not obviously uncomfortable with homosexuals. The suggestion that transsexuals are denying their homosexual inclinations is sometimes supported by the observation that some transsexuals go out of their way to avoid any contact or association with homosexual men or women. However, some of Chris's friends were homosexual men and women. One of his previous lovers, Lynn, was bisexual and had been living with another woman when they met.

Etiological Considerations

It is not clear why some people develop gender identity disorders. In fact, the process by which anyone develops a sense of masculine or feminine identity is a matter of considerable interest and dispute (Gangestad, Bailey, & Martin, 2000; Herman-Jeglinska et al., 2002). As in other areas of human behavior, alternative explanations invoke the ubiquitous nature/nurture controversy. Is gender identity determined genetically prior to the infant's birth, or is it largely determined by biological or social factors that the individual encounters in his or her environment? Explanations for the development of transsexualism have taken both sides of this argument.

Some investigators and clinicians have emphasized the importance of the parents and family in the etiology of the disorder. Stoller (1985), for example, placed principal emphasis in male transsexualism on the absence (either physical or psychological) of the father and the presence of a close-binding, dominant mother. A different family pattern was identified in cases of female transsexualism. In these families, according to Stoller, the mothers are prone to depression. Rather than providing support and care for their spouses, the fathers are presumably aloof and uninvolved. Thus, the daughter is forced to fill the supportive, masculine role vacated by her father. Other masculine behaviors are also reinforced by the father, but femininity is discouraged.

Chris's experience was not consistent with Stoller's hypothesis. His mother was not depressed while Chris was a child, and he was not expected to take the place of his father. Chris's parents were not close to each other, but they did not involve the children in their disagreements. His masculine gender identity was clearly fixed several years before his parents' conflict became known to the children. Although he did not spend a great deal of time with his mother, they did have a good relationship; they spoke to each other openly—including several talks about the fact that Chris felt more like a boy than a girl—and cared very much for each other.

Green (1987) proposed a multifaceted model for the development of feminine behavior in boys and masculine behavior in girls. His view places considerable emphasis on learning principles such as modeling and social reinforcement. According to Green, gender identity disturbances are likely to develop when the parent of the opposite sex is dominant and provides the most salient model for the child's social behavior. The same-sexed parent is presumably retiring or unavailable. When the child begins to imitate cross-role behaviors, rather than objecting, the parents provide attention and praise. Peer relations also play a role in Green's model; feminine boys prefer and spend more time with girls while masculine girls spend more time with boys. This combination of parental and peer support enhances the process of identification with the opposite sex. Eventually, this process of socialization becomes an obstacle to any attempt to change the pattern and integrate the child with members of his or her own sex.

In Chris's case, his father certainly provided reinforcement for playing masculine games. Chris spent a great deal of time in rough, competitive play with boys. His father also discouraged open displays of emotion, such as crying. It is difficult to say, however, that the social reinforcement he provided was definitely responsible for Chris's gender identity disorder, particularly since so many other girls are treated in similar ways without becoming transsexual.

Relatively little empirical evidence is available regarding the influence of environmental events in the development of transsexualism. A few research studies have compared people with gender identity disorders and control subjects in terms of their recollections of their parents' behavior. One study found that male-to-female transsexuals remembered their fathers as having been less warm and more rejecting in comparison to the way in which control subjects remembered their fathers (Cohen-Kettenis, & Arrindell, 1990). It is important to note, however, that these data were collected after the people with gender identity disorder were adults and had sought treatment for their condition. It is not clear that the styles of interaction that were reported by these people preceded or contributed to the original development of their problems in gender identity. Interactions between the parents and their transsexual sons and daughters may have been determined, at least in part, by a reaction to the gender identity problems of the children. Prospective data, collected prior to the onset of gender identity problems, have not been reported on this issue.

Case studies provide the basis for much speculation regarding the possible influence of environmental and biological factors in the etiology of transsexualism. For example, Garden and Rothery (1992) described one pair of 13-year-old female monozygotic (MZ) twins who were discordant for gender identity disorder. The authors hypothesized that differences between the girls in terms of their social upbringing were responsible for the discrepancy in their gender identities. Their father had problems with alcohol dependence and played little, if any, role in the family. Their anxious and depressed mother seemed to treat the transsexual twin as a confidante. This pattern is consistent with Stoller's hypothesis. The fact that these genetically identical individuals were discordant for the condition indicates that genetic factors do not account for all of the variance in its etiology. That is, of course, not a particularly surprising result because concordance rates in MZ twins do not approach 100 percent for any form of mental disorder. Analyses based on large samples of MZ and DZ twin pairs indicate that genetic factors make a larger contribution than environmental factors in the development of gender identity disorder (Coolidge, Thede, & Young, 2002).

There is, in fact, good reason to believe that certain aspects of gender identity are influenced by biological as well as environmental factors (Zucker, 2001). Speculation regarding biological considerations has also been fueled by case studies. One example involves the extraordinary experiences of several members of a single extended family in the Dominican Republic (Imperato-McGinley, Guerrero, Gautier, & Peterson, 1974). These individuals are unable to produce dihydrotestosterone, a hormone that is responsible, in the male fetus, for shaping the penis and scrotum. In the absence of this hormone, the children are born with external genitalia that are ambiguous in appearance, including a very small, clitoral-like penis, a scrotum that looks like labial folds, and a blind vaginal pouch. Of the 24 cases described in the initial report, 18 were raised as girls. Then, when they reached puberty, everything changed in response to an increase in testosterone. Each child's "clitoris" enlarged and became a penis—just as it would have in utero if the appropriate hormone had been present—and testicles descended into a scrotum. Their voices deepened and the muscle mass of their bodies increased to produce a masculine appearance. Quite remarkably, 17 of the 18 quickly developed a male gender identity; they consider themselves to be men and are sexually attracted to women.

The cases of the Dominican children suggest that the effects of the postnatal environment may not be as salient as many investigators concerned with transsexualism have suggested. The children were raised as girls, but they were able to alter their gender identities promptly and with considerable success when their anatomy changed. If their interactions with parents, siblings, and peers during childhood were of primary importance, how could this transformation have been accomplished? Strictly environmental views of gender identity have obvious difficulty dealing with this problem. An alternative account, favored by more biologically minded investigators (e.g., Diamond & Sigmundson, 1997), holds that gender identity is one characteristic that may be shaped very early, during the development of the human embryo, by exposure to male hormones.

The latter possibility suggests that Chris's masculine gender identity is, at least in part, the product of a fundamental, biological process. Viewed from a subtle neurological perspective, and regardless of the shape of his external sexual characteristics, this argument would hold that Chris's brain is essentially masculine. Unfortunately, although there is considerable reason to believe that there are reliable group differences between men and women in terms of brain structure and function, there are no valid tests that would be useful in this regard at an individual level. The issue is, therefore, unresolved.

Treatment

There are two obvious solutions to problems that involve gender identity conflict: Change the person's gender identity to match his or her anatomy, or change the anatomy to match the person's gender identity. Various forms of psychotherapy have been used in an attempt to alter the gender identity of transsexual patients, but the success of these interventions has been limited. Some positive results have been reported by Barlow, Abel, and Blanchard (1979), who used behavioral procedures to shape and maintain masculine sex-role behaviors in three male transsexual patients. Uncontrolled followup reports indicate that behavior therapy can be beneficial for prepubescent boys who exhibit symptoms of gender identity disorder. Rekers, Kilgus, and Rosen (1990) studied a group of 29 boys approximately four years after the end of treatment. Greatest improvement was found among those boys who had been treated at younger ages.

As an alternative to trying to change the transsexual's gender identity, some physicians have used surgical procedures to transform transsexuals' bodies so that they will match their gender identities. Surgical procedures can be used to alter and construct both male and female genitalia. Some of these methods were initially developed for the treatment of problems such as traumatic loss or congenital abnormalities. An artificial penis can be constructed from abdominal tissue that is transplanted and formed into a tube. The goals of such surgery may include cosmetic considerations (i.e., the construction of an organ that resembles a penis) as well as physiological criteria (e.g., passing urine in a standing position, accomplishing intercourse, and sensing stimulation). Although it is not possible to construct a completely functional penis that will become erect in response to sexual stimulation, erection can be achieved through the use of removable implants made of bone, cartilage, or silicone. In the case of female-to-male transsexuals, the labia are fused, but the clitoris is left intact and remains the primary receptor for sexual stimulation. Prostheses can be inserted to resemble testicles in a scrotum.

Surgical procedures for transsexuals can become quite complex and involve several areas of the body in addition to the genitals. Surgery for male-to-female transsexuals may include breast augmentation as well as changing the size of the nose and shaving the larnyx. Surgery for female-to-male transsexuals can involve a series of steps, including removal of the ovaries, Fallopian tubes, uterus, and breast tissue.

The sporadic use of sex change surgery can be traced back to 1882 (see Bullough & Bullough, 1993). Such procedures did not become widely used or attract the attention of the general public until Hamburger, Sturup, and Dahl-Iverson (1953) reported the case of Christine Jorgensen, a male-to-female transsexual who had received surgery in Copenhagen in 1951. This case differed from many of the previous reports in that the patient was treated with large doses of female sex hormones for several months prior to the surgical removal of his penis and the construction of female genitalia. Subsequent to this report, a number of gender identity clinics were established at medical schools in Europe and the United States. One of the best known was begun at the Johns Hopkins University in 1965. Sexreassignment surgery was performed frequently throughout the 1960s and 1970s. Exact figures are not available regarding the numbers of men and women who have received this radical treatment, but reports suggest that they must number in the thousands.

Clinical impressions regarding the success of these procedures have been positive. Case studies suggest that most patients are pleased with the results of the surgery and relieved finally to have the body they desire. Many are able to adjust to life as a member of the opposite sex, and some report adequate sexual functioning and marriage (Smith, van Goozen, Kuiper, & Cohen-Kettenis, 2005). Almost no one reports postsurgical grief over the loss of his sexual organ, although isolated cases have occurred. The most frequent complaints center on requests for further medical and surgical procedures. In the case of male-to-female transsexuals, these requests include improvements in genital appearance and functioning, increased breast size, and inhibition of beard growth. Followup reports suggest that at least 80 percent of patients are considered generally satisfied by their surgeons. Most patients who have gone through sex reassignment surgery are satisfied with the results. The vast majority report reduced levels of anxiety and depression and believe that they do not have any trouble passing as a member of their newly assumed gender (Bodlund & Kullgren, 1996; Rehman et al., 1999).

Although these results seem rather encouraging, there are some limitations associated with the data that have been used to evaluate the outcome of sex reassignment surgery. Postsurgical adjustment is often assessed in terms of the surgeon's global, subjective impression of the patient's adjustment rather than specific measures of occupational and social functioning made by people who do not know that the patient had received surgery. Appropriate control groups are seldom employed, and followup periods are often rather short. It should not be surprising, therefore, that some reports provide a more pessimistic picture of surgical outcome (Lindemalm, Korlin, & Uddenberg, 1986; Meyer & Reter, 1979). These studies demonstrate, for example, that the social and occupational functioning of many transsexuals does not improve following surgery in spite of the fact that the patients are subjectively satisfied with the results of the operation. Partially in response to data of this sort and questions that were raised about the value of surgery, the Gender Identity Clinic at Johns Hopkins stopped providing sex reassignment surgery for transsexuals in 1979. There are, however, many other centers that continue to perform these procedures (Petersen & Dickey, 1995).

Surgery and psychotherapy are not the only options available to people with gender identity disorders. Chris was already well-adjusted in his personal and professional roles without surgery. It seems unlikely that the surgical alteration of his body would lead to an even better adjustment. Like Chris, many transsexuals forego surgery but still cross-dress and live full time as a member of the opposite gender with the help of hormone therapy. This alternative has become a more reasonable and appealing option as the law and popular opinion have become somewhat more tolerant of people with gender identity disorders (Green, 1994; Michel et al., 2002). People who are considering treatment for gender identity disorders and the mental health professionals who want to help them should consider carefully the many thoughtful recommendations that are included in a set of standards of care for gender identity disorders, written by an international committee of experts on these problems (Levine, 1999).

CHAPTER 16

Eating Disorder: Anorexia Nervosa

Joan was a 38-year-old woman with a good job and family life. She lived with her second husband, Mike; her 16-year-old son, Charlie, from her first marriage; and her husband's 18-year-old daughter from a previous marriage. Joan was employed as a secretary at a university, and Mike was a temporary federal employee. Joan was 5'3" and weighed approximately 125 pounds. Although she was concerned about her weight, her current attitudes and behaviors were much more reasonable than they had been a few years earlier, when she had been diagnosed with anorexia nervosa.

Joan had struggled with a serious eating disorder from the ages of 29 to 34. She was eventually hospitalized for a period of 30 days. The treatment that she received during that hospital stay had finally helped her overcome her eating problems. Four years later, her condition remained much improved. In the following pages we trace the history of Joan's problems from her childhood and adolescence through their eventual resolution in adulthood.

Social History

Joan was born in a suburb on the outskirts of a large northeastern city. She had one brother, two years younger than she. Her father held various jobs, including that of a supervisor for an aircraft subcontractor. Joan's mother stayed at home while the children were young and then worked parttime for a number of years as a waitress and bookkeeper. Both parents were of average weight.

Joan's early childhood was quite ordinary. She was an above-average student and enjoyed school. She and her brother bickered, but their disagreements did not extend beyond the usual sibling rivalry. Her family lived in a large neighborhood filled with lots of children. Joan was somewhat heavy during elementary school. She had high personal standards and strove to be a perfect child. She always did what was right and conformed completely to the wishes of her parents.

When Joan was 14 and entering the ninth grade, tragedy struck her family and forever changed her home life. She and her 12-year-old brother had been left home alone while her parents went to work. Although her brother was too old to require baby-sitting, she was supposed to keep an eye on him. Joan had a friend over, and the two girls were upstairs in her room. Joan heard some loud noise outside and looked out the window. She saw her brother lying dead in the road. He had been run over by a car. Although the feeling became less intense as years passed, Joan continued to feel guilty about her brother's death well into adulthood.

After the accident, Joan's parents changed. They became extremely overprotective, and Joan felt as if she "had a leash on all of the time." From age 14 on, she no longer had a normal childhood. She could not hang out with friends, be away from the house for long periods of time, or go out in cars. Her parents wanted to know where she was and what she was doing, and they set a strict curfew. Joan knew that if she were late, her parents would worry, so she always tried to be home early. She made a special effort to do exactly as she was told. Joan did not go out much because she felt the need to stay near her parents so that they would know that she was alive and well.

The rest of high school was unremarkable. Joan received reasonably good grades and got along well with the other students. During the summer after her brother's death, when Joan was 15, she met and began to date a boy who was two years older than she. Joan's parents were initially unhappy with this relationship, in part because Randy owned a car, and they didn't want her to ride around with him. Joan had to meet Randy secretly for the first few months. As her parents got to know him better, they grew to like him, and the young couple no longer had to sneak around. During this time, Joan continued to feel guilty when she was in cars because she was reminded of her brother's death. She frequently stayed home because she knew that her parents would suffer horribly if anything happened to her.

After high school, Joan attended a two-year business school and became engaged to Randy. The couple was married after Joan graduated. She was 19 years old as she began her marriage and her first full-time job as a secretary in a medical office. Prior to this time, Joan's father had never allowed her to hold even a part-time job. He insisted on providing for all of her needs.

Although this marriage lasted legally for six years, it became clear within nine months that the relationship was in trouble. Joan cared for her husband, but she did not love him. She soon realized that she had used Randy as an escape route from her parents' home. She felt as if she had simply jumped from one dependent relationship into another. When she had been at home, her parents provided everything. Now Randy was taking care of her. Joan worried that she did not know how to take care of herself. In spite of these negative feelings, Joan and Randy tried to make the marriage work. They bought a home one year after their wedding. Two years later, Joan accidentally became pregnant.

Joan gained 80 pounds during the course of her pregnancy. When Charlie was born, she weighed 200 pounds. Over the next few months, Joan found it difficult to lose weight but eventually got down to 140 pounds. Although it was hard for her to adjust to this weight gain, she did not try to change her weight because it felt "safe" to her. Joan and Randy were legally separated two years after Charlie was born. They continued to see each other occasionally and sought marital counseling at various times during the next couple of years. They could not reconcile their differences, however, and Randy eventually moved to another state. The divorce was finalized when Joan was 25 years old.

Shortly after she and Randy were separated, Joan stopped working and went on welfare. With financial help from her father, she managed to keep up the mortgage payments on her house for several months. She and Charlie continued to live on their own, but Joan fell further into debt while she and Randy tried to work things out. She was forced to sell her home when the divorce became final. Although she came to regret the decision, she moved back into her parents' home. Living there was stressful for Joan. Although she was 25 years old, she felt like a child. Her parents once again took care of Joan, and now they also provided for her son. In this submissive role, Joan started to feel more like Charlie's older sister than his mother.

Joan lost some weight after she and Charlie were involved in a serious car accident, six months after moving back to live with her parents. Charlie was not hurt, but Joan's left hip and leg were broken. She spent a month in the hospital. She was immobile when she came home, and her mother had to take even greater care of her and Charlie. Joan needed repeated surgery on her knee, as well as extensive physical therapy, and she had to relearn how to walk. During her recovery, she had little appetite, was nauseated, and did not eat much, but she was not consciously dieting. Joan's weight went down to about 110 pounds, which she considered to be a reasonable weight.

While she was recovering from her injuries, Joan became involved with a man named Jack, whom she met in one of the hospital's rehabilitation programs. She was now 27 years old. In order to escape her parents' overly protective home, she decided to take Charlie and move in with Jack. This move actually created more problems than it solved, in large part because Jack had a serious problem with alcohol. Joan had never been a heavy drinker. In the beginning of their relationship, she drank only during the weekend. After she started living with Jack, drinking became a daily activity. Much of their relationship and socializing revolved around alcohol. On the average weekday, Joan consumed a couple of beers and some wine, or perhaps a glass or two of bourbon. On weekends, she drank considerably more. Charlie was increasingly left at day-care centers and with baby-sitters. Joan eventually recognized the destructive nature of this relationship and ended it after a few months. She reluctantly moved back into her parents' home. After leaving Jack, Joan stopped drinking, except occasionally when she was out socializing.

Onset of the Eating Disorder

After breaking up with Jack, Joan lived with her parents for two more years. When she was 29 years old, almost three years after her accident, Joan returned to the hospital for more surgery on her leg. After being discharged, she began the diet that set the stage for five years of serious eating problems and nearly destroyed her life. Joan had gained a few pounds while she was drinking heavily and now weighed 125 pounds. She was concerned that she would start to gain more weight while she was inactive, recovering from surgery.

Joan's diet was strict from the beginning: She measured and weighed all of her food. Within a year, she weighed less than 100 pounds. Her food intake was severely restricted. During the day she consumed only coffee with skim milk and an artificial sweetener. Occasionally, she ate a piece of fruit or a bran muffin. When she and Charlie ate dinner with her parents, Joan took a normal amount of food on her plate but played with it rather than eating it. After dinner, she usually excused herself to go to the bathroom where she took laxatives in an effort to get rid of what little food she had eaten. Joan hardly ate any meats, breads, or starches. She preferred fruits and vegetables because they consist mainly of water and fiber. Although she did not allow herself to eat, Joan still felt hungry; in fact, she was starving most of the time. She thought about food constantly, spent all of her time reading recipe and health books, and cooked elaborate meals for the family.

Although she weighed less than 100 pounds, Joan still felt overweight and believed that she would look better if she lost more weight. She had an overwhelming fear of getting fat, because she believed that gaining weight would mean that she was not perfect. She tried to be a model young adult and struggled to be what she imagined everybody else wanted. She gave little thought to what she would want for herself. It seemed to Joan that everything in her life was out of control and that her weight and body were the only things over which she could be in charge. The demonstration of strict self-control with regard to eating was a source of pride and accomplishment to Joan.

As she lost weight, Joan experienced several of the physical effects that accompany starvation. Her periods stopped; she had problems with her liver; her skin became dry and lost its elasticity; her hair was no longer healthy; and she would often get dizzy when she stood up. At this time, Joan was working as a secretary in a university medical school. Some of her coworkers noticed the drastic change in her appearance and became concerned. An internist in her department recognized her symptoms as those of anorexia nervosa and tried to get Joan to seek help. Joan agreed to attend an eating disorders support group and even went to some outpatient therapy sessions, mostly in an attempt to appease her friends. She also consulted a dietician at the university hospital and worked on an eating plan. There were moments when Joan considered the possibility that her behavior was not normal, but most of the time she viewed her ability to control her weight and appetite as a sign of strength. When she was transferred to a different department within the university, she left therapy and returned to her restrictive dieting.

Joan's parents were also acutely aware of their daughter's abnormal patterns of eating and her excessive weight loss. They were extremely worried about her health. The more they tried to talk to Joan about this issue, the more resistant she became to their pleadings. Arguments about eating became frequent, and the level of tension in the home escalated dramatically.

A year and a half after the onset of her eating disorder, Joan moved with Charlie into an apartment of their own. Her decision was prompted in large part by the aversive nature of her interactions with her parents. She continued to diet and now weighed about 90 pounds. Charlie's diet had also become restricted, in part because there was very little food in the house. Joan could hardly bring herself to go to the grocery store. Once there, she made an effort to behave normally and went through the store putting food into her shopping cart. When it came time to pay, however, she would not actually buy anything. She believed that food was bad and that it was a waste of money. Instead of purchasing anything, she would wander up and down the aisles, eating much of what was in her shopping cart. Her reasoning was that it made no sense to pay for food that could be eaten while you were in the store.

This type of binge eating also happened whenever she did manage to buy something. In one afternoon, she would occasionally eat two dozen donuts, a five-pound box of candy, and some ice cream. After this, Joan took 20 to 30 laxatives to rid herself of the food. At times she made herself vomit by sticking a toothbrush down her throat, but she preferred to take laxatives. Some weeks she did not binge at all, others once or twice. On the days in between binges, she ate only a little fruit and drank some liquids.

Joan's eating problems persisted for the next five years. Her weight fluctuated between 90 and 105 pounds during this period. At times she ate more normally, but then she would eat practically nothing for months. She tried therapy, though she was not seriously or consistently committed to changing her behavior. Her life seemed like a roller coaster, as she cycled back and forth between relatively healthy patterns of eating, severe restricting, and bingeing and purging. Most of her diet consisted of liquids such as diet soda, water, and coffee. Occasionally she drank beer, seeking the numbing effect it had on her appetite. She was pleased with her weight when it was very low, but she felt horrible physically. She was weak most of the time, and other people constantly told her that she was too thin. In Joan's mind, however, she was still too heavy.

When she was 32 years old, almost three years after the onset of her eating problems, Joan met Mike at a church group she was attending. They began to date on a regular basis. Mike was different from all of the other men in Joan's past. He genuinely cared about her, and he also liked her son. Her weight was at one of its peaks when they met, somewhere between 100 and 105 pounds, so her eating problems were not immediately obvious to him.

Unfortunately, soon after they began dating, Joan once again began to restrict her eating, and her weight quickly dropped to another low point. Mike noticed the obvious change in her behavior and appearance. His reaction was sympathetic. As their relationship grew stronger, Mike seemed to help Joan feel differently about herself. They talked frequently about her weight and how little she ate. Mike expressed great concern about her health, pleading gently with her to gain weight, but her restrictive patterns of eating persisted in spite of the other psychological benefits that accompanied the development of this relationship. One year after she started dating Mike, Joan needed major abdominal surgery to remove two cysts from her small intestine. During the operation, the surgeon saw that she had other problems and reconstructed her entire bowel system. When she left the hospital, Joan's weight had fallen to 85 pounds. She ate reasonably well at first, trying to regain her strength. After two months, she was feeling better, returned to work, and went back on a restrictive diet. This time, however, Mike and her friends would not let her continue this prolonged pattern of self-imposed starvation.

Treatment

Mike and one of Joan's friends from the medical school sought help for her. Realizing that she would never be free of her problems unless she faced them, Joan agreed to contact an eating disorder specialist. Though it was one of the hardest decisions she ever made, Joan had herself committed to a 30-day stay in a psychiatric ward. She was now 34 years old.

Joan's diet was completely controlled in the hospital. She was started on a 1500-calorie-a-day diet and was required to eat three meals a day in the presence of a staff member. Privileges such as use of the phone, visitors, and outings were made contingent upon eating. Specific goals were set for weight gain, and caloric intake was increased gradually. There were also daily individual therapy sessions in which a staff psychologist explored with Joan how she felt about herself.

At first, hospitalization was difficult for Joan. The amount of food that she was required to eat for breakfast (two pancakes, a bowl of cereal, a glass of milk, one piece of fruit, and a piece of toast) would previously have lasted her for several days. She was initially rebellious, refusing to eat or giving her food away to other patients. She didn't earn any privileges in the first 10 days of her hospital stay. Unaccustomed to eating, she experienced severe constipation, bloating, and indigestion. At times she tried to vomit to get rid of the food, but she was not successful. She eventually accepted the fact that she had no choice and allowed herself to gain 15 pounds. She felt stronger physically but was still troubled. Joan convinced herself that she would lose that weight as soon as she was released from the hospital.

An important turning point in her attitude came during the third week of treatment when Joan received a pass to go home. Outside the hospital, she felt out of control, as if she were too weak to take care of herself. She asked Mike to take her back to the hospital immediately. Safely back in her hospital room, she cried and felt as though she would never get better. This wrenching experience helped Joan recognize that she would, indeed, need to change her eating behavior as well as her attitudes regarding weight control and physical appearance. Somehow at the end of 30 days, Joan found the strength to leave the hospital. She was frightened at first, but with support from Mike and her family, she was able to maintain a normal pattern of eating. She remained in therapy for six more months and was able to gain another 15 pounds.

While she was in the hospital, Joan learned that her own attitudes about eating and her body were the principal problem, and she had become her own worst enemy. She learned that she could control her weight without becoming extremely restrictive in her eating. She began to feel differently about herself and food. Joan could not pinpoint exactly what had happened, but she had become a different person who was no longer preoccupied with dieting and weight control.

Discussion

Anorexia nervosa and bulimia nervosa (discussed in the next chapter) are the two principal eating disorders described in *DSM-IV-TR* (APA, 2000). Anorexia nervosa is a condition characterized by extreme weight loss. Ninety to ninety-five percent of anorexics are female. Current estimates of prevalence vary, but approximately 1 in 100 adolescent girls is affected by this disorder. The course of the disorder can be chronic, and 5 percent of patients with anorexia starve to death (Nielsen, 2001; Steinhausen, 2002). Deaths also occur from physical complications of the illness and from suicide. Complications such as osteoporosis, anemia, and compromised immune function are common (Misra, Aggarwal, Miller, Almazan, Worley, Soyka et al., 2004). The *DSM-IV-TR* (APA, 2000, p. 589) diagnostic criteria are as follows:

A. Refusal to maintain body weight at or above a minimally normal weight for age and height (e.g., weight loss leading to maintenance of body weight less than 85 percent of that expected; or failure to make expected weight gain during a period of growth, leading to body weight less than 85 percent of that expected)

B. Intense fear of gaining weight or becoming fat, even though underweight

C. Disturbance in the way in which one's body weight or shape is experienced, undue influence of body weight or shape on self-evaluation, or denial of the seriousness of the current low body weight

D. In postmenarcheal females, amenorrhea, that is, the absence of at least three consecutive menstrual cycles.

The *DSM-IV-TR* (APA, 2000) specifies two types of anorexia nervosa. Individuals are considered to be the *restricting type* if during the episode of anorexia nervosa they do not regularly engage in eating binges or purge themselves of the food they have eaten during a binge (whether through vomiting or laxative misuse). The *binge-eating/purging* type, which is consistent with Joan's behavior, involves the regular occurrence of binge eating or purging behavior during the episode of anorexia. This approach to subclassification of eating disorders recognizes the frequent appearance of overlapping symptoms. Approximately one-half of patients with anorexia also have bulimic symptoms, and roughly one-third of patients with bulimia have a history of anorexia. The distinction between subtypes of anorexia nervosa should not be taken too literally, however. When patients are followed over a period of several years, many people who originally fit the description for restricting type have changed over to the binge-eating/purging type (Eddy et al., 2002).

Research has revealed some important differences between the two subtypes of anorexia nervosa. Anorexics who also binge and purge tend to have weighed more before their illness, are more sexually experienced, are more outgoing, tend to have reduced impulse control, are more likely to abuse drugs or steal, and have more variable moods than restrictors (Casper & Troiani, 2001). The presence of bingeing and purging is also thought to be a sign of greater psychological disturbance and an indication of a poorer prognosis (van der Ham, 1997).

Anorexia nervosa is often comorbid with several other disorders, including substance abuse, obsessive-compulsive disorder, and several personality disorders (O'Brien & Vincent, 2003). The disorder that is most frequently comorbid with anorexia is major depression. These two conditions actually share many of the same symptoms such as insomnia, disturbed sleep, weight loss, constipation, loss of interest in sex, indecisiveness, poor concentration, and social withdrawal. Studies have also shown an increased prevalence of mood disorders in the relatives of patients with anorexia. However, some have suggested that comorbid disorders may not be as common among anorexics who do not seek treatment, and therefore, studies may have overestimated rates of comorbidity because they have often relied upon clinical samples (Perkins, Klump, Iacono, & McGue, 2005).

Patients with anorexia are often characterized as being obsessional, conforming, and emotionally reserved. The research evidence supports this impression, but also indicates that many different personality styles are also found (Thornton & Russell, 1997). Many researchers and clinicians have described perfectionism as common among people with anorexia (Franco-Paredes, Mancilla-Díaz, Vázquez-Arévalo, López-Aguilar, & Álvarez-Rayón, 2005). A frequent feature of anorexia is overactivity. Patients are often restless, fidgety, and engage in excessive exercise (Klein & Walsh, 2004).

Joan met the diagnostic criteria for anorexia nervosa, binge-eating/purging type. She experienced a drastic, self-induced loss of weight, was intensely afraid of becoming fat, could not recognize the true size of her body or the seriousness of her condition, and was no longer menstruating. In addition to her severe restriction of food intake, Joan would also periodically eat large amounts of food and then try to rid herself of the unwanted calories through vomiting and laxatives. She also experienced many of the physical and psychological side effects that accompany starvation. These include constipation, hypotension, skin changes, bloating, abdominal pains, dehydration, and lanugo (downy hair growth).

It is important to recognize that some of the psychological symptoms of anorexia nervosa are produced by the lack of food and are not necessarily inherent aspects of the anorexic's personality. For example, people who are starving become preoccupied with food and eating. Like Joan, they will often cook for others, read recipe books, and may even develop peculiar food rituals. Obsessive behaviors, such as hoarding, may also appear. There is often an exaggeration of previous personality traits, such as increased irritability, avoidance and social withdrawal, and a narrowing of interests (Kaye, Strober, & Rhodes, 2002).

Etiological Considerations

Various biological factors have been considered in the search for the causes of anorexia nervosa. Some speculation has focused on the possible influence of a dysfunctional hypothalamus, a part of the brain that plays a crucial role in the regulation of feeding behavior (Stoving et al., 1999). Hypothalamic irregularities have been observed among anorexic patients, but it is likely that these problems are the result, rather than the cause, of the eating disorder. Furthermore, a hypothalamic problem would not easily account for the intense fear of being fat that is found in anorexia. It does seem likely that biological factors—including hormones and neurotransmitters that regulate metabolism and mediate perceptions of satiety—are involved in the etiology of anorexia nervosa. The specific nature of these factors and their role in pathways leading to the disorder have not been determined (Ferguson & Pigott, 2000; Halmi, 1996).

Because the onset of anorexia nervosa typically occurs during adolescence, many theories discuss anorexia in terms of maturational problems that are sparked by the physical, emotional, and cognitive changes that occur at this time. Some clinicians view anorexia as the product of resistance to sexual and psychological maturity, or more broadly as trouble with individuation and separation from the family

(Shoebridge & Gowers, 2000). The family often plays a role to the extent that parents may set high performance demands and may actively resist attempts by their children to gain independence. Parents of anorexic adolescents have been described as being enmeshed (overly involved in their children's lives), overprotective, and unable to solve problems (Blair, Freeman, & Cull, 1995). Of course, these characteristics may be a response to having a child with a severe eating disorder rather than a reason for the original onset of the child's disorder. Patterns of family interaction may contribute to the development of anorexia among adolescents who also have other predisposing factors, including preoccupation with weight and appearance, body dissatisfaction, and low self-esteem (Leung, 1996).

Joan's case was atypical, in the sense that her eating problems appeared when she was 29 years old. Nevertheless, her family situation did fit the "anorexic profile." After the death of her brother, her parents became overly protective. When she returned to their home after her divorce, she felt as if she were a child again. Joan's parents conscientiously provided for her needs, but by not allowing her to work, they may have contributed to her feelings of ineffectiveness and inadequacy. These aspects of Joan's situation fit the theoretical perspective outlined by Hilde Bruch (1973, 1981), who described anorexia nervosa as the product of fundamental deficits in ego functioning. According to this theory, patients with anorexia suffer from low self-esteem, a sense of personal ineffectiveness, and a lack of trust in their internal states and emotions. Mastery over the body becomes a means of achieving a sense of control.

Cultural attitudes and standards are also thought to play an important role in the development of anorexia nervosa (Bordo, 1997; Simpson, 2002). Culture has a strong influence on standards for what is considered to be the ideal female shape. In Western society, for example, the feminine ideal has shifted from the buxom figure of the early 1900s, to the thin flapper of the 1920s, to the hourglass shape of the 1950s, and more recently, back to a thin body shape. This ideal shape is more than a "look." It takes on additional meaning and comes to symbolize other attributes such as success, beauty, and self-control.

At the same time that contemporary cultural standards have emphasized thinness, women's body weight has been increasing as a result of improved health and nutrition. These circumstances have created a conflict between the ideal shape and a woman's actual shape. The conflict typically leads to prolonged or obsessive dieting, which is often a prelude to the development of anorexia nervosa (Hsu, 1996). As might be expected given this line of reasoning, the prevalence of anorexia nervosa has increased as the thin feminine ideal took hold, and the prevalence of anorexia nervosa is especially high among women who are under intense pressure to be thin, such as dancers and models. Of course, not all dieting develops into anorexia nervosa. It is hypothesized that sociocultural pressures are part of a larger model of development, which includes other predisposing factors such as problems with autonomy, rapid physical change at puberty, premorbid obesity, personality traits, cognitive style, perceptual disturbances, and interpersonal and familial difficulties (Polivy & Herman, 2002).

The role of sexuality in the development of anorexia is not clear (Ghizzani & Montomoli, 2000; Wiederman, 1996). Although some experienced clinicians have described the disorder as a retreat from maturity, sexual issues are not necessarily the central problem. Rather, the patient with anorexia may be focused more specifically on achieving control of her body and diet. Attempts to examine a possible causal connection between sexual behavior and eating disorders is also made more complicated by the need to consider additional variables, such as personality traits and negative body image.

For some women, sexual abuse is an important factor in the development of an eating disorder. Nevertheless, there does not appear to be a specific relation between eating disorders and exposure to sexual trauma (Wonderlich et al., 1997). It has been estimated that 30 percent of women with eating disorders were sexually abused as children, but this seems to be a more important risk factor for bulimia nervosa than for anorexia nervosa (Jacobi, Hayward, de Zwaan, Kraemer, & Agras, 2004). Sexual abuse does not explain the development of most cases of anorexia nervosa, but it is one important risk factor for eating disorders as well as other forms of psychological disturbance.

Some researchers have proposed the *adapted to flee famine hypothesis*, which explains anorexia nervosa symptoms as an adaptive mechanism that evolved to protect our ancestors from starvation in famine conditions (Guisinger, 2003). This mechanism would occur when body weight became too low (which now would be due to a diet rather than famine) and only among certain individuals with the genes for it, and would then trigger restlessness, energy, and cognitive distortions about the emaciated state of one's body to enable the starving individual to have both the courage and energy to travel to new locations where food might be more plentiful. More research is needed to evaluate this interesting hypothesis.

Treatment

Research on anorexia has not identified one form of treatment that is consistently more effective than others. Various forms of psychotherapy are employed by clinicians, with most using cognitive-behavioral therapy or a combination of cognitive-behavioral and psychodynamic techniques (Peterson & Mitchell, 1999).

A number of steps are typically followed in the treatment of anorexia nervosa. The first step is often hospitalization. This may be necessary in cases in which weight loss is extreme, suicidal thoughts are present, the patient is still denying her illness, or previous outpatient therapy has been ineffective (Andersen, 1997). Weight restoration must occur before any psychological treatment can begin. This is necessary to alleviate the psychological symptoms of starvation as well as to confront the patient with the body size that she fears. Although there is no single best way to restore weight, the key is to elicit as much cooperation as possible and to be sensitive to the patient's concerns. It is important to work with the patient to set a target weight, usually 90 percent of the average weight for a particular age and height. Behavioral techniques, such as those used with Joan, are often used to facilitate immediate weight gain.

Various types of medication are used to treat patients with eating disorders. Antidepressant drugs are employed most frequently, perhaps because anorexic and bulimic patients are often depressed. Selective serotonin reuptake inhibitors (SSRIs), such as fluoxetine (Prozac®), have been beneficial in individual case studies. Only one controlled outcome study has supported the efficacy of these drugs in the treatment of anorexia nervosa, so more research is needed (Pederson, Roerig, & Mitchell, 2003).

After the person's weight is restored to a normal level, dysfunctional attitudes toward food and body shape can be addressed in psychotherapy. This aspect of treatment can be especially challenging because patients with anorexia are usually not self-referred, and most are resistant to treatment. Establishing a connection with the patient and building a therapeutic relationship are particularly important in working with severe cases of anorexia nervosa (Strober, 1997). The therapist's goal is to build a trusting relationship within which other interventions can be employed. Cognitive distortions, superstitious thinking, trouble with expressing emotion, body-image misperceptions, self-esteem, and autonomy are some of the issues that need to be addressed (Cooper, Todd, & Wells, 2002). When the patient is under the age of 16 and is still living at home, family therapy is often recommended.

Joan's treatment followed parts of this approach. During her hospitalization various behavioral techniques were used to restore her weight to a healthy level. Because Joan was older and living on her own, she was treated individually, rather than in family therapy. Consistent with a cognitive approach, Joan's ways of viewing the world and herself were challenged directly. Cognitive therapy procedures can be applied in the treatment of anorexia nervosa. This process involves several steps: (1) learning to be more aware of thoughts and beliefs; (2) exploring and clarifying the connection between the dysfunctional beliefs and maladaptive behaviors; (3) examining the truth of those beliefs; (4) learning to replace the dysfunctional beliefs with more realistic ones; and (5) eventually changing the underlying assumptions that are creating the dysfunctional beliefs (Kleifield, Wagner, & Halmi, 1996).

The prognosis for patients with anorexia nervosa is mixed. Approximately 50 percent relapse after hospitalization. Five percent die as a direct result of the biological effects of self-imposed starvation. Those who have a relatively good outcome often continue to have difficulties with attitudes toward weight and eating (Eckert et al., 1995). Some people are able to recover without professional intervention, but usually this involves the support, encouragement, empathy, and practical help of a parent or close friend (Woods, 2004). One long-term followup study of women who had recovered from anorexia investigated the subjective experience of this process. The women were interviewed 20 years after the onset of their disorder. They reported that "personality strength," "self-confidence," and "being understood" were the most important factors in their sustained health (Hsu, Crisp, & Callender, 1992). Joan had some of these factors working in her favor. She was fortunate to have Mike and close friends as sources of support. She may have also had the advantage of psychological maturity because she was already an adult when she developed her eating disorder. Although she was initially resistant to treatment, she decided to admit herself to the hospital and was determined to change her behavior. These factors may have played an important role in her eventual recovery.

CHAPTER 17

Eating Disorder: Bulimia Nervosa

Tracy was a 22-year-old junior in college when she was referred to the group therapy program for people with eating disorders. She had entered individual psychotherapy at the Student Health Center three months earlier, hoping that her therapist could help her deal more successfully with the stress of university life. Their sessions had focused on the development of better study skills and on issues surrounding Tracy's low self-esteem. Although she was very bright and had managed to earn a 3.2 grade point average, Tracy's academic performance was slipping. Planning and organization were not among her strengths. She attended classes only sporadically and regularly found herself staying up all night in order to finish writing papers or to prepare for tests.

Her depressed mood and pattern of increasing social isolation were also a source of some concern, perhaps more to her therapist than to Tracy. She lived by herself in an apartment near the campus. Relatively few activities gave her any pleasure. She had developed a small circle of both male and female friends during her two years at the university. She had gone out with several different men but had not been involved in a serious romantic relationship for almost three years. Her feelings about these dating experiences were largely ambivalent. Occasional casual sexual encounters were more a source of puzzlement than pleasure for her. She couldn't understand why these men found her attractive. Further discussion of this issue revealed Tracy's pervasive concerns about her appearance and her strong, negative feelings about her body. She told the therapist that she had tried to lose weight for several years. It eventually became apparent that Tracy had a serious eating disorder. After several extended conversations with her therapist, she finally agreed to join an eating disorders group while she continued her individual psychotherapy sessions.

During her first meeting with the woman who ran the therapy group, Tracy was obviously self-conscious and embarrassed while describing the nature of her eating problems. She was a reserved, attractive young woman, dressed neatly in casual clothes. Her graceful, athletic build (5'6" tall and 135 pounds) gave the impression of a person who might be more comfortable with her body than she actually was. Her muscular hips and thighs were especially upsetting to her. She thought they were ugly and said that she very much wanted to lose 15 pounds. Tracy reluctantly provided more complete descriptions of her problems with food as the conversation continued. For the past two years, she had been going on private eating binges in which she consumed very large quantities of food and then forced herself to throw up. These episodes currently happened three to four times per week. At its worst, this binge/purge cycle had occurred 8 to 10 times per week.

Tracy took four to six diet pills each day in a largely unsuccessful effort to control her appetite. She hoped that the pills would prevent her binge eating, but they did not. She also took laxatives on a regular basis, usually once a day. This practice was based on her erroneous assumption that the laxatives would decrease her body's absorption of food.[1] Taking the laxatives made Tracy feel that she was somehow losing most of the food that she consumed.

Tracy's notion of an appropriate diet bordered on the concept of starvation. She tried not to eat all day long. After skipping breakfast and lunch, she would invariably experience intense hunger pains during the afternoon. Not trusting these signals from her body, she would manage to fight them throughout the rest of the day. Tracy usually returned to her apartment around 7 or 8 o'clock at night after a hectic day of classes, meetings, and work. By that point, she would be starving. That was the point at which her binges were most likely to occur.

A typical binge would begin with a trip to the nearby grocery store. Tracy would buy a whole chicken and take it home to prepare. The process usually began with a glass of wine, which made her feel more relaxed (particularly on an empty stomach). As she sipped her wine, Tracy would bake the chicken and prepare a large batch of stuffing and mashed potatoes—almost like a Thanksgiving dinner. Then she would order two large sausage pizzas to be delivered from a local restaurant. While she was waiting for the chicken to bake and the pizzas to be delivered, she would eat cookies and potato chips while finishing her bottle of wine. Whenever she started to feel full, she would go in the bathroom and make herself throw up. This lengthy process of eating and regurgitation would continue until all the food was consumed.

Tracy felt helpless and out of control during these binges, which often lasted two and sometimes as much as three hours. Once the process started, it seemed to demand completion. Tracy seldom ate sitting at a table. She ate quickly, pacing about her apartment. At times she felt as if she were outside of her body, watching the process unfold. She usually took the phone off the hook so that she wouldn't be interrupted by calls from any of the few friends she still had.

After purging, her mood would go from bad to worse. Tracy felt awful about herself, particularly at these moments. Her stomach hurt, but physical pain was not as debilitating as the psychological consequences of the episode. She invariably felt disgusted by her own behavior and deeply ashamed of her complete inability to control her binge eating. She felt guilty both because she had eaten so much and also because she didn't have the control that others had. Tracy had read extensively about anorexia nervosa and now told her therapist that she envied the control that those women had over their appetites. If only she could do that!

She began to experience several harmful physical effects from the repeated vomiting. Her dentist noticed that the enamel had begun to erode on the inner surface of her front teeth. He had asked Tracy about the pattern at her last checkup. She denied any eating problems, but the concern that she detected in his voice left her feeling even more unsettled about her problem. The skin over the knuckles on

---

[1] Laxatives actually have no effect on calorie absorption. Weight loss associated with their use is transient and based on water loss.

her right hand was now scarred; she put those fingers down her throat to stimulate the gag reflex when she wanted to throw up. She knew that her throat was beginning to suffer, as indicated by recurrent hoarseness and sore throats. Perhaps most alarming was the fact that she had begun throwing up blood on occasion, a sign that the walls of her esophagus were tearing.

The wine that Tracy consumed at the outset of her binges was also a source of some considerable concern and reflected a drinking problem that intensified and complicated her eating disorder. Tracy found it annoying that some of her friends had begun to criticize her drinking, but she privately shared the feeling that she ought to cut back. She often drank quite heavily when she went out socially with other people, and she sometimes engaged in casual sexual relations that contributed to her already ample feelings of guilt, confusion, and lack of control. This aspect of her interpersonal relationships seemed particularly self-destructive.

Social History

Tracy's parents were divorced when she was 2 years old. Their separation was messy and painful for everyone. Her father had been awarded custody of Tracy because of her mother's substance-use problems and because she abandoned the family to live with her boyfriend. That relationship didn't last much longer than the divorce proceedings, but her mother did eventually remarry and had two additional children, a girl and a boy.

Tracy grew up living with her father, who provided her with a comfortable home. Unfortunately, he was so preoccupied with his job that he spent little time with her. While she was in elementary school, she was supervised by a housekeeper who lived with Tracy and her father. This woman was fond of Tracy, but was also rather rigid and aloof. Tracy spent most of her time alone when she returned home after school. She watched TV and played games until her father got home from work at 8 or 9 o'clock. She looked forward to his arrival because that was when he would spend time with her. Unfortunately, he didn't show much interest in her life. They would fix a meal of frozen dinners and snacks and desserts, then sit down and watch TV together.

When Tracy was 13 years old, her mother—who was now 36—suddenly reappeared. She and her second family had moved back to the city in which Tracy lived. She wanted to spend time with Tracy and become friends with her. Tracy's father was understandably opposed to this idea, but the original divorce agreement had stipulated that Tracy could see her mother on weekends. That agreement was still in effect, even though her mother had never before followed through on the plan. In fact, Tracy had always been curious about her mom and was now anxious to meet her. They agreed to meet for lunch on a couple of occasions.

Tracy was initially struck by her mother's stunning appearance. She was beautiful—still very thin and exquisitely dressed. Tracy was charmed by her mother's warm and friendly manner as well as her physical appearance.

Her mother was intrigued by Tracy's interests, her accomplishments, and her friends. This concern was a welcome change from the indifference that her father had always shown her. Tracy and her mother began to spend more time together on weekends and holidays. She admired her mother. It was fun to have a mom who would take her out to lunch and dote on her. As they got to know each other better, however, Tracy's mother became more intrusive and critical of Tracy's behavior and appearance. She began to tell Tracy that it wouldn't hurt for her to lose a few pounds. Tracy's younger half-sister was also very thin, like their mother. She and Tracy soon found themselves competing for their mother's attention.

Like most other teenagers, Tracy was self-conscious about her body and the changes that she was going through at this time. Whatever doubts she already had about her own figure and appearance were seriously exacerbated by these competitive interactions with her mother and half-sister. Tracy was built more like her father—muscular and stocky. At her mother's suggestion, Tracy started to experiment with various kinds of diets. Her mother recommended a sequence of diets that had worked for her. Unfortunately, nothing worked for very long when Tracy tried it. If she did manage to lose 10 pounds, she would gain it back within three months. Her weight fluctuated for the next few years between 120 and 145 pounds.

Tracy eventually found herself spending time moving back and forth between her mother's and father's homes. Her patterns of eating became even more inconsistent, perhaps largely because there were different ways to eat in these different places. Her dad lived on packaged cereal, snack food, and late, precooked dinners. Her mom's family ate carefully prepared, nutritious meals that emphasized low-fat foods, including lots of fruits and vegetables. The latter pattern was obviously more healthy, but the atmosphere at these meals frequently made Tracy uncomfortable. Her half-sister seemed to be able to eat more than Tracy without gaining weight. She and her half-sister and stepfather were always given bigger servings than Tracy, as her mother reminded her to watch what she ate. Whenever Tracy expressed an interest in having a light dessert, her mother would smile at her and ask, "Do you really think you should do that?" For obvious reasons, Tracy experienced a lot of negative emotional responses—guilt, shame, and anger—when she ate with her mother's family.

Like many of her peers, Tracy was rebellious as a teenager. Her father was quite lenient with her as she entered adolescence, allowing her to run with a crowd of wild boys and girls. Her friends were unconventional and viewed themselves as outsiders in their high school. Their group drank alcohol and smoked marijuana regularly, beginning in their early teens. Her father's house was occasionally the site for these gatherings because he was seldom around to supervise. After smoking marijuana, Tracy and her friends would get "the munchies" and consume large quantities of snacks and desserts (such as chips and cookies, which were in abundant supply at her father's house). This pattern of sporadic binge eating subverted more than one of her diet plans. Her weight increased noticeably.

Although some of her friends skipped classes and used drugs at school, Tracy did not. She didn't study very much, but she was smart enough to be a good student. She did feel that she was subjected to unfair criticism and scrutiny from teachers and administrators because of her friends. Her academic talents were underdeveloped as she became more alienated from the school.

Tracy found her first serious boyfriend at age 16. She fell head-over-heels in love with Jerome, who was 21 years old and working as a clerk at the video store where Tracy and her friends rented movies and games. Their relationship quickly became sexual, which was both exciting and anxiety provoking for Tracy, who had not had any previous sexual experience. When Tracy's father found out that she was dating Jerome, he became angry. He told her mother, and soon everyone was embroiled in the conflict over this new romance. Tracy felt increasingly alienated from both of her parents and from her friends, who somewhat paradoxically shared her parents' concern about her choice of boyfriends.

When Tracy was 17 years old, she dropped out of high school in her senior year and moved to southern California to be with Jerome. He had moved there three months before she decided to go. Their romance had actually faded in recent months. Her decision to leave was perhaps more motivated by the desire to avoid high school and her family than by her feelings for Jerome. Once she'd arrived in California, Tracy realized that he no longer cared for her. She started to feel depressed when it became apparent that Jerome did not want to spend much time with her. She realized that she now had no family, no friends, and no job. One night, after she had spent an entire day sitting alone in their small apartment, Tracy told Jerome that she felt like she might be better off dead. His only response was to say, "If that's how you feel, go ahead and kill yourself."

Tracy's binge eating and purging evolved gradually while she was living with Jerome in California. As she became more seriously depressed, she often ate snack foods to make herself feel better. Within two months, she had gained eight more pounds. Renewed concern about her appearance and guilt about her inability to control her snacking caused a further decline in her mood. In an attempt to lose the new weight, Tracy went back to some of her earlier diets. Nothing seemed to work. Increased efforts to control what she ate seemed to produce a paradoxical increase in her consumption of food. One day, after eating two large bags of pretzels, Tracy began to feel nauseated. Rather than waiting to find out whether she would vomit spontaneously, she decided to go to the bathroom and stick her fingers down her throat. The process itself was upsetting, but she felt much better after it was over. Then it dawned on her: Maybe self-induced vomiting was a way to avoid gaining weight. It was easy to do. Because she didn't have a job, she was usually all alone with plenty of time and privacy. She couldn't control what she ate, but she could be sure that it didn't sit on her stomach. At first she only threw up once or twice a week. The frequency progressed slowly over the next year.

Three months after she had moved to California, Tracy returned to live with her father. It was difficult to admit that she had made a mistake, but she was shocked by Jerome's lack of concern for her feelings and disgusted by the dismal quality of their relationship. She returned in a better mood than when she left. Her decision to leave Jerome had given her new energy and confidence. She got a part-time job and went back to high school classes at night. She was able to earn her high school equivalency degree and went on to school at a local community college. From there, she transferred to the university.

Unfortunately, Tracy also returned home in the early stages of an expanding eating disorder. She was already starting to experience some physical consequences from throwing up repeatedly. She had severe stomach pains. One of her friends commented on the fact that she frequently had very bad breath. As her secret problem escalated, she became more embarrassed and ashamed.

Although she had managed to pass all her classes since entering the university, Tracy knew that she was falling behind. She was taking courses in the School of Commerce, which was a very demanding curriculum. Pressure from assignments was becoming overwhelming. Her feelings of depression were beginning to return. Tracy's father suggested to her that she might find it useful to see a psychologist at the Student Health Center, in the hope that psychotherapy would help her cope with stress. She was not enthusiastic about going to see a psychologist, and she wasn't willing to acknowledge the severity of her eating problems. When Tracy did finally make an appointment with a psychologist, she said that she wanted to develop her study skills. Her goal was presumably to become a more effective student. She spent several weeks in treatment before she and her therapist eventually recognized the nature of her eating disorder.

Conceptualization and Treatment

Tracy's individual therapist referred her to a group for people suffering from bulimia nervosa. The group was based on a cognitive-behavioral approach to treatment outlined by Fairburn (1995) in his book, *Overcoming Binge Eating*. The book provides a useful summary of information about the disorder and can also serve as a self-help manual for those people who are able to change without entering professional treatment. This is an important option because the secretive nature of this problem causes many people to be reluctant to seek help. The short-term approach represents a blend of cognitive procedures that were originally used to treat depression and behavioral approaches for the treatment of obesity. The cognitive elements of the program are aimed at factors such as low self-esteem and extreme concern about body size and shape. The behavioral elements are designed to alter maladaptive patterns of eating.

The group included Tracy and four other women who also suffered from bulimia. Led by a clinical psychologist who specialized in the treatment of eating disorders, they met once a week for 10 weeks and followed a prearranged sequence of topics.

Week 1: Self-Monitoring

The psychologist began their first session by acknowledging the difficulty that they all must have had in deciding to participate in this process. Up to this point, the most common reaction that they had all had from friends and family members involved accusations of weakness and provocation of guilt. Most had been asked over and over again, "Why can't you just stop?" as if it were actually quite simple. This group would be a place where they could all share their feelings with people who understood quite clearly why they couldn't stop.

The first step of the program involved self-monitoring. Participants were asked to keep a careful, daily record of everything they ate or drank. The record included information about binge eating and purging. This information would be used as a baseline against which subsequent progress could be measured. The instructions were to keep a careful record but not to change anything about her eating. The psychologist also asked each woman to begin weighing herself once a week (and no more than once a week).

Tracy was more reserved than the other group members during this first session. She had trouble connecting to the other women. The others felt good about being in the group, but Tracy did not. She said that she did want to stop binge eating and purging, but she also insisted that she still needed to lose five pounds before she would be happy with her body.

Week 2: Cues and Consequences

During the second session, group members discussed their self-monitoring records from the preceding week. Did they notice any situations or foods that regularly triggered their binges? Most found it relatively easy and helpful to share their experiences with the group. One woman said that, if she ate one french fry, she would say to herself, "Now it's over." Another said that her binges were set off by fights with her boyfriend. Still another said that her first binge of the week happened immediately after she got off the phone with her mother, who said something critical to her about her attempt to change her eating problems (when she really needed reassurance and support).

Unfortunately, Tracy reported that she had experienced trouble with the assignment. She claimed that she was too busy to keep detailed records of her eating. In fact, the biggest problem was that she was not comfortable sharing descriptions of her binges with the group. She had been struck by the intensity of her negative feelings around binge eating. She was also beginning to understand how negatively she thought about herself.

The psychologist also asked the women to generate a list of other activities that could be used to replace binges. They generated many options, including calling friends on the phone, going for a walk or swimming, going to a movie, reading a book, taking baths or showers, and doing a relaxation exercise. Passive activities would clearly be less effective. For example, watching television did not seem like a useful option because many said that they usually ate while watching TV. Each person was asked to create her own list of alternative activities and to have that list ready for moments when she was tempted to start a binge. The therapist explained that by doing something active in response to an urge to binge, the person is also likely to reduce the duration of any strong, negative feelings that are associated.[2]

For the next week, each woman was encouraged to begin replacing binges with a pattern of regular eating throughout each day. This pattern would include

---

[2] This argument is based on the hypothesis proposed by Nolen-Hoeksema (1990), who suggests that women are more likely than men to engage in ruminative thinking during a depressed mood (see Chapter 6).

breakfast, lunch, and dinner as well as a planned snack within two or three hours after each meal. The women were urged not to skip any planned meals or snacks, and also not to eat any unplanned foods. This step was discussed at great length because it is, in fact, the most important element in the treatment program.

Eating on a schedule struck some as being a bad idea. Tracy expressed concern that she should only eat when her body told her that she was hungry. The problem with this argument is that hunger signals are often disrupted in people who have been involved in binge eating and purging. The therapist explained that until they had returned to normal patterns of eating for a substantial period of time, it would be better to eat at prearranged times.

The therapist noted that eating regular meals and snacks everyday could have an effect on each person's weight. As before, they were encouraged to weigh themselves only once each week. And they were asked to take a leap of faith—to let their weight fluctuate to wherever it was supposed to be, given a regular pattern of eating. This could mean that their weight would go up or down a little bit, even in the first week or two.

Week 3: Thoughts, Feelings, and Behaviors

Tracy called the group's leader before this session to say that she would have to miss the meeting because she had a lot of work to do. She apologized and explained that school had been especially stressful this week. In truth, she had not been doing her self-monitoring and had not been able to begin a regular pattern of eating—even at breakfast. She was too embarrassed to tell the other group members that her binge eating and purging had continued unabated. Tracy was not yet committed to the treatment program.

Everyone else spent the session talking about distorted patterns of thinking. These are cognitive events that are presumably responsible for many forms of emotional distress. Cognitive therapists assume that if a person is extremely upset, she may not be aware that certain thoughts could have produced her negative emotional state. For example, the women were asked to suppose that they had just eaten a piece of cake that was not on their meal plan. What do you think to yourself? Some volunteered that they would say, "Now I just ruined everything. One piece of cake is as good as a binge. I hate myself! I screwed up, and now I should just finish the binge. I'll start being 'good' again tomorrow." The goal of this session was to help them learn to revise the consequences of this type of event by interrupting the chain that leads from distorted, self-deprecating thoughts to negative feelings and then to bingeing and purging behavior.

It is important to discuss the cognitive basis of strong negative emotions for several reasons. Intense feelings of sadness, anger, and fear often trigger binge episodes. And the binges are often employed to blunt or control these feelings. As people make progress in following a regular pattern of eating, their binges become less frequent, and they may find themselves faced with the experience of rather intense negative emotional responses.

Week 4: Perfectionism and All-or-Nothing Thinking

At the beginning of the fourth session, the other members of the group asked Tracy about her absence from the previous meeting. She initially tried to tell them that she was too busy to attend, but they didn't buy her excuse. She finally confided tearfully, and with great difficulty, that she had become increasingly depressed over the past two weeks. Frustrated and disappointed with her inability to engage with the program, she wondered openly whether she would ever be able to eat normally. Tracy confessed that she had stopped monitoring completely and had not been able to follow even the simplest elements of regular eating. She was engaging in binge eating and purging at least as often as before she entered the group. Having disclosed these secrets to the rest of the group, Tracy was overwhelmed with feelings of shame and guilt. She got up and quietly walked out of the room, halfway through the session. She went home to her apartment and immediately ordered food to be delivered. While she was waiting for it to arrive, she had a glass of wine and wrote in her previously empty self-monitoring journal about feelings of giving up.

The other members of the group had mixed reactions to Tracy's message and her early departure. They all sympathetic, but some also expressed mild disappointment at her lack of commitment to the therapy process. Some were concerned that the therapist should follow her when she left the room, but most recognized the importance of her commitment to stay with the others. There was also a feeling of failure and rejection associated with their own apparent inability to make Tracy feel that they could help her succeed in the treatment program. These emotional reactions were discussed at length before the therapist continued with their planned agenda for the week.

The remaining portion of this session was devoted to a further discussion of personality traits and distorted thinking patterns that are often associated with binge eating. Examples were, "I need to be thin in order to be liked and successful" and "If I eat regular meals, I will turn into a blimp." Another example followed from Tracy's current distress: "If I don't succeed in the first two weeks of treatment, it means that I will never be able to change." Group members were asked to discuss a series of questions: Are these thoughts really accurate? How can they be tested? Will you *really* be unhappy for the rest of your life if you don't fit in the smallest dress size? Do you *have* to be perfect in everything that you do? And do you plan to make yourself miserable unless every aspect of your appearance is perfect?

Week 5: Assertive Behavior

To some people's surprise, Tracy appeared on time for the group's next meeting. She was composed and cheerful, in stark contrast to the state in which she had fled their last session. Tracy explained that, two days after their last session, she had an experience that promised to change her entire outlook on her eating disorder.

The fateful event took place while she was babysitting for a neighbor's little girl. The next day was the girl's fifth birthday. A party was planned, with 20 of the little girl's best friends scheduled to attend. Her mother had ordered a special birthday cake and left it in the refrigerator. Tracy hadn't eaten all day when she arrived to babysit. She was starving. As soon as she saw the cake, she knew it was going to be a serious problem. The girl talked about the cake all night, telling Tracy how beautiful it was and what a nice party she was going to have the next day. She repeatedly took Tracy to the refrigerator to look at the cake and talk about its decorations. Tracy resisted the temptation to eat a piece of the cake for two hours after the little girl went to sleep. Then she completely lost control. Before she realized what she was doing, Tracy had eaten the whole cake. Horrified and ashamed by what she had done, she quickly found herself in the bathroom. She sobbed uncontrollably as she threw up in the toilet. When she finally stood up, she was staring directly at her face in the mirror. Tears were streaming down her face. Tracy told the group that at that moment she finally acknowledged the reality and the severity of her eating problems. Her eating was so far out of control that she could devour a child's birthday cake the day before her party. Tracy knew then that she would have to take responsibility for changing her own feelings and behavior.

Tracy had not binged or purged since that night. She started monitoring what she ate the next morning and had not missed a day. Although she had not previously kept written records, the discussions in weeks 1 and 2 had been enough to help her recognize that, in her own case, she would have to start eating regularly throughout the day if she wanted to control her late-night binges. She forced herself to eat at least a small breakfast on each of the remaining days. She still skipped lunch on most days, but she did eat a regular evening meal without escalating into a binge. Her decision to avoid having a glass of wine when she arrived home was undoubtedly one important part of that success.

The group listened to her story with rapt attention. Some cried, knowing that they could easily have done the same thing if they found themselves in the same situation. They praised her lavishly for the positive changes that she had already accomplished. Their sympathetic responses helped Tracy to feel that she had finally become part of the group.

For the remaining time in the session, the group returned to a discussion of the topics that had originally been planned: assertive behavior. This issue represents a logical extension of the preceding discussions of negative emotional triggers for binge eating. For some people, anger can be a stimulus for uncontrolled eating. By training the women to behave more assertively, the psychologist hoped that they would be able to solve interpersonal problems more effectively and minimize emotional distress.

For the first time, Tracy participated actively and constructively in this discussion. The relevance to her own situation was quite apparent. Throughout adolescence, she had been afraid to stand up for herself. She received frequent critical messages from her parents, teachers, and peers. For example, her mother's criticism of her appearance and weight had been a common source of irritation and embarrassment. She role-played with the group ways in which she could tell her mother that these critical remarks made her feel bad, without becoming rude or hostile.

Week 6: Body Image

This session was devoted to a discussion of the women's images of their own bodies. The women had already made it clear to one another that their lives were, in many ways, dominated by concerns about their appearance and their weight. Some said they believed that, unless they found a way to keep themselves thin, they would be depressed and lonely for the rest of their lives.

In an effort to help group members identify and challenge their own negative feelings about their bodies, the therapist reviewed a number of facts about physiology. For example, women need a certain amount of body fat to enable reproduction. Their bodies need more fat than men's bodies. Women also have a lower resting metabolism rate than men. Dieting suppresses metabolism even further.

Each member of the group was asked to write down five things about her body that she *liked*. These were not to be aspects of her appearance. Rather, they were to list things that their bodies did for them. This became a very challenging exercise. Tracy was unable to think of a single thing. Others were able to generate a few items, such as "My body allows me to run for 30 minutes every day. It makes me feel strong." The difficulty that the women had in constructing this particular list helped them realize the extent of the distorted and imbalanced views that they had come to hold about their own bodies.

The session ended with each person reporting her own progress toward the introduction of regular patterns of eating. Tracy noted that she was now eating three regular meals and two scheduled snacks each day. She had completely eliminated her late-night binges. When she experienced an urge to have a glass of wine or bake a batch of cookies, she would record the urge in her journal and then distract herself by doing "stomach crunches." The exercise made her feel better about herself, and she found that the urge to binge usually passed by the time she was finished.

Week 7: Dieting and Other Causal Factors

In the first portion of this session, the group discussed the relation between different types of dieting and the onset of binge eating. Dieting plays a crucial role in most cases of bulimia. Sometimes people begin with dieting and progress to binge eating and purging. In other cases, overeating in childhood and/or obesity precede the onset of dieting, which then leads to bulimia. People who set dietary restraints make themselves feel food deprived. When they do eat, they are more likely to binge.

There are many forms of dieting. The women were instructed to identify any food groups that they had been trying to avoid. All said that they avoided sweet desserts. Others stayed away from dairy foods, fatty meats, and simple carbohydrates. The psychologist told them that they should gradually introduce small amounts of each type of food into their planned meals and snacks. This process was designed to diminish the probability of further binges by eliminating extreme forms of dietary restraint.

The remainder of this session was devoted to a review of information about causes of bulimia. Emphasis was placed on the notion that no single factor is responsible for all cases of eating disorder. The pathways to bulimia are complex, and the symptoms of the disorder can vary over time.

Several family issues were discussed, including traumatic events such as deaths, divorce, parental conflict, and childhood sexual abuse. One woman in the group reported that she had been secretly abused for several years by an older stepbrother. These prolonged, terrifying experiences had many far-reaching negative effects in her life. They contributed to her early feelings of shame about her body. She experienced intense negative emotions such as fear and rage, but she was unable to express these feelings to anyone. The abuse also made her feel that she was not in control of her own body and its sensations.

Week 8: Problem Solving and Stress Reduction

The women's self-monitoring records indicated clearly that their binge episodes did not occur at random. Rather, their binges were much more likely to occur during moments of increased stress. Their next discussion focused on the development of problem-solving skills that might then serve to decrease the frequency of future binge eating. They began by talking about ways of spotting problems before they became unmanageable. Warning signals would include the onset of negative mood states (particularly sadness or anger) as well as particular situations, such as being alone with nothing to do. After recognizing the presence of a problem situation, the psychologist worked with them on ways to generate a large number of potential solutions to the problem. These alternatives could then be compared in terms of their likely advantages and disadvantages.

Week 9: Healthy Exercise and Relapse Prevention

In their next-to-last session, the women worked on two topics that would help them maintain progress once the group treatment was completed. First, they talked about the benefits of *healthy* exercise. The women listed several considerations, including stress reduction, mood elevation, social interaction with friends, and the regulation of metabolism. The damaging effects of compulsive exercise were also discussed. Exercise should be pleasurable, not a punishment for overeating. The discussion turned up several faulty beliefs that the women had used to force themselves into compulsive and unpleasant exercise patterns (which often perpetuated negative mood states). For example, one woman had been telling herself, "If I skip a single day, I may never start again." This is a classic example of all-or-nothing thinking. Another seemed to be operating on the belief that "Exercise can make my body perfect." She had been feeling frustrated and guilty because, no matter how hard she worked at it, some parts of her body still seemed to be soft and fleshy. The therapist encouraged them to set realistic exercise goals, emphasizing the point that these activities should be fun and accomplished easily.

The second half of this session was devoted to the prevention of relapse. Minor setbacks are virtually inevitable in this type of program. It may be unrealistic to assume that, after a person has recovered from binge eating, she will never overeat again. The women acknowledged that eating problems might be their Achilles' heel for the rest of their lives. Particularly during stressful times, they would still be tempted to binge. How would they react when that happened? How would they feel and how would they behave if they did overeat? They were encouraged to distinguish between temporary lapses and full-blown relapses. By overreacting, they could contribute to an escalation of the problem. If they did slip up, it would not mean that they were back where they had started before the group. It would simply mean that they should address the problem right away and reinstate those aspects of the program that had been most successful initially.

Week 10: Coping with Future Events

The final session was devoted to a review of earlier steps and a discussion of ways that they could reduce their vulnerability to future binge eating. What kinds of situations might contribute to their own relapse? One crucial consideration was obviously the continuation of eating regular meals and avoiding all forms of dieting. They also discussed methods that they had learned to use when coping with stressful events, negative emotions, and self-defeating thoughts. The group leader recommended a few books that might be useful to them, including *Making Peace with Food* (Susan Kano, 1989) and *Feeling Good: The New Mood Therapy* (David Burns, 1992).

By the time the group ended, Tracy had made significant improvements with regard to her eating problems. She had eaten regular meals on a daily basis for five weeks. She had not binged or purged since the traumatic night when she ate the birthday cake, and she had stopped taking diet pills and laxatives. Somewhat to her surprise, her weight had remained fairly steady for the first couple of weeks and then leveled off at five pounds less than it had been when she entered the group. Her mood was much improved, but she still experienced periods of marked sadness and loneliness. Her concerns about drinking as well as difficulties in relationships with boyfriends and her parents had not been resolved. She continued to discuss these issues with her individual therapist.

Discussion

Tracy's disorder, bulimia nervosa, is one of two eating disorders described in *DSM-IV-TR* (APA, 2000). The other eating disorder is anorexia nervosa: an intense fear of becoming obese resulting in reduced intake of food and severe weight loss. The key to the diagnosis of bulimia nervosa is recurrent episodes of binge eating coupled with compensatory behavior, such as vomiting, to prevent weight gain. Literally, bulimia means "ox hunger," or voracious appetite, but it now refers to binge eating and purging. Although many people report occasional binges, the *DSM-IV-TR* (APA, 2000) diagnosis requires at least two binges per week for at least three months. The binges, which are often triggered by stress, typically involve eating high-calorie, easily ingested food in a short period of time (e.g., two hours) and in secret. During the binges, the person feels out of control and may consume 2000 to 4000 calories, more than someone would usually eat in an entire day. The binges end when the person becomes uncomfortably full or when the person is interrupted or falls asleep. Vomiting frequently follows the binge, either terminating it or allowing further eating to take place. Heavy laxative use and excessive exercise are other ways of trying to compensate for the large number of calories that have been consumed.

People suffering from bulimia are usually intensely concerned about their weight and fear becoming fat. They realize that their eating is abnormal but report that they cannot control themselves. Their inability to control their eating often leads to feelings of depression, guilt, and low self-esteem (Garner & Magana, 2002).

The exact prevalence of bulimia is not known, principally because it is a secretive problem. Probably about 2 percent of the college-aged population has the disorder. The disorder typically begins in the late teens and is much more common in women than men (Garvin & Streigel-Moore, 2001; Hsu, 1996). Little information is available on the prognosis for bulimia. The average duration of the disorder is five to six years, suggesting a chronic course for many patients (Keel & Mitchell, 1997).

Bulimia can occur either by itself, as in Tracy's case, or as an accompanying symptom of anorexia nervosa. About 50 percent of patients with anorexia also have episodes of binge eating. The frequency of binges and vomiting in these patients, however, is less than was true for Tracy. Bulimia also is comorbid with several other diagnoses, including personality disorders (especially borderline personality disorder), anxiety disorders, and depression (O'Brien & Vincent, 2003; van Hanswijck et al., 2003).

Several serious physical complications may result from bulimia (Johnson, Spitzer, & Williams, 2001; Mickley, 2001). Tracy experienced several of these problems, including sore throat, swollen salivary glands, and destruction of dental enamel, which occur as a result of the frequent presence of stomach acid in these areas. Repeated vomiting can also lead to potassium depletion, which, in turn, can produce seizures. Urinary infections and kidney failure also occur in some patients. Menstrual irregularity is also common.

Etiological Considerations

Bulimia nervosa is undoubtedly the product of a complex interaction among biological, psychological, and social factors. These include various sorts of antecedent conditions and predispositions to the disorder, such as negative self-evaluations and fear of gaining weight. In the presence of these vulnerability factors, the stress of dieting often triggers the full-blown symptoms of the disorder and sets off a cascade of related biological reactions (Halmi, 1997; Polivy & Herman, 2002).

Biological Factors. Supporting the possible importance of genetics, bulimia nervosa clearly runs in families. Data from twin studies also show higher concordance for monozygotic than for dizygotic twins (Kay et al., 2004; Sullivan, Bulik, & Kendler, 1998).

At a neurochemical level, interest has focused on the neurotransmitter serotonin (Kaye, Strober, & Klump, 2002). Several factors make serotonin an appealing variable to play a role in bulimia. First, drugs that block serotonin receptors lead to increased food intake and appear to do so by reducing feelings of being satiated after eating. Patients with bulimia binge, of course, and also report less satiety after eating. Second, low levels of serotonin are associated with both depression and increased impulsivity. Depression is often found in patients with bulimia, and their binge eating could well be regarded as reflecting a high level of impulsivity. Studies of serotonin in patients with bulimia provide more direct support. Research has found a low level of serotonin in patients with bulimia. Furthermore, studies in which patients with bulimia take drugs that affect serotonin have found that patients with bulimia show smaller responses than normals, again demonstrating the importance of this variable (Ferguson & Pigott, 2000; Jimerson et al., 1997).

Psychological Factors. A fear of being fat is a primary feature of the eating disorders, including bulimia. This fear is likely to lead to dieting, which is an important precursor of bulimia (Austin, 2001; Brewerton et al., 2000). Fear of being fat arises from several sources. First, there are sociocultural influences. Over the past several decades, there has been a steady progression toward thinness as the ideal shape, although this trend now seems to have leveled off (Wiseman et al, 1992). We know that this ideal has been internalized by large numbers of women because many normal-weight women perceive themselves to be overweight. At the same time that society was becoming preoccupied with being thin, the prevalence of bulimia increased markedly (Hoek, 2003). This cultural influence has had greater impact on women than men and may thus account for the gender difference in the prevalence of bulimia. As would be expected if cultural effects are important, the frequency of eating disorders is particularly high among women, such as gymnasts and dancers, who are under extreme pressure to keep their weight down.

Several other factors also contribute to fear of being fat. For example, being overweight or having overweight parents are risk factors for bulimia. Being teased by peers or criticized by parents about being overweight can also contribute (Fairburn et al., 1997). In Tracy's case, her mother's persistent comments about Tracy's weight undoubtedly contributed to her own exaggerated concerns about being fat, as well as her low self-esteem. A distorted view of the size of one's body is another risk factor. For example, in one study, women with bulimia were shown silhouettes of very thin to very obese women. They were asked to select the one closest to their own body size and the one they would most like to be. The women with bulimia overestimated their current body size and chose thinner ideal body sizes than control women (Williamson, Cubic, & Gleaves, 1993).

One psychological explanation for the development of bulimia nervosa suggests that the disorder is a combination of extreme weight concerns and dieting practices (Byrne & McLean, 2002; Lowe, 1996). Fear of becoming fat leads to restricting food intake, which then sets the stage for the development of the binge-purge cycle. Dietary restraint paradoxically *increases* the likelihood of binge eating when the person is stressed (Heatherton & Polivy, 1992). Emotional arousal increases eating among people who are trying to restrict their food intake. The binge-eating pattern for patients with bulimia is similar but more extreme. Dieting frequently precedes the onset of bulimia, and it also appears to be triggered by episodes of stress. After the binge, the patient with bulimia feels anxious and the purge is then a way of reducing this anxiety.

What function did binge eating serve for Tracy? Several processes could be involved. First, Tracy was afraid of becoming fat and did often restrain her eating, for example, by skipping breakfast and lunch. Second, Tracy's early binges seemed, at least in part, to be stress related. Binge eating could have been established as a way of coping with stress. Her binges may have filled up a life that was devoid of many other pleasurable activities.

Considerable speculation has surrounded the relationship between sexual abuse and eating disorders (Cooper, Todd, & Wells, 2002; Steiger et al., 2001; Wooley, 1995). One woman in Tracy's group reported that she had been abused by her stepbrother. Many other case studies suggest the impact of similar experiences, but the research literature is ambiguous on this point. The link to eating disorders is apparently not specific. Empirical data indicate that sexual abuse can lead to many different types of mental disorders, ranging from anxiety disorders (such as post-traumatic stress disorder [PTSD] and panic disorder) to depression, borderline personality disorder, and sexual dysfunction.

Treatment

Many patients with eating disorders do not seek treatment for their disorder because they do not believe that anything is wrong (Fairburn et al., 1996). Others fail to enter therapy because they are ashamed of their condition or feel hopeless about it. When patients with bulimia do enter therapy, they are treated with both biological and psychological treatments.

Because bulimia is often comorbid with depression, it is not surprising that it has been treated with antidepressant medication, especially SSRIs. Medication is beneficial for some patients, but up to one-third of bulimic patients drop out of therapy because of unpleasant drug side effects, and relapse is the rule when medication is discontinued (Krueger & Kennedy, 2000; Narash-Eisikovits et al., 2002; Romano et al., 2002).

The major psychological intervention, as was the case with Tracy, is cognitive-behavior therapy. Patients are encouraged to question society's standards for physical attractiveness and learn that normal weight can be achieved without extreme dieting. Patients must also learn that dieting can trigger a binge and that all is not lost by eating a high-calorie afternoon snack. Another crucial step involves determining the situations that elicit binges and developing alternative ways of coping with them. The goal, then, is to establish a normal pattern of eating three meals a day and even snacks between meals. Regular meals control hunger and thus make it less likely that a person will binge and then become anxious and purge. Results from these cognitive-behavioral interventions are more favorable than those from treatment with antidepressant medication (Hsu et al., 2001; Lundgren et al., 2004;

Ricca et al., 2000). For some patients, the optimal treatment may involve a combination of both drugs and cognitive-behavior therapy.

Unfortunately, only about half of bulimic patients improve significantly during treatment. One year after the end of treatment, only one-third are maintaining their treatment gains (Anderson & Maloney, 2001; Keel & Mitchell, 1997). What factors might explain these high rates of treatment failure? Desire to change is obviously one crucial element in any program aimed at the treatment of eating disorders. Relatively little is known about factors that influence these patients' ability to appreciate the severity of their problems (Fairburn, 1995). Some people seem to accept their binge eating and adjust their lives around it. They are not motivated to change. Tracy was unable to benefit from her experience in group therapy until the dramatic evening when she devoured the birthday cake and found herself staring in the mirror of her neighbor's bathroom. This event clearly played a crucial role in her subsequent recovery.

The *abstinence violation effect* can also contribute to continued binge eating and relapse in bulimia nervosa (Johnson et al., 1995). This phenomenon was initially observed among people who are recovering from substance dependence. A single violation of abstinence is often sufficient to wipe out totally any treatment gains that had occurred. When a person violates his or her commitment to stop using drugs, a state of dissonance is created between the behavior and the self-image of the person. This dissonance motivates attempts to reduce it, for example, by changing the self-image: "I guess I haven't really recovered." Furthermore, the transgression is attributed to personal weakness and thus the person is likely to expect future failures.

Recognition of the impact of the abstinence violation effect led to the inclusion of relapse prevention elements in the type of group therapy that Tracy received. Tracy and the other members of her group were trained to recognize situations that could create pressure for them. Furthermore, she was given specific training in coping with stress, including skills to handle problematic life situations and ways to deal with negative emotional states. Finally, she was told that minor lapses were likely and that they would not indicate that the treatment had failed or that she was a weak person. Within this framework, she was instructed on ways to cope with a single binge to reduce the likelihood that a single abstinence violation would lead to a complete resumption of her old pattern.

CHAPTER 18

Paranoid Personality Disorder

This case study is based on personal, rather than clinical, experience. Joe Fuller was in treatment for a brief period of time, but he terminated the relationship well before a therapy plan was formulated. This pattern is, in fact, characteristic of this type of person; people who are paranoid seldom seek professional services and, when they do, are difficult to work with. One of the authors was well acquainted with Joe during high school and college and has stayed in contact with him throughout subsequent years.

Social History

Joe was the third of four children. He had two older brothers and a younger sister. His father was a steamfitter and his mother was a homemaker. The family lived in a lower-middle-class neighborhood in a large, northeastern city. Joe's grandmother also lived with them, beginning when Joe was 11 years old. She was an invalid and could not care for herself after Joe's grandfather died.

Our first information about Joe comes from his high school years. Unlike his older brothers, Joe was an exceptionally bright student. On the basis of his performance in elementary school and entrance examinations, he was admitted to a prestigious public high school. The school was widely recognized for academic excellence. More than 90 percent of the graduating seniors went on to college; most went to Ivy League schools. The school was also known as a "pressure cooker." All of the students were expected to meet very high standards; those who failed were denigrated by their peers. Joe thrived in this intellectually competitive environment. He usually received the highest test scores in his classes, particularly in science. These achievements were based on a combination of intelligence and hard work. Joe was clearly very bright, but so were most of the other students in this school. Joe was a serious student who seemed to be driven by a desire to succeed. While many of the other students worried about examinations and talked to one another about their fear of failure, Joe exuded self-confidence. He knew that the teachers and other students viewed him as one of the best students; he often made jokes about people who "couldn't make the grade." This critical attitude was not reserved for other students alone. Whenever a teacher made a mistake in class, Joe was always the first to laugh and make a snide comment. His classmates usually laughed along with him, but they also noticed a sneering, condescending quality in Joe's humor that set him apart from themselves.

Joe was a classic example of the critic who could "dish it out but couldn't take it." He was extremely sensitive to criticism. It did not seem to matter whether the criticism was accurate or justified; Joe was ready to retaliate at the slightest provocation. He argued endlessly about examinations, particularly in mathematics and science classes. If he lost points on any of his answers, even if he had gotten an "A" on the exam, he would insist that his answer was correct, the question was poorly written, or the teacher had not adequately explained the topic prior to the exam. He never admitted that he was wrong.

His sensitivity was also evident in interpersonal relationships. Most people are able to laugh at themselves, but Joe could not. His family background was a particularly sore spot. Many of the other students in his school were from wealthy homes. Their parents were mostly professionals with advanced degrees. Joe seemed to be self-conscious about his father's lack of formal education and the fact that his family did not live in a large, modern house. He never admitted it openly, but the topic led to frequent arguments. The following example was a typical instance of this sort. Joe had been arguing in class about his grade on a chemistry examination. After class, he overheard another student say to one of his friends, "I don't know why some people have to work so hard for everything." The other boy's father happened to be a successful businessman. Joe took his comment to mean that Joe was trying to compensate for the fact that his family did not have a lot of money. This implied insult, which may or may not have been a simple comment about Joe's aggressive behavior, infuriated him. Two nights later, while everyone else was watching a school basketball game, Joe sneaked out into the parking lot and poured sugar into the gas tank of the other boy's car so that the engine would be ruined.

Joe did not participate in organized sports or student organizations, and he tended to avoid group activities. He did have a small circle of friends and was particularly close to two other boys. They were people whom he had judged to be his intellectual equals, and they were the only people in whom he could confide. He was interested in women, but his attitude toward them and his interactions with them struck his friends as being somewhat odd. The issues of dependence and control seemed to be of central importance to Joe. Whenever one of his friends spent a lot of time with a girlfriend or went out with her instead of a group of guys, Joe accused him of being spineless or "on a tight leash."

Joe seldom dated the same woman twice. He usually insisted that she was weird or boring, but, if the truth were known, most of them would not have gone out on another date with him if he had asked. They found Joe to be rude and arrogant. Conversations with him were one-sided, with Joe trying to impress his date with his intelligence and simultaneously implying that she was barely worthy of his company. He was not interested in being friends; his sole purpose was to make a sexual conquest. He often bragged about having sex with many women, but his closest friends suspected that he was still a virgin.

In most respects, Joe's relationship with his family was unremarkable. They were not a tight-knit family, but he respected his parents and got along well with his older brothers and his sister. His principal problem at home centered on his grandmother, whom he hated. He complained about her continuously to his friends, saying that she was old and crippled, and he wished that his parents would ship her off to a nursing home. Her inability to care for herself and her dependence on Joe's parents seemed to be particularly annoying to him. He noted on several occasions that if he was ever in a similar situation, he hoped that someone would put him out of his misery.

After graduating from high school, Joe enrolled at an Ivy League university, where he majored in chemistry and maintained a straight-A average throughout his first two years. He seemed to study all the time; his friends described him as a workaholic. Everything he did became a preoccupation. If he was studying for a particular course, he concentrated on that topic day and night, seven days a week. If he was involved in a laboratory project, he practically lived in the laboratory. Relaxation and recreation were not included in his schedule. Even if he had the time, there were few leisure activities that Joe enjoyed. He had never been particularly athletic and was, in fact, clumsy. He hated to lose at anything and was also afraid of being ridiculed for looking awkward, so he avoided sports altogether. He was also uninterested in art and films. Joe argued that these activities were a waste of time and a sign of weakness and effeminacy.

Joe's first steady relationship with a woman began during his sophomore year. Carla was a student at a small liberal arts college in upstate New York. They happened to meet at a small party while she was visiting friends in New York City. Several weeks later, Joe drove to spend the weekend with her. They continued to see each other once or twice a month throughout the spring semester. From Joe's point of view, this was an ideal relationship. He liked Carla; she shared his sarcastic, almost bitter, sense of humor, and they got along well sexually. Perhaps most important, the fact that she was not in the same city meant that she could not demand a great deal of his time and could not try to control his schedule or activities.

Unfortunately, the relationship ended after a few months when Carla told Joe that she had another boyfriend. Although he was shocked and furious, he made every effort to seem calm and rational. He had always taken pride in his ability to avoid emotional reactions, particularly if they were expected. In discussing the situation with friends, Joe maintained that he had never really cared for Carla and said that he was interested only in her body. Nevertheless, he was clearly interested in revenge. His first plan was to win her back so that he could then turn the tables and drop her. Presumably this process would demonstrate to everyone that he, not Carla, had been in control of the relationship. When this effort failed, he settled for spreading rumors about Carla's promiscuous sexual behavior.

After his breakup with Carla, Joe became more deeply involved in his laboratory work. He would disappear for days at a time and seldom saw any of his friends. The experiments he was running were apparently based on his own ideas. His assigned work and routine studying were largely ignored; consequently, his academic performance began to deteriorate.

The experience with Carla also contributed to an increase in Joe's already cynical attitude toward women. He described her behavior as treacherous and deceitful and took the rejection as one more piece of evidence proving that he could not trust anyone, particularly a woman. He continued to go out on dates, but he was extremely suspicious of women's intentions and obviously jealous of their attention to other men. On one occasion, he went to a party with a woman he met in one of his classes. They arrived together, but Joe chose to ignore her while he chatted with some male friends in the kitchen. When he later discovered his date talking with another man in the living room, he became rude and offensive. He insulted the woman, made jokes about her clothes and the makeup she was wearing, and suggested that her friend was gay. As might be expected, they never saw each other again. Another time, after he had dated a woman once, he sat in his parked car outside her apartment and watched the entrance for two nights to determine whether one of his friends was also seeing her.

Later Adjustment

After receiving his B.S. degree, Joe stayed on at the same university to do graduate work in biochemistry. He continued to work very hard and was considered one of the most promising students in the department. His best work was done in the laboratory, where he was allowed to pursue independent research. Classroom performance was more of a problem. Joe resented being told what to do and what to read. He believed that most faculty members were envious of his intellect. Highly structured reading lists and laboratory assignments, which were often time consuming, were taken by Joe to be efforts to interfere with his professional advancement.

In one case, Joe became convinced that a professor had cheated him on a final examination. The professor had, in fact, gone out of her way to avoid bias in scoring the examinations; every answer had been typewritten and identified only by social security number. When Joe received a "B+" instead of an "A," he argued that the entire process had been designed to cover up the professor's effort to cheat him. He said that the examination booklets had been decoded *prior* to being read! When his friends asked him why the system was used, he pointed out that the professor was not stupid and, knowing that Joe would discover the plot, had devised a means to make it look as though she had been fair. The chemistry faculty was concerned by this incident but decided to tolerate Joe's eccentricity because he was doing creative work and did not present any other problems.

In his second year of graduate school, Joe began dating an undergraduate woman in one of his study sections. Ruth was unremarkable in every way. His friends described her as plain, bland, and mousy. They were surprised that Joe was even interested in her, but in retrospect, she had one general feature that made her perfect for Joe—she was not at all threatening. He made all the decisions in the relationship, and she acquiesced to his every whim and fancy. Other men were not interested in her. In fact, they seldom noticed her, so Joe did not have to remain constantly alert to the possibility of desertion. They were perfect complements to each other and were married within a year.

Joe's first job after getting his Ph.D. was as a research chemist for a major drug company. At the beginning, it seemed like an ideal position. He was expected to work somewhat independently doing basic biochemical research. There was no question that he was intellectually capable of the work, and his willingness to work long hours would be beneficial to his advancement, which was closely tied to productivity. Joe expected to be promoted rapidly and was confident that he would be the head of a division within five years.

When Joe began working in the company laboratory, he quickly evaluated all the employees and their relationship to his own position. There were several young Ph.D.s like himself, three supervisors, and the head of the laboratory, Dr. Daniels, a distinguished senior investigator. Joe admired Dr. Daniels and wanted to impress him. He did not think much of his young colleagues and particularly resented the supervisors, whom he considered to be his intellectual inferiors. He believed that they had been promoted because they were "yes-men," not because they were competent scientists. He often complained about them to his peers and occasionally laughed openly about their mistakes. When they asked him to perform a specific experiment, particularly if the task was tedious, he was arrogant and resentful, but he usually complied with the request. He hoped that the quality of his work would be noticed by Dr. Daniels, who would then allow him to work more independently. He also worried, however, that the others would notice that he was being subservient in an effort to gain Dr. Daniel's favor. He became more and more self-conscious and was constantly alert to signs of disdain and rejection from the others in the laboratory. The others gradually came to see him as rigid and defensive, and he eventually became isolated from the rest of the group. He interpreted their rejection as evidence of professional jealousy.

Joe's initial work did gain some recognition, and he was given greater independence in his choice of projects. He was interested in the neurochemical basis of depression and spent several months pursuing a series of animal experiments aimed at specific details of his personal theory. Very few people knew what he was doing. He refused to discuss the research with anyone other than Dr. Daniels; even then he was careful to avoid the description of procedural details. His principal concern was that other people might get credit for his ideas. He wanted to impress Dr. Daniels, but he also wanted to take over Dr. Daniels's job. The quickest way to do that was to make a major breakthrough in the laboratory, one for which he alone would receive credit.

Dr. Daniels and the other supervisors recognized that Joe was exceptionally bright and a talented, dedicated scientist. They liked his early work at the company but were dissatisfied with the independent work that he was pursuing. It seemed overly ambitious and, more important, highly esoteric. There were no immediate, practical implications to this line of research, and it did not promise to lead to any commercial results in the near future. Consequently, Joe was told that his work was not acceptable and that he would have to return to doing work that was more closely supervised.

Joe's response to this criticism was openly hostile. He complained bitterly about the imbeciles in company management and swore that he would no longer tolerate their jealousy and stupidity. He was certain that someone had learned about his ideas and that Dr. Daniels and the others were trying to force him out of the company so that they could then publish the theory without giving him credit. Their insistence that he discontinue his work and return to more menial tasks was clear proof, from Joe's point of view, that they wanted to slow down his progress so that they could complete the most important experiments themselves. His paranoid ideas attracted considerable attention. Other people began to avoid him, and he sometimes noticed that they gave him apprehensive glances. It did not occur to him that these responses were provoked by his own hostile behavior; he took their behavior as further evidence that the whole laboratory was plotting against him. As the tension mounted, Joe began to fear for his life.

The situation soon became intolerable. After three years with the firm, Joe was told that he would have to resign. Dr. Daniels agreed to write him a letter of reference so that he could obtain another position as long as he did not contest his termination. Joe considered hiring a lawyer to help him fight for his job, but he became convinced that the plot against him was too pervasive for him to win. He also had serious doubts about being able to find a lawyer he could trust. He therefore decided to apply for other positions and eventually took a job as a research associate working with a faculty member at a large state university.

In many ways the new position was a serious demotion. His salary was considerably less than it had been at the drug company, and the position carried much less prestige. Someone with Joe's academic credentials and experience should have been able to do better, but he had not published any of his research. He was convinced that this lack of professional success could be attributed to interference from jealous, incompetent administrators at the drug company. A more plausible explanation was that his work had never achieved publishable form. Although the ideas were interesting and his laboratory techniques were technically skillful, Joe was not able to connect the two facets of his work to produce conclusive results. He was also a perfectionist. Never satisfied with the results of an experiment, he insisted on doing followup after followup and could not bring himself to consider a piece of work finished. The thought of submitting an article and having it rejected by a professional journal was extremely anxiety provoking. Thus, despite his recognized brilliance and several years of careful research, Joe was not able to land anything better than this job as a research associate.

Joe did not like the new job, partly because he thought it was beneath him and also because his activity was even more highly structured than it had been at the drug company. He was working on a research grant in which all the experiments had been planned in advance. Although he complained a good deal about the people who had ruined his career and expressed a lack of interest in the new line of work, he did high-quality work and was tolerated by the others in the laboratory. The salary was extremely important to Joe and Ruth because they now had a young daughter, who was 2 years old. There were also some other features about the job that were attractive to Joe. Much of his work was planned, but he was allowed to use the laboratory in his spare time to pursue his own ideas. It was an active research program, and the department included a number of well-known faculty members. Joe believed that these people, particularly his boss, Dr. Willner, would soon recognize his talent and that he would eventually be able to move into a faculty position.

Things did not work out the way Joe had planned. After he had been working at the university for one year, Dr. Willner asked him to curtail his independent research. He explained that these outside experiments were becoming too expensive and that the main research funded by the grant would require more of the laboratory's time. Joe did not accept this explanation, which he considered to be an obvious excuse to interfere with his personal work. He believed that Dr. Willner had pretended to be disinterested in Joe's work while he actually kept careful tabs on his progress. In fact, he took this interference to indicate that Dr. Willner believed Joe's research was on the verge of a breakthrough. Joe continued to work independently when he had the opportunity and became even more secretive about his ideas. Several weeks after these developments, Dr. Willner hired another research associate and asked Joe to share his office with the new person. Joe, of course, believed that the new person was hired and placed in his office solely to spy on his research.

As the tension mounted at work, Joe's relationship with Ruth became severely strained. They had never had a close or affectionate relationship and now seemed on the verge of open conflict. Ruth recognized that Joe was overreacting to minor events; she did not want him to lose another job. She often tried to talk rationally with him in an effort to help him view these events from a more objective perspective. These talks led to arguments, and Joe finally accused her of collaborating with his enemies. He suggested that the people from the drug company and from the university had persuaded her to help them steal his ideas and then get rid of him. As Joe became more paranoid and belligerent, Ruth became fearful for her own safety and that of her daughter. She eventually took their daughter with her to live with Ruth's parents and began divorce proceedings. Her desertion, as Joe viewed it, provided more evidence that she had been part of the plot all along.

Two weeks after Ruth left, Joe began to experience panic attacks. The first one occurred while he was driving home from work. He was alone in the car, the road was familiar, and the traffic pattern was not particularly congested. Although the temperature was cool, Joe noticed that he was perspiring profusely. His hands and feet began to tingle, and his heart seemed to be beating irregularly. When he began to feel dizzy and faint, he had to pull the car off the road and stop. His shirt was now completely soaked with perspiration, and his breathing was rapid and labored. At the time, he thought that he was going to smother. All in all, it was a terrifying experience. The symptoms disappeared as quickly as they had appeared; within 10 minutes he was able to get back on the road and drive home. He experienced three such incidents within a two-week period and became so concerned about his health that he overcame his distrust of physicians and made an appointment for a physical examination.

The physician was unable to discover any medical disorder and recommended that Joe consult a psychiatrist about his anxiety. Joe reluctantly agreed that a psychiatrist might be of help and arranged an appointment with Dr. Fein. The issue of Joe's paranoid thinking did not come up during his conversations with Dr. Fein because Joe did not consider it to be a problem. Furthermore, he knew that other people thought that he was overly suspicious and that some people would consider him to be mentally ill. He therefore carefully avoided talking about the efforts to steal his ideas and did not mention the plot involving his wife and former colleagues. He simply wanted to know what was causing the panic attacks and how he could control them. At the end of his second session, Dr. Fein suggested that Joe begin taking imipramine (Tofranil®), an antidepressant drug that has also been effective in treating panic anxiety. This suggestion precipitated an extended conversation about the physiological action of mood-stabilizing drugs that escalated into a heated argument.

Joe had been disappointed with Dr. Fein; he did not believe that Dr. Fein understood his problem (i.e., the panic attacks) and resented the many open-ended, probing questions that he asked about Joe's personal life. Dr. Fein believed that he was trying to complete a thorough assessment that would allow him to place this specific problem in an appropriate context, but Joe considered this line of inquiry an invasion of privacy regarding matters for which he had not sought advice. The prospect of taking antidepressant drugs further aroused Joe's suspicions. He began asking Dr. Fein about the neurological mechanisms affected by this drug—a topic with which he was intimately familiar because of his own research at the drug company. He was obviously better versed on this subject than Dr. Fein and concluded that Dr. Fein was therefore incompetent because he recommended a treatment that he could not explain completely. Joe finally ended the conversation by telling Dr. Fein that he thought he was a quack. He stormed out of the office and did not return.

The panic attacks continued at the approximate rate of one a week for the next three months. Joe also noticed that he frequently felt physically ill and nauseated, even on days when he did not experience a panic attack. Searching for an explanation for these escalating problems, and considering his conviction that other people were trying to harm him, he finally borrowed some equipment from another department and checked the radiation levels in his laboratory. He claimed that he found an unusually high level of radiation coming from a new balance that Dr. Willner had recently purchased. That was the final piece of evidence he needed. He believed that the people who were conspiring against him, including Dr. Willner, the people from the drug company, and his wife, had planted the radioactive balance in his laboratory so that he would eventually die from radiation poisoning. It struck him as a clever plot. He spent much more time in the laboratory than anyone else and would therefore receive very high doses of radiation. The others were presumably wearing special clothing to screen them from the radiation, thus further reducing their own risk.

Joe confronted Dr. Willner with this discovery; as expected, Dr. Willner denied any knowledge of radioactivity emanating from the balance. He suggested that Joe should take some time away from the laboratory. He had obviously been under a lot of strain lately, considering the divorce proceedings, and could benefit from the rest. Joe was certain that this was a ruse to allow the conspirators to remove the evidence of what he now called the assassination attempt. He refused to take time off and insisted that he would not let the others steal his ideas. The following day he went to the office of the president of the university to demand a formal investigation. An informal series of meetings was eventually arranged involving various members of the laboratory and representatives of the university administration. Joe also contacted the government agency that funded Dr. Willner's research, which conducted its own investigation. The result of this time-consuming process was that Joe lost his job. No one was able to find any evidence of a conspiracy to harm Joe or steal his ideas. Both investigations concluded that Joe should seek professional help to deal with his unwarranted suspicions.

When he left the university, Joe took a job driving a cab. This final fiasco had ruined his chances of obtaining another research position. No one would write him letters of recommendation. He was, of course, convinced that he had been black-listed and did not consider the possibility that his problems were created by his own antagonistic behavior. In many ways, the change in occupations led to positive changes in Joe's adjustment. He seemed to love driving a cab. He worked late at night, when most other cabbies were sleeping, and was thus in a noncompetitive situation. The people with whom he interacted were not threatening to his sense of intellectual superiority; in fact, he derived considerable enjoyment from telling his friends stories about the derelicts and imbeciles that rode in his cab. Joe was quite content with the situation. He lived by himself in a small apartment, maintained a small circle of friends, and planned to continue working as a cab driver. He was still arrogant and resented his past treatment but seemed resigned to his status as a martyr in the world of chemistry. The need for constant vigilance was greatly reduced because he no longer had access to a laboratory and could not continue to work on his ideas.

Fifteen-Year Followup

Joe had found an occupational and social niche in which he was able to function on a relatively stable basis. He continued to live in the same community, working as a cab driver. Still convinced that Ruth had betrayed him, Joe never tried to contact her again. He had no further contact with his daughter. He remained grandiose, suspicious, and frequently contemptuous of others, but his condition did not deteriorate any further. In fact, he functioned relatively well, given his maladaptive personality traits. His small and rather loose-knit circle of friends afforded him some support and enough companionship to suit his modest needs. Because he did not see himself as having any psychological problems, Joe did not seek additional treatment after his brief encounter with Dr. Fein.

Five years after Ruth left him, Joe developed a relationship with a new girlfriend. Wendy worked as a dispatcher for the cab company. Like his former wife, she was quiet and shy—a perfect complement to his narcissism. Wendy was infatuated with Joe, and he loved to show off for her. He was obviously different in many ways from the other people who worked for the company. Having only a limited education, Wendy was easily impressed by his intelligence and apparent knowledge of the world. She treated him with extreme deference. At work, she helped him to receive special privileges with the hours and routes that he was scheduled to drive (often to the dismay of his fellow drivers). In their blossoming social relationship, Wendy acquiesced to all his interests and demands. They dated for several months, and she eventually moved into his apartment.

Joe hadn't lost his intellectual curiosity or his passion for natural science. He was still fascinated by theoretical issues in chemistry, especially those related to the quality of the environment (our supply of air and water). Wendy encouraged him to pursue these interests and was happy to give him plenty of time on his own to think and write papers. It is not clear whether this activity is best described as an eccentric hobby or the work of a dissident scholar who had been spurned and persecuted by his jealous peers. Joe certainly favored the latter explanation. Because he didn't have access to a lab, his papers were entirely theoretical in nature. The quality of these papers remained unknown because they were never submitted to professional journals. Joe enjoyed these intellectual pursuits and was satisfied by sharing the general outlines of his theory with the nonthreatening people in his nonacademic world—his girlfriend and the customers who rode in his cab.

Joe's grandiosity was still readily apparent to anyone who met him, but his most pronounced paranoid thoughts, such as his concern about the balance in the chemistry lab, were in remission for several years. He privately viewed the grievous end of his professional career as the product of laboratory intrigue and professional jealousies, but he was no longer preoccupied with these thoughts. His competitive instincts were under control because he was not working in an intellectual environment. He did not read professional journals or attend academic meetings. His self-esteem was no longer threatened on a daily basis by comparisons with other people in his field.

Joe's paranoid thoughts were suddenly rekindled by an unexpected news event. One day, while driving his cab, he heard on the radio that the Nobel Prize in chemistry had been awarded to a professor at the university where he had received his bachelor's and doctoral degrees. The recipient, a faculty member in that department for 35 years, had been a member of Joe's dissertation committee when he was in graduate school. Everyone in his field considered this man to be a genius of enormous achievement. He was also known as a man who did not "suffer fools gladly" and could respond sharply when he disagreed with an idea. He had, in fact, criticized part of Joe's dissertation plan in front of the other members of the committee. Although the man was only trying to be helpful, Joe had felt enormous anger and embarrassment. Since that incident, Joe had always described this professor as "a simple-minded, unimaginative charlatan." No one else shared this view, but others hadn't been able to change Joe's bizarre opinion. Joe always considered his own mentor, a senior person who was also a Nobel laureate in chemistry, to be far superior to this other man.

The most shocking aspect of this news story, from Joe's point of view, was the topic of the work for which the prize was awarded: atmospheric chemistry. This subject had been of great interest to Joe for many years. In fact, he had written two lengthy theoretical papers about it while he was still working for the drug company. Joe had presumably developed a revolutionary new theory regarding the ozone layer and the future of the Earth's atmosphere. He believed that, if only anyone would listen, his ideas would dramatically affect the future of the human race. Unfortunately (from his point of view), most other scientists were too stupid to appreciate his ideas. Those who could understand were the people who plotted against him.

Ruminating about the prize, Joe remembered that he had mailed copies of these papers to the chemistry department at his alma mater when he was leaving his job at the drug company and had been desperate for employment. He had applied for a postdoctoral position in another laboratory. Although he was always reluctant to share his ideas with others in the field, he had mailed copies of these papers in the hope of impressing the head of the lab. He hadn't gotten the job. Surely, he reasoned, this other professor (who had now won the Nobel Prize) had obtained the papers, stolen Joe's ideas, and gone on to conduct brilliant research while pretending that the ideas were his own. Once again, Joe believed that he had been cheated—this time out of the world's most prestigious scientific award.

Unfortunately, little could be done. Joe complained bitterly and continuously to his girlfriend, who believed his story and was as sympathetic and supportive as she could be. He knew that he couldn't complain to any of his peers from graduate school or his former colleagues at the university. They hadn't believed him before, and he was certain that they would not support him now. Joe was undoubtedly correct in this appraisal of the situation. He wisely chose not to take action on this grievance or to file any formal complaints with the university. He was quite upset about this story for several weeks, but he also had enough perspective on his own suspicions to know that other people thought he was irrational. He resigned himself once again to living the life of an exile from the scientific community.

Discussion

Personality disorders (PDs) are defined in terms of stable, cross-situational patterns of behavior that lead to impairment in social and occupational functioning or subjective distress. These response patterns are exhibited in a rigid and inflexible manner, despite their maladaptive consequences (Oltmanns & Okada, 2005). The principal features of a paranoid personality are unwarranted suspicion and mistrust of other people. People with this personality disorder are often seen by others as cold, guarded, and defensive; they refuse to accept blame, even if it is justified, and they tend to retaliate at the slightest provocation. *DSM-IV-TR* (APA, 2000, p. 694) lists the following criteria for paranoid personality disorder:

1. A pervasive distrust and suspiciousness of others such that their motives are interpreted as malevolent, beginning by early adulthood and present in a variety of contexts, as indicated by four (or more) or the following:

   A. Suspects, without sufficient basis, that others are exploiting, harming, or deceiving him or her

   B. Is preoccupied with unjustified doubts about the loyalty or trustworthiness of friends or associates

   C. Is reluctant to confide in others because of unwarranted fear that the information will be used maliciously against him or her

   D. Reads hidden demeaning or threatening meanings into benign remarks or events

   E. Persistently bears grudges (for example, is unforgiving of insults, injuries, or slights)

   F. Perceives attacks on his or her character or reputation that are not apparent to others and is quick to react angrily or to counterattack

    G. Has recurrent suspicions, without justification, regarding fidelity of spouse or sexual partner

2. Does not occur exclusively during the course of schizophrenia, a mood disorder with psychotic features, or another psychotic disorder

These characteristics are not limited to periods of acute disturbance; they are typical of the person's behavior over a long period of time.

    Personality disorders are among the most controversial categories included in *DSM-IV-TR* (Kendell, 2002; Potter, 2004). Part of the controversy derives from a debate regarding personality traits and situational specificity of behavior. Social learning theorists have argued that human behavior is largely determined by the context in which it occurs and not by internal personality characteristics. It has been demonstrated, however, that ratings of personality traits are useful predictors of behavior, especially when the ratings are made by several observers, the observers are thoroughly familiar with the people who are being rated, observations are made on a number of occasions, and the ratings are made on dimensions that are publicly observable (Funder, 1999). The definition of paranoid personality disorder does not assume that people so diagnosed will always be suspicious, guarded, or tense, regardless of the context, but it does assume that they *often* behave in this manner and that they are *more likely* than nonparanoid people to behave in this manner.

    Two other issues also contribute to the controversial status of the personality disorders. One involves reliability. For many years, interrater reliability for personality disorders was considerably lower than it was for many other disorders. This situation has improved, partly because of the introduction of structured interview schedules aimed specifically at personality disorders. Several studies have evaluated the reliability of diagnostic decisions based on these interviews. Mean interrater reliabilities (measured using the kappa statistic and averaged across several studies) are all higher than .60 for specific personality disorder categories (Clark & Harrison, 2001; Zanarini et al., 2000; Zimmerman, 1994).[1] Lowest reliability is often found for paranoid personality disorder (average of .62), and higher reliability tends to be associated with antisocial personality disorder (average of .77). These results indicate that some personality disorders can be diagnosed reliably by trained clinicians who use structured diagnostic interviews. But the fact that kappa values for some categories are consistently below .70 suggests that skepticism is still warranted with regard to the reliability of diagnosing personality disorders.

    Another issue that must be mentioned with regard to the personality disorders is the overlap between diagnostic categories (Grant et al., 2005). Many patients meet the criteria for more than one form of personality disorder. Among people who meet the criteria for paranoid personality disorder, the most frequent comorbid conditions are schizotypal, narcissistic, borderline, and avoidant personality disorders (Bernstein, Useda, & Siever, 1995). Extensive overlap among Axis II categories

---

[1] The statistic known as kappa takes into account the probability of agreement by chance. A kappa value of zero indicates agreement that is no better than chance. A kappa of +1.0 would indicate perfect agreement between raters. Although there is no single criterion for interpreting this statistic, kappa values greater than .70 are often considered to indicate a good level of agreement.

indicates that the specific types of personality disorder listed in *DSM-IV-TR* (APA, 2000) may not be the most efficient or meaningful way to describe this particular type of abnormal behavior.

Joe's case illustrates the overlap among different types of personality disorders. In addition to paranoid PD, Joe also met the *DSM-IV-TR* (APA, 2000, p. 717) criteria for narcissistic PD, which requires that the person exhibit five (or more) of the following features:

1. Has a grandiose sense of self-importance (for example, exaggerates achievements and talents, expects to be recognized as superior without commensurate achievements)

2. Is preoccupied with fantasies of unlimited success, power, brilliance, beauty, or ideal love

3. Believes that he or she is "special" and unique, and can only be understood by, or should associate with, other special or high-status people (or institutions)

4. Requires excessive admiration

5. Has a sense of entitlement (that is, unreasonable expectations of especially favorable treatment or automatic compliance with his or her expectations)

6. Is interpersonally exploitative (that is, takes advantage of others to achieve his or her own ends)

7. Lacks empathy: is unwilling to recognize or identify with the feelings and needs of others

8. Is often envious of others or believes that others are envious of him or her

9. Shows arrogant, haughty behaviors or attitudes

Joe's inflated sense of his own intellectual abilities and scientific accomplishments clearly fits the pattern for narcissistic personality disorder. He also exhibited the lack of empathy and feelings of entitlement that are described in these criteria. In addition to these characteristics, his behavior was arrogant and occasionally exploitative.

The principal issue regarding differential diagnosis and paranoid PD concerns the distinction between this category and delusional disorder, in which the patients exhibit persistent persecutory delusions or delusional jealousy. Delusional disorder is listed on Axis I, while paranoid personality is listed on Axis II. The paranoid ideas in paranoid personality disorders are presumably not of sufficient severity to be considered delusional, but the criteria to be used in making this distinction are not entirely clear. When does pervasive suspicion and mistrust become a paranoid belief? The two categories may be etiologically distinct, but it has not been demonstrated that they carry different treatment implications. *DSM-IV-TR* (APA, 2000) lists the categories separately, but the reliability and validity of the two categories remain open questions (Bernstein, Useda, & Siever, 1995).

Personality disorders seem to be among the most common forms of abnormal behavior. It is difficult to provide empirical support for that claim, however, be-

cause the existing epidemiological data are inconsistent. The overall lifetime prevalence of Axis II disorders (i.e., having at least one type of PD) varies between 10
and 14 percent in samples of adults who are not in treatment for a mental disorder
(Samuels et al., 2002; Torgersen, Kringlen, & Cramer, 2001). Rates for specific
disorders vary from one study to the next, depending on the type of assessment procedure that was used and the way in which the sample of subjects was identified.
Several studies that used structured interviews with community residents have reported a lifetime prevalence of approximately 1 percent for paranoid personality
disorder (Mattia & Zimmerman, 2001).

Followup studies indicate that delusional disorder and paranoid personality
characteristics are typically long-term problems that change relatively little over
time (Seivewright, Tyrer, & Johnson, 2002; Stephens, Richard, & McHugh, 2000).
For many patients, their paranoid beliefs become more pronounced over time.

Psychological Theories

Several theories have been proposed that attempt to account for the development of
paranoid ideas (Fenigstein, 1996; Miller et al., 2001). Perhaps the earliest hypothesis regarding paranoia was suggested by Freud (1909, 1925) in his analysis of the
memoirs of Daniel Paul Schreber, an accomplished lawyer who had spent close to
14 years of his life in mental hospitals. Schreber's problems centered on an elaborate set of persecutory and grandiose delusions, including the notion that he would
be transformed into a woman. Following this transformation, Schreber believed that
he would become God's mate and that they would produce a better and healthier
race of people. Freud argued that the content of Schreber's delusions revealed the
presence of an unconscious homosexual wish-fantasy. This hidden desire was taken
to be the core of the conflict motivating paranoid ideas. The process presumably
begins with the unacceptable thought that "I (a man) love him (a man)." To avoid
the anxiety associated with the conscious realization of this idea, the thought is
transformed to its opposite: "I do not love him—I *hate* him because he persecutes
me."

At least two aspects of Joe's case might be consistent with this psychodynamic
model. He occasionally made comments about other men's sexual orientation, particularly when he was trying to embarrass them. We might infer from these remarks
that he was concerned about his own sexual desires, but we do not have any direct
evidence to validate this conclusion. His only sexual experiences had been with
women, and he did not express ambivalence about his interest in women. Joe's
panic attacks might also fit into Freud's model, which suggests that Joe was using
the defense mechanism of projection to avoid the anxiety associated with unconscious homosexual impulses. It could be argued that the panic attacks represented a
spilling over of excess anxiety that was not being handled efficiently by projection
and other secondary defense mechanisms such as repression. Once again, the
model seems plausible, but it cannot be tested directly.

An alternative explanation for the development of paranoid delusions was proposed by Cameron (1959). He argued that predelusional patients are anxious, fear-

ful, socially withdrawn, and reluctant to confide in other people. This suggestion is consistent with recent evidence indicating that people with paranoid personality disorder are more likely than other people to have experienced anxiety disorders when they were children (Kasen et al., 2001). Cameron went on to point out that social isolation leads to a deficiency in social skills. In particular, he argued that predelusional patients are less adept than others in understanding the motivations of other people. They are therefore more likely to misinterpret other people's behavior and, having done so, are also less able to elicit disconfirming evidence from their peers. From time to time, most of us have thought that someone else was angry with us or trying to do us harm when, in fact, they were not. We usually come to realize our mistake by talking to our friends about what happened. Cameron's argument was that predelusional patients are even more likely to misinterpret other people's behavior and, given an instance of misinterpretation, are also less able to correct the mistake through interaction with other people. According to Cameron's hypothesis, this cycle is perpetuated by the paranoid person's subsequent behavior. For example, someone who believes that his relatives are plotting against him is likely to behave in a hostile, defensive manner when his relatives are present. They, in turn, may become angry and irritable in response to his apparently unprovoked hostility, thus confirming the paranoid person's original suspicion that they are out to get him. Thus, Cameron's formulation allows for a complex interaction of personality traits, social skills, and environmental events.

Several elements of Cameron's theory seem applicable in Joe's case. He was not particularly withdrawn and fearful, but he was reluctant to confide in other people. He tended to be a "loner" and felt awkward in social situations such as parties. His habit of laughing at people and provoking arguments would indicate that he was not sensitive to their feelings and point of view, as suggested by Cameron. Perhaps most important is the effect that Joe's behavior had on other people. He was completely unable to consider the possibility that other people talked about him and avoided him because he was initially hostile and belligerent.

Colby (1975, 1977) proposed an information-processing view of paranoid thinking in which the principal feature is sensitivity to shame and humiliation. The model focuses exclusively on verbal interactions. In the "paranoid mode" of processing, people presumably scan linguistic input for comments or questions that might lead to the experience of shame (defined as "a rise in the truth value of a belief that the self is inadequate"). Faced with the threat of humiliation, the person in the paranoid mode responds by denying personal inadequacy and blaming others. The theory implies that paranoia is associated with low self-esteem and that episodes of paranoid behavior may be triggered by environmental circumstances that increase the threat of shame (e.g., failure, ridicule). Other negative emotions, most notably fear and anger, are presumably not likely to elicit paranoid responses. Some indirect support for this hypothesis comes from the observation that the family members of patients with paranoid disorders are more likely than people in the general population to exhibit feelings of inferiority (Kendler & Hays, 1981; Webb & Levinson, 1993).

Colby's model provides a plausible explanation for Joe's problems at the drug company and the university laboratory; his paranoid comments provided a rationale for his own failure to succeed. Joe was a brilliant chemist, but he had not developed a successful, independent line of research. The limitations of his work were particularly evident after he had been allowed some independence at the drug company. Joe's supervisors finally became so disappointed with his progress that he was reassigned to more structured projects. Shortly after this demotion, his suspicions began to reach delusional proportions. Colby would probably argue that Joe chose to blame his colleagues' interference for failures that would otherwise indicate his own professional inadequacy. The shame-humiliation model also accounts for Joe's later improvement following his change of occupations. As a cab driver, Joe was removed from the field of professional competition in which he was continually exposed to threatening messages. He was reasonably successful as a cab driver, and his self-esteem did not suffer in comparison to the people with whom he usually interacted. There was therefore little need for him to behave in a hostile or defensive manner. His paranoid beliefs did emerge again, however, when he heard about the professor who won the Nobel Prize. This man's success may have, once again, reminded him of his own disappointing career.

Treatment

Psychotherapy can be beneficial for patients with various kinds of personality disorder (Beck, Freeman, & Davis, 2004; Robins & Chapman, 2004). Unfortunately, relatively little evidence is available with regard to the effects of treatment for paranoid PD. Clinical experience suggests that therapy is often of limited value with paranoid patients because it is so difficult to establish a trusting therapeutic relationship with them (Bernstein, 2001). Joe's case is a good example. He expected the therapist to help him cope with his anxiety but was unwilling to discuss his problems at anything other than a superficial level. This defensive attitude would hamper most attempts to engage in traditional, insight-oriented psychotherapy. The client-centered approach developed by Carl Rogers might be more effective with paranoid clients because it fosters a nonthreatening environment. The therapist must also be careful to avoid the display of excessive friendliness or sympathy, however, because it might be interpreted as an attempt to deceive the patient (Akhtar, 1992). From Colby's point of view, Rogers's emphasis on the provision of accurate empathy and unconditional positive regard would also be likely to bolster the paranoid's fragile self-esteem and thereby reduce his or her sensitivity to potential embarrassment. Unfortunately, there are no data available to support this type of speculation.

Cameron's model might lead to a more directive form of intervention focused on the development of specific social skills. For example, various situations might be constructed in order to demonstrate to the client the manner in which his or her behavior affects other people. Similarly, the therapist might practice various social interactions with the client in an effort to improve his or her ability to discuss initial social impressions. It might also be possible to improve the client's ability to read social cues. This behavioral approach would be used in an effort to expand the client's repertoire of appropriate social behaviors so that the client could respond more flexibly to specific situational demands.

Cognitive therapy also has interesting applications for the treatment of paranoid patients. The central assumption of this approach is that personality disorders are associated with deeply ingrained, maladaptive beliefs (Beck et al., 2004). In the case of paranoid personality, these include thoughts such as "people cannot be trusted" and "if I get close to people, they will find out my weaknesses and hurt me." The therapist works with the client to identify and recognize these cognitive distortions and their influence on the person's behavior. The paranoid person is encouraged to test the validity of these maladaptive thoughts. Over time, the goal is to help the person learn to replace them with more adaptive thoughts and more accurate attributions (Kinderman, 2001).

When paranoid ideas reach delusional proportions, the use of antipsychotic medication may also be considered. These drugs are effective in the treatment of schizophrenia, but their effect has usually been measured in terms of global improvement ratings; it is not clear if they have an equally positive effect on all of the symptoms of schizophrenia. In fact, a few studies have examined changes in specific symptoms and concluded that antipsychotic drugs are most likely to have a positive effect on auditory hallucinations and disorganized speech. Paranoid delusions are among the *least* responsive symptoms (Manschreck, 1992). Thus, in the absence of other schizophrenic symptoms, patients with paranoid delusions are not likely to benefit from drug treatment.

CHAPTER 19

Borderline Personality Disorder

Amanda Siegel was 22 years old when she reluctantly agreed to interrupt her college semester and admit herself for the eighth time to a psychiatric hospital. Her psychologist, Dr. Swenson, and her psychiatrist, Dr. Smythe, believed that neither psychotherapy nor medication was controlling her symptoms and that continuing outpatient treatment would be too risky. Amanda was experiencing brief but terrifying episodes in which she felt that her body was not real. She sometimes reacted by cutting herself with a knife in order to feel pain, so she would feel real. During the first part of the admission interview at the hospital, Amanda angrily denied that she had done anything self-destructive. The anger dissolved, however, and she was soon in tears as she recounted her fears that she would fail her midterm examinations and be expelled from college. The admitting psychiatrist also noted that at times Amanda behaved in a flirtatious manner, asking inappropriately personal questions such as whether any of the psychiatrist's girlfriends were in the hospital.

When she arrived at the inpatient psychiatric unit, Amanda once again became quite angry. She protested loudly, using obscene and abusive language when the nurse searched her luggage for illegal drugs and sharp objects, even though Amanda was very familiar with this routine procedure. These impulsive outbursts of anger were quite characteristic of Amanda. She would often express anger at an intensity level that was out of proportion to the situation. When she became this angry, she would typically do or say something that she later regretted, such as verbally abusing a close friend or breaking a prized possession. In spite of the negative consequences of these actions and Amanda's ensuing guilt and regret, she was unable to stop losing control of her anger.

That same day Amanda filed a "three-day notice," a written statement expressing an intention to leave the hospital within 72 hours. Dr. Swenson told Amanda that if she did not agree to remain in the hospital voluntarily, he would initiate legal proceedings for her involuntary commitment on the grounds that she was a threat to herself. Two days later, Amanda retracted the three-day notice, and her anger seemed to subside.

Over the next two weeks, Amanda appeared to be getting along rather well. Despite some complaints of feeling depressed, she was always well dressed and groomed, in contrast to many of the other patients. Except for occasional episodes when she became verbally abusive and slammed doors, Amanda appeared and acted like a staff member. She began to adopt a "therapist" role with the other patients, listening intently to their problems and suggesting solutions. She would often serve as a spokesperson for the more disgruntled patients, expressing their concerns and complaints to the administrators of the treatment unit. With the help of her therapist, Amanda also wrote a contract stating that she would not hurt herself and that she would notify staff members if she began to have thoughts of doing so. Since her safety was no longer as big of a concern, she was allowed a number of passes off the unit with other patients and friends.

Amanda became particularly attached to several staff members and arranged one-to-one talks with them as often as possible. She used these talks to flatter and compliment the staff members and tell them that they were one of the few who truly understood her and could help her, and she also complained to them about alleged incompetence and lack of professionalism among other staff members. Some of these staff members Amanda was attached to had trouble confronting Amanda when she broke the rules. For example, when she was late returning from a pass off grounds, it was often overlooked. If she was confronted, especially by someone with whom she felt she had a special relationship, she would feel betrayed and, as if an emotional switch had flipped, would lash out angrily and accuse that person of being "just like the rest of them."

By the end of the third week of hospitalization, Amanda no longer appeared to be in acute distress, and the staff began to plan for her discharge. At about this time, Amanda began to drop hints in her therapy sessions with Dr. Swenson that she had been withholding some kind of secret. Dr. Swenson addressed this issue in therapy and encouraged her to be more open and direct if there was something she needed to talk about. She then revealed that since her second day in the hospital, she had been receiving illegal street drugs from two friends who visited her. Besides occasionally using the drugs herself, Amanda had been giving them to other patients on the unit. This situation was quickly brought to the attention of all the other patients on the unit in a meeting called by Dr. Swenson. During the meeting, Amanda protested that the other patients had forced her to bring them drugs and that she actually had no choice in the matter. Dr. Swenson didn't believe Amanda's explanation and instead thought that Amanda had found it intolerable to be denied approval and found it impossible to say no.

Soon after this meeting, Amanda experienced another episode of feeling as if she were unreal and cut herself a number of times across her wrists with a soda can she had broken in half. The cuts were deep enough to draw blood but were not life threatening. In contrast to previous incidents, she did not try to hide her injuries and several staff members therefore concluded that Amanda was exaggerating the severity of her problems to avoid discharge from the hospital. The members of Amanda's treatment team then met to decide the best course of action.

Not everyone agreed about Amanda's motivation for cutting herself. Amanda was undoubtedly self-destructive and possibly suicidal. Therefore, she needed further hospitalization. But she had been sabotaging the treatment of other patients and could not be trusted to refrain from doing so again. With the members of her treatment team split on the question of whether or not Amanda should be allowed to remain in the hospital, designing a coherent treatment program would prove difficult at best.

Social History

Amanda was the older of two daughters born to a suburban middle-class family. She was 2 years old when her sister Megan was born. Amanda's mother and father divorced four years later, leaving the children in their mother's custody. The family had significant financial difficulties because Amanda's father provided little child support. He remarried soon afterward and was generally unavailable to his original family. He never remembered the children on birthdays or holidays. When Amanda was 7 years old, her mother began working as a waitress in a neighborhood restaurant. Neighbors would check in on Amanda and Megan after school, but the children were left largely unattended until their mother returned home from work in the evening. So at a very early age, Amanda assumed a caregiver role toward her younger sister. Over the next few years, Amanda took on a number of household responsibilities, like regular meal preparation and shopping, that were more appropriate for a teenager. She did not complain about the situation and behaved well at home and in school. However, she remained distressed about the absence of her father. Had she somehow had something to do with the divorce? How much better would her life have been if her father were with her?

When Amanda was 13 years old, her mother married a man she had been dating for about three months. The man, Arthur Siegel, had a 16-year-old son named Michael who joined the household on a somewhat sporadic basis. Michael had been moving back and forth between his mother's and father's houses since their divorce four years earlier. His mother had legal custody but could not manage his abusive and aggressive behaviors, so she frequently sent him to live with his father for several weeks or months. Because Amanda still secretly hoped that her mother and father would remarry, she resented the intrusion of her stepfather and stepbrother into the household and was quite upset when her mother changed her and her children's last name to Siegel. She also resented the loss of some of her caregiving responsibilities, which were now shared with her mother and stepfather.

Soon after her mother and stepfather married, Michael began sexually abusing Amanda. Michael told Amanda that it was important for her to learn about sex and after raping her threatened that if she ever told anyone he would tell all her friends that she was a "slut." When this occurred, she had not been sexually active with anyone. This pattern of abuse continued on numerous occasions whenever Michael was living with his father. Even though Amanda was traumatized by the abuse, she felt unable to refuse participation or to let anyone know what was occurring.

Amanda's behavior began to deteriorate. She had been doing very well academically in the seventh grade and then began to skip classes. Her grades fell precipitously over the course of a semester, and she began spending time with peers who were experimenting with alcohol and street drugs. Amanda became a frequent user of these drugs, even though she experienced some frightening symptoms after taking them (e.g., vivid visual hallucinations and strong feelings of paranoia). By the end of the eighth grade, Amanda's grades were so poor and her school attendance so erratic that it was recommended that she be evaluated by a psychologist and possibly held back for a year. Amanda was given a fairly extensive battery of intelligence, achievement, and projective tests. She was found to be extremely intelligent, with an IQ of 130. Projective test results (Rorschach, Thematic Apperception Test) were interpreted as reflecting a significant degree of underlying anger, which was believed to be contributing to Amanda's behavioral problems. Of more concern was that Amanda gave a number of bizarre and confused responses on the projective tests. For example, when people report what they "see" in the famous Rorschach inkblots, it is usually easy for the tester to share the client's perception. Several of Amanda's responses, however, just didn't match any discernible features of the inkblots. The psychologist, although having no knowledge of Amanda's home life, suspected that her problems may have reflected her difficulties at home and recommended family therapy at a local community mental health center.

Several months later Amanda and her mother and sister had their first appointment with a social worker at the mental health center. Mr. Siegel was distrustful of the prospect of therapy and refused to attend, stating, "No shrink is going to mess with my head!" In the ensuing therapy, the social worker first took a detailed family history. She noticed that Amanda appeared very guarded and was reluctant to share any feelings about or perceptions of the events of her life. The next phase of family therapy was more educational in nature, consisting of teaching Mrs. Siegel more effective methods of discipline and helping Amanda to see the importance of attending school on a regular basis.

Family therapy ended after three months with only marginal success. Although Mrs. Siegel had been a highly motivated client and diligently followed the therapist's suggestions, Amanda remained a reluctant participant in the therapy and was unwilling to open up. She never disclosed the sexual abuse she was experiencing. She felt depressed and guilty, with a very low opinion of herself.

When Amanda was 15 years old, her mother and Mr. Siegel divorced, ending the abuse at the hands of Michael. When Amanda began high school, she continued her association with the same peer group she had known in junior high. They all regularly abused drugs. Amanda had her first experiences of feeling unreal and dissociated from her surroundings while under the influence of drugs. She felt as though she were ghostlike, that she was transparent and could pass through objects or people.

Amanda also began a pattern of promiscuous sexual activity. As happened when she was being abused by her stepbrother, she felt guilty for engaging in sex but was unable to turn down sexual advances, from either men or women. She was particularly vulnerable when under the influence of drugs and would, under some circumstances, participate in various sadomasochistic sexual activities. For example, Amanda was sometimes physically abused, such as being punched in the face, by her sexual partners while having sex. She didn't protest and, after a while, expected such violence. Sometimes Amanda's sexual partners would ask her to inflict some kind of pain on them during sexual activity, for example, biting during fellatio or digging her nails into her partner's buttocks. Even though these activities left Amanda with a sense of shame and guilt, she felt unable either to set limits, to break off these relationships or her friendships with people in that group, or to avoid those whose sexual activities upset her.

By the time Amanda was 16 years old, she never wanted to be alone. She was often bored and depressed, particularly if she had no plans for spending time with anyone else. An important incident occurred at about this time. One night while cruising in a car with friends, they were pulled over by the police because the car had been stolen by one of her friends. Street drugs were also found in the car. Amanda claimed that she had not known that the car was stolen. The judge who heard the case was concerned about the progressive deterioration in Amanda's academic performance and social functioning. Because previous outpatient treatment had failed, he recommended inpatient treatment to help her gain some control over her impulses and prevent future legal and psychological problems. Amanda was being offered a choice between being prosecuted as an accessory to car theft and for possession of illegal substances, or signing into a mental hospital. Reluctantly, she chose the hospitalization.

During her first hospitalization, Amanda's mood swings seemed to intensify. She vacillated between outbursts of anger and feelings of emptiness and depression. She showed signs of depression, such as lack of appetite and insomnia. Antidepressant medication was tried for several weeks and found to be ineffective. Amanda spent most of her time with a male patient in the hospital. To any observer, their relationship would not have seemed to have a romantic component. They watched TV together, ate together, and played various games that were available on the ward. After only a couple of meetings with him, Amanda had revealed the most intimate details of her life. There was no physical contact or romantic talk. Nonetheless, Amanda idealized the man and had fantasies of marrying him. When he was discharged from the hospital and broke off the relationship, Amanda had her first nondrug-induced episode of feeling unreal (derealization) and subsequently cut herself with a kitchen knife in order to feel real. She began making suicide threats over the telephone to the former patient, saying that if he did not take her back she would kill herself. She was given a short trial of an antipsychotic medication, which proved as ineffective as the antidepressants had.

While in the hospital, Amanda started individual psychotherapy, which was continued after her discharge from the hospital. The therapy was psychodynamically oriented and focused on helping Amanda to establish a trusting relationship with a caring adult (her therapist). The therapist also attempted to help Amanda understand the intrapsychic conflicts that had started very early in her life. For example, the therapist hypothesized that her biological parents' divorce, and Amanda's idea that she was somehow responsible for it, led to her fear of being abandoned by people who were important to her. One of the therapist's goals was to show Amanda that he would still be available and would not leave her regardless of how she behaved. It was hoped that this would help Amanda to feel more secure in her interpersonal relationships.

Despite these therapy sessions, which she thought were helpful, Amanda continued to experience problems with drug abuse, promiscuity, depression, feelings of boredom, episodes of intense anger, suicide threats, derealization, and self-injurious behavior, such as cutting herself. Several hospitalizations were required when Amanda's threats and self-injurious behavior became particularly intense or frequent. These were usually precipitated by stressful interpersonal events, such as breaking up with a boyfriend, or discussing emotionally charged issues, such as the sexual abuse by Michael in psychotherapy. Most of the hospitalizations were relatively brief, lasting one to two weeks, and Amanda was discharged after the precipitating crisis had been resolved. She received a number of diagnoses during these hospitalizations, including brief psychotic disorder, major depressive episode, atypical anxiety disorder, adjustment disorder with mixed emotional features, substance use disorder, adjustment disorder with mixed disturbances of emotion and conduct, and borderline personality disorder.

During one of these hospitalizations, Amanda decided that she wanted to change therapists, and after careful consideration her treatment team decided to grant her request. When Amanda was 19 years old, she was introduced to Dr. Swenson, a psychologist, and she began individual behaviorally oriented psychotherapy with him.

Conceptualization and Treatment

As opposed to Amanda's previous therapist, Dr. Swenson's approach was more focused and more directive, concentrating on helping Amanda solve specific problems and behave in ways that would be more personally rewarding. At the same time, Dr. Swenson did not try to force change on her. He was empathic and accepting, and gave her the opportunity to identify areas that she wanted to work on. Over a number of sessions, Amanda and Dr. Swenson identified several problem areas: (1) lack of direction or goals, (2) feelings of depression, (3) poor impulse control, and (4) excessive and poorly controlled anger. Specific interventions were designed for each of these areas. Concerning the first problem, Amanda had done so poorly in her schoolwork and was so far behind that going back to high school to graduate was not realistic. Amanda therefore decided to study to take an examination for a General Equivalency Diploma, which would then allow her to pursue further education or job training. Amanda passed the exam after studying for approximately four months. This success enhanced her self-esteem because she had never before maintained the self-discipline necessary to accomplish any but the most short-term goals.

Because antidepressants had not helped Amanda in the past, her depression was treated with cognitive therapy based on the assumption that a person's thoughts can influence her mood. In order to help Amanda become more aware of the thoughts that might make her more vulnerable to depression, she was asked to keep a written record of her mood three times daily. Next to her mood she wrote down what she was thinking, particularly those thoughts that involved predictions about how a given situation might turn out. Through this exercise Amanda came to realize that she often made negative predictions about how events would turn out and subsequently felt sad and depressed.

In order to learn to restructure or "talk back" to these negative thoughts, Amanda was given another exercise. When faced with an anxiety-provoking situation, Amanda was asked to write three different scenarios for the situation: (1) a worst-case scenario in which everything that could go wrong did go wrong, (2) a best-case scenario in which events turned out just as she wanted, and (3) a scenario that she believed was most likely to occur. The actual outcome was then compared with the three different predicted outcomes. More often than not, the actual events were markedly different from either the best- or worst-case predictions. With time, this exercise helped Amanda control some of her more negative thoughts and replace them with more adaptive and realistic ways of thinking that were based on her own experiences.

One example of the use of cognitive therapy had to do with Amanda's difficulties keeping a job. She held numerous part-time jobs that lasted for one or two months before she quit or was fired for not showing up to work. She typically believed that people at work, especially her supervisors, did not like her to begin with and were looking for excuses to fire her. After the smallest of negative interactions with someone at work, Amanda assumed that she was about to be fired. She then stopped showing up to work, creating a self-fulfilling prophecy. Through monitoring her mood, she came to see that the predominant emotion she experienced in these situations was fear that she would be rejected by either her coworkers or supervisors. In order to prevent that, she typically rejected them first. After Amanda obtained a part-time job in a supermarket, her therapist had her write out the three scenarios mentioned, prior to actually starting work. Her scenarios were as follows:

[worst case] I'll show up to work and nobody will like me. Nobody will show me how to do my job, and they will probably make fun of me because I'm new there. I'll probably quit after one day.

[best case] This will be a job that I can finally do well. It will be the kind of work I have always wanted, and I'll be promoted quickly and earn a high salary. Everyone at work will like me.

[most likely] I'm new at work, but everyone else was new at one time, too. Some people may like me, and some may not, but that's the way it is with everyone. Some conflict with other people is inevitable. I can still do my job even if everyone does not like me. One bad day at work does not mean I have to quit.

Amanda was instructed to rehearse mentally the "most likely" scenario daily, especially when she felt like quitting. This helped her to keep the part-time job in the supermarket for 18 months, substantially longer than she had kept previous jobs.

Amanda had a number of problems with impulsiveness, drug abuse, self-mutilation, promiscuity, and anger. Dr. Swenson convinced her to join Narcotics Anonymous (NA), a nonprofessional self-help group for drug addicts based on the same principles as Alcoholics Anonymous. Whenever Amanda had an impulse to use drugs, she was to use a technique called time delay. This involves a commitment not to use drugs for at least 15 minutes and during that time to engage in an alternative activity. This alternative activity could be telephoning another member of NA for help in controlling the impulse to use drugs. A similar approach was taken with Amanda's self-mutilating behaviors; she was instructed to telephone Dr. Swenson or go to a hospital emergency room if she thought she could not control the impulse on her own. Since Amanda's problems with anger concerned the impulsive manner in which she acted it out, this too was handled with similar procedures. Dr. Swenson attempted to help Amanda see anger not as a negative emotion but as a positive emotion that becomes destructive only when it is too intense. He then taught Amanda time-delay procedures to help her wait before expressing anger. During the waiting period the intensity of the emotion declined, and she had an opportunity to think over different ways of dealing with the situation, possibly resulting in a more appropriate expression of anger.

Amanda made noticeable progress over the first few months of therapy with Dr. Swenson, showing a marked decline in her symptoms. She felt optimistic for the first time in a long while. However, this optimism soon deteriorated in the face of conflicts at home. For example, Amanda did not want to help maintain the household, either financially or by doing work around the house. She insisted that it was her mother's responsibility to take care of her. She also wanted her boyfriends to be able to spend the night with her, which her mother would not allow. Amanda's mother then asked her to move out of the house, but Amanda refused. Instead, she threatened suicide, superficially cut her wrists with a razor blade, and had to be rehospitalized. Amanda followed this same pattern over the next few years, making apparent gains in therapy for a month or so and then falling back in the face of interpersonal conflict. Each time her problems returned, they seemed increasingly stressful for Amanda because she usually came to believe during her periods of relative stability that her problems had been "cured."

When Amanda was 22 years old, she decided to attend college on a full-time basis while living at home. Dr. Swenson was opposed to this because Amanda had not shown enough psychological stability to complete even a semester of college, let alone a degree program. She went to college anyway and soon became sexually involved with another student. As with previous relationships, Amanda idealized this boyfriend and became quite dependent on him. She had to be the sole focus of his attention and couldn't tolerate the times when they were apart. After an argument in which Amanda smashed plates and glasses on the floor, her boyfriend left her. Amanda once again became suicidal and self-destructive. This episode led to the hospitalization described at the beginning of this chapter.

Amanda's treatment team at the hospital noted that none of the therapeutic interventions attempted with Amanda (e.g., medication, insight-oriented psychotherapy, behavior therapy) had had any lasting impact. Amanda had a poor employment history and showed little evidence that she would be able to support herself independently in the foreseeable future. It was also feared that she might continue to deteriorate, perhaps winding up in a state hospital on a long-term basis. It was decided that Dr. Swenson needed help in working with Amanda, especially because her symptoms tended to worsen after dealing with difficult issues in therapy. She was referred to a day-treatment program at a local hospital, where she would have regular access to staff members who could provide therapy and support, while living outside the hospital and possibly working part-time at an entry-level unskilled job. The treatment team realized that it would require a great deal of work to convince Amanda to accept these recommendations because accepting them would be an admission that she was more seriously disturbed than she cared to admit. Even if she did follow the recommendations, Amanda's prognosis was guarded.

Discussion

As an Axis II diagnosis in *DSM-IV-TR* (APA, 2000), borderline personality describes a set of inflexible and maladaptive traits that characterize a person's long-term functioning. A person with borderline personality disorder has instability in relationships, behavior, mood, and self-image (Sanislow, Grilo, & McGlashen, 2000). For example, attitudes and feelings toward other people may vary considerably and inexplicably over short periods of time. Emotions are also erratic and can shift abruptly, particularly to anger. People with borderline personality disorder are argumentative, irritable, and sarcastic. Their unpredictable and impulsive behavior, such as suicide attempts, gambling, spending, sex, and eating sprees, is potentially self-damaging. They have not developed a clear and coherent sense of self and remain uncertain about their values, loyalties, and choice of career. They cannot bear to be alone and have fears of abandonment. They tend to have a series of intense one-on-one relationships that are usually stormy and transient, alternating between idealization (the other person is perfect and can do no wrong) and devaluation (the other person is horrible, worthless). Subject to chronic feelings of depression and emptiness, they make manipulative attempts at suicide. Paranoid ideation and dissociative symptoms may appear during periods of high stress. Amanda's interpersonal relationships were both intense and unstable. She was very impulsive, couldn't control her anger, and had an unstable self-image. She clearly met the diagnostic criteria for borderline personality disorder.

A voluminous literature on patients with borderline personality disorder has been published over the last few decades. Although this category was not included in the first or second edition of the *DSM* (APA, 1952, 1968), it was still widely used in certain areas of the country. Originally, the diagnosis implied that the person was on the borderline between neurosis and psychosis. The term no longer has this connotation.

Borderline personality disorder has a lifetime prevalence of 1 to 2 percent and may be somewhat more prevalent among women than men (Bohus, Schmahl, & Lieb, 2004). Though the *DSM-IV-TR* (APA, 2000) reported 75 percent of those diagnosed with the disorder are women, this is likely due to the greater numbers of women seeking treatment and the actual prevalence by gender is unclear (Skodol & Bender, 2003). The disorder typically begins in adolescence (McGlashan, 1983). Borderline personality disorder often occurs with other disorders, especially major depression, eating disorders, post-traumatic stress disorder, and substance abuse (Lieb, Zanarini, Schmahl, Linehan, & Bohus, 2004). On several occasions, Amanda met the diagnostic criteria for an episode of major depression with depressed mood, suicidal thoughts, insomnia, poor appetite, and feelings of self-reproach and guilt. About 75 percent of those diagnosed with borderline personality disorder attempt suicide, and about 10 percent eventually do commit suicide (Black, Blum, Pfohl, & Hale, 2004). Borderline personality disorder, like the other personality disorders, has high levels of comorbidity with several other personality disorders, including antisocial, histrionic, narcissistic, and schizotypal (Becker, Grilo, Edell, & McGlashen, 2000; Skodol, Oldham, & Gallaher, 1999).

Both environmental and biological variables have been studied in an attempt to discover the etiology of borderline personality disorder, and a diathesis-stress theory appears promising (e.g., Linehan, 1993). The main stressors appear to lie in family relations. Patients with borderline personality disorder report that their families were low in support and closeness and high in conflict (Klonsky, Oltmanns, Turkheimer, & Fiedler, 2000). As with Amanda's case, they also report high levels of physical and sexual abuse (Silk, Lee, Hill, & Lohr, 1995), which have been validated in one report (Johnson, Cohen, Brown Smailes, & Bernstein, 1999). Patients with borderline personality disorder have often experienced separation from parents or lack of parental support during childhood (Sansone & Levitt, 2005). Linehan (1993) proposes that the key factor is what she calls an invalidating environment. In an invalidating environment, a person's needs and feelings are disrespected, and efforts to communicate feelings are ignored or punished.

A number of studies have explored the neurobiology of borderline personality disorder, especially focusing on emotional instability and impulsivity (Bohus et al., 2004). Abnormalities in serotonin activity have been found in prefrontal and limbic areas of the brain that may be related to these symptom constellations. The hypothalamic-pituitary-adrenal axis being sensitized by childhood trauma, particularly in the form of abuse, may also be important in the neurobiology of this disorder.

Many researchers have argued that borderline personality disorder runs in families, suggesting it may have a genetic component, but studies have methodological limitations (White, Gunderson, Zanarini, & Hudson, 2003). One of the characteristics that may be inherited is neuroticism, a tendency to easily become anxious. Borderline patients are high in neuroticism; this trait is a key feature of borderline personality disorder and is known to be heritable (Morey & Zanarini, 2000). Problems regulating emotions may be another key component that could be genetically transmitted (White et al., 2003). A diathesis-stress theory may provide a way of conceptualizing borderline personality disorder, with childhood experiences providing the stressors and an inherited component, the diathesis (Zanarini & Frankenburg, 1997).

Treatment

A number of drugs have been tried in the pharmacotherapy of borderline personality disorder, including antidepressants and atypical antipsychotic medications (Zanarini, 2004). Double-blind, placebo-controlled trials have shown that many of the different drugs do help in treating problems managing emotions and controlling impulsiveness and aggression. Research also suggests that dietary supplementation with omega-3 fatty acids may also reduce depression and aggression in patients with borderline personality disorder (Raj, 2004).

Object Relations Psychotherapy.   Object relations theory, a branch of psycho-analytic theory, deals with the nature and development of mental representations of the self and others. It includes not only the representations themselves but also the fantasies and emotions attached to these representations and how these variables mediate interpersonal functioning. The object relations of borderlines are often described as malevolent. Analyses of borderline patients' responses to projective tests indicate that they view other people as capricious and destructive for no reason (Nigg, Lohr, Westen, Gold, & Silk, 1992). This theory has been particularly important in the field of personality disorders. The leading contemporary object relations theorist is Otto Kernberg, who has written extensively about the borderline personality.

Kernberg (1985) operates from the basic assumption that borderline personalities have weak egos and therefore experience inordinate difficulty tolerating the regression (probing of childhood conflicts) that occurs in psychoanalytic treatment. The weak ego fears being flooded by primitive primary process thinking of the id. Kernberg's modified analytic treatment has the overall goal of strengthening the patient's weak ego. Therapy involves analysis of a principal defense of the border-line person, namely, splitting, or dichotomizing into all good or all bad and not in-tegrating positive and negative aspects of a person into a whole. Splitting is the re-sult of an inability to form complex object representations that do not fit a simple good/bad dichotomy. That is, the person with borderline personality disorder does not see people as fairly complex and capable of both good and bad behavior. This causes extreme difficulty in regulating emotions because the person sees the world in black-and-white terms. Other people and even the self are either all good or all bad; there is no middle ground. We saw many examples of this in Amanda, as when she idolized her boyfriend but could then turn on a dime and hate him. This thera-peutic approach is currently being compared with dialectical behavior therapy (see below) and a supportive therapy control in a long-term, randomized control trial that is now in progress to determine which is most effective (Clarkin, Levy, Len-zenweger, & Kernberg, 2004).

Dialectical Behavior Therapy.   An approach to treating borderline personality disorder that combines client-centered empathy with behavioral problem solving was developed by Marsha Linehan (1993). Dialectical behavior therapy (DBT) centers on the therapist's full acceptance of people with borderline personalities with all their contradictions and acting out, empathically validating their (distorted) beliefs with a matter-of-fact attitude toward their suicidal and other dysfunctional behavior. This total acceptance is necessary, argues Linehan, because the patient is extremely sensitive to criticism and rejection and will pull away from therapy if any hint of a possible rejection is perceived. This acceptance is a dialectical (or polar opposite) of the goal of bringing about change in the patient.

The behavioral aspect of the treatment involves helping patients learn to solve problems, that is, to acquire more effective and socially acceptable ways of han-dling their daily living problems and controlling their emotions. Work is also done on improving their interpersonal skills and in controlling their anxieties. After many months of intensive treatment, limits are set on their behavior. This is consistent with what Kernberg advocates. Patients have to commit to one year of intensive treatment as part of DBT (Smith & Peck, 2004).

Linehan and her associates have reported the results of the first randomized, controlled study of a psychological intervention of borderline personality disorder (Linehan, Armstrong, Suarez, Allmon, & Heard, 1991). Patients were randomly assigned either to dialectical behavior therapy or to treatment-as-usual, meaning any therapy available in the community. At the end of one year of treatment and again six and twelve months later, patients in the two groups were compared on a variety of measures (Linehan, Heard, & Armstrong, 1992). Findings immediately after treatment revealed the significant superiority of DBT on the following measures: less intentional self-injurious behavior, including fewer suicide attempts, fewer dropouts from treatment, and fewer inpatient hospital days. At the followups, superiority was maintained, and in addition, DBT patients reported less anger and were judged as overall better adjusted than the comparison therapy patients.

This study has generated a great deal of interest in this approach to borderline personality disorder. Workshops and seminars have been offered around the country, and the therapy is becoming rather widely used. Other studies examining the effectiveness of DBT have indicated that it shows promise in improving functioning and reducing some of the symptoms of borderline personality disorder (Robins & Chapman, 2004). Others have shown that a three-month inpatient treatment program using DBT was effective in reducing depression, anxiety, and self-injury and in improving interpersonal functioning (Bohus, Haaf, Simms, Limberger, Schmahl, Unckel, et al., 2004).

Amanda's therapists faced a common dilemma encountered with borderline patients: Should treatment be aimed at structural intrapsychic change or simply better adaptation to the environment? Waldinger and Gunderson (1984) found in a retrospective study that relatively few borderline patients complete the process of intensive psychotherapy, often terminating when an impasse in therapy occurs. When Amanda decided to change therapists, a decision had to be made as to whether or not she was seeking change in order to avoid working through a difficult impasse in therapy. It was determined that this may have been the case, but that she was unlikely to remain in therapy if her request was not granted.

Although Amanda's treatment seemed largely unsuccessful, it should not be assumed that all borderlines are equally impaired. For example, McGlashan (1986) has reported on a 15-year followup of patients in several diagnostic groups. As a group, patients with borderline personality disorder fared considerably better than those with schizotypal personality disorder. Indeed, there is a great deal of heterogeneity within the domain of borderline personality disorder. Many patients can be maintained in outpatient psychotherapy without ever being admitted to a hospital, and the outcome of therapy is not invariably negative. One of the major differences between hospitalized and nonhospitalized borderlines is that the latter group is involved in significantly fewer incidents of self-mutilation (Koenigsberg, 1982). Clearly, not all borderline patients are as self-destructive as Amanda. Nevertheless, they present a daunting challenge to anyone who treats them.

CHAPTER 20

Antisocial Personality Disorder: Psychopathy

This case differs from most of the others in this book because Bill was never in therapy. One of the authors was acquainted with Bill during his childhood and adolescence. The following case history is based on this personal experience.

Bill was the third child in the Wallace family. His parents, originally from Europe, had immigrated when Bill was 9 years old. They rented an apartment on the upper floor of a house in a middle-class neighborhood, and Bill's father got a job in a local factory. His mother worked part time in a supermarket. No information is available concerning the family's history when they lived in Europe.

Bill and his older brother, Jack, quickly became part of the neighborhood group and participated in all the activities, including baseball, football, and outings to the beach. Jack became a leader in the group and Bill, although not as well liked as his brother, was always included.

I began to get to know Bill well. We were the same age; most of the other boys were older. Although we became friends, our relationship was also characterized by a good deal of conflict. When things did not go Bill's way, his response was simple and direct—a fight. My first fight with Bill was during a baseball game at a park. We were on opposing teams and were involved in a close play at second base. He slid into the base; I tagged and called "out," and Bill jumped up swinging his fists. Although he lost these fights as often as he won them, fighting became a consistent pattern in his relationships, both with me and with other neighborhood children. Not even an older and obviously stronger opponent could get Bill to back down.

Bill's aggressiveness was not really what made him seem different as we grew up together. His escalating daredevil and antisocial behavior seemed more peculiar. One of the first of these episodes occurred when Bill organized a window-breaking competition. He explained to me and three other boys that he had recently been walking neighborhood streets at night, throwing rocks through windows. With great enthusiasm, he described the excitement this created and how he had easily eluded the few residents who had come out to try to catch him. Bill wanted the four of us to compete in a window-breaking contest. He had worked out a detailed point system—the larger the window, the more points—and wanted to start that night. We all agreed to meet at 7:30 P.M. in front of his house.

We met as planned and first filled our pockets with stones. The competition soon began, with Bill clearly in the role of leader, encouraging the rest of us and pointing out windows that would yield many points. My own reaction as all this began was extreme fear. All I could think of was, "What if we get caught?" Bill, in contrast, showed no signs of apprehension. Indeed, he seemed ecstatic and was virtually bubbling over with enthusiasm. His only negative reaction of the evening was directed toward me when, after "missing" several windows, I emptied my pockets and withdrew from the competition. "You gutless chicken," he called as I went down the street toward home. The other two boys went along with Bill. They also seemed frightened, but they looked up to Bill and may have been more concerned by his disapproval. Although I was excluded from subsequent nights of competition, Bill eagerly kept me informed of the results. After several months, he was declared the winner when he broke all the large windows of the supermarket where his mother worked.

At age 10, petty theft replaced window breaking as Bill's major source of excitement. It seemed to me that he always stole something whenever I was in a store with him. He would steal anything—candy, fruit, clothing, toys—not just things he wanted. In fact, he often threw away the things he had stolen. He seemed more interested in the excitement than in any actual material gain. He had discovered several ways of getting money. The first was a Roman Catholic church that had two easy sources of cash—a poor box and a container for donations left by worshippers who had lit a candle. Bill cleaned out both on a regular basis. His second source was a restaurant that had a wishing well located in a rear garden, whose proceeds went to the Salvation Army. Although the wishing well was covered with a metal grate, Bill found an opening just large enough to get his hand through. Every couple of weeks, armed with a flashlight and a long stick, he would sneak into the garden at night, move the coins to the right spot, and collect them. Because he often had money, he had to lie regularly to his parents about how he got it, inventing a series of odd jobs he held around the neighborhood. Finally, he regularly stole milk money from various neighborhood homes. Bill even stole the milk money from my home. The first time our money was missing, I went directly after him and accused him of the theft. He denied it. The second time, he admitted the theft and offered to cut me in if I would keep quiet!

One other incident, which occurred when Bill and I were both 12, crystallized for me how Bill was somehow different. About a 15-minute walk from our homes was a river that had many expensive houses along its banks. A tremendous rainstorm caused a flood, and, tragically, more than 100 people were killed. Early the next morning, with the news of the disaster in the papers and on the radio, Bill set out for the scene. Because the victims were wealthy, Bill reasoned, he might strike it rich if he could be the first one to find some bodies and take their wallets, watches, and jewelry. He went alone and returned later in the day, proudly displaying his loot—six watches and several hundred dollars. He had found several dead bodies and stolen their possessions. He returned to the river several more times over the next few days, and although he came back empty handed, he would enthusiastically relate his experiences to anyone who would listen. The excitement and danger seemed more important than the valuables he found.

During these three years, most of the neighborhood youngsters had also received more than a glimpse of the Wallaces' family life. Bill's father was frequently out of work and seemed to have trouble holding a job for more than several months at a stretch. He drank heavily. While we played street ball, we often saw him returning home, obviously drunk. At the first glimpse of their drunken father, Bill and Jack would get out of his sight as quickly as possible. Both boys reported frequent beatings, particularly when their father had been drinking. At the same time, Bill's father allowed him to get away with things, such as staying out late at night, which none of the other neighborhood children were allowed to do. Bill and Jack both reported that their father was unpredictable in his punishments. Their father and mother also fought often, and his mother may well have been physically abused. On many occasions, our play was interrupted by yelling and the sound of loud crashes from their apartment.

The Wallaces eventually moved to an apartment in another area of the city, about a 30-minute bus ride from their first home. Bill and I were no longer close friends, but I kept track of him through Jack, his older brother. According to Jack, Bill's pattern of antisocial behavior escalated. He continued to steal regularly, even from members of his family. He frequently skipped school and got into very serious trouble for hitting a teacher who had tried to break up a fight between him and another boy. Jack was very concerned about Bill and attempted to talk to him several times. Jack reported that during these talks, Bill would genuinely seem to agree that he had to change and would express shame and regret about whatever he had done most recently. However, within a few days the old pattern would be back in full force. Jack eventually came to see Bill's contrition as a con.

We were both 15 the next time I met Bill. Through my continued contacts with Jack, I had learned that Bill had been sent to reform school. I did not know any of the details because Jack had been so ashamed of his brother's behavior that he would not talk about it. One evening shortly after dinner, the doorbell rang. I answered, and Bill motioned me outside. He had escaped from reform school and wanted me to buy him a meal and loan him some money. We went to a local restaurant where I bought him a hamburger and Cokes for both of us. He told me he had been convicted of car theft and rape the previous year. He had been stealing cars regularly and taking them on joyrides. He was caught when he decided to keep a stolen car, one that had particularly caught his fancy. The third day he had the car, he had parked in a deserted place with a 12-year-old girl he knew from school, where he raped her.

As Bill related the story, he became visibly disgusted, not at himself, but at the girl. As he explained it, he was only trying to have some fun and had picked this particular girl because she was only 12 years old and not likely to get pregnant. From his perspective, it was an ideal situation. With pregnancy impossible, she should have just lain back and enjoyed it. He obviously had no concern at all for the feelings of his victim.

I never saw Bill again but through Jack learned what happened to him over the next several years. A few weeks after our meeting, he was apprehended by the police. He had again stolen a car; while driving drunk, he had smashed into a telephone pole. After a short stay in a hospital, he was returned to the reform school, where he spent two years. When he was released, Bill had changed greatly. It seemed to Jack that he had now become a real criminal. Car thefts were no longer for joyrides but for profit. Bill became involved in selling stolen cars to others who stripped them to sell their parts. He briefly returned to high school but with no friends there and little real interest, he soon dropped out. He became a regular at the racetrack and lost money there and with several bookmakers. As had happened before, Jack tried to talk to his younger brother about the trouble for which he seemed headed. But now even the charade of shame and guilt was gone. Bill expressed an "I'll take what I want when I want it" attitude. When Jack tried to point out the likely negative consequences of his behavior, Bill simply shrugged it off, saying that he was too smart to ever end up in jail.

Shortly after his eighteenth birthday, Bill attempted a bank robbery, armed with a .38-caliber automatic pistol. Bill was driving a stolen car. On seeing what he thought was a bank, he impulsively decided to rob it. In his rush he had actually undertaken to rob an office of the electric company. Seeing the people lined up at tellers' windows to pay their bills had made him think it was a bank. Once inside, although recognizing his mistake, he decided to go through with the holdup anyway and had several tellers empty their cash drawers into a sack. A patrol car passed by the office as the holdup was in progress, and seeing what was happening, the policemen stopped to investigate. Bill ran out of the office directly into the police and was easily arrested. He was tried, convicted, and sentenced to 10 years in the penitentiary.

Discussion

The terms *antisocial personality disorder* and *psychopathy* (and sometimes *sociopathy* as well) are often used interchangeably, although there are important differences between the two. The current *DSM-IV-TR* (APA, 2000) concept of antisocial personality disorder involves two major components. The first refers to antisocial behavior before the age of 15. Criteria include truancy, running away from home, frequent lying, theft, arson, and deliberate destruction of property. The second part of the *DSM-IV-TR* (APA, 2000) definition refers to the continuation of this pattern of antisocial behavior in adulthood. Adults with antisocial personality disorder show irresponsible and antisocial behavior by not working consistently, breaking laws, being irritable and physically aggressive, defaulting on debts, and being reckless. They are impulsive and fail to plan ahead. In addition, they show no regard for truth or remorse for their actions.

In a large, nationally representative study, 3.63 percent of adult Americans met the criteria for antisocial personality disorder (Grant, Hasin, Stinson, Dawson, Chou, Ruan, & Pickering, 2004). They found that three times as many men as women had the disorder. It was more likely among Native Americans, less likely among Asian Americans, and less likely among older rather than younger age groups. There is no significant difference between African Americans and European Americans (whites) on the level of psychopathy (Skeem, Edens, Camp, & Colwell, 2004). The disorder is frequently comorbid with substance abuse (Smith & Newman, 1990). Pimps, confidence artists, murderers, and drug dealers are by no means the only antisocial personalities. Business executives, professors, politicians, physicians, plumbers, salespeople, carpenters, and bartenders can have antisocial personality traits as well. Adult antisocial personalities have a history of behavior problems and conduct disorder in childhood (Paris, 2004). Their symptoms tend to fade some during middle age, and a number of people with antisocial personalities die prematurely.

The concept of psychopathy is closely linked to the writings of Hervey Cleckley and his classic book *The Mask of Sanity* (1976). On the basis of his vast clinical experience, Cleckley formulated a set of criteria by which to recognize the disorder. Unlike the *DSM* criteria for antisocial personality disorder, Cleckley's criteria for psychopathy refer less to antisocial behavior per se and more to the psychopath's personality. For example, one of the key characteristics of the psychopath is poverty of emotions, both positive and negative. Psychopaths have no sense of shame, and even their seemingly positive feelings for others are merely an act. The psychopath is superficially charming and manipulates others for personal gain. The lack of some negative emotions, especially anxiety, may make it impossible for psychopaths to learn from their mistakes, and the lack of positive emotions leads them to behave irresponsibly toward others. Another key point is that Cleckley describes the antisocial behavior of the psychopath as "inadequately motivated;" it is not due, for example, to a need for something like money but is performed impulsively, as much for thrills as anything else.

Currently, most researchers identify psychopaths using a checklist developed by Hare and his associates (Hare et al., 1990). The checklist identifies two major clusters of psychopathic behaviors. The first, referred to as emotional detachment, describes a selfish, remorseless individual who exploits others (descriptors of this cluster include lack of remorse or guilt, callous lack of empathy, and conning/manipulative). The second characterizes an antisocial lifestyle (parasitic lifestyle, pathological lying, history of juvenile delinquency). The degree of psychopathy among adolescents who had committed a crime was a strong predictor of their likelihood to continue involvement in criminal activities into adulthood, particularly violent offenses (Gretton, Hare, & Catchpole, 2004).

The two categories—antisocial personality disorder and psychopathy—are related but not identical. This sometimes complicates integrating the findings of research in this area because the clinical features are defined in different ways. Bill's behavior during childhood and adolescence clearly meets many of Cleckley's criteria. He was unreliable, untruthful, lacking in any feelings of shame about his misconduct, and totally without anxiety. His antisocial behavior (such as stealing) was not motivated by any genuine desire to possess the stolen objects, but rather to get some sort of thrill. And he often displayed poor judgment, particularly in his escapades of late adolescence. His poverty of emotion was amply demonstrated by his thefts from the homes of his friends and by the attitude he had toward the victim of his rape, which was completely lacking in empathy.

Etiological Considerations

What causes behavior like Bill's? As with most disorders, the search for the causes of psychopathy has considered both biological and psychological variables. We will describe research efforts in several areas—the role of the family, emotion, genetics, and impulsivity.

The Role of the Family. Children who grow up in physically abusive or neglectful homes are at increased risk for antisocial behavior in adolescence and adulthood (Cicchetti & Toth, 2004). Authoritarian parenting characterized by punitiveness and restrictiveness, as well as low warmth, has been linked to antisocial behavior in children (Smith & Farrington, 2004). In addition, conflict and violence between parents increases a child's antisociality. The harsh yet inconsistent disciplinary practices of Bill's father, as well as the conflict between his parents, mesh well with these findings. The link between parents with antisocial traits and children with antisocial traits may be partly due to harsh, inconsistent, or rejecting parenting behaviors (Barnow, Lucht, & Freyberger, 2005).

Contemporary research on the role of the family has taken a more interactional view, recognizing that while parents indeed influence their children, children also influence their parents. For example, Moffitt (1993) proposes that persistent antisocial behavior begins with deficits in neurological functions, such as attention and impulsivity. These deficits make the child difficult for the parents to handle and can produce the type of disciplinary practices that were found by the early studies on parenting and psychopathic behavior.

Growing up in poverty is also a risk factor for the development of antisocial traits in children. Macmillan, McMorris, and Kruttschnitt (2004) found that when families living in poverty were able to escape the poverty, their children's antisocial behavior was reduced. Long-term exposure to poverty was most harmful.

Emotion and Psychopathy. In defining psychopathy, Cleckley pointed out the inability of these persons to learn from experience. In particular, they seem to feel no need to avoid the negative consequences of social misbehavior. Cleckley also remarked that they were not neurotic and seldom anxious. From these clinical descriptions, Lykken (1957) deduced that psychopaths may have few inhibitions about committing antisocial acts because they experience no anxiety. Because avoidance learning is assumed to be mediated by anxiety, one of Lykken's tests of this hypothesis involved learning to avoid electric shocks. As expected, psychopaths were poor at learning to avoid the shocks.

Because of the role of the autonomic nervous system in emotion, investigators have examined psychopaths for both their resting levels of autonomic activity and their patterns of autonomic reactivity to various classes of stimuli. Psychopaths have lower than normal levels of skin conductance, are less autonomically reactive when stressful or aversive stimuli are presented, and have lower resting heart rates (Lorber, 2004). These results are consistent with clinical descriptions of psychopaths as being nonanxious, and with research using other measures of emotion, showing that psychopaths are generally less emotionally reactive than normals (Herpetz et al., 2001; Patrick, Bradley & Lang, 1993).

Neurobiological investigations have suggested abnormalities in the functioning of the amygdala (a part of the brain involved in aversive conditioning and responses to facial expressions depicting fear and sadness) among people with high psychopathy (Blair, 2003). Some studies have shown that they have smaller amygdalas, and others have shown reduced amygdala responses. The reasons for these brain differences, though, are unknown.

Overall, the research literature is consistent with the idea that it is difficult to arouse negative emotions in psychopaths. This may well be an important determinant of their repetitive antisocial behavior. But it is also important to consider that arousing negative emotions is not the whole story of socialization. Empathy, being aware of and in tune with the emotions of others, could be equally important. The idea that psychopaths lack empathy has been tested by comparing their skin conductance responses to those of normals while viewing slides of varying content. Consistent with the idea that psychopaths lack empathy, they showed smaller responses to slides showing people in distress (Blair, Jones, Clark, & Smith, 1997).

Behavior Genetic Research.   How do psychopaths acquire this pattern of low anxiety and reduced electrodermal response? Research suggests that both criminality and antisocial personality have heritable components (Hicks, Krueger, Iacono, McGue, & Patrick, 2004). Twin studies of twins reared apart show that genetics plays a role in the likelihood that a person will commit a criminal act (Gottesman & Goldsmith, 1994). For antisocial personality disorder, twin studies show higher concordance for monozygotic than dizygotic pairs (Lyons, True, Eisen, Goldbert, Meyer et al., 1995), and adoption studies show higher rates of antisocial behavior in the adopted children of biological parents with antisocial personality disorder (Cadoret, Yates, Troughton, Woodworth, & Stewart, 1995b). A recent report documented that the monoamine oxidase A gene, previously implicated in risk for antisocial behavior, only increased antisocial behavior when the adolescent was raised in an environment characterized by parental neglect, exposure to violence between parents, and inconsistent parental discipline (Foley, Eaves, Wormley, Silberg, Maes, Kuhn, & Riley, 2004). Genes may only be expressed in certain types of environments, and interactions between genes and environments must be considered.

Researchers have found a link between prenatal exposure to cigarette smoking of the mother and later antisocial behavior. Research has shown this link to be stronger the more cigarettes that were used, even when genetic risks for antisocial behavior were controlled (Maughan, Taylor, Caspi, & Moffitt, 2004). However, investigators cautioned that the effects could be due to some other difference in the environment that has not been controlled. More research is needed to find out whether cigarette smoking during pregnancy increases the child's later antisocial behavior.

Impulsivity and Psychopathy.   Gorenstein and Newman (1980) proposed that a key feature of psychopathy is impulsivity and an inability to sustain goal-directed behavior. In one study demonstrating this phenomenon, participants viewed playing cards on a computer screen (Newman, Patterson, & Kosson, 1987). If a face card appeared, the participant won 5 cents: if a nonface card appeared, he lost 5 cents. After each trial, the participant could either continue or quit the game. The probability of losing was controlled by the experimenter and started at 10 percent, but increased by 10 percent every 10 cards until it reached 100 percent. The psychopaths continued to play the game much longer than the control participants. Nine out of twelve psychopaths continued to play the game even after they had lost money on 19 of the last 20 trials. They appeared unable to alter a maladaptive response. When the same game was played with a five-second waiting period imposed after each trial, the psychopaths markedly reduced the number of trials for which they played the game. Enforcing a delay may force psychopaths to reflect on their behavior and thus be less impulsive.

These findings seem particularly applicable to Bill. The fear that might prevent stealing, breaking windows, and looting seemed totally absent in him. From his own statements we can conclude that he felt little shame or remorse about his transgressions. Indeed, he seemed proud of them. He clearly had little or no empathy for his victims. Finally, Bill also displayed characteristics similar to those revealed in the study by Newman and colleagues, not reflecting on the negative consequences of his antisocial behavior.

Treatment

There is general agreement that treatment is unsuccessful for psychopaths. Cleckley (1976, pp.438-439) summarized his clinical impressions as follows:

> Over a period of many years I have remained discouraged about the effect of treatment on the psychopath. Having regularly failed in my own efforts to help such patients, . . . I hoped for a while that treatment by others would be more successful. I have had the opportunity to see patients of this sort who were treated by psychoanalysis, by psychoanalytically oriented psychotherapy, by group and milieu therapy . . . None of these measures impressed me as achieving successful results . . . I have now, after more than three decades, had the opportunity to observe a considerable number of patients who, through commitment or the threat of losing their probation status or by other means, were kept under treatment . . . for years. The therapeutic failure in all such patients leads me to feel that we do not at present have any kind of psychotherapy that can be relied on to change the psychopath fundamentally.

Empirical evaluations of the many treatments that have been employed with psychopaths—psychoanalysis, milieu therapy, group therapy, various medications, aversive conditioning, psychosurgery—reach conclusions quite similar to Cleckley's (Palmer, 1984). Some forms of therapy may even have negative effects on psychopaths. Rice, Harris, and Cormier (1992) compared the results of a therapeutic community to standard institutionalization in a sample of prison inmates. While the special program reduced recidivism in nonpsychopaths, it actually increased it among psychopaths. The inability of psychopaths to form an honest, trusting relationship with a therapist may be a major reason for the ineffectiveness of psychotherapy. A person who lies, cares little for the feelings of others, and has few regrets about personal misconduct is certainly a poor candidate for most forms

280 Case Studies in Abnormal Psychology

of psychotherapy. One experienced clinician (Lion, 1978) has suggested the following guidelines:

> First, the therapist must be continually vigilant with regard to manipulation on the part of the patient. Second, he must assume, until proved otherwise, that information given to him by the patient contains distortions and fabrications. Third, he must recognize that a working alliance develops, if ever, exceedingly late in any therapeutic relationship.

Because many psychopaths spend time in prison, the discouraging results of imprisonment and rehabilitation of convicts are relevant to the treatment of psychopathy. Prisons operate more as schools for crime (as for Bill) than for rehabilitation. An interesting argument in favor of the incarceration of psychopaths, however, is that psychopaths tend to settle down in middle age (Hare et al., 1988). Prisons, then, may protect society from the antisocial behavior of "active" psychopaths.

Preventing some cases of antisocial personality disorder may be possible through programs designed to address situations that put individuals at risk for developing the disorder. For example, programs to reduce child abuse might prevent later antisocial behavior among the children at risk for abuse (Harrington & Bailey, 2004). Also, targeting groups of children and adolescents known to be at high risk for antisocial behavior, such as those with attention-deficit/hyperactivity disorder, might be effective. And even though the outlook is not optimistic for the treatment of adult antisocial personalities, multisystemic treatment, a treatment approach for juvenile offenders that focuses on family and home interventions, shows promise (Curtis, Ronan, & Borduin, 2004). The treatment focuses on making changes in the family, school, and community settings to reduce their contributions to problem behaviors. A recent meta-analysis found that adolescents who received the treatment had better functioning than 70 percent of those who did not receive the treatment. This raises the hope that specific types of early intervention may reduce the severity and cost of future adult antisocial personality disorder.

CHAPTER 21

Autistic Disorder

Sam Williams was the second child of John and Carol Williams. The couple had been married for 5 years when Sam was born; John was a lawyer, and Carol a homemaker. Sam weighed 7 pounds, 11 ounces at birth, which had followed an uncomplicated, full-term pregnancy. Delivered by Caesarean section, he came home six days after the delivery.

His parents reported that Sam's early development seemed quite normal. He was not colicky, and he slept and ate well. During his first two years, there were no childhood illnesses except some mild colds. By Sam's second birthday, however, his parents began to become concerned. He had been somewhat slower than his older sister in achieving some developmental milestones (such as sitting up alone and crawling). Furthermore, his motor development seemed uneven. He would crawl normally for a few days and then not crawl at all for a while. Although he made babbling sounds, he had not developed any speech and did not even seem to understand anything his parents said to him. Simple requests such as, "Come" or, "Do you want a cookie?" elicited no response.

Initially, the Williamses thought that Sam might be deaf. Later they vacillated between this belief and the idea that Sam was being stubborn. They reported many frustrating experiences in which they tried to force him to obey a command or say "Mama" or "Dada." Sometimes Sam would go into a tantrum during one of these situations, yelling, screaming, and throwing himself to the floor. That same year, the Williamses' pediatrician told them that Sam might be mentally retarded.

As he neared his third birthday, Sam's parents noticed him engaging in more and more strange and puzzling behavior. Most obvious were his repetitive hand movements. Many times each day, he would suddenly flap his hands for several minutes (activities like this are called self-stimulatory behaviors). Other times he rolled his eyes around in their sockets. He still did not speak, but he made smacking sounds and sometimes he would burst out laughing for no apparent reason. He was walking now and often walked on his toes. Sam had not been toilet trained, although his parents had tried to do so.

Sam's social development was also beginning to concern his parents. Although he would let them hug and touch him, he would not look at them and generally seemed indifferent to their attention. He also did not play at all with his older sister, seeming to prefer being left alone. Even his solitary play was strange. He did not really play with his toys—for example, pretending to drive a toy car into a gas station. Instead, he was more likely just to manipulate a toy, such as a car, holding it and repetitively spinning its wheels. The only thing that really seemed to interest him was a ceiling fan in the den. He was content to sit there for as long as permitted, watching intently as the fan spun around and around. He would often have temper tantrums when the fan was turned off.

At the age of 3, the family's pediatrician recommended a complete physical and neurological examination. Sam was found to be in good health, and the neurological examination revealed nothing remarkable. A psychiatric evaluation was performed several months later. Sam was brought to a treatment facility specializing in behavior disturbances of childhood and was observed for a day. During that time the psychiatrist was able to see firsthand most of the behaviors that Sam's parents had described—hand flapping, toe walking, smacking sounds, and preference for being left alone. When the psychiatrist evaluated Sam, she observed that a loud slapping noise did not elicit a startle response as it does in most children. The only vocalization she could elicit that approximated speech was a repetitive "nah, nah." Sam did, however, obey some simple commands such as "Come" and "Go get a potato chip." She diagnosed Sam as having autistic disorder and recommended placement in a day-treatment setting.

Conceptualization and Treatment

Sam was 4 years old by the time there was an opening for him at the treatment center. He attended the special school 5 days a week, spending the remainder of his time at home with his parents and sister. The school provided a comprehensive educational program conducted by specially trained teachers. The program was organized mainly along operant conditioning principles. In addition, Sam's parents attended classes once a week to learn operant conditioning so they could continue the school program at home. The school's personnel conducted another evaluation of Sam, observing him in the school and later at home. Interviews with the parents established that they were both well adjusted and that their marriage was stable. Both parents were, however, experiencing considerable stress from having to cope with Sam on a day-to-day basis and from their fears that Sam's condition might have been caused by something they had done.

One of the first targets of the training program was Sam's eye contact. When working with Sam, his teacher provided small food rewards when Sam spontaneously looked at him. The teacher also began requesting eye contact and again rewarded Sam when he complied. Along with this training, the teacher worked on having Sam obey other simple commands. The teacher would wait for a time when Sam seemed attentive and would then, establishing eye contact, say the command and model the desired behavior by demonstrating it. For example, the teacher would say, "Sam, stretch your arms up like this," lifting Sam's arms up and rewarding him with praise and a small amount of food, such as a grape. This procedure was repeated several times. Once Sam began to become more skilled at following the command, the teacher stopped raising Sam's arms for him and had him do it himself. These training trials were conducted daily. As Sam's response to a particular command became well established, the teacher would expand his learning to following commands in other situations and by other people. Sam's progress was slow. It often took weeks of training to establish his response to a simple command.

After his first year in the school, he did respond reliably to several simple requests such as "Come," "Give it to me," and "Put on your coat."

At the same time that Sam was learning to respond to commands, other aspects of the training program were also being implemented. While Sam was in the classroom, his teacher worked with him on trying to develop skills that would be important in learning, for example, sitting in his seat, maintaining eye contact, and listening and working for longer periods of time. His teacher used the same reward strategy to teach Sam each activity.

As these skills became better established, the teacher also began working on expanding Sam's vocabulary by teaching him the words for pictures of common objects. A picture of one object, such as an orange, was placed on a table in front of Sam. Once Sam had looked at the object, the teacher said, "This is an orange. Point to the orange." When Sam pointed to the orange, he was rewarded. If necessary, the teacher would move his hand for him at first. Next another picture, such as a cat, was selected and the same procedure followed. Then the two pictures were placed in front of Sam and the teacher asked him to point to one of them: "Point to the orange." If Sam pointed correctly, he was rewarded. If he did not, the teacher moved his hand to the correct object. After Sam had correctly pointed to the orange several times in a row, the teacher asked him to point to the cat. With that response established, the teacher switched the position of the pictures and repeated the process. When Sam had begun to point correctly to the orange and the cat, a third picture was introduced and the training procedure was started anew. During one year of training, Sam learned the names of 38 common objects with this procedure.

Sam's speech therapist, whom he saw daily, was also working with him on language skills. Initially, they worked on getting Sam to imitate simple sounds. Sitting across a table from Sam and waiting until Sam was looking (or prompting him to look by holding a piece of food near his mouth), the teacher would say, "Say this, ah," taking care to accentuate the movements required for this sound. At first, Sam was rewarded for making any sound. Subsequently, rewards were given when Sam approximated more and more closely the required sound. As sounds were mastered, Sam was trained to say simple words in a similar fashion. Over the course of a year, Sam learned a few words—"bye-bye," "no more," and "mine," but overall, his verbal imitation remained poor.

Teaching Sam to dress and undress himself was another target during the first year. Initially, his teacher helped him through the entire sequence, describing each step as they did it. Next, they would go through the sequence again, but now Sam had to do the last step himself (taking off his shoes, putting on his shoes). More difficult steps (tying shoes) were worked on individually to give Sam more practice on them. Once some progress was being made, this aspect of the treatment was carried out by the parents. They first observed the teacher working with Sam and then discussed the procedure and were shown how to make a chart to record Sam's progress. Over a period of weeks, the number of steps that Sam had to complete by himself was gradually increased, moving from the last toward the first. Sam was rewarded each time he dressed or undressed, usually with a special treat, such as a favorite breakfast food. In this case, the training was quite successful. By midyear, Sam had mastered dressing and undressing.

Toilet training was another area that Sam's parents and teachers tackled. At home and at school, Sam was rewarded for using the toilet. He was checked every hour to see if his pants were dry. If they were, he was praised and reminded that when he went to the toilet he would get a reward. Shortly thereafter, Sam would be taken to the toilet, where he would remove his pants and sit. If he urinated or defecated, he was given a large reward. If not, he was given a small reward just for sitting. As this training was progressing, Sam was also taught to associate the word "potty" with going to the toilet. Progress was slow at first, and there were many "accidents," which both teachers and parents were instructed to ignore. But Sam soon caught on and began urinating or defecating more and more often when he was taken to the bathroom. Then the parents and teachers began working on having Sam tell them when he had to go. When they checked to see if his pants were dry, they would tell him to say "potty" when he had to go to the toilet. Although there were many ups and downs in Sam's progress, by the end of the year he was having an average of fewer than two accidents per week.

Sam's temper tantrums slowed his progress during his first year in the special school. They occurred sometimes when he was given a command or when a teacher interrupted something he was doing. Not getting a reward during a training session also led to tantrums. Sam would scream loudly at the top of his voice, throw himself to the ground, and flail away with his arms and legs. Several interventions were tried. Sam's tantrums usually led to getting his own way, particularly at home. For example, a tantrum had often resulted in getting his parents to keep the ceiling fan on, even when they wanted to turn it off. Ignoring the tantrum was the first approach. Sam's teachers and parents simply let the tantrum play itself out, acting as if it had not happened. This did not reduce the number of tantrums, so "time-out" was tried. Every time a tantrum started, Sam was picked up, carried to a special room, and left there for 10 minutes or until the screaming stopped. This procedure also failed to have much of an effect on the tantrums and screaming, even with several modifications such as lengthening the time-out period.

During Sam's second year of treatment, many of the first year's programs were continued. Sam, now 6 years old, was responding to more commands, and his ability to recognize and point to simple objects increased. In speech therapy, he learned to imitate more sounds and some new words ("hello," "cookie," and "book"), but his progress was slow and uneven. He would seem to master some sound or word and then somehow lose it. He was still dressing and undressing himself and using the toilet reliably.

Feeding skills were one of the first targets for the second-year program. Although his parents had tried to get him to use a knife, fork, and spoon, Sam resisted and ate with his fingers or by licking the food from his plate. Drinking from a cup was also a problem. He still used a baby cup with only a small opening at the top. The feeding skills program was implemented by both Sam's teachers and parents and involved a combination of modeling and operant conditioning. Training sessions conducted at mealtime first involved getting Sam to use a spoon. Sam was shown how to hold the spoon; then the teacher picked up the spoon, saying, "Watch me. You push the spoon in like this and then lift it up to your mouth." Sam did not initially imitate, so the teacher had to guide him through the necessary steps:

moving his hand and spoon to pick up food, raising his arm until the spoon was at his mouth, telling him to open his mouth, and guiding the spoon in. Praise was provided as each step in the chain was completed. After many repetitions, Sam was required to do the last step by himself. Gradually, more and more of the steps were done by Sam himself. Successes were followed by praise and failures by saying "no" or removing his meal for a short time. When eating with a spoon was well established, the training was expanded to using a fork and drinking from a cup. In several months, Sam was eating and drinking well.

Sam's failure to play with other children was also a major focus during the second year. The first step was to get Sam to play near other children. Most of his playtime was spent alone, even when other children were in the playroom with him. His teacher watched Sam carefully and rewarded him with small bits of food whenever he was near another child with autistic disorder. A procedure was also used to force Sam to interact with another child. Sam and another child would be seated next to each other and given the task of stacking some blocks. Each child was, in turn, given a block and prompted to place it on the stack. In addition to praising them individually as they stacked each block, both children were rewarded with praise and food when they had completed their block tower. After repeating this process several times, the program was expanded to include the cooperative completion of simple puzzles. "Sam, put the dog in here. Okay now, Hannah, put the cat here." Gradually the prompts were faded out, and the children were simply rewarded for their cooperative play. Although this aspect of therapy progressed well, transferring these skills to the natural play environment proved difficult. Attempts were made to have Sam and another child play together with toys such as a farm set or a small train. The teacher encouraged them to move the objects around, talking to them about what they were doing and rewarding them for following simple commands. Although Sam would usually follow these commands, his play remained solitary, with little eye contact or cooperation with the other child.

Sam's self-stimulatory behavior was a final target of the second year. Sam's hand flapping and eye rolling had already decreased somewhat over the past year, perhaps because more of his day was being filled with constructive activities. Now a specific intervention, to be used by Sam's teachers and his parents, was planned. Whenever Sam began hand flapping, he was stopped and told to hold his hands still, except when told to move them, for 5 minutes. During the five-minute period, he was told to hold his hands in several different positions for periods of 30 seconds. If he did not follow the command, the teacher or parent moved his hands into the desired position; if he did not maintain the position for 30 seconds, the teacher or parent held his hands still. Food rewards were provided for successful completion of each 30-second period. Gradually, the teachers and parents were able to get Sam to comply without moving his hands for him or holding him. Then they turned to the eye rolling and implemented a similar program, having Sam fix his gaze on certain objects around his environment whenever he began to roll his eyes. Over a period of several months of training, Sam's self-stimulatory behavior decreased by about 50 percent.

At the beginning of his third year in school, Sam, now 7 years old, was given an intelligence test and achieved an IQ of 30, a score reflecting severe mental retardation. The language and speech training continued, as did the attempts to reduce the frequency of his self-stimulatory behavior. His tantrums, which had not responded to previous interventions, were becoming worse. In addition to screaming and throwing himself on the floor, he now became violent at times. On several occasions, he had either punched, bitten, or kicked his sister. His parents reported that during these tantrums he became so out of control that they feared he might seriously injure someone. Similar episodes occurred in school, usually when an ongoing activity was interrupted or he failed at some task.

Trouble had also emerged on the school bus. All children were required to wear seat belts, but Sam would not do so and was often out of his seat. Twice in one week, the bus driver stopped the bus and tried to get Sam buckled back into his seat. She was bitten once the first time and twice the second. The bus company acted quickly and suspended service for Sam. In an initial attempt to resolve the problem, Sam was put on haloperidol (Haldol®), a drug widely used in the treatment of schizophrenia in adults. But after a month of the drug and no apparent effect, it was stopped. In the meantime, Sam's mother had to drive him to and from school. He was beginning to miss days or be late when his mother had schedule conflicts.

The seriousness of the tantrum problem and the fact that other treatments had not worked led to the implementation of a punishment system. Because Sam's tantrums and violent outbursts were almost always preceded by loud screaming, it was decided to try to break up the usual behavior sequence and punish the screaming. Whenever Sam began to scream, a mixture of water and Tabasco sauce was squirted into his mouth. The effect of this procedure, which was used by both his teachers and parents, was dramatic. The first day of the treatment, Sam began screaming and was squirted six times. His response to the Tabasco mixture was one of shock and some crying, which stopped quickly after he was allowed to rinse out his mouth. The next day, he was squirted with the Tabasco twice. The third and fourth days, he did not scream at all. The fifth day, he had one screaming episode; thereafter, he neither screamed nor had a severe temper tantrum again for the rest of the year.

Sam's progress in other areas was not so dramatic. He continued to expand his vocabulary slowly, learning to say more words and recognize more and more objects. But his performance remained highly variable from day to day. His self-stimulatory behavior continued, although at a level below that which had been present earlier. He still remained isolated, preferring to be alone rather than with other children.

Discussion

Autistic disorder was first described in 1943 by a psychiatrist at Harvard, Leo Kanner, who noticed a group of disturbed children that behaved in ways that were not common in children with mental retardation or with schizophrenia. He named the syndrome early infantile autism because he observed that they had an extreme autistic aloneness that shut out anything from the outside. Kanner considered autistic aloneness the most fundamental symptom, but he also found that these children had been unable from the beginning of life to relate to other people, were severely limited in language, and had an obsessive desire that everything about them remain exactly the same. Despite its early description by Kanner and others, the disorder was not accepted into official diagnostic nomenclature until the publication of *DSM-III* in 1980 (APA). In *DSM-IV-TR* (APA, 2000) *autistic disorder* is classified as one of the Pervasive Developmental Disorders.

A major feature of autistic disorder is abnormality in social development (Volkmar, Chawarska, & Klin, 2005). Children with autistic disorder have a lack of interest in or difficulty relating to people, which is found from the very beginning of life. Infants with autistic disorder are often reported to be "good babies" because they do not place any demands on their parents. They do not fret or demand attention, nor do they reach out or smile or look at their mothers when being fed. When they are picked up or cuddled, they often arch their bodies away from their caretakers instead of molding themselves against the adult as other babies do. They are content to sit quietly in their playpens for hours, never even noticing other people. After infancy, they do not form attachments with people but may become extremely attached to mechanical objects such as refrigerators or vacuum cleaners. They rapidly fall behind their peers in development. Clearly, this feature was very characteristic of Sam. Although he did not actively avoid human contact or develop an attachment with a mechanical object, he was almost totally asocial.

Communication deficits are a second major feature of autism. Even before the period when language is usually acquired, infants with autistic disorder show deficits in communication. Babbling, an early stage of language development characterized by infants repeating sounds such as ba-ba-ba, is less frequent in those with autistic disorder and conveys less information than it does with other children (Ricks, 1972). Older children with autistic disorder also have difficulties with language. Mutism—complete absence of speech—is prevalent, as was true with Sam. About 50 percent of all children with autistic disorder never learn to speak (Paul, 1987). When they do speak, peculiarities are often found, including echolalia, where children echo, usually with remarkable fidelity, what they have heard another person say. In delayed echolalia, the child may not repeat the sentence or phrase until hours or weeks after hearing it. Another abnormality common in the speech of children with autistic disorder is pronoun reversal. They refer to themselves as "he," "you," or by their own proper names; they seldom use the pronouns "I" or "me" and then only when referring to others.

The ability or inability to speak is often an effective means of predicting the later adjustment of children with autistic disorder, an additional indication of the central role of language. Eisenberg and Kanner (1956) followed up a sample of 80 children with autistic disorder classified according to whether or not they had learned to speak by age five. Fifty percent of the children who had been able to speak at this age were later rated as showing fair or good adjustment, but only three percent of the nonspeaking children were so rated. Other studies have also shown a close link between the acquisition of language and later adjustment (Gillberg, 1991). Based on these findings, we would predict a relatively poor outcome for Sam.

288 Case Studies in Abnormal Psychology

A third major feature of autistic disorder is restricted or stereotyped interests (Volkmar et al., 2005), including compulsive and ritualistic activity, such as a fascination with spinning objects, as shown by Sam. Furthermore, children with autistic disorder often become extremely upset over changes in daily routine and their surroundings. An offer of milk in a different drinking cup or a rearrangement of furniture may make them cry or bring on a temper tantrum. Even common greetings must not vary. In play, they may continually line up toys or construct intricate patterns out of household objects. They engage in much less symbolic or make-believe play than either normal or mentally retarded children of the same mental age (Sigman, Ungerer, Mundy, & Sherman, 1987). They may become preoccupied with train schedules, subway routes, or number sequences. Clearly, Sam displayed many of these behaviors.

In addition to the three major signs just described, many children with autistic disorder have problems in eating, often refusing food or eating only one or a few kinds of food. They may also have difficulty walking but be quite proficient at twirling and spinning objects and in performing ritualistic hand movements. Other rhythmic movements, such as endless body rocking, seem to please them. They may also become preoccupied with manipulating a mechanical object and be very upset when interrupted. Often the children have sensory problems. Like Sam, some children with autistic disorder are first thought to be deaf because they never respond to any sound; some even seem to be insensitive to sound or light. Bowel training is frequently delayed, and head banging and other self-injurious behaviors are common (Rutter, 1974).

Autistic disorder is being diagnosed more frequently (Barbaresi, Katusic, Colligan, Weaver & Jacobsen, 2005). From 1980 to 1983, the incidence was 5.5 per 100,000 children, but for 1995 to 1997, it was 44.9 per 100,000, an 8.2-fold increase. The increase was most noticeable after the publication of the *DSM-III-R* in 1988 (APA), which broadened the diagnostic criteria, and increased awareness of autism. It is probable that the increase in cases is at least in part due to these changes rather than to an actual increase in the disorder.

Boys have rates of autistic disorder that are 3 to 4 times higher than girls (Volkmar et al., 2005). There is a high comorbidity with seizure disorders. There has been a growing interest in autism spectrum disorders, particularly in Asperger syndrome. There is controversy about whether the spectrum disorders are really separate disorders, and the diagnostic criteria are not well-defined (Volkmar, Lord, Bailey, Schultz, & Klin, 2004). Without clearly defined criteria, such disorders, especially Asperger syndrome, are likely to be overdiagnosed. Clinicians must be cautious about doing this because labeling a child who may just have poor social skills as having an autistic disorder could have negative implications for the child and family.

About 75 to 80 percent of people with autistic disorder are mentally retarded (Kabot, Masi, & Segal, 2003). A very small number of individuals with autistic disorder have the rare savant syndrome, a discrete area of outstanding ability such as calendar calculation or art, music, or memory skills in some very specific area (Heaton & Wallace, 2004). Savant syndrome is associated with autistic disorder but is not understood.

What happens to such severely disturbed children when they reach adulthood? Kanner (1973) reported the adult status of some of the children whom he had described in his original paper. Two developed epileptic seizures; by 1966, one of them had died and the other was in a state mental hospital. Four others had spent most of their lives in institutions. One had remained mute, but was working on a farm and as an orderly in a nursing home. The last two made at least somewhat satisfactory recoveries. Although both still lived with their parents and had little social life, they were gainfully employed and had some recreational interests. From his review of early followup studies, Lotter (1978) concluded that only 5 to 17 percent of autistic children had a relatively good outcome in adulthood. Most of the remaining children had a poor outcome, and 50 percent were institutionalized. Recent studies have reached similar conclusions (Nordin & Gillberg, 1998).

Etiological Considerations

Investigators believe that neurobiological factors are the cause of autistic disorder (Volkmar et al., 2005). A number of neurological abnormalities have been documented. Toddlers with autistic disorder have heads that are 10 percent larger in volume than those without autistic disorder (Volkmar et al., 2004). This difference is not present at birth, and the overgrowth during toddlerhood and childhood tends to level off so that differences are not so marked during adulthood. The reason for these differences is not yet understood. Abnormalities are also found in the amygdala, hippocampus, and cerebellum; the nature and causes of these abnormalities are being investigated. Furthermore, the prevalence of autism in children whose mothers had rubella during the prenatal period is approximately 10 times higher than in the general population of children.

Genetic factors in the etiology of autistic disorder are well-established. Siblings of children with autistic disorder have a 2 percent chance of also having the disorder (McBride, Anderson, & Shapiro, 1996). Although this is a small percentage, it represents a fiftyfold increase in risk as compared to the morbidity risk in the general population. Further evidence of the importance of genetic factors in autistic disorder is provided by twin studies. Monozygotic twins have concordance rates of over 60 percent while dizygotic twins have concordance rates of 0 percent (Muhle, Trentacoste, & Rapin, 2004). At least three to four but maybe as many as ten different genes are believed to interact to result in the phenotype of autistic disorder (Volkmar et al., 2004).

Family studies reveal delayed language acquisition and social deficits in the nonautistic relatives of index cases with autistic disorder (Piren, Palmer, Jacobi, Childress, & Arndt, 1997). Taken together, the evidence from family and twin studies supports a genetic basis for autistic disorder. In Sam's case, there was no evidence of any neurological abnormality, nor was there any family history of autism. However, Sam's older sister did have a learning disability.

Genetic factors alone may not be the only etiological contributor to autistic disorder. It is possible that genes create a susceptibility to environmental factors, such as toxins (Lawler, Croen, Grether, & Van de Water, 2004). However, there is no definitive evidence at this time that any specific toxin or teratogen is related. There has been tremendous focus in the media on vaccines, specifically thimerosal, a preservative used in vaccines, as playing a role in autistic disorder, following a research report published in 1998 that speculated about such a link. However, that report was retracted because it was based on insufficient evidence and because one of the authors had a financial incentive in a lawsuit against the vaccine manufacturers (Fleck, 2004). A flurry of research on vaccines followed, and no link with autistic disorder has been found (Parker, Schwartz, Todd, & Pickering, 2004). Unfortunately, many parents have withheld vaccines for their children out of fear due to the media reports, and as a result, many children are at risk for those infectious diseases.

Treatment

Numerous biological therapeutic approaches have been tried with autistic disorder, most commonly the same kinds of medication (e.g., haloperidol) that are used to treat adult patients who have psychotic disorders, and also with selective serotonin reuptake inhibitors (Palermo & Curatolo, 2004). Some improvement is found with these medications in reducing stereotyped motor behavior, social withdrawal, and aggression. However, positive effects are not found for language impairment and social deficits (McBride et al., 1996). There has also been some interest in two other drugs—fenfluramine, an amphetamine derivitive, and naltrexone, a drug that blocks the brain's opioid receptors. Both may lead to some improvement, although neither appears to alter the core symptoms of the disorder (Kolmen, Feldman, Handen, & Janosky, 1995; Rapin, 1997).

The major psychological treatment for autism is behavior therapy. As we saw in Sam's case, it requires a great expenditure of time and effort. Furthermore, these children have several problems that make teaching them difficult. They have difficulty adjusting to changes in routine, such as substitute teachers. Their self-stimulatory behavior interferes with effective teaching, and finding reinforcers that motivate autistic children can be difficult.

In general, behavior therapists focus on reliably assessed, observable behaviors and manipulate the consequences these behaviors elicit from the environment. As in Sam's case, desirable behaviors (e.g., speech, playing with other children) are rewarded, and undesirable ones (e.g., hand flapping, screaming) are either ignored or punished. The desired behaviors are broken down into smaller elements that are learned first and then assembled into a whole. A good example of this procedure was seen in the procedures used to try to get Sam to speak. Modeling is a frequent adjunct in these operant behavior therapy programs.

Many aspects of autistic disorder can be improved with behavioral programs. Self-care skills, social behavior, and language have all shown improvements in controlled studies (e.g., Koegel, Schreibman, Britten, Burke, & O'Neill, 1982). Undesirable behaviors such as self-stimulation and self-injurious behavior have been decreased (Ross & Nelson, 1979). Ivar Lovaas developed an intensive behavior therapy program with very young (under 4 years) children with autistic disorder

(Lovaas, 1987). Therapy encompassed all aspects of the children's lives for more than 40 hours a week for more than 2 years. Parents were trained extensively so that treatment could continue during almost all waking hours of the children's lives. Nineteen youngsters receiving this intensive treatment were compared to 40 control children who received a similar treatment for less than 10 hours per week. All children were rewarded for being less aggressive, more compliant, and more socially appropriate, including talking and playing with other children.

The results were quite dramatic and encouraging for the intensive therapy group. Their measured IQs averaged 83 in first grade (after about 2 years in the intensive therapy) compared to about 55 for the controls; 12 of the 19 reached the normal range as compared to only 2 (of 40) in the control group. Furthermore, 9 out of the 19 intensives were promoted to second grade in a normal public school, whereas only one of the much larger control group achieved this level of normal functioning. A four-year followup showed that they had maintained their gains (McEachin, Smith, & Lovaas, 1993). A recent randomized control trial of this treatment approach confirmed that it was more effective than a parent training control group, although the gains were not as impressive as those reported originally above (Volkmar et al., 2004). Moreover, other types of treatment have been shown to be effective as well.

This ambitious study confirms the need for heavy involvement of both professionals and parents in dealing with the extreme challenge of autistic disorder. Although such intensive treatment is expensive and time-consuming, the long-term dependence and loss of productive work in less intensively treated children with autistic disorder represent a greater cost to society than a treatment that enables some of these children to achieve a normal level of functioning. However, even with intensive early intervention, most children will not recover or have normal functioning, but will continue to have significant symptoms and impairment (Shea, 2004).

CHAPTER 22

Attention-Deficit/Hyperactivity Disorder

Ken's mother contacted the clinic in the middle of November about her 7-year-old son, a first-grader. She explained that Ken was having trouble at school, both academically and socially. The school psychologist had said that he was hyperactive. An initial appointment was scheduled for Ken and both parents.

Social History

The case was assigned to a clinical psychology intern who met the family in the clinic's waiting room. After a brief chat with all of them, he explained that he would first like to see the parents alone and later spend some time with Ken.

Mr. and Mrs. Wilson had been married for 12 years. He was a business manager and she was a homemaker. Ken was the middle of three children; his older sister was 9 and his younger brother, 4. There were no apparent problems with either sibling. Mrs. Wilson had a full-term pregnancy with Ken. The delivery was without complication, although labor was fairly long. The therapist explained that he would like to get an overview of the problem as it existed now.

According to his parents, Ken's current problems began in kindergarten. His teacher frequently sent notes home about disciplinary problems in the classroom. In fact, there had been concerns about promoting Ken to the first grade. The final result was a "trial promotion." Everyone hoped that Ken would mature and do much better in first grade, but his behavior became even more disruptive. Ken's mother stated that she had received negative reports about him from his teacher several times over the first two months of school. Ken's teacher complained about his failure to get work done, classroom disruption, and aggressiveness.

The therapist then asked about the parents' perception of Ken at home and his developmental history. They described him as a difficult infant, much more so than his older sister. He cried frequently and was described as a colicky baby by their pediatrician. He did not eat well, and his sleep was often fitful and restless. As Ken grew, his mother reported even more difficulties with him. He was into everything. Verbal reprimands, which had been effective in controlling his sister's behavior, seemed to have no effect on him. When either parent tried to stop him from doing something dangerous, like playing with an expensive vase or turning the stove off and on, he would often have a temper tantrum that included throwing things, breaking toys, and screaming. His relationship with his sister was poor. He bit her on several occasions and seemed to take delight in trying to get her into trouble.

His parents described a similar pattern of aggressiveness in Ken's behavior with the neighborhood children. Many of the parents no longer allowed their children to play with Ken. Ken's parents also reported that he had low frustration tolerance and a short attention span. Ken could not stay with puzzles and games for more than a few minutes and often reacted angrily when his brief efforts did not produce success. Going out for dinner had become impossible because of Ken's misbehavior in restaurants. Even mealtimes at home had become unpleasant. Indeed, Ken's parents had begun to argue frequently about how to deal with him.

Toward the end of the first session, the therapist brought Ken to his office while his parents remained in the clinic waiting room. Ken initially maintained that he did not understand why he was at the clinic, but later he admitted that he was getting into a lot of trouble at school. He agreed that it would probably be a good idea to try to do something about his misbehavior.

Ken and his parents were brought together for the final minutes of the first session. The therapist explained that the next several sessions would be devoted to conducting a more thorough assessment, including visits to the Wilsons' home and Ken's school. The parents signed release forms so the therapist could obtain information from their pediatrician and the school. The following information was gathered through these sources and from further interviews with the parents.

The Current Problem

School records generally corroborated his parents' description of Ken's behavior in kindergarten. His teacher described him as being "distractible, moody, aggressive," and a "discipline problem." Toward the end of kindergarten, his intelligence and academic achievement were tested. Although his IQ was placed at 120, he did not perform very well on reading and mathematics achievement tests. An interview with Ken's first-grade teacher provided information that agreed with other reports. Ken's teacher complained that he was frequently out of his seat, seldom sat still when he was supposed to, did not complete assignments, and had poor peer relations. Ken seemed indifferent to efforts at disciplining him. Ken's teacher also completed a short form of the Conners Rating Scale (Sprague, Cohen, & Werry, 1974) about Ken's behavior. The instrument verified the picture of hyperactive behavior that had already emerged (see Table 21.1).

The therapist arranged to spend a morning in Ken's classroom. During that time Ken was out of his seat inappropriately six times. On one occasion he jumped up to look out the window when a noise, probably a car backfiring, was heard. He went to talk to other children three times. Ken got up twice and just began walking quickly around the classroom. Even when he stayed seated, he was often not working and instead was fidgeting or bothering other children. Any noise, even another child coughing or dropping a pencil, distracted him from his work. When his teacher

Table 2.1   Teacher's Ratings of Ken's Behavior on the Short Form of the Conners Rating Scale

Observation: Classroom Behavior	Degree of Activity			
	(0) Not at All	(1) Just a Little	(2) Pretty Much	(3) Very Much
Constantly fidgeting			X	
Demands must be met immediately—easily frustrated				X
Restless or overactive				X
Excitable, impulsive			X	
Inattentive, easily distracted				X
Fails to finish things he starts—short attention span				X
Cries often and easily		X		
Disturbs other children		X		
Mood changes quickly and drastically		X		
Temper outbursts, explosive and unpredictable behavior				X

Source: Sprague, Cohen, and Werry (1974)

spoke to him, he did not seem to hear; it was not until the teacher had begun yelling at him that he paid any attention.

Subsequent sessions with Ken's parents focused on his current behavior at home. The pattern that had begun earlier in Ken's childhood continued. He still got along poorly with his sister, had difficulty sitting still at mealtimes, and reacted with temper tantrums when demands were made of him. His behavior had also taken on a daredevil quality, as illustrated by his climbing out of his second-story bedroom window and racing his bicycle down the hill of a heavily trafficked local street. Indeed, his daring acts seemed to be the only way he could get any positive attention from his neighborhood peers, who seemed to be mostly afraid of him. He had no really close friends.

Mr. Wilson missed two of these sessions because of his business schedule. Most days he had to commute to work, a two-hour train trip each way. During a session he missed, Mrs. Wilson hinted that they had marital problems. When this was brought up directly, she agreed that their marriage was not as good now as it once had been. Their arguments centered on how to handle Ken. Mrs. Wilson had come to believe that severe physical punishment was the only answer. She described an active, growing dislike of Ken and feared that he might never change.

The next time Mr. Wilson was present, the therapist asked him about his child-rearing philosophy. He admitted that he took more of a "boys will be boys" approach. In fact, he reported that as a child he was like Ken. He had "grown out of it" and expected Ken would, too. As a result, he let Ken get away with things for which Mrs. Wilson would have punished him. The couple's arguments, which had recently become more heated and frequent, usually occurred after Mr. Wilson had arrived home from work. Mrs. Wilson, after a particularly exasperating day with Ken, would try to get Mr. Wilson to discipline Ken. "Just wait until your father gets home" was a familiar refrain. But Mr. Wilson would refuse and accuse his wife of overreacting; the battle would then begin.

The next week, the therapist visited the Wilson home, arriving just before Ken and his sister got home from school. The first part of the visit was uneventful, but at about 4:30 P.M., Ken and his sister got into a fight over who was winning a game. Ken broke the game, and his sister came crying to her mother, who began shouting at Ken. Ken tried to explain his behavior by saying that his sister had been cheating. His mother ordered him to his room; shortly thereafter, when she heard him crying, she went up and told him he could come out.

The children ate their dinner at 5:30 P.M.; Mrs. Wilson planned to wait until her husband came home later to have hers. The meal began with Ken complaining that he did not like anything on his plate. He picked at his food for a few minutes and then started making faces at his sister. Mrs. Wilson yelled at him to stop making the faces and eat his dinner. When she turned her back, he began shoving food from his plate onto his sister's. As she resisted, Ken knocked over his glass of milk, which broke on the floor. Ken's mother was enraged at this point. She looked as if she was ready to hit Ken, but she calmed herself, perhaps because of the therapist's presence. Although she told Ken that he would be in big trouble when his father got home, nothing happened. When Mr. Wilson came home, he made light of the incident and refused to punish Ken. Even though Mrs. Wilson's exasperation was obvious, she said nothing.

Conceptualization and Treatment

The therapist conceptualized Ken's problem in an operant-conditioning framework. Although open to possible biological causes of Ken's behavior, the therapist believed that a structured program of rewards and punishments—contingency management—would help. Treatment would then involve trying to increase the frequency of positive behaviors (complying with parental requests, interacting positively with his sister, staying in his seat in the classroom) by providing positive consequences for them. Similarly, undesirable behaviors should be followed by negative consequences. It was explained to Ken's parents that many of these undesirable behaviors had actually been producing positive results for him. His tantrums, for example, frequently allowed him to have his own way. The complicating feature was the attitude of Ken's parents. Would either of them be willing to engage in the considerable effort required to make a contingency management system work? To try to counter this potential problem, the therapist, after explaining the results of his overall assessment and the broad outlines of his treatment plan, asked both parents to try to put aside their current attitudes for a brief period while they implemented a simple, scaled-down version of the overall plan. The hope was that a simple intervention, directed at only a couple of problem areas, would produce visible, quick results. This small change might be sufficient to increase the parents' enthusiasm and allow a complete therapeutic package to be instituted later.

Two target behaviors were selected—leaving his seat in the classroom and inappropriate behavior at mealtimes at home. Mealtime behavior problems were defined as complaining about the food served; kicking his sister under the table; not staying in his chair; and laughing, giggling, or making faces. During the next week the parents were instructed to record the frequency of disruptive behavior at mealtimes as well as several other target behaviors (temper tantrums, fights with siblings, and noncompliance with parental requests) that could be targets for later interventions. The next day, Ken's teacher was contacted. He agreed to keep a record of the number of times Ken was out of his seat each day.

During the next session, an intervention was planned. The records of the past week indicated that every meal had been problematic. Ken had also been out of his seat when he was supposed to be working at his desk for an average of nine times per day. The therapist explained to Ken and his parents that in the next week daily rewards would be made available if Ken was not disruptive at mealtimes and if he reduced the number of times he was out of his seat at school. Everyone agreed that Ken would be allowed to select an extra half hour of television watching, a favorite dessert, or a game to be played with one of his parents if his behavior met an agreed-on criterion. The initial criterion was being out of his seat less than five times per day at school and being nondisruptive for at least one of the two meals eaten at home each day. The therapist showed Ken's parents how to make a chart that was to be posted on the refrigerator. Ken's teacher would send a daily note home indicating how many times he was out of his seat and that number, along with checks for a "good" meal, would be entered on the chart. Ken's teacher was contacted after the session, and the program was explained. He agreed to send home a daily record of the number of times Ken was out of his seat.

Ken's parents were obviously pleased at the beginning of the next session. They had brought their chart with them; some changes had obviously occurred. Ken had met criterion on six of the seven days. The average number of times he was out of his seat went from 9 to 3.6, and he had been unpleasant at mealtimes only five times (two of these occurred on Saturday, resulting in his single failure to obtain a reward). During the next several sessions, the parents and the therapist worked on expanding the program. Temper tantrums, fighting with his siblings, and noncompliance with parental requests had all been frequent the previous week. Ken's parents now were eager to attempt to deal with them.

Of the three targets, noncompliance proved to be the most difficult to address. It presented such a large array of possibilities that a specific description of a criterion was problematic. A program was developed that involved the following components: Temper tantrums would lead to a time-out procedure in which Ken would have to go to his room and stay quietly for 10 minutes. Fighting was handled first by a simple request to stop. If that was ineffective, the time-out procedure would be employed. To try to get Ken to comply with parental requests such as going to bed or to stop teasing his sister, his parents were instructed to make the requests calmly and clearly to be sure he heard them. If he did not comply, they were to give him one reminder, again in a calm fashion; if that failed, he would be sent to his room. The therapist stressed to the parents that their requests to stop or do something had to be made calmly and that time-out should also be administered calmly. Finally, the parents were instructed to provide social reinforcement for cooperative play and being pleasant at meals by simply telling Ken how pleased they were when they saw him playing nicely with his siblings.

Based on the records from the previous weeks, it looked as though Ken would have experienced about 20 time-outs if the new system had been in effect. It was therefore decided that if Ken was sent to his room fewer than 10 times, he would receive a special end-of-week reward, a trip to the theater to see a film. The meal-time procedure was kept in effect, and as before, a chart was to be completed showing school behavior, mealtimes, and frequency of time-outs. This time, the parents were also asked to keep a log of the number of times they praised Ken and of the specific details of instances of noncompliance. The latter feature was included to make sure the parents' requests were not unreasonable.

Meanwhile, the therapist contacted Ken's teacher and increased the scope of the school program. The teacher was asked to maintain his recordkeeping of Ken's being out of his seat, but he was also to praise Ken as often as possible when he was working appropriately. The daily report card was expanded to include the number of assignments completed and the number of aggressive interactions with peers, defined broadly to include both physical and verbal aggression. Other instances of disruptive behavior (being noisy, making faces) were also to be recorded. The records from this week were to be used in planning another intervention during the next session with the parents.

At the session following the implementation of the time-out procedure, the parents were decidedly less enthusiastic than they had been the previous week. Although the improvement in mealtime behavior had been maintained, Ken had been sent to his room 17 times over the course of the week and thus did not get his Sunday trip to the movie. It seemed that time-out was not an effective consequence for Ken. The therapist asked the parents for more details on how they were using the procedure. It turned out that Ken had lots of toys in his room, so the therapist decided to change the system. In an effort to increase the effectiveness of time-out, Ken's toys were put away so that time-out consisted of sitting on his bed with no toys to play with or books to look at. Furthermore, all the at-home targets were linked to a daily reward (one of the three described earlier). Specifically, Ken was to get 2 points for each pleasant meal, 2 points if he had only one time-out before dinner, and 2 points for none after dinner.

The expanded school program was also converted to a point system. The teacher's records for the previous week indicated that Ken had been out of his seat an average of three times per day, had completed 55 percent of his assignments, and was either aggressive or disruptive five times during the average day. A set of new criteria was adopted for school and linked to points: 2 points for being out of his seat less than three times per day, 2 points for completing 70 percent or more of his assignments, and 2 points for reducing the frequency of aggressive behavior or disruptiveness to less than three times per day. Thus, Ken could earn 12 points on each school day and 6 on weekends. The criterion for one of the daily rewards was set at 8 points on a school day and 4 points on weekends. In addition, a weekly total of 54 points would result in Ken's being taken to see a movie.

The system now appeared to be working well. During one typical week Ken earned 58 points and thus got his trip to the movie. In addition, he met the criterion for a daily reward each day. At home he averaged only one time-out per day, and 12 of 14 meals had been without incident. At school he was out of his seat slightly less than twice per day, completed an average of 70 percent of his assignments, and was either aggressive or disruptive fewer than three times per day.

For the following week, the criteria for school behavior were increased again. Points could be earned for being out of his seat less than twice per day, completing 80 percent of his assignments, and being aggressive or disruptive less than twice per day. At home, the point system was left unchanged. The criterion for a daily reward was raised to 10 for school days and 6 on weekends; the criterion for the end-of-week reward was raised to 66. In addition, a new daily reward was added to the program—a bedtime story from Ken's father. The parents were also encouraged to continue providing praise for good behavior. The therapist called Ken's teacher to discuss a similar tactic for the classroom.

The program continued to evolve over the next few weeks, and Ken made steady progress. By the fourteenth week, it was clear that Ken's behavior had dramatically changed and his academic performance was improving. At this point, sessions were held only once every two weeks, and the family was followed for three more months. Increased emphasis was placed on teaching Ken's parents the general principles that they had been following so that when problems arose they would be able to handle them on their own by modifying the system.

Both Ken's parents and his teacher were also reporting changes in Ken that had not been targets of the intervention. He was described as being less moody, more pleasant, and more able to deal with frustration. He had also begun to form some friendships and was being invited to other children's homes to play. Although Ken was still somewhat difficult to handle, his parents now believed that they had some skills they could use. Ken's mother reported that she now felt much more positive toward him. The couple also indicated that their arguments had become much less frequent. Two steps remained. First, the daily rewards were phased out. Instead, the parents were to provide social reinforcement for good behavior during the day. The rewards were still provided, but in a less formal manner in which they were not linked explicitly to the number of points earned during the day.

Finally, the formal contingency aspect of the weekend reward was dropped. A "good week" still led to a special treat or activity but was not linked specifically to a particular criterion. Ken's behavior remained stable, and treatment was concluded.

Discussion

According to *DSM-IV-TR* (APA, 2000), Ken meets criteria for attention-deficit/hyperactivity disorder (ADHD), one of the subcategories in the manual's section headed "Disorders Usually First Diagnosed in Infancy, Childhood, or Adolescence." This large section encompasses disorders of the intellect (e.g., mental retardation), overt behavior (e.g., attention-deficit/hyperactivity disorder, conduct disorder), and pervasive disorders of development (e.g., autistic disorder, discussed in Chapter 21).

The term *attention-deficit/hyperactivity disorder* reflects the prevailing view that problems in attention are the principal aspect of the disorder. These difficulties include failure to finish tasks, not listening, being easily distracted, and having problems concentrating and maintaining attention. This description fits Ken well. Overactivity and restlessness are reflected in his problems staying seated in school, fidgeting when seated, and being described as "always on the go." Hyperactivity is especially evident in any situation that requires controlling activity level, such as school and mealtimes.

DSM-IV-TR (APA, 2000) lists three types of ADHD: (1) the primarily inattentive type in which poor attention predominates, (2) the predominately hyperactive type in which hyperactivity and impulsivity are primary, and (3) the combined type in which both hyperactivity and inattention are prominent. Overall, the combined type is most common, but among girls, the inattentive type predominates (Biederman, Mick, Faraone, et al., 2002). Ken's formal diagnosis was ADHD, combined type, because he met the criteria for both the inattention and hyperactivity components.

In addition to their core problems, children with ADHD have a number of other difficulties. As evidenced by poor academic and test performance (Barkley, DuPaul, & McMurray, 1990), between 20 and 25 percent have learning problems. Children with ADHD also have difficulties getting along with peers and making friends (Hinshaw & Melnick, 1995). As many as 50 percent also meet the diagnostic criteria for conduct disorder, behavior that violates the rights of others and basic social norms, for example, being aggressive toward people, lying, stealing, and damaging property (Flory & Lynam, 2003). Oppositional-defiant disorder and learning disabilities are also common comorbid disorders. Distinguishing between conduct disorder and ADHD can be difficult because of the overlap of the symptoms of each disorder. In conduct disorder, however, it is thought that the antisocial behavior does not arise from attention deficits or impulsiveness. Therefore, although Ken showed some features of conduct disorder, he was diagnosed with ADHD because his antisocial behavior seemed due to impulsivity. People who have both ADHD and conduct disorder appear to be at particularly high risk for substance abuse in adulthood.

Between 5 and 10 percent of elementary school children have ADHD, with 2 to 3 times as many boys meeting the diagnostic criteria as girls (Willoughby, 2003). It is much more common in boys than girls in samples seeking treatment, but the gender difference in prevalence appears to be much smaller in community samples (McGee & Feehan, 1991).

The first symptoms typically appear early in toddlerhood, and most children with the hyperactive or combined subtypes are considered to be having serious problems by the time they are 7 years old (Voeller, 2004). Recently there has been a trend to diagnose adolescents and adults with ADHD. However, a recent review of the research concluded that ADHD symptoms generally improve with age (Willoughby, 2003). Nonetheless, childhood ADHD constitutes a risk for poor educational, occupational, and psychosocial outcomes. Longitudinal studies begun in the 1980s have shown that children with ADHD continue to have adjustment problems throughout adolescence and into young adulthood. In one study, over 70 percent of children with ADHD still met diagnostic criteria for the disorder in adolescence (Barkley, Fischer, Edelbrock, & Smallish, 1990). In adulthood, some with ADHD, mostly men, are more likely to abuse alcohol, display antisocial behavior, and have deficits in social and occupational behavior (Mannuzza, Klein, Bessler, Malloy, & LaPadula, 1993). Unfavorable outcomes are related to a high level of aggressiveness in childhood (Paternite & Loney, 1980).

Etiological Considerations

Research indicates a strong genetic component in ADHD. Heritability estimates for ADHD are between 60 and 90 percent (Kent, 2004). Biederman, Faraone, Mick, et al. (1995) have found that when parents have ADHD, 50 percent of their children also have ADHD. Similarly, Goodman and Stevenson (1989) found concordance for clinically diagnosed hyperactivity in 51 percent of monozygotic twins and 33 percent of dizygotic twins. Adoption studies further support the importance of a genetic predisposition to ADHD (van den Oord, Boomma, & Verhulst, 1994). Reports from Ken's father mentioned earlier indicate that he may have had ADHD as a child.

What do children with ADHD inherit? Research into brain structures has been guided by the idea that ADHD reflects impulsivity; children with ADHD are unable to inhibit activity when the environment calls for it and cannot inhibit attention from distracting stimuli (Quay, 1997). Evidence has accumulated that there may be some impairment in the frontal lobes of the brain, which are known to play an important role in allowing people to inhibit behavioral responses. For example, Castellanos, Giedd, Marsh, Hamburger, Vaituzis, et al. (1996) studied children with ADHD with magnetic resonance imaging (MRI) scans and found that they had smaller frontal lobes than controls. Evidence of the poorer performance of children with ADHD on neuropsychological tests of frontal lobe functioning (such as inhibiting behavioral responses) provides further support for the theory that a basic deficit in this part of the brain may be related to the symptoms of the disorder (Nigg, 2001).

Other biological risk factors that may be linked to ADHD include low birth weight and birth complications (Ben Amor, Grizenko, Schwartz, Lageix, Baron, Ter-Stepanian, et al., 2005; Tannock, 1998). Maternal smoking during pregnancy may also be important. Millberger, Biederman, Faraone, Chen, & Jones (1996) found that 22 percent of the children of mothers who smoked a pack or more of cigarettes a day could be diagnosed with ADHD as compared to only 8 percent in a control sample. Animal research has shown that nicotine interferes with brain development during gestation. Brain injury due to trauma, stroke, or encephalitis can sometimes lead to symptoms of ADHD (Voeller, 2004).

A mother's emotional state during her pregnancy also may affect her child's risk for behavior problems. High levels of anxiety during early pregnancy may affect the developing brain through stress hormones. Van den Bergh and Marcoen

(2004) found that maternal levels of anxiety early in pregnancy predicted ADHD symptoms in children when they were 8 and 9 years old. The anxiety levels during early pregnancy were more predictive than those after the birth, which is consistent with the pregnancy hormonal environment programming brain development.

Other environmental causes have been investigated as well. Watching a lot of television at 1 and 3 years of age has been linked to later attentional problems (Christakis, Zimmerman, DiGiuseppe, & McCarty, 2004). Television's fast-paced events and changing images may affect the developing brain, shortening attention span. However, it is not yet clear whether this association is causal, or whether some other variable is linked to both. Being raised in chaotic or impoverished environments may lead to difficulties regulating attention and controlling impulses (Voeller, 2004). Bettelheim (1973) suggested that ADHD develops when a predisposition to the disorder is coupled with ineffective parenting strategies. A child with a disposition toward overactivity and moodiness is stressed further by a mother who easily becomes impatient and resentful. The child is unable to cope with the mother's demands for obedience; the mother becomes more and more negative and disapproving, and the mother-child relationship becomes a battleground. With a disruptive and disobedient pattern already established, the demands of school cannot be handled, and the behavior of the child is often in conflict with the rules of the classroom.

A longitudinal study of child development generated some evidence that is consistent with Bettelheim's position (Battle & Lacey, 1972). Mothers of children with ADHD were found to be critical of them and relatively unaffectionate, even during the children's infancy. These mothers continued to be disapproving of their children and dispensed severe penalties for disobedience. More recently, maternal warmth was found to predict teachers' ratings of ADHD symptoms in a sample of low-birth-weight children who were at risk for behavioral problems (Tully, Arseneault, Caspi, Moffitt, & Morgan, 2004).

The parent-child relationship, however, is bidirectional; the behavior of each is determined by the actions and reactions of the other. While parents of children with ADHD give them more commands and have negative interactions with them, children with ADHD have also been found to be less compliant and more negative in their interactions with their parents (Barkley, Karlsson, & Pollard, 1985). As indicated later in the section on treatment, stimulant medication has been shown to reduce hyperactivity and increase compliance in ADHD children. Significantly, when such medication is used, the parent's commands and negative behavior also decrease (see Barkley, 1990), suggesting that the child's behavior influenced that of the parents. In Ken's case it seemed that his mother's negative attitude toward him was principally a response to his disruptive behavior. Nevertheless, her negative attitude, coupled with the inconsistent disciplinary practices of the parents, may have exacerbated Ken's disorder.

Treatment

The most common therapy for children with ADHD is stimulant medication such as methylphenidate (Ritalin®) and amphetamine (Adderall®). Although it may seem strange to stimulate further a child who may already be having problems with overactivity, research indicates that these drugs improve attention and lower activity level in both normal and ADHD children (Rapoport, Buchsbaum, Weingartner, Zahn, Ludlow, & Mikkelsen, 1980). The main therapeutic effect may be to improve attention or to increase the child's sensitivity to rewards (Barkley, 1990); activity level then decreases because the child is able to stay with various activities for longer periods of time and is more strongly reinforced by them.

The available research clearly indicates that stimulants, particularly methyl-phenidate, are partially effective (Gillberg, Melander, von Knorring, Janols, Thernlund, et al. 1997). The drugs reduce aggression and hyperactivity and improve concentration, classroom behavior, and social interactions. One ingenious study even demonstrated that Ritalin helped children with ADHD who were playing soft-ball to assume the ready position in the outfield and keep track of the status of the game. Children given placebos, in contrast, frequently threw or kicked their gloves while the pitch was in progress (Pelham, McBurnett, Harper, Milich, Murphy, Clinton, & Thiele, 1990). Short-term side effects of stimulant treatment, principally insomnia and loss of appetite, usually disappear quickly.

The benefits of the drugs are lost, however, if they are discontinued. Therefore, long-term treatment is indicated, but the possible long-term risks of treatment with stimulants have not been well researched, so the decision to use them should be weighed carefully. Furthermore, although the drugs cause improvement, they do not lead to fully normal functioning. For example, Whalen, Henker, Buhrmester, Hinshaw, Huber, & Laski (1989) found significantly better peer appraisals during treatment, but the ADHD boys were still liked less than average. The effect of drugs on academic performance also remains controversial, with some studies revealing positive changes and others none (Henker & Whalen, 1989). Finally, there have been concerns that stimulants are being overused and given to children who do not have ADHD. Prescriptions for stimulants have certainly increased in the last decade (Zito, Safer, dosReis, et al., 2000). Furthermore, in a study conducted in Virginia, 18 to 20 percent of fifth grade boys were on stimulants, a figure much higher than the number expected given the prevalence of ADHD (LeFever, Dawson, & Mor-row, 1999). Increasing numbers of preschool children have been prescribed stimu-lant medication, even though there is little data available for this age group (Kra-tochvil, Greenhill, March, Burke, & Vaughan, 2004). Some professionals have been concerned that using stimulant medication in childhood would increase the risk of substance abuse in adulthood, but research has shown that it actually de-creases the risk, possibly by reducing ADHD symptoms (Wilens, Faraone, Bieder-man, & Gunawardene, 2003).

A variety of psychological therapies have been used for ADHD, but the most thoroughly studied is an operant learning or contingency management approach such as that used in Ken's case. Positive reinforcement is used to increase on-task behavior such as remaining in one's seat and engaging in positive interactions with peers, teachers, and parents. Negative consequences follow undesirable behaviors such as being disruptive in the classroom.

The comparative effectiveness of different treatments for ADHD has been evaluated in a large-scale, carefully conducted study (MTA Cooperative Group,

1999). Children with ADHD were randomly assigned to one of four groups: (1) stimulant medication, (2) behavioral treatment, (3) medication plus behavioral treatment, and (4) standard community care. In terms of reducing symptoms and increasing positive functioning, the combined treatment was best but only slightly better than medication alone. However, children in the combined treatment group needed less medication, a potential advantage given the possible side effects of drugs. Results for the behavioral treatment were not as positive in this study as in prior research. On certain outcomes such as harsh and ineffective disciplines, combined medication and behavioral treatment was superior to medication alone (Chronis, Chacko, Fabiano, Wymbs, & Pelham, 2004). Behavioral treatment alone is recommended as the first treatment approach for preschool children, when the parents are reluctant to use medication, and for milder forms of ADHD (Root & Resnick, 2003).

CHAPTER 23

Separation Anxiety Disorder: School Phobia

Mr. and Mrs. Berg had taken Robert to physicians and clinics many times. One Sunday night they even took him to the emergency room after they found him panic-stricken, writhing in bed with pain. An attractive, curly haired, underweight 8-year-old, Robert, in second grade, had always been afraid of school. Recently, his fears were becoming tinged with a morbid depression that alarmed his parents.

The child sat in an overstuffed chair in the office of the family's doctor, who did not take an especially psychological approach in treating her patients. She asked the skeptical Robert whether the warm chocolate milk she had suggested helped, but he shook his head sheepishly, looking all the while to his mother. She was sitting nearby with an expression of desperation and love that only made the boy feel even more guilty about the pain he was causing his family. If only he could stop being a baby, Robert thought to himself, as the doctor and his mother discussed the latest pattern of school morning and evening difficulties.

Without fail, Sunday through Thursday evenings found the boy eating little at dinner, staring morosely at his plate, picking idly at his food, and wondering whether it was really worth eating, since he would probably be vomiting it all up an hour or two later. His skinny little body was beset with a host of twitches and rituals that became more pronounced if noticed. Robert felt ill-equipped to resist them and helpless to control the anxiety that worsened as the evening wore on.

Bedtime offered little solace. If he was still awake after 9:30 P.M., he would sometimes break into tears that brought his mother into bed with him. In a fruitless effort to distract his worrying mind and ease him into sleep, she told Robert fanciful stories and promised him rewards if he would manage to go to school the following day without the usual somatic complaints and pitiful entreaties that he be allowed to stay home "just for today."

But it was the morning that really threw the household into total chaos. Rising by 6 A.M., Robert would pace the floor of the small apartment, causing the boards to creak and usually waking his older brother. By 7 A.M., everyone was awake whether they wanted to be or not. While preparations for the day occupied everyone else, Robert spent the time groaning in a corner of the kitchen, rubbing his stomach, and occasionally dashing into the bathroom to throw up in the toilet. His mother would plead, cajole, and insist that he at least drink a glass of milk for breakfast, but he would refuse, whining that it would only make him vomit more.

When it was time to leave for school, Robert had to be pushed out of the apartment. His tearful pleading and complaints of stomach upset and body pains led his

his mother many times to relent and allow him to stay home. Robert was unusually bright and did not get much out of school academically, and his mother had come to use this to justify her frequent decision to let him stay with her instead of insisting he go to school. Much of the time, however, Robert's pleading was rebuffed, especially when his stern father had not yet left for work. Robert would make his way miserably to school, trying to hide his tears from other children.

Once there, Robert usually settled down by lunchtime, but not without a visit from his mother, who would come to the schoolyard at recess with encouraging and loving words to her little boy and a container of milk and some cookies. This midmorning contact with mother was an implicit part of the deal Robert had struck with her for his going off to school. She continued these visits even though she knew they were probably not in her son's best interests, because she would otherwise be nervous and upset about his well-being in her absence.

Robert's peer relationships were surprisingly good. He was well liked by his classmates and by neighborhood friends, in spite of his fear of going to school. Although thin and almost emaciated in appearance from all the vomiting and his generally lackluster appetite, Robert was healthy and a good athlete. Even if he could not get to school without crying and vomiting, he could at least play ball with enthusiasm and distinction.

But he had no way to express adequately to anyone, even to his mother, how school terrified him. It was not just the separation from home that frightened him— although, to be sure, he never went far from his neighborhood or even spend much time at friends' houses. There was something particular about *school*. His second-grade teacher was not especially warm, but was always nice to Robert, both out of concern and out of appreciation for how good a student he was. The building itself seemed to him as cheery and attractive as a haunted house, and the authoritarian atmosphere did little to make him feel better. It is not an exaggeration to say that Robert's sorrowful walk to school in the morning resembled that of a convicted murderer as he was led from his cell to be put to death.

Social History

Robert was the younger of two sons; his brother was six years older. His parents were third-generation Jewish immigrants from Russia, and Mr. Berg was a self-employed insurance broker. He had graduated from a business school and worked for several years in a large agency downtown before striking out on his own. Mrs. Berg had not attended college. She married soon after her graduation from high school and became pregnant three months later. During an argument some years into the marriage, Mr. Berg angrily told her that he would have gone into another line of work if he had not been saddled so quickly with family responsibilities. For some time, Mrs. Berg blamed herself for having prevented her husband from pursuing the work he wanted.

Money was a constant worry. Dinner conversation revolved around things the family needed but could not afford, and around the importance of higher education for the two boys. It was never a question of *whether* Robert and his brother would go to college and to professional or graduate school afterward but, of *which* college and which type of postgraduate training. For many lower-middle-class Jewish families, education was viewed as *the* golden opportunity for advancement. Even though it had been 90 years since Robert's great-grandparents fled from Russia to the United States to escape tsarist pogroms, he had already incorporated these values and anxiety-laden goals. Robert and his older brother were very different from each other—Robert tense and nervous much of the time, his older brother jovial and optimistic, at least outwardly. They were, however, both highly intelligent and serious about their schooling.   Years later, Robert recalled that he viewed kindergarten as the first difficult and challenging step to making his way in life.

Both boys received a boundless outpouring of love from grandparents and parents alike, especially from their mother.   She constantly hugged and kissed her two boys, showering praise and food on them whenever they were near her, which was often. Robert's brother seemed to respond positively to this affection (and his rotund, cherubic appearance attested to his enjoyment of the food), but somehow Robert experienced it as yet another source of tension. In his worrying mind, every display of love and every word of approval only reminded him of the possibility of *not* having the love and approval. Even though praise and affection seemed to be constantly available, Robert began, even in earliest childhood, to worry whether his mother would still love him if he were not "good." When he began school, there suddenly seemed to be countless hoops to be jumped through in an unending effort to retain the closeness and reassurance that he had developed a strong need for, especially from his mother.

Robert was constantly comparing the modest, lower-middle-class surroundings of his family and the relative affluence of his cousins. His maternal uncle was an extroverted lawyer who had built a lucrative practice. As far back as Robert could remember, the visits to his cousins' home were a mixture of gleeful enjoyment of expensive and elaborate toys and a spacious house, and a brooding envy and resentment that they were not his. The return to the small, crowded apartment on Sunday evening, after an afternoon of temporary immersion in wealth, upset Robert and made him feel tense, angry, inferior, and hurt.

Robert was afraid of school from the beginning. His extreme fear and avoidance, however, were almost less remarkable than his incredible seriousness, an attitude that was apparent on the days he managed to get to school. His kindergarten teacher noted to herself the first few days of school that Robert behaved more like a goal-oriented first-year medical student than a 5-year-old child. He always sat with his hands tightly folded on the table in front of him looking attentively at the teacher, eager to do her bidding, even trying to anticipate her wishes—anything to be patted on the head, assured that he was a good and smart boy, not prone to make mistakes or to give cause for a cross word or rebuke. So sensitive had he become by then to criticism and disapproval that it would wound him deeply even when another child was reprimanded. He was on edge continuously, fearful that he would fall short in the teacher's eyes or that a classmate would be disciplined.

This pattern persisted until the middle of second grade, when a visit to the family doctor—who by now was at her wits' end with Robert—resulted in a promising referral. At the nearby university, a professor visiting from another country was teaching a seminar on child psychotherapy, and was seeking referrals of children with psychological problems for the graduate students to treat under the supervision. This referral led to the following intervention.

Conceptualization and Treatment

Exposure to the School Setting

The way therapy was planned and implemented was unusual in that Robert's case was discussed intensively in the clinical seminar of Professor Long. The more behavioral members of the group argued that Robert's school phobia be handled straightforwardly, as a fear and avoidance of school, and therefore, amenable to a graduated exposure therapy regimen. A counterconditioning approach—whereby an undesirable response is replaced by a more desirable one by encouraging its performance—is appropriate in the earliest stages of treatment, when fear and avoidance are so high that virtually no approach responses are being performed. The strategy is to expose the child gradually to school, all the while trying to induce states antagonistic to anxiety with comforting and hugging, even if it means reinforcing avoidance. Later on, as the child is more and more able to attend school, rewards can be made contingent on varying degrees of school attendance.

But the less behaviorally oriented students suggested a more complex and less strictly behavioral intervention. First, it was noted that Robert was subject to anxieties other than those surrounding school, although his school phobia was obviously a dominating problem. He showed anxiety and extreme reluctance about venturing far from home for *any* reason unless in the company of a family member, especially his mother. His mother seemed to need to have him overly dependent on her. She acceded too readily to his demands to stay home, and, if he made it to school, she would visit during recess and lovingly hand milk and cookies to Robert through the bars of the school fence. In addition, Robert's unusual seriousness and perfectionism seemed to play a part in the phobia. For Robert, school was a grave and weighty matter at an age when most children have fun and enjoy the simple pleasures of childhood. Robert's resentment and envy of his wealthy uncle also seemed relevant, perhaps highlighting the benefits that awaited those who would work instead of play. Finally, since the household had been organized around Robert's fearfulness, adjustments would be necessary in order to support whatever improvement Robert might show in going to school regularly.

Therapy proceeded along several fronts, often simultaneously—an intensive approach that was possible because it was a teaching case for the graduate students. Professor Long and one of his students conducted office sessions with Robert alone, with Robert accompanied by his parents, and with the parents by themselves; another student worked with the boy directly on the school phobia every weekday.

The latter, as the most straightforward and behavioral aspect of the treatment program, can be described first. The overall goal was to expose Robert gradually and steadily to more and more of the school situation. For the first few mornings, the student-therapist came to the apartment 30 minutes before Robert's scheduled departure, talk soothingly with him, trying to point out the fun aspects of school. Robert knew, in other words, that he would not attend school the first few days but would just practice walking in the company of the therapist (whom he grew quickly to like). By the end of the week, Robert felt he was ready to enter the schoolyard with the therapist and decide only then whether to proceed to the classroom. By this point, the school administration and Robert's teacher knew about the therapy and that he would be accompanied by the therapist. It was also explained to the other children in his class that Robert's "friend" was someone who was trying to make him more at ease in school. The children showed understanding and support. They liked Robert, even with his occasional vomiting and erratic attendance, and hoped that the therapist would succeed in making him more comfortable in school.

After two weeks, Robert was able to leave his house alone, walk to school, and enter the schoolyard knowing that the therapist was waiting for him. A few days later, he was able to make it into the classroom with the therapist waiting for him there; two weeks after that he could remain at school all day, meeting the graduate student as he left the building for the walk home. During these weeks the emphasis was on rewarding approximations to school attendance; his mother was cautioned against coming to school at recess or allowing Robert to stay home if asked. Dealing with the mother's reluctance to stay away from school at recess was the focus of other members of the therapist team.

A breakthrough occurred seven weeks after the beginning of therapy. The therapist was waiting at the end of the school day for the boy to come out of the school building and then accompany him home, when Robert appeared with several classmates who lived in his neighborhood. In a serious manner, more appropriate for a child several years older, Robert asked the therapist if he would mind not walking him home because he would rather be with his friends.

Family Sessions with the Parents

Without necessarily implicating the mother as the cause of the boy's dependency and school avoidance, Professor Long and his student cotherapists decided that her attitudes and needs should be examined. Perhaps Mrs. Berg derived something positive from Robert's fearfulness; at the very least, she put up with monumental disruption in her own life just to cater to Robert's wishes and anxieties.

The first few sessions in Professor Long's office were with Robert and his parents. The therapists asked each of them for their perspectives on what was going on and what might help the situation. Robert was fairly uncommunicative, looking frequently at his parents for help in answering even the simplest and most mundane questions, such as what his teacher's name was and how many students were in his class. The mother sighed a great deal during the sessions, occasionally weeping and declaring that she would lay her life down for Robert, and would do anything "just to make my little boy happy." The father was distant in the sessions, acutely uncomfortable about discussing emotional issues. They had a very traditional marriage, and the raising of the children was considered entirely Mrs. Berg's responsibility. In the case of Mrs. Berg, it became more and more clear that this was a responsibility she treasured and was reluctant to share with her husband, even though she complained that he did not take enough of an interest in the children.

Individual Cognitive-Behavioral Therapy with the Boy

Two sessions were spent with Robert alone, and the therapists were pleasantly surprised at how loquacious and insightful he was when his parents were absent. He was able to express that he dreaded making a mistake at school, that he desperately needed the approval of his teacher even as he needed that of his mother, that "perfect" performance at school seemed to him the best and most reliable way to obtain praise from his parents, without which existence itself seemed doubtful. In Robert's eyes, entrance into college also depended very much on his work in second grade. The pressure this created made going to school a dreaded and awesome task. At the same time, Robert expressed a vague sense that his mother was almost as anxious about his leaving her side as he was. Even when she pleaded with him to go to school or to play in a friend's house on a Saturday morning, he somehow felt that she would rather he not do so and felt confused about what she actually wanted. Not wishing to disappoint her, the boy was made even more nervous by this ambiguity. He also wondered how she could be so accepting of his frequent vomiting and complaining. He saw himself as a burden and found it hard to believe that she did not occasionally resent his behavior (several weeks into therapy, Robert got his mother to admit that, indeed, she had often been angry at him for his dependency and angry at herself as well for needing it).

The therapist who saw Robert alone considered the boy intelligent enough to attempt some cognitive-behavioral therapy:

Therapist: Okay, Robert, can you tell me what makes you nervous when Ms. Fine returns the test papers?

Robert: I dunno . . . maybe it's because my grade won't be good.

Therapist: How good is good?

Robert (smiling sheepishly): Well . . . kind of like . . . uh . . . having everything right.

Therapist: That must be hard to do all the time.

Robert: Naw, not that hard, not if I think real well on the test.

Therapist: But can't it happen that you make a mistake?

Robert: Yup, I once did.

Therapist (restraining himself from laughing): Well, what happened?

Robert: I felt really awful when I saw my paper.

Therapist: What did the teacher say? Did she say anything to you as she handed it to you?

Robert: No, she kind of smiled. But I just knew she was disappointed in me. That's why she smiled.

Therapist: Is that the only reason she could have smiled?

Robert: Well . . . yeah, I think so.

Therapist: Okay, I'm going to play a little game with you about things we say to ourselves. Will you do it with me?

Robert (unenthusiastically): I guess so, if we have to.

Therapist: Well, I think it might help you. So let's give it a try. Let's pretend I'm your teacher, and I am smiling at you while I hand you a test that you made a mistake on. What I want you to do is talk out loud about whatever comes into your mind. You know, tell me what you are saying to yourself.

Robert: Isn't it nutty to talk to yourself?

Therapist: Nope, I do it all the time. Don't you?

Robert: Hmm, yeah. But I didn't know if it was normal.

Therapist: Sure it is. Everyone does it. And the kind of stuff I'm learning from Professor Long shows me that what people talk about with themselves has a lot to do with how they feel. Does that make any sense to you, Robert?

Robert: Yeah, I guess so.

Therapist (not wanting to push the issue): Okay, let's just see what comes up. (pretends to hand Robert his test that has an error on it)

Robert (forehead furrowed): Oy, I made a mistake. She thinks I'm a jerk, a dope. She doesn't like me anymore. I can't stand this.

Therapist: Hmm, that's heavy stuff, little friend. Is that what you'd really think to yourself?

Robert: Well, I think so. I give myself a hard time when I make a mistake, and I'm sure other people think I'm a jerk.

Therapist: Do you think other people are jerks when they make mistakes?

Robert: Well, sometimes I do. I mean, if you're careful about what you do, won't you always be right?

Therapist: I don't think so. I make lots of mistakes, but I don't think I'm a jerk for doing that. That's part of being a human being. Aren't you one of those? (pokes Robert playfully in the ribs)

Robert (laughs in spite of himself): Yeah, I guess so. I'm sure no angel!

Therapist: That would be kind of boring, don't you think?

Robert: I guess so.

Therapist: Listen, Robert. I think that the kind of hard time you give yourself when you make a mistake is what makes you feel bad. Ms. Fine's smile can't make you feel bad, can it?

Robert: No, I guess not.

Therapist: And even if she frowned at you, would that make you a total jerk? Wouldn't there be good things about you, like all the other things you do nicely? And how nice you are to other kids? And other stuff?

Robert: Well, I guess so.

Therapist: Let's try this. I'm going to pretend I'm your teacher again, giving you back that same test. This time, instead of telling me what you'd usually think, I want you to try to tell yourself something that might make you not feel so bad. Can you try?

Robert: Okay. (takes imaginary test paper from Therapist) Oy—I mean, oh. A mistake. Poo. I don't like making mistakes. Hmm. She's smiling at me. Maybe she likes me even though I made a mistake. Come to think of it, she always tells us kids that as long as we do our best, she isn't going to be disappointed or mad.

Therapist: How do you feel?

Robert: A little better, I guess. But I don't think I can do that at school.

Therapist: Well, we'll do lots of practice here, and you can try these new things out at school, and at home, and anywhere you like. And we can see how it works for you.

More Family Therapy Sessions

Such dialogues were repeated many times in the six sessions the therapist had alone with Robert and were also discussed in the conjoint family sessions with Robert's parents. It required a fair amount of explaining for the parents to accept the therapeutic approach.

In the family sessions, the mother's needs and fears also came up for discussion. The professor and his cotherapist encouraged her to talk about how she felt on mornings that Robert left the house for school. At first insisting that she was grateful and delighted to have him out of the house, she slowly came to admit that her own anxieties would mount within minutes of Robert's departure. "What if he falls down? What if some bully picks on my little Robert? What if Robert begins to vomit—will he be okay? What if he gets upset by something the teacher says?" She began to see how she was getting herself worked up by dwelling on these remote negative possibilities. She also came to realize that there was an emptiness in her life at home. An intelligent woman, she had not attended college but instead, married right out of high school and quickly became pregnant with Robert's older brother. Her home life was not terribly exciting. Her husband worked long hours and played a very small role in household activities. The marital relationship was impoverished, and Mrs. Berg lavished her considerable affection on her boys, especially little Robert who, "after all," needed extra love and affection.

After several sessions that included Robert, it was decided that the parents come without him to work on improving their communication. There turned out to be a number of unresolved issues in their marriage, among them Mr. Berg's feelings of having let his family down by not earning as much money as he felt he should, Mrs. Berg's guilt about having (in her eyes) deprived Mr. Berg of a more satisfying career by getting married early and beginning a family right away, and other problems that had developed over the years and contributed to the remoteness each felt from the other.

These marital therapy sessions took place at the same time Robert began to show significant improvement in school attendance. His mother was thus able to support Robert's leaving the house in the morning and endure not seeing him again until he returned home. The midmorning visits to the school seemed less necessary to Mrs. Berg as her relationship with her husband improved. She even began to go to his office several mornings a week to help out with some clerical chores, which brought them together in new way and rekindled their interest in each other.

An interesting development took place regarding Robert's love-hate attitudes toward his wealthy uncle. Mrs. Berg would complain periodically at dinner about the family's marginal financial picture. Mr. Berg's reaction would be to withdraw into sullen silence. Robert's anxieties would mount, fearing that a disaster was about to befall the household. His reaction would quickly turn to anger at what was viewed to be an unfair attack on his father—anger, however, of which he was barely aware, so quickly was it avoided or repressed by his love for his mother. How could his beloved mother do anything so wrong as attack his father?

For Robert, these feelings took the form of violent envy of his uncle's affluence tinged with resentment at the uncle and at his father as well. These revelations emerged at one of the closing individual sessions the boy had with the therapist in which his fears of failing at school were linked to the belief that he had to do well at this early stage of his education if he were to succeed financially later in life. Non-directive discussions helped Robert elaborate on these concerns and see their origins more clearly. At the last therapy session, a conjoint one with Robert and his parents, each family member talked openly about the financial worries each had been harboring for several years. Ironically, it turned out that Robert's father was doing a lot better in his insurance business than the mother or Robert believed. Robert was becoming less anxious about his need to succeed in elementary school; the treatment helped him view things in general as less serious and forbidding.

Outcome of the Multifaceted Treatment

Two months after beginning treatment, Robert was attending school regularly with only an occasional bout of nervousness in the morning. When he did report reluctance to leave for school, his mother matter-of-factly informed him that she would not be able to look after him at home because of a prior commitment, usually to go to Mr. Berg's office. Robert's father did not leave for work until Robert had left for school, enabling him to support his wife in the firm decision that weekday mornings were a time for children to go to school and parents to begin their own activities. There was overall much less tension in the household as the parents' relationship improved. This improvement in emotional tone lessened Robert's general anxiety level and helped him regard school as less threatening, even as inviting. Robert's brother, who was not very involved in the treatment, proved to be helpful in providing rewards to his younger brother, such as taking him to a nearby park on Friday afternoons after a week of regular school attendance.

This story has a happy ending. By chance we learned many years later that the positive outcomes of Robert's therapy were maintained for the rest of his schooling. Ironically, that schooling included a Master's degree in education and a successful career as a secondary school teacher of social science and geography. We were able in fact to talk to him recently, and he indicated that his earlier struggles with school phobia had helped him to become a more empathic and more competent teacher. As he put it, while most of his students did not suffer from the kind of morbid fear he had endured and then been treated for, the great majority of them from time to time experienced insecurities and anxieties that interfered with their ability to fulfill their potential. His own emotional struggles made him more aware of these factors in children and contributed to greater effectiveness as a teacher.

Discussion

Most children experience fears and worries as part of the normal course of development. Common fears, most of which are outgrown, include fear of the dark and of imaginary creatures (in children under five years old) and fear of being separated from parents (in children under 10 years old). In general, as with adults, fears and phobias are reported more often for girls than for boys (Lichtenstein & Annas, 2000), though this sex difference may be due at least in part to social pressures against boys admitting that they are afraid of things. For fears and worries to be classified as disorders, children's functioning must be impaired. Between 5 to 18 percent of children have an anxiety disorder, making them the most common disorders of childhood (Arnold et al., 2003). Although most unrealistic childhood fears dissipate over time, most anxious adults can trace their problems back to childhood.

Even though Robert sometimes felt that he was the only child with such a problem, school phobia is not uncommon. Unlike other childhood fears, school phobia is not typically outgrown without treatment. But the intervention itself does not have to be professional; many school phobic children get over the problem if they are somehow forced to attend school, regardless of their misery. Repeated exposures to school, as is the case with most fears, tend to extinguish the fear if nothing traumatic occurs during an exposure.

School phobia, often referred to as school refusal, is not a separate category in *DSM-IV-TR* (APA, 2000), and its nature is a subject of continuing debate (Kearney, 2003; Kearney & Silverman, 1996). It is seen as one facet of separation anxiety disorder. The essential feature of separation anxiety disorder, which typically has its onset in childhood, is excessive anxiety about separation from home or loved ones which lasts more than four weeks. Children with this disorder often fear for the well-being of their parents when separated from them, become extremely homesick, are afraid of becoming lost and never reunited with their parents or other attachment figures, and may refuse to go to school. Sometimes their anxieties are expressed as anger or depression.

Between 1 and 5 percent of all school-aged children have school refusal, which is distinct from truancy, which is associated with antisocial behavior and not associated with anxiety about school (Egger, Costello, & Angold, 2003). The disorder is equally common among boys and girls and is most common when children are 5, 6, 10, and 11 years old (Fremont, 2003). Somatic symptoms such as vomiting, diarrhea, chest pains, dizziness, and back pains are frequent and tend to worsen over time if the child is allowed to stay home. School refusal is comorbid with a wide variety of diagnostic categories, among which are social phobia, oppositional-defiant disorder, agoraphobia, major depression, and attention-deficit/hyperactivity disorder (Kearney, 1992, cited in Kearney & Silverman, 1996). In one community study, pure anxious school refusal had the highest comorbidity with depression and separation anxiety disorder, and pure truancy had the highest comorbidity with oppositional-defiant disorder, conduct disorder, and depression, and 88 percent of the children with a mixture of truancy and anxious school refusal had a psychiatric disorder (Egger et al., 2003). Others have found high rates of comorbid specific phobias, mood disorders, oppositional-defiant disorder, and functional enuresis among children with separation anxiety disorder (Verduin & Kendall, 2003). Children with comorbid depression and social phobia had poorer treatment outcome three years after treatment, particularly in terms of their partici-pation in school (McShane, Walter, & Rey, 2004).

Children with anxious school refusal often have difficulty in getting along with other children at school; they are significantly more shy, are more likely to be teased or bullied, and have more conflict with their peers. McShane et al. (2004) found that intervention was particularly effective in the short term with children with school refusal who were experiencing bullying.

As the person grows into adulthood, separation anxiety disorder can take the form of having difficulties handling new situations, like getting married or moving, and being overly preoccupied with the safety of one's own children. It is a problem that warrants attention because not attending school regularly places children at risk for such adult problems as marital conflict (Hibbett & Fogelman, 1990), occupa-tional difficulties (Hibbett, Fogelman, & Manor, 1990), anxiety and depression (Tyrer & Tyrer, 1974), and alcohol abuse and criminal behavior (Robins & Ratcliffe, 1980). Children who were treated for separation anxiety disorder during childhood are more likely to be diagnosed with phobia, obsessive-compulsive disorder, or posttraumatic or acute stress disorder in adulthood, particularly if the separation anxiety disorder was severe (Aschenbrand, Kendall, Webb, Safford, & Flannery-Schroeder, 2003). Spotty school attendance also carries with it major financial disadvantages because of limited advanced educational opportunities (Kearney & Silverman, 1996). Not only do children with school phobia suffer from the intense unpleasantness of being anxious, they may also lose out on mastering developmental tasks at various stages of their young lives. The diagnostic descrip-tion clearly characterizes Robert, who was reluctant to be away from his mother under many circumstances. School itself becomes a serious issue because it is a regular event, and children are expected to go.

Cognitive, family systems, and attachment theorists have recently begun to contribute to understanding the etiology of separation anxiety disorder and school phobia. Below, various theories are reviewed.

Psychoanalytic Theories

Psychoanalytic or psychodynamic theories on school phobia and separation anxiety disorder focus on unconscious conflicts driving the symptoms. A wide range of techniques, such as free association, dream analysis, and interpretation, is used by analysts and also, to some extent, by ego analysts or psychodynamic therapists. For most young children, clinicians employ play therapy. Children are less able and often less willing to express their concerns verbally to adults, and themes and behaviors in the play may reveal unconscious conflicts or concerns (Klein, 1932; A. Freud, 1946). A play therapy room is equipped with toys that allow such expression, such as dolls, puppets, sand, and water. Carefully implemented inter-pretations by the therapist may be powerful in helping the child overcome symp-toms (O'Connor, 2002).

Therapists from other theoretical orientations also employ play therapy. In nondirective play therapy, for example, instead of interpreting the child's play as symbolic expressions of unconscious conflicts and concerns, the client-centered therapist responds to the child's words and actions in an empathic manner, demonstrating unconditional acceptance (Axline, 1964). Behavior therapists also use the play therapy setting, but with a different focus: One report used short-term puppet play as a modeling procedure to help reduce anxiety in children about to undergo surgery (Cassell, 1965). Therapists often use the playroom at least to establish a relationship with a child client and to determine, from what the child says and does with toys, the youngster's perspective on the problem. Evidence on the effectiveness of play therapy in general is equivocal (Barret, Hampe, & Miller, 1978; Phillips, 1985). Nonetheless, it is a well-established and popular technique, and some argue for its effectiveness (Hall, Kaduson, & Schaefer, 2002).

Behavioral and Cognitive Theories

Behavioral theorists have proposed that phobias are acquired by classical conditioning, as seems to have happened in the case of Little Albert (Watson & Rayner, 1920). A variation of straightforward classical conditioning might provide a better account of how phobias develop. People are physiologically predisposed, or prepared, to acquire classically conditioned fear responses to certain types of events. Preparedness is described more fully in Chapter 4. Perhaps children are prepared to learn phobias relating to separation from caregivers.

Another behavioral view hypothesizes that phobic reactions can be learned by imitating others or modeling. Research confirms that a wide range of behaviors and emotions can be acquired through modeling but, as with the classical conditioning view, there is little evidence that modeling accounts for the origins of most phobias. In Robert's case, for example, the therapists did not find instances of other school phobic children whom Robert knew. The youngster with whom he had the closest relationship, his older brother, seemed to be an unusually happy child, not one who could provide a model for fearfulness. On the other hand, Robert's mother seemed to be an overly anxious person, and there is evidence that anxiety problems are often found in the families of school phobic children (Bernstein & Garfinckel, 1988). One study found that 75 percent of children with school phobia had mothers who had this problem in childhood (Last & Strauss, 1990). Others also found that the majority of children with school refusal had a parent who had been in treatment for a psychological problem (McShane et al., 2004). It may be that parents can communicate to their child their own separation anxieties, which would implicate modeling, and they may also unwittingly reinforce their child's dependent and avoidant behavior, through operant conditioning.

The third behavioral hypothesis, operant conditioning, proposes that phobic avoidance is directly rewarded. Kearney and Albano (2004) found that for children with school refusal behavior, three subtypes could be identified: those with anxiety and/or depression, those with separation anxiety disorder, and those with oppositional-defiant disorder. They found that the anxiety/depression group had school refusal behavior that was more likely to be negatively reinforced, those with separation anxiety disorder were more likely to engage in attention-seeking behavior, and those with oppositional-defiant disorder were more likely to be seeking tangible rewards outside of school, like going out with friends instead of going to school. So for the anxiety/depression group, for whatever reason, the child begins to shy away from school, and this behavior is reinforced by the parents. There is suggestive evidence for this in Robert's case—his mother seemed to give in readily to Robert's pleas to remain by her side instead of going to school. And even when he made it to school, she would visit during recess, perhaps communicating to the boy that leaving the school situation would be okay. But such an account does not explain the initial avoidance of school, nor does it help us understand the great fear that accompanies the avoidance of a school phobic child.

Cognitive theories are increasingly applied in efforts to understand phobias. One view is that people with phobias, including someone like Robert, attend to negative events in their environment and also believe that such events are very likely to occur in the future (Mathews & MacLeod, 1994; Turk et al., 2001). Some have found that negative life experiences, such as attending a dangerous school, are more likely among children with school refusal (Egger et al., 2003). Other cognitive theories emphasize the way people construe events. For example, people with a social phobia may be prone to think that the world is coming to an end if others disapprove of them. We saw this in Robert, whose excessive concern about his teacher's approval seemed to be central to his overall fear and avoidance of school.

Attachment and Family Systems Theories

According to attachment theory (Ainsworth, 1989; Bowlby, 1973), children form attachments to adults who care for them. This nature of this attachment can be secure or insecure. There are two general types of insecure attachments: anxious or ambivalent, and avoidant. Anxious attachments are characterized by extreme distress in the child upon separation, and ambivalent reactions when reunited with the caregiver (clingy one moment, angry and punishing the next). Infants go through a normal developmental phase of showing some distress at separation, but as children enter their fourth or fifth year of life, such behavior is not considered adaptive or normal and may indicate an anxious attachment.

What can disrupt the formation of a secure attachment with caregivers? One possibility is that the parent interacts with the child based on the parent's needs rather than the child's needs. This apparently random nurturing leaves the child preoccupied with or uncertain of the trustworthiness of the caregiver. The parent may be ambivalent toward the child. The causal relationship may be reciprocal: A "clingy" child may place such demands on the parent that being with the child becomes aversive, leading the parent to sometimes reject the child (or at least not providing enough emotional support to satisfy normal attachment needs). Such withdrawal or rejection further strengthens the child's insecurity. We saw evidence for this in Robert's mother, who, despite her initial protestations, admitted during conjoint therapy that she sometimes found Robert's excessive dependency a burden.

Research supports the notion that attachment problems in infancy and preschool-age children are associated with school refusal problems (Routh & Bernholtz, 1991). Others have found that adolescents with ambivalent attachments reported higher levels of depression and anxiety (Brown & Wright, 2003).

Family systems researchers have also focused on family factors and interactional styles in the etiology of separation anxiety and school phobia. Family systems theory argues that children's symptoms are reflective of interaction patterns in the family. Sometimes a child's symptoms may serve a purpose of maintaining harmony or avoiding conflict between other family members. Family systems approaches have been successful in alleviating school refusal (Cerio, 1997). Researchers have explored other family factors and found that adverse life events or stressors such as having a parent with psychological difficulties or living in a single parent home are more likely among children with school refusal or separation anxiety disorder (Cronk, Slutske, Madden, Bucholz, & Heath, 2004; Kearney, Sims, Pursell, & Tillotson, 2003). Researchers have linked school refusal with overdependency among family members, communication problems, and problems with the rigidity of family roles and problems with cohesiveness among family members (Fremont, 2003) and with conflictual, detached, and isolated families (Kearney & Silverman, 1995). Kearney et al. (2003) found that children's separation anxiety disorder severity was correlated with reports of family disharmony and parental inconsistency. When a family component was added to cognitive-behavioral therapy for treatment of a child's anxiety disorder (separation anxiety disorder, overanxious disorder, or social phobia), at one-year followup 96 percent of the combination group no longer had the anxiety disorder, compared to 70 percent of the cognitive-behavioral therapy only group (Barrett, Dadds, & Rapee, 1996).

In addition to sharing environmental factors, biologically related families share genes. Researchers studying twin pairs have examined genetic and shared environmental influences on separation anxiety disorder. They estimated that 47 percent of the variance in symptoms was accounted for by genetic influences, and 21 percent was accounted for by shared environment (Feigon, Waldman, Levy, & Hay, 2001). They concluded that anxiety disorders are moderately heritable.

Treatment

Behavior therapies have been successful in treating phobias (Chorpita, Albano, Heimberg, & Barlow, 1996; Davison, Neale & Kring, 2004), but many argue for the superiority of the combined behavioral and cognitive aspects of cognitive-behavioral therapy, which incorporates psychoeducation, management of bodily sensations of anxiety, cognitive restructuring, problem solving, and exposure, and which has substantial empirical support to indicate its effectiveness in treating separation anxiety disorder and school refusal (Gosschalk, 2004; Moffitt, Chorpita, & Fernandez, 2003; Velting, Setzer, & Albano, 2004). Robert's treatment contains a number of elements combined to provide a broad-spectrum cognitive-behavioral approach to the several facets of his problem.

Children with school phobia often have other fears as well. Robert fit this description with his extreme need for approval and perfection. Indeed, the therapy team thought that Robert's fear of school was related to his extreme sensitivity to criticism and his inordinate desire to do well and not to make mistakes, so he would be successful in life. Thus, while Robert experienced anxiety whenever he had to be away from a family figure, especially his mother, the therapists also addressed his fears of making mistakes because they believed that improvement in that area would complement other efforts to get him to attend school without distress.

Robert's individual treatment accomplished the essential component of exposing him to what he feared (Thyer, 1991) and also dealt with particular sensitivities that could be seen as contributing to the phobia—in Robert's case, the demands he placed on himself never to err. Exposure to school was accomplished by gradually bringing Robert into more and more contact with the school situation, initially while trying to reduce his anxiety (through the comforting presence of the therapist). In the later stages of treatment, when Robert seemed capable of actually approaching the school and remaining there on his own, attendance was treated more as an operant, reinforced by praise from his parents and the therapist.

Robert's perfectionism was conceptualized as the result of self-statements that it was catastrophic to make a mistake. Others have found in their casework a recurring theme in children with school refusal of fear of failure and criticism (Brand & O'Conner, 2004). Robert's therapy also focused on misinterpretations he was making of events around him. With respect to his perfectionism, the therapist taught Robert to challenge his belief that it was essential to perform flawlessly in order to feel comfortable and avoid crippling fears of rejection and disapproval. Robert was encouraged to analyze and challenge the accuracy of some of his judgments, such as the teacher not liking him if he did not get every answer correct. Coupled with the graduated in vivo exposure regimen, Robert's fear and avoidance of school diminished over the two months of intensive therapy.

Sometimes medication is used in the treatment of school refusal, usually in conjunction with other types of therapy, particularly antidepressant medications, but sometimes also benzodiazepines, which include a number of side effects and should only be used briefly (Fremont, 2003). When imipramine (a tricyclic antidepressant) is used in conjunction with cognitive-behavioral therapy, the treatment outcome is better than when a placebo is used (Layne, Bernstein, Egan, & Kushner, 2003). Other types of treatment include relaxation training for children, establishing set routines in the family, and communication skills training (Kearney, 2003).

The therapy team did not overlook the separation anxiety component of the phobia. The initial interviews with Robert and his parents suggested that Mrs. Berg was, as it were, conspiring to keep Robert near her, both because of her own morbid fears of something dreadful befalling him and because he had become the center of her existence. Her relationship with her husband was found wanting, especially in honesty and depth of communication. Several sessions of teaching Mr. and Mrs. Berg to express their concerns and feelings to each other helped reestablish the intimacy that was once there and shifted Mrs. Berg's attentions to someone other than Robert, namely, to her husband and to herself. This seemed to help the boy in another way. He had been finding it hard to believe that his mother did not resent his fearfulness at least a little, and her protestations that she would do *anything* for Robert's well-being were as suspicious to Robert as they were false to the mother herself. Her increased honesty with him helped solidify the gains in his attending school because she was better able to resist his pleas to stay at home with her; she now had other things to turn to and felt more justified in asserting her own needs. Fortunately for Robert, the satisfaction of those needs was inconsistent with his remaining at home from school. Mrs. Berg's constant availability had, it seemed, undermined Robert's attempts to get himself to school.

For many years, mothers have been blamed for their children's psychopathology (Davison et al., 2004). Neglectful, emotionally distant mothers were thought at one time to be the cause of autistic disorder (Ferster, 1961). Mothers have also been blamed for causing schizophrenia. Schizophrenia is now thought to be linked to a genetic predisposition and not to parenting behaviors. However, the way parents interact with children is likely to be important, if not in the genesis of a disorder then at least in its course. In Robert's case the therapists hypothesized that Mrs. Berg's own dependency on Robert and the exclusive focus he provided in her otherwise uninteresting life were reducing whatever inclination and capacity the boy had to make it to school. The reinforcement she provided for avoidance would be expected to help maintain the problem by diminishing Robert's opportunities to be exposed to the school situation. The therapists realized that Mrs. Berg would have to change her reactions to Robert's early morning activities if therapy was to proceed. She would have to stop relenting when Robert pleaded with her to stay at home, and she would have to allow the therapist to apply some pressure as well as encouragement in getting the youngster out of the apartment and to school.

On the surface this seems straightforward, but it is not. The graduated exposure regimen, as benign and gentle as it was, nonetheless required Robert to do things that he would have preferred not to do. It would have been easier for him to fall back and stay at home. On some mornings, the therapist did not easily get him to leave the house; the conduct of treatment seldom is as smooth as it sometimes appears to be in case reports. On one morning in particular, Robert's mother tugged at the therapist's sleeve, her eyes moist, and whispered to him that Robert be allowed to remain at home "just this one more time." The therapist empathized with her pain but saw it as his professional responsibility to apply more pressure than the mother would. Not being as emotionally involved with the boy as the mother, he was able to overlook the boy's sad and pained begging and nudge him out the door (it is not without good reason that most professionals avoid treating their own family members—there is such a thing as caring too much). However, mental health professionals, especially if they themselves have never raised children, must appreciate parents' torment when a child suffers, whether psychologically or physically.

When a child is referred for treatment, the motivation usually comes from an adult, because children do not usually know the benefits or even the possibility of treatment. Children are designated as the "identified patient," the one with the problem in need of fixing. If the therapists in this case had only treated Robert without involving the parents at all, Robert might have been rid of his school phobia. But it seems unlikely that this would have worked because he was enmeshed in the parents' relationship. The therapists considered how other issues in the family might be affecting Robert's difficulties. Treatment could have been initiated by the parents for their marital problems, with Robert's phobia of school regarded as a secondary problem that would have responded to improvement in the parents' relationship, but some attention to Robert would probably have been needed. Child therapy usually involves the child's caregivers, who are most often the parents. To intervene only with a child, keeping the parents uninvolved in or even ignorant of the treatment, is not seen by most child clinicians as effective.

Robert's school phobia was eliminated during the two months of treatment, but it is not possible to know which aspect of the multifaceted therapy was most important. Would Robert have fared as well without the conjoint and individual therapy sessions? Like many clinicians, the team decided that family factors should be considered. Robert's mother seemed so dependent on him—in some ways even more than Robert was dependent on her—that the concern was that she might undermine Robert leaving home each morning. As much as she sincerely wished for him to attend school, his presence at home seemed so reinforcing to her that denying her that without helping her find a substitute might have failed.

One benefit of being involved in a teaching case was that the intensive therapy was provided at no charge. Over the two months of treatment, about 25 hours of professional time were devoted to the Berg family, which would cost thousands of dollars today. Even with health insurance, this cost might have been beyond the family's means.

REFERENCES

Abbott, M. J., & Rapee, R. M. (2004). Post-event rumination and negative self-appraisal in social phobia before and after treatment. *Journal of Abnormal Psychology, 113,* 136–144.

Abouesh, A., & Clayton, A. (1999). Compulsive voyeurism and exhibitionism: A clinical response to paroxetine. *Archives of Sexual Behavior, 28,* 23–30.

Abramowitz, J. S. (1997). Effectiveness of psychological and pharmacological treatments for obsessive-compulsive disorder: A quantitative review. *Journal of Consulting and Clinical Psychology, 65,* 44–52.

Abramowitz, J. S., Franklin, M. E., Street, G. P., Kozak, J. M., & Foa, E. B. (2000). Effects of comorbid depression on response to treatment for obsessive-compulsive disorder. *Behavior Therapy, 31,* 517–528.

Abramowitz, J. S., Brigidi, B. D., & Roche, K. R. (2001). Cognitive-behavioral therapy for obsessive-compulsive disorder: A review of the treatment literature. *Research on Social Work Practice, 11,* 357–372.

Abrams, R. (2002). *Electroconvulsive therapy* (4th edition). New York: Oxford University Press.

Abramson, L. Y., Seligman, M. E. P., & Teasdale, J. (1978). Learned helplessness in humans: Critique and reformulation. *Journal of Abnormal Psychology, 87,* 49–74.

Acocella, J. (1999). *Creating hysteria: Women and Multiple Personality Disorder.* San Francisco, CA: Jossey-Bass.

Agras, W. S., Schneider, J. A., Arnow, B., Raeburm, S. D., & Telch, C. F. (1989). Cognitive-behavioral and response prevention treatments for bulimia nervosa. *Journal of Consulting and Clinical Psychology, 57,* 215–221.

Ainsworth, M. D. S. (1989). Attachments beyond infancy. *American Psychologist, 44,* 709–716.

Akhtar, S. (1990). Paranoid personality disorder: A synthesis of developmental, dynamic and descriptive features. *American Journal of Psychotherapy, 44,* 5–25.

Akhtar, S. (1992). *Broken Structures: Severe Personality Disorders and Their Treatment.* Northvale, NJ: Jason Aronson.

Akiskal, H. S. (1981). Subaffective disorders: Dysthymic, Cyclothymic, and Bipolar II Disorders in the "borderline" realm. *Psychiatric Clinics of North America, 4,* 25–46.

Akyuez, G., Dogan, O., Sar, V., Yargic, L. I., & Tutkun, J. (1999). Frequency of dissociative identity disorder in the general population in Turkey. *Comprehensive Psychiatry, 40,* 151–159.

Allen, J. J. B., & Iacono, W. G. (2001). Assessing the validity of amnesia in dissociative identity disorder. *Psychology, Public Policy, and Law, 7,* 311–344.

Alexander, F. (1950). *Psychosomatic medicine.* New York: Norton.

Alexander, F., & French, T. M. (1946). *Psychoanalytic Therapy.* New York: Ronald Press.

Alloy, L. B., Abramson, L. Y., Gibb, B. E., Crossfield, A. G., Pieracci, A. M., Spaso-jevic, J., & Steinberg, J. A. (2004). Developmental antecedents of cognitive vulner-ability to depression: Review of findings from the cognitive vulnerability to depres-sion project. *Journal of Cognitive Psychotherapy, 18,* 115–133.

Alloy, L. B., Reilly-Harrington, N., Fresco, D. M., Whitehouse, W. G., & Zechmeister, J. S. (1999). Cognitive styles and life events in subsyndromal unipolar and bipolar dis-orders. *Journal of Cognitive Psychotherapy, 13,* 21–40.

American Psychiatric Association. (1952). *Diagnostic and statistical manual of mental disorders: First edition (DSM-I).* Washington, DC: American Psychiatric Associa-tion.

American Psychiatric Association. (1968). *Diagnostic and statistical manual of mental disorders: Second edition (DSM-II).* Washington, DC: American Psychiatric Asso-ciation.

American Psychiatric Association. (1980). *Diagnostic and statistical manual of mental disorders: Third edition (DSM-III).* Washington, DC: American Psychiatric Association.

American Psychiatric Association. (1987). *Diagnostic and statistical manual of mental disorders: Third edition revised (DSM-III-R).* Washington, DC: American Psychiat-ric Association.

American Psychiatric Association. (1994). *Diagnostic and statistical manual of mental disorders: Fourth edition (DSM-IV).* Washington, DC: American Psychiatric Asso-ciation.

American Psychiatric Association. (2000). *Diagnostic and statistical manual of mental disorders: Fourth edition, Text revision (DSM-IV-TR).* Washington, DC: American Psychiatric Association.

Andersen, A. E. (1997). Inpatient treatment of anorexia nervosa. In D. M. Garner & P. E. Garfinkel (Eds.), *Handbook of Treatment for Eating Disorders* (2nd ed., pp. 327–353). New York: Guilford.

Andersen, B. L., & Cyranowski, J. C. (1995). Women's sexuality: Behaviors, responses, and individual differences. *Journal of Consulting and Clinical Psychology, 63,* 891–906.

Anderson, D. A., & Maloney, K. C. (2001). The efficacy of cognitive-behavioral therapy on the core symptoms of bulimia nervosa. *Clinical Psychology Review, 21,* 971–988.

Anderson, N. B., & Armstead, C. A. (1995). Toward understanding the association of socioeconomic status and health: A new challenge for the biopsychosocial approach. *Psychosomatic Medicine, 57,* 213–225.

Andreasen, N. C., Arndt, S., Alliger, R., Miller, D., & Flaum, M. (1995). Symptoms of schizophrenia: Methods, meanings, and mechanisms. *Archives of General Psychia-try, 52,* 341–351.

Andreasen, N. C., Ehrhardt, J. C., Swayze, V. W., Alliger, R. J., Yuh, W. T. C., Cohen, G., & Ziebell, S. (1990). Magnetic resonance imaging of the brain in schizophrenia: The pathophysiologic significance of structural abnormalities. *Archives of General Psychiatry, 47,* 35–44.

Andrews, B., Brewin, C. R., & Rose, S. (2003). Gender, social support, and PTSD in victims of violent crime. *Journal of Traumatic Stress, 16,* 421–427.

Angst, J., Sellaro, R., & Angst, F. (1998). Long-term outcome and mortality of treated versus untreated bipolar and depressed patients: A preliminary report. *International Journal of Psychiatry in Clinical Practice, 2,* 115–119.

Appelbaum, P. S., Robbins, P. C., & Monahan, J. (2000). Violence and delusions: Data from the MacArthur Violence Risk Assessment Study. *American Journal of Psy-chiatry, 157,* 566–572.

Arieti, S. (1979). New views on the psychodynamics of phobias. *American Journal of Psychotherapy, 33,* 82–95.

Arnold, P. A., Banerjee, S. P., Bhandari, R., Lorch, E., Ivey, J., Rose, M., & Rosenberg, D. R. (2003). Childhood anxiety disorders and developmental issues in anxiety. *Current Psychiatry Reports, 5,* 252–265.

Arnold, P. D., Zai, G., & Richter, M. A. (2004). Genetics of anxiety disorders. *Current Psychiatry Reports, 6,* 243–254.

Aschenbrand, S., Kendall, P. C., Webb, A., Safford, S. M., & Flannery-Schroeder, E. (2003). Is childhood separation anxiety disorder a predictor of adult panic disorder and agoraphobia? A seven-year longitudinal study. *Journal of the American Academy of Child and Adolescent Psychiatry, 42,* 1478–1485.

Atkinson, D. R. (1983). Ethnic similarity in counseling psychology: A review of research. *The Counseling Psychologist, 11,* 79–92.

Atkinson, D. R. (1985). A meta-review of research on cross-cultural counseling and psychotherapy. *Journal of Multicultural Counseling and Development, 13,* 138–153.

Atkinson, D. R., Maruyama, M., & Matsui, S. (1978). The effects of counselor race and counseling approach on Asian Americans' perception of counselor credibility and utility. *Journal of Counseling Psychology, 25,* 76–83.

August, G. J., Stewart, M. A., & Tsai, L. (1981). The incidence of cognitive disabilities in the siblings of autistic children. *British Journal of Psychiatry, 138,* 416–422.

Austin, S. B. (2001). Population-based prevention of eating disorders: An application of the Rose prevention model. *Preventive Medicine, 32,* 268–283.

Averill, P. M., Reas, D. L., Shack, A., Shah, N. N., Cowan, K., Krajewski, K., Kopecky, C., & Guynn, R. W. (2004). Is schizoaffective disorder a stable diagnostic category? A retrospective examination. *Psychiatric Quarterly, 75,* 215–227.

Axline, V. M. (1964). *Dibs: In Search of Self.* New York: Ballantine.

Baastrup, P. D., & Schou, M. (1967). Lithium as a prophylactic agent against recurrent depressions and manic-depressive psychosis. *Archives of General Psychiatry, 16,* 162–172.

Bach, A. K., Wincze, J. P., & Barlow, D. H. (2001). Sexual dysfunction. In D. H. Barlow (Ed.). *Clinical Handbook of Psychological Disorders: A Step-By-Step Treatment Manual* (3rd ed., pp. 562–608). New York: Guilford.

Baer, J. S., Sampson, P. D., Barr, H. M., Connor, P. D., & Streissguth, A. P. (2003). A 21-year longitudinal analysis of the effects of prenatal alcohol exposure on young adult drinking. *Archives of General Psychiatry, 60,* 377–385.

Baer, L., & Jenike, M. A. (1992). Personality disorders in obsessive compulsive disorder. *Psychiatric Clinics of North America, 15,* 803–812.

Baethge, C. (2003). Long-term treatment of schizoaffective disorder: Review and recommendations. *Pharmacopsychiatry, 36,* 45–56.

Baker, B., Szalai, J. P., Paquette, M., & Tobe, S. (2003). Marital support, spousal contact, and the course of mild hypertension. *Journal of Psychosomatic Research, 55,* 229–233.

Baker, C. A., & Morrison, A. P. (1998). Cognitive processes in auditory hallucinations: Attributional biases and metacognition. *Psychological Medicine, 28,* 1199–1208.

Bakker, A., van Kesteren, P. J. M., Gooren, L. J. G., & Bezemer, P. D. (1993). The prevalence of transsexualism in the Netherlands. *Acta Psychiatrica Scandinavica, 87,* 237–238.

Ballenger, J. C. (1997). Panic disorder in the medical setting. *Journal of Clinical Psychiatry, 58* (*Suppl. 2*), 13–17.

Ballenger, J. C., Davidson, J. R. T., Lecrubier, Y., Nutt, D. J., Borkovec, T. D., Rickels, K., Stein, D. J., & Wittchen, H. U. (2001). Consensus statement on generalized anxiety disorder from the International Consensus Group on Depression and Anxiety. *Journal of Clinical Psychiatry, 62,* 53–58.

Ballenger, J. C., Davidson, J. R. T., Lecrubier, Y., Nutt, D. J., Foa, E. B., Kessler, R. C., & McFarlane, A. C. (2000). Consensus statement on posttraumatic stress disorder from the international consensus group on depression and anxiety. *Journal of Clinical Psychiatry, 61 (Suppl. 5),* 60–66.

Bancroft, J. (1997). Sexual problems. In D. M. Millar & C. G. Fairburn (Eds.), *Science and Practice of Cognitive Behaviour Therapy* (pp. 243–257). New York: Oxford University Press.

Bandura, A., & Rosenthal, T. L. (1966). Vicarious classical conditioning as a function of arousal level. *Journal of Personality and Social Psychology, 3,* 54–62.

Barbaresi, W. J., Katusic, S. K., Colligan, R. C., Weaver, A. L., & Jacobsen, S. J. (2005). The incidence of autism in Olmsted County, Minnesota, 1976–1997: Results from a population-based study. *Archives of Pediatrics and Adolescent Medicine, 159,* 37–44.

Barkley, R. A. (1990). *Attention-deficit hyperactivity disorder: A handbook for diagnosis and treatment.* New York: Guilford.

Barkley, R. A., DuPaul, G. J., & McMurray, M. B. (1990). A comprehensive evaluation of attention deficit disorder with and without hyperactivity defined by research criteria. *Journal of Consulting and Clinical Psychology, 58,* 775–789.

Barkley, R. A., Fischer, M., Edelbrock, C. S., & Smallish, L. (1990). The adolescent outcome of hyperactive children diagnosed by research criteria: I. An 8-year prospective follow-up. *Journal of the American Academy of Child and Adolescent Psychiatry, 29,* 546–557.

Barkley, R. A., Karlsson, J., & Pollard, S. (1985). Effects of age on the mother-child interactions of hyperactive children. *Journal of Abnormal Child Psychology, 13,* 631–638.

Barlow, D. H. (1986). Causes of sexual dysfunction: The role of anxiety and cognitive interference. *Journal of Consulting and Clinical Psychology, 54,* 140–148.

Barlow, D. H. (1997). Cognitive-behavioral therapy for panic disorder: Current status. *Journal of Clinical Psychiatry, 58 (Suppl. 2),* 32–35.

Barlow, D. H. (2002). *Anxiety and its disorders: The nature and treatment of anxiety and panic* (2nd ed.). New York: Guilford.

Barlow, D. H., Abel, G. G., & Blanchard, E. B. (1979). Gender identity change in transsexuals: Follow-up and replications. *Archives of General Psychiatry, 36,* 1001–1007.

Barlow, D. H., Craske, M. G., Cerny, J. A., & Klosko, J. S. (1989). Behavioral treatment of panic disorder. *Behavior Therapy, 20,* 261–282.

Barlow, D. H., Gorman, J. M., Shear, M. K., & Woods, S. W. (2000). Cognitive-behavioral therapy, imipramine, or their combination for panic disorder: A randomized controlled trial. *Journal of the American Medical Association, 283,* 2529–2536.

Barlow, D. H., Raffa, S. D., & Cohen, E. M. (2002). Psychosocial treatments for panic disorders, phobias, and generalized anxiety disorder. In P. E. Nathan & J. M. Gorman (Eds.), *A guide to treatments that work* (2nd ed., pp. 301–335). London, England: Oxford University Press.

Barnes, M. F. (1995). Sex therapy in the couples context: Therapy issues of victims of sexual trauma. *American Journal of Family Therapy, 23,* 351–360.

Barnow, S., Lucht, M., & Freyberger, H. J. (2005). Correlates of aggressive and delinquent conduct problems in adolescence. *Aggressive Behavior, 31,* 24–39.

Baron, M. (1995). Genes and psychosis: Old wine in new bottles? *Acta Psychiatrica Scandinavica, 92*, 81–86.

Baron, M., Risch, N., Hamburger, R., et al. (1987). Genetic linkage between X chromosome markers and manic depression. *Nature, 326*, 806–808.

Barrett, C. L., Hampe, E., & Miller, L. (1978). Research on psychotherapy with children. In S. L. Garfield & A. E. Bergin (Eds.), *Handbook of Psychotherapy and Behavior Change: An Empirical Analysis* (2nd ed.). New York: Wiley.

Barrett, P. M., Dadds, M. R., & Rapee, R. M. (1996). Family treatment of childhood anxiety: A controlled trial. *Journal of Consulting and Clinical Psychology, 64*, 333–342.

Bartak, L., Rutter, M., & Cox, A. (1975). A comparative study of infantile autism and specific developmental language disorders: I. The children. *British Journal of Psychiatry, 126*, 127–145.

Basoglu, M., & Mineka, S. (1992). The role of uncontrollable and unpredictable stress in post-traumatic stress responses in torture survivors. In M. Basoglu (Ed.), *Torture and Its Consequences: Current Treatment Approaches* (pp. 182–225). Cambridge, England: Cambridge University Press.

Basoglu, M., & Paker, M. (1995). Severity of trauma as predictor of long-term psychological status in survivors of torture. *Journal of Anxiety Disorders, 9*, 339–350.

Basoglu, M., & Paker, M., Paker, O., Ozmen, E. et al. (1994). Psychological effects of torture: A comparison of tortured with nontortured political activists in Turkey. *American Journal of Psychiatry, 151*, 76–81.

Bass, C., Peveler, R., & House, A. (2001). Somatoform disorders: Severe psychiatric illnesses neglected by psychiatrists. *British Journal of Psychiatry, 179*, 11–14.

Basson, R., Berman, J., Burnett, A., Derogatis, L., Ferguson, D., Fourcroy, J., et al. (2000). Report of the international consensus development conference on female sexual dysfunction: Definitions and classifications. *Journal of Urology, 163*, 888–899.

Bates, G. W., Campbell, I. M., & Burgess, P. M. (1990). Accessment of articulated thoughts in social anxiety: Modification of the ATSS procedure. *British Journal of Clinical Psychology, 29*, 91–98.

Battle, E. S., & Lacey, B. (1972). A context for hyperactivity in children over time. *Child Development, 43*, 757–773.

Bebbington, P. E. (1998). Epidemiology of obsessive-compulsive disorder. *British Journal of Psychiatry, 173 (Suppl. 35)*, 2–6.

Bebbington, P. E., Brugha, T., MacCarthy, B., Potter, J., et al. (1988). The Camberwell Collaborative Depression Study: I. Depressed probands: Adversity and the form of depression. *British Journal of Psychiatry, 152*, 754–765.

Beck, A. T. (1967). *Depression: Causes and Treatment*. Philadelphia, PA: University of Pennsylvania Press.

Beck, A. T. (1987). Cognitive models of depression. *Journal of Cognitive Psychotherapy, 1*, 5–37.

Beck, A. T., Butler, A. C., Brown, G. K., Dahlsgaard, K. K., Newman, C. F., & Beck, J. S. (2001). Dysfunctional beliefs discriminate personality disorders. *Behaviour Research and Therapy, 39*, 1213–1225.

Beck, A. T., Freeman, A., & Davis, D. D. (2004). *Cognitive Therapy of Personality Disorders* (2nd edition). New York: Guilford.

Becker, D. F., Grilo, C. M., Edell, W. S., & McGlashen, T. H. (2000). Comorbidity of borderline personality disorder with other personality disorders in hospitalized adolescents and adults. *American Journal of Psychiatry, 157*, 2011–2016.

Becker, J. V., & Kaplan, M. S. (1991). Rape victims: Issues, theories, and treatment. *Annual Review of Sex Research, 2*, 267–292.

Bellack, A. S., Mueser, K. T., Gingerich, S., & Agresta, J. (1997). *Social skills training for schizophrenia: A step-by-step guide.* New York: Guilford.

Ben Amor, L., Grizenko, H., Schwartz, G. Lageix, P., Baron, C., Ter-Stepanian, M., et al. (2005). Perinatal complications in children with attention-deficit hyperactivity disorder and their unaffected siblings. *Review of Psychiatry and Neuroscience, 30,* 120–126.

Benjamin, J., Ben-Zion, I. K., Karbofsky, E., & Dannon, P. (2000). Double-blind-placebo-controlled pilot study of paroxetine for specific phobia. *Psychopharmacology, 149,* 194–196.

Bernstein, A. (2001). Problems in treating paranoia: A case illustration. *Modern Psychoanalysis, 26,* 237–247.

Bernstein, D. P., Useda, D., & Siever, L. J. (1993). Paranoid personality disorder: Review of the literature and recommendations for DSM-IV. *Journal of Personality Disorders, 7,* 53–62.

Bernstein, D. P., Useda, D., & Siever, L. J. (1995). Paranoid personality disorder. In W. J. Livesley (Ed.), *The DSM-IV Personality Disorders* (pp. 45–57). New York: Guilford.

Bernstein, G. A., & Garfinkel, B. D. (1988). Pedigrees, functioning, and psychopathology in families of school phobic children. *American Journal of Psychiatry, 145,* 70–74.

Berrettini, W. H. (2000). Genetics of psychiatric disease. *Annual Review of Medicine, 51,* 465–479.

Berrios, G. E., & Chiu, H. (1989). Obsessive-compulsive disorders in Cambridgeshire: A follow-up study of up to 20 years. *British Journal of Psychiatry, 154 (Suppl. 4),* 17–20.

Bertelsen, A., & Gottesman, I. I. (1995). Schizoaffective psychoses: Genetical clues to classification. *American Journal of Medical Genetics, 60,* 7–11.

Bettelheim, B. (1967). *The Empty Fortress.* New York: Free Press.

Bettelheim, B. (1973). Bringing up children. *Ladies Home Journal, 90,* 28.

Beutler, L. E., Machado, P. P. P., & Neufeldt, S. A. (1994). Therapist variables. In A. E. Bergin & S. L. Garfield (Eds.), *Handbook of Psychotherapy and Behavior Change* (4th ed., pp. 229–269). New York: Wiley.

Biederman, J., Faraone, S. V., Keenan, K., et al. (1992). Further evidence for family-genetic risk factors in attention deficit hyperactivity disorder: Patterns of comorbidity in probands and relatives in psychiatrically and pediatrically referred samples. *Archives of General Psychiatry, 49,* 728–738.

Biederman, J., Faraone, S., Mick, E., et al. (1995). High risk for attention deficit hyperactivity disorder among children of parents with childhood onset of the disorder. *American Journal of Psychiatry,* 152, 431–435.

Biederman, J., Mick, E., Faraone, S. V., et al. (2002). Influence of gender on attention deficit hyperactivity disorder in children referred to a psychiatric clinic. *American Journal of Psychiatry, 159,* 36–42.

Biederman, J., Rosenbaum, J., Hirschfeld, D., Faraone, S., Bolduc, E., et al. (1990). Psychiatric correlates of behavioral inhibition in young children of parents with and without psychiatric disorders. *Archives of General Psychiatry, 47,* 21–26.

Binik, Y. M. (2005). Should dyspareunia be retained as a sexual dysfunction in DSM-V? *Archives of Sexual Behavior, 34,* 11–21.

Binik, Y. M., Reissing, E., Pukall, C., Flory, N., Payne, K. A., & Khalife, S. (2002). The female sexual pain disorders: Genital pain or sexual dysfunction? *Archives of Sexual Behavior, 31,* 425–431.

Bischof, G., Rumpf, H. J., Meyer, C., & John, U. (2003). Types of natural recovery from alcohol dependence: A cluster analytic approach. *Addiction, 98,* 1737–1746.

Bitran, S., & Barlow, D. H. (2004). Etiology and treatment of social anxiety: A commentary. *Journal of Clinical Psychology, 60*, 881–886.

Black, D. W., Blum, N., Pfohl, B., & Hale, N. (2004). Suicidal behavior in borderline personality disorder: Prevalence, risk factors, prediction, and prevention. *Journal of Personality Disorders, 18*, 226–239.

Blackwood, D. H. R., Visscher, P. M., & Muir, W. J. (2001). Genetic studies of bipolar affective disorder in large families. *British Journal of Psychiatry, 178 (Suppl. 41)*, S134–S136.

Blair, C., Freeman, C., & Cull, A. (1995). The families of anorexia nervosa and cystic fibrosis patients. *Psychological Medicine, 25*, 985–993.

Blair, R. J. R. (2003). Neurobiological basis of psychopathy. *British Journal of Psychiatry, 182*, 5–7.

Blair, R. J. D., Jones, L., Clark, F., & Smith, M. (1997). The psychopathic individual: A lack of responsiveness to distress cues. *Psychophysiology, 34*, 192–198.

Blanchard, E. (1990). Biofeedback treatments of essential hypertension. *Biofeedback and Self-Regulation, 15*, 209–228.

Blanchard, E. E., Eisele, G., Vollmer, A., Payne, A., et al. (1996). Controlled evaluation of thermal biofeedback in treatment of elevated blood pressure in unmedicated mild hypertension. *Biofeedback and Self-Regulation, 21*, 167–190.

Blanchard, R., & Clemmensen, L. H. (1988). A test of the DSM-III-R's implicit assumption that fetishistic arousal and gender dysphoria are mutually exclusive. *Journal of Sex Research, 25*, 426–432.

Bleuler, E. (1950). *Dementia Praecox or the Group of Schizophrenias*. New York: International Universities Press. (Originally published 1911.)

Bliss, E. L. (1986). *Multiple personality, allied disorders and hypnosis*. Oxford: Oxford University Press.

Bodlund, O., & Kullgren, G. (1996). Transsexualism—general outcome and prognostic factors: A five-year follow-up study of nineteen transsexuals in the process of changing sex. *Archives of Sexual Behavior, 25*, 303–316.

Bögels, S. M., & Mansell, W. (2004). Attention processes in the maintenance and treatment of social phobia: Hypervigilance, avoidance, and self-focused attention. *Clinical Psychology Review, 24*, 827–856.

Bögels, S. M., & Tarrier, N. (2004). Unexplored issues and future directions in social phobia research. *Clinical Psychology Review, 24*, 731–736.

Bohus, M., Haaf, B., Simms, T., Limberger, M. F., Schmahl, C., Unckel, C., et al. (2004). Effectiveness of inpatient dialectical behavioral therapy for borderline personality disorder: A controlled trial. *Behaviour Research and Therapy, 42*, 487–499.

Bohus, M., Schmahl, C., & Lieb, K. (2004). New developments in the neurobiology of borderline personality disorder. *Current Psychiatry Reports, 6*, 43–50.

Boon, S., & Draijer, N. (1993). Multiple personality disorder in the Netherlands: A clinical investigation of 71 patients. *American Journal of Psychiatry, 150*, 489–494.

Bordo, S. (1997). Anorexia nervosa: Psychopathology as the crystallization of culture. In M. M. Gergen & S. N. Davis (Eds.), *Toward a New Psychology of Gender* (pp. 423–453). New York: Routledge.

Borkovec, T. D., & Costello, E. (1993). Efficacy of applied relaxation and cognitive-behavioral therapy in the treatment of generalized anxiety disorder. *Journal of Consulting and Clinical Psychology, 61*, 611–619.

Bosworth, H. B., Bartash, R. M., Olsen, M. K., & Steffens, DC (2003). The association of psychosocial factors and depression with hypertension among older adults. *International Journal of Geriatric Psychiatry, 18*, 1142–1148.

Bower, H. (2001). The gender identity disorder in the DSM-IV classification: A critical evaluation. *Australian and New Zealand Journal of Psychiatry, 35*, 1–8.

Bowlby, J. (1973). *Separation: Anxiety and Anger.* New York: Basic Books.

Bradford, D., Stroup, S., & Lieberman, J. (2002). Pharmacological treatments for schizophrenia. In P. E. Nathan & J . M. Gorman (Eds.), *A Guide to Treatments that Work* (2nd ed., pp. 169–199). London, England: Oxford University Press.

Bradford, J. M. (2001). The neurobiology, neuropharmacology, and pharmacological treatment of the paraphilias and compulsive sexual behavior. *Canadian Journal of Psychiatry, 46,* 26–34.

Bradley, R., Greene, J., Russ, E., Dutra, L., & Westen, D. (2005). A multidimensional meta-analysis of psychotherapy for PTSD. *American Journal of Psychiatry, 162,* 214–227.

Bradley, S. J., & Zucker, K. J. (1997). Gender identity disorder: A review of the past 10 years. *Journal of the American Academy of Child and Adolescent Psychiatry, 36,* 872–880.

Braham, L. G., Trower, P., & Birchwood, M. (2004). Acting on command hallucinations and dangerous behavior: A critique of the major findings in the last decade. *Clinical Psychology Review, 24,* 513–528.

Brand, C., & O'Conner, L. (2004). School refusal: It takes a team. *Children & Schools, 26,* 54–64.

Bretschneider, J. G., & McCoy, N. L. (1988). Sexual interest and behavior in healthy 80- to 102-year-olds. *Archives of Sexual Behavior, 17,* 109–129.

Brewerton, T. D., Dansky, B. S., Kilpatrick, D. G., & O'Neil, P. M. (2000). Which comes first in the pathogenesis of bulimia nervosa: Dieting or bingeing? *International Journal of Eating Disorders, 20,* 259–264.

Brewin, C. R., Andrews, B., & Gotlib, I. H. (1993). Psychopathology and early experience: A reappraisal of retrospective reports. *Psychological Bulletin, 113,* 82–98.

Brondolo, E., Rieppi, R., Kelly, K. P., & Gerin, W. (2003). Perceived racism and blood pressure: A review of the literature and conceptual and methodological critique. *Annals of Behavioral Medicine, 25,* 55–65.

Brooks, F. (2001). Substance abuse and violence: A coexisting issue. In D. S. Sandhu (Ed.). *Faces of Violence: Psychological Correlates, Concepts, and Intervention Strategies* (pp. 171–190). Huntington, NY: Nova Science Publishers.

Brown, A. S., & Susser, E. S. (2002). In utero infection and adult schizophrenia. *Mental Retardation and Developmental Disabilities Research Reviews, 8,* 51–57.

Brown, D., Frischholz, E. J., & Scheflin, A. W. (1999). Iatrogenic dissociative identity disorder—An evaluation of the scientific evidence. *Journal of Psychiatry and Law, 27,* 549–637.

Brown, G. W. (2002). Social roles, context and evolution in the origins of depression. *Journal of Health and Social Behavior, 43,* 255–276.

Brown, G. W., & Harris, T. (1978). *Social Origins of Depression: A Study of Psychiatric Disorder in Women.* New York: Free Press.

Brown, L. S., & Wright, J. (2003). The relationship between attachment strategies and psychopathology in adolescence. *Psychology and Psychotherapy: Theory, Research, and Practice, 76,* 351–367.

Bruch, H. (1973). *Eating Disorders: Obesity, Anorexia Nervosa, and the Person Within.* New York: Basic Books.

Bruch, H. (1981). Developmental considerations of anorexia nervosa and obesity. *Canadian Journal of Psychiatry, 26,* 212–217.

Bryant, R. A. (1995). Autobiographical memory across personalities in dissociative identity disorder: A case report. *Journal of Abnormal Psychology, 104,* 625–631.

Bullough, V. L., & Bullough, B. (1993). *Cross Dressing, Sex, and Gender.* Philadelphia, PA: University of Pennsylvania Press.

Burns, A. S., Rivas, D. A., & Ditunno, J. F. (2001). The management of neurogenic bladder and sexual dysfunction after spinal cord injury. *Spine, 26*, S129–S136.

Burns, D. D. (1992). *Feeling Good: The New Mood Therapy*. New York: Avon.

Bustillo, J. R., Lauriello, J., Horan, W. P., & Keith, S. J. (2001). The psychosocial treatment of schizophrenia: An update. *American Journal of Psychiatry, 158*, 163–175.

Butzlaff, R. L., & Hooley, J. M. (1998). Expressed emotion and psychiatric relapse. *Archives of General Psychiatry, 55*, 547–552.

Byrne, S. M., & McLean, N. J. (2002). The cognitive-behavioral model of bulimia nervosa: A direct evaluation. *International Journal of Eating Disorders*.

Cade, J. F. J. (1949). Lithium salts in the treatment of psychotic excitement. *Medical Journal of Australia, 36*, 349–352.

Cadoret, R. J., Yates, W. R., Troughton, E., Woodworth, G., & Stewart, M. A. (1995a). Adoption study demonstrating two genetic pathways to drug abuse. *Archives of General Psychiatry, 52*, 42–52.

Cadoret, R. J., Yates, W. R., Troughton, E., Woodworth, G., & Stewart, M. A. (1995b). Genetic-environment interaction in the genesis of aggressivity and conduct disorders. *Archives of General Psychiatry, 52*, 916–924.

Caldwell, D. (1949). Psychopathia transsexualis. *Sexology, 16*, 274–280.

Calhoun, K. S., & Wilson, A. E. (2000). Rape and sexual aggression. In L. T. Szuchman & F. Muscarella (Eds.), *Psychological Perspectives on Human Sexuality* (pp. 573–602). New York: Wiley.

Cameron, N. (1959). The paranoid pseudo-community revisited. *American Journal of Sociology, 65*, 52–58.

Campbell, M. (1988). Fenfluramine treatment of autism. *Journal of Child Psychology and Psychiatry, 29*, 1–10.

Campbell, M., Anderson, L. T., & Small, A. M. (1990). Pharmacotherapy in autism: A summary of research at Bellevue/New York University. *Brain Dysfunction, 3*, 299–307.

Campbell, M., Anderson, L. T., Small, A. M., Locascio, L. L., Lynch, N. S., & Choroco, M. C. (1990). Naltrexone in autistic children: A double-blind and placebo controlled study. *Psychopharmacology Bulletin, 26*, 130–135.

Campo, J., Nijman, H., Merckelbach, H., Evers, C. (2003). Psychiatric comorbidity of gender identity disorders: A survey among Dutch psychiatrists. *American Journal of Psychiatry, 160*, 1332–1336.

Cannon, T. D., Kaprio, J., Loennqvist, J., Huttunen, M., & Koskenvuo, M. (1998). The genetic epidemiology of schizophrenia in a Finnish twin cohort: A population-based modeling study. *Archives of General Psychiatry, 55*, 67–74.

Cappeliez, P. (1988). Some thoughts on the prevalence and etiology of depressive conditions in the elderly. Special Issue: Francophone research in gerontology in Canada. *Canadian Journal on Aging, 7*, 431–440.

Casper, R. C., Eckert, H. A., Halmi, S. C., Goldberg, S. C., & Davis, J. M. (1980). Bulimia. *Archives of General Psychiatry, 37*, 1030–1035.

Casper, R. C., & Troiani, M. (2001). Family functioning in anorexia nervosa differs by subtypes. *International Journal of Eating Disorders, 30*, 338–342.

Cassell, S. (1965). Effect of brief puppet therapy upon the emotional responses of children undergoing cardiac catheterization. *Journal of Consulting Psychology, 29*, 1–8.

Castellanos, F. X., Giedd, J. N., Marsh, W. L., Hamburger, S. D., Vaituzis, A. C., et al. (1996). Quantitative brain magnetic resonance imaging in attention-deficit/hyperactivity disorder. *Archives of General Psychiatry, 53*, 607–616.

Cerio, J. (1997). School phobia: A family systems approach. *Elementary School Guidance & Counseling, 31*, 180–192.

Chambers, K. C., & Bernstein, I. L. (2003). Conditioned flavor aversions. In R. L. Doty (Ed.), *Handbook of Clinical Olfaction and Gustation* (2nd ed.). New York: Marcel Dekker.

Chambless, D. L., Cherney, J., Caputo, G. C., & Rheinstein, B. J. (1987). Anxiety disorders and alcoholism: A study with inpatient alcoholics. *Journal of Anxiety Disorders, 1,* 29–40.

Chartier, M. J., Walker, J. R., & Stein, M. B. (2003). Considering comorbidity in social phobia. *Social Psychiatry and Psychiatric Epidemiology, 38,* 728–734.

Chassin, L., Pitts, S. C., DeLucia, C., & Todd, M. (1999). A longitudinal study of children of alcoholics: Predicting young adult substance use disorders, anxiety, and depression. *Journal of Abnormal Psychology, 108,* 106–119.

Cheung, P., Schweitzer, I., Crowley, K., & Tuckwell, V. (1997). Violence in schizophrenia: Role of hallucinations and delusions. *Schizophrenia Research, 26,* 181–190.

Chioqueta, A. P., & Stiles, T. C. (2004). Suicide risk in patients with somatization disorder. *Crisis, 25,* 3–7.

Chivers, M. L., & Bailey, J. M. (2000). Sexual orientation of female-to-male transsexuals: A comparison of homosexual and nonhomosexual types. *Archives of Sexual Behavior, 29,* 259–278.

Chorpita, B. F., Albano, A. M., Heimberg, R. G., & Barlow, D. H. (1996). A systematic replication of the prescriptive treatment of school refusal behavior in a single subject. *Journal of Behavior Therapy and Experimental Psychiatry, 27,* 281–290.

Chrichton, P. (1996). First-rank symptoms or rank-and-file symptoms? *British Journal of Psychiatry, 169,* 537–540.

Christakis, D. A., Zimmerman, F. J., DiGiuseppe, D. L., & McCarty, C. A. (2004). Early television exposure and subsequent attentional problems in children. *Pediatrics, 113,* 708–713.

Christensen, P. N., Stein, M. B., & Means-Christensen, A. (2003). Social anxiety and interpersonal perception: A social relations model analysis. *Behavior Research and Therapy, 41,* 1355–1371.

Chronis, A. M., Chacko, A., Fabiano, G. A., Wymbs, B. T., & Pelham, W. E. (2004). Enhancements to the behavioral parent training paradigm for families of children with ADHD: Review and future directions. *Clinical Child and Family Psychology Review, 7,* 1–27.

Churchill, D. W. (1969). Psychotic children and behavior modification. *American Journal of Psychiatry, 125,* 1585–1590.

Cicchetti, D., & Toth, S. L. (2004). Child maltreatment. Annual Reviews in Clinical Psychology, *Reviews in Advance, 1,* 1–30.

Citronme, L., & Volavka, J. (2000). Management of violence in schizophrenia. *Psychiatric Annals, 30,* 41–52.

Clark, D. M., Salkovskis, P. M., Ost, L. G., Breitholtz, E., Koehler, K., Westling, B. E., et al. (1997). Misinterpretation of body sensations in panic disorder. *Journal of Consulting and Clinical Psychology, 65,* 203–213.

Clark, L. A., & Harrison, J. A. (2001). Assessment instruments. In W. J. Livesley (Ed.), *Handbook of Personality Disorders: Theory, Research, and Treatment* (pp. 277–306). New York: Guilford.

Clark, L. A., Livesley, W. J., & Morey, L. (1997). Personality disorder assessment: The challenge of construct validity. *Journal of Personality Disorders, 11,* 205–231.

Clark, R. E., Bartels, S. J., Mellman, T. A., & Peacock, W. J. (2002). Recent trends in antipsychotic combination therapy of schizophrenia and schizoaffective disorders: Implications for state mental health policy. *Schizophrenia Bulletin, 28,* 75–84.

Clarkin, J. F., Levy, K. N., Lenzenweger, M. F., & Kernberg, O. F. (2004). The Personality Disorders Institute/Borderline Personality Disorder Research Foundation randomized control trial for borderline personality disorder: Rationale, methods, and patient characteristics. *Journal of Personality Disorders, 18,* 52–72.

Clayton, A. H., & West, S. G. (2003). The effects of antidepressants on human sexuality. *Primary Psychiatry, 10,* 62–70.

Cleckley, H. E. (1976). *The Mask of Sanity.* St. Louis: Mosby.

Cloninger, C. R., Bohman, M., & Sigvardsson, S. (1981). Inheritance of alcohol abuse: Cross-fostering analysis of adopted men. *Archives of General Psychiatry, 38,* 861–868.

Cloninger, C. R., Sigvardsson, S., Gilligan, S. B., von Knorring, A., et al. (1988). Genetic heterogeneity and the classification of alcoholism. *Advances in Alcohol and Substance Abuse, 7,* 3–16.

Cohen, A. N., Hammen, C., Henry, R. M., & Daley, S. E. (2004). Effects of stress and social support on recurrence in bipolar disorder. *Journal of Affective Disorders, 82,* 143–147.

Cohen, S., & Herbert, T. B. (1996). Health psychology: Psychological factors and physical disease from the perspective of human psychoneuroimmunology. In J. T. Spence, J. M. Darley, & D. J. Foss (Eds.), *Annual Review of Psychology* (pp. 123–142). Stanford, CA: Stanford University Press.

Cohen-Kettenis, P. T., & Arrindell, W. A. (1990). Perceived parental rearing style, parental divorce and transsexualism: A controlled study. *Psychological Medicine, 20,* 613–620.

Colby, K. M. (1975). *Artificial Paranoia: A Computer Simulation of Paranoid Processes.* New York: Pergamon.

Colby, K. M. (1977). Appraisal of four psychological theories of paranoid phenomena. *Journal of Abnormal Psychology, 86,* 54–59.

Cole, J. O., & Davis, J. M. (1969). Antipsychotic drugs. In L. Bellak & L. Loeb (Eds.), *The schizophrenic syndrome.* New York: Grune and Stratton.

Comas-Diaz, L. (1992). The future of psychotherapy with ethnic minorities. *Psychotherapy, 29,* 88–94.

Compton, A. (1992). The psychoanalytic view of phobias: III. Agoraphobia and other phobias of adults. *Psychoanalytic Quarterly, 61,* 400–425.

Cooks, J., Schotte, D. E., & McNally, R. J. (1992). Emotional arousal and overeating in restrained eaters. *Journal of Abnormal Psychology, 101,* 348–351.

Coolidge, F. L., Thede, L. L., & Young, S. E. (2002). The heritability of gender identity disorder in a child and adolescent twin sample. *Behavior Genetics, 32,* 251–257.

Coons, P. M., Bowman, E. S., & Milstein, V. (1988). Multiple personality disorder: A clinical investigation of 50 cases. *Journal of Nervous and Mental Disease, 176,* 519–527.

Cooper, M. J., Todd, G., & Wells, A. (2002). Content, origins, and consequences of dysfunctional beliefs in anorexia nervosa and bulimia nervosa. In R. L. Leahy & E. T. Dowd (Eds.). *Clinical Advances in Cognitive Psychotherapy: Theory and Application* (pp. 399–417). New York: Springer.

Cooper, M. L., Frone, M. R., Russell, M., & Mudar, P. (1995). Drinking to regulate positive and negative emotion: A motivational model of alcoholism. *Journal of Personality and Social Psychology, 69,* 961–971.

Coryell, W., Scheftner, W., Keller, M., Endicott, J., et al. (1993). The enduring psychosocial consequences of mania and depression. *American Journal of Psychiatry, 150,* 720–727.

Courchesne, E., Yeung-Courchesne, R., Press, G. A., Hesselink, J. R., & Jernigan, T. L. (1988). Hypoplasia of cerebellar vermal lobules VI and VII in autism. *New England Journal of Medicine, 318*, 1349–1354.

Cowan, P. A., Hoddinott, G. A., & Wright, B. A. (1965). Compliance and resistance in the conditioning of autistic children: An exploratory study. *Child Development, 36*, 913–923.

Coyne, J. C. (1992). Cognition in depression: A paradigm in crisis. *Psychological Inquiry, 3*, 232–235.

Coyne, J. C., Downey, G., & Boergers, J. (1993). Depression in families: A systems perspective. In D. Cichetti & S. L. Toth (Eds.), *Rochester symposium on developmental psychopathology: Vol. 4. Developmental approaches to the affective disorders.* Rochester, NY: University of Rochester.

Coyne, J. C., & Gotlib, I. H. (1983). The role of cognition in depression: A critical appraisal. *Psychological Bulletin, 94*, 472–505.

Craig, T. K. J., Boardman, A. P., Mills, K., Daly-Jones, O., & Drake, H. (1993). The South London Somatisation Study: I. Longitudinal course and the influence of early life experiences. *British Journal of Psychiatry, 163*, 579–588.

Craig, T. K. J., Drake, H., Mills, K., & Boardman, A. P. (1994). The South London Somatisation Study: II. Influence of stressful life events, and secondary gain. *British Journal of Psychiatry, 165*, 248–258.

Craighead, W. E., & Miklowitz, D. J. (2000). Psychosocial interventions for bipolar disorder. *Journal of Clinical Psychiatry, 61 (Suppl. 13)*, 58–64.

Craske, M. G., & Barlow, D. H. (2001). Panic disorder and agoraphobia. In D. H. Barlow (Ed). *Clinical Handbook of Psychological Disorders: A Step-by-Step Treatment Manual* (3rd ed.). New York: Guilford. 1–59.

Crimlisk, H. L., Bhatia, K. P., Cope, H., David, A. S., Marsden, D., & Ron, M. A. (2000). Patterns of referral in patients with medically unexplained motor symptoms. *Journal of Psychosomatic Research, 49*, 217–219.

Cronk, N. J., Slutske, W. S., Madden, P. A. F., Bucholz, K. K., & Heath, A. C. (2004). Risk for separation anxiety disorder among girls: Paternal absence, socioeconomic disadvantage, and genetic vulnerability. *Journal of Abnormal Psychology, 113*, 237–247.

Crow, T. J., Ferrier, I. N., & Johnstone, E. C. (1986). The two-syndrome concept and neuroendocrinology of schizophrenia. *Psychiatric Clinics of North America, 9*, 99–113.

Crowe, R. R. (1984). Current concepts: Electroconvulsive therapy—a current perspective. *New England Journal of Medicine, 311*, 163–167.

Crowther, J. H., Kichler, J. C., Sherwood, N. E., & Kuhnert, J. E. (2002). The role of familial factors in bulimia nervosa. *Eating Disorders: The Journal of Treatment and Prevention, 10*, 141–151.

Cunningham, J. A., Blomqvist, J., Koski-Jännes, A., & Cordingley, J. (2005). Maturing out of drinking problems: Perceptions of natural history as a function of severity. *Addiction Research and Theory, 13*, 79–84.

Curtis, N. M., Ronan, K. R., & Borduin, C. M. (2004). Multisystemic treatment: A meta-analysis of outcome studies. *Journal of Family Psychology, 18*, 411–419.

Dalal, B., Larkin, E., Leese, M., & Taylor, P. J. (1999). Clozapine treatment of long-standing schizophrenia and serious violence: A two-year follow-up study of the first 50 patients treated with clozapine in Rampton high security hospital. *Criminal Behaviour and Mental Health, 9*, 168–178.

Dandescu, A., & Wolfe, R. (2003). Considerations on fantasy use by child molesters and exhibitionists. *Sexual Abuse: A Journal of Research and Treatment, 15*, 297–305.

Davidson, J. R. T. (1997). Use of benzodiazepines in panic disorder. *Journal of Clinical Psychology, 58 (Suppl. 2)*, 26–31.

Davison, G. C. (1968). Elimination of a sadistic fantasy by a client-controlled counter-conditioning technique. *Journal of Abnormal Psychology, 73*, 84–90.

Davison, G. C., & Lazarus, A. A. (1994). Clinical innovation and evaluation: Integrating practice with inquiry. *Clinical Psychology: Science and Practice, 1*, 157–168.

Davison, G. C., & Neale, J. M. (1994). *Abnormal Psychology* (6th ed.). New York: Wiley.

Davison, G. C., Neale, J. M., & Kring, A. (2004). *Abnormal Psychology* (9th ed.). New York: Wiley.

Davison, G. C., Williams, M. E., Nezami, E., Bice, T. L., & DeQuattro, V. (1991). Relaxation, reduction in angry articulated thoughts, and improvements in borderline essential hypertension and heart rate. *Journal of Behavioral Medicine, 14*, 453–468.

Davison, G. C., & Zighelboim, V. (1987). Irrational beliefs in the articulated thoughts of college students with social anxiety. *Journal of Rational-Emotive Therapy, 5*, 238–254.

Davison, J. R. T. (1997). Use of benzodiazepines in panic disorder. *Journal of Clinical Psychiatry, 58 (Suppl. 2)*, 26–28.

De Gucht, V., & Heiser, W. (2003). Alexithymia and somatisation: A quantitative review of the literature. *Journal of Psychosomatic Research, 54*, 425–434.

Dell, P. F. (2001). Why the diagnostic criteria for dissociative identity disorder should be changed. *Journal of Trauma and Dissociation, 2*, 7–37.

DeMyer, M. K., Pontius, W., Norton, J. A., Barton, S., Allen, J., & Denhoff, E. (1973). The natural history of children with minimal brain dysfunction. *Annals of the New York Academy of Sciences, 205*, 188–205.

Deniker, P. (1970). Introduction of neuroleptic chemotherapy into psychiatry. In F. J. Ayd & B. Blackwell (Eds.), *Discoveries in biological psychiatry*. Philadelphia, PA: Lippincott.

De Silva, P. (1999). Sexual consequences of non-sexual trauma. *Sexual and Marital Therapy, 14*, 143–150.

Diamond, M., & Sigmundson, H. K. (1997). Sex reassignment at birth. Long-term, review and clinical implications. *Archives of Pediatrics and Adolescent Medicine, 151*, 298–304.

Dorahy, M. J. (2001). Dissociative identity disorder and memory dysfunction: The current state of experimental research and its future directions. *Clinical Psychology Review, 21*, 771–795.

Drake, R. E., & Mueser, K. T. (2000). Psychosocial approaches to dual diagnosis. *Schizophrenia Bulletin, 26*, 105–118.

Dressler, W. W. (2004). Culture and the risk of disease. *British Medical Bulletin, 69*, 21–31.

Dubbert, P. (1995). Behavioral (life style) modification in the prevention and treatment of hypertension: *Clinical Psychology Review, 15*, 187–216.

Dunsieth, N. W., Nelson, E. B., Brusman-Lovins, L. A., Holcomb, J. L., Beckman, D., Welge, J. A., et al. (2004). Psychiatric and legal features of 113 men convicted of sexual offenses. *Journal of Clinical Psychiatry, 65*, 293–300.

Eaton, W., & Harrison, G. (2001). Life chances, life planning, and schizophrenia: A review and interpretation of research on social deprivation. *International Journal of Mental Health, 30*, 58–81.

Eaton, W. W., Anthony, J. C., Romanoski, A., Tien, A., Gallo, J., Cai. G., Neufeld, K., Schlaepfer, T., Laugharne, J., & Chen, L. S. (1998). Onset and recovery from panic disorder in the Baltimore Epidemiologic Catchment Area follow-up. *British Journal of Psychiatry, 173*, 501–507.

Eaton, W. W., Kramer, M., Anthony, J. C., Dryman, A., Shapiro, S., et al. (1989). The incidence of specific DIS/DSM-III mental disorders: Data from the NIMH Epidemiologic Catchment Area Programs. *Acta Psychiatrica Scandinavica, 79,* 163–178.

Eckert, E. D., Halmi, K. A., Marchi, P., Grove, W., et al. (1995). Ten-year-follow-up of anorexia nervosa: Clinical course and outcome. *Psychological Medicine, 25,* 143–156.

Eddy, K. T., Keel, P. K., Dorer, D. J., Delinsky, S. S., Franko, D. L., & Herzog, D. B. (2002). Longitudinal comparison of anorexia nervosa subtypes. *International Journal of Eating Disorders, 20,* 191–201.

Eddy, K. T., Dutra, L., Bradley, R., & Westen, D. (2004). A multidimensional meta-analysis of psychotherapy and pharmacotherapy for obsessive-compulsive disorder. *Clinical Psychology Review, 24,* 1011–1030.

Egeland, J. A., Gerhard, D. S., Pauls, D. L., Sussex, J. N., et al. (1987). Bipolar affective disorders linked to DNA markers on chromosome 11. *Nature, 325,* 783–787.

Egger, H. L., Costello, E. J., & Angold, A. (2003). School refusal and psychiatric disorders: A community study. *Journal of the American Academy of Child and Adolescent Psychiatry, 42,* 797–807.

Eich, E., Macaulay, D., Loewenstein, R. J., & Dihle, P. H. (1997). Memory, amnesia, and dissociative identity disorder. *Psychological Science, 8,* 417–422.

Eisen, J. L., Phillips, K. A., & Rasmussen, S. A. (1999). Obsessions and delusions: The relationship between obsessive-compulsive disorder and the psychotic disorders. *Psychiatric Annals, 29,* 515–522.

Eisenberg, L., & Kanner, L. (1956). Early infantile autism. *American Journal of Orthopsychiatry, 26,* 556–566.

Ellason, J. W., & Ross, C. A. (1997). Two-year follow-up of inpatients with dissociative disorder. *American Journal of Psychiatry, 154,* 832–839.

Elliott, D. M., Mok, D. S., & Briere, J. (2004). Adult sexual assault: Prevalence, symptomatology, and sex differences in the general population. *Journal of Traumatic Stress, 17,* 203–211.

Emmers-Sommer, T. M., Allen, M., Bourhis, J., Sahlstein, E., Laskowski, K., Falato, W. I., et al. (2004). A meta-analysis of the relationship between social skills and sexual offenders. *Communication Reports, 17,* 1–10.

Eronen, M. (1995). Mental disorders and homicidal behavior in female subjects. *American Journal of Psychiatry, 152,* 1216–1218.

Evans, J. D., Heaton, R. K., Paulsen, J. S., McAdams, L. A., Heaton, S. C., & Jeste, D. V. (1999). Schizoaffective disorder: A form of schizophrenia or affective disorder? *Journal of Clinical Psychiatry, 60,* 874–882.

Faber, S. D., & Burns, J. W. (1996). Anger management style, degree of expressed anger, and gender influence cardiovascular recovery from interpersonal harassment. *Journal of Behavioral Medicine, 19,* 31–53.

Fahy, T. A. (1988). The diagnosis of multiple personality disorder: A critical review. *British Journal of Psychiatry, 153,* 597–606.

Fahy, T. A., Abas, M., & Brown, J. C. (1989). Multiple personality: A symptom of psychiatric disorder. *British Journal of Psychiatry, 154,* 99–101.

Fairburn, C. (1981). A cognitive-behavioral approach to the treatment of bulimia. *Psychological Medicine, 11,* 707–711.

Fairburn, C. (1995). *Overcoming Binge Eating.* New York: Guilford.

Fairburn, C. G., & Beglin, S. J. (1990). Studies of the epidemiology of bulimia nervosa. *American Journal of Psychiatry, 147,* 401–498.

Fairburn, C. G., Jones, R., Peveler, R. C., Hope, R. A., & O'Connor, M. (1993). Psychotherapy and bulimia nervosa: Longer term effects of interpersonal psychotherapy, behavior therapy, and cognitive therapy. *Archives of General Psychiatry, 50,* 419–428.

Fairburn, C. G., Peveler, R. C., Jones, R., Hope, R. A., & Doll, H. A. (1993). Predictors of twelve-month outcome in bulimia nervosa and the influence of attitudes to shape and weight. *Journal of Consulting and Clinical Psychology, 61,* 696–698.

Fairburn, C. G., Welch, S. L., Doll, H. A., Davies, B. A., & O'Connor, M. E. (1997). Risk factors for bulimia nervosa: A community-based case-control study. *Archives of General Psychiatry, 54,* 509–517.

Fairburn, C. G., Welch, S. L., Norman, P. A., O'Connor, M. E., et al. (1996). Bias and bulimia nervosa: How typical are clinic cases? *American Journal of Psychiatry, 153,* 386–391.

Falloon, I. R. H., Held, T., Coverdale, J. H., Roncone, R., & Laidlaw, T. M. (1999). Family interventions for schizophrenia: A review of long-term benefits of international studies. *Psychiatric Rehabilitation Skills, 3,* 268–290.

Farag, N. H., & Mills, P. J. (2004). What's next in behavioral hypertension research? *Annals of Behavioral Medicine, 27,* 1–2.

Fazel, S., & Danesh, J. (2002). Serious mental disorder in 23,000 prisoners: A systematic review of 62 surveys. *Lancet, 359,* 545–550.

Fedora, O., Reddon, J. R., & Yeudall, L. T. (1986). Stimuli eliciting sexual arousal in genital exhibitionists: A possible clinical application. *Archives of Sexual Behavior, 15,* 417–427.

Feeny, N. C. (2000). Exploring the roles of emotional numbing, depression, and dissociation in PTSD. *Journal of Traumatic Stress, 13,* 489–498.

Feeney, S. L. (2004). The cognitive-behavioral treatment of social phobia. *Clinical Case Studies, 3,* 124–146.

Feigon, S. A., Waldman, I. D., Levy, F., & Hay, D. A. (2001). Genetic and environmental influences on separation anxiety disorder symptoms and their moderation by age and sex. *Behavior Genetics, 31,* 403–411.

Feldman, P. J., Ullman, J. B., & Dunkel-Schetter, C. (1998). Women's reactions to rape victims: Motivational processes associated with blame and social support. *Journal of Applied Social Psychology, 28,* 469–503.

Fenichel, O. (1945). *The Psychoanalytic Theory of Neuroses.* New York: Norton.

Fenigstein, A. (1996). Paranoia. In C. G. Costello (Ed.), *Personality Characteristics of the Personality Disordered* (pp. 242–275). New York: Wiley.

Ferguson, C. P., & Pigott, T. A. (2000). Anorexia and bulimia nervosa: Neurobiology and pharmacotherapy. *Behavior Therapy, 31,* 237–263.

Fernander, A. F., Durán, R. E. F., Saab, P. G., & Schneiderman, N. (2004). John Henry active coping, education, and blood pressure among urban blacks. *Journal of the National Medical Association, 96,* 246–255.

Ferster, C. B. (1961). Positive reinforcement and behavior deficits in autistic children. *Child Development, 32,* 437–456.

Fine, C. G. (1999). The tactical-integration model for the treatment of dissociative identity disorder and allied dissociative disorders. *American Journal of Psychotherapy, 53,* 361–376.

Fink, P. (1992). Surgery and medical treatment in persistent somatizing patients. *Journal of Psychosomatic Research, 36,* 439–447.

Finney, J. W., & Moos, R. H. (1998). Psychosocial treatments for alcohol use disorders. In P. E. Nathan & J. M. Gorman (Eds.), *A Guide to Treatments that Work* (pp. 156–166). New York: Oxford University Press.

Fireman, B., Koran, L. M., Leventhal, J. L., & Jacobson, A., (2001). The prevalence of clinically recognized obsessive-compulsive disorder in a large health maintenance organization. *American Journal of Psychiatry, 158*, 1904–1910.

Fischer, M. (1973). Genetic and environmental factors in schizophrenia: A study of schizophrenic twins and their families. *Acta Psychiatrica Scandinavica (Suppl. 238)*.

Fischetti, M., Curran, J. P., & Wessberg, H. W. (1977). Sense of timing: A skill deficit in heterosexual-socially anxious males. *Behavior Modification, 1*, 179–194.

Fleck, F. (2004). MMR controversy raises questions about publication ethics. *Bulletin of the World Health Organization, 82*, 311–312.

Flory, K., & Lynam, D. R. (2003). The relation between attention deficit hyperactivity disorder and substance abuse: What role does conduct disorder play? *Clinical Child and Family Psychology Review, 6*, 1–16.

Foa, E. B., Dancu, C. V., Hembree, E. A., Jaycox, L. H., Meadows, E. A., & Street, G. P. (1999). A comparison of exposure therapy, stress inoculation training, and their combination for reducing posttraumatic stress disorder in female assault victims. *Journal of Consulting and Clinical Psychology, 67*, 194–200.

Foa, E. B., & Franklin, M. E. (2001). Obsessive-compulsive disorder. In D. H. Barlow (Ed). *Clinical Handbook of Psychological Disorders: A Step-by-Step Treatment Manual* (3rd ed., pp. 209–263.). New York: Guilford.

Foa, E. B., & Kozak, M. J. (1995). DSM-IV field trial: Obsessive-compulsive disorder. *American Journal of Psychiatry, 152*, 90–96.

Foa, E. B., Kozak, M. J., Steketee, G. S., & McCarthy, P. R. (1992). Treatment of depressive and obsessive-compulsive symptoms in OCD by imipramine and behaviour therapy. *British Journal of Clinical Psychology, 31*, 279–292.

Foa, E. B., & Riggs, D. S. (1995). Posttraumatic stress disorder following assault: Theoretical considerations and empirical findings. *Current Directions in Psychological Science, 4*, 61–65.

Foa, E. B., Riggs, D. S., & Gershuny, B. S. (1995). Arousal, numbing, and intrusion: Symptom structure of PTSD following assault. *American Journal of Psychiatry, 152*, 116–120.

Foa, E. B. (1997). Trauma and women: Course, predictors, and treatment. *Journal of Clinical Psychology, 58 (Suppl. 9)*, 25–28.

Foa, E. B., & Rothbaum, B. O. (1997). *Treating the trauma of rape: Cognitive-behavioral therapy for PTSD*. New York: Guilford.

Foa, E. B., Rothbaum, B. O., Riggs, D. S., & Murdock, T. B. (1991). Treatment of posttraumatic stress disorder in rape victims: A comparison between cognitive-behavioral procedures and counseling. *Journal of Consulting and Clinical Psychology, 59*, 715–723.

Foa, E. B., & Steketee, G. (1989). Behavioral/cognitive conceptualization of posttraumatic stress disorder. *Behavior Therapy, 20*, 155–176.

Foley, D. L., Eaves, L. J., Wormley, B., Silberg, J. L., Maes, H. H., Kuhn, J., & Riley, B. (2004). Childhood adversity, monoamine oxidase A genotype, and risk for conduct disorder. *Archives of General Psychiatry, 61*, 738–744.

Folstein, M. F., Marshal, F., Bassett, S. S., et al. (1991). Dementia: A case ascertainment in a community survey. *Journal of Gerontology, 46*, 132–138.

Fontana, A. F. (1966). Familial etiology of schizophrenia: Is a scientific methodology possible? *Psychological Bulletin, 66*, 214–227.

Forgac, G. E., & Michaels, E. J. (1982). Personality characteristics of two types of male exhibitionists. *Journal of Abnormal Psychology, 91*, 287–293.

Forrest, K. A. (2001). Toward an etiology of dissociative identity disorder: A neurodevelopmental approach. *Consciousness and Cognition, 10*, 259–293.

Forth, A. E., & Hare, R. D. (1989). The contingent negative variation in psychopaths. *Psychophysiology, 26,* 676–682.

Frances, A., First, M. B., & Pincus, H. A. (1995). *DSM-IV Guidebook.* Washington, D C: American Psychiatric Press.

Franco-Paredes, K., Mancilla-Díaz, J. M., Vázquez-Arévalo, R., López-Aguilar, X., & Álvarez-Rayón, G. (2005). Perfectionism and eating disorders: A review of the literature. *European Eating Disorders Review, 13,* 61–70.

Frank, E. (1996). Long-term treatment of depression: Interpersonal psychotherapy with and without medication. In C. Mundt, M. J. Goldstein, K. Hahlweg & P. Fiedler (Eds.), *Interpersonal Factors in the Origin and Course of Affective Disorders* (pp. 303–315). London, England: Gaskell/Royal College of Psychiatrists.

Frank, E., Swartz, H. A., & Kupfer, D. J. (2000). Interpersonal and social rhythm therapy: Managing the chaos of bipolar disorder. *Biological Psychiatry, 48,* 593–604.

Franklin, M. E., Abramowitz, J. S., Kozak, M. J., Levitt, J. T., & Foa, E. B. (2000). Effectiveness of exposure and ritual prevention for obsessive-compulsive disorder: randomized compared with nonrandomized samples. *Journal of Consulting and Clinical Psychology, 68,* 594–602.

Freeman, C., Sinclair, F., Turnbull, J., & Annandale, A. (1985). Psychotherapy for bulimia: A controlled study. Conference on Anorexia Nervosa and Related Disorders. *Journal of Psychiatric Research, 19,* 473–478.

Fremont, W. P. (2003). School refusal in children and adolescents. *American Family Physician, 68,* 1555–1560.

Freud, A. (1946). *The Psychoanalytic Treatment of Children: Lectures and Essays.* London: Imago.

Freud, S. (1925). Mourning and melancholia. In *Sigmund Freud, Collected Papers, Volume IV* (Alix and James Strachey, trans.). London: Hogarth Press. (Originally published in *Zeitschrift,* 1917.)

Freud, S. (1925). Psycho-analytic notes upon an autobiographical account of a case of paranoia (dementia Paranoides). In *Sigmund Freud, Collected Papers, Volume III* (Alix and James Strachey, trans.). London: Hogarth Press. (Originally published in *Jahrbuch für psychoanalytische und psychopathologische Forschungen,* 1909.)

Freund, K., & Watson, R. (1990). Mapping the boundaries of courtship disorder. *Journal of Sex Research, 27,* 589–606.

Friedman, R. A., & Kocsis, J. H. (1996). Pharmacotherapy for chronic depression. *Psychiatric Clinics of North America, 19,* 121–132.

Fritz, G. K., Fritsch, S., & Hagino, O. (1997). Somatoform disorders in children and adolescents: A review of the past 10 years. *Journal of the American Academy of Child and Adolescent Psychiatry, 36,* 1329–1338.

Funder, DC (1999). *Personality Judgment: A Realistic Approach to Person Perception.* San Diego, CA: Academic Press.

Gabbard, G. O. (1992). Psychodynamics of panic disorder and social phobia. *Bulletin of the Menninger Clinic, 56 (Suppl. A),* 3–13.

Gangestad, S. W., Bailey, J. M., & Martin, N. G. (2000). Taxometric analyses of sexual orientation and gender identity. *Journal of Personality and Social Psychology, 78,* 1109–1121.

Garden, G. M., & Rothery, D. J. (1992). A female monozygotic twin pair discordant for transsexualism: Some theoretical implications. *British Journal of Psychiatry, 161,* 852–854.

Gardner, H. (1997, January 19). Review of the creation of Dr. B. *Los Angeles Times Book Review,* p. 3.

Garfinkel, P. E., & Kaplan, A. S. (1986). Anorexia nervosa: Diagnostic conceptualizations. In K. D. Brownell & J. P. Foreyt (Eds.), *Handbook of Eating Disorders*. New York: Basic Books.

Garfinkel, P. E., Moldofsky, H., & Garner, D. M. (1980). The heterogeneity of anorexia nervosa. *Archives of General Psychiatry, 37,* 1036–1040.

Garner, D. M. (1986). Cognitive therapy for anorexia nervosa. In K. D. Brownell & J. P. Foreyt (Eds.), *Handbook of Eating Disorders*. New York: Basic Books.

Garner, D. M., & Magana, C. (2002). Bulimia nervosa. In M. Hersen & L. K. Porzelius (Eds.). *Diagnosis, Conceptualization, and Treatment Planning for Adults: A Step-by-Step Guide* (pp. 251–269). Mahwah, NJ: Erlbaum.

Garvin, V., & Streigel-Moore, R. H. (2001). Health services research for eating disorders in the United States: A status report and a call to action. In R. H. Striegel-Moore & L. Smolak (Eds.). *Eating Disorders: Innovative Direction in Research and Practice* (pp. 135–152). Washington, DC: American Psychological Association.

Gearson, J. S., Kaltman, S. I., Brown, C., & Bellack, A. S. (2003). Traumatic life events and PTSD among women with substance use disorders and schizophrenia. *Psychiatric Services, 54,* 523–528.

Geddes, J. R., Burgess, S., Hawton, K., Jamison, K., & Goodwin, G. M. (2004). Long-term lithium therapy for bipolar disorder: Systematic review and meta-analysis of randomized controlled studies. *American Journal of Psychiatry, 161,* 217–222.

Gelernter, C. S., Uhde, T. W., Cimbolic, P., Arnkoff, D. B., Vittone, B. J., et al. (1991). Cognitive behavioral and pharmacological treatments of social phobia: A controlled study. *Archives of General Psychiatry, 48,* 938–945.

Gerlach, A. L., Wilhelm, F. H., Gruber, K., & Roth, W. T. (2001). Blushing and physiological arousability in social phobia. *Journal of Abnormal Psychology, 110,* 247–258.

Ghizzani, A., & Montomoli, M. (2000). Anorexia nervosa and sexuality in women: A revew. *Journal of Sex Education and Therapy, 25,* 80–88.

Gillberg, C. (1991). Outcome in autism and autistic-like conditions. *Journal of the American Academy of Child and Adolescent Psychiatry, 30,* 375–382.

Gillberg, C., Melander, H., von Knorring, A-L., Janols, L-A., Thernlund, G., et al. (1997). Long-term stimulant treatment of children with attention-deficit hyperactivity disorder symptoms: A randomized, double-blind, placebo-control trial. *Archives of General Psychiatry, 54,* 85–864.

Gilligan, C. (1982). *In a different Voice: Psychological Theory and Women's Development*. Cambridge, MA: Harvard University Press.

Gleaves, D. H. (1996). The sociocognitive model of dissociative identity disorder: A reexamination of the evidence. *Psychological Bulletin, 120,* 42–59.

Gleaves, D. H., May, M. C., & Cardena, E. (2001). An examination of the diagnostic validity of dissociative identity disorder. *Clinical Psychology Review, 21,* 577–608.

Goldfried, M. R., & Davison, G. C. (1976). *Clinical Behavior Therapy.* New York: Holt, Rinehart, & Winston.

Goldfried, M. R., & Davison, G. C. (1994). *Clinical Behavior Therapy.* Expanded edition. New York: Wiley.

Goldfried, M. R., Padawer, W., & Robins, C. (1984). Social anxiety and the semantic structure of heterosocial interactions. *Journal of Abnormal Psychology, 93,* 87–97.

Goldman, D., & Mazzanti, C. (2002). From phenotype to gene and back: A critical appraisal of progress so far. In J. Benjamin & R. P. Ebstein (Eds.). *Molecular Genetics and the Human Personality* (pp. 273–291). Washington, DC: American Psychiatric Press.

Goodman, R., & Stevenson, J. (1989). A twin study of hyperactivity: II. The aetiological role of genes, family relationships, and perinatal adversity. *Journal of Child Psychology and Psychiatry, 30,* 691–709.

Goodwin, D. W. (1979). Alcoholism and heredity: A review and hypothesis. *Archives of General Psychiatry, 36,* 57–61.

Goodwin, R. D. (2002). Anxiety disorders and the onset of depression among adults in the community. *Psychological Medicine, 32,* 1121–1124.

Gordon, C. T., State, R. C., Nelson, J. E., Hamburger, S. D., & Rapoport, J. L. (1993). A double-blind comparison of clomipramine, desipramine, and placebo in the treatment of autistic disorder. *Archives of General Psychiatry, 50,* 441–447.

Gordon, P., & Ahmed, W. (1988). A comparison of two group therapies for bulimia. *British Review of Bulimia and Anorexia Nervosa, 3,* 17–31.

Gore, S., Aseltine, R. H., Jr., & Colten, M. E. (1993). Gender, social-relational involvement, and depression. *Journal of Research on Adolescence, 3,* 101–125.

Gorenstein, E. E., & Newman, J. P. (1980). Disinhibitory psychopathology: A new perspective and a model for research. *Psychological Review, 87,* 301–315.

Gossop, M., Harris, J., Best, D., Man, L. H., Manning, V., Marshall, J. et al. (2003). Is attendance at Alcoholics Anonymous meetings after inpatient treatment related to improved outcomes? A 6–month follow-up study. *Alcohol and Alcoholism, 38,* 421–426.

Gosschalk, P. O. (2004). Behavioral treatment of acute onset school refusal in a 5-year old girl with separation anxiety disorder. *Education and Treatment of Children, 27,* 150–160.

Gotlib, I. H., & Neubauer, D. L. (2000). Information-processing approaches to the study of cognitive biases in depression. In S. L. Johnson & A. M. Hayes (Eds.), *Stress, Coping, and Depression* (pp. 117–143). Mahwah, NJ: Erlbaum Associates.

Gottesman, I. I. (1991). *Schizophrenia Genesis: The Origins of Madness.* New York: Freeman.

Gottesman, I. I., & Goldsmith, H. H. (1994). Developmental psychopathology of antisocial behavior: Inserting genes into its ontogenesis and epigenesis. In C. A. Nelson (Ed.), *Threats to Optimal Development.* Hillsdale, NJ: Erlbaum Associates.

Goyette, C. H., & Conners, C. K. (1977). *Food Additives and Hyperactivity.* Paper presented at the 85th annual convention of the American Psychological Association.

Grant, B. F., Hasin, D. S., Stinson, F. S., Dawson, D. A., Chou, S. P., Ruan, W. J., & Pickering, R. P. (2004). Prevalence, correlates, and disability of personality disorders in the United States: Results from the National Epidemiological Survey and Alcohol and Related Conditions. *Journal of Clinical Psychiatry, 65,* 948–958.

Grant, B. F., Stinson, F. S., Dawson, D. A., Chou, S. P., & Ruan, W. J. (2005). Co-occurrence of DSM-IV personality disorders in the United States: Results from the National Epidemiologic Survey on Alcohol and Related Conditions. *Comprehensive Psychiatry, 46,* 1–5.

Greaves, G. B. (1980). Multiple personality: 165 years after Mary Reynolds. *Journal of Nervous and Mental Disease, 168,* 577–596.

Green, R. (1974). *Sexual Identity Conflict in Children and Adults.* New York: Basic Books.

Green, R. (1987). *The "Sissy Boy Syndrome" and the Development of Homosexuality.* New Haven, CT: Yale University Press.

Green, R. (1994). Transsexualism and the law. *Bulletin of the American Academy of Psychiatry and the Law, 22,* 511–517.

Greene, B. A. (1985). Considerations in the treatment of black patients by white therapists. *Psychotherapy, 22,* 115–122.

Grenier, G., & Byers, E. S. (1995). Rapid ejaculation: A review of conceptual, etiological, and treatment issues. *Archives of Sexual Behavior, 24,* 447–472.

Gretton, H. M., Hare, R. D., & Catchpole, R. E. H. (2004). Psychopathy and offending from adolescence to adulthood: A 10-year follow-up. *Journal of Consulting and Clinical Psychology, 72,* 636–645.

Gruenewald, D. (1984). On the nature of multiple personality. Comparisons with hypnosis. *International Journal of Clinical and Experimental Hypnosis, 32,* 170–190.

Guisinger, S. (2003). Adapted to flee famine: Adding an evolutionary perspective on anorexia nervosa. *Psychological Review, 110,* 745–761.

Gunderson, J. G., & Sabo, A. N. (1993). The phenomenological and conceptual interface between borderline personality disorder and PTSD. *American Journal of Psychiatry, 150,* 19–27.

Gunderson, J. G., & Singer, M. T. (1975). Defining borderline patients: An overview. *American Journal of Psychiatry, 132,* 1–10.

Gureje, O., Simon, G. E., Ustun, T. B., & Goldberg, D. P. (1997). Somatization in cross-cultural perspective: A World Health Organization study in primary care. *American Journal of Psychiatry, 154,* 989–995.

Hacking, I. (1995). *Rewriting the Soul: Multiple Personality and the Sciences of Memory.* Princeton, NJ: Princeton University Press.

Haffey, M., & Cohen, P. M. (1992). Treatment issues for divorcing women. *Families in Society, 73,* 142–148.

Hall, T. M., Kaduson, H. G., & Schaefer, C. E. (2002). Fifteen effective play therapy techniques. *Professional Psychology: Research and Practice, 33,* 515–522.

Halmi, K. A. (1996). The psychobiology of eating behavior in anorexia nervosa. *Psychiatry Research, 62,* 23–29.

Halmi, K. A. (1997). Models to conceptualize risk factors for bulimia nervosa. *Archives of General Psychiatry, 54,* 507–508.

Hamburger, C., Sturup, G. K., & Dahl-Iverson, E. (1953). Transvestism: Hormonal, psychiatric and surgical treatment. *Journal of the American Medical Association, 152,* 391–396.

Hamilton, J. A., & Jensvold, M. (1992). Personality, psychopathology, and depression in women. In L. S. Brown & M. Ballou (Eds.), *Personality and psychopathology: Feminist reappraisals* (pp. 116–143). New York: Guilford.

Hammen, C. (1997). *Depression.* East Sussex, UK: Psychology Press.

Hammen, C. (2005). Stress and depression. *Annual Review of Clinical Psychology, 55,* 11. 1–11. 27.

Harburg, E., Erfurt, J. C., Hauenstein, L. S., Chape, C., Schull, W. J., & Schork, M. A. (1973). Socioecological stress, suppressed hostility, skin color and black—white male blood pressure: Detroit. *Psychosomatic Medicine, 35,* 276–296.

Hardy, K. V., & Laszloffy, T. A. (1995). Therapy with African-Americans and the phenomenon of rage. *In Session: Psychotherapy in Practice, 1,* 57–70.

Hare, R. D., Harpur, T. J., Hakstian, R. A., et al. (1990). The revised Psychopathy Checklist: Reliability and factor structure. *Psychological Assessment, 2,* 338–341.

Hare, R. D., McPherson, L. M., & Forth, A. E. (1988). Male psychopaths and their criminal careers. *Journal of Consulting and Clinical Psychology, 56,* 710–714.

Harrington, R., & Bailey, S. (2004). Prevention of antisocial personality disorder: Mounting evidence on optimal timing and methods. *Criminal Behaviour and Mental Health, 14,* 75–81.

Harris, B. (1979). Whatever happened to Little Albert? *American Psychologist, 34,* 151–160.

Harris, T. O. (1989). Disorders of menstruation. In G. W. Brown & T. O. Harris (eds.), *Life Events and Illness,* New York: Guilford Press, pp. 261–294.

Harrow, M., Grossman, L. S., Herbener, E. S., & Davies, E. W. (2000). Ten-year outcome: Patients with schizoaffective disorders, schizophrenia, affective disorders and mood-incongruent psychotic symptoms. *British Journal of Psychiatry, 177,* 421–426.

Hart, S. D., & Hare, R. D. (1989). Discriminant validity of the Psychopathy Checklist in a forensic psychiatric population. *Psychological Assessment, 1,* 211–218.

Hastrup, J. L., Light, K. C., & Obrist, P. A. (1982). Parental hypertension and cardiovascular response to stress in healthy young adults. *Psychophysiology, 19,* 615–622.

Hawley, C., & Buckley, R. (1974). Food dyes and the hyperkinetic child. *Academic Therapy, 10,* 27–32.

Hay, P. J., Sachdev, P. S., Cumming, S., Smith, J. S., et al. (1993). Treatment of obsessive-compulsive disorder by psychosurgery. *Acta Psychiatrica Scandinavica, 87,* 197–207.

Heatherton, T. F., & Polivy, J. (1992). Chronic dieting and eating disorders: A spiral model. In J. Crowther, E. Hobfall, M. A. P. Stephens, & D. L. Tennenbaum (Eds.), *The Etiology of Bulimia: The Individual and Familial Context* (pp. 135–155). Washington, DC: Hemisphere.

Heaton, P., & Wallace, G. L. (2004). Annotation: The savant syndrome. disorders. *Journal of Child Psychology and Psychiatry, 45,* 899–911.

Heberbrand, J. (1992). A critical appraisal of X-linked bipolar illness. Evidence for the assumed mode of transmission is lacking. *British Journal of Psychiatry, 160,* 7–11.

Heiden, W., & Hafner, H. (2000). The epidemiology of onset and course of schizophrenia. *European Archives of Psychiatry and Clinical Neuroscience, 250,* 292–303.

Heiman, J., LoPiccolo, L., & LoPiccolo, J. (1988). *Becoming Orgasmic: A Sexual Growth Program for Women.* Englewood Cliffs, NJ: Prentice-Hall.

Heimberg, R. G., & Juster, H. R. (1994). Treatment of social phobia in cognitive-behavioral groups. *Journal of Clinical Psychiatry, 55,* 38–46.

Heimberg, R. G., Liebowitz, M. R., Hope, D. A., Scneier, F. R. Holt, C. S., Welkowitz, L. A., Juster, H. R., Campeas, R., Bruch, M. A., Cloitre, M., Fallon, B., & Klein, D. F. (1998). Cognitive behavioral group therapy vs phenelzine therapy for social phobia: 12-week outcome. *Archives of General Psychiatry, 55,* 1133–1141.

Heinssen, R. K., Liberman, R. P., & Kopelowicz, A. (2000). Psychosocial skills training for schizophrenia: Lessons from the laboratory. *Schizophrenia Bulletin, 26,* 21–46.

Helmes, E., & Landmark, J. (2003). Subtypes of schizophrenia: A cluster analytic approach. *Canadian Journal of Psychiatry, 48,* 702–708.

Helzer, J. E., Robins, L., & McEvoy, L. (1987). Post-traumatic stress disorder in the general population: Findings of the Epidemiological Catchment Area Survey. *New England Journal of Medicine, 317,* 1630–1634.

Henker, B., & Whalen, C. K. (1989). Hyperactivity and attention deficits. Special Issue: Children and their development: Knowledge base, research agenda, and social policy application. *American Psychologist, 44,* 216–223.

Herman-Jeglinska, A., Grabowska, A., & Dulko, S. (2002). Masculinity, femininity, and transsexualism. *Archives of Sexual Behavior, 31,* 527–534.

Herpetz, S. C., Werth, U., Lukas, G., et al. (2001). Emotion in criminal offenders with psychopathic personality disorder. *Archives of General Psychiatry, 58,* 737–745.

Herzog, D. B. (1982). Bulimia: The secretive syndrome. *Psychosomatics, 23,* 481–483.

Heston, L. L. (1966). Psychiatric disorders in foster home reared children of schizophrenic mothers. *British Journal of Psychiatry, 112,* 819–825.

Hettema, J. M., Neale, M. C., & Kendler, K. S. (2001). A review and meta- analysis of the genetic epidemiology of the anxiety disorders. *American Journal of Psychiatry, 158,* 1568–1578.

Hewett, F. M. (1965). Teaching speech to an autistic child through operant conditioning. *American Journal of Orthopsychiatry, 33,* 927–936.

Heyne, D., King, N. J., Tonge, B. J., Rollings, S., Young, D., Pritchard, M., & Ollendick, T. H. (2002). Evaluation of child therapy and caregiver training in the treatment of school refusal. *Journal of the American Academy of Child and Adolescent Psychiatry, 41,* 687–695.

Hibbett, A., & Fogelman, K. (1990). Future lives of truants: Family formation and health-related behavior. *British Journal of Educational Psychology, 60,* 171–179.

Hibbett, A., Fogelman, K., & Manor, O. (1990). Occupational outcomes of truancy. *British Journal of Educational Psychology, 60,* 23–26.

Hicks, B. M., Krueger, R. F., Iacono, W. G., McGue, M., & Patrick, C. J. (2004). Family transmission and heritability of externalizing disorders. *Archives of General Psychiatry, 61,* 922–928.

Hill, M. N., Han, H. R., Dennison, C. R., Kim, M. T., Roary, M. C., Blumenthal, R. S., et al. (2003). Hypertension care and control in underserved urban African American men: Behavioral and physiologic outcomes at 36 months. *American Journal of Hypertension, 16,* 906–913.

Hiller, W., Fichter, M. M., & Rief, W. (2003). A controlled treatment study of somatoform disorders including analysis of healthcare utilization and cost-effectiveness. *Journal of Psychosomatic Research, 54,* 369–380.

Hinshaw, S. P., & Melnick, S. M. (1995). Peer relationship with boys with attention-deficit hyperactivity disorder with and without comorbid aggression. *Development and Psychopathy, 7,* 627–647.

Hirschfeld, R. M. A. (2001). Antidepressants in the United States: Current status and future needs. In M. M. Weissman (Ed.), *Treatment of Depression: Bridging the 21st Century* (pp. 123–134). Washington, DC: American Psychiatric Press

Hoch, P., & Polatin, P. (1949). Pseudoneurotic forms of schizophrenia. *Psychiatric Quarterly, 23,* 248–276.

Hodapp, V., Weyer, G., & Becker, J. (1976). Situational stereotype in essential hypertension patients. *Journal of Psychosomatic Research, 19,* 113–121.

Hoek, H. W., & van Hoeken, D. (2003). Review of the prevalence and incidence of eating disorders. *International Journal of Eating Disorders, 34,* 383–396.

Hofland, B. F. (1988). Autonomy in long term care: Background issues and a programmatic response. *The Gerontologist, 28 (Suppl.),* 3–9.

Hofmann, S. G., Moscovitch, D. A., Kim, H. J., & Taylor, A. N. (2004). Changes in self-perception during treatment of social phobia. *Journal of Consulting and Clinical Psychology, 72,* 588–596.

Hogan, B. E., & Linden, W. (2004). Anger response styles and blood pressure: At least don't ruminate about it! *Annals of Behavioral Medicine, 27,* 38–49.

Hokanson, J. E., & Burgess, M. (1962). The effects of three types of aggression on vascular processes. *Journal of Abnormal and Social Psychology, 65,* 446–449.

Holder, H., Longabaugh, R., Miller, W. R., & Rubonis, A. V. (1991). The cost-effectiveness of treatment for alcoholism: A first approximation. *Journal of Studies on Alcohol, 52,* 517–540.

Hollander, E., & Allen, A. (2001). Serotonergic drugs and the treatment of disorders related to obsessive-compulsive disorder. In M. T. Pato and J. Zohar (Eds). *Current Treatments of Obsessive-Compulsive Disorder* (2nd edition pp. 193–220) Washington, DC: USic Association.

Hollon, S. D., Thase, M. E., & Markowitz, J. C. (2002). Treatment and prevention of depression. *Psychological Science in the Public Interest, 3,* 39–77.

Holm, V. A., & Varley, C. K. (1989). Pharmacological treatment of autistic children. In G. Dawson (Ed.), *Autism: Nature, Diagnosis, Treatment* (pp. 386–404). New York: Guilford.

Hooley, J. M. (1985). Expressed emotion: A review of the critical literature. *Clinical Psychology Review, 5*, 119–139.

Hoover, C. F., & Insel, T. R. (1984). Families of origin in obsessive-compulsive disorder. *Journal of Nervous and Mental Disease, 172*, 207–215.

Hope, D. A., Heimberg, R. G., & Bruch, M. A. (1995). Dismantling cognitive-behavioral group therapy for social phobia. *Behaviour Research and Therapy, 33*, 637–650.

Hornstein, N. L., & Putnam, F. W. (1996). Abuse and the development of dissociative symptoms and dissociative identity disorder. In C. R. Pfeffer (Ed.), *Severe Stress and Mental Disturbance in Children* (pp. 449–473). Washington, DC: American Psychiatric Press.

Horley, K., Williams, L. M., Gonsalvez, C., & Gordon, E. (2004). Face to face: Visual scanpath evidence for abnormal processing of facial expressions in social phobia. *Psychiatry Research, 127*, 43–53.

Hsu, L. K. G. (1987). Are eating disorders becoming more common in blacks? *International Journal of Eating Disorders, 6*, 113–124.

Hsu, L. K. G. (1990). *Eating Disorders*. New York: Guilford.

Hsu, L. K. G. (1996). Epidemiology of the eating disorders. *Psychiatric Clinics of North America, 19*, 681–700.

Hsu, L. K. G., Crisp, A. H., & Callender, J. S. (1992). Recovery in anorexia nervosa: The patient's perspective. *International Journal of Eating Disorders, 11*, 341–350.

Hsu, L. K. G., Rand, W., Sullivan, S., Liu, D. W., Mulliken, B., McDonagh, B., & Kaye, W. H. (2001). Cognitive therapy, nutritional therapy and their combination in the treatment of bulimia nervosa. *Psychological Medicine, 31*, 871–879.

Hudziak, J. J., van Beijsterveldt, C. E. M., Althoff, R. R., Stanger, C., Rettew, DC, Nelson, E. C., Todd, R. D., Bartels, M., & Boomsma, D. I. (2004). Genetic and environmental contributions to the child behavior checklist obsessive-compulsive scale: A cross-cultural twin study. *Archives of General Psychiatry, 61*, 608–616.

Hughlings-Jackson, J. (1931). In J. Taylor (Ed.), *Selected writings*. London: Hodder & Stoughton.

Huppert, J. D., Roth, D. A., & Foa, E. B. (2003). Cognitive-behavioral treatment of social phobia: New advances. *Current Psychiatry Reports, 5*, 289–296.

Hurwitz, T. A. (2004). Somatization and conversion disorder. *Canadian Journal of Psychiatry, 49*, 172–178.

Husain, S. S., Kevan, I. M., Linnell, R., & Scott, A. I. F. (2004). Electroconvulsive therapy in depressive illness that has not responded to drug treatment. *Journal of Affective Disorders. 83*, 121–126.

Hussong, A. M., Hicks, R. E., Levy, S. A., & Curran, P. J. (2001). Specifying the relations between affect and heavy alcohol use among young adults. *Journal of Abnormal Psychology, 110*, 449–461.

Imperato-McGinley, J., Guerrero, L., Gautier, T., & Peterson, R. E. (1974). Steroid 5a-reductase deficiency in man: An inherited form of male pseudohermaphroditism. *Science, 186*, 1213–1215.

Iwamasa, G. Y. (1993). Asian Americans and cognitive-behavioral therapy. *The Behavior Therapist, 16*, 233–235.

Jackson, A. M. (1973). Psychotherapy: Factors associated with the race of the therapist. *Psychotherapy: Theory, Research, and Practice, 10*, 273–277.

Jacobi, C., Hayward, C., de Zwaan, M., Kraemer, H. C., & Agras, W. S. (2004). Coming to terms with risk factors for eating disorders: Application of risk terminology and suggestions for a general taxonomy. *Psychological Bulletin, 130*, 19–65.

Jacobson, E. (1938). *Progressive relaxation*. Chicago: University of Chicago Press.

James, D. (1998). Multiple personality disorder in the courts: A review of the North American experience. *Journal of Forensic Psychiatry, 9*, 339–361.

Janicak, P. G., Keck, P. E., Davis, J. M., Kasckow, J. W., Tugrul, K., Dowd, S. M., Strong, J., Sharma, R. P., & Strakowski, S. M. (2001). A double-blind, randomized, prospective evaluation of the efficacy and safety of risperidone versus haloperidol in the treatment of schizoaffective disorder. *Journal of Clinical Psychopharmacology, 21*, 360–368.

Jenike, J. A. (1998). Neurosurgical treatment of obsessive-compulsive disorder. *British Journal of Psychiatry, 173*, 79–90.

Jenike, M. A., Baer, L., & Minichiello, W. E. (Eds.) (1986). *Obsessive-compulsive disorders: Theory and management*. Littleton, MA: PSG.

Jimerson, DC, Wolfe, B. E., Metzger, E. D., Finkelstein, D. M., Cooper, T. B., & Levine, J. M. (1997). Decreased serotonin function in bulimia nervosa. *Archives of General Psychiatry, 54*, 529–534.

Johns, L. C., Hemsley, D., & Kuipers, E. (2002). A comparison of auditory hallucinations in a psychiatric and non-psychiatric group. *British Journal of Clinical Psychology, 41*, 81–86.

Johns, L. C., Rossell, S., Frith, C., Ahmad, F., Hemsley, D., Kuipers, E., & McGuire, P. K. (2001). Verbal self-monitoring and auditory verbal hallucinations in patients with schizophrenia. *Psychological Medicine, 31*, 705–715.

Johnson, J. G., Cohen, P., Brown, J., Smailes, E. M., & Bernstein, D. P. (1999). Childhood maltreatment increases risk for personality disorders during early childhood. *Archives of General Psychiatry, 56*, 600–606.

Johnson, J. G., Spitzer, R. L., & Williams, J. B. W. (2001). Health problems, impairment and illnesses associated with bulimia nervosa and binge eating disorder among primary care and obstetric gynaecology patients. *Psychological Medicine, 31*, 1455–1466.

Johnson, S. L., & Kizer, A. (2002). Bipolar and unipolar depression: A comparison of clinical phenomenology and psychosocial predictors. In I. H. Gotlib and C. L. Hammen (Eds.), *Handbook of Depression* (pp. 141–165). New York: Guilford.

Johnson, S. L., & Roberts, J. E. (1995). Life events and bipolar disorder: Implications from biological theories. *Psychological Bulletin, 117*, 434–449.

Johnson, S. L., Sandrow, D., Meyter, B., Winters, R., Miller, I., Solomon, D., & Keitner, G. (2000). Increases in manic symptoms after life events involving goal attainment. *Journal of Abnormal Psychology, 109*, 721–727.

Johnson, W. G., Schlundt, D. G., Barclay, D. R., Carr-Nangle, R. E., et al. (1995). A naturalistic functional analysis of binge eating. *Behavior Therapy, 26*, 101–118.

Joiner, T., Coyne, J. C., & Blalock, J. (1999). On the interpersonal nature of depression: Overview and synthesis. In T. Joiner & J. C. Coyne (Eds.), *The Interactional Nature of Depression* (pp. 3–20). Washington, DC: American Psychological Association.

Jones, P., & Cannon, M. (1998). The new epidemiology of schizophrenia. *Psychiatric Clinics of North America, 21*, 1–25.

Jones, S. (2004). Psychotherapy of bipolar disorder: A review. *Journal of Affective Disorders, 80*, 101–114.

Kabot, S. Masi, W., & Segal, M. (2003). Advances in the diagnosis and treatment of autism spectrum disorders. *Professional Psychology: Research and Practice, 34*, 26–33.

Kafka, M. P., & Hennen, J. (2002). A DSM-IV Axis I comorbidity study of males (n=120) with paraphilias and paraphilia-related disorders. *Sexual Abuse: A Journal of Research and Treatment, 14*, 349–366.

Kagan, J., Snidman, N, Zentner, M., & Peterson, E. (1999). Infant temperament and anxious symptoms in school age children. *Development & Psychopathology, 11*, 209–224.

Kahler, C. W., Read, J. P., Stuart, G. L., Ramsey, S. E., McCrady, B. S., & Brown, R. A. (2004). Motivational enhancement for 12–step involvement among patients undergoing alcohol detoxification. *Journal of Consulting and Clinical Psychology, 72*, 736–741.

Kane, J. M. (1996). Treatment-resistant schizophrenic patients. *Journal of Clinical Psychiatry, 57 (Suppl. 9)*, 35–40.

Kane, J. M. (2001). Long-term therapeutic management in schizophrenia. In A. Breier & P. V. Tran (Eds.), *Current Issues in the Psychopharmacology of Schizophrenia* (pp. 430–446). Philadelphia, PA: Lippincott, Williams and Wilkins.

Kane, J. M. (2004). Tardive dyskinesia rates with atypical antipsychotics in adults: Prevalence and incidence. *Journal of Clinical Psychiatry, 65*, 16–20.

Kanner, L. (1943). Autistic disturbances of affective contact. *Nervous Child, 2*, 217–250.

Kanner, L. (1973). Follow-up of eleven autistic children originally reported in 1943. In L. Kanner (Ed.), *Childhood Psychosis: Initial Studies and New Insights*. Washington, DC: Winston/Wiley.

Kano, S. (1989). *Making Peace with Food*. New York: HarperCollins.

Kapur, S., & Remington, G. (2001). Atypical antipsychotics: New directions and new challenges in the treatment of schizophrenia. *Annual Review of Medicine, 52*, 503–517.

Karno, M., & Golding, J. M. (1991). Obsessive compulsive disorder. In L. N. Robins & D. A. Regier (Eds.), *Psychiatric disorders in America: The Epidemiologic Catchment Area Study* (pp. 204–219). New York: Free Press.

Karpman, B. (1954). *The sexual offender and his offenses*. New York: Julian Press.

Karvonen, J. T., Veijola, J., Jokelainen, J., Läksy, K., Järvelin, M. R., & Joukamaa, M. (2004). Somatization disorder in young adult population. *General Hospital Psychiatry, 26*, 9–12.

Kasen, S., Cohen, P., Skodol., A. E., Johnson, J. G., Smailes, E., & Brook, J. S. (2001). Childhood depression and adult personality disorder: Alternative pathways of continuity. *Archives of General Psychiatry, 58*, 231–236.

Kasl, S. V., & Cobb, S. (1970). Blood pressure changes in men undergoing job loss: A preliminary report. *Psychosomatic Medicine, 6*, 95–106.

Katon, W. (1996). Panic disorder: Relationship to high medical utilization, unexplained physical symptoms, and medical costs. *Journal of Clinical Psychiatry, 57 (Suppl. 10)*, 11–17.

Kay, W. H., Devlin, B., Barbarich, N., Bulik, C. M., Thornton, L. Bacanu, S., Fichter, M. M., Halmi, K. A. Kaplan, A. S., Strober, M., et al. (2004). Genetic analysis of bulimia nervosa: Methods and sample description. *International Journal of Eating Disorders, 35*, 556–570.

Kavahagh, D. J., McGrath, J., Saunders, J. B., Dore, G., & Clark, D. (2002). Substance misuse in patients with schizophrenia: Epidemiology and management. *Drugs, 62*, 743–755.

Kaye, W. H., Strober, M., & Klump, K. L. (2002). Serotonin neuronal function in anorexia nervosa and bulimia nervosa. In F. Lewis-Hall & T. S. Williams (Eds.), *Psychiatric Illness in Women: Emerging Treatments and Research* (pp. 557–575). Washington, DC: American Psychiatric Publishing.

Kaye, W. H., Strober, M., & Rhodes, L. (2002). Body image disturbance and other core symptoms in anorexia and bulimia nervosa. In D. J. Castle & K. A. Phillips (Eds.). *Disorders of Body Image* (pp. 67–82). Petersfield, England: Wrightson Biomedical Publishing.

Keane, T. M. (1985). Defining traumatic stress: Some comments on the current terminological confusion [Letter to the editor]. *Behavior Therapy, 16*, 419–423.

Keane, T. M., Fisher, L. M., Krinsley, K. E., & Niles, B. L. (1994). Posttraumatic stress disorder. In M. Hersen & R. T. Ammerman (Eds.), *Handbook of Prescriptive Treatments for Adults* (pp. 237–260). New York: Plenum.

Kearney, C. A. (1992). Prescriptive treatment for school refusal behavior. Symposium at annual meeting of the Association for Advancement of Behavior Therapy, Boston.

Kearney, C. A., & Silverman, W. K. (1996). The evolution and reconciliation of taxonomic strategies for school refusal behavior. *Clinical Psychology: Science and Practice, 3*, 339–354.

Kearney, C. A. (2003). Bridging the gap among professionals who address youths with school absenteeism: Overview and suggestions for consensus. *Professional Psychology: Research and Practice, 34*, 57–65.

Kearney, C. A., & Albano, A. M. (2004). The functional profiles of school refusal behavior. *Behavior Modification, 28*, 147–161.

Kearney, C. A., & Silverman, W. K. (1995). Family environments of youngsters with school refusal behavior: A synopsis with implications for assessment and treatment. *The American Journal of Family Therapy, 23*, 59–72.

Kearney, C. A., Sims, K. E., Pursell, C. R., & Tillotson, C. A. (2003). Separation anxiety disorder in young children: A longitudinal and family analysis. *Journal of Clinical Child and Adolescent Psychology, 32*, 593–598.

Keel, P. K., & Mitchell, J. E. (1997). Outcome in bulimia nervosa. *American Journal of Psychiatry, 154*, 313–321.

Keith, S. J., Regier, D. A., & Rae, D. S. (1991). Schizophrenic disorders. In L. N. Robins & D. A. Regier (Eds.), *Psychiatric disorders in America: The Epidemiologic Catchment Area Study* (pp. 33–52). New York: Free Press.

Kelly, M. P., Strassberg, D. S., & Turner, C. M. (2004). Communication and associated relationship issues in female anorgasmia. *Journal of Sex & Marital Therapy, 30*, 263–276.

Kendell, R. E. (2002) The distinction between personality disorder and mental illness. *British Journal of Psychiatry, 180*, 110–115.

Kendler, K. S., & Diehl, S. R. (1993). The genetics of schizophrenia: A current, genetic-epidemiologic perspective. *Schizophrenia Bulletin, 19*, 261–285.

Kendler, K. S., & Hays, P. (1981). Paranoid psychosis (delusional disorder) and schizophrenia: A family history study. *Archives of General Psychiatry, 38*, 547–551.

Kendler, K. S., Hettema, J. M., Butera, F., Gardner, C. O., & Prescott, D. A. (2003). Life event dimensions of loss, humiliation, entrapment, and danger in the prediction of onsets of major depression and generalized anxiety. *Archives of General Psychiatry, 60*, 789–796.

Kendler, K. S., McGuire, J., Gruenberg, A. M., & Walsh, D. (1994). Outcome and family study of the subtypes of schizophrenia in the west of Ireland. *American Journal of Psychiatry, 151*, 849–856.

Kent, L. (2004). Recent advances in the genetics of of attention deficit hyperactivity disorder. *Current Psychiatry Reports, 6*, 143–148.

Kernberg, O. F. (1985). *Borderline Conditions and Pathological Narcissism*. Northvale, NJ: Jason Aronson.

Kessler, R. C. (2002). Epidemiology of depression. In I. H. Gotlib & C. L. Hammen (Eds.), *Handbook of Depression*. New York: Guilford.

Kessler, R. C., McGonagle, K. A., Zhao, S., Nelson, C. B., Hughes, M., Eshleman, S., Wittchen, H., & Kendler, K. S. (1994). Lifetime and 12–month prevalence of DSM-III-R psychiatric disorders in the United States. *Archives of General Psychiatry, 51,* 8–19.

Kessler, S., & McKenna, W. (2000). Who put the "trans" in transgender? Gender theory and everyday life. *International Journal of Transgenderism, 4,* http://www.sypmposium.com/ ijt/gilbert/kessler.htm.

Kessler, R., Sonnega, A., Bromet, E., et al. (1995). Posttraumatic stress disorder in the National Comorbidity Survey. *Archives of General Psychiatry, 52,* 1048–1060.

Kessler, R. C., Sonnega, A., Bromet, E., Hughes, M., Nelson, D. B., & Breslau, N. (1999). Epidemiological risk factors for trauma and PTSD. In R. Yehuda (Ed.), *Risk Factors for Posttraumatic Stress Disorder* (pp. 23–59). Washington, DC: American Psychiatric Press.

Kety, S. S., Rosenthal, D., Wender, P. H., & Schulsinger, F. (1971). Mental illness in the biological and adoptive families of adopted schizophrenics. *American Journal of Psychiatry, 128,* 82–86.

Kilpatrick, D. G., & Acierno, R. (2003). Mental health needs of crime victims: Epidemiology and outcomes. *Journal of Traumatic Stress, 16,* 119–132.

Kilpatrick, D. G., Saunders, B. E., Veronen, L. J., Best, C. L., & Von, J. M. (1987). Criminal victimization: Lifetime prevalence, reporting to police, and psychological impact. *Crime and Delinquency, 33,* 479–489.

Kilpatrick, D. G., Resick, H. S., Saunders, B. E., & Best, C. L. (1998). Rape, other violence against women, and posttraumatic stress disorder. In B. P. Dohrenwend (Ed.), *Adversity, Stress, and Psychopathology* (pp 161–176). London: Oxford University Press.

Kilpatrick, D. G., Veronen, L. J., & Resick, P. A. (1979). Assessment of the aftermath of rape: Changing patterns of fear. *Journal of Behavioral Assessment, 1,* 133–148.

Kim, M. T., Han, H. R., Hill, M. N., Rose, L., & Roary, M. (2003). Depression, substance use, adherence behaviors, and blood pressure in urban hypertensive black men. *Annals of Behavioral Medicine, 26,* 24–31.

Kinderman, P. (2001). Changing causal attributions. In P. W. Corrigan & D. L. Penn (Eds.), *Social Cognition and Schizophrenia* (pp. 195–215). Washington, DC: American Psychological Association.

Kinzie, J. D. (1985). Overview of clinical issues in the treatment of Southeast Asian refugees. In T. C. Owan (Ed.), *Southeast Asian mental health treatment, prevention services, training, and research.* Washington, DC: National Institute of Mental Health.

Kirmayer, L. J., Groleau, D., Looper, K. J., & Dao, M. D. (2004). Explaining medically unexplained symptoms. *Canadian Journal of Psychiatry, 49,* 663–672.

Kirmayer, L. J., & Young, A. (1998). Culture and somatization: Clinical, epidemiological, and ethnographic perspectives. *Psychosomatic Medicine, 60,* 420–430.

Kleifield, E. I., Wagner, S., & Halmi, K. A. (1996). Cognitive-behavioral treatment of anorexia nervosa. *Psychiatric Clinics of North America, 19,* 715–737.

Klein, D. A., & Walsh, B. T. (2004). Eating disorders: Clinical features and pathophysiology. *Physiology & Behavior, 81,* 359–374.

Klein, D. F. (1981). Anxiety reconceptualized. In D. F. Klein & J. Rabkin (Eds.), *Anxiety: New Directions and Changing Concepts.* New York: Raven Press.

Klein, D. F. (1993). False suffocation alarms, spontaneous panics, and related conditions: An integrative hypothesis. *Archives of General Psychiatry, 50,* 306–317.

Klein, M. (1932). *The psychoanalysis of children.* London: Hogarth Press.

Kleindienst, N., & Greil, W. (2000). Differential efficacy of lithium and carbamazepine in the prophylaxis of bipolar disorder. *Neuropsychobiology, 42,* 2–10.

Klonsky, E. D., Oltmanns, T. F., Turkheimer, E., & Fiedler, E. R. (2000). Recollections of conflict with parents and family support in the personality disorders. *Journal of Personality Disorders, 14,* 327–338.

Kluft, R. P. (1991). Clinical presentations of multiple personality disorder. *Psychiatric Clinics of North America, 14,* 605–629.

Kluft, R. P. (1995). The confirmation and disconfirmation of memories of abuse in DID patients: A naturalistic clinical study. *Dissociation: Progress in the Dissociative Disorders, 8,* 253–258.

Kluft, R. P. (1996). Treating the traumatic memories of patients with dissociative identity disorder. *American Journal of Psychiatry, 153 (Suppl.),* 103–110.

Kluft, R. P. (1999). An overview of the psychotherapy of dissociative identity disorder. *American Journal of Psychotherapy, 53,* 289–319.

Knight, R. (1953). Borderline states. *Bulletin of the Menninger Clinic, 17,* 1–12.

Knox, S., Burkard, A. W., Johnson, A. J., Suzuki, L. A., & Ponterotto, J. G. (2003). African American and European American therapists' experiences of addressing race in cross-racial psychotherapy dyads. *Journal of Counseling Psychology, 50,* 466–481.

Koegel, R. L., Schreibman, L., Britten, K. R., Burke, J. C., & O'Neill, R. E. (1982). A comparison of parent training to direct child treatment. In R. L. Koegel, A. Rincover, & A. L. Egel (Eds.), *Educating and Understanding Autistic Children.* San Diego, CA: College-Hill.

Koenigsberg, H. W. (1982). A comparison of hospitalized and nonhospitalized borderline patients. *American Journal of Psychiatry, 139,* 1292–1297.

Kohn, M. L. (1968). Social class and schizophrenia: A critical review. In D. Rosenthal & S. S. Kety (Eds.), *The transmission of schizophrenia.* New York: Pergamon.

Kolarsky, A., & Madlafousek, J. (1983). The inverse role of preparatory erotic stimulation in exhibitionists: Phallometric studies. *Archives of Sexual Behavior, 12,* 123–148.

Kolmen, B. K., Feldman, H. E., Handen, B. L., & Janosky, H. E. (1995). Naltrexone in young autistic children: A double-blind, placebo-controlled crossover study. *Journal of the American Academy of Child and Adolescent Psychiatry, 34,* 223–231.

Kopelowicz, A., Liberman, R. P., Mintz, J., & Zarate, R. (1997). Comparison of efficacy of social skills training for deficit and nondeficit negative symptoms in schizophrenia. *American Journal of Psychiatry, 154,* 424–425.

Koss, M. P., & Burkhart, B. R. (1989). A conceptual analysis of rape victimization. *Psychology of Women Quarterly, 13,* 27–40.

Koss, M. P., Gidycz, C. A., & Wisniewski, N. (1987). The scope of rape: Incidence and prevalence of sexual aggression and victimization in a national sample of higher education students. *Journal of Consulting and Clinical Psychology, 55,* 162–170.

Kraepelin, E. (1971). *Dementia Praecox and Paraphrenia* (R. M. Barclay, trans.). Huntington, NY: Krieger. (Originally published 1919.)

Kratochvil, C. J., Greenhill, L. L., March, J. S., Burke, W. J., & Vaughan, B. S. (2004). The role of stimulants in the treatment of preschool children with of attention-deficit/hyperactivity disorder. *CNS Drugs, 18,* 957–966.

Kreuger, R. B., & Kaplan, M. S. (1997). Frotteurism: Assessment and treatment. In D. R. Laws & W. O'Donohue (Eds.), *Sexual Deviance.* New York: Guilford.

Kringlen, E. (1970). Natural history of obsessional neurosis. *Seminars in Psychiatry, 2,* 403–419.

Kroenke, K., West, S. L., Gilsenan, A., Eckert, G. J., Dolor, R., Stang, P., Zhou, X., Hays, R., & Weinberger, M. (2001). Similar effectiveness of paroxetine, fluoxetine, and sertraline in primary care: A randomized trial. *Journal of the American Medical Association, 286,* 2947–2955.

Krueger, S., & Kennedy, S. H. (2000). Psychopharmacotherapy of anorexia nervosa, bulimia nervosa and binge-eating disorder. *Journal of Psychiatry and Neuroscience, 25*, 497–508.

Kuiper, B., & Cohen-Kettenis, P. (1988). Sex reassignment surgery: A study of 141 Dutch transsexuals. *Archives of Sexual Behavior, 17*, 439–457.

Kuipers, L., & Bebbington, P. (1988). Expressed emotion research in schizophrenia: Theoretical and clinical implications. *Psychological Medicine, 18*, 893–909.

Kushner, M. G., Abrams, K., & Borchardt, C. (2000). The relationship between anxiety disorders and alcohol use disorders: A review of major perspectives and findings. *Clinical Psychology Review, 20*, 149–171.

Kushner, M. G., Riggs, D. S., Foa, E. B., & Miller, S. M. (1992). Perceived controllability and the development of posttraumatic stress disorder (PTSD) in crime victims. *Behaviour Research and Therapy, 31*, 105–110.

Kuzma, J. M., & Black, D. W. (2004). Integrating pharmacotherapy and psychotherapy in the management of anxiety disorders. *Current Psychiatry Reports, 6*, 268–273.

Labott, S. M., & Wallach, H. R. (2002). Malingering dissociative identity disorder: Objective and projective assessment. *Psychological Reports, 90*, 525–538.

Ladwig, K. H., Marten-Mittag, B., Erazo, N., & Gündel, H. (2001). Identifying somatization disorder in a population-based health examination survey: Psychosocial burden and gender differences. *Psychosomatics, 42*, 511–518.

Lambert, D., & Waters, C. H. (1998). Sexual dysfunction in Parkinson's disease. *Clinical Neuroscience, 5*, 73–77.

Landen, M., Walinder, J., & lundstrom, B. (1996). Prevalence, incidence and sex ratio of transsexualism. *Acta Psychiatrica, 93*, 221–223.

Langenbucher, J. W., & Chung, T. (1995). Onset and staging of DSM-IV alcohol dependence using mean age and survival-hazard methods. *Journal of Abnormal Psychology, 104*, 346–354.

Larkin, K. T., & Zayfert, C. (2004). Anger expression and essential hypertension: Behavioral response to confrontation. *Journal of Psychosomatic Research, 56*, 113–118.

LaRue, A., Dessonville, C., & Jarvik, L. F. (1985). Aging and mental disorders. In J. E. Birren & K. W. Schaie (Eds.), *Handbook of Psychology of Aging* (2nd ed.). New York: Van Nostrand Reinhold.

Last, C. G., & Strauss, C. C. (1990). School refusal in anxiety-disordered children and adolescents. *Journal of the American Academy of Child and Adolescent Psychiatry, 29*, 31–35.

Latimer, P. R. (1995). Tardive dyskinesia: A review. *Canadian Journal of Psychiatry, 40 (Suppl. 2)*, S49–54.

Lauer, J., Black, D. W., & Keen, P. (1993). Multiple personality disorder and borderline personality disorder: Distinct entities or variations on a common theme? *Annals of Clinical Psychiatry, 5*, 129–134.

Laumann, E. O., Gagnon, J. H., Michael, R. T., & Michaels, S. (1994). *The Social Organization of Sexuality: Sexual Practices in the United States.* Chicago: University of Chicago Press.

Lawler, C. P., Croen, L. A., Grether, J. K., & Van de Water, J. (2004). Identifying environmental contributions to autism: Provocative clues and false leads. *Mental Retardation and Developmental Disabilities Research Reviews, 10*, 292–302.

Layne, A. E., Bernstein, G. A., Egan, E. A., & Kushner, M. G. (2003). Predictors of treatment response in anxious-depressed adolescents with school refusal. *Journal of the American Academy of Child and Adolescent Psychiatry, 42*, 319–326.

Lee, D., DeQuattro, V., Cox, T., Pyter, L., Foti, A., Allen, J., Barndt, R., Azen, S., & Davison, G. C. (1987). Neurohormonal mechanisms and left ventricular hypertrophy: Effects of hygienic therapy. *Journal of Human Hypertension, 1*, 147–151.

Lee, J. K. P., Jackson, H. J., Pattison, P., & Ward, T. (2002). Developmental risk factors for sexual offending. *Child Abuse & Neglect, 26,* 73–92.

LeFever, G. B., Dawson, K. V., & Morrow, A. L. (1999). The extent of drug therapy for attention deficit-hyperactivity disorder among children in public schools. *American Journal of Public Health,* 89, 1359–1364.

Leff, J., Sartorius, N., Jablensky, A., Korten, A., & Ernberg, G. (1992). The International Pilot Study of Schizophrenia: Five-year follow-up findings. *Psychological Medicine, 22,* 131–145.

Leibbrand, R., Hiller, W., & Fichter, M. M. (2000). Hypochondriasis and somatization: Two distinct aspects of somatoform disorders? *Journal of Clinical Psychology, 56,* 63–72.

Leonard, H. L., Swedo, S. E., Rapoport, J. L., Koby, E. V., Lenane, M. C., Cheslow, D. L., & Hamburger, S. D. (1989). Treatment of obsessive-compulsive disorder with clomipramine and desipramine in children and adolescents: A double-blind crossover comparison. *Archives of General Psychiatry, 46,* 1088–1092.

Leonard, L. M., & Follette, V. M. (2002). Sexual functioning in women reporting a history of child sexual abuse: Review of the empirical literature and clinical implications. *Annual Review of Sex Research, 13,* 346–388.

Letourneau, E. J., & O'Donohue, W. (1997). Classical conditioning of female sexual arousal. *Archives of Sexual Behavior, 26,* 63–78.

Leue, A., Borchard, B., & Hoyer, J. (2004). Mental disorders in a forensic sample of sexual offenders. *European Psychiatry, 19,* 123–130.

Leung, F. (1996). Testing a dual-process family model in understanding the development of eating pathology: A structural equation modeling analysis. *International Journal of Eating Disorders, 20,* 367–375.

LeVay, S., & Valente, S. M. (2003). *Human Sexuality.* Sunderland, MA: Sinauer Associates.

Levine, S. B. (1999). The newly revised standards of care for gender identity disorders. *Journal of Sex Education and Therapy, 24,* 117–127.

Levinson, D. F., Umapathy, C., & Musthaq, M. (1999). Treatment of schizoaffective disorder and schizophrenia with mood symptoms. *American Journal of Psychiatry, 156,* 1138–1148.

Lewins, F. (2002). Explaining stable partnerships among FTMs and MTFs: A significant difference? *Journal of Sociology, 38,* 76–88.

Lewinsohn, P. M., Rohde, P., Fischer, S. A., & Seeley, J. R. (1991). Age and depression. Unique and shared effects. *Psychology and Aging, 6,* 247–260.

Lewis, C. E. (2002). Impact of substance abuse and dependence on patients with schizophrenia. In J. G. Csernansky (Ed.), *Schizophrenia: A New Guide for Clinicians* (pp. 267–283). New York: Marcel Dekker.

Lichtenstein, P., & Annas, P. (2000). Borderline personality disorder. *Journal of Child Psychology and Psychiatry, 41,* 927–937.

Lidbeck, J. (2003). Group therapy for somatization disorders in primary care: Maintenance of treatment goals of short cognitive-behavioural treatment one-and-a-half year follow-up. *Acta Psychiatrica Scandinavia, 107,* 449–456.

Lieb, K. Zanarini, M. C., Schmahl, C., Linehan, M. M., & Bohus, M. (2004). Borderline personality disorder. *Lancet, 364,* 453–461.

Light, K. C., Dolan, C. A., Davis, M. R., & Sherwood, A. (1992). Cardiovascular responses to an active coping challenge as predictors of blood pressure patterns 10 to 15 years later. *Psychosomatic Medicine, 54,* 217–230.

Lilienfeld, S. O., Lynn, S. J., Kirsch, I., Chaves, J. F., Sarbin, T. R., & Powell, R. A. (1999). Dissociative identity disorder and the sociocognitive model: Recalling the lessons of the past. *Psychological Bulletin, 125,* 507–523.

Lilienfeld, S. O., & Lynn, S. J. (2003). Dissociative identity disorder: Multiple personalities, multiple controversies. In S. O. Lilienfeld and S. J. Lynn (Eds). *Science and Pseudoscience in Clinical Psychology.* New York: Guilford. pp. 109–142.

Lindeman, G., Korlin, D., & Uddenberg, N. (1986). Long-term follow-up of "sex change" in 13 male-to-female transsexuals. *Archives of Sexual Behavior, 15,* 187–210.

Linden, W. (2003). Psychologic treatment for hypertension can be efficacious. *Preventive Cardiology, 6,* 48–53.

Lindenmayer, J. P., Eerdekens, E., Berry, S. A., & Eerdekens, M. (2004). Safety and efficacy of long-acting risperidone in schizophrenia: A 12–week, multicenter, open-label study in stable patients switched from typical and atypical oral antipsychotics. *Journal of Clinical Psychiatry, 65,* 1084–1089.

Linehan, M. M. (1993). *Cognitive Behavioral Treatment of Borderline Personality Disorder: The Dialectics of Effective Treatment.* New York: Guilford.

Linehan, M. M., Armstrong, H. E., Suarez, R. A., Allmon, D., & Heard, H. L. (1991). Cognitive-behavioral treatment of chronically parasuicidal borderline patients. *Archives of General Psychiatry, 48,* 1060–1064.

Linehan, M. M., Heard, H. L., & Armstrong, H. E. (1992). Naturalistic follow-up of a behavioral treatment for chronically parasuicidal borderline patients. Unpublished manuscript, University of Washington.

Link, B. G., Monahan, J., Stueve, A., & Cullen, F. T. (1999). Real in their consequences: A sociological approach to understanding the association between psychotic symptoms and violence. *American Sociological Review, 64,* 316–332.

Link, G., Phelan, J. C., Bresnahan, M., Stueve, A., & Pescosolido, B. A. (1999). Public conceptions of mental illness: Labels, causes, dangerousness, and social distance. *American Journal of Public Health, 89,* 1328–1333.

Lion, J. R. (1978). Outpatient treatment of psychopaths. In W. H. Reid (Ed.), *The Psychopath: A Comprehensive Study of Antisocial Disorders and Behaviors.* New York: Brunner/Mazel.

Lipsitz, J. D., & Markowitz, J. C. (1999). Open trial of interpersonal psychotherapy for the treatment of social phobia. *American Journal of Psychiatry, 156,* 1814–1816.

Litt, M. D., Kadden, R. M., Cooney, N. L., & Kabela, E. (2003). Coping skills and treatment outcomes in cognitive-behavioral and interactional group therapy for alcoholism. *Journal of Consulting and Clinical Psychology, 71,* 118–128.

Liu, I. C., Blacker, D. L., Xu, R., Fitzmaurice, G., Lyons, M. J., & Tsuang, M. T. (2004). Genetic and environmental contributions to the development of alcohol dependence in male twins. *Archives of General Psychiatry, 61,* 897–903.

Locke, H. J., & Wallace, K. M. (1959). Short marital adjustment and prediction tests: Their reliability and validity. *Marriage and Family Living, 21,* 251–255.

Looper, K. J., & Kirmayer, L. J. (2002). Behavioral medicine approaches to somatoform disorders. *Journal of Consulting and Clinical Psychology, 70,* 810–827.

LoPiccolo, J., & Stock, W. E. (1986). Treatment of sexual dysfunction. *Journal of Consulting and Clinical Psychology, 54,* 158–167.

Loranger, A. W., Oldham, J. M., & Tulis, E. H. (1983). Familial transmission of DSM-III borderline personality disorder. *Archives of General Psychiatry, 40,* 795–799.

Lorber, M. F. (2004). Psychophysiology of aggression, psychopathy, and conduct problems: A meta-analysis. *Psychological Bulletin, 130,* 531–552.

Lotter, V. (1978). Follow-up studies. In M. Rutter & E. Schopler (Eds.), *Autism: A Reappraisal of Concepts and Treatment.* New York: Plenum.

Lovaas, O. I. (1987). Behavioral treatment and normal educational and intellectual functioning in young autistic children. *Journal of Consulting and Clinical Psychology, 55,* 3–9.

Lowe, M. R. (1996). Restraint, dieting, and the continuum model of bulimia nervosa. *Journal of Abnormal Psychology, 105*, 508–517.

Luczak, S. E., Wall, T. L., Cook, T. A. R., Shea, S. H., & Carr, L. G. (2004). *ALDH2* status and conduct disorder mediate the relationship between ethnicity and alcohol dependence in Chinese, Korean, and White American college students. *Journal of Abnormal Psychology, 113*, 271–278.

Lukoschek, P. (2003). African Americans' beliefs and attitudes regarding hypertension and its treatment: A qualitative study. *Journal of Health Care for the Poor and Underserved, 14*, 566–585.

Lundgren, J. D., Danoff-Burg, S., & Anderson, D. A. (2004). Cognitive behavioral therapy for bulimia nervosa: An empirical analysis of clinical significance. *International Journal of Eating Disorders, 35*, 262–274.

Lykken, D. T. (1957). A study of anxiety in the sociopathic personality. *Journal of Abnormal and Social Psychology, 55*, 6–10.

Lyons, M. J., True, W. S., Eisen, A., Goldberg, J., Meyer, J. M., et al. (1995). Differential heritability of adult and juvenile traits. *Archives of General Psychiatry, 52*, 906–915.

Macmillan, R., McMorris, B. J., & Kruttschnitt, C. (2004). Linked lives: Stability and change in maternal circumstances and trajectories of antisocial behavior in children. *Child Development, 75*, 205–220.

Magee, W. J., Eaton, W. W., Wittchern, H. U., McGonagle, K. A., & Kessler, R. C. (1996). Agoraphobia, simple phobia and social phobia in the National Comorbidity Survey. *Archives of General Psychiatry, 53*, 159–168.

Mai F. (2004). Somatization disorder: A practical review. *Canadian Journal of Psychiatry, 49*, 652–662.

Maldonado, J. R., Butler, L. D., & Spiegel, D. (2002). Treatments for dissociative disorders. In P. E. Nathan & J. M. Gorman (Eds.), *A Guide to Treatments that Work* (2nd ed., pp. 463–496). London, England: Oxford University Press.

Maletzky, B. M. (1997). Exhibitionism: Assessment and treatment. In D. R. Laws & W. O'Donohue (Eds.), *Sexual Deviance*. New York: Guilford.

Manari, A. P., Preedy, V. R., & Peters, T. J. (2003). Nutritional intake of hazardous drinkers and dependent alcoholics in the UK. *Addiction Biology, 8*, 201–210.

Mann, K. (2004). Pharmacotherapy of alcohol dependence: A review of the clinical data. *CNS Drugs, 18*, 485–504.

Mannuzza, S., Klein, R. G., Bessler, A., Malloy, P., & LaPadula, M. (1993). Adult outcome of hyperactive boys: Educational achievement, occupational rank, and psychiatric status. *Archives of General Psychiatry, 50*, 563–551.

Manschreck, T. C. (1992). Delusional disorders: Clinical concepts and diagnostic strategies. *Psychiatric Annals, 22*, 241–251.

Marks, I. M. (1969). *Fears and Phobias*. New York: Academic Press.

Marks, I. M. (1986). Epidemiology of anxiety. *Social Psychiatry, 21*, 167–171.

Marks, I. M. (1987). *Fears, Phobias, and Rituals: Panic, Anxiety, and Their Disorders*. New York: Oxford University Press.

Marks, I. M. (1995). Advances in behavioral-cognitive therapy of social phobia. *Journal of Clinical Psychiatry, 56*, 25–31.

Marlatt, G. A. (1985). Controlled drinking: The controversy rages on. *American Psychologist, 40*, 374–375.

Marlatt, G. A. (1996). Taxonomy of high-risk situations for alcohol relapse: Evolution and development of a cognitive-behavioral model. *Addiction, 91 (Suppl.)*, S37–S49.

Marshall, J. (1998). Dual-diagnosis: Co-morbidity of severe mental illness and substance misuse. *Journal of Forensic Psychiatry, 9*, 9–15.

Marshall, W. L., Eccles, A., & Barbaree, H. E. (1991). The treatment of exhibitionism: A focus on sexual deviance versus cognitive and relationship factors. *Behavior Research and Therapy, 29*, 129–135.

Marshall, W. L., Jones, R., Ward, T., Johnston, P., & Barabee, H. E. (1991). Treatment outcomes with sex offenders. *Clinical Psychology Review*, 11, 465–485.

Masters, W. H., & Johnson, V. E. (1966). *Human Sexual Response*. Boston: Little, Brown.

Masters, W. H., & Johnson, V. E. (1970). *Human Sexual Inadequacy*. Boston: Little, Brown.

Masters, W. H., & Johnson, V. E., & Kolodny, R. C. (1985). *Human Sexuality* (2nd ed.). Boston: Little, Brown.

Mathew, S. J., Yudofsky, S. C., McCullough, L. B., Teasdale, T. A., & Jankovic, J. (1999). Attitudes toward neurosurgical procedures for Parkinson's disease and obsessive-compulsive disorder. *Journal of Neuropsychiatry and Clinical Neurosciences, 11*, 259–267.

Matthews, A., & MacLeod, C. (1994). Cognitive approaches to emotion and emotional disorders. In L. W. Porter, & M. Rosenzweig (Eds.), *Annual Review of Psychology* (pp. 25–50). Stanford, CA: Stanford University Press.

Matthews, K. A., & Rakacky, C. J. (1987). Familial aspects of Type A behavior and physiologic reactivity to stress. In T. Dembroski & T. Schmidt (Eds.), *Behavioral Factors in Coronary Heart Disease*. Heidelberg: Springer-Verlag.

Mattia, J. I., & Zimmerman, M. (2001). Epidemiology. In W. J. Livesley (Ed.), *Handbook of Personality Disorders: Theory, Research, and Treatment* (pp. 107–123). New York: Guilford.

Maughan, B., Taylor, A., Caspi, A., & Moffitt, T. E. (2004). Prenatal smoking and early childhood conduct problems. *Archives of General Psychiatry, 61*, 836–843.

May, P. R. A., Van Putten, T., Yale, C., Potepan, P., Jenden, D. J., Fairchild, M. D., Goldstein, M. J., & Dixon, W. J. (1976). Predicting individual responses to drug treatment in schizophrenia: A test dose model. *Journal of Nervous and Mental Disease, 162*, 177–183.

Mayer, E. A., Craske, M., & Naliboff, B. D. (2001). Depression, anxiety, and the gastrointestinal system. *Journal of Clinical Psychiatry, 62 (Suppl. 8)*, 28–36.

McBride, P. A., Anderson, G. M., Hertzig, M. E., Sweeney, J. A., et al. (1989). Serotonergic responsivity in male young adults with autistic disorder: Results of a pilot study. *Archives of General Psychiatry, 46*, 213–221.

McBride, P. A., Anderson, G. M., & Shapiro, T. (1996). Autism research: Bringing together approaches to pull apart the disorder. *Archives of General Psychiatry, 53*, 980–983.

McCabe, M. P. (2001). Evaluation of a cognitive behavior therapy program for people with sexual dysfunction. *Journal of Sex and Marital Therapy, 27*, 259–271.

McCarthy, B. W. (2004). An integrative cognitive-behavioral approach to understanding, assessing, and treating female sexual dysfunction. *Journal of Family Psychotherapy, 15*, 19–35.

McConaghy, N. (1994). Sexual deviations. In M. Hersen & R. T. Ammerman (Eds.) *Handbook of aggressive and destructive behavior in psychiatric patients*. New York: Plenum Press.

McConaghy, N. (2005). Sexual dysfunctions and disorders. In J. E. Maddux and B. A. Winstead (Eds.) *Psychopathology: Foundations for a Contemporary Understanding*. Mahwah, NJ: Erlbaum. pp. 255–280.

McDougle, C. J. Price, L. H., Volkmar, F. R., Goodman, W. K., et al. (1992). Clomipramine in autism: Preliminary evidence of efficacy. *Journal of the American Academy of Child and Adolescent Psychiatry, 31*, 746–750.

McEachin, J. J., Smith, T., & Lovaas, O. I. (1993). Long-term outcome for children with autism who receive early intensive behavioral treatment. *American Journal on Mental Retardation, 97*, 359–372.

McElroy, S. L., Keck, P. E., & Strakowski, S. M. (1999). An overview of the treatment of schizoaffective disorder. *Journal of Clinical Psychiatry, 60 (Suppl. 5),* 16–21.

McEwen, B. S. (1998). Protective and damaging effects of stress mediators. *New England Journal of Medicine, 338*, 171–179.

McGee, R., & Feehan, M. (1991). Are girls with problems of attention underrecognized? *Journal of Psychopathology and Behavioral Assessment, 13*, 187–198.

McGlashan, T. H. (1986). Schizotypal personality disorder: Chestnut Lodge follow-up study. *Archives of General Psychiatry, 43*, 329–334.

McGlashan, T. H., & Williams, P. V. (1990). Predicting outcome in schizoaffective psychosis. *Journal of Nervous and Mental Disease, 178*, 518–520.

McGlashan, T. M. (1983). The borderline syndrome: I. Testing three diagnostic systems. *Archives of General Psychiatry, 40*, 1311–1318.

McGrady, A., Nadsady, P. A., & Schumann-Brzezinski, C. (1991). Sustained effects of biofeedback-assisted relaxation in essential hypertension. *Biofeedback and Self-Regulation, 16*, 399–411.

McGue, M., & Gottesman, I. I. (1989). A single dominant gene still cannot account for the transmission of schizophrenia. *Archives of General Psychiatry, 46*, 478–480.

McGue, M., Pickens, R. W., & Suikis, D. S. (1992). Sex and age effects on the inheritance of alcohol problems: A twin study. *Journal of Abnormal Psychology, 101*, 3–17.

McGuffin, P., Rijsdijk, F., Andrew, M., Sham, P., Katz, R., & Cardno, A. (2003). The heritability of bipolar affective disorder and the genetic relationship to unipolar depression. *Archives of General Psychiatry, 60*, 497–502.

McLean, P. D., Whittal, J. L., Thordarson, D. S., Taylor, S., Sochting, I., Koch, W. J., Paterson, R., & Anderson, K. W. (2001). Cognitive versus behavior therapy in the group treatment of obsessive-compulsive disorder. *Journal of Consulting and Clinical Psychology, 69*, 205–214.

McMahon, F. J., Simpson, S. G., McInnis, M. G., Badner, J. A., MacKinnon, D. F., & DePaulo, J. R. (2001). Linkage of bipolar disorder to chromosome 18q and the validity of bipolar II disorder. *Archives of General Psychiatry, 58*, 1025–1031.

McNally, R. J. (1994a). *Panic Disorder: A Critical Analysis*. New York: Guilford.

McNally, R. J. (1994b). Preparedness and phobias: A review. *Psychological Bulletin, 101*, 283–303.

McNally, R. J. (2003). Progress and controversy in the study of posttraumatic stress disorder. *Annual Review of Psychology, 54*, 229–252.

McNeil, D. E., Eisner, J. P., & Binder, R. L., (2000). The relationship between command hallucinations and violence. *Psychiatric Services, 51,* 1288–1292.

McShane, G., Walter, G., & Rey, J. M. (2004). Functional outcome of adolescents with 'school refusal. ' *Clinical Child Psychology and Psychiatry, 9,* 53–60.

Meehl, P. E. (1964). Manual for use with checklist of schizotypic signs. Unpublished manuscript, University of Minnesota Medical School, Minneapolis.

Menza, M., Lauritano, M., Allen, L., Warman, M., Ostella, F., Hamer, R. M., et al. (2001). Treatment of somatization disorder with nefazodone: A prospective, open-label study. *Annals of Clinical Psychiatry, 13,* 153–158.

Merskey, H. (1992). The manufacture of personalities: The production of multiple personality disorder. *British Journal of Psychiatry, 160*, 327–340.

Merskey, H. (2004). Somatization, hysteria, or incompletely explained symptoms? *Canadian Journal of Psychiatry, 49,* 649–651.

Meyer, J. K. (1974). Clinical variants among sex reassignment applicants. *Archives of Sexual Behavior, 3*, 527–558.

Meyer, J. K., & Reter, D. J. (1979). Sex reassignment: Follow-up. *Archives of General Psychiatry, 36*, 1010–1015.

Meyer, W. J., Cole, C., & Emory, E. (1992). Depo provera treatment for sex offending behavior: An evaluation of outcome. *Bulletin of the American Academy of Psychiatry and the Law, 20*, 249–259.

Michel, A., Ansseau, M., Legros, J. J., Pitchot, W., & Mormont, C. (2002). The transsexual: What about the future. *European Psychiatry, 17*, 353–362.

Mickley, D. W. (2001). Medical aspects of anorexia and bulimia. In B. P. Kinoy (Ed.), *Eating Disorders: New Directions in Treatment and Recovery* (2nd ed., pp. 7–16). New York: Columbia University Press.

Miklowitz, D. J., Frank, E., & George, E. L. (1996). New psychosocial treatments for the outpatient management of bipolar disorder. *Psychopharmacology Bulletin, 32*, 613–621.

Miklowitz, D. J., Goldstein, M. J., & Nuechterlein, K. H. (1995). Verbal interactions in the families of schizophrenic and bipolar affective patients. *Journal of Abnormal Psychology, 104*, 268–276.

Miklowitz, D. J., Goldstein, J. J., Nuechterlein, K. H., Snyder, K. S., & Mintz, J. (1988). Family factors and the course of bipolar affective disorder. *Archives of General Psychiatry, 45*, 225–231.

Millberger, S., Biederman, J., Faraone, S. V., Chen, L., & Jones, J. (1996). Is maternal smoking during pregnancy a risk factor for attention deficit hyperactivity in children? *American Journal of Psychiatry, 153*, 1138–1142.

Miller, M. B., Useda, J. D., Trull, T. J., Burr, R. M., & Minks-Brown, C. (2001). Paranoid, schizoid, and schizotypal personality disorders. In P. B. Sutker & H. E. Adams (Eds.), *Comprehensive Handbook of Psychopathology* (3rd ed., pp. 535–559.). New York: Kluwer Academic/Plenum.

Miller, R. G., Palkes, H. S., & Stewart, M. A. (1973). Hyperactive children in suburban elementary schools. *Child Psychiatry and Human Development, 4*, 121–127.

Mineka, S., & Zinbarg, R. (1995). Conditioning and ethological models of social phobia. In R. G. Heimberg, M. R. Liebowitz, D. A. Hope, & F. R. Schneier (Eds.), *Social Phobia: Diagnosis, Assessment, and Treatment* (pp. 134–162). New York: Guilford.

Mineka, S., & Zinbarg, R. (1996). Conditioning and ethological models of anxiety disorders: Stress-in-dynamic-context anxiety models. In D. A. Hope (Ed.). *Nebraska Symposium on Motivation*. Lincoln: University of Nebraska Press, pp. 135–210.

Mishler, E. G., & Waxler, N. E. (1968). *Interaction in Families: An Experimental Study of Family Processes and Schizophrenia*. New York: Wiley.

Misra, M., Aggarwal, A., Miller, K. K., Almazan, C., Worley, M., Soyka, L. A. et al. (2004). Effects of anorexia nervosa on clinical, hematologic, biochemical, and bone density parameters in community-dwelling adolescent girls. *Pediatrics, 114*, 1574–1583.

Modestin, J. (1992). Multiple personality disorder in Switzerland. *American Journal of Psychiatry, 149*, 88–92.

Moffitt, C. E., Chorpita, B. F., & Fernandez, S. N. (2003). Intensive cognitive-behavioral treatment of school refusal behavior. *Cognitive and Behavioral Practice, 10*, 51–60.

Moffitt, T. E. (1993). Adolescence-limited and life-course-persistent antisocial behavior: A developmental taxonomy. *Psychological Review, 100*, 674–701.

Mohr, J. W., Turner, R. E., & Jerry, M. B. (1964). *Pedophilia and Exhibitionism*. Toronto: University of Toronto Press.

Monahan, J. (2001). Major mental disorders and violence: Epidemiology and risk assessment. In G. Pinard & L. Pagani (Eds.), *Clinical Assessment of Dangerousness: Empirical Contributions* (pp. 89–102). New York: Cambridge University Press.

Monroe, S. M., & Harkness, K. L. (2005). Life stress, the "kindling" hypothesis, and the recurrence of depression: Considerations from a life stress perspective. *Psychological Review, 112*, 417–445.

Morey, L. C., & Zanarini, M. C. (2000). Borderline personality: Traits and disorder. *Journal of Abnormal Psychology, 109*, 733–737.

Morrison, A. P., Wells, A., & Nothard, S. (2000). Cognitive factors in predisposition to auditory and visual hallucinations. *British Journal of Clinical Psychology, 39*, 67–78.

Mowrer, O. H. (1947). On the dual nature of learning: A reinterpretation of "conditioning" and "problem-solving. " *Harvard Educational Review, 17*, 102–148.

MTA Cooperative Group. (1999). Moderators and mediators of treatment response for children with attention-deficit-hyperactivity disorder. *Archives of General Psychiatry, 56*, 1088–1096.

Mufson, L., Dorta, K. P., Wickramaratne, P., Nomura, Yl, Olfson, M., & Weissman, M. M. (2004). A randomized effectiveness trial of interpersonal psychotherapy for depressed adolescents. *Archives of General Psychiatry, 61*, 577–584.

Muhle, R., Trentacoste, S. V., & Rapin, I. (2004). The genetics of autism. *Pediatrics, 113*, 472–486.

Munjack, D. J. (1984). The onset of driving phobias. *Journal of Behavior Therapy and Experimental Psychiatry, 15*, 305–308.

Murphy, J. K., Stoney, C. M., Alpert, B. S., & Walker, S. S. (1995). Gender and ethnicity in children's cardiovascular reactivity: 7 years of study. *Health Psychology, 14*, 48–55.

Murphy, W. D. (1997). Exhibitionism: Psychopathology and theory. In D. R. Laws & W. O'Donohue (Eds.), *Sexual Deviance*. New York: Guilford.

Myrick, H., & Anton, R. (2004). Recent advances in the pharmacotherapy of alcoholism. *Current Psychiatry Reports, 6*, 332–338.

Narash-Eisikovits, O., Dierberger, A., & Westen, D. (2002). A multidimensional meta-analysis of pharmacotherapy for bulimia nervosa: Summarizing the range of outcomes in controlled clinical trials. *Harvard Review of Psychiatry, 10*, 193–211.

Narrow, W. E., Rae, D. S., Robins, L. N., & Regier, D. A. (2002). Revised prevalence estimates of mental disorders in the United States. *Archives of General Psychiatry, 59*, 115–123.

Neal, J. A., & Edelmann, R. J. (2003). The etiology of social phobia: Toward a developmental profile. *Clinical Psychology Review, 23*, 761–786.

Neighbors, H. W., & Jackson, J. S. (1996). *Mental Health in Black America*. Thousand Oaks, CA: Sage Publications.

Nelson, E., & Rice, J. (1997). Stability of diagnosis of obsessive-compulsive disorder in the Epidemiologic Catchment Area Study. *American Journal of Psychiatry, 154*, 826–831.

Nestor, P. G. (2002). Mental disorder and violence: Personality dimensions and clinical features. *American Journal of Psychiatry, 159*, 1973–1978.

Neumann, C. S., Grimes, K., Walker, E. F., & Baum, K. (1995). Developmental pathways to schizophrenia: Behavioral stereotypes. *Journal of Abnormal Psychology, 104*, 558–566.

Newlin, D. B., & Thompson, J. B. (1990). Alcohol challenge with the sons of alcoholics: A review and analysis. *Psychological Bulletin, 108*, 383–402.

Newman, J. P., & Kosson, D. S. (1986). Passive avoidance learning in psychopathic and nonpsychopathic offenders. *Journal of Abnormal Psychology, 95*, 257–263.

Newman, J. P., Kosson, D. S., & Patterson, D. S. (1992). Delay of gratification in psychopathic and nonpsychopathic offenders. *Journal of Abnormal Psychology, 101*, 630–636.

Newman, J. P., Patterson, C. M., & Kosson, D. S. (1987). Response perseveration in psychopaths. *Journal of Abnormal Psychology, 96*, 145–149.

Newman, L. K. (1991). Sex, gender and culture: Issues in the definition, assessment and treatment of gender identity disorder. *Clinical Child Psychology and Psychiatry, 7*, 352–359.

Nguyen, S. D. (1985). Mental health services for refugees and immigrants in Canada. In T. C. Owen (Ed.), *Southeast Asian Mental Health: Treatment, Prevention, Services, Training, and Research* (pp. 261–282). Washington, DC: National Institute of Mental Health.

Nielsen, S. (2001). Epidemiology and mortality of eating disorders. *Psychiatric Clinics of North America, 24*, 201–214.

Nigg, J. T. (2001). Is ADHD an inhibitory disorder? *Psychological Bulletin, 127*, 571–598.

Nigg, J. T., Lohr, N. E., Westen, D., Gold, L. J., & Silk, K. R. (1992). Malevolent object representations in borderline personality and major depression. *Journal of Abnormal Psychology, 101*, 61–67.

Nolen-Hoeksema, S. (1995). Epidemiology and theories of gender differences in unipolar depression. In M. V. Seeman (Ed.), *Gender and psychopathology* (pp. 63–88). Washington, DC: American Psychiatric Press.

Nolen-Hoeksema, S. (1990). Gender differences in depression. In I. H. Gotlib and C. L. Hammen (Eds.) *Handbook of depression.* New York: Guilford.

Nolen-Hoeksema, S. (2002). *Sex Differences in Depression.* Stanford, CA: Stanford University Press.

Nordin, V., & Gillberg, C. (1998). The long-term course of autistic disorders: Update on follow-up studies. *Acta Psychiatrica Scandinavica, 97*, 99–108.

North, C. S., Thompson, S. J., Pollio, D. E., Ricci, D. A., et al. (1997). A diagnostic comparison of homeless and nonhomeless patients in an urban mental health clinic. *Social Psychiatry and Psychiatric Epidemiology, 32*, 236–240.

Notman, M. T., & Nadelson, C. C. (1995). Gender, development, and psychopathology: A revised psychodynamic view. In M. V. Seeman (Ed.), *Gender and psychopathology* (pp. 1–16). Washington, DC: American Psychiatric Press.

Novaco, R. W. (1995). Clinical problems of anger and its assessment and regulation through a stress coping skills approach. In W. O'Donohue & L. Krasner (Eds.), *Handbook of psychological skills training: Clinical techniques and applications* (pp. 320–338). Boston, MA: Allyn & Bacon.

Nunes, E. V., & Levin, F. R. (2004). Treatment of depression in patients with alcohol or other drug dependence: A meta-analysis. *Journal of the American Medical Association, 291*, 1887–1896.

Nurnberger, J. I., Wiegand, R., Bucholz, K., O'Connor, S., Meyer, E. T., Reich, T., et al. (2004). A family study of alcohol dependence. *Archives of General Psychiatry, 61*, 1246–1256.

O'Brien, K. M., & Vincent, N. K. (2003). Psychiatric comorbidity in anorexia and bulimia nervosa: Nature, prevalence, and causal relationships. *Clinical Psychology Review, 23*, 57–74.

O'Connor, K. (2002). The value and use of interpretation in play therapy. *Professional Psychology: Research and Practice, 33*, 523–528.

O'Donohue, W., & Geer, J. H. (1993). *Handbook of sexual dysfunctions: Assessment and treatment.* Boston: Allyn & Bacon.

O'Donohue, W. T., Swingen, D. N., Dopke, C. A., & Regev, L. G. (1999). Psychotherapy for male sexual dysfunction: A review. *Clinical Psychology Review, 18*, 591–630.

Ogata, S. N., Silk, K. R., Goodrich, S., et al. (1990). Childhood sexual and physical abuse in adult patients with borderline personality disorder. *American Journal of Psychiatry, 147*, 1008–1013.

Ogedegbe, G., Harrison, M., Robbins, L., Mancuso, C. A., & Allegrante, J. P. (2004). Barriers and facilitators of medication adherence in hypertensive African Americans: A qualitative study. *Ethnicity and Disease, 14*, 3–12.

Ohayon, M. M. (2000). Prevalence of hallucinations and their pathological associations in the general population. *Psychiatry Research, 97*, 153–164.

O'Leary, D. S., Flaum, M., Kesler, M. L., Flashman, L. A., Arndt, S., & Andreasen, N. C. (2000). Cognitive correlates of the negative, disorganized, and psychotic symptom dimensions of schizophrenia. *Journal of Neuropsychiatry and Clinical Neuroscience, 12*, 4–14.

Oltmanns, T. F., & Okada, M. (in press). Paranoia. In J. E. Fisher and W. O'Donohue (Eds.), *Practitioner's Guide to Evidence-Based Psychotherapy*. Kluwer Academic.

Olsson, S., & Moller, A. R. (2003). On the incidence and sex ratio of transsexualism in Sweden, 1972–2002. *Archives of Sexual Behavior, 32*, 381–386.

Opler, L. A., White, L., Caton, C. L. M., Dominguez, B., Hirshfield, S., & Shrout, P. E. (2001). Gender differences in the relationship of homelessness to symptom severity, substance abuse, and neuroleptic noncompliance in schizophrenia. *Journal of Nervous and Mental Disease, 189*, 449–456.

Orne, M. T., Dinges, D. F., & Orne, E. C. (1984). On the differential diagnosis of multiple personality in the forensic case. *International Journal of Clinical and Experimental Hypnosis, 32*, 118–169.

Osborn, I. (1998). *Tormenting Thoughts and Secret Rituals*. New York: Dell Publishing.

Ost, L. G. (1987). Age of onset in different phobias. *Journal of Abnormal Psychology, 96*, 223–229.

Ozer, E. J., & Weiss, D. S. (2004). Who develops posttraumatic stress disorder? *Current Directions in Psychological Science, 4*, 169–172.

Palmer, T. (1984). Treatment and the role of classification: Review of basics. *Crime and Delinquency, 30*, 245–267.

Palermo, M. T., & Curatolo, P. (2004). Pharmacologic treatment of autism. *Journal of Child Neurology, 19*, 155–164.

Paris, J. (2004). Personality disorders over time: Implications for psychotherapy. *American Journal of Psychotherapy, 58*, 420–429.

Parker, S. K., Schwartz, B., Todd, J., & Pickering, L. K. (2004). Thimerosal-containing vaccines and autistic spectrum disorder: A critical review of published original data. *Pediatrics, 114*, 793–804.

Parmet, S., Glass, T. J., & Glass, R. M. (2004). Obsessive-compulsive disorder. *Journal of the American Medical Association, 292*, 2040.

Paternite, C. E., & Loney, J. (1980). Childhood hyperkinesis: Relationships between symptomatology and home environment. In C. K. Whalen & B. Henker (Eds.), *Hyperactive Children*. New York: Academic Press.

Patrick, C. J., Bradley, M. M., & Lang, P. J. (1993). Emotion in the criminal psychopath: Startle reflex modulation. *Journal of Abnormal Psychology, 102*, 82–92.

Paul, R. (1987). Communication. In D. J. Cohen, A. M. Donellan, & R. Paul (Eds.), *Handbook of Autism and Pervasive Developmental Disorders* (pp. 61–84). New York: Wiley.

Pauls, D. L., Alsobrook, J. P., Goodman, W., Rasmussen, S., et al. (1995). A family study of obsessive-compulsive disorder. *American Journal of Psychiatry, 152*, 76–84.

Pederson, K. J., Roerig, J. L., & Mitchell, J. E. (2003). Towards the pharmacotherapy of eating disorders. *Expert Opinions in Pharmacotherapy, 4,* 1659–1678.

Pelham, W. E., McBurnett, K., Harper, G. W., Milich, R., Murphy, D. A., Clinton, J., & Thiele, C. (1990). Methylphenidate and baseball playing in ADHD children: Who's on first? *Journal of Consulting and Clinical Psychology, 58,* 130–133.

Perkins, D. O. (2002). Predictors of noncompliance in patients with schizophrenia. *Journal of Clinical Psychiatry, 63,* 1121–1128.

Perkins, P. S., Klump, K. L., Iacono, W. G., & McGue, M. (2005). Personality traits in women with anorexia nervosa: Evidence for a treatment-seeking bias? *International Journal of Eating Disorders, 37,* 32–37.

Perris, C. (1992). Bipolar-unipolar distinction. In E. S. Paykel (Ed.), *Handbook of Affective Disorders* (2nd ed., pp. 57–75). New York: Guilford.

Pescosolida, B. A., Monahan, J., Link, B., Stueve, A., & Kikuzawa, S. (1999). The public's view of the competence, dangerousness, and need for legal coercion of persons with mental health problems. *American Journal of Public Health, 89,* 1339–1345.

Peterson, C. B., & Mitchell, J. E. (1999). Psychosocial and pharmacological treatment of eating disorders: A review of research findings. *Journal of Clinical Psychology, 55,* 685–697.

Peterson, D. R. (1954). The diagnosis of subclinical schizophrenia. *Journal of Consulting Psychology, 18,* 198–200.

Petersen, M. E., & Dickey, R. (1995). Surgical sex reassignment: A comparative survey of international centers. *Archives of Sexual Behavior, 24,* 135–156.

Phillips, R. D. (1985). Whistling in the dark? A review of play therapy research. *Psychotherapy, 22,* 752–760.

Pilling, S., Bebbington, P., Kuipers, E., Garety, P., Geddes, J., Martindale, B., Orbach, G., & Morgan, C. (2002). Psychological treatments in scizophrenia: II. Meta-analyses of randomized controlled trials of social skills training and cognitive remediation. *Psychological Medicine, 32,* 783–791.

Piper, A., & Merskey, H. (2004). The persistence of folly: A critical examination of dissociative identity disorder. Part 1. The excesses of an improbable concept. *Canadian Journal of Psychiatry, 49,* 592–600.

Piren J., Palmer, P., Jacobi, D., Childress, D., & Arndt, S. (1997). Broader autism phenotype: Evidence from a family history study of multiple-incidence autism families. *American Journal of Psychiatry, 154,* 185–190.

Polivy, J., & Herman, C. P. (2002). Causes of eating disorders. *Annual Review of Psychology, 53,* 187–213.

Pollard, T. M., & Schwartz, J. E. (2003). Are changes in blood pressure and total cholesterol related to changes in mood? An 18–month study of men and women. *Health Psychology, 22,* 47–53.

Potter, N. N. (2004). Perplexing issues in personality disorders. *Current Opinion in Psychiatry, 17,* 487–492.

Powers, P. S., Schulman, R. G., Gleghorn, A. A., & Prange, M. E. (1987). Perceptual and cognitive abnormalities in bulimia. *American Journal of Psychiatry, 144,* 1456–1460.

Putnam, F. W. (1989). *Diagnosis and Treatment of Multiple Personality Disorder.* New York: Guilford.

Putnam, F. W. (1991). Recent research on multiple personality disorder. *Psychiatric Clinics of North America, 14,* 489–502.

Putnam, F. W. (1993). Diagnosis and clinical phenomenology of multiple personality disorder: A North American perspective. *Dissociation, 6,* 80–86.

Putnam, F. W., Guroff, J. J., Silberman, E. K., Barban, L., & Post, R. M. (1986). The clinical phenomenology of multiple personality disorder: Review of 100 recent cases. *Journal of Clinical Psychiatry, 47,* 285–293.

Pyle, R. L., Mitchell, J. E., & Eckert, E. D. (1981). Bulimia: A report of 34 cases. *Journal of Clinical Psychology, 42,* 60–64.

Quay, H. C. (1997). Inhibition and attention deficit hyperactivity disorder. *Journal of Abnormal Child Psychology, 25,* 7–13.

Rabinowitz Greenberg, S. R., Firestone, P., Bradford, J. M., & Greenberg, D. M. (2002). Prediction of recidivism in exhibitionists: Psychological phallometric, and offense factors. *Sexual Abuse: A Journal of Research and Treatment, 14,* 329–347.

Rachman, S. J. (2002). A cognitive theory of compulsive checking. *Behaviour Research and Therapy, 40,* 625–639.

Rachman, S. J., & Hodgson, R. J. (1980). *Obsessions and Compulsions.* Englewood, Cliffs, NJ: Prentice-Hall.

Raine, A., O'Brien, M., Chan, C. J., et al. (1990). Reward learning in adolescent psychopaths. *Journal of Abnormal Child Psychology, 18,* 451–463.

Raj, Y. P. (2004). Psychopharmacology of borderline personality disorder. *Current Psychiatry Reports, 6,* 225–231.

Rapee, R. M., & Barlow, D. H. (1988). Cognitive-behavioral treatment of panic disorder. *Psychiatric Annals, 18,* 473–477.

Rapee, R. M., & Spence, S. H. (2004). The etiology of social phobia: Empirical evidence and an initial model. *Clinical Psychology Review, 24,* 737–767.

Rapin, I. (1997). Autism. *New England Journal of Medicine, 337,* 97–104.

Rapoport, J. L., Buchsbaum, M. S., Weingartner, H., Zahn, T. P., Ludlow, C., & Mikkelsen, E. J. (1980). Dextroamphetamine: Its cognitive and behavioral effects in normal and hyperactive boys and normal men. *Archives of General Psychiatry, 37,* 933–943.

Rasmussen, A. M., & Charney, D. S. (1997). Animal models of relevance to PTSD. *Annals of the New York Academy of Sciences, 821,* 332–351.

Rasmussen, S. A., & Eisen, J. L. (1992). The epidemiology and clinical features of obsessive compulsive disorder. *Psychiatric Clinics of North America, 15,* 743–758.

Rehman, J., Lazer, S., Benet, A. E., Schaefer, L. C., & Melman, A. (1999). The reported sex and surgery satisfactions of 28 postoperative male-to-female transsexual patients. *Archives of Sexual Behavior, 28,* 71–89.

Rekers, G. A., Kilgus, M., & Rosen, A. C. (1990). Long-term effects of treatment for gender identity disorder of childhood. *Journal of Psychology and Human Sexuality, 3,* 121–153.

Resick, P. A. (1993). The psychological impact of rape. *Journal of Interpersonal Violence, 8,* 223–255

Resick, P. A., & Calhoun, K. S. (1996). Post-traumatic stress disorder. In C. G. Lindemann (Ed.), *Handbook of the Treatment of the Anxiety Disorders* (2nd ed., pp. 191–216). Northvale, NJ: Jason Aronson.

Resick, P. A., & Schnicke, M. K. (1992). Cognitive processing therapy for sexual assault victims. *Journal of Consulting and Clinical Psychology, 60,* 748–756.

Restak, R. M. (1979). The sex-change conspiracy. *Psychology Today, 13,* 20–24.

Ricca, V., Mannucci, E., Zucchi, T., Rotella, C. M., & Faravelli, C. (2000). Cognitive-behavioural therapy for bulimia nervosa and binge eating disorder: A review. *Psychotherapy and Psychosomatics, 69,* 287–295.

Rice, M. E., Harris, G. T., & Cormier, C. A. (1992). An evaluation of a maximum security therapeutic community for psychopaths and other mentally disordered offenders. *Law and Human Behavior, 16,* 399–412.

Ricks, D. M. (1972). The beginning of vocal communication in infants and autistic children. Unpublished dissertation, University of London.

Rieber, R. W. (1999). Hypnosis, false memory and multiple personality: A trinity of affinity. *History of Psychiatry, 10*, 3–11.

Rief, W., Pilger, F., Ihle, D., Verkerk, R., Scharpe, S., & Maes, M. (2004). Psychobiological aspects of somatoform disorders: Contributions of monoaminergic transmitter systems. *Neuropsychobiology, 49*, 24–29.

Riggs, D. S., Dancu, C. V., Gershuny, B. S., Greenberg, D., & Foa, E. B. (1992). Anger and post-traumatic stress disorder in female crime victims. *Journal of Traumatic Stress, 5*, 613–625.

Ritvo, E. R., Freeman, B. J., Geller, E., & Yuwiler, A. (1983). Effects of fenfluramine on 14 outpatients with the syndrome of autism. *Journal of the American Academy of Child Psychiatry, 22*, 549–558.

Robins, C. J., & Chapman, A. L. (2004). Dialectical behavior therapy: Current status, recent developments, and future directions. *Journal of Personality Disorders, 18*, 73–89.

Robins, L. N., Helzer, J. E., Weissman, M. M., et al. (1984). Lifetime prevalence of specific psychiatric disorders in three sites. *Archives of General Psychiatry, 41*, 942–949.

Robins, L. N., & Ratcliffe, K. S. (1980). The long-term outcome of truancy. In L. Fersov & I. Berg (Eds.), *Out of School* (pp. 65–83). New York: Wiley.

Robins, L. N., & Regier, D. A. (Eds.). (1991). *Psychiatric Disorders in America: The Epidemiologic Catchment Area Study*. New York: Free Press.

Rodin, J., & Langer, E. J. (1977). Long-term effects of a control-relevant intervention with the institutionalized aged. *Journal of Personality and Social Psychology, 35*, 897–902.

Rogers, C. R. (1951). *Client-Centered Therapy*. Boston: Houghton Mifflin.

Romano, S. J., Halmi, K. A., Sarkar, N. P., Koke, S., & Lee, J. S. (2002). A placebo-controlled study of fluoxetine in continued treatment of bulimia nervosa after successful acute fluoxetine treatment. *American Journal of Psychiatry, 159*, 96–102.

Room, R., Babor, T., & Rehm, J. (2005). Alcohol and public health. *Lancet, 365*, 519–530.

Root, R. W., & Resnick, R. J. (2003). An update on the diagnosis and treatment of attention-deficit/hyperactivity disorder in children. *Professional Psychology: Research and Practice, 34*, 34–41.

Rosen, R. C., & Leiblum, S. R. (1995). Treatment of sexual disorders in the 1990s: An integrated approach. *Journal of Consulting and Clinical Psychology, 63*, 877–890.

Rosenbloom, M., Sullivan. E. V., & Pfefferbaum, A. (2003). Using magnetic resonance imaging and diffusion tensor imaging to assess brain damage in alcoholics. *Alcohol Research and Health, 27*, 146–152.

Rosenthal, T. L, & Bandura, A. (1978). Psychological modeling: Theory and practice. In S. L. Garfield & A. E. Bergin (Eds.), *Handbook of Psychotherapy and Behavior change: An Empirical Analysis* (2nd ed.). New York: Wiley.

Ross, A. O., & Nelson, R. (1979). Behavior therapy. In H. S. Quay & J. S. Werry (Eds.), *Psychopathological Disorders of Childhood*. New York: Wiley.

Ross, C. A. (1991). Epidemiology of multiple personality disorder and dissociation. *Psychiatric Clinics of North America, 14*, 503–517.

Ross, C. A. (1997a). *Dissociative Identity Disorder: Diagnosis, Clinical Features, and Treatment of Multiple Personality* (2nd ed.). New York: Wiley.

Ross, C. A. (1997b). Cognitive therapy of dissociative identity disorder. In P. S. Appelbaum & L. A. Uyehara (Eds.), *Trauma and Memory: Clinical and Legal Controversies* (pp. 360–377). New York: Oxford University Press.

Roth, W. T., Wilhelm, F. H., & Pettit, D. (2005). Are current theories of panic falsifiable? *Psychological Bulletin, 131*, 171–192.

Rothbard, A. B., Schinnar, A. P., Hadley, T. P., Foley, K. A., & Kuno, E. (1998). Cost comparison of state hospital and community-based care for seriously mentally ill adults. *American Journal of Psychiatry, 155*, 523–529.

Rothbaum, B. O., Foa, E. B., Riggs, D. S., Murdock, T., & Walsh, W. (1992). A prospective examination of post-traumatic stress disorder in rape victims. *Journal of Traumatic Stress, 5*, 455–475.

Routh, D. K., & Bernholtz, J. E. (1991). Attachment, separation, and phobias. In J. L. Gewirtz & W. M. Kurtines (Eds.), *Intersections with Attachment* (pp. 295–309). Hillsdale, N J: Erlbaum Associates.

Russell, G. (1979). Bulimia nervosa: An ominous variant of anorexia nervosa. *Psychological Medicine, 9*, 429–448.

Rutledge, T., & Linden, W. (2003). Defensiveness and 3-year blood pressure levels among young adults: The mediating effect of stress-reactivity. *Annals of Behavioral Medicine, 25*, 34–40.

Rutter, M. (1967). Psychotic disorders in early childhood. In A. J. Cooper (Ed.), Recent developments in schizophrenia. *British Journal of Psychiatry, 1*, Special Publication.

Rutter, M. (1974). The development of infantile autism. *Psychological Medicine, 4*, 147–163.

Sachs, G., Anderer, P., Dantendorfer, K., & Saletu, B. (2004). EEG mapping in patients with social phobia. *Psychiatry Research: Neuroimaging, 131*, 237–247.

Saleh, F. M., & Berlin, F. S. (2003). Sexual deviancy: Diagnostic and neurobiological considerations. *Journal of Child Sexual Abuse, 12*, 53–76.

Saleh, F. M., Niel, T., & Fishman, M. J. (2004). Treatment of paraphilia in young adults with leuprolide acetate: A preliminary case report series. *Journal of Forensic Sciences, 49*, 1343–1348.

Salkovskis, P. M. (1999). Understanding and treating obsessive-compulsive disorder. *Behaviour Research and Therapy, 37*, S29–S52.

Salkovskis, P. M., & Forrester, E. (2002). Responsibility. In R. O. Frost and G. Steketee (Eds.). *Cognitive Approaches to Obsessions and Compulsions: Theory, Assessment, and Treatment*. Amsterdam, Netherlands. Pergamon. pp. 45–61.

Salmon, P., Peters, S., & Stanley, I. (1999). Patients' perceptions of medical explanations for somatisation disorders: Qualitative analysis. *British Medical Journal, 318*, 372–376.

Salmon, P. Skaife, K., & Rhodes, J. (2003). Abuse, dissociation, and somatization in irritable bowel syndrome: Towards an explanatory model. *Journal of Behavioral Medicine, 26*, 1–18.

Samelson, F. (1980). J. B. Watson's Little Albert, Cyril Burt's twins, and the need for a critical science. *American Psychologist, 35*, 619–625.

Samuels, J., Eaton, W. W., Bienvenu, O. J., Brown, C., Costa, P. T., & Nestadt, G. (2002). Prevalence and correlates of personality disorders in a community sample. *British Journal of Psychiatry, 180*, 536–542.

Sanislow, C. A., Grilo, C. M., & McGlashan, T. H. (2000). Factor analysis of the *DSM-III-R* borderline personality criteria in psychiatric inpatients. *American Journal of Psychiatry, 157*, 1629–1633.

Sansone, R. A., & Levitt, J. L. (2005). Borderline personality and eating disorders. *Eating Disorders, 13*, 71–83.

Scherrer, J. F., Xian, H., Bucholz, K. K., Eisen, S. A., Lyons, M. J., Goldberg, J., et al. (2003). A twin study of depression symptoms, hypertension, and heart disease in middle-aged men. *Psychosomatic Medicine, 65*, 548–557.

Schiffman, J., Abrahamson, A., Cannon, T., LaBrie, J., Parnas, J., Schulsinger, F., & Mednick, S. (2001). Early rearing factors in schizophrenia. *International Journal of Mental Health, 30*, 3–16.

Schneider, K. (1959). *Clinical psychopathology.* New York: Grune and Stratton.

Schooler, N. R., Keith, S. J., Severe, J. B., Matthews, S. M., Bellack, A. S., Glick, I. D., et. al. (1997). Relapse and rehospitalization during maintenance treatment of schizophrenia. The effects of dose reduction and family treatment. *Archives of General Psychiatry, 54*, 453–463.

Schreiber, F. (1973). *Sybil.* Chicago: Henry Regnery. (Reprinted by Warner Paperback Library, New York, 1974)

Schuckit, M. A. (1994). Low level of response to alcohol as a predictor of future alcoholism. *American Journal of Psychiatry, 151*, 41–49.

Schuckit, M. A., & Smith, T. L. (1996). An 8-year follow-up of 450 sons of alcoholic and control subjects. *Archives of General Psychiatry, 53*, 202–210.

Schuckit, M. A., Smith, T. L., Danko, G. p., Bucholz, K. K., Reich, T., & Bierut, L. (2001). Five-year clinical course associated with *DSM-IV* alcohol abuse or dependence in a large group of men and women. *American Journal of Psychiatry, 158*, 1084–1090.

Schulsinger, F. (1972). Psychopathy: Heredity and environment. *International Journal of Mental Health, 1*, 190–206.

Schum, J. L., Jorgensen, R. S., Verhaeghen, P., Sauro, M., & Thibodeau, R. (2003). Trait anger, anger expression, and ambulatory blood pressure: A meta-analytic review. *Journal of Behavioral Medicine, 26*, 395–415.

Schwalberg, M. D., Barlow, D. H., Alger, S. A., & Howard, L. J. (1992). Comparison of bulimics, obese binge eaters, social phobics, and individuals with panic disorder on comorbidity across *DSM-III* anxiety disorders. *Journal of Abnormal Psychology, 101*, 675–682.

Schweizer, E., Rickels, K., Case, G., & Greenblatt, D. J. (1990). Long-term therapeutic use of benzodiazapines: Effects of gradual taper. *Archives of General Psychiatry, 47*, 908–915.

Seivewright, H., Tyrer, P., & Johnson, T. (2002). Change in personality status in neurotic disorders. *Lancet, 359*, 2253–2254.

Seligman, M. E. P. (1975). *Helplessness: On depression, development, and death.* San Francisco: Freeman.

Seto, M. C., & Kuban, M. (1996). Criterion related validity of phallometric tests for paraphilic rape and sadism. *Behaviour Research and Therapy, 34*, 175–183.

Shaner, R. (2000). Benzodiazepines in psychiatric emergency settings. *Psychiatric Annals, 30*, 268–275.

Shea, V. (2004). A perspective on the research literature related to early intensive behavioral intervention (Lovaas) for young children with autism. *Autism, 8*, 349–367.

Sher, K. J., & Levenson, R. W. (1982). Risk for alcoholism and individual differences in the stress-response-dampening effect of alcohol. *Journal of Abnormal Psychology, 91*, 350–367.

Sher, K. J., Walitzer, K. S., Wood, P. K., & Brent, E. F. (1991). Characteristics of children of alcoholics: Putative risk factors, substance use and abuse, and psychopathology. *Journal of Abnormal Psychology, 100*, 427–448.

Shergill, S. S., Brammer, M. J., Williams, S. C. R., Murray, R. M., & McGuire, P. K. (2000). Mapping auditory hallucinations in schizophrenia using functional magnetic imaging. *Archives of General Psychiatry, 57*, 1033–1038.

Sherman, J. A. (1994). John Henryism and the health of African-Americans. *Cultures, Medicine, and Psychiatry, 18*, 163–182.

Shoebridge, P. J., & Gowers, S. G. (2000). Parental high concern and adolescent-onset anorexia nervosa: A case-control study to investigate direction of causality. *British Journal of Psychiatry, 176*, 132–137.

Siegel, D. J. (1996). Cognition, memory, and dissociation. *Child and Adolescent Psychiatric Clinics of North America, 5*, 509–536.

Sigman, M., Ungerer, J. A., Mundy, P., & Sherman, T. (1987). Cognition in autistic children. In D. J. Cohen, A. M. Donellan, & R. Paul (Eds.). *Handbook of Autism and Pervasive Developmental Disorders.* New York: Wiley.

Silk, K. R., Lee, S., Hill, E. M., & Lohr, N. (1995). Borderline personality disorder symptoms and severity of sexual abuse. *American Journal of Psychiatry, 152*, 1053–1057.

Simon, G. E., & Gureje, O. (1999). Stability of somatization disorder and somatization symptoms among primary care patients. *Archives of General Psychiatry, 56*, 90–95.

Simon, G. E., VonKorff, M., Piccinelli, M., Fullerton, C., & Ormel, J. (1999). An international study of the relation between somatic symptoms and depression. *New England Journal of Medicine, 341*, 1329–1335.

Simon, N. M., & Pollack, M. H. (2000). The current status of the treatment of panic disorder: pharmacotherapy and cognitive-behavioral therapy. *Psychiatric Annals, 30*, 689–696.

Simons, J. S., & Carey, M. P. (2001). Prevalence of the sexual dysfunctions: Results from a decade of research. *Archives of Sexual Behavior, 30*, 177–219.

Simpson, K. J. (2002). Anorexia nervosa and culture. *Journal of Psychiatric and Mental Health Nursing, 9*, 65–71.

Skeem, J. L., Edens, J. F., Camp, J., & Colwell, L. H. (2004). Are there ethnic differences in levels of psychopathy? A meta-analysis. *Law and Human Behavior, 28*, 505–527.

Skodol, A. E., & Bender, D. S. (2003). Why are women diagnosed borderline more than men? *Psychiatric Quarterly, 74*, 349–360.

Skoog, G., Oldman, J. M., & Gallager, P. E. (1999). Axis II comorbidity of substance use disorders among patients referred for treatment of personality disorders. *American Journal of Psychiatry, 156*, 733–738.

Smith, C. A., & Farrington, D. P. (2004). Continuities in antisocial behavior and parenting across three generations. *Journal of Child Psychology and Psychiatry, 45*, 230–247.

Smith, L. D., & Peck, P. L. (2004). Dialectical behavior therapy: A review and call to research. *Journal of Mental Health Counseling, 26*, 25–38.

Smith, S. S., & Newman, J. P. (1990). Alcohol and drug dependence in psychopathic and nonpsychopathic criminal offenders. *Journal of Abnormal Psychology, 99*, 430–439.

Smith, Y. L. S., Van Goozen, S. H. M., Kuiper, A. J., & Cohen-Kettenis, P. T. (2005). Sex reassignment: Outcomes and predictors of treatment for adolescent and adult transsexuals. *Psychological Medicine, 35*, 89–99.

Snyder, S. H. (1974). *Madness and the brain.* New York: McGraw-Hill.

Sobell, M. B., & Sobell, L. C. (1976). Second-year treatment outcome of alcoholics treated by individualized behavior therapy: Results. *Behavior Research and Therapy, 14*, 195–215.

Sobell, M. B., & Sobell, L. C. (1993). *Problem Drinkers: Guided Self-Change Treatment.* New York: Guilford.

Somers, J. M., Goldner, E. M., Waraich, P., & Hsu, L. (2004). Prevalence studies of substance-related disorders: A systematic review of the literature. *Canadian Journal of Psychiatry, 49*, 373–384.

Spanos, N. P. (1996). *Multiple Identities and False Memories: A Sociocognitive Perspective.* Washington, DC: American Psychological Association.

Spanos, N. P., Weekes, J. R., & Bertrand, L. D. (1985). Multiple personality: A social psychological perspective. *Journal of Abnormal Psychology, 94*, 362–376.

Spiegel, D. (2001). Deconstructing the dissociative disorders: For whom the Dell tolls. *Journal of Trauma and Dissociation, 2*, 51–57.

Sprague, R. L., Cohen, M., & Werry, J. S. (1974). *Normative Data on the Conners Teacher Rating Sale and Abbreviated Scale*. Technical Report. Children's Research Center, University of Illinois, Urbana.

Stanley, M. A., & Turner, S. M. (1995). Current status of pharmacological and behavioral treatment of obsessive-compulsive disorder. *Behavior Therapy, 26*, 163–186.

St. Clair, H. R. (1951). Psychiatric interview experience with Negroes. *American Journal of Psychiatry, 108*, 113–119.

Steadman, H. J., Mulvey, E. P., Monahan, J., Robbins, P. C., Appelbaum, P. S., Grisso, T., Roth, L., & Silver, E. (1998). Violence by people discharged from acute psychiatric inpatient facilities and by others in the same neighborhoods. *Archives of General Psychiatry, 55*, 393–401.

Steele, C. M., & Josephs, R. A. (1988). Drinking your troubles away: II. An attention-allocation model of alcohol's effects on psychological stress. *Journal of Abnormal Psychology, 97*, 196–205.

Steffenburg, S., Gillberg, C., Hellgren, L., Andersson, L., et al. (1989). A twin study of autism in Denmark, Finland, Iceland, Norway and Sweden. *Journal of Child Psychology and Psychiatry and Allied Disciplines, 30,* 405–416.

Steiger, H., Gauvin, L., Israel, M., Koerner, N., Ng Ying Kin, N. M. K., Paris, J., & Young, S. N. (2001). Association of serotonin and cortisol indices with childhood abuse in bulimia nervosa. *Archives of General Psychiatry, 58*, 837–843.

Steinhausen, H. (2002). The outcome of anorexia nervosa in the 20th century. *American Journal of Psychiatry, 159*, 1284–1293.

Steketee, G. (1994). Behavioral assessment and treatment planning with obsessive compulsive disorder: A review emphasizing clinical application. *Behavior Therapy, 25*, 613–633.

Stekette, G., Eisen, J., Dyck, I., Warshaw, M., & Rasmussen, S. (1999). Predictors of course in obsessive-compulsive disorder. *Psychiatry Research, 89,* 229–238.

Stephens, J. H., Richard, P., & McHugh, P. R. (2000). Long-term follow-up of patients with a diagnosis of paranoid state and hospitalized, 1913 to 1940. *Journal of Nervous and Mental Disease, 188*, 202–208.

Steptoe, A., & Willemsen, G. (2004). The influence of low job control on ambulatory blood pressure and perceived stress over the working day in men and women from the Whitehall II cohort. *Journal of Hypertension, 22*, 915–920.

Stern, J., Murphy, M., & Bass, C. (1993). Personality disorders in patients with somatisation disorder: A controlled study. *British Journal of Psychiatry, 163*, 785–789.

Stock, W. (1993). Inhibited female orgasm. In W. O'Donohue & J. H. Geer (Eds.), *Handbook of Sexual Dysfunctions: Assessment and Treatment* (pp. 253–277). Needham Heights, MA: Allyn & Bacon.

Stoller, R. J. (1985). *Presentations of gender*. New Haven, CT: Yale University Press.

Stoller, R. J., & Herdt, G. H. (1985). Theories of the origin of male homosexuality: A cross-cultural look. *Archives of General Psychiatry, 42,* 399–404.

Stoving, R. K., Hangaard, J., Hansen-Nord, M., & Hagen, C. (1999). A review of endocrine changes in anorexia nervosa. *Journal of Psychiatric Research, 33*, 139–152.

Striegel-Moore, R. H., Silberstein, L. R., & Rodin, J. (1993). The social self in bulimia nervosa: Public self-consciousness, social anxiety, and perceived fraudulence. *Journal of Abnormal Psychology, 102*, 297–304.

Strober, M. (1986). Anorexia nervosa: History and psychological concepts. In K. D. Brownell & J. P. Foreyt (Eds.), *Handbook of Eating Disorders*. New York: Basic Books.

Strober, M. (1997). Consultation and therapeutic engagement in severe anorexia nervosa. In D. M. Garner & P. E. Garfinkel (Eds.), *Handbook of Treatment for Eating Disorders* (2nd ed., pp. 229–247). New York: Guilford.

Stuart, H. L., & Arboleda-Florez, J. E. (2001). A public health perspective on violent offenses among persons with mental illness. *Psychiatric Services, 52*, 654–659.

Suddath, R. L., Christison, G. W., Torrey, E. F., Casanova, M. R., & Weinberger, D. R. (1990). Anatomical abnormalities in the brains of monozygotic twins discordant for schizophrenia. *New England Journal of Medicine, 322*, 789–794.

Sue, D. W., & Sue, D. (1999). *Counselling the Culturally Different*. New York: Wiley.

Sugarman, P., Dumughn, C., Saad, K., Hinder, S., & Bluglass, S. (1994). Dangerousness in exhibitionists. *Journal of Forensic Psychiatry, 5*, 287–296.

Sullivan, P. F., Bulik, C. M., & Kendler, K. S. (1998). The genetic epidemiology of binging and vomiting. *British Journal of Psychiatry, 173*, 75–79.

Summerfield, D. (2001). The invention of post-traumatic stress disorder and the social usefulness of a psychiatric category. *British Medical Journal, 322*, 95–98.

Swanson, J. W., Borum, R., Swartz, M. S., & Monahan, J. (1996). Psychotic symptoms and disorders and the risk of violent behaviour in the community. *Criminal Behaviour and Mental Health, 6*, 309–3269.

Swanson, J., Estroff, S., Swartz, M., Borum, R., et al. (1997). Violence and severe mental disorder in clinical and community populations: The effects of psychotic symptoms. *Psychiatry: Interpersonal and Biological Processes, 60*, 1–22.

Swendsen, E. J., King, D. W., King, L. A., Wolfe, J., Erickson, D. J., & Stokes, L. R. (2000). Mood and alcohol consumption: An experience sampling test of the self-medication hypothesis. *Journal of Abnormal Psychology, 109*, 198–204.

Szatmari, P., Offord, D. R., & Boyle, M. H. (1989). Ontario Child Health Study: Prevalence of attention deficit disorder with hyperactivity. *Journal of Child Psychology and Psychiatry and Allied Disciplines, 30*, 219–230.

Talbot, P. S. (2004). The molecular neuroimaging of anxiety disorders. *Current Psychiatry Reports, 6*, 274–279.

Tan, Y., & Zhong, Y. (2001). Chinese style psychoanalysis—assessment and treatment of paraphilias: Exhibitionism, frotteurism, voyeurism, and fetishism. *International Journal of Psychotherapy, 6*, 297–314.

Tannock, R. (1998). Attention deficit hyperactivity disorder: Advances in cognitive, neurobiological, and genetic research. *Journal of Child Psychology and Psychiatry, 39*, 65–96.

Tardiff, K. (2001). Axis II disorders and dangerousness. In G. Pinard & L. Pagani (Eds.), *Clinical Assessment of Dangerousness: Empirical Contributions* (pp. 103–120). New York: Cambridge University Press.

Tarrier, N., Pilgrim, H., Sommerfield, C., Faragher, B., Reynolds, M., Graham, E., & Barrowclough, C. (1999). A randomized trial of cognitive therapy and imaginal exposure in the treatment of chronic posttraumatic stress disorder. *Journal of Consulting and Clinical Psychology, 67*, 13–18.

Taylor, S., Thordarson, D. S., Maxfield, L., Fedoroff, I. C., Lovell, K., & Ogrodniczuk, J. (2003). Comparative efficacy, speed, and adverse effects of three PTSD treatments: Exposure therapy, EMDR, and relaxation training. *Journal of Consulting and Clinical Psychology, 71*, 330–338.

Tennant, C. (1988). Parental loss in childhood: Its effect in adult life. *Archives of General Psychiatry, 45*, 1045–1050.

Teplin, L. A., Abram, K. M., & McClelland, G. M. (1996). Prevalence of psychiatric disorders among incarcerated women: Pretrial jail detainees. *Archives of General Psychiatry, 53*, 505–512.

Terao, T., & Nakamura, J. (2000). Exhibitionism and low-dose trazodone treatment. *Human Psychopharmacology: Clinical and Experimental, 15,* 347–349.

Thigpen, C. H., & Cleckley, H. M. (1957). *The Three Faces of Eve.* New York: McGraw-Hill.

Thigpen, C. H., & Cleckley, H. M. (1984). On the incidence of multiple personality disorder. *International Journal of Clinical and Experimental Hypnosis, 32*, 63–66.

Thomas, A. (2001). Factitious and malingered dissociative identity disorder: Clinical features observed in 18 cases. *Journal of Trauma & Dissociation, 2*, 59–77.

Thomas, J. A., & Dobbins, J. E. (1986). The color line and social distance in the genesis of essential hypertension. *Journal of the National Medical Association, 78*, 532–536.

Thomson, L. D. G., Bogue, J. P., Humphreys, M. S., & Johnstone, E. C. (2001). A survey of female patients in high security psychiatric care in Scotland. *Criminal Behaviour and Mental Health, 11*, 86–93.

Thornton, C., & Russell, J. (1997). Obsessive compulsive comorbidity in the dieting disorders. *International Journal of Eating Disorders, 21*, 83–87.

Thyer, B. A. (1991). Diagnosis and treatment of child and adolescent anxiety disorders. *Behavior Modification, 15*, 310–325.

Tollison, C. D., & Adams, H. E. (1979). *Sexual Disorders: Treatment, Theory, Research.* New York: Gardner.

Tomasson, K., Kent, D., & Coryell, W. (1991). Somatization and conversion disorders: Comorbidity and demographics at presentation. *Acta Psychiatrica Scandinavia, 84*, 288–293.

Torgersen, S., Kringlen, E., & Cramer, V. (2001). The prevalence of personality disorders in a community sample. *Archives of General Psychiatry, 58*, 590–596.

Tsuang, M. T. (1991). Morbidity risks of schizophrenia and affective disorders among first-degree relatives of patients with schizoaffective disorders. *British Journal of Psychiatry, 158*, 165–170.

Tsuang, M. T., Glatt, S. J., & Faraone, S. V. (2003). Genetics and genomics in schizophrenia. *Primary Psychiatry, 10*, 37–40.

Tully, L. A., Arseneault, L., Caspi, A., Moffitt, T. E., & Morgan, J. (2004). Does maternal warmth moderate the effects of birth weight on twins' attention-deficit/ hyperactivity disorder (ADHD) symptoms and low IQ? *Journal of Consulting and Clinical Psychology, 72,* 218–226.

Turk, C. L., Heimberg, R. G., & Hope, D. A. (2001). Social anxiety disorder. In D. H. Barlow (Ed.), *Clinical Handbook of Psychological Disorders* (pp. 114–153). New York: Guilford.

Turner, S. M., Beidel, DC, & Cooley-Quille, M. R. (1995). Two-year follow-up of social phobics treated with Social Effectiveness Therapy. *Behaviour Research and Therapy, 33*, 553–555.

Twentyman, C. T., & McFall, R. M. (1975). Behavioral training of social skills in shy males. *Journal of Consulting and Clinical Psychology, 43*, 384–395.

Tyrer, P., & Tyrer, S. (1974). School refusal, truancy, and adult neurotic illness. *Psychological Medicine, 6*, 313–332.

Ullman, S. E., & Filipas, H. H. (2001). Predictors of PTSD symptom severity and social reactions in sexual assault victims. *Journal of Traumatic Stress, 14*, 369–389.

Vaillant, G. E. (1996). A long-term follow-up of male alcohol abuse. *Archives of General Psychiatry, 53,* 243–249.

Vaillant, G. E. (2003). A 60-year follow-up of alcoholic men. *Addiction, 98,* 1043–1051.

Van Amerigen, M. A., Lane, R. M., Walker, J. R., et al. (2001). Sertreline treatment of generalized social phobia: A 20-week, double-blind, placebo-controlled study. *American Journal of Psychiatry, 158*, 275–281.

Van den Bergh, B. R. H., & Marcoen, A. (2004). High antenatal maternal anxiety is related to ADHD symptoms, externalizing problems, and anxiety in 8- and 9-year-olds. *Child Development, 75,* 1085–1097.

Van den Heuvel, O. A., van de Wetering, B. J. M., Veltman, D. J., & Pauls, D. L. (2000). Genetic studies of panic disorder: A review. *Journal of Clinical Psychiatry, 61,* 756–766.

Van den Oord, E. J., Boomsma, D. I., & Verhulst, F. C. (1994). A study of problem behaviors in 10- to 15-year old biologically related and unrelated international adoptees. *Behavior Genetics, 24,* 193–205.

Van der Ham, T. (1997). Empirically based subgrouping of eating disorders in adolescents: A longitudinal perspective. *British Journal of Psychiatry, 170*, 363–368.

Van Hanswijck, J. P., van Furth, E. F., Lacey, J. H., & Waller, G. (2003). The prevalence of DSM-IV personality pathology among individuals with bulimia nervosa, binge eating disorder and obesity. *Psychological Medicine, 33*, 1311–1317.

Velting, O. N., Setzer, N. J., & Albano, A. M. (2004). Update on and advances in assessment and cognitive-behavioral treatment of anxiety disorders in children and adolescents. *Professional Psychology: Research and Practice, 35,* 42–54.

Verduin, T. L., & Kendall, Ph. C. (2003). Differential occurrence of comorbidity within childhood anxiety disorders. *Journal of Clinical Child and Adolescent Psychology, 32,* 290–295.

Verschoor, A. M., & Poortinga, J. (1988). Psychosocial differences between Dutch male and female transsexuals. *Archives of Sexual Behavior, 17*, 173–178.

Voeller, K. K. S. (2004). Attention-deficit hyperactivity disorder (ADHD). *Journal of Child Neurology, 19,* 798–814.

Volkmar, F. R., Chawarska, K., & Klin, A. (2005). Autism in infancy and early childhood. *Annual Review of Psychology, 56,* 315–336.

Volkmar, F. R., Lord, C., Bailey, A., Schultz, R. T., & Klin, A. (2004). Autism and pervasive developmental disorders. *Journal of Child Psychology and Psychiatry, 45,* 135–170.

Wade, T. D., Treloar, S. A., & Martin, N. G. (2001). A comparison of family functioning, temperament, and childhood conditions in monozygotic twin pairs discordant for lifetime bulimia nervosa. *American Journal of Psychiatry, 158*, 1155–1157.

Walden, J., Mormann, C. l., Langosch, J., Berger, J., & Grunze, H. (1998). Differential treatment of bipolar disorder with old and new antiepileptic drugs. *Neuropsychobiology, 38,* 181–184.

Waldinger, M. D., Zwinderman, A. H., & Olivier, B. (2001). Antidepressants and ejaculation: A double-blind, randomized, placebo-controlled, fixed dose study with paroxetine, sertraline, and nefazodone. *Journal of Clinical Psychopharmacology, 21,* 293–297.

Waldinger, R. J., & Gunderson, J. G. (1984). Completed psychotherapies with borderline patients. *American Journal of Psychotherapy, 38,* 190–202.

Walker, E., Kestler, L., Bollini, A., & Hochman, K. M. (2004). Schizophrenia: Etiology and course. *Annual Review of Psychology, 55,* 401–430.

Walker, E. F., Lewine, R. R. J., & Newmann, C. (1996). Childhood behavioral characteristics and adult brain morphology in schizophrenia. *Schizophrenia Research, 22*, 93–101.

Wallace, S. T., & Alden, L. E. (1997) Social phobia and positive social events: The price of success. *Journal of Abnormal Psychology, 106(3),* 416–424.

Walsh, E., Gilvarry, C., Samele, C., Harvey, K., Manley, C., Tattan, T., Tyrer, P., Creed, F., Murray, R., & Fahy, T. (2004). Predicting violence in schizophrenia: A prospective study. *Schizophrenia Research, 67*, 247–252.

Wang, J. L., & El-Guebaly, N. (2004). Sociodemographic factors associated with comorbid major depressive episodes and alcohol dependence in the general population. *Canadian Journal of Psychiatry, 49*, 37–44.

Waraich, P., Goldner, E. M., Somers, J. M., & Hsu, L. (2004). Prevalence and incidence studies of mood disorders: A systematic review of the literature. *Canadian Journal of Psychiatry, 49*, 124–138.

Warnock, J. K. (2002). Female hypoactive sexual desire disorder: Epidemiology, diagnosis and treatment. *CNS Drugs, 16*, 745–753.

Warshaw, R. (1988). *I Never Called It Rape: The Ms. Report on Recognizing, Fighting, and Surviving Acquaintance Rape.* New York: Harper & Row.

Watson, J. B., & Rayner, R. (1920). Conditioned emotional reactions. *Journal of Experimental Psychology, 3*, 1–14.

Watt, N. F., & Lubensky, A. (1976). Childhood roots of schizophrenia. *Journal of Consulting and Clinical Psychology, 44*, 363–375.

Webb, C. T., & Levinson, D. F. (1993). Schizotypal and paranoid personality disorder in the relatives of patients with schizophrenia and affective disorders: A review. *Schizophrenia Research, 11*, 81–92.

Wegner, D. M. (1994). Ironic processes of mental control. *Psychological Review, 101*, 34–52.

Weissberg, M. (1993). Multiple personality disorder and iatrogenesis: The cautionary tale of Anna O. *International Journal of Clinical and Experimental Hypnosis, 41*, 15–34.

Weissman, M. M., & Markowitz, J. C. (1994). Interpersonal psychotherapy: Current status. *Archives of General Psychiatry, 51*, 599–606.

Werry, J. S., Weiss, G., & Douglas, V. (1964). Studies on the hyperactive child: I. Some preliminary findings. *Canadian Psychiatric Association Journal, 9*, 120–130.

Whalen, C. K., Henker, B., Buhrmester, D., Hinshaw, S. P., Huber, A., & Laski, K. (1989). Does stimulant medication improve the peer status of hyperactive children? *Journal of Consulting and Clinical Psychology, 57*, 545–549.

Whelton, P. K., Appel, L. J., Espeland, M. A., Applegate, W. B., Ettinger, W. H., Kostis, J. B., Kumanyika, S., et al. (1998). Sodium reduction and weight loss in treatment of hypertension in older persons: A randomized controlled trial of nonpharmacologic interventions in the elderly. *Journal of the American Medical Association, 279*, 839–846.

White, C. N., Gunderson, J. G., Zanarini, M. C., & Hudson, J. I. (2003). Family studies of borderline personality disorder: A review. *Harvard Review of Psychiatry, 11*, 8–19.

Whitfield, J. B., Zhu, G., Madden, P. A., Neale, M. C., Heath, A. C., & Martin, N. G. (2004). The genetics of alcohol intake and of alcohol dependence. *Alcoholism: Clinical and Experimental Research, 28*, 1153–1160.

Wickramsekara, I. (1977). The application of learning theory to the treatment of a case of exhibitionism. In J. Fischer & H. Gochros (Eds.), *Handbook of Behavior Therapy with Sexual Problems.* New York: Pergamon.

Widiger, T. A. (2001). Official classification systems. In W. J. Livesley (Ed.), *Handbook of Personality Disorders: Theory, Research, and Treatment* (pp. 60–83). New York: Guilford.

Widiger, T. A., Frances, A., Spitzer, R., & Williams, J. (1988). The DSM-III-R personality disorders: An overview. *American Journal of Psychiatry, 145*, 786–795.

Widiger, T. A., Frances, A., & Trull, T. J. (1987). A psychometric analysis of the social-interpersonal and cognitive-perceptual items for the schizotypal personality disorder. *Archives of General Psychiatry, 44*, 741–745.

Widiger, T. A., Trull, T. J., Hurt, S., Clarkin, J., & Francis, A. (1987). A multidimensional scaling of the DMS-III personality disorders. *Archives of General Psychiatry, 44*, 557–566.

Wiederman, M. W. (1996). Women, sex, and food: A review of research on eating disorders and sexuality. *Journal of Sex Research, 33*, 301–311.

Wiegel, M., Wincze, J. P., & Barlow, D. H. (2002). Sexual dysfunction. In M. M. Antony & D. H. Barlow (Eds.), *Handbook of Assessment and Treatment Planning for Psychological Disorders* (pp. 481–522). New York: Guilford.

Wilcox, D. T., & Sosnowski, D. E. (2005). Polygraph examination of British sexual offenders: A pilot study on sexual history disclosure testing. *Journal of Sexual Aggression, 11*, 3–25.

Wilens, T. E., Faraone, S. V., Biederman, J., & Gunawardene, S. (2003). Does stimulant therapy of attention-deficit/hyperactivity disorder beget later substance abuse? A meta-analytic review of the literature. *Pediatrics, 111*, 179–185.

Williams, R. B., Barefoot, J. C., & Schneiderman, N. (2003). Psychosocial risk factors for cardiovascular disease: More than one culprit at work. *Journal of the American Medical Association, 290*, 2190–2192.

Williamson, D. A., Cubic, B. A., & Gleaves, D. H. (1993). Equivalence of body image disturbance in anorexia and bulimia nervosa. *Journal of Abnormal Psychology, 120*, 173–176.

Willoughby, M. T. (2003). Developmental course of ADHD symptomatology during the transition from childhood to adolescence: A review with recommendations. *Journal of Child Psychology and Psychiatry, 44*, 88–106.

Wilson, G. T., Fairburn, C. C., Agras, W. S., Walsh, B. T., & Kraemer, H. (2002). Cognitive-behavioral therapy for bulimia nervosa: Time course and mechanisms of change. *Journal of Consulting and Clinical Psychology, 70*, 267–274.

Wise, T. N., & Meyer, J. K. (1980). The border area between transvestism and gender dysphoria: Transvestitic applicants for sex reassignment. *Archives of Sexual Behavior, 9*, 327–342.

Wiseman, C. V., Gray, J. J., Moismann, J. E., & Arhens, A. H. (1992). Cultural expectations of thinness in women: An update. *International Journal of Eating Disorders, 11*, 85–89.

Wittchen, H., Schuster, P., & Lieb, R. (2001). Comorbidity and mixed anxiety-depressive disorder: Clinical curiosity or pathophysiological need? *Human Psychopharmacology, 16 (Suppl. 1)*, S21–S30.

Witzig, J. S. (1968). The group treatment of male exhibitionists. *American Journal of Psychiatry, 125*, 75–81.

Wolff, M., Alsobrook, J. P., & Pauls, D. L. (2000). Genetic aspects of obsessive-compulsive disorder. *Psychiatric Clinics of North America, 23*, 535–544.

Wolpe, J., & Rowan, V. C. (1988). Panic disorder: A product of classical conditioning: *Behavior Research and Therapy, 26*, 441–450.

Wolpe, J. P. (1958). *Psychotherapy by Reciprocal Inhibition*. Stanford, CA: Stanford University Press.

Wonderlich, S. A., Brewerton, T. D., Jocic, Z., Dansky, B. S., et al. (1997). Relationship of childhood sexual abuse and eating disorders. *Journal of the American Academy of Child and Adolescent Psychiatry, 36*, 1107–1115.

Wood, D. L., Sheps, S. G., et al. (1984). Cold pressor test as a predictor of hypertension. *Hypertension, 6*, 301–306.

Woodruff, P. W. R. (2004). Auditory hallucinations: Insights and questions from neuroimaging. *Cognitive Neuropsychiatry, 9*, 73–91.

Woods, S. (2004). Untreated recovery from eating disorders. *Adolescence, 39*, 361–371.

Wooley, S. C. (1995). Sexual abuse and eating disorders: The concealed debate. In P. Fallon, M. A. Katzman, & S. C. Wooely (Eds.), *Feminist Perspectives on Eating Disorders* (pp. 171–21). New York: Guilford.

World Almanac and Book of Facts 1993. (1992). New York: Pharos Books.

World Health Organization. (1990). *International Classification of Diseases and Related Health Care Problems* (10th ed.). Geneva.

Yalom, I. D., & Lieberman, M. A. (1971). A study of encounter group casualties. *Archives of General Psychiatry, 25*, 16–30.

Yan, L. L., Liu, K., Matthews, K. A., Daviglus, M. L., Ferguson, T. F., & Kiefe, C. I. (2003). Psychosocial factors and risk of hypertension: The Coronary Artery Risk Development in Young Adults (CARDIA) Study. *Journal of the American Medical Association, 290,* 2138–2148.

Yates, A. (1990). Current perspectives on the eating disorders: II. Treatment, outcome, and research directions. *Journal of the American Academy of Child and Adolescent Psychiatry, 29*, 1–9.

Yeager, C. A., & Lewis, D. O. (1997). False memories of cult abuse. *American Journal of Psychiatry, 154*, 435.

Yehuda, R. (2002). Current concepts: Post-traumatic stress disorder. *New England Journal of Medicine, 346*, 108–114.

Yung, P. M., & Keltner, A. A. (1996). A controlled comparison of the effects of muscle and cognitive relaxation procedures on blood pressure: Implications for the behavioural treatment of borderline hypertensives. *Behaviour Research and Therapy, 34*, 821–826.

Zanarini, M. C. (2004). Update on pharmacotherapy of borderline personality disorder. *Current Psychiatry Reports, 6,* 66–70.

Zanarini, M. C., & Frankenburg, F. R. (1997). Pathways to the development of borderline personality disorder. *Journal of Personality Disorders, 11*, 93–104.

Zanarini, M. C., Gunderson, J. G., Marino, M. F., et al. (1988). DSM-III disorders in the families of borderline outpatients. *Journal of Personality Disorders, 2*, 292–302.

Zanarini, M. C., Skodol, A. E., Bender, D., Dolan, R., Sanislow, C., Schaefer, E., Morey, L. C., Grilo, C. M. Shea, M. T., McGlashan, T. H., & Gunderson, J. C. (2000). The Collaborative Longitudinal Personality Disorders Study: Reliability of axis I and II diagnoses. *Journal of Personality Disorders, 14*, 291–299.

Zarit, S. H. (1980). *Aging and mental disorders: Psychological Approaches to Assessment and Treatment*. New York: Free Press.

Zaubler, T. S., & Katon, W. (1998). Panic disorder in the general medical setting. *Journal of Psychosomatic Research, 44*, 25–42.

Zimmerman, M. (1994). Diagnosing personality disorders: A review of issues and research methods. *Archives of General Psychiatry, 51*, 225–245.

Zito, J. M., Safer, D. J., dosReis, S., et al. (2000). Trends in the prescribing of psychotropic medication to preschoolers. *JAMA, 283,* 1025–1030.

Zohar, A. H., Apter, A., King, R. A., Pauls, D. L., Leckman, J. F., & Cohen, D. J. (1999). Epidemiological studies. In J. F. Leckman & D. J. Cohen (Eds.). *Tourette's Syndrome–Tics, Obsessions, Compulsions: Developmental Psychopathology and Clinical Care* (pp. 177–193). New York: Wiley.

Zohar, J., Kaplan, Z., & Benjamin, J. (1994). Compulsive exhibitionism successfully treated with fluvoxamine: A controlled case study. *Journal of Clinical Psychiatry, 55*, 86–88.

Zucker, K. J. (2001). Biological differences on psychosexual differentiation. In R. K. Under (Ed.),. *Handbook of the Psychology of Women and Gender* (pp. 101–115). New York: Wiley.

Zucker, K. J., & Bradley, S. J. (1995). *Gender Identity Disorder and Psychosexual Problems in Children and Adolescents*. New York: Guilford.

Zucker, K. J., & Bradley, S. J. (2000). Gender identity disorder. In C. H. Zeanah (Ed.), *Handbook of Infant Mental Health* (2nd ed., pp. 412–424). New York: Guilford.

Zucker, K. J., & Green, R. (1992). Psychosexual disorders in children and adolescents. *Journal of Child Psychology and Psychiatry, 33*, 107–151.

INDEX